The
PORTABLE
MBA
in
FINANCE and
ACCOUNTING

The

PORTABLE
MBA
in
FINANCE and
ACCOUNTING
FOURTH EDITION

Edited by

Theodore Grossman and
John Leslie Livingstone

WILEY

John Wiley & Sons, Inc.

ISBN 978-0-470-48130-1

Printed in the United States of America.

10 9 8 7 6 5 4 3 2 1

Contents

List of Downloadable Materials

For access to the following list of downloadable materials for *The Portable MBA in Finance and Accounting, Fourth edition*, please visit www.wiley.com/go/ portablembainfinance

Understanding Financial Statements Balance Sheet: Liabilities + Equity

Analyzing Financial Statements: Direct Competitor Comparison Worksheet

Analyzing Financial Statements: Financial Statement Ratio Analysis

Adjustment Worksheet for Sustainable Earnings Base

Adjustment Worksheet for Sustainable Earnings Base, Pfizer, Inc.

Discounted Cash Flow: Using Excel to Solve Financial Formulas

Discounted Cash Flow Web

Capital Structure Problems and Solutions

The Integrity of Financial Accounting: Sarbanes-Oxley and Fraudulent Financial Reporting

Information about the Sarbanes-Oxley Act and Corporate Governance and Financial Reporting

Ethics and the Golden Rule

Information Technology and You

Information Technology and the Firm

Syllabus

How Chapter Topics in This Book Track the Core MBA Curriculum

If one were to review the core curriculum for first-year students offered by most of the major MBA programs, one would find, in one form or another, the following courses:

- Financial Accounting
- Management Accounting
- Financial Management
- Business Law and Business Entities
- Planning and Strategy
- Information Systems
- Operations Management
- Decision Support or Management Sciences
- Marketing
- Managerial Economics
- Organizational Behavior
- Entrepreneurial Thinking

Of course this varies from school to school; however, the vast majority follow this pattern, including Harvard University, the University of Michigan, Babson College, Stanford University, Columbia University, and many others.

While this book makes no attempt to cover the entire core curriculum, it does cover most, if not all, of the accounting and finance topics, as well as several others. The following table compares the chapter topics with the typical courses that would be in an MBA program.

Financial Accounting	Financial Management	Business Entities	Management Accounting	Planning and Strategy	Advanced Topics
Chapter 1. Understanding Financial Statements	Chapter 4. Discounted Cash Flow	Chapter 8. Choosing a Business Form	Chapter 11. Forecasts and Budgeting	Chapter 14. Business Planning	Chapter 19. Information Technology and You
Chapter 2. Analyzing Financial Statements	Chapter 5. Capital Structure	Chapter 9. Taxes and Business Decisions	Chapter 12. Cost Structure Analysis, Profit Planning, and Value Creation	Chapter 15. Financial Management of Risks	Chapter 20. Information Technology and the Firm
Chapter 3. Analyzing Business Earnings	Chapter 6. Planning Capital Expenditure	Chapter 10. The Integrity of Financial Reporting	Chapter 13. Activity-Based Costing	Chapter 16. Business Valuation	Chapter 21. Careers in Finance
	Chapter 7. Global Finance			Chapter 17. Profitable Growth by Acquisition	
				Chapter 18. Outsourcing	

Preface

Since the third edition of this book was published in late 2001, much has happened to reshape the business world as we now know it. Our financial system almost collapsed. Stalwarts like Lehman Brothers and Merrill Lynch ceased to exist because they had assumed huge risk in financial instruments that were vastly overvalued. The mortgage market collapsed and along with it went a host of financial companies and banks that had invested in subprime mortgage-backed securities. Bernie Madoff went from obscurity to become a household name after allegedly bilking investors out of approximately $50 billion in the largest-ever Ponzi scheme. The stock market lost 35% of its value. Personal 401(k) retirement accounts were devastated, and people had to rethink their retirement plans. Companies planning to use their stock to finance the purchase of acquisitions found that the value of their stock had plunged. Credit became tight and financing difficult.

As a result of the Enron scandal, corporate governance has become a hot topic, with potential liability for CEOs and CFOs and with much increased and highly expensive and cumbersome added requirements for internal control imposed by the 2002 Sarbanes-Oxley Act.

All of these issues have created a new financial world that requires special skills for a manager to succeed. Do you have those skill sets?

Do you know how to accomplish these important business tasks?

- Understand financial statements.
- Measure liquidity of a business.
- Analyze business profitability.
- Differentiate between regular income and extraordinary items.
- Predict future bankruptcy for an enterprise.
- Prepare a budget.
- Do a break-even analysis.
- Figure out return on investment.
- Compute the cost of capital.
- Put together a business plan.
- Legitimately minimize income taxes payable by you or your business.
- Decide what your obligations are as an officer or director of the company.

- Determine the implications of outsourcing a product, a function, or a project either domestically or internationally.
- Manage foreign currency exposure.
- Evaluate a merger or acquisition target.
- Serve as a director of a corporation.
- Build a successful e-business.
- Understand and use financial derivatives.
- Use information technology for competitive advantage.
- Value a business.

These are some of the key topics explained in this book. It is a book designed to help you learn the basics in finance and accounting, without incurring the considerable time and expense of a formal MBA program. The book consists of valuable, practical how-to information, applicable to an entire range of businesses, from the smallest start-up to the largest corporations in the world. Each chapter of the book has been written by an outstanding expert in the subject matter of that particular chapter. Some of these experts are full-time practitioners in the real world, and others are business school professors with substantial real-world experience who also serve as part-time management consultants. Most of these professors are on the faculty of Babson College, which is famous for its major contributions to the field of entrepreneurship, and which year after year is at the top of the annual list of leading independent business schools compiled by *U.S. News & World Report* and the University of Maryland's University College, a leading Internet university with 100,000 students, including 3,000 MBA students.

The first edition of this book was published in 1992, the second edition in 1997, and the third in 2001. All of the editions, hardback and paperback, have been highly successful, and have sold many, many copies. In addition, the book has been translated into Chinese (Cantonese and Mandarin), Indonesian, Portuguese, Russian, and Spanish. We are delighted that so many readers in various countries have found this book useful. Now, the entire book has been updated for the fourth edition. New chapters have been added on the following subjects:

- Discounted Cash Flow.
- Analyzing Financial Statements.
- Capital Structure.
- The Integrity of Financial Reporting.
- Outsourcing.
- Careers in Finance.

Also, there are six new authors, substantial revisions of several chapters, and complete updates of the remaining chapters.

Some of the chapters include additional online materials that will reinforce the materials contained in the chapters. Please go to www.wiley.com/go/portablembainfinance.com to access the online materials that are designated for this book.

This book can be read, and reread, with a great deal of profit. Also, it can be kept handy on a nearby shelf so you can pull it down and look up answers to questions as they occur. Further, this book will help you to work with finance and accounting professionals on their own turf and in their own jargon. You will know what questions to ask, and you will better understand the answers you receive, without being confused or intimidated.

Who can benefit from this book? Many different people, such as:

- Managers wishing to improve their business skills.
- Engineers, attorneys, chemists, scientists, and other technical specialists preparing to take on increased management responsibilities.
- People already operating their own businesses, or thinking of doing so.
- Businesspeople in nonfinancial positions who want to be better versed in financial matters.
- BBA or MBA alumni who want a refresher in finance and accounting.
- People in many walks of life who need to understand more about financial matters.

Whether you are in one, some, or even none of these categories, you will find much of value in this book, and the book is reader-friendly. Frankly, most finance and accounting books are technically complex, boringly detailed, or just plain dull. This book emphasizes clarity to nonfinancial readers, using many helpful examples and a bright, interesting style of writing. Learn, and enjoy!

THEODORE GROSSMAN
JOHN LESLIE LIVINGSTONE

Acknowledgments

A book like this can result only from the contributions of many talented people. We would like to thank the chapter authors who make up this book for their clear and informative explanations of the powerful concepts and tools of finance and accounting. These people dedicate their lives to educating others in the complexities of their disciplines. In this ever-changing world of technology, strategy, economic cycles, geopolitical events, and the Internet, while most of the underlying concepts remain fixed, the applications are ever changing, requiring the authors to constantly rededicate themselves to their professions. We thank our editor, Michael Grossman, for his reviewing of the materials from the perspective of an MBA student.

We dedicate this book to our wives, Ruthie Grossman and Trudy Livingstone, and to our children and grandchildren. They provide the daily inspiration to diligently perform our work and to have undertaken this project.

T. G.
J. L. L.

About the Contributors

Richard T. Bliss has been involved in corporate financial analysis since 1987 and is currently on the finance faculty at Babson College. He teaches at the undergraduate, MBA, and executive levels, specializing in the areas of corporate financial strategy and entrepreneurial finance. Prior to coming to Babson, Dr. Bliss was on the faculty at Indiana University, and he has also taught extensively in Central and Eastern Europe, including at the Warsaw School of Economics, Warsaw University, and the University of Ljubljana in Slovenia.

With publications in the areas of corporate finance, emerging markets, entrepreneurship, and banking, Dr. Bliss has an active research agenda. His work on the impact of bank mergers on CEO compensation has been cited in *Fortune* magazine and numerous other business publications and was published in the *Journal of Financial Economics*.

Dr. Bliss holds a PhD in finance from Indiana University. He also received his MBA in finance/real estate from Indiana University and graduated with honors from Rutgers University, earning a BS degree in engineering and a BA degree in economics.

Ralph J. Constantino is associate director of the MBA Center for Career Development, F.W. Olin Graduate School of Business, Babson College. He has had over 30 years of senior-level professional experience in the financial services industry. Prior to joining Babson, he served as the managing director for strategic marketing and product development for State Street Global Advisors, where he drove international initiatives in Hong Kong and Australia and played a leading role in the formation of CitiStreet LLC, a joint venture between State Street and CitiCorp. He was also the senior vice president and chief investment officer for the Schoolhouse Capital business unit that built solutions for the 529 college savings marketplace. Before his tenure at State Street Corporation, he held senior-level positions with the Abu Dhabi Investment Authority, Chase Consulting Group, Mercer Meidenger Hanson, Equitable Capital Management Company, Smilen and Safian, and Citibank. Aside from his corporate experience, Mr. Constantino has also served as a member of the adjunct faculty at New York University, Loyola University, the American Institute of Banking, and Bentley University. He is also a featured speaker at professional conferences in the United States, Europe, and Asia. He has also appeared on the *Nightly Business Report* and major print media. He holds a BS degree in economics and business administration from Wagner College as well as a master's degree in economics from Rutgers University.

Michael A. Crain, CPA/ABV, CFA, ASA, CFE, MBA, is a practitioner specializing mostly in business valuation and forensic accounting in Fort Lauderdale, Florida. He holds several certifications related to valuation: Chartered Financial Analyst awarded by the CFA Institute, Accredited Senior Appraiser in business valuation from the American Society of Appraisers, and Accredited in Business Valuation awarded by the American Institute of Certified Public Accountants (AICPA). Mr. Crain is a past chairman of the AICPA business valuation committee, and he has been a member of the committee that develops the examination given to CPAs who seek the AICPA's certification in business valuation. He teaches a business valuation course at Florida Atlantic University. Mr. Crain has received several awards, including the AICPA *Journal of Accountancy* Lawler Award for best article of the year, and has been inducted into the AICPA business valuation hall of fame. His articles have been published in practitioner journals, and he has spoken to national audiences. He is currently working on doctorate research at the Manchester Business School, University of Manchester, England.

Dawna Travis Dewire is a member of the full-time faculty at Babson College in Massachusetts. She teaches courses in information systems design, database development, and process reengineering. Ms. Dewire is the author of five books and has been the editor of *The James Martin Report*, the *Year 2000 Practitioner*, and the quarterly *Journal of Information Systems Management*. Prior to joining Babson College, she was on the full-time faculty at Bentley College. Ms. Dewire's professional experience includes positions with Information Resources, Inc., TRW United-Carr Division, Blue Cross/Blue Shield, and the State of New York. Ms. Dewire holds a BS in mathematics and an MS in computer science from the University at Albany–State University of New York and an MBA from Northeastern University.

James A. Elfter currently resides in East Seaham, a suburb of Newcastle, New South Wales, Australia. Jim has an MBA from the University of Maryland University College and an undergraduate degree from Governors State University in Illinois. Since 2006, he has been working for the University of Maryland's Graduate School of Management and Technology as a graduate faculty assistant. Jim retired from General Motors after more than 30 years of service in various managerial capacities and international assignments. He has lived and worked in Greece, Egypt, Yugoslavia, Brazil, Canada, and Australia, where he is enjoying semiretirement.

Steven P. Feinstein is an associate professor of finance at Babson College. He has earned a PhD in economics from Yale University and a BA degree in economics from Pomona College, and he also holds the Chartered Financial Analyst (CFA) designation. His research and teaching specialties are in the fields of investments and capital markets. In addition to his teaching and research, Professor Feinstein provides consulting services and expert testimony on a variety of financial topics, most frequently securities litigation. Past and present clients include the United States Securities and Exchange Commission, the National Association of Securities Dealers, the Internal Revenue Service, the attorney general of the State of Illinois, State Street Bank, and numerous law firms.

Theodore Grossman is a member of the faculty of Babson College, where he teaches information technology and accounting. He lectures on various information technology topics such as Web technologies, e-commerce, strategic information systems, managing information technology, and systems analysis and design. He also performs extensive consulting for food and nonfood retailers and suppliers of technology products to the retail industry. He is called on frequently to act as an expert witness in complex litigation in matters relating to technology and cyber law. Prior to joining Babson College, he was the founder and CEO of a computer software company for the retail industry. He holds a BS degree in engineering from the University of New Hampshire and an MS in management from Northeastern University. Mr. Grossman was a contributor to the second edition of this book and is an editor of both the third and fourth editions.

Robert F. Halsey has a BA, MBA, and PhD from the University of Wisconsin–Madison. During his business career, Dr. Halsey managed the commercial lending division of a large Midwestern bank and served as the chief financial officer of a privately held retailing and manufacturing company. Prior to joining the faculty of Babson College, he taught at the University of Wisconsin–Madison, where he received the Douglas Clarke Memorial teaching award. His teaching and research interests are in the area of financial reporting and include firm valuation, financial statement analysis, and disclosure issues. Dr. Halsey is the author of *Advanced Financial Accounting* (forthcoming in 2009 by Cambridge Business Publishers) and a co-author of *Financial Accounting for MBAs*, *third* edition (Cambridge Business Publishers), *MBA Financial & Managerial Accounting* (Cambridge Business Publishers), and *Financial Statement Analysis, ninth* edition (McGraw-Hill). He has published in *Advances in Quantitative Analysis of Finance and Accounting*, the *Journal of the American Taxation Association*, and *Issues in Accounting Education*.

William C. Lawler is the leadership professor, strategy and accounting, F.W. Olin Graduate School of Business, Babson College. He is also the director of the Consortium for Executive Development at Babson Executive Education. His teaching and research focus on two areas: financial footprints of business unit strategy and the impact of new technologies on cost systems design. Dr. Lawler has written several papers and given numerous professional presentations. His primary focus is on aiding operational managers in understanding the financial consequences of their decisions. He has run seminars on this topic for such diverse groups as telecom managers in China, production managers in the Czech Republic, and R&D managers in the United States. Dr. Lawler consults with a number of companies, ranging from small biotechs to Fortune 100 technology companies, concerning the design and use of cost information systems for management decision support rather than external financial reporting. His most recent publications in this area are a chapter, "Understanding the Financial Footprint of Strategy," in *Strategy, Innovation, and Change* (Oxford University Press, 2008), and chapters on activity-based costing and profit planning in the fourth edition of *The Portable MBA in Finance and Accounting*.

Les Livingstone is the MBA Program Director in Economics, Finance and Accounting at the University of Maryland University College, a leading Internet university with 100,000 students, including 3,000 MBA students. (http://www.umuc.edu/index.shtml). He earned MBA and PhD degrees at Stanford University and is a CPA (licensed in

New York and Texas). Since 1991 he has directed his own consulting firm, specializing in damage estimation for large-scale commercial litigation and in business valuation. He has served as a consulting or testifying expert in many cases, and has testified in federal and state courts in Arizona, California, Florida, Georgia, Illinois, Massachusetts, New York, Rhode Island, and Texas. He has also testified before federal government agencies, including the Federal Trade Commission (FTC) Federal Energy Regulatory Commission (FERC), as well as the Public Utilities Commission of Texas. Web site http://leslivingstone.com.

Richard P. Mandel is associate dean of the Undergraduate School and associate professor of law at Babson College, where he teaches a variety of courses in business law and taxation on the undergraduate, graduate, and executive education levels and has served as chair of the finance division and acting dean of the Undergraduate School. He is also of counsel to the law firm of Bowditch and Dewey, of Worcester, Framingham, and Boston, Massachusetts, where he specializes in the representation of growing businesses and their executives. Mr. Mandel has written a number of articles regarding legal issues encountered by small businesses. He holds an AB in government and meteorology from Cornell University and a JD from Harvard Law School.

Tracee Petrillo is director, MBA Center for Career Development, and assistant dean, F. W. Olin Graduate School of Business, Babson College. She has over 15 years of corporate and higher education experience. Prior to receiving her MBA at Babson in 2000, she had been in operations management, business development, and corporate sales in the hospitality industry working for organizations such as Disney, Doubletree, and Sheraton. After her Babson MBA, she worked at Keane Consulting Group as an operations consultant. She returned to Babson as program manager of the two-year MBA program in 2003. Subsequently she became the director of the office of program management before becoming assistant dean of the graduate school. During this time, she led the transition of the experiential learning function to the graduate school leading the corporate business development program for the experiential learning programs, and implemented new processes for both programs. In addition to her Babson MBA, she holds a BA degree from Union College. She is proficient in Spanish and German, and has traveled extensively, including time living abroad in both Germany and Spain. In Madrid, she studied at Sampere Language School.

Michael J. Riley is a professor at the University of Maryland University College, teaching MBAs. He is a board member of Church Mutual Insurance Company and chairs the audit committee of the Architect of the Capitol, an agency of the U.S. Congress. Previously, Dr. Riley earned his doctorate of business administration from Harvard University (1977), his MBA from the University of Southern California (1972), and his BS from the United States Naval Academy (1965). Dr. Riley has served as CFO of the United States Postal Service, CFO of Lee Enterprises, CFO of United Airlines, and treasurer of Michigan Bell Telephone Company. During his tenure, the Postal Service posted the largest increase in profits of any organization in the world (1995) and remained consistently profitable during the remainder of his service. He has consulted with companies, government agencies, and a major union. He has taught at Harvard University, Boston University, the University of Connecticut, the University of Michigan, and George Mason University.

His articles have appeared in major magazines and newspapers, including the *Wall Street Journal*. Dr. Riley began his career as a Navy pilot, earning the Air Medal for service in Vietnam.

Virginia Earll Soybel teaches financial accounting and financial statement analysis in both the graduate and undergraduate programs at Babson College. She earned her MBA and PhD at Columbia University and taught at the Amos Tuck School of Business at Dartmouth College before coming to Babson in 1995. Professor Soybel's research focuses on the effects of alternate reporting methods on corporate financial statements and ratios, the time series behavior of financial ratios, and the political process of accounting standard-setting. Her publications include articles in *Strategic Management Journal* and in the *Journal of Accounting and Public Policy*.

Craig A. Stephenson has been a member of the faculty at Babson College since 1997. He has experience in the CFO organizations of Phillips Petroleum, Texas Instruments, and Dell. He teaches in the undergraduate, graduate, and executive education programs, and he specializes in corporate finance and financial strategy. He has also been on the faculty at the University of Colorado, the University of Wisconsin, and MIT's Sloan School of Management. Professor Stephenson received his PhD from the University of Arizona, his MBA from the University of Texas, and his BS from the University of Colorado. He is also the recipient of an honorary degree from the Babson College graduating class of 2004, awarded to the undergraduate professor of the year. He is a member of the Institute of Management Accountants, and is a certified management accountant.

Andrew Zacharakis is the John H. Muller Jr. chair in entrepreneurship and the director of the Babson College Entrepreneurship Research Conference, the leading academic conference on entrepreneurship worldwide. He previously served as chair of the entrepreneurship department at Babson College from 2003 to 2005 and as acting director of the Arthur M. Blank Center for Entrepreneurship at Babson College from 2003 to 2004. In addition, Dr. Zacharakis was the president of the Academy of Management, entrepreneurship division, an organization with 1,800 members, from 2004 to 2005. He also served as an associate editor at the *Journal of Small Business Management* (2003–2006). His primary research areas include the venture capital process and entrepreneurial growth strategies. Dr. Zacharakis is the co-author of five books, *The Portable MBA in Entrepreneurship, third edition; Business Plans That Work*; *How to Raise Capital*; *Entrepreneurship, The Engine of Growth*; and a forthcoming textbook titled *Entrepreneurship*. The editors of *Journal of Small Business Management* selected "Differing Perceptions of New Venture Failure" as the 1999 best article. His dissertation *The Venture Capital Investment Decision* received the 1995 Certificate of Distinction from the Academy of Management and Mr. Edgar F. Heizer, recognizing outstanding research in the field of new enterprise development. Dr. Zacharakis has been interviewed in newspapers nationwide, including the *Boston Globe*, the *Wall Street Journal*, and *USA Today*. He has also appeared on the *Bloomberg Small Business Report* and been interviewed on National Public Radio. He has taught seminars to leading corporations, such as Boeing, Met Life, Lucent, and Intel. He has also taught executives in countries worldwide, including Spain, Chile,

Costa Rica, Mexico, Australia, China, Turkey, and Germany. Dr. Zacharakis received a BS (finance/marketing) from the University of Colorado, an MBA (finance/international business) from Indiana University, and a PhD (strategy and entrepreneurship/cognitive psychology) from the University of Colorado. Professor Zacharakis actively consults with entrepreneurs and small business startups. His professional experience includes positions with The Cambridge Companies (investment banking/venture capital), IBM, and Leisure Technologies.

Part I

Financial Accounting

1

Understanding Financial Statements

Les Livingstone

What Are Financial Statements? A Case Study

Gail was applying for a bank loan to start her new business: Nutrimin, a retail store selling nutritional supplements, vitamins, and herbal remedies. She described her concept to Hal, a loan officer at the bank.

Hal: How much money will you need to get started?

Gail: I estimate $80,000 for the beginning inventory, plus $36,000 for store signs, shelves, fixtures, counters, and cash registers, plus $24,000 working capital to cover operating expenses for about two months. That's a total of $140,000 for the start-up.

Hal: How are you planning to finance the investment of $140,000 for the start-up?

Gail: I can put in $100,000 from my savings, and I'd like to borrow the remaining $40,000 from the bank.

Hal: Suppose the bank lends you $40,000 on a one-year note, at 15% interest, secured by a lien on the inventory. Let's put together projected financial statements from the figures you gave me. Your beginning balance sheet would look like what you see on the computer screen:

Nutrimin			
Projected Balance Sheet as of January 1, 20XX			
Assets		**Liabilities and Equity**	
Cash	$ 24,000	Bank loan	$ 40,000
Inventory	80,000		
Current assets	104,000	Current liabilities	40,000
Fixed assets:		Equity:	
Equipment	36,000	Owner capital	100,000
Total assets	$140,000	Liabilities and equity	$140,000

The left side shows Nutrimin's investment in assets. It classifies the assets into "current" (which means turning into cash in a year or less) and "noncurrent" (not turning into cash within a year). The right side shows how the assets are to be financed: partly by the bank loan and partly by your equity as the owner.

Gail: Now I see why it's called a "balance sheet." The money invested in assets must equal the financing available—it's like two sides of the same coin. Also, I see why the assets and liabilities are classified as "current" and "noncurrent"—the bank wants to see if the assets turning into cash in a year or less will provide enough cash to repay the one-year bank loan. Well, in a year there should be cash of $104,000. That's enough cash to pay off more than twice the $40,000 amount of the loan. I guess that guarantees approval of my loan!

Hal: We're not quite there yet. We need some more information. First, tell me: How much do you expect your operating expenses will be?

Gail: For year 1, I estimate as follows:

Store rent	$36,000	
Phone and utilities	14,400	
Assistants' salaries	40,000	
Interest on the loan	6,000	(15% on $40,000)
Total	$96,400	

Hal: We also have to consider depreciation on the store equipment. It probably has a useful life of 10 years. So each year it depreciates 10% of its cost of $36,000. That is $3,600 a year for depreciation. So operating expenses must be increased by $3,600 a year from $96,400 to $100,000. Now, moving on, how much do you think your sales will be this year?

Gail: I'm confident that sales will be $720,000 or even a little better. The wholesale cost of the items sold will be $480,000, giving a markup of $240,000—which is 33⅓% on the projected sales of $720,000.

Hal: Excellent! Let's organize this information into a projected income statement. We start with the sales, and then deduct the cost of the items sold to arrive at the gross profit. From the gross profit we deduct your operating expenses, giving us the income before taxes. Finally we deduct the income tax expense in order to get the famous "bottom line," which is the net income. Here is the projected income statement shown on my computer screen:

Nutrimin

Projected Income Statement for the Year Ending December 31, 20XX

Sales		$720,000
Less cost of goods sold		480,000
Gross profit		240,000
Less expenses		
Salaries	$40,000	
Rent	36,000	
Phone and utilities	14,400	
Depreciation	3,600	
Interest	6,000	100,000
Income before taxes		140,000
Income tax expense (40%)		56,000
Net income		$ 84,000

Gail, this looks very good for your first year in a new business. Many business start-ups find it difficult to earn income in their first year. They do well just to limit their losses and stay in business. Of course, I'll need to carefully review all your sales and expense projections with you, in order to make sure that they are realistic. But first, do you have any questions about the projected income statement?

Gail: I understand the general idea. But what does "gross profit" mean?

Hal: It's the usual accounting term for sales less the amount that your suppliers charged you for the goods that you sold to your customers. In other words, it represents your markup from the wholesale cost you paid for goods to the price for which you sold those goods to your customers. It is called "gross profit" because your operating expenses have to be deducted from it. In accounting, the word *gross* means "before deductions." For example, "gross sales" means sales before deducting goods returned by customers. Sales after deducting goods returned by customers are referred to as "net sales." In accounting, the word *net* means "after deductions." So, "gross profit" means income before deducting operating expenses. By the same token, "net income" means income after deducting operating expenses and income taxes. Now, moving along, we are ready to figure out your projected balance sheet at the end of your first year in business. But first, I need to ask you: How much cash do you plan to draw out of the business as your compensation?

Gail: My present job pays $76,000 a year. I'd like to keep the same standard of compensation in my new business this coming year.

Hal: Let's see how that works out after we've completed the projected balance sheet at the end of year 1. Here it is on my computer screen:

		Nutrimin		
		Projected Balance Sheet as of December 31, 20XX		
Assets			**Liabilities and Equity**	
Cash		$ 35,600	Bank loan	$ 40,000
Inventory		80,000		
Current assets		115,600	Current liabilities	40,000
Fixed assets:			Equity:	
Equipment	$36,000		Capital: Jan. 1	100,000
Less depreciation	3,600		Add net income	84,000
Net equipment	$32,400	32,400	Less drawings	(76,000)
			Capital: Dec. 31	108,000
Total assets		$148,000	Liabilities and equity	$148,000

Gail, let's go over this balance sheet together. It has changed, compared to the balance sheet as of January 1. On the "Liabilities and Equity" side of the balance sheet, the net income of $84,000 has increased capital to $184,000 (because earning income adds to the owner's capital), and deducting drawings of $76,000 has reduced capital to $108,000 (because drawings take capital out of the business). On the "Assets" side, notice that the equipment now has a year of depreciation deducted, which writes it down from the original $36,000 to a net (there's that word "net" again) $32,400 after depreciation. The equipment had an expected useful life of

10 years, now reduced to a remaining life of nine years. Last, but not least, notice that the cash has increased by only $11,600 from $24,000 at the beginning of the year to $35,600 at year-end. This leads to a problem: The bank loan of $40,000 is due for repayment on December 31. But there is only $35,600 of cash available on December 31. How can the loan be paid off when there is not enough cash to do so?

Gail: I see the problem. But I think it's bigger than just paying off the loan. The business will also need to keep about $25,000 cash on hand to cover two months' operating expenses and income taxes. So, with $40,000 to repay the loan, plus $25,000 for operating expenses, the cash requirements add up to $65,000. But there is only $35,600 cash on hand. This leaves a cash shortage of almost $30,000 ($65,000 less $35,600). Do you think that will force me to cut down my drawings by $30,000, from $76,000 to $46,000? Here I am, opening my own business, and it looks as if I have to go back to what I was earning five years ago!

Hal: That's one way to do it. But here's another way that you might like better. After your suppliers get to know you, and do business with you for a few months, you can ask them to open credit accounts for Nutrimin. If you get the customary 30-day credit terms, then your suppliers will be financing one month's inventory. That amounts to one-twelfth of your $480,000 annual cost of goods sold, or $40,000. This $40,000 will more than cover the cash shortage of $30,000.

Gail: That's a perfect solution! Now, can we see how the balance sheet would look in this case?

Hal: Sure. When you pay off the bank loan, it vanishes from the balance sheet. It is replaced by accounts payable of $40,000. Then the balance sheet looks like this:

Nutrimin				
Projected Balance Sheet as of December 31, 20XX				
Assets			**Liabilities and Equity**	
Cash		$ 35,600	Accounts payable	$ 40,000
Inventory		80,000		
Current assets		115,600	Current liabilities	40,000
Fixed assets:			Equity:	
Equipment	$36,000		Capital: Jan. 1	100,000
Less depreciation	3,600		Add net income	84,000
Net equipment	$32,400	32,400	Less drawings	(76,000)
			Capital: Dec. 31	108,000
Total assets		$148,000	Liabilities and equity	$148,000

Now the cash position looks a lot better. But it hasn't been entirely solved: there is still a gap between the accounts payable of $40,000 and the cash of $35,600. So, you will need to cut your drawings by about $5,000 in year 1. But that's still much better than the cut of $30,000 that had seemed necessary before. In year 2, the bank loan will be gone, so the interest expense of $6,000 will be saved. Then you can use $5,000 of this savings to restore your drawings back up to $76,000 again.

Gail: That's good news. I'm beginning to see how useful projected financial statements are for business planning. Can we look at the revised projected balance sheet now?

Hal: Of course. Here it is:

Nutrimin

Projected Balance Sheet as of December 31, 20XX

Assets			Liabilities and Equity	
Cash		$ 40,600	Accounts payable	$ 40,000
Inventory		80,000		
Current assets		120,600	Current liabilities	40,000
Fixed assets:			Equity:	
Equipment	$36,000		Capital: Jan. 1	100,000
Less depreciation	3,600		Add net income	84,000
Net equipment	$32,400	32,400	Less drawings	(71,000)
			Capital: Dec. 31	113,000
Total assets		$153,000	Liabilities and equity	$153,000

As we see, cash is increased by $5,000 to $40,600—which is sufficient to pay the accounts payable of $40,000. Drawings are decreased by $5,000 to $71,000, which provided the $5,000 increase in cash.

Gail: Thanks. That makes sense. I really appreciate everything you've taught me about financial statements.

Hal: I'm happy to help. But there is one more financial statement to discuss. A full set of financial statements consists of more than the balance sheet and the income statement. It also includes a cash flow statement. Here is the projected cash flow statement:

Nutrimin

Projected Cash Flow Statement for the Year Ending December 31, 20XX

Sources of Cash

From operations:

Net income	$ 84,000
Add depreciation	3,600
Add increase in current liabilities	40,000
Total cash from operations (a)	$127,600

From financing:

Drawings	$(71,000) *Negative cash*
Bank loan repaid	(40,000) *Negative cash*
Net cash from financing (b)	(111,000) *Negative cash*
Total sources of cash (a + b)	$ 16,600 *($127,600 cash from operations less $111,000 negative cash from financing)*

Uses of Cash

Total uses of cash	0
Total sources less total uses of cash	$ 16,600 Net cash increase
Add cash at beginning of year	24,000
Cash at end of year	$ 40,600

Gail, do you have any questions about this cash flow statement?

Gail: Actually, it makes sense to me. I realize that there are only two sources that a business can tap in order to generate cash: internal (by earning income) and external (by obtaining cash from outside sources, such as bank loans). In our case the internal sources of cash are represented by the "Cash from Operations" section of the cash flow statement, and the external sources are represented by the "Cash from Financing" section of the cash flow statement. It happens that the "Cash from Financing" is negative, because no additional outside financing is received for the year 20XX, but cash payments are incurred for drawings and for repayment of the bank loan. I also understand that there are no "Uses of Cash" because no extra equipment was acquired. In addition, I can see that the total sources of cash less the total uses of cash must equal the net cash increase, which in turn is the cash at the end of the year less the cash at the beginning of the year. But I am puzzled by the "Cash from Operations" section of the cash flow statement. I can understand that earning income produces cash. However, why do we add back depreciation to the net income in order to calculate cash from operations?

Hal: This can be confusing, so let me try to explain as clearly as I can. Certainly net income increases cash, but first an adjustment has to be made in order to convert net income to a cash basis. Depreciation was deducted as an expense in figuring net income. So adding back depreciation to net income just reverses the charge for depreciation expense. We back it out because depreciation is *not* a cash outflow. Remember that depreciation represents just one year's use of the equipment. The cash outflow for purchasing the equipment was incurred back when the equipment was first acquired, and amounted to $36,000. The equipment cost of $36,000 is spread out over the 10-year life of the equipment at the rate of $3,600 per year, which we call depreciation expense. So, it would be double counting to recognize the $36,000 cash outflow for the equipment when it was originally acquired, and then to recognize it again a second time when it shows up as depreciation expense. We do not write a check to pay for depreciation each year, because it is not a cash outflow.

Gail: Thanks. Now I understand that depreciation is not a cash outflow. But I don't see why we also added back the increase in current liabilities to the net income in order to calculate cash from operations. Can you explain that to me?

Hal: Of course. The increase in current liabilities is caused by an increase in accounts payable. Accounts payable is amounts owed to our suppliers for our purchases of goods for resale in our business. Purchasing goods for resale from our suppliers on credit is not a cash outflow. The cash outflow occurs only when the goods are actually paid for by writing out checks to our suppliers. That is why we added back the increase in current liabilities to the net income in order to calculate cash from operations. In the future, the increase in current liabilities will, in fact, be paid in cash. But that will take place in the future, and is not a cash outflow in this year. Going back to the cash flow statement, notice that it ties in neatly with our balance sheet amount for cash. It shows how the cash at the beginning of the year plus the net cash increase equals the cash at the end of the year.

Gail: Now I get it. Am I right that you are going to review my projections and then I'll hear from you about my loan application?

Hal: Yes, I'll be back to you in a few days. By the way, would you like a printout of the projected financial statements to take with you?

Gail: Yes, please. I really appreciate your putting them together and explaining them to me. I picked up some financial skills that will be very useful to me as an aspiring entrepreneur.

Points to Remember about Financial Statements

When Gail arrived home, she carefully reviewed the projected financial statements, and then made notes about what she had learned.

1. The basic form of the balance sheet is Assets = Liabilities + Owner Equity.

2. Assets are the expenditures made for items such as inventory and equipment that are needed to operate the business. The liabilities and owner equity reflect the funds that financed the expenditures for the assets.

3. Balance sheets show the financial position of a business at a given moment of time.

4. Balance sheets change as transactions are recorded.

5. Every transaction is an exchange, and both sides of each transaction are recorded. For example, when a bank loan is made, there is an increase in cash, which is matched by an increase in a liability entitled "Bank loan." When a bank loan is repaid, there is a decrease in cash, which is matched by a decrease in a liability entitled "Bank loan." After every transaction, the balance sheet stays in balance.

6. Income increases owner equity, and drawings decrease owner equity.

7. The income statement shows how the income for the period was earned.

8. The basic form of the income statement is:
   a. Sales − Cost of Goods Sold = Gross Income.
   b. Gross Income − Expenses = Net Income.

9. The income statement is simply a detailed explanation of the increase in owner equity represented by net income. It shows how the owner equity increased from the beginning of the year to the end of the year on account of the net income.

10. Net income contributes to cash from operations, after it has been adjusted to a cash basis.

11. Not all expenses are cash outflows: for instance, depreciation.

12. Changes in current assets (except cash) and current liabilities are not cash outflows or inflows, respectively, in the period under consideration. They represent future, rather than present, cash flows.

13. Cash can be generated internally by operations, or externally from outside sources such as lenders (or equity investors).

14. The cash flow statement is simply a detailed explanation of how cash at the start developed into cash at the end by virtue of cash inflows, generated internally and externally, less cash outflows.

15. As previously noted:
    a. The income statement is an elaboration of the change in owner equity in the balance sheet caused by earning income.
    b. The cash flow statement is an elaboration of the balance sheet change in beginning and ending cash.
        Therefore, all three financial statements are interrelated, or, to use the technical term, "articulated." They are mutually consistent, and that is why they are referred to as a "set" of financial statements. The three-piece set consists of a balance sheet, income statement, and cash flow statement.
16. A set of financial statements can convey much valuable information about the enterprise to anyone who knows how to analyze financial statements. This information goes to the core of the organization's business strategy and the effectiveness of its management.

While Gail was making her notes, Hal was carefully analyzing the Nutrimin projected financial statements in order to make his recommendation to the bank's loan committee about the Nutrimin loan application. He paid special attention to the cash flow statement, keeping handy the bank's guidelines on cash flow analysis, which included issues such as the following:

- Is cash from operations positive? Is it growing over time? Is it keeping pace with growth in sales? If not, why not?
- Are cash withdrawals by owners only a small portion of cash from operations? If cash withdrawals by owners are a large share of cash from operations, then the business is conceivably being milked of cash, and may not be able to finance its future growth.
- Of the total sources of cash, how much is being internally generated by operations versus obtained from outside sources? Normally, it is wiser to rely more on internally generated cash for growth than on external financing.
- Of the outside financing, how much is derived from equity investors and how much is borrowed money? Normally, it is preferable to rely more on equity than on debt financing.
- What kinds of assets is the company acquiring with the cash being expended? Is it likely that that these asset expenditures will be profitable? How long will it take for these assets to repay their cost, and then to earn a reasonable return?

Hal reflected carefully on these issues, and then finalized his recommendation, which was to approve the loan. It turned out that the bank's loan committee accepted Hal's recommendation, and even went further. They authorized Hal to tell Gail that—if she met all of her responsibilities in regard to the loan throughout the year—the bank would renew the loan at the end of the year and even increase the amount. Hal called Gail with the good news. Their conversation included the following dialogue:

Hal: In order to renew the loan, the bank will ask you for new projected financial statements for the subsequent year. Also, the loan agreement will want you to submit financial statements for the year just past—that is, not projected, but actual financial statements. The bank will require that these actual financial statements have been reviewed by an independent CPA.

Gail: Let me be sure I understand: Projected financial statements are forward-looking, whereas actual financial statements are backward-looking. Is that correct?

Hal: Yes, that's right.

Gail: Next, what is an independent CPA?

Hal: As you probably know, a CPA is a certified public accountant, a professional trained in finance and accounting, and licensed by the state. *Independent* means a CPA who is not an employee of yours, or a relative. It means someone in public practice in a CPA firm. In other words, it is someone outside, objective and unbiased.

Gail: And what does *reviewed* mean?

Hal: Good question. CPAs offer three levels of service relating to financial statements:

1. An *audit* is a thorough in-depth examination of the financial statements and tests of the supporting records. The result is an audit report, which states whether the financial statements are free of material misstatements (whether caused by error or by fraud). A "clean" audit report provides assurance that the financial statements are free of material misstatements. A "modified" report gives no such assurance, and is cause for concern. Financial professionals always read the auditor's report first, before even looking at any financial statement, in order to see if the report is clean. If it is not clean, there is no assurance that the financial statements are free of material misstatements. The auditor is a watchdog, and this watchdog barks by issuing a modified audit report. By law, all companies that have publicly traded securities must have their financial statements audited, as a protection to investors, creditors, and other financial statement users. Private companies are not required by law to have audits. But sometimes audits are required for private companies by agreement with particular investors or creditors. An audit provides the highest level of assurance that a CPA can provide. Audits are also the most expensive level of service. There are less expensive and less thorough levels of service, such as the following.

2. A *review* is a less extensive, and less expensive, level of financial statement inspection by a CPA. Since it is less extensive and less expensive, it provides a lower level of assurance that the financial statements are free of material misstatements.

3. Finally, there is the lowest level of service, which is called a *compilation*, where the outside CPA puts together the financial statements from the client company's books and records but does not examine them in much depth. A compilation provides the least assurance and is the least expensive level of service.

So the bank is asking you for the middle level of assurance when it requires a review by an independent CPA. Banks usually require a review from borrowers that are smaller private businesses.

Gail: Thanks. That makes it very clear.

We now leave Gail and Hal to their successful loan transaction, and move on.

Financial Statements: Who Uses Them and Why

Here is a brief list of who uses financial statements and why. This list gives only 14 examples, and is by no means complete.

1. Existing equity investors and lenders, to monitor their investments and to evaluate the performance of management.
2. Prospective equity investors and lenders, to decide whether to invest.
3. Investment analysts, money managers, and stockbrokers to make buy/sell/hold recommendations to their clients.
4. Rating agencies (such as Moody's Investors Service, Standard & Poor's, and Fitch Ratings), to assign credit ratings, or Dun & Bradstreet, to obtain business information reports.
5. Major customers and suppliers, to evaluate the financial strength and staying power of the company as a dependable resource for their business.
6. Labor unions, to gauge how much of a pay increase a company is able to afford in upcoming labor negotiations.
7. The board of directors, to review the performance of management.
8. Management, to assess its own performance.
9. Corporate raiders, to seek hidden value in companies with underpriced stock.
10. Competitors, to benchmark their own financial results.
11. Potential competitors, to assess how profitable it may be to enter an industry.
12. Government agencies responsible for taxing, regulating, or investigating the company.
13. Politicians, lobbyists, issue groups, consumer advocates, environmentalists, think tanks, foundations, media reporters, and others who are supporting or opposing any particular issue.
14. Actual or potential joint venture partners, franchisors or franchisees, and other business interests that have a reason to be informed about the company and its financial situation.

This brief list shows how many people use and rely on financial statements for a large variety of business purposes. It shows how important financial statements are in business.

It also shows how essential it is to master the understanding, analysis, and use of financial statements in order to be successful in the business world.

Financial Statement Format

Financial statements have a standard format. This format is similar whether an enterprise is as small as Nutrimin or as large as a major corporation. For example, a recent set of financial statements for a large public corporation can be summarized (in millions of dollars) as follows:

Income Statement

Years Ended June 30	XXX1	XXX2	XXX3
Revenue	$15,262	$19,747	$22,956
Cost of revenue	2,460	2,814	3,002
Research and development	2,601	2,970	3,775
Other expenses	3,787	4,035	5,242
Total expenses	$ 8,848	$ 9,819	$12,019
Operating income	$ 6,414	$ 9,928	$10,937
Investment income	703	1,963	3,338
Income before income taxes	7,117	11,891	14,275
Income taxes	2,627	4,106	4,854
Net income	$ 4,490	$ 7,785	$ 9,421

Note what this income statement tells us:

- Revenue increased each year, by $4,485 in XXX2 and by $3,209 in XXX3. These increases are good news, but note that the amount of increase has dropped in year XXX3.

- Total expenses have also increased each year, but by a smaller amount than revenue.

- As a result, net income increased each year, by $3,295 in XXX2 and by $1,636 in XXX3. Again, this is good news, but note that the amount of increase has dropped in year XXX3.

Cash Flow Statement

Years Ended June 30	XXX1	XXX2	XXX3
Operations			
Net income	$ 4,490	$ 7,785	$ 9,421
Adjustments to convert net income to a cash basis	3,943	5,352	4,540
Cash from operations	$ 8,433	$ 13,137	$ 13,961
Financing			
Stock repurchased, net	$(1,509)	$ (1,600)	$ (2,651)
Stock warrants sold	538	766	472
Preferred stock dividends	(28)	(28)	(13)
Cash from financing	$ (999)	$ (862)	$ (2,192)
Investing			
Additions to property and equipment	$ (656)	$ (583)	$ (879)
Net additions to Investments	(6,616)	(10,608)	(11,048)
Net cash invested	$(7,272)	$(11,191)	$(11,927)
Net change in cash	162	1,084	(158)

Note what this cash flow statement tells us:

- Cash from operations increased each year, by $4,704 in XXX2 and by $824 in XXX3. These increases are good news, but note that the amount of increase has dropped in year XXX3.

- Cash from financing is negative each year. The corporation has not increased its outside financing, but rather has reduced it—mainly by repurchasing its own stock.

- Net cash invested increased each year, by $3,919 in XXX2 and by $736 in XXX3. Again, this is good news, because investment is needed to grow the company. But note that the amount of increase has dropped in year XXX3.

- Cash from operations has been sufficient to provide for the company's investment needs, and even to reduce outside financing. That shows a company with sufficient growth and profitability to keep investing for further growth. It generates sufficient cash from operations to cover all investment needs while also reducing outside financing.

Balance Sheet		
Years Ended June 30	**XXX2**	**XXX3**
Current Assets		
Cash and equivalents	$ 4,975	$ 4,846
Short-term investments	12,261	18,952
Accounts receivable	2,245	3,250
Other	2,221	3,260
Total current assets	$21,702	$30,308
Property and equipment, net	$ 1,611	$ 1,903
Investments	15,312	19,939
Total fixed assets	$16,923	$21,842
Total assets	$38,625	$52,150
Current Liabilities		
Accounts payable	$ 874	$ 1,083
Other	7,928	8,672
Total current liabilities	8,802	9,755
Noncurrent liabilities	1,385	1,027
Total liabilities	$10,187	$10,782
Preferred stock	$ 980	
Common stock	13,844	$23,195
Retained earnings	13,614	18,173
Total equity	$28,438	$41,368
Total liabilities and equity	$38,625	$52,150

Note what this balance sheet tells us:

- This company grew its total assets by $13,525, from $38,625 to $52,150.
- But total liabilities increased only by $595, from $10,187 to $10,782.

- Therefore net assets grew by $13,525 less $595, which is $12,930.
- This $12,930 is the same amount by which total equity increased from $28,438 to $41,368, because, as we know: Total Assets = Total Liabilities + Owner Equity.

You may have observed that there are only two years of balance sheets but three years of income statements and cash flow statements. This is because these public company financial statements were obtained from filings with the U.S. Securities and Exchange Commission (SEC), and the SEC requirements for corporate annual report filings are two years of balance sheets, plus three years of income statements and cash flow statements.

These corporate financial statements contain numbers very much larger than those for Nutrimin. But there is no difference in the general format of these two sets of financial statements.

Guide to SEC Filings

The SEC requires all public companies in the United States to disclose certain financial information in filings with the SEC, which can be viewed online. The main filings include:

- *Form 8-K.* Disclosure of significant financial events—for example, resignation or termination of auditor, a new borrowing of material amount, a material merger or acquisition, or a material divestment.
- *Form 10-Q.* Quarterly financial statements.
- *Form 10-K.* Annual report for the fiscal year. Typical Table of Contents:

  Item 1. Brief Description of Company Business

  Item 1A. Risk Factors

  Item 1B. Unresolved Staff Comments

  Item 2. Properties

  Item 3. Legal Proceedings

  Item 4. Submission of Matters to a Vote of Security Holders

  Item 5. Market for Registrant's Common Equity, Related Stockholder Matters and Issuer, Purchases of Equity Securities

  Item 6. Selected Financial Data

  Item 7. Management's Discussion and Analysis of Financial Condition and Results of Operations (often abbreviated as MD&A)

  Item 7A. Quantitative and Qualitative Disclosures about Market Risk

  Item 8. Financial Statements and Supplementary Data

  Item 9. Changes in and Disagreements with Accountants on Accounting and Financial Disclosure

  Item 9A. Controls and Procedures

  Item 9B. Other Information

  Item 10. Directors and Executive Officers of the Registrant

  Item 11. Executive Compensation

Item 12. Security Ownership of Certain Beneficial Owners and Management and Related Stockholder Matters

Item 13. Certain Relationships and Related Transactions

Item 14. Principal Accountant Fees and Services

Item 15. Exhibits and Financial Statement Schedules

The Notes to the Financial Statements

In addition to the three financial statements, there are the notes to the financial statements, which are regarded as an integral part of the three statements. (See Exhibit 1.1.)

Financial Accounting Standards

It is no accident that financial statements have a standard format. There are financial accounting standards that require uniformity in financial statement presentation, in order that financial statements can be compared:

- From period to period for the same organization.
- From organization to organization for the same period.

This comparability is essential because accounting is the language of business, so it is important that all businesses use the same language. How is this uniformity established?

Since 1973, the Financial Accounting Standards Board (FASB) has been the designated organization in the private sector for establishing standards in financial accounting

Exhibit 1.1 Notes to financial statements.

The Notes provide detailed information about the items in the financial statements and also supplementary information. This detailed and supplementary information is of substantial value and importance. It includes details such as the following:

1. Summary of Significant Accounting Policies
2. Recent Accounting Developments
3. Acquisition of Certain Assets
4. Commitments
5. Accrued Liabilities
6. Revolving Credit Facility
7. Long-Term Debt
8. Leases
9. Project Early Departure
10. Derivative and Financial Instruments
11. Comprehensive Income
12. Common Stock
13. Stock Plans
14. Employee Retirement Plans
15. Income Taxes
16. Net Income per Share
17. Contingencies

and reporting. Those standards govern the preparation of financial reports, and are known as generally accepted accounting principles (GAAP). They are officially recognized as authoritative by the Securities and Exchange Commission (SEC) (Financial Reporting Release No. 1, Section 101, and reaffirmed in its April 2003 Policy Statement) and the American Institute of Certified Public Accountants (AICPA) (Rule 203, Rules of Professional Conduct, as amended May 1973 and May 1979). The main purpose of GAAP is to make financial statements uniform and comparable in form and content from organization to organization and from period to period. Such standards are essential to the efficient functioning of the economy, because investors, creditors, auditors, and others rely on credible, transparent, and comparable financial information.

The Securities and Exchange Commission has statutory authority to establish financial accounting and reporting standards for publicly held companies under the Securities Exchange Act of 1934. Throughout its history, however, the SEC's policy has been to rely on the private sector for this function to the extent that the private sector demonstrates ability to fulfill the responsibility in the public interest.

From GAAP to IFRS

While GAAP has served the United States for many years, other countries have developed their own accounting standards. With increasing globalization it becomes more important to be able to read, understand, and compare financial statements for firms in many different countries. In order to do so it is necessary for the various financial accounting standards of different countries to be replaced with a single set of worldwide financial accounting standards. That development is currently proceeding under the name of International Financial Reporting Standards (IFRS).

Adoption of IFRS has already taken place in more than 100 countries, including the European Union. In addition, China, Japan, India, and Canada are all committed to following the EU's lead in 2011. The SEC is planning to phase IFRS into the U.S. system as a replacement for GAAP in stages over the next few years. This is not a simple task, and will encounter substantial difficulties and require major adjustments. In essence, GAAP and IFRS are based on very different and conflicting concepts.

GAAP is a vast collection of rules that set out in detail how financial information must be compiled and disclosed in financial statements. In brief, GAAP is rule-based. In contrast, IFRS is much less detailed and much less specific. It lays out broad general principles, and leaves the specific details to the discretion of users, so long as they keep within the broad general principles. In brief, IFRS is principles-based rather than rules-based. As a result, there are many disagreements and disputes between proponents of GAAP and proponents of IFRS. However, while the resolutions of these disputes remain unclear, one thing seems absolutely certain: In a few years IFRS will replace U.S. GAAP.

Summary and Conclusions

Financial statements contain critically important business information, and are used for many different purposes by many different parties inside the business and outside of the business. Clearly, all successful businesspeople should have a good basic understanding of financial statements and of the main financial ratios, such as profit margin, asset turnover, return on assets, and return on equity. Beyond the present chapter, this book contains further information and explanations relating to financial statements:

Chapter 2: Analyzing Financial Statements

Chapter 3: Analyzing Business Earnings

Chapter 10: The Integrity of Financial Reporting

Downloadable Resources for this chapter available at www.wiley.com/go/portablembainfinance

Understanding Financial Statements Balance Sheet: Liabilities + Equity

Internet Links

You can access an excellent 45-minute tutorial on understanding financial statements at www.baruch.cuny.edu/tutorials/statements/.

Here are short videos about each of the financial statements:

"What Is a Balance Sheet?"
www.youtube.com/watch?v=v_EpPu5tiXY&feature=related

"What Is an Income Statement?"
www.youtube.com/watch?v=KqNEvgT71l8& feature=related

"What Is a Cash Flow Statement?"
www.youtube.com/watch?v=-eietCf5nNI& feature=related

The following Web site provides a great deal of information on financial statements and related topics, plus many useful links: http://CPAclass.com/arp/.

Guidance on understanding financial statements from IBM Corporation is available at www.ibm.com/investor/tools/guides.phtml.

Notes and exercises on financial and managerial accounting are at www.middlecity.com/index.shtml.

For Further Reading

Horngren, Charles T., Gary L. Sundem, John A. Elliott, and Donna Philbrick, *Introduction to Financial Accounting*, Charles T. Horngren Series in Accounting (Upper Saddle River, NJ: Prentice-Hall, 2005).

Ingram, Robert W., and Thomas L. Albright, *Financial Accounting: Information for Decisions* (Florence, KY: South-Western College Publishing, 2007).

Stickney, Clyde P., and Roman L. Weil, *Financial Accounting: An Introduction to Concepts, Methods and Uses* (Florence, KY: South-Western College Publishing, 2006).

Weygandt, Jerry J., Donald E. Kieso, and Paul D. Kimmel, *Accounting Principles*, 7th ed., with PepsiCo Annual Report (Hoboken, NJ: John Wiley & Sons, 2004).

Wild, John J., *Financial Accounting: Information for Decisions*, 4th ed. (New York: McGraw-Hill, 2006).

Analyzing Financial Statements

Les Livingstone

How to Analyze Financial Statements

Imagine that you are a health professional, such as a nurse or a physician, and that you work in the emergency room of a busy hospital. Patients arrive with all kinds of serious injuries or illnesses, some barely alive or perhaps even dead. Others arrive with less urgent problems, or minor complaints, or only vaguely suspected ailments. Your training and experience have taught you to perform a quick triage, in order to identify and prioritize the most endangered patients by means of vital signs, such as respiration, pulse, blood pressure, temperature, and reflexes. Next, there follows a more detailed diagnosis, based on appropriate medical tests.

We check the financial health of a company in much the same fashion, by analyzing the financial statements. The vital signs are tested mostly by various financial ratios, which are calculated from the financial statements. The financial vital signs can be classified into three main categories:

1. Short-term liquidity.
2. Long-term solvency.
3. Profitability.

Next, we explain each of these three categories in turn.

Short-Term Liquidity

In the emergency room, the first question is: Can this patient survive? By the same token, the first issue in analyzing financial statements is: Can this company survive? Business survival means being able to pay the bills, meet the payroll, and come up with the rent. In other words, is there enough liquidity to provide the cash needed to pay the current financial commitments? "Yes" means survival. "No" means bankruptcy. The importance and urgency of this question are the reasons why current assets (which are expected to turn into cash within a year) and current liabilities (which are expected to be paid in cash within a year) are shown separately on the balance sheet. Net current assets (current assets less current liabilities) are known as *working capital*. Most businesses cannot operate without positive working capital. Therefore, the question of whether current assets exceed current liabilities is crucial.

When current assets are greater than current liabilities, there is sufficient liquidity to enable the enterprise to survive. However, when current liabilities are greater than current assets, the enterprise may well be in imminent danger of bankruptcy. The financial ratio used to measure this risk is current assets divided by current liabilities, and is known as the *current ratio*. It is expressed as (for example) 2.5 to 1 or 2.5:1 or just 2.5. A current ratio greater than 1 is the bare minimum to indicate survival, but it lacks any margin of safety. We will explain why financial ratios are only rough approximations, not precise indicators, and why it is therefore important to allow for a reasonable margin of safety, or cushion. For this reason, a current ratio of 1 is not at all impressive evidence of liquidity. In most cases, from a practical point of view, a current ratio of 2 or more just begins to provide credible evidence of liquidity. An example of a current ratio can be found in the current sections of a balance sheet shown earlier in Chapter 1:

Nutrimin			
Selected Sections of Projected Balance Sheet as of December 31, 20XX			
	Assets	**Liabilities and Equity**	
Cash	$ 40,600	Accounts payable	$40,000
Inventory	80,000		
Current assets	$120,600	Current liabilities	$40,000

The current ratio is $120,600 divided by $40,000, which is a ratio of about 3. This is only a rough approximation for several reasons. One reason is that a company can, quite legitimately, improve its current ratio. In the Nutrimin example, let us assume that the business wanted its balance sheet to reflect a higher current ratio. One perfectly legitimate way to do so would be to pay off $20,000 on the bank loan on December 31. This would reduce current assets to $100,600 and also reduce current liabilities to $20,000. Then the current ratio is changed to $100,600 divided by $20,000, which is a ratio of about 5. By totally legitimate means, the current ratio has been improved from 3 to 5. This technique is widely used by companies who want to put their best foot forward in the balance sheet, and it always works, provided that the current ratio was greater than 1 to start with.

Current assets usually include:

- Cash and cash equivalents.
- Securities expected to become liquid by maturing or being sold within a year.
- Accounts receivable (which Nutrimin did not have, because it did not sell to its customers on credit).
- Inventory.

Current liabilities usually include:

- Accounts payable.
- Other current payables, such as taxes, wages, or insurance.
- The current portion of long-term debt.

Some items included in current assets need further explanation. These are:

- Cash equivalents are near-cash securities, such as U.S. Treasury bills maturing in three months or less.

- Accounts receivable are amounts owed by customers, and should be reported on the balance sheet at "realizable value," which means at the amount reasonably expected to be collected in cash. Any accounts whose collectability is in doubt must be reduced to realizable value by deducting an allowance for doubtful debts.

- Inventories in some cases may not be liquid in a crisis situation (except at fire sale prices). This condition is especially likely for goods of a perishable, seasonal, high-fashion, or trendy nature, or items subject to technological obsolescence, such as computers. Since inventory can readily lose value, it must be reported on the balance sheet at the "lower of cost or market value." This means that the amount reported for inventory on the balance sheet is what it cost to acquire (including freight and insurance) or—if lower—the cost of replacement or the expected selling price less costs of sale.

Despite these requirements designed to report inventory at a realistic amount, inventory is regarded as an asset subject to inherent liquidity risk, particularly in difficult economic times, and especially for items that are subject to obsolescence, theft, or deterioration. For these reasons, the current ratio is often modified by excluding inventory, so that the modified ratio is current assets excluding inventory, divided by current liabilities. This modified ratio is known as the *quick ratio* or the *acid test* ratio. In the case of Nutrimin, it is $40,600 divided by $40,000, which is about 1, as of December 31. This indicates that Nutrimin has a barely adequate quick ratio, with no margin of safety at all. It is a red flag, or warning signal.

The current ratio and the quick ratio deal with all or most of the current assets and current liabilities. There are also short-term liquidity ratios that focus more narrowly on individual components of current assets and current liabilities.

These are the *turnover ratios*, which consist of:

- Accounts receivable turnover.
- Inventory turnover.
- Accounts payable turnover.

Turnover is a key factor in liquidity. Faster turnover allows a company to do more business without increasing assets. Increased turnover means that less cash is tied up in assets, and that improves liquidity. By the same token, slower turnover of liabilities conserves cash and thereby increases liquidity. Or, more simply, achieving better turnover of working capital can significantly improve liquidity. Therefore, turnover ratios provide valuable information. The working capital turnover ratios are described next.

Accounts Receivable Turnover

For accounts receivable turnover, the calculation is as follows:

$$\text{Accounts Receivable Turnover} = \frac{\text{Credit Sales}}{\text{Accounts Receivable}}$$

So, if credit sales are $120,000 and accounts receivable are $30,000, then:

$$\text{Accounts Receivable Turnover} = \frac{\$120,000}{\$30,000} = 4$$

This shows that, on average, accounts receivable turn over four times a year, or every 91 days.

The 91-day turnover period is found by dividing a year, 365 days, by the accounts receivable turnover ratio of 4, to get the average of 91 days. This is how long on average it takes to collect accounts receivable. That is fine if our credit terms call for payment 90 days from invoice. But it is not fine if credit terms are 60 days, and it is alarming if credit terms are 30 days.

Accounts receivable, unlike vintage wines or antiques, do not improve with age. Accounts receivable turnover should be in line with credit terms, and it signals increasing danger to liquidity as turnover gets further out of line with credit terms.

Inventory Turnover

Inventory turnover is computed in the following manner:

$$\text{Inventory Turnover} = \frac{\text{Cost of Goods Sold}}{\text{Inventory}}$$

If cost of goods sold is $100,000 and inventory is $20,000, then:

$$\text{Inventory Turnover} = \frac{\$100,000}{\$20,000} = 5$$

This shows that, on average, inventory turns over five times a year, or about every 70 days.

In the case of accounts receivable turnover, the numerator was Credit Sales. But for inventory turnover, the numerator is Cost of Goods Sold. The reason is that both accounts receivable and sales are measured in terms of the selling price of the goods involved. That makes the accounts receivable turnover a consistent ratio where the numerator and the denominator are both expressed at selling prices, in an apples-to-apples manner. By the same token, inventory turnover is an apples-to-apples comparison, where the numerator, Cost of Goods Sold, and the denominator, Inventory, are both expressed in terms of the cost, not the selling price, of the goods.

In our example, the inventory turnover is 5, or about every 70 days. In the auto retailing industry or the furniture manufacturing industry, that would be an acceptable result. However, in the supermarket business or in gasoline retailing, it would be extremely unsatisfactory, in comparison with their norms of about 25 times a year, or roughly every two weeks. Inventory turnover is usually evaluated in terms of what is typical for the industry in question. Just as was the case for accounts receivable turnover, an inventory turnover ratio that is out of line is a red flag.

Accounts Payable Turnover

Accounts payable turnover is measured as follows:

$$\text{Accounts Payable Turnover} = \frac{\text{Cost of Goods Sold}}{\text{Accounts Payable}}$$

If cost of goods sold is \$100,000 and accounts payable is \$16,600, then:

$$\text{Accounts Payable Turnover} = \frac{\$100,000}{\$16,600} = \text{about } 6$$

This shows that, on average, accounts payable turn over six times a year, or around every 60 days.

Again, note the consistency of the numerator and denominator, which are both stated at the cost of the goods purchased. Accounts payable turnover is evaluated by comparison with industry norms. An accounts payable turnover that turns out to be appreciably faster than the industry norm is fine, provided that liquidity is satisfactory, because prompt payments to suppliers usually earn cash discounts, which, in turn, lower the cost of goods sold and thus lead to higher income. However, accounts payable turnover that is faster than the industry norm diminishes liquidity, and is therefore not wise when liquidity is tight. By the same token, accounts payable turnover that is slower than the industry norm enhances liquidity, and is therefore wise when liquidity is tight, but inadvisable when liquidity is fine, because it sacrifices cash discounts from suppliers and thus reduces the resulting income.

This concludes our survey of the ratios relating to short-term liquidity. By way of summary, the five ratios are:

1. The current ratio.
2. The quick, or acid test, ratio.
3. Accounts receivable turnover.
4. Inventory turnover.
5. Accounts payable turnover.

If these ratios are seriously deficient, our diagnosis may be complete. The subject business may be almost insolvent, and even desperate measures may be insufficient to revive it. In contrast, if these ratios are favorable, short-term liquidity does not appear to be threatened, and the financial doctor should proceed to the next set of tests, which measure long-term solvency.

However, it is worth noting that there are some rare exceptions to these guidelines. For example, large gas and electric utilities typically have current ratios of less than 1, and quick ratios of less than 0.5. This is due to exceptional characteristics of those utility companies:

- They usually require deposits before providing service to customers, and they can shut off service to customers who do not pay on time. Customers are reluctant to go without necessities such as gas and electricity, and therefore tend to pay their utility bills ahead of most other bills. These factors sharply reduce the risk of uncollectible accounts receivable for gas and electric utility companies.

- Inventories of gas and electric utility companies are not subject to much risk from changing fashion trends, deterioration, or obsolescence.

- Under regulation, gas and electric utility companies are steady, low-risk businesses, largely free from competition and consistently profitable.

- These reduced risks and increased predictability of gas and electric utility companies make short-term liquidity less crucial, and make safety margins less necessary. In turn, the ratios indicating short-term liquidity become less important. Short-term survival is not a significant concern for these businesses.

Long-Term Solvency

Long-term solvency focuses on a firm's ability to pay the interest and principal on its long-term debt. There are two commonly used ratios relating to servicing long-term debt. One ratio measures the ability to pay the interest, while the other reflects the ability to repay the principal.

The ratio for interest compares the amount of income available for paying interest with the amount of the interest expense. This ratio is called *interest coverage* or *times interest earned*.

The amount of income available for paying interest is simply earnings before interest and income taxes are paid (bear in mind that business interest expense is deductible for income tax purposes, and therefore income taxes are based on earnings after interest, otherwise known as earnings before income taxes). Earnings before both interest and taxes are known as EBIT.

$$\text{Interest Coverage or Times Interest Earned} = \frac{\text{EBIT}}{\text{Interest Expense}}$$

For instance, assume that EBIT is \$120,000 and interest expense is \$60,000. Then:

$$\text{Interest Coverage or Times Interest Earned} = \frac{\$120,000}{\$60,000} = 2$$

This shows that the subject business has EBIT sufficient to cover two times the interest expense. The cushion, or margin of safety, is therefore quite substantial. Whether or not the interest coverage ratio is acceptable depends on the industry. Different industries have different degrees of year-to-year fluctuations in EBIT. Interest coverage of two times may be satisfactory for a steady and mature firm in an industry with stable earnings, such as regulated gas and electricity supply. However, when the same industry experiences the uncertain forces of deregulation, earnings may become volatile, and interest coverage of 2 may prove to be inadequate. Also, in the more turbulent industries, such as movie studios and Internet retailers, interest coverage of 2 may be regarded as insufficient.

The long-term solvency ratio that reflects a firm's ability to repay principal on long-term debt is the *debt-to-equity ratio*. The long-term capital structure of a firm is made up principally of two types of financing: (1) long-term debt and (2) owner equity. There are some hybrid forms of financing that mix some characteristics of both debt and equity. But these hybrids usually can be classified as mainly debt or mainly equity in nature, so the distinction between debt and equity is normally clear.

The debt-to-equity relationship is usually measured as:

$$\text{Debt-to-Equity Ratio} = \frac{\text{Long-Term Debt}}{(\text{Long-Term Debt} + \text{Equity})}$$

If long-term debt is $150,000 and equity is $300,000, then:

$$\frac{\$150,000}{(\$150,000 + \$300,000)} = 33\frac{1}{3}\%$$

Long-term debt is frequently secured by liens on property, and has priority on payment of periodic interest and repayment of principal. In contrast, there is no priority for equity in regard to dividend payments or return of capital to owners. Holders of long-term debt have a high degree of security with respect to receiving full and punctual payments of interest and principal, but they are not entitled to receive any more than these fixed amounts. In good times or bad, that is all that is due to them. In consequence, they can expect the same income, whether the company's fortunes are good or bad. They have reduced their risk of loss in exchange for more certainty. Owners of equity enjoy no such certainty. They are entitled to nothing, except if and when any dividends might be declared, and, in the case of bankruptcy, to whatever funds might be left over after all obligations have been paid. Theirs is a totally at-risk investment. They prosper in good times, and suffer in bad times. They accept these risks, in the hope that in the long run gains will substantially exceed losses.

From the firm's point of view, long-term debt obligations are a burden that must be carried in times when incomes are low, or absent—or even worse, negative. But long-term debt obligations are a blessing when incomes are lush, since they receive no more than their fixed payments, even if incomes soar. The greater the proportion of long-term debt and the smaller the proportion of equity in the capital structure, the more the incomes of the equity holders will fluctuate according to how good or bad the times are. The proportion of long-term debt to equity is known as leverage.

The higher the proportion of long-term debt to equity, the more leveraged the firm is considered to be. The more leveraged the firm is, the more equity holders prosper in good times, and the worse they fare in bad times. It has been said that leverage is like alcohol, because it makes the good times better, but the bad times worse. Since increased leverage leads to increased volatility of incomes, increased leverage is regarded as an indicator of increased risk. A moderate degree of leverage is considered desirable. But excessive leverage is regarded as incurring an excessive degree of risk.

The debt-to-equity ratio is evaluated relative to the industry in question and to the customary volatility of earnings in that industry. For example, a debt-to-equity ratio of 80% would be considered conservative in banking (where leverage is customarily above 80%), but would be regarded as extremely risky for toy manufacturing or designer apparel (where earnings are volatile). The well-known "junk bonds" are an example of long-term debt securities where leverage is considered too high in relation to earnings volatility. It is the increased risk associated with junk bonds that explains their higher interest yields. This illustrates the general financial principle that the greater the risk, the higher the expected return.

In summary, the two ratios used to assess long-term solvency are:

1. Interest coverage.
2. Long-term debt to equity.

Next, we consider the ratios for analyzing profitability.

Profitability

Profitability is the lifeblood of a business. Businesses that earn incomes can survive, grow, and prosper. Businesses that incur losses cannot stay in operation, and will last only until their cash runs out. Therefore, in order to assess business viability, it is important to analyze profitability.

Analyzing profitability is usually done in two phases, which are:

- Profitability in relation to sales.
- Profitability in relation to investment.

Profitability in Relation to Sales

The analysis of profitability in relation to sales recognizes the fact that:

$$Income = Sales - Expenses$$

or, rearranging terms:

$$Sales = Expenses + Income$$

Therefore, expenses and income are measured in relation to their sum total, which is sales. The expenses, in turn, may be broken down by line item. As an example, we use the Chapter 1 Nutrimin income statement for the first year of operation, along with its statements for the second and third years.

Nutrimin			
Income Statements for Years Ended December 31			
	Year 1	**Year 2**	**Year 3**
Sales	$720,000	$800,000	$900,000
Less cost of goods sold	480,000	530,000	600,000
Gross profit	$240,000	$270,000	$300,000
Less expenses			
Salaries	$ 40,000	$ 49,600	$ 69,000
Rent	36,000	49,400	54,400
Phone and utilities	14,400	19,400	26,000
Depreciation	3,600	3,600	3,600
Interest	6,000	6,000	6,000
Total expenses	$100,000	$128,000	$159,000
Income before taxes	$140,000	$142,000	$141,000
Income tax expense (40%)	56,000	56,800	56,400
Net income	$ 84,000	$ 85,200	$ 84,600

These income statements show a steady increase in sales and gross profits each year. But, despite this favorable result, the net income has remained almost unchanged at from $84,000 to $85,200 for each year. It is not obvious from these income statements why this is the case. However, when expenses and income are converted to percentages of sales, it becomes much clearer. The income statements converted to percentages of sales are known as "common size" income statements, and are as follows:

Common Size Income Statements for Years Ended December 31

	Year 1	Year 2	Year 3	*Change Years 1–3*
Sales	100.0%	100.0%	100.0%	*0.0%*
Less cost of goods sold	66.7	66.2	66.7	*0.0*
Gross profit	33.3%	33.8%	33.3%	*0.0%*
Less expenses				
Salaries	5.6%	6.2%	7.7%	*2.1%*
Rent	5.0	6.2	6.0	*1.0*
Phone and utilities	2.0	2.4	2.9	*0.9*
Depreciation	0.5	0.4	0.4	*–0.1*
Interest	0.8	0.8	0.7	*–0.1*
Total expenses	13.9%	16.0%	17.7%	*3.8%*
Income before taxes	19.4%	17.8%	15.6%	*–3.8%*
Income tax expense (40%)	7.8	7.2	6.2	*–1.6*
Net Income	11.6%	10.6%	9.4%	*–2.2%*

From these percentage figures it is easy to see why the net income failed to increase, despite the substantial growth in sales and gross profit. The clear reason is that, relative to sales, total expenses rose by 3.8 percentage points, from 13.9% of sales in year 1 to 17.7% of sales in year 3. In particular, the increase in total expenses relative to sales was driven mainly by increases in salaries (2.1 percentage points), rent (1 percentage point), and phone and utilities (0.9 percentage point). As a result of the relative increases in these items of expense, the bad news is that income before taxes, relative to sales, fell by 3.8 percentage points from year 1 to year 3. The good news is that the drop in income before taxes caused a reduction of income tax expense, relative to sales, of 1.6 percentage points from year 1 to year 3. The net effect was a drop in net income, relative to sales, of 2.2 percentage points from year 1 to year 3.

This information is useful. It shows four things:

1. The profit stagnation is not related to sales or gross profit causes.
2. It is entirely due to the disproportionate increase in total expenses.
3. Specific causes are the expenses for salaries, rent, and phone and utilities.
4. Action to correct the profit slump requires an analysis of these particular expense categories.

The use of percentage of sales ratios is a simple but powerful technique for analyzing profitability. The main ratios that are generally used are:

- Gross profit.
- Operating expenses:
  - In total.
  - Individually.

- Selling, general, and administrative expenses (often called just SG&A).
- Operating income.
- Income before taxes.
- Net income.

The second category of profitability ratios is profitability in relation to investment.

Profitability in Relation to Investment

In order to earn profits, it is usually necessary to invest capital in items such as plant, equipment, inventory, or research and development. Up to this point we have analyzed profitability without considering invested capital. That was a useful simplification in the beginning. But, since profitability is highly dependent on the investment of capital, it is now time to bring invested capital into the analysis of profitability.

We start with the balance sheet. Recall that working capital is current assets less current liabilities. So we can simplify the balance sheet by including a single category for working capital in place of the separate categories for current assets and current liabilities. Here is an example of a simplified balance sheet:

Example Company

Simplified Balance Sheet as of December 31, 20XX

Assets		Liabilities and Equity	
Working capital	$ 40,000	Long-term debt	$ 30,000
Fixed assets, net	80,000	Equity	90,000
Total assets	$120,000	Liabilities and equity	$120,000

A simplified income statement for Example Company for the year 20XX is summarized next:

Income before interest and taxes (EBIT)	$36,000
Less interest expense	3,000
Income before income taxes	33,000
Less income taxes (40%)	13,200
Net income	$19,800

The first ratio we will consider is earnings before interest and taxes (EBIT, also known as operating profit) to total assets. This ratio is often referred to as return on total assets (ROTA), and it can be expressed as either before tax (which is usual) or after tax (which is less usual). From Example Company, the calculations are:

Return on Total Assets	Before Tax	After Tax
EBIT/Total Assets = $36,000/$120,000	30%	
EBI/Total Assets = $21,600/$120,000		18%

This ratio indicates the raw (or basic) earning power of the business. Raw earning power is independent of whether the assets are financed by equity or debt. This independence exists because of two facts:

1. The numerator (EBIT or EBI) is free of interest expense.
2. The denominator, Total Assets, is equal to total capital regardless of how much capital is equity and how much is debt.

Independence is important, because it allows the ratio to be measured and compared:

- For any business, from one period to another.
- For any period, from one business to another.

These comparisons remain valid, even if the debt-to-equity ratio may vary from one period to the next and from one business to another.

Now that we have measured basic earning power, regardless of the debt-to-equity ratio, our next step is to take the debt-to-equity ratio into consideration. First, it is important to note that long-term debt is normally a less expensive form of financing than equity for two reasons:

1. Dividends paid to stockholders are not a tax deduction for the paying company. But interest expense paid on long-term debt *is* deductible for tax purposes. Therefore the net after-tax cost of interest is reduced by the related tax deduction. But this is not the case for dividends, which are not deductible.
2. Debt is senior to equity, which means that debt obligations for interest and principal must be paid in full before making any payments on equity, such as dividends. This makes debt less risky than equity to the investors, and so debt holders are willing to accept a lower rate of return than holders of the more risky equity securities.

This can be seen from the simplified financial statements of Example Company. The interest of $3,000 on the long-term debt of $30,000 is 10% before tax. But, after the 40% tax deduction, the interest after tax is only $1,800 ($3,000 − 40% tax on $3,000), and this interest after tax of $1,800 represents an after-tax interest rate of 6% on the long-term debt of $30,000. In comparison, let us turn to rate of return on the equity. The return on the equity is the net income. The net income is $19,800, which represents a 22% rate of return on the equity of $90,000. This 22% rate of return is a financial ratio known as return on equity, sometimes abbreviated as ROE. Return on equity is an important and widely used financial ratio.

There is much more to be said about return on equity, but first it may be helpful to recap briefly the main points we have covered about profitability in relation to investment.

The EBIT of $36,000 represented a 30% return on total assets, before income tax, and this $36,000 was shared by three parties:

1. Long-term debt holders received interest of $3,000, representing an interest cost of 10% before income tax, and 6% after income tax.
2. Governments at city, state, and/or federal levels received income taxes of $13,200.
3. Stockholder equity increased by the net income of $19,800, which represented 22% return on equity.

If there had been no long-term debt, there would have been no interest expense. The EBIT of $36,000, less income tax at 40%, would provide net income of $21,600, which is larger than the prior net income of $19,800 by $1,800. This $1,800 represents the $3,000 amount of interest before tax, less 40% tax, which is $1,200. In the absence of long-term debt, the total assets would have been funded entirely by equity, which would have required equity to be $120,000. In turn, with net income of $21,600, the revised return on equity would be:

$$\frac{\text{Net Income}}{\text{Equity}} = \frac{\$21,600}{\$120,000} = 18\%$$

The increase in the return on equity from this 18% to 22% was attributable to the use of long-term debt. The long-term debt, after tax, had a cost of only 6% versus the return on assets, after tax, of 18%. When a business earns 18% after tax, it is profitable to borrow at 6% after tax. This, in turn, improves the return on equity, raising it from 18% to 22%, which illustrates the advantage of leverage: that a business earning 18% on assets can, with a little leverage, earn 22% on equity.

But what if EBIT is only $3,000? The entire $3,000 would be used up to pay the interest of $3,000 on the long-term debt. The net income would be $0, resulting in a 0% return on equity. This illustrates the disadvantage of leverage. Without long-term debt, the EBIT of $3,000, less 40% tax, would result in net income of $1,800. In turn, return on equity would be $1,800 divided by equity of $120,000, which is 1.5%. A return on equity of 1.5% may not be impressive, but it is certainly better than the 0% return on equity that prevailed with long-term debt.

Leverage is a fair-weather friend: It boosts return on equity when earnings are robust, but it depresses return on equity when earnings are poor. As previously mentioned, leverage makes the good times better, but the bad times worse. Therefore, it should be used in moderation, and in businesses with stable earnings. It should be used sparingly and cautiously in businesses with volatile earnings.

We have now described all of the main financial ratios, and they are summarized in Exhibit 2.1.

Using Financial Ratios

Some important points to keep in mind when using financial ratios are:

- All balance sheet numbers are end-of-period numbers, but all income statement numbers relate to the entire period. For example, when calculating the ratio for accounts receivable turnover, we use a numerator of Credit Sales (which is an entire-period number from the income statement) and a denominator of Accounts Receivable (which is an end-of-period number from the balance sheet). This is not an apples-to-apples ratio, with an entire-period number in the numerator but an end-of-period number in the denominator. Accounts receivable can be represented by an average of the beginning-of-year and end-of-year figures for accounts receivable. This average is closer to a midyear estimate of accounts receivable and therefore is more comparable to the entire-period numerator, Credit Sales. Using averages of the beginning-of-year and end-of-year figures for balance sheet numbers helps

Exhibit 2.1 Summary of main financial ratios.

Ratio	Numerator	Denominator
Short-Term Liquidity		
Current ratio	Current assets	Current liabilities
Quick ratio (acid test)	Current assets (excluding inventory)	Current liabilities
Receivables turnover	Credit sales	Accounts receivable
Inventory turnover	Cost of sales	Inventory
Payables turnover	Cost of sales	Accounts payable
Long-Term Solvency		
Interest coverage	EBIT	Interest on long-term debt
Debt to capital	Long-term debt	Long-term debt + Equity
Profitability on Sales		
Gross profit ratio	Gross profit	Sales
Operating expense ratio	Operating expenses	Sales
SG&A expense ratio	SG&A expenses	Sales
EBIT ratio	EBIT	Sales
Pretax income ratio	Pretax income	Sales
Net income ratio	Net income	Sales
Profitability on Investment		
Return on total assets:		
Before tax	EBIT	Total assets[a]
After tax	EBIT × (1 − Tax rate)	Total assets[b]
Return on equity	Net income: common[c]	Common equity

[a]Total Assets = Fixed Assets + Working Capital (Current Assets − Current Liabilities).
[b]Total Assets = Fixed Assets + Working Capital (Current Assets − Current Liabilities).
[c]Net Income − Preferred Dividends.

to make ratios more of an apples-to-apples comparison. For this reason, averages should be used for all balance sheet numbers when calculating financial ratios.

- Financial ratios are no more reliable than the data from which the ratios were calculated. The most reliable data is from audited financial statements, provided that the audit reports are clean and unqualified.

- Financial ratios cannot be fully considered without yardsticks of comparison. The simplest yardsticks are comparisons of financial ratios for an enterprise with the financial ratios for the same enterprise in previous periods. Companies often provide this type of information in their financial reporting. For example, Apple Computer Inc. recently disclosed the following financial quarterly information (dollars in millions):

This table compares four successive quarters of information, which makes it possible to see the latest trends in such important items as sales, as well as gross margin and operating income percentages.

Quarter	4	3	2	1
Net sales	$1,870	$1,825	$1,945	$2,343
Gross margin	$1,122	$1,016	$1,043	$1,377
Gross margin %	25%	30%	28%	28%
Operating costs	$ 383	$ 375	$ 379	$ 409
Operating income	$ 64	$ 168	$ 170	$ 100
Operating income %	4%	9%	9%	4%

Other types of comparisons of financial ratios include:

- *Comparisons with competitors.* For example, the financial ratios of Apple Computer could be compared with those of Hewlett-Packard, Dell, or Gateway.

- *Comparisons with industry composites.* Industry composite ratios can be found from a number of sources, such as:

  - *The Almanac of Business and Industrial Financial Ratios*, by Leo Troy, published annually by Prentice Hall (Paramus, NJ). This publication uses Internal Revenue Service data for 4.6 million U.S. corporations, classified into 179 industries, divided into categories by firm size, and reporting 50 different financial ratios.

  - *Risk Management Associates: Annual Statement Studies.* This is a database compiled by bank loan officers from the financial statements of more than 150,000 commercial borrowers, representing more than 600 industries, classified by business size, and reporting 16 different financial ratios. Available on the Internet at www.rmahq.org.

  - Financial ratios can also be obtained from other firms that specialize in financial information, such as Dun & Bradstreet, Moody's, and Standard & Poor's.

Combining Financial Ratios

Up to this point we have considered financial ratios one at a time. However, there is a useful method for combining financial ratios known as DuPont[1] analysis. In order to explain it, we first need to define some financial ratios, together with their abbreviations:

Ratio	Calculation	Abbreviation
Profit margin[2]	Net Income/Sales	NI/S
Asset turnover	Sales/Total Assets	S/TA
Return on assets[3]	Net Income/Total Assets	NI/TA
Leverage	Total Assets/Common Equity	TA/CE
Return on equity	Net Income/Common Equity	NI/CE
Book to market	$\dfrac{\text{Book Value of Common Equity}}{\text{Market Value of Common Equity}}$	CE/MV
Earnings to price	$\dfrac{\text{Earnings per Common Share}}{\text{Price per Common Share}}$	EPS/MVPS

Now, these financial ratios can be combined in the following manner:

$$\text{Profit Margin} \times \text{Asset Turnover} = \text{Return on Assets}$$
$$\text{NI/S} \times \text{S/TA} = \text{NI/TA}$$
$$\text{Return on Assets} \times \text{Leverage} = \text{Return on Equity}$$
$$\text{NI/TA} \times \text{TA/CE} = \text{NI/CE}$$
$$\text{Return on Equity} \times \text{Book to Market} = \text{Earnings to Price}$$
$$\text{NI/CE} \times \text{CE/MV} = \text{NI/MV}$$

In summary:

$$\text{NI/S} \times \text{S/TA} \times \text{TA/CE} \times \text{CE/MV} = \text{NI/MV}$$

The DuPont equation says that the earnings-to-price ratio is the result of:

$$\text{Profit Margin} \times \text{Asset Turnover} \times \text{Leverage} \times \text{Book to Market}$$

The earnings-to-price ratio is the inverse of the well-known price-earnings (P/E) ratio.

So DuPont analysis reveals the links between the price-earnings ratio and the ratios for profit margin, asset turnover, leverage, and book to market value of equity.

Also, this equation provides a financial approach to business strategy. It recognizes that the ultimate objective of business strategy is to maximize stockholder value (i.e., the market price of the common stock). In turn, this requires maximizing the price-earnings ratio of the common equity. The DuPont equation breaks the return on common equity into its four component parts: profit margin (net income/sales), asset turnover (sales/total assets), leverage (total assets/common equity), and book to market value of the common stock. If any one of these four ratios can be improved (without harm to the remaining ratios), then the price-earnings ratio of the common equity will increase. This provides specific strategic targets:

- Profit margin improvement can be pursued in a number of ways. On the one hand, revenues might be increased or costs decreased by:
  - Raising prices, perhaps by improving product quality or offering extra services. This has been successfully done by makers of luxury cars that provide free roadside assistance and loaner cars when customer cars are being serviced.
  - Maintaining prices, but reducing the quantity of product in the package. This is a method often used by candy bar manufacturers and other makers of packaged foods.
  - Initiating or increasing charges for ancillary goods or services. For example, banks have substantially increased their charges to stop checks, and for checks written with insufficient funds. Distributors of computers and software have instituted fees for providing technical assistance on their help lines, and fees for restocking returned items.
  - Improving the productivity and efficiency of operations.
  - Cutting costs in a variety of ways.

- Asset turnover may be improved in ways such as:
  - Speeding up the collection of accounts receivable.
  - Increasing inventory turnover, perhaps by adopting just-in-time inventory methods.
  - Slowing down payments to suppliers, and thus increasing accounts payable.
  - Reducing idle capacity of plant and equipment.
- Leverage may be increased, within prudent limits, by means such as:
  - Using long-term debt rather than equity to fund additions to plant, property, and equipment.
  - Repurchasing previously issued common stock of the enterprise in the open market.

The chief advantage of using the DuPont formula is to focus attention on specific initiatives that will improve return on equity by means of enhancing profit margins, increasing asset turnover, or employing greater financial leverage within prudent limits.

In addition to the DuPont formula, there is another way to combine financial ratios in order to serve a useful purpose. This purpose is the prediction of solvency or bankruptcy for a given enterprise. It uses what is known as the Z-Score.

The Z-Score

Financial ratios are useful not only to assess the past or present condition of an enterprise, but also to reliably predict its future solvency or bankruptcy. This type of information is of critical importance to present and potential creditors and investors. There are several different methods of analysis for obtaining this predictive information. The best known is the Z-Score, developed for publicly traded manufacturing firms by Professor Edward Altman of New York University, which has stood the test of time. Its reliability can be expressed in terms of the two types of errors to which all predictive methods are vulnerable, namely:

1. Type I error: predicting solvency when in fact a firm becomes bankrupt (a false positive).
2. Type II error: predicting bankruptcy when in fact a firm remains solvent (a false negative).

The predictive error rates for the Altman Z-Score have been found to be as follows:

Years Prior to Bankruptcy	% False Positives	% False Negatives
1	6%	3%
2	18%	6%

Given the inherent difficulty of predicting future events, these error rates are relatively low, and therefore the Altman Z-Score is generally regarded as a reasonably reliable bankruptcy predictor. The Z-Score is calculated from financial ratios in the following manner:

$$Z = 1.2 \times \frac{\text{Working Capital}}{\text{Total Assets}}$$
$$+ 1.4 \times \frac{\text{Retained Earnings}}{\text{Total Assets}}$$
$$+ 3.3 \times \frac{\text{EBIT}}{\text{Total Assets}}$$
$$+ 0.6 \times \frac{\text{Equity at Market Value}}{\text{Debt}}$$
$$+ 1.0 \times \frac{\text{Sales}}{\text{Total Assets}}$$

A Z-Score above 2.99 predicts solvency, and a Z-Score below 1.81 predicts bankruptcy. Z-Scores between 1.81 and 2.99 are in a gray area, with scores above 2.675 suggesting solvency and scores below 2.675 suggesting bankruptcy.

Since the Z-Score uses equity at market value, it is not applicable to private firms, which do not issue marketable securities. A variation of the Z-Score for private firms has been developed. It is known as the Z′ Score, and uses the book value of equity rather than the market value. Due to this modification, the multipliers in the formula have changed from those in the original Z-Score, and so have the scores that indicate solvency, bankruptcy, or the gray area. For firms that are not manufacturers but are in the service sector, a further variation in the formula has been developed. It omits the variable for asset turnover, and is known as the Z″ Score. Once again, the multipliers in the formula have changed from those in the Z′ Score and the original Z-Score, and so have the scores that indicate solvency, bankruptcy, or the gray area.

Professor Altman later developed a more refined bankruptcy predictor than the Z-Score and named it ZETA. ZETA uses financial ratios for times interest earned, return on assets (the average and the standard deviation), and debt to equity. Other details of ZETA have not been made public. ZETA is proprietary and is made available to users for a fee.

Summary and Conclusions

Financial ratios contain critically important business information and are used for many different purposes by many different parties inside the business and outside of the business. Clearly all successful businesspeople should have a good basic understanding of the main financial ratios. Beyond the present chapter, this book contains further information and explanations relating to financial ratios:

Chapter 3, Analyzing Business Earnings

Chapter 10, The Integrity of Financial Reporting

Chapter 16, Business Valuation

On this book's Web site you will find an Excel file named DrugstoreChains.xls. This file contains a complete financial ratio analysis for two national drugstore chains. It illustrates all of the ratios and analyses discussed in this chapter.

Downloadable Resources for this chapter available at www.wiley.com/go/portablembainfinance

Analyzing Financial Statements: Direct Competitor Comparison Worksheet

Analyzing Financial Statements: Financial Statement Ratio Analysis

Internet Links

There are several Web sites where you can find the financial statements of U.S. public companies, and from which financial ratios can be obtained or computed. Probably the most convenient are MSN Money and Yahoo! Finance. Go to MSN Money or Yahoo! Finance, provide the stock symbols for each company (for example: FDX for FedEx and UPS for UPS, or KO for Coca-Cola and PEP for PepsiCo),[4] and all the relevant financial information will become available on-screen. Industry information can also be found in MSN Money and Yahoo! Finance.

The financial statements in MSN Money and Yahoo! Finance are displayed in standard uniform formats, and can differ slightly from the actual financial statements, which are in the Securities and Exchange Commission (SEC) Forms 10-K of the respective companies (accessible from MSN Money and Yahoo! Finance) and on the various corporate Web sites.

Other helpful sites include:

- Teach Me Finance (http://teachmefinance.com/). This Web site presents basic finance concepts.

- Introductory Finance Lectures, University of Arizona (www.studyfinance.com/).

- Tools and Resources for Financial Executives (www.CFO.com/). Useful information about news and current events of interest to financial executives, how-to tips, and career advice.

- Java Financial Ratio Calculators (www.dinkytown.net/java/Ratios.html). Calculate 10 financial ratios.

- Wachowicz's Web World (http://web.utk.edu/~jwachowi/wacho_world.html). A very large collection of useful links to Web sites on financial topics, techniques, and information.

- Web site for the American Institute of Certified Public Accountants (www.aicpa.org).

- Risk Management Association (RMA) (www.rmahq.org). This Web site contains financial ratios, classified by size of firm, for more than 600 industries.

Notes

1. The name comes from its original use at the DuPont Corporation.
2. After income taxes.
3. After income taxes.
4. MSN Money and Yahoo! Finance allow you to look up stock symbols by using company names.

For Further Reading

Penman, Stephen, *Financial Statement Analysis and Security Valuation* (New York: McGraw-Hill/Irwin, 2006).

Peterson, Pamela P., and Frank J. Fabozzi, *Analysis of Financial Statements*, Frank J. Fabozzi Series (Hoboken, NJ: John Wiley & Sons, 2006).

Stickney, Clyde P., Paul Brown, and James M. Wahlen, *Financial Reporting, Financial Statement Analysis, and Valuation: A Strategic Perspective (with Thomson One Access Code)* (Florence, KY: South-Western College Publishing, 2006).

Subramanyam, K. R., and John J. Wild, *Financial Statement Analysis* (New York: McGraw-Hill/Irwin, 2008).

Analyzing Business Earnings

Virginia Earll Soybel

More than a decade ago, a special committee of the American Institute of Certified Public Accountants (AICPA) concluded the following about earnings and user needs:

> Users want information about the portion of a company's reported earnings that is stable or recurring and that provides a basis for estimating sustainable earnings.[1]

While users may want information about the stable or recurring portion of a company's earnings, firms remain under no obligation to provide this earnings series. However, there are generally accepted accounting principles (GAAP) requirements for separate disclosure of selected nonrecurring revenues, gains, expenses, and losses on the face of the income statement or in notes to the financial statements. Further, the Securities and Exchange Commission (SEC) requires the disclosure of material nonrecurring items.

The prominence given the demand by users for information on nonrecurring items in the AICPA report is, no doubt, driven in part by the explosive growth in nonrecurring items over the past two decades. The acceleration of change, together with a passion for rightsizing and cyclical needs for downsizing, has fueled this growth. The issuance by the Financial Accounting Standards Board (FASB) of a number of new accounting statements, which require recognition of previously unrecorded expenses and more timely recognition of declines in asset values, has also contributed to the increase in nonrecurring items.

In October 2008, the FASB and the International Accounting Standards Board (IASB) issued a joint discussion paper proposing new requirements with respect to the presentation of financial statements.[2] This step is only the first in a long deliberation process, but if adopted, income statements in future years will be more detailed, and the identification of nonrecurring items may become simpler. For the foreseeable future, though, users of financial statements must analyze the financial statements and footnotes meticulously to identify the effects of anomalous transactions on earnings, and this chapter offers a systematic structure to support that analysis.

A limited number of firms do provide, on a voluntary basis, schedules that show their results with nonrecurring items removed. However, in March 2003 the SEC issued Regulation G—an implementation of part of the Sarbanes-Oxley legislation—which limits the use of some non-GAAP measures and requires a formal reconciliation of any non-GAAP income measure with its GAAP version.[3] Panera Bread Company provides an example of this disclosure. Exhibit 3.1 includes a schedule that adjusts reported net

Exhibit 3.1   Non-GAAP net income: Panera Bread Company, year ended December (in thousands).

	2007	2006	2005
GAAP net income	$57,456	$58,849	$52,183
Investment write-down and discontinued product (net of tax)	1,090	—	—
One-time acquisition charge (net of tax)	—	1,072	—
Stock-based compensation expense (net of tax)	—	—	(4,115)
Non-GAAP net income	$58,546	$59,921	$48,068

Source: Panera Bread Co., annual report, December 2007.

income to a revised earnings measure, offering greater comparability across the three-year period.

Several studies have found that companies' use of non-GAAP measures in financial reporting has decreased since the SEC rule (Regulation G) took effect.[4] Some companies have found other ways to disclose nonrecurring or unpredictable items without specific reference to non-GAAP measures. Exhibit 3.2 shows a table from an annual report of Coca-Cola Enterprises, Inc., providing detailed reasons for *changes* in its operating income.

Exhibit 3.2   Analysis of changes in operating income: Coca-Cola Enterprises, Inc., year ended December 31, 2007.

During 2007, we had operating income of $1.5 billion compared to an operating loss of $1.5 billion in 2006. The following table summarizes the significant components of the change in our 2007 operating income (loss) (in millions; percentages rounded to the nearest 0.5 percent):

	Amount	Change Percent of Total
Changes in operating income (loss):		
Impact of bottle and can price, cost, and mix on gross profit	$ 128	8.5%
Impact of bottle and can volume on gross profit	(85)	(5.5)
Impact of bottle and can selling day shift on gross profit	28	2.0
Impact of Jumpstart funding on gross profit	(39)	(2.5)
Selling, delivery, and administrative expenses	(46)	(3.0)
Net impact of restructuring charges	(55)	(3.5)
Gain on sale of land in 2007	20	1.0
Franchise impairment charge in 2006	2,922	195.5
Currency exchange rate changes	54	3.5
Other changes	16	1.0
Change in operating income (loss)	$2,965	198.5%

Source: Coca-Cola Enterprises, Inc., annual report, December 2007.

Note that this disclosure includes both core business issues, such as product mix and price/cost shifts, and nonrecurring effects, such as restructuring and impairment charges.

To varying degrees, typically in footnotes or in the textual discussion of financial results, companies provide information regarding the effects of idiosyncratic events and transactions on net income. However, the often formidable task of determining a firm's sustainable or core earnings—a process sometimes called "normalizing earnings"—remains the responsibility of the financial statement user. The central goal of this chapter is to help users develop the background and skills to perform this critical aspect of earnings analysis. The chapter covers income statement formats and the nature of nonrecurring items, and it outlines efficient approaches for locating them in financial statements and associated notes. Throughout the chapter, information drawn from the financial statements of many companies is used for illustration. A summary exercise offers a comprehensive example of removing all nonrecurring items from reported results in order to arrive at a sustainable earnings series.

The Nature of Nonrecurring Items

It is difficult to provide a comprehensive definition of nonrecurring items. *Unusual* or *infrequent in occurrence* are qualities that are often cited in defining nonrecurring items. Donald Kieso, Jerry Weygandt, and Terry Warfield, in their popular intermediate accounting text, use the term *irregular* to describe what most statement users would consider nonrecurring items.[5] For our purposes, irregular or nonrecurring revenues, gains, expenses, and losses are not consistent contributors to results, in terms of either their presence or their amount. This is the manner in which we use the term *nonrecurring items* throughout this chapter.

From a security valuation perspective, nonrecurring items could be characterized as items having a smaller impact on share price than recurring elements of earnings. Some items can often be identified as nonrecurring simply by their basic nature (e.g., restructuring charges, litigation settlements, flood losses, product recall costs, embezzlement losses, and insurance settlements). Other items may affect net income every year, but vary widely in sign (revenue versus expense, gain versus loss) and amount. For example, the following gains on the sale of marketable securities were reported over a number of years by Archer Daniels Midland Company:[6]

2004	$ 24 million
2005	113 million
2006	40 million
2007	393 million
2008	38 million

The gains averaged about $122 million over the five years ending in 2008, but obviously varied substantially from one year to the next. It would be difficult to characterize these gains as nonrecurring, but they are certainly irregular in amount.

There are at least three different ways to handle this line item in revising results for the purpose of identifying sustainable or recurring earnings. The first—and the most common—approach is simply to eliminate the item altogether. This solution is persuasive in the illustration because Archer Daniels Midland is a food processor, and transactions related to its portfolio of marketable securities are not associated with its core business. But consider a different example. Northwest Airlines reported the following gains (losses) on the disposition of property and equipment.[7]

2002	($ 41) million
2003	113 million
2004	95 million
2005	80 million
2006	(16) million

Again, these amounts are both irregular and unpredictable, and eliminating them from measures of sustainable earnings is a common technique. In this case, however, some users would see these transactions as part of Northwest's ongoing operations. While an airline is not in the business of selling airplanes, its business does require that it manage its aircraft fleet. So we would expect these dispositions to recur. Rather than eliminate them altogether, an alternative would be to smooth them by including an average value (e.g., $46 million for Northwest for the period 2002 to 2006) over some period of time. A third approach is to attempt to acquire information on planned aircraft dispositions that would make possible a better prediction of the effects of aircraft dispositions on future results. While the last approach may appear to be the most appealing, it may prove to be difficult to implement due to lack of information, and it may also be less attractive when viewed from a cost-benefit perspective. Unless the amounts are consistently substantial, most financial statement users either remove the gains (losses) or use a recent average value in making earnings projections.

First Solar, Inc., offers another example of the impact of a recurring but irregular item on the evaluation of earnings performance. Listed in Exhibit 3.3 are First Solar's foreign currency gains (losses) and their effects on pretax profit margins.

As with Northwest Airlines, it may seem questionable to classify as nonrecurring foreign currency gains (losses) that appear repeatedly. However, in line with the definition

Exhibit 3.3 First Solar, Inc., foreign currency gains (losses) and effects on pretax profit margins, years ended December (in thousands).

	2007	2006	2005
Income (loss) before income taxes	$155,962	$ 9,180	($6,551)
Foreign currency gain (loss)	1,881	5,544	(1,715)
Income (loss) before income taxes and foreign currency gain (loss)	154,081	3,636	(4,836)
Net sales revenue	503,976	134,974	48,063
Pretax profit margin:			
As reported	30.9%	6.8%	(13.6%)
As adjusted before foreign currency gain (loss)	30.6%	2.7%	(10.1%)

Source: First Solar, Inc., annual report, December 2007.

of the key characteristics of nonrecurring items given earlier, First Solar's foreign currency effects are irregular in amount, direction, and significance, and they are unlikely to be consistent contributors to results in future years. In 2006 more than half of First Solar's pretax earnings were generated by foreign currency gains, a proportion that is unlikely to be repeated.

Other examples of irregular items of revenue, gain, expense, and loss abound. For example, the recent loss of liquidity in the credit markets affected more than financial services firms. Bristol-Myers Squibb reported a $225 million write-down of its investments in auction-rate securities (ARS) in 2007 when the ARS market froze.[8] Natural disasters may also affect corporate earnings. Whole Foods Market recorded a $16.5 million charge in 2005 for the loss of its stores caught in the path of Hurricane Katrina and then $7.2 million in income the next year from insurance proceeds.[9] Temporary revenue increases have been associated with expanded television sales due to World Cup soccer and the Olympic Games. Temporary expense increases have resulted from adjustments to loan-loss provisions in economic downturns.

The identification of nonrecurring or irregular items is not a mechanical process; it calls for the exercise of judgment and involves both line items as well as the period-to-period behavior of individual income statement items.

The Process of Identifying Nonrecurring Items

Careful analysis of past financial performance, aimed at removing the effects of nonrecurring items, is a more formidable task than one might suspect. This task would be fairly simple if there were general agreement on just what constitutes a nonrecurring item and if most nonrecurring items were prominently displayed on the face of the income statement. However, this is not the case. Some research suggests that fewer than one-fourth of nonrecurring items are likely to be found separately disclosed in the income statement.[10] Providing guidance to aid in the location of the remaining three-fourths is a key goal of this chapter.

Identifying Nonrecurring Items: An Efficient Search Procedure

The search sequence outlined in Exhibit 3.4 locates a high cumulative percentage of material nonrecurring items and does so in a cost-effective manner. Search cost, mainly analyst time, is an important consideration because financial analysis is an economic activity that should be conducted in an efficient manner. Further, time devoted to this task is not available for other tasks and, therefore, there is an *opportunity cost* to consider. The discussion that follows is organized around this recommended search sequence.

Nonrecurring Items in the Income Statement

An examination of the income statement, the first step in the search sequence, requires an understanding of the design and content of contemporary income statements. This calls for a review of the generally accepted accounting principles (GAAP) that determine the structure and content of the income statement. Some nonrecurring items are prominently displayed on separate lines and readily recognizable in the statement. Further, leads to other nonrecurring items, disclosed elsewhere, may be discovered during this process. For example, a line item that summarizes items of other income and expense may include an associated note reference detailing its contents. These notes should always be reviewed

Exhibit 3.4   Efficient search sequence for nonrecurring items.

Search Step	Search Location
1.	Income statement.
2.	Statement of cash flows—operating activities section.
3.	Inventory note, generally assuming that the firm employs the last in, first out (LIFO) inventory method.
	However, even with non-LIFO firms, inventory notes may reveal inventory write-downs.
4.	Income tax note, with attention focused on the tax rate reconciliation schedule.
5.	Other income (expense) note in cases where this amount is not detailed on the face of the income statement.
6.	Management's Discussion & Analysis (MD&A) of Financial Condition and Results of Operations—Item 7 of the annual report, Form 10-K, filed with the SEC.
7.	Other notes that often include nonrecurring items:

Note		*Nonrecurring items revealed*
a.	Property and equipment	Gains and losses on asset sales
b.	Long-term debt	Gains and losses on debt retirement
c.	Foreign currency	Foreign currency gains and losses
d.	Restructuring	Current and prospective impact of restructuring activities
e.	Acquisitions and dispositions	Mergers and acquisitions (M&A) costs, gains and losses on sale of businesses
f.	Intangible assets	Impairment charges
g.	Contingencies	Prospective revenues and expenses
h.	Segment data	Various nonrecurring items
i.	Quarterly data	Various nonrecurring items

(step 5 in the search sequence), because they often reveal a wide range of nonrecurring items.

Alternative Income Statement Formats

Examples of the two principal income statement formats under current GAAP are presented here. The income statement of Dow Chemical Company in Exhibit 3.5 is *single-step*, and that of Adobe Systems, Inc., in Exhibit 3.6 is in the *multistep* format. An annual survey of financial statements conducted by the American Institute of Certified Public Accountants (AICPA) reveals that about 14% of the 600 companies in its survey use the single-step format.[11] The distinguishing feature of the multistep statement is that it provides intermediate earnings subtotals that are designed to measure operating performance. In principle, operating income should be composed almost entirely of recurring items of revenue and expense that result from the main operating activities of the firm. In practice, numerous material nonrecurring items may be included in operating income. For example, restructuring charges are often included in operating income.

Exhibit 3.5 Consolidated single-step statements of income: Dow Chemical Company, years ended December 31 (in millions).

	Year Ended		
	2007	**2006**	**2005**
Net sales	$53,513	$49,124	$46,307
Cost of sales	46,400	41,526	38,276
Research and development expense	1,305	1,164	1,073
Selling, general, and administrative expense	1,864	1,663	1,545
Amortization of intangibles	72	50	55
Restructuring charges	578	591	114
Purchased in-process research and development charges	57	—	—
Asbestos-related credit	—	177	—
Equity in earnings of unconsolidated affiliates	1,122	959	964
Sundry income—net	324	137	755
Interest income	130	185	138
Interest expense and amortization of debt discount	584	616	702
Income before income taxes and minority interests	4,229	4,972	6,399
Provision for income taxes	1,244	1,155	1,782
Minority interests' share in income	98	93	82
Income before cumulative effect of accounting change	2,887	3,724	4,535
Cumulative effect of change in accounting principle	—	—	(20)
Net income	$ 2,887	$ 3,724	$ 4,515

Note: Per-share amounts omitted.
Source: Dow Chemical Company, annual report, December 2007.

The Dow Chemical single-step income statement does not partition results into intermediate subtotals. For example, there are no line items identified as either "gross profit" or "operating income." Rather, all revenues and expenses are separately listed, and "income before income taxes and minority interests" is computed in a single step, as total expenses are deducted from total revenues. However, the Adobe Systems multistep income statement provides both gross profit and operating income subtotals.

Note that Dow Chemical has several nonrecurring items in its income statements. While they vary in size, the following would normally be considered to be nonrecurring: restructuring charges, purchased in-process research and development (IPR&D) charges, and asbestos-related credit.

More nonrecurring items are usually lurking in other statements or footnotes. Note the varying amounts of sundry income (net) across the three years. Also, Dow Chemical's income taxes in 2006 were unusual. The effective tax rate ($1,155 divided by $4,972) is only about 23%, noticeably lower than the 28% or 29% of the other years.

Nonrecurring Items Located in Income from Continuing Operations

Whether a single or multistep format is used, the composition of income from continuing operations is the same. It includes all items of revenue, gain, expense, and loss, with the

Exhibit 3.6 Consolidated multistep statements of income: Adobe Systems, Inc. (in thousands).

	Year Ended		
	Nov. 30 2007	Dec. 1 2006	Dec. 2 2005
Revenue:			
Products	$3,019,524	$2,484,710	$1,923,278
Services and support	138,357	90,590	43,043
Total revenue	3,157,881	2,575,300	1,966,321
Cost of revenue:			
Products	270,818	226,506	89,942
Services and support	83,876	65,951	22,636
Total cost of revenue	354,694	292,457	112,578
Gross profit	2,803,187	2,282,843	1,853,743
Operating expenses:			
Research and development	613,242	539,684	365,328
Sales and marketing	984,388	867,145	593,323
General and administrative	274,982	234,597	166,658
Restructuring and other charges	555	20,251	—
Amortization of purchased intangibles and incomplete technology	72,435	69,873	—
Total operating expenses	1,945,602	1,731,550	1,125,309
Operating income	857,585	551,293	728,434
Non-operating income:			
Investment gain (loss), net	7,134	61,249	(1,310)
Interest and other income, net	82,471	67,185	38,643
Total non-operating income	89,605	128,434	37,342
Income before income taxes	947,190	679,727	765,776
Provision for income taxes	223,383	173,918	162,937
Net income	$ 723,807	$ 505,809	$ 602,839

Note: Per-share amounts omitted.
Source: Adobe Systems, Inc., annual report, November 2007.

exception of those (1) identified with discontinued operations, (2) meeting the definition of extraordinary items, and (3) resulting from the cumulative effect of changes in accounting principles. Because income from continuing operations excludes only these three items, it follows that all other nonrecurring items of revenues or gains and expenses or losses are included in this key profit subtotal.

The Nature of Operating Income

Operating income is not defined under GAAP, and is often considered equivalent to earnings before interest and taxes (EBIT). More specifically, operating income is designed to reflect the revenues, gains, expenses, and losses that are related to the fundamental operating activities of the firm independent of capital structure and income tax environment. However, notice that the Adobe Systems operating income in both 2006 and 2007 is reported after restructuring charges. While operating income or loss may include only operations-related items, some of these items may be nonrecurring. Hence, operating income is often not the "sustainable" earnings measure called for by the AICPA Special Committee on Financial Reporting. Even at this early point in the income statement, nonrecurring items have been introduced that will require adjustment in order to arrive at an earnings base "that provides a basis for estimating sustainable earnings."[12] Note also that "operating income" in a multistep format is an earlier subtotal than "income from continuing operations." Operating income is a pretax measure, but income from continuing operations is after tax. A more extensive sampling of items included in operating income is provided next.

Nonrecurring Items Included in Operating Income

A review of recent corporate annual reports reveals that the inclusion in operating income of nonrecurring revenues, gains, expenses, and losses is common. A sample of nonrecurring items included in the operating income section of multistep income statements is provided in Exhibit 3.7. As is typical, nonrecurring expenses and losses are more numerous than nonrecurring revenues and gains. This disparity is due in part to the conservatism principle underlying GAAP, which requires recognizing certain unrealized losses (e.g., asset impairments), but prohibits the recognition of most unrealized gains.

Many of the nonrecurring expense or loss items involve the recognition of declines in the value of specific assets. Restructuring charges are among the most common items in this section of the income statement. These charges involve asset write-downs and liability accruals for costs such as severance expenses that will be paid off in future years and are typically described in detail in a note.

There is substantial variety in the nonrecurring expenses and losses included in operating income. Some of the listed items appear to be closely linked to operations; inventory write-downs, for example, are integral to operating a retail business. However, some items appear to be at the fringes of normal operating activities. Examples related to expenses and losses would include the expropriated asset impairment charges of ConocoPhillips, Warner Music's loss on termination of management, and Hewlett-Packard's pension settlement charges. Among the gains, the Alliant Energy and Iron Mountain gains on selling fixed assets would seem to be candidates for inclusion further down in the income statement, as would Humana's investment income (since Humana is not a financial services firm).

Once the items included in operating income are compared to those that are excluded, it is apparent that management exercises considerable judgment in its classification of these items. Clearly, operating income, when reported, may not be a reliable measure of ongoing operating performance, given the wide range of nonrecurring items that are included in its determination.

Nonrecurring Items Excluded from Operating Income

Unlike the multistep format, the single-step income statement does not include a subtotal representing operating income. Nonrecurring items of revenue or gain and expense or loss are either presented as separate line items within the listing of revenues or gain and expense or loss or are included in an "other income (expense)" line. Multistep

Exhibit 3.7 Nonrecurring items of revenue or gain and expense or loss included in operating income.

Company	Nonrecurring Item
Expenses or Losses	
Abbott Laboratories (2007)	Purchased in-process R&D charges
Adobe Systems (2007)	Restructuring charges
AGCO, Inc. (2007)	Goodwill impairment charge
Amazon.com (2005)	Patent lawsuit settlement charge
ConocoPhillips (2007)	Expropriated assets impairment charge
FedEx Corporation (2007)	Trademark impairment charge
Hewlett-Packard (2007)	Pension curtailments and settlements
Interface, Inc. (2007)	Loss on sale of a subsidiary
Kimberly-Clark Corporation (2007)	Asset impairments
Limited Brands, Inc. (2007)	Loss on divestiture of Limited Stores
McDonald's Corporation (2007)	Loss on sale of interest to licensee
Navigant Consulting, Inc. (2006)	Litigation charge
Northrop Grumman Corporation (2005)	Hurricane Katrina charge
Novartis, Inc. (2007)	Environmental remediation charge
Pacific Sunwear of California (2006)	Inventory write-down
Sprint Nextel Corp. (2007)	Severance, exit costs, and asset impairments
United Natural Foods (2007)	Impairment on assets held for sale
Warner Music Group Corp. (2005)	Loss on termination of management
Weyerhaeuser Company (2006)	Facilities closure charge
Revenues or Gains	
Alliant Energy Corporation (2007)	Gain on sale of electric transmission assets
Humana, Inc. (2006)	Investment income
Iron Mountain (2007)	Gain on sale of property, plant, and equipment
Limited Brands, Inc. (2007)	Gain on divestiture of Express
McDonald's Corporation (2007)	Gain on transfer of interest to licensee
Southwest Airlines (2007)	Fuel hedge gains
Weyerhaeuser Company (2006)	Reversal of litigation accrual
Yum! Brands, Inc. (2007)	Refranchising gains

Sources: Companies' annual reports. The year following each company name designates the annual report from which each example was drawn.

income statements may also include an "other income (expense)" item, typically after the calculation of operating income. A sampling of nonrecurring items found in the "other income (expense)" category of the multistep income statements of a number of companies is provided in Exhibit 3.8.

A comparison of the items in two exhibits reveals some potential for overlap in these two categories. The first, nonrecurring items in operating income, should be dominated by items closely linked to company operations. The nonrecurring items in the second, below operating income, should fall outside the operations area of the firm. Notice

Exhibit 3.8   Nonrecurring items of revenue or gain and expense or loss excluded from operating income.

Company	Nonrecurring Item
Expenses or Losses	
Abbott Laboratories (2007)	Foreign exchange loss
Advanced Micro Devices, Inc. (2005)	Foreign currency transaction loss
Electronic Arts (2007)	Losses on strategic investments
Iron Mountain, Inc. (2006)	Loss on early extinguishment of debt
Northrop Grumman Corporation (2007)	Litigation charges
Revenues or Gains	
Alliant Energy Corporation (2006)	Gain on sale of investment
EMC Corporation (2007)	Gain on sale of VMware stock to Cisco
Magma Design Automation, Inc. (2006)	Gain on extinguishment of debt
Motorola, Inc. (2007)	Gains on sales of investments and businesses
Sprint Nextel Corporation (2007)	Gain on sale of investments
Starbucks Corporation (2006)	Income on unredeemed value card balances
Tektronix, Inc. (2005)	Gain on sale of investment

Sources: Companies' annual reports. The year following each company name designates the annual report from which each example was drawn.

that there is a litigation charge included in operating income (Exhibit 3.7, Navigant Consulting) as well as litigation charges excluded from operating income (Exhibit 3.8, Northrop Grumman). Gains on the sale of investments are found far less frequently within operating income. Firms may have a reluctance to classify these nonrecurring gains within operating income because it may create unrealistic expectations for earnings in subsequent periods. It is common to see foreign currency gains and losses classified below operating income. This is somewhat difficult to rationalize, because currency exposure is an integral part of operations when a firm does business with foreign customers and/or has foreign operations, but the volatility of these effects may justify their separation.

The goal of the operating income subtotal should be to develop a measure of the basic profitability of a firm's operations. It is far from a net earnings number, because its location in the income statement is above a number of other non-operating revenues, gains, expenses, and losses, as well as interest charges and income taxes. Clearly, the range and complexity of nonrecurring items creates the need for judgment calls in implementing this concept of operating income. There is also the possibility that management may use this flexibility to manage the operating income number. That is, the classification of items either within or outside of operating income could be influenced by the goal of maintaining stable growth in this key performance measure. Earnings management incentives heighten the importance of careful analysis of nonrecurring items.

Nonrecurring Items Located below Income from Continuing Operations

The region in the income statement below income from continuing operations has a standard organization and is the same for both the single and the multistep income statement. This format is outlined in Exhibit 3.9. The income statement of Eastman

Exhibit 3.9 Income statement format with special items.

Income from continuing operations	$000
Discontinued operations	000
Extraordinary items	000
Cumulative effect of changes in accounting principles	000
Net income	000
Other comprehensive income	000
Comprehensive income	$000

Sources: Key guidance is found in Accounting Principles Board Opinion No. 30, *Reporting the Results of Operations* (1973); Financial Accounting Standards Board, Statement of Financial Accounting Standards No. 130, *Reporting Comprehensive Income* (1997); Financial Accounting Standards Board, Statement of Financial Accounting Standards No. 144, *Accounting for the Impairment or Disposal of Long-lived Assets* (2001); and Financial Accounting Standards Board, Statement of Financial Accounting Standards No. 154, *Accounting Changes and Error Corrections—A Replacement of APB Opinion No. 20 and FASB Statement No. 3* (2005).

Kodak Corporation, shown in Exhibit 3.10, illustrates this format. Each of the special line items (e.g., discontinued operations and changes in accounting principles) is discussed along with illustrative examples in the following sections. All of these items are presented in the income statement on an after-tax basis.

Discontinued Operations

The discontinued operations section is designed to enhance time series comparability of the income statement by separating the results of continuing operations from those that have been, or are in the process of being, discontinued. The discontinued business may be a segment (as defined by Statement of Financial Accounting Standards No. 131) or may be a smaller component of the firm, as long as the component "comprises operations and cash flows that can be clearly distinguished, operationally and for financial reporting purposes, from the rest of the entity."[13]

Some examples of operations that have been viewed as separable components and, therefore, classified as "discontinued operations" are provided in Exhibit 3.11.

For the financial statement user, the separation of discontinued operations offers income statement data for a consistent entity across the three years presented in an annual report and thus enhances comparability.

Extraordinary Items

Income statement items are considered extraordinary if they are *both* (1) unusual and (2) infrequent in occurrence.[14] Unusual items are not related to the typical activities or operations of the firm. Infrequency of occurrence simply implies that the item is not expected to recur in the foreseeable future. In practice, the strict application of the joint requirement of "unusual and nonrecurring" results in very few extraordinary items. In fact, in 2006 only four companies in a survey of 600 reported an extraordinary item.[15] One of those was Hampshire Group, Ltd., an apparel company, which completed an acquisition at a purchase price that was lower than the net asset value acquired and, as required under SFAS No. 141, reported the difference as an extraordinary gain.[16]

Exhibit 3.10   Consolidated statements of income: Eastman Kodak Corporation, years ended December 31 (in millions).

	2007	2006	2005
Net sales	$10,301	$10,568	$11,395
Cost of goods sold	7,785	8,159	8,864
Gross profit	2,516	2,409	2,531
Selling, general, and administrative expenses	1,764	1,950	2,240
Research and development costs	535	578	739
Restructuring costs and other	543	416	665
Other operating (income) expenses, net	(96)	(59)	(40)
Loss from continuing operations before interest, other income (charges), net, and income taxes	(230)	(476)	(1,073)
Interest expense	113	172	139
Other income (charges), net	87	65	4
Loss from continuing operations before income taxes	(256)	(583)	(1,208)
(Benefit) provision for income taxes	(51)	221	449
Loss from continuing operations	(205)	(804)	(1,657)
Earnings from discontinued operations, net of income taxes	881	203	451
Loss from cumulative effect of accounting change, net of income taxes	—	—	(55)
Net earnings (loss)	$ 676	$ (601)	$ (1,261)

Note: Per-share amounts omitted.
Source: Eastman Kodak Corporation, annual report, December 2007.

Exhibit 3.11   Examples of discontinued operations.

Company	Principal Business	Discontinued Operation
Campbell Soup Company (2008)	Branded convenience foods	Godiva chocolates
Cardinal Health, Inc. (2007)	Pharma wholesaler	Pharma technology and services
Interface, Inc. (2007)	Modular carpet	Fabrics
Monster Worldwide, Inc. (2006)	Online employment agent	Advertising
Motorola, Inc. (2006)	Communications technology	Automotive electronics
Pfizer, Inc. (2006)	Pharmaceutical	Consumer health care

Sources: Companies' annual reports. The year following each company name designates the annual report from which each example was drawn.

Natural disasters and civil unrest may trigger the recognition of extraordinary items. In 1980, Weyerhaeuser Company reported an extraordinary loss due to the Mount St. Helens eruption. But note from examples of nonrecurring items discussed earlier that Whole Foods Markets and Northrop Grumman included the effects of Hurricane Katrina in their income from continuing operations. For ConocoPhillips, even the expropriation of assets by Venezuela was not treated as extraordinary.

The task of locating all nonrecurring items of revenue or gain and expense or loss is aided only marginally by the presence of the extraordinary category in the income statement, because the extraordinary classification is employed so sparingly. Identifying most nonrecurring items calls for careful review of other parts of the income statement, other statements, and notes to the financial statements.

Changes in Accounting Principles

Until 2006, the cumulative effects (catch-up adjustments) of changes in accounting principles were also reported below income from continuing operations as in Exhibits 3.9 and 3.10. Most changes in accounting principles result from the adoption of new standards or interpretations issued by the FASB or the SEC. Under SFAS No. 154, however, since 2007 changes in accounting principles are applied retrospectively with the cumulative effect captured in the beginning balance of retained earnings and therefore bypassing the income statement altogether. If practical, all three years of income should be restated using the new principle to provide comparability. However, the most frequent example of principle changes since 2006 involves the application of FASB Interpretation No. 48 (FIN 48), which most companies have implemented only in the year of adoption, presumably because restatement to earlier years was impractical. In its annual report for the year ending June 30, 2008, the Procter & Gamble Company made the following disclosure in Note 1:

> On July 1, 2007, we adopted FASB Interpretation No. 48, "Accounting for Uncertainty in Income Taxes—an interpretation of FASB statement No. 109" (FIN 48). FIN 48 addresses the accounting and disclosure of uncertain tax positions. FIN 48 prescribes a recognition threshold and measurement attribute for the financial statement recognition and measurement of a tax position taken or expected to be taken in a tax return. The difference between the tax benefit recognized in the financial statements for a position in accordance with FIN 48 and the tax benefit claimed in the tax return is referred to as an unrecognized tax benefit.
>
> The adoption of FIN 48 resulted in a decrease to retained earnings as of July 1, 2007, of $232, which was reflected as a cumulative effect of a change in accounting principle, with a corresponding increase to the net liability for unrecognized tax benefits. The impact primarily reflects the accrual of additional statutory interest and penalties as required by FIN 48, partially offset by adjustments to existing unrecognized tax benefits to comply with FIN 48 measurement principles.[17]

Exhibit 3.12 lists the accounting principle changes seen most often through 2006. Companies may also change estimates, such as depreciable useful lives, but those changes are treated prospectively, as discussed next.

Changes in Estimates

Whereas changes in accounting principles are handled retrospectively and—when practical—with restatement, changes in accounting estimates are handled on a

Exhibit 3.12   Accounting changes.

Subject of Change	Number of Companies		
	2006	2005	2004
Stock-based compensation (SFAS 123R)	437	36	16
Defined benefit pension and postretirement plans (SFAS 158)	304	—	—
Asset retirement obligation	29	93	9
Inventories	8	7	4

Source: American Institute of Certified Public Accountants, *Accounting Trends and Techniques* (New York: AICPA, 2007), Table 1-8.

prospective basis. For example, beginning on July 1, 2004, Netflix, Inc., changed the estimated useful life of its back-catalog DVD library. The company disclosed the change in estimate in the following note of its annual report for the year ending December 31, 2004:

> Prior to July 1, 2004, the Company amortized the cost of its entire DVD Library . . . over one year. However, based on a periodic evaluation of both new release and back-catalogue utilization for amortization purposes, the Company determined that back-catalogue titles have a significantly longer life than previously estimated. As a result, the Company revised the estimate of useful life for the back-catalogue DVD library from a "sum of the months" accelerated method using a one-year life to the same accelerated method of amortization using a three-year life. The purpose of this change was to more accurately reflect the productive life of these assets. In accordance with Accounting Principles Board Opinion No. 20, Accounting Changes ("APB 20"), the change in life has been accounted for as a change in accounting estimate on a prospective basis from July 1, 2004. . . . As a result of the change in the estimated life of the back-catalogue library, total cost of revenues was $10.9 million lower, net income was $10.9 million higher and net income per diluted share was $0.17 higher for the year ended December 31, 2004.[18]

The $10.9 million reduction in 2004 DVD amortization expense was not set out separately in the income statement. Netflix reported pretax earnings of $21.8 million in 2004 and pretax earnings of $6.5 million in 2003. On an as-reported basis, Netflix's pretax earnings in 2004 increased by over 300%. However, without the $10.9 million benefit from the increase in DVD back-catalog useful life, the pretax earnings increase in 2004 would have been 68%. Locating this accounting change in estimate and isolating its effect on income are essential steps in evaluating the 2004 financial performance of Netflix, Inc.

Nonrecurring Items in the Statement of Cash Flows

After the income statement, the operating activities section—using the indirect method—of the statement of cash flows is an excellent secondary source for locating nonrecurring items (step 2 in the search sequence outlined in Exhibit 3.4). The diagnostic value of this section of the statement of cash flows results from two factors needed to reconcile net income to net operating cash flows. First, gains and losses on the sale of investments and fixed assets must be removed from net income in deriving cash flow from operating activities, since all cash inflows from these transactions must be reported in the investing activities section of the statement of cash flows. Second, noncash items of revenue or gain and expense or loss must also be removed from net income to derive net operating cash flows. Both types of adjustments typically involve nonrecurring items that may not appear separately on the income statement.

The partial statement of cash flows of Baxter International, Inc., in Exhibit 3.13 illustrates the disclosure of nonrecurring items in the operating activities section of the statement of cash flows. The nonrecurring items would appear to be (1) infusion pump charges, (2) hemodialysis instrument charge, (3) average wholesale pricing litigation charge, (4) acquired in-process and collaboration research and development, and (5) restructuring charge (adjustments). Of these five items, only the last—restructuring charge (adjustments)—was disclosed on Baxter's income statement. The first, second, and fifth items all involved asset write-downs, which are added back to net income because they did not involve cash outflows. The acquisition of in-process R&D is added back in the operating section because the entire cash outflow to acquire another company

Exhibit 3.13   Nonrecurring items disclosed in the statement of cash flows: Baxter International, Inc., partial consolidated statements of cash flows, years ended December 31.

	2007	2006	2005
Cash flows from operations:			
Net income (loss)	$1,707	$1,397	$ 956
Adjustments to reconcile net income (loss) to net cash provide from (used in) operating activities:			
Depreciation and amortization	581	575	580
Deferred income taxes	126	8	201
Stock compensation	136	94	9
Infusion pump charges	—	76	126
Hemodialysis instrument charge	—	—	50
Average wholesale pricing litigation charge	56	—	—
Acquired in-process and collaboration research and development	61	—	—
Restructuring charge (adjustments)	70	—	(109)
Other	(5)	34	48
Changes in balance sheet items:			
Accounts and other current receivables	(278)	(16)	178
Inventories	(211)	(35)	88
Accounts payable and accrued liabilities	1	1	(325)
Restructuring payments	(27)	(42)	(117)
Other	88	91	(135)
Cash flows from operations	$2,305	$2,183	$1,550

Source: Baxter International, Inc., annual report, December 31, 2007.

Exhibit 3.14   Disclosure of nonrecurring items in both the income statement and the operating activities section of the statement of cash flows.

Company	Nonrecurring Item
Separately disclosed in both the income statement and statement of cash flows	
Baxter International (2007)	Restructuring charge
Eastman Kodak (2007)	Restructuring charges
eBay (2007)	Impairment of goodwill
Limited Brands (2007)	Gain on sale of Express
Merck & Company (2007)	U.S. Vioxx settlement agreement charge
New York Times Company (2007)	Loss on sale of assets
Office Depot (2006)	Asset impairments
Separately disclosed only in the statement of cash flows	
Baxter International (2006)	Infusion pump charges
Denny's Corporation (2007)	Loss on early extinguishment of debt
Eastman Kodak (2007)	Gains on sales of businesses
Limited Brands (2007)	Gains on sales of assets
Office Depot (2005)	Facility closure costs and impairment charges
Pfizer (2007)	Intangible asset impairments
TJX Companies (2007)	Losses on property disposals
Under Armour (2007)	Foreign currency exchange gains
United States Steel (2005)	Property tax settlement gain
Yahoo! (2007)	Gains on sales of investments

Sources: Companies' annual reports. The year following each company name designates the annual report from which the example was drawn.

must be reported in the investing section. The litigation charge is added back because it is a provision, and no cash payments were made in 2007.

    Examples of nonrecurring items disclosed in the operating activities sections of a number of different companies are presented in Exhibit 3.14. Frequently, nonrecurring items appear in both the income statement and operating activities section of the statement of cash flows. However, some nonrecurring items are disclosed in the statement of cash flows but not the income statement. Exhibit 3.14 provides examples of both types of disclosure.

Interpreting Information in the Operating Activities Section

The statement of cash flows is an important additional source of information on nonrecurring items, as it may reveal nonrecurring items that are not disclosed separately in the income statement. To realize the diagnostic value of the statement of cash flows, it is crucial to determine which items in the operating activities section of the statement of cash flows are nonrecurring. The mere appearance in the operating section of the statement of cash flows as either an addition to or deduction from net income or loss does not signify that the item is nonrecurring. Some entries in this section simply reflect the noncash character of certain items of revenue, gain, expense, and loss. For

Exhibit 3.15   Investing cash flows: Baxter International, Inc., partial investing cash flows section, years ended December 31.

	2007	2006	2005
Cash flows from investing activities:			
Acquisitions of and investments in businesses and technologies	($112)	($5)	($47)

Source: Baxter International, Inc., annual report, December 31, 2007.

example, depreciation and amortization are added back to Baxter's net income or loss (Exhibit 3.13) because they are not cash expenses.[19] The asset write-down charges are likewise added back to net income or loss because of their noncash character. However, a separate judgment may also be made that, unlike depreciation, these two items are *both* noncash *and* nonrecurring.

Not all add-backs to net income involve noncash charges. Acquired in-process R&D, for example, is part of investing transactions involving cash outflows, as shown in a portion of the investing section in Exhibit 3.15.

Nonrecurring Items in the Inventory Disclosures of LIFO Firms

The carrying values of inventories maintained under the last in, first out (LIFO) method are sometimes significantly understated in relation to their replacement cost. For public companies, the difference between the LIFO carrying value and replacement cost—frequently approximated by the first in, first out (FIFO) method—is a required disclosure under Securities and Exchange Commission regulations.[20] An example of a substantial difference between LIFO and current replacement value is found in a summary of the inventory disclosures of Winnebago Industries in Exhibit 3.16.

Exhibit 3.16   LIFO inventory valuation differences: Winnebago Industries, Inc. inventory footnote (in thousands).

	Year Ended August 25, 2007	Year Ended August 26, 2006
Inventories consist of the following:		
Finished goods	$ 45,489	$33,420
Work in process	41,417	35,166
Raw materials	37,007	40,080
	133,913	108,666
LIFO reserve	(32,705)	(31,585)
	$101,208	$77,081

The above value of inventories, before reduction for the LIFO reserve, approximates replacement cost at the respective dates.

Source: Winnebago Industries, Inc., annual report, 2007, Note 3.

The inventory value on Winnebago's 2007 balance sheet is $101,208, as measured using LIFO, while the replacement cost of the same inventory is $133,913—32% higher than reported.

A reduction in the physical inventory quantities of a LIFO inventory is called a *LIFO liquidation*. With a LIFO liquidation, a portion of the firm's cost of sales for the year will be made up of the carrying values associated with the liquidated units. These costs are typically lower than current replacement costs, resulting in increased profits or reduced losses. As with the differences between the LIFO cost and the replacement value of the LIFO inventory, Securities and Exchange Commission regulations also call for disclosures of the effect of LIFO liquidations.[21] Winnebago Industries had a LIFO liquidation in both 2006 as reported in the following disclosure:

> During Fiscal 2006, inventory quantities were reduced. This reduction resulted in a liquidation of LIFO inventory values, the effect of which decreased cost of goods sold by $4.0 million and increased net income by $2.6 million or $0.08 per share.[22]

Including the effects of the LIFO liquidations, Winnebago reported after-tax income from continuing operations in 2006 of $68.2 million, but would have reported $65.6 million without the LIFO liquidation, a 4% decrease. Given that the LIFO liquidation is nonrecurring, we would adjust 2006 earnings accordingly. Conceptually, the profit improvements resulting from LIFO liquidations represent the realization of an undervalued asset, not sustainable core earnings. The effect is analogous to the gain associated with the disposition of an undervalued investment, piece of equipment, or plot of land.

Nonrecurring Items in the Income Tax Note

Income tax notes are among the more challenging of the disclosures found in annual reports. However, they can be a rich source of information on nonrecurring items. Fortunately, one key schedule found in the standard income tax note helps us to identify nonrecurring increases and decreases in income tax expense. The schedule reconciles the actual tax expense or tax benefit with the amount that would have resulted if all pretax results had been taxed at the statutory federal rate (currently 35% in the United States). This disclosure for PepsiCo, Inc., is presented in Exhibit 3.17.

Exhibit 3.17   Reconciliation of statutory and actual tax rates: PepsiCo, Inc., years ended December 31.

	2007	2006	2005
U.S. federal statutory rate	35.0%	35.0%	35.0%
State income taxes, net of U.S. federal benefit	0.9	0.5	1.4
Lower taxes on foreign results	(6.5)	(6.5)	(6.5)
Tax settlements	(1.7)	(8.6)	—
Taxes on American Jobs Creation Act repatriation	—	—	7.0
Other (net)	(1.8)	(1.1)	(0.8)
Effective tax rate	25.9%	19.3%	36.1%

Source: PepsiCo, Inc., annual report, 2007, Note 5.

Notice that PepsiCo's effective tax rate was reduced in 2006 by 8.6% and in 2007 by 1.7% as a result of a redetermination of taxes in prior years. The percentage effects are expressed in terms of the ratio of the reduction in income tax expense to income from continuing operations before taxes. In 2007 PepsiCo's pretax income from continuing operations was $7,631 million, and its total tax provision was $1,973 million. The 2007 effective tax rate, disclosed in Exhibit 3.17, is derived by dividing the total tax provision by income from continuing operations before taxes: $1,973 divided by $7,631 equals 25.9%. To determine the dollar, as opposed to percentage, tax savings from tax settlements in 2007, multiply 1.7% times the 2007 pretax earnings: $7,631 million times .017 equals $129.7 million. PepsiCo explained in its note: "In 2007, we recognized $129 million of non-cash tax benefits related to the favorable resolution of certain foreign tax matters."[23] The tax settlement effects in both 2006 and 2007 appear to be nonrecurring. In contrast, lower tax rates on foreign operations are noticeably consistent, suggesting that PepsiCo's effective tax rate will continue to be lower than the U.S. federal rate.

PepsiCo's 2005 effective tax rate was increased by 7.0% as a result of repatriating earnings under the American Jobs Creation Act (AJCA)—congressional legislation that triggered many one-time repatriations. Using the reconciliation from statutory to effective tax rates, we might estimate PepsiCo's sustainable effective tax rate as 35% plus 1% for state income tax effects less 6.5% for foreign tax effects, equaling 29.5%.

The PepsiCo disclosures provide one example of nonrecurring tax effects. Exhibit 3.18 provides a sampling of other nonrecurring tax benefits and tax charges that were found in recent company tax notes.

The tax benefits to Amazon.com result from utilizing loss carryforwards for which benefits had not previously been recognized. Taxable losses in earlier periods produced the tax savings recognized in 2004. Because the likelihood of their realization was not sufficiently high, the potential tax savings of the losses were not recognized in the income statements in the years in which these losses were incurred. The subsequent realization of these benefits occurs when the operating and capital loss carryforwards are used to shield operating earnings and capital gains, respectively, from taxation. These benefits

Exhibit 3.18   Examples of nonrecurring income tax charges and benefits.

Company	Nonrecurring Charge or Benefit
Alliant Energy (2005)	Nonconventional fuel credits
Amazon.com, Inc. (2004)	Benefit from recognition of net operating loss carryforward
Boston Scientific (2007)	Charge for valuation allowance increase
Eli Lilly & Company (2007)	Benefit from operations in Puerto Rico
First Solar (2007)	Research and development tax credits
McDonald's Corporation (2007)	Higher rate due to nondeductibility of asset write-down
Monster Worldwide (2007)	Benefit from valuation allowance decrease
Motorola (2006)	Benefit from charitable contributions
Wyeth (2007)	Benefits from research tax credits

Sources: Companies' annual reports. The year following each company name designates the annual report from which the example was drawn.

should be treated as nonrecurring in analyzing earnings performance for the year in which the benefits are realized. In the case of Amazon.com, the tax benefit increased earnings by 65% in 2004.

Both Wyeth and First Solar reduced their effective tax rates as a result of benefits from research and development tax credits. This feature of the tax law is designed to encourage R&D spending in areas such as specific pharmaceuticals and alternative energy sources. As with all other tax credits, continuation of this source of tax reduction requires that the provision continue to be part of the tax law and that companies make the R&D expenditures necessary to earn future benefits.

The nonrecurring items of Boston Scientific and Monster Worldwide both result from adjustments to their deferred tax asset valuation allowances. The allowance balances represent the portion of tax benefits that have been judged unlikely to be realized.[24] Increasing or decreasing this balance will create a nonrecurring tax charge or benefit, respectively. The prospects for realization of the tax benefit must have declined for Boston Scientific but improved for Monster Worldwide, although these changes are highly discretionary.

Eli Lilly has a tax reduction that is associated with operations located in Puerto Rico. It is also common to see such tax benefits produced by firms with operations in other countries. These benefits are designed to encourage companies, typically manufacturing companies, to locate in foreign countries. In many cases these benefits are for a limited period of time, though renewals of the benefit are sometimes possible. As a result, while the benefits are real, there remains a possibility that they will cease at some point in time. Eli Lilly reports in its tax note:

> We have a subsidiary operating in Puerto Rico under a tax incentive grant. The current tax incentive grant will not expire prior to 2017.

When a company reports tax benefits due to the location of operations in other countries, the possibility that the benefits might end or be reduced should be considered. In this case, however, we would treat the effect as recurring at least for the next 10 years.

Nonrecurring Items in the Other Income and Expense Note

An "other income (expense), net" or equivalent line item is commonly found in both the single and the multistep income statements. In the case of the multistep format, the composition of other income and expenses is sometimes detailed on the face of the income statement. In both the multistep and single-step formats, the most typical presentation is a single line item. Even though a note detailing the contents of other income and expense may exist, guidance is typically not provided as to its specific location. Where present, other income and expense notes tend to be toward the end of the notes to the financial statements.

Colgate-Palmolive Company uses a multistep format income statement and includes "other (income) expense, net" in operating income. The supporting note is provided in Exhibit 3.19.

Although these net amounts are small relative to Colgate-Palmolive's operating income (over $2.6 billion in 2007), the volatility invites a closer look at the components. While some are recurring and steady, note the uneven effects of restructuring charges, gains on sales of product lines, and investment losses (income), and the nonrecurring effects

Exhibit 3.19 Composition of an other income and expense note: Colgate-Palmolive Company, years ended December 31 (millions).

	2007	2006	2005
Minority interest	$ 67.1	$ 57.5	$ 55.3
Amortization of intangible assets	18.2	16.3	15.6
Equity (income)	(3.7)	(3.4)	(2.0)
Gains on sales of noncore product lines, net	(48.6)	(46.5)	(147.9)
2004 restructuring program	55.6	153.1	80.8
Pension and other retiree benefits SFAS 88 charges	15.4	—	34.0
Hill's limited voluntary recall	12.6	—	—
Investment losses (income)	(1.5)	(5.7)	19.7
Other, net	6.2	14.6	13.7
Total other (income) expense, net	$121.3	$185.9	$ 69.2

Source: Colgate-Palmolive Company, annual report, December 2007, Note 15.

of the voluntary product recall and SFAS 88 charges. Although the amounts are modest, on an adjusted basis, 2006 operating income increased by $60 million instead of the reported decrease of $55 million. In both 2005 and 2007 the nonrecurring items are largely offsetting, a common smoothing technique.

Nonrecurring Items in Management's Discussion and Analysis (MD&A)

Management's discussion and analysis (MD&A) of financial condition and results of operations is an annual and a quarterly Securities and Exchange Commission reporting requirement. Provisions of this regulation have a direct bearing on the goal of locating nonrecurring items. As part of the MD&A, the Securities and Exchange Commission requires registrants to:

> Describe any unusual or infrequent events or transactions or any significant economic changes that materially affected the amount of reported income from continuing operations and, in each case, indicate the extent to which income was so affected. In addition, describe any other significant components of revenues and expenses that, in the registrant's judgment, should be described in order to understand the registrant's results of operations.[25]

Complying with these requirements will require some firms to identify and discuss items that may have already been listed in other financial statements and notes. In reviewing the MD&A with a view to locating nonrecurring items, attention should be focused on the section dealing with results of operations. Here management presents a comparison of results over the most recent three years, with the standard pattern involving discussion of, for example, 2007 with 2006 and 2006 with 2005.

Locating nonrecurring items in MD&A is somewhat more difficult than locating these items in other places. Often, the nonrecurring items in MD&A are discussed in text and are not set out in schedules or statements. However, a small number of firms do summarize nonrecurring items in schedules within MD&A. These tend to be more comprehensive and user-friendly than piecemeal disclosures embedded in text.

Exhibit 3.20 Effects of divestitures/impairment charges on income from continuing operations by segment included in MD&A of financial condition and results of operations: H.J. Heinz Company, year ended May 3, 2006 (in millions).

Business or Product Line	Segment	Pretax	After-Tax
Loss on sale of seafood business in Israel	Other operating	$ (15.9)	$ (15.9)
Impairment charge on Portion Pac bulk product line	U.S. Foodservice	(21.5)	(13.3)
Impairment charge on U.K. frozen and chilled product lines	Europe	(15.2)	(15.2)
Impairment charge on European production assets	Europe	(18.7)	(18.7)
Impairment charge on noodle product line in Indonesia	Asia/Pacific	(15.8)	(8.5)
Impairment charge on investment in Zimbabwe business	Other operating	(111.0)	(105.6)
Other	Various	(1.5)	0.5
Total		$(199.6)	$(176.7)

Note: Of the above pretax amounts, $74.1 million was recorded in cost of products sold, $15.5 million in SG&A, $111.0 million in asset impairment charges for cost and equity investments, and $(1.0) million in other expense.

Source: H.J. Heinz Company, annual report, May 2006, 17.

The disclosure presented earlier in Exhibit 3.1 provided a restatement of the as-reported net income of Panera Bread Company. This restatement removed the effects of items considered by Panera to be nonrecurring and was disclosed in Panera's MD&A. An additional example of the disclosure of nonrecurring items from the MD&A of H.J. Heinz Company is presented in Exhibit 3.20. This schedule is not a comprehensive list of nonrecurring items, but is focused on the effects that exiting certain businesses has had on specific business segments.

As a result of the finalization of the strategic reviews related to the portfolio realignment, certain noncore businesses and product lines were sold in fiscal 2006 or are anticipated to be sold in fiscal 2007, and, accordingly, the relevant gains (losses) or noncash asset impairment charges have been recorded in continuing operations during fiscal 2006.

The presentation within the MD&A of information on nonrecurring items in schedules is still a fairly limited practice, but some companies list items that affect time series comparability. Conagra Foods, Inc., provided the following list in its May 2008 MD&A:

> Items of note impacting comparability for fiscal 2008 included the following:
>   Reported within Continuing Operations
>
> - charges totaling $45 million ($28 million after tax) related to product recalls,
> - charges totaling $26 million ($16 million after tax) under the Company's restructuring plans, and

- net tax benefits of approximately $19 million related to changes in the Company's legal entity structure, favorable settlements, and changes in estimates.

  Items of note impacting comparability for fiscal 2007 included the following:
    Reported within Continuing Operations

- charges totaling $103 million ($64 million after tax) under the Company's 2006–2008 restructuring plan,
- charges totaling $66 million ($41 million after tax) related to the peanut butter recall,
- gains of approximately $21 million ($13 million after tax) related to the divestiture of an oat milling business and other non-core assets,
- benefits of $13 million ($8 million after tax) resulting from favorable legal settlements,
- a benefit of approximately $7 million ($5 million after tax) resulting from a favorable resolution of franchise tax matters,
- net tax charges of approximately $6 million related to unfavorable settlements and changes in estimates, and
- a gain of approximately $4 million resulting from the sale of an equity investment in a malt business, and related income tax benefits of approximately $4 million, resulting in an after tax gain of approximately $8 million.[26]

Though helpful in locating nonrecurring items, such schedules must be viewed as useful complements to, but not substitutes for, a complete search and restatement process.

The discussion to this point has taken us through the first six steps in the nonrecurring items search process that was outlined in Exhibit 3.4. This last step illustrates how additional nonrecurring items may be located in other selected notes to the financial statements.

Nonrecurring Items in Other Selected Notes

Typically, most material nonrecurring items will have been located by proceeding through the first six steps of the search sequence outlined in Exhibit 3.4. However, additional nonrecurring items or further details may be located in other notes. In fact, nonrecurring items can surface in virtually any note to the financial statements. Three selected notes that frequently contain other nonrecurring items are now discussed. These include notes on foreign currency exchange, restructuring, and quarterly and segment financial data. Recall that inventory, income tax, and other income and expense notes were discussed in steps 3 to 5.

Foreign Currency Exchange Notes

Foreign exchange gains and losses can result from both transaction and translation exposure. Transaction gains and losses result from either unhedged or partially hedged foreign currency exposure.[27] This exposure is created by items such as accounts receivable and accounts payable that are denominated in foreign currencies. These foreign currency balances result from sales and purchases denominated in foreign currencies. As foreign currency exchange rates change, the value of the foreign currency assets and liabilities will expand and contract. This results, in turn, in foreign currency transaction gains and losses. This is the essence of the concept of currency exposure.

Translation gains and losses result from either unhedged or partially hedged exposure associated with foreign subsidiaries. Translation exposure depends on the mix of assets and liabilities of the foreign subsidiary. In addition, the character of the operations of the foreign subsidiary and features of the foreign economy are also factors in determining both exposure and the translation method applied. There are two possible statement translation methods, and of the two only one results in translation gains or losses that appear as part of net income. With the other method, the translation adjustment will be reported as part of other comprehensive income.[28]

Foreign currency gains and losses can also result from the use of various currency contracts such as forwards, futures, options, and swaps for purposes of both hedging and speculation. It is not uncommon to observe foreign exchange gains and losses year after year in a company's income statement. However, it is also the case that the amounts of these items, as well as whether they are gains or losses, are often very irregular, making them candidates for nonrecurring classification.

To illustrate this, a portion of a note titled "Financial Instruments—Other Derivatives" from the 2007 annual report of Hewlett-Packard Company is reproduced here:

HP recognizes the gains or losses on foreign currency forward contracts used to hedge balance sheet exposures in interest and other, net in the same period as the remeasurement gain and loss of the related foreign currency denominated assets and liabilities. Interest and other, net, included net foreign currency exchange gains of approximately $86 million in fiscal 2007, gains of approximately $54 million in fiscal 2006, and gains of approximately $70 million in fiscal 2005.[29]

While appearing in each of the past three years, Hewlett-Packard's foreign currency exchange gains and losses are irregular. At 1% to 2% of pretax income during these years, the amounts are less material than the effects for First Solar described in Exhibit 3.3. The significance of foreign currency gains to First Solar's financial results explains why they appear on the face of its income statement and are discussed in the MD&A, while for Hewlett-Packard, the only disclosure is in the foreign currency section of the note on financial instruments.

Restructuring Notes

Throughout business cycles, but especially in economic contractions, companies continuously tinker with their product lines, geographic reach, and organizational structure. Different firms call the process by different names (e.g., streamlining, downsizing, rightsizing, redeploying, or strategic repositioning), but the result is that firms often record nonrecurring—or at least irregular—charges for these activities. The size and scope of these activities ensures that they leave their tracks throughout the statements and notes. Notes on restructuring charges are among the most common of the transaction-specific notes. An example of a restructuring note is provided in Exhibit 3.21.

Exhibit 3.21   Restructuring note: Kimberly-Clark Corporation, year ended December 31, 2007 (in millions).

In July 2005, the Corporation authorized a multi-year plan to further improve its competitive position by accelerating investments in targeted growth opportunities and strategic cost reductions aimed at streamlining manufacturing and administrative operations, primarily in North America and Europe.

The strategic cost reductions commenced in the third quarter of 2005 and are expected to be substantially completed by December 31, 2008. Based on current estimates, the strategic cost reductions are expected to result in cumulative charges of approximately $880 to $910 million before tax ($610 to $630 million after tax) over that three-and-one-half-year period.

By the end of 2008, it is anticipated there will be a net workforce reduction of about 10 percent, or approximately 6,000 employees. Since the inception of the strategic cost reductions, a net workforce reduction of approximately 4,700 has occurred. Approximately 24 manufacturing facilities are expected to be sold, closed, or streamlined. As of December 31, 2007, charges have been recorded related to the cost reduction initiatives for 23 facilities. To date, 14 facilities have been disposed of and 3 additional facilities have been closed and are being marketed for sale.

Strategic Cost Reduction Plan

The following pretax charges were incurred in connection with the strategic cost reductions:

	Year Ended December 31		
	2007	**2006**	**2005**
Noncash charges	$ 60.0	$264.8	$179.7
Charges for workforce reductions	8.8	161.9	35.6
Other cash charges	29.9	44.6	11.0
Charges for special pension and other benefits	8.5	13.1	2.3
Total pretax charges	$107.2	$484.4	$228.6

Source: Kimberly-Clark Corporation, annual report, December 2007, Note 2.

Kimberly-Clark's note provides further details, listing asset impairment charges for each year and describing the pattern of actual cash payments. Then the note provides the following schedule, which identifies where the restructuring charges are reflected on the income statement:

	Year Ended December 31		
	2007	**2006**	**2005**
Cost of products sold	$ 89.4	$342.4	$201.6
Marketing, research, and general expenses	31.8	134.0	27.0
Other (income) and expense, net	(14.0)	8.0	—
Pretax charges	$107.2	$484.4	$228.6

Using this information, and more provided in the note, we can identify and assess the effects of the restructuring charges on individual expenses, on pretax income, and on after-tax income from continuing operations. Although discussed in the MD&A, these charges are not revealed on any of the financial statements. The note is critical to our understanding of these activities.

Historically, firms have exhibited a tendency to overaccrue restructuring charges. Companies facing a poor year already may decide to take a "big bath" and recognize excessive amounts of restructuring costs. By accelerating these costs, the company relieves future profits of this burden and will, therefore, look stronger. Other companies seem more inclined to spread these charges out over several years, minimizing their effects and reflecting the longer-term nature of some restructuring plans. Because of their common recurrence, these charges are sometimes dubbed "cockroach" charges—from the old saying that if you see one cockroach, there are more where it came from. Still, even when recurring as for Kimberly-Clark, they remain irregular and unpredictable and should at least be isolated from core measures of ongoing operating profitability.

For some companies, disclosure of restructuring charges is so prominent that it would be difficult to miss them. In its 2007 annual report, The Hershey Company reported its restructuring charges in at least four separate locations:

1. On a separate line item of the income statement (step 1 in the nonrecurring items search sequence).
2. Within the operating activities section of the statement of cash flows, with the noncash portion of the charges added back to net earnings or loss (step 2 in the search sequence).
3. In the section of the MD&A dealing with earnings (step 6 in the search sequence).
4. In a separate note to the financial statements on restructuring charges (step 7d in the search sequence).

Quarterly and Segmental Financial Data

Quarterly and segmental financial disclosures frequently reveal nonrecurring items, sometimes as footnotes to the schedules to support the assessment of profitability trends by quarter or by segment. E.I. du Pont de Nemours and Company, for example, reported the effects of a litigation charge and an asset impairment charge on the 2007 pretax earnings of its Performance Materials segment.[30] Quarterly financial data of Bristol-Myers Squibb Company included a schedule of items affecting comparability, such as downsizing charges of $37 million in the first quarter, a $247 million gain on the sale of property in the third quarter, and its $275 million auction rate securities impairment charge in the fourth quarter.[31]

The last item to consider before we illustrate the collection of information on nonrecurring items and the development of the sustainable earnings series is other comprehensive income that companies must disclose in addition to net income.

Earnings Analysis and Other Comprehensive Income

As part of the disclosure of its statement of shareholders' equity, the Walt Disney Company included the table shown in Exhibit 3.22.

Exhibit 3.22   Comprehensive income: The Walt Disney Company, year ended September 29, 2007 (in millions).

Comprehensive Income (Loss)	Year Ended September		
	2007	2006	2005
Net income	$4,687	$3,374	$2,533
Market value adjustments for investments and hedges	(71)	(2)	92
Foreign currency translation and other	77	(19)	20
Minimum pension liability adjustment, increase (decrease) (see Note 9)	106	585	(448)
Comprehensive income	$4,799	$3,938	$2,197

Source: The Walt Disney Corporation, annual report, September 2007, Statement of Shareholders' Equity.

This disclosure is required by SFAS No. 130, *Reporting Comprehensive Income*, which expanded the concept of income to include specific nonrecurring items.[32] Traditional net income is combined with other comprehensive income to produce a complete bottom line (i.e., comprehensive income).

The principal elements of other comprehensive income are listed in the other comprehensive income section of the Walt Disney Company's comprehensive income statement (Exhibit 3.23). They include:

- Foreign currency translation adjustments.[33]
- Unrealized gains and losses on certain securities.
- Pension adjustments.[34]

Unrealized gains and losses on available-for-sale securities will make their way into the income statement when they are realized through sales. Unrealized gains and losses on derivatives will move into the income statement at their settlement dates. Foreign currency translation and pension adjustments will generally not be recognized in net income, but will remain in other comprehensive income indefinitely.

SFAS No. 130 permitted other comprehensive income to be reported in three different ways. The preferred alternative was to include it as a section of the income statement.[35] However, reporting other comprehensive income in a separate statement is also permitted. A third option permitted is to report other comprehensive income as part of the statement of shareholders' equity. It should come as no surprise that most firms have elected this third option. Firms have an aversion to including items in the income statement that have the potential to increase the volatility of earnings. Hence, given the option, firms have generally chosen to avoid the income statement.[36]

There is scant evidence at this point in time that statement users pay much attention to information on other comprehensive income, except as it affects total shareholders' equity. Other comprehensive income is not included in discussions by companies about their earnings performance. It is not commented on in the financial press when earnings are announced. Earnings per share statistics do not incorporate other comprehensive income. There is no focus on other comprehensive income as part of earnings analysis, particularly since most of its components are irregular and unpredictable.

With the structure of the income statement and relevant GAAP now reviewed, the nature of nonrecurring items considered, and methods of locating nonrecurring items outlined and illustrated, we can now turn to the task of developing the sustainable earnings series.

Summarizing Nonrecurring Items and Determining Sustainable Earnings

The work to this point has laid out important background and provided specific examples, but it is not complete. Still required is a device to assist in summarizing information discovered in nonrecurring items so that new measures of sustainable earnings can be developed. The balance of this chapter is devoted to presenting a worksheet designed to summarize nonrecurring items and illustrating its use using a case study.[37]

The Sustainable Earnings Base Worksheet: Downloadable Exhibit 3.23

The sustainable earnings base (SEB) worksheet is shown in Exhibit 3.23. Detailed instructions on completing the worksheet follow:

1. Net income or loss as reported is recorded on the top line of the worksheet.

2. All identified items of nonrecurring expense or loss, which were included in the income statement on a pretax basis, are recorded on the "add" lines provided. Where a prelabeled line is not listed in the worksheet, a descriptive phrase should be recorded on one of the "other" lines and the amounts recorded there. In practice, the processes of locating nonrecurring items and recording them on the worksheet would take place at the same time. However, effective use of the worksheet calls for the background provided earlier in the chapter. This explains the separation of these steps in this chapter.

3. When all pretax, nonrecurring expenses and losses have been recorded, subtotals should be computed. These subtotals are then multiplied times 1 minus a representative combined federal, state, and foreign income tax rate. This puts these items on an after-tax basis so that they are stated on the same basis as net income or net loss.

4. The results from step 3 should be recorded on the line titled "tax-adjusted additions."

5. All after-tax nonrecurring expenses or losses are next added separately. These items are either tax items or special income statement items that are disclosed on an after-tax basis under GAAP (e.g., discontinued operations, extraordinary items, or the cumulative effect of accounting changes). The effects of LIFO liquidations are sometimes presented before tax and sometimes after tax. Note that a line item is provided for the effect of LIFO liquidations in both the pretax and the after-tax additions section of the worksheet.

Exhibit 3.23   Adjustment worksheet for sustainable earnings base.

	Year	Year	Year
Reported net income or (loss)	_____	_____	_____
Nonrecurring Expenses and Losses			
Add			
Pretax LIFO liquidation losses	_____	_____	_____
Losses on sales of fixed assets	_____	_____	_____
Losses on sales of investments	_____	_____	_____
Losses on sales of other assets	_____	_____	_____
Restructuring charges	_____	_____	_____
Investment write-downs	_____	_____	_____
Inventory write-downs	_____	_____	_____
Other asset write-downs	_____	_____	_____
Foreign currency losses	_____	_____	_____
Litigation charges	_____	_____	_____
Losses on patent infringement suits	_____	_____	_____
Exceptional bad-debt provisions	_____	_____	_____
Nonrecurring expense increases	_____	_____	_____
Temporary revenue reductions	_____	_____	_____
Other	_____	_____	_____
Other	_____	_____	_____
Other	_____	_____	_____
Subtotal	_____	_____	_____
Multiply by			
(1 – combined federal, state tax rates)	_____	_____	_____
Tax-adjusted additions	_____	_____	_____
Add			
After-tax LIFO liquidation losses	_____	_____	_____
Increases in deferred tax valuation allowances	_____	_____	_____
Other nonrecurring tax charges	_____	_____	_____
Losses on discontinued operations	_____	_____	_____
Extraordinary losses	_____	_____	_____
Losses/cumulative-effect accounting changes	_____	_____	_____
Other	_____	_____	_____
Other	_____	_____	_____
Other	_____	_____	_____
Subtotal	_____	_____	_____
Total additions	_____	_____	_____

Exhibit 3.23 *(Continued)*

	Year	Year	Year
Nonrecurring Revenues and Gains			
Deduct			
Pretax LIFO liquidation gains	_____	_____	_____
Gains on fixed asset sales	_____	_____	_____
Gains on sales of investments	_____	_____	_____
Gains on sales of other assets	_____	_____	_____
Reversals of restructuring accruals	_____	_____	_____
Investment write-ups (trading account)	_____	_____	_____
Foreign currency gains	_____	_____	_____
Litigation revenues	_____	_____	_____
Gains on patent infringement suits	_____	_____	_____
Temporary expense decreases	_____	_____	_____
Temporary revenue increases	_____	_____	_____
Reversals of bad-debt allowances	_____	_____	_____
Other	_____	_____	_____
Other	_____	_____	_____
Other	_____	_____	_____
Subtotal	_____	_____	_____
Multiply by			
(1 – combined federal, state tax rates)	_____	_____	_____
Tax-adjusted deductions	_____	_____	_____
Deduct			
After-tax LIFO liquidation gains	_____	_____	_____
Reductions in deferred tax valuation allowances	_____	_____	_____
Loss carryforward benefits from prior years	_____	_____	_____
Other nonrecurring tax benefits	_____	_____	_____
Gains on discontinued operations	_____	_____	_____
Extraordinary gains	_____	_____	_____
Gains/cumulative-effect accounting changes	_____	_____	_____
Other	_____	_____	_____
Other	_____	_____	_____
Other	_____	_____	_____
Subtotal	_____	_____	_____
Total deductions	_____	_____	_____
Sustainable earnings base	_____	_____	_____

6. Changes in deferred-tax valuation allowances are recorded in the tax-adjusted additions (or deductions) section only if such changes affected net income or net loss for the period. Evidence of an income statement impact will usually take the form of an entry in the income tax rate-reconciliation schedule.

7. The next step is to subtotal the entries for after-tax additions and then combine this subtotal with the amount labeled "tax-adjusted additions." The result is then recorded on the "total additions" line.

8. Completion of the next section of the worksheet, for nonrecurring revenues and gains, follows exactly the same steps as those outlined for nonrecurring expenses and losses.

9. With the completion of section two, the sustainable earnings base for each year is computed by adding the "total additions" line item to net income (loss) and then deducting the "total deductions" line item.

Role of the Sustainable Earnings Base

The sustainable earnings base (SEB) provides earnings information from which the distorting effects of nonrecurring items have been removed. Some analysts refer to such revised numbers as representing "core" or "underlying" earnings. *Sustainable* is used here in the sense that earnings devoid of nonrecurring items of revenue, gain, expense, and loss are much more likely to be maintained in the future, other things being equal. *Base* implies that the sustainable earnings provide the most reliable foundation or starting point for projections of future results. The more reliable such forecasts become, the less likely it is that earnings surprises will result.

Application of the Sustainable Earnings Base Worksheet: Pfizer, Inc.

This example of using the SEB worksheet is based on the 2007 annual report of Pfizer, Inc. and its results for 2005 to 2007. The income statement, statement of cash flows, management's discussion and analysis (MD&A) of results of operations, and selected notes are provided on the pages that follow in Exhibits 3.24 through 3.37.

Much of the content of the Pfizer financial statements as well as relevant footnote and other textual information is provided. This is designed to make the exercise as realistic as possible.

Exhibit 3.24 Consolidated statements of income: Pfizer, Inc., years ended December 31 (in millions).

	2007	2006	2005
Revenues	$48,418	$48,371	$47,405
Costs and expenses:			
Cost of sales	11,239	7,640	7,232
Selling, informational, and administrative expenses	15,626	15,589	15,313
Research and development expenses	8,089	7,599	7,256
Amortization of intangible asset	3,128	3,261	3,399
Acquisition-related in-process research and development charges	283	835	1,652
Restructuring charges and acquisition-related costs	2,534	1,323	1,356
Other (income)/deductions, net	(1,759)	(904)	397
Income from continuing operations before provision for taxes on income, minority interests, and cumulative effect of a change in accounting principles	9,278	13,028	10,800
Provision for taxes on income	1,023	1,992	3,178
Minority interests	42	12	12
Income from continuing operations before cumulative effect of a change in accounting principles	8,213	11,024	7,610
Discontinued operations:			
Income (loss) from discontinued operations, net of tax	(3)	433	451
Gains/(losses) on sales of discontinued operations, net of tax	(66)	7,880	47
Discontinued operations, net of tax	(69)	8,313	498
Income before cumulative effect of a change in accounting principles	—	—	(23)
Net income	$ 8,144	$19,337	$ 8,085

Note: Per-share amounts omitted.
Source: Pfizer, Inc., annual report, December 2007.

Exhibit 3.25 Consolidated statements of cash flows (operating activities only): Pfizer, Inc., years ended December 31 (in millions).

	2007	2006	2005
Operating activities:			
Net income	$ 8,144	$19,337	$ 8,085
Adjustments to reconcile net income to net cash provided by operating activities:			
Depreciation and amortization	5,200	5,293	5,576
Share-based compensation expense	437	655	157
Acquisition-related in-process research and development charges	283	835	1,652
Intangible asset impairments and other associated noncash charges	2,220	320	1,240
Gains on disposals	(326)	(280)	(172)
(Gains)/losses on sales of discontinued operations	168	(10,243)	(77)
Cumulative effect of a change in accounting principles	—	—	40
Deferred taxes from continuing operations	(2,788)	(1,525)	(1,465)
Other deferred taxes	—	(420)	8
Other noncash adjustments	815	606	486
Changes in assets and liabilities, net of effect of businesses acquired and divested:			
Accounts receivable	(320)	(172)	(803)
Inventories	720	118	72
Prepaid and other assets	(647)	314	615
Accounts payable and accrued liabilities	1,509	(450)	(1,054)
Income taxes payable	(2,002)	2,909	254
Other liabilities	(60)	297	119
Net cash provided by operating activities	$13,353	$17,594	$14,722

Source: Pfizer, Inc., annual report, December 2007.

Exhibit 3.26   Income tax note—excerpts: Pfizer, Inc., years ended December 31 (in millions).

Taxes on Income

Income from continuing operations before provision for taxes on income, minority interests, and the cumulative effect of a change in accounting principles consists of the following:

	2007	2006	2005
United States	$ 242	$ 3,266	$ 985
International	9,036	9,762	9,815
Total	$9,278	$13,028	$10,800

The decrease in domestic income from continuing operations before taxes in 2007 compared to 2006 is due primarily to the volume and geographic mix of product sales and restructuring charges in 2007 compared to 2006, as well as the impact of charges associated with Exubera (see *Note 4. Asset Impairment Charges and Other Costs Associated with Exiting Exubera*), partially offset by lower IPR&D charges in 2007 of $283 million, primarily related to our acquisitions of Biorexis and Embrex, compared to IPR&D charges in 2006 of $835 million, primarily related to our acquisitions of Rinat and PowderMed.

The increase in domestic income from continuing operations before taxes in 2006 compared to 2005 is due primarily to IPR&D charges in 2005 of $1.7 billion, primarily related to our acquisitions of Vicuron and Idun, the Bextra impairment and changes in product mix, among other factors, partially offset by IPR&D charges recorded in 2006 of $835 million, primarily related to our acquisitions of Rinat and PowderMed, and a 2006 charge of $320 million related to the impairment of the Depo-Provera intangible asset.

The provision for taxes on income from continuing operations before minority interests and the cumulative effect of a change in accounting principles consists of the following:

	2007	2006	2005
United States			
Taxes currently payable			
Federal	$ 1,393	$ 1,399	$ 2,572
State and local	243	205	108
Deferred income taxes	(1,986)	(1,371)	(1,295)
Total U.S. tax (benefit)/provision	(350)	233	1,385
International			
Taxes currently payable	2,175	1,913	1,963
Deferred income taxes	(802)	(154)	(170)
Total international tax provision	1,373	1,759	1,793
Total provision for taxes on income	$ 1,023	$ 1,992	$ 3,178

(*continued*)

Exhibit 3.26 *(Continued)*

In 2006, we were notified by the Internal Revenue Service (IRS) Appeals Division that a resolution had been reached on the matter that we were in the process of appealing related to the tax deductibility of an acquisition-related breakup fee paid by the Warner-Lambert Company in 2000. As a result, we recorded a tax benefit of approximately $441 million related to the resolution of this issue. . . . Also in 2006, we recorded a decrease to the 2005 estimated U.S. tax provision related to the repatriation of foreign earnings, due primarily to the receipt of information that raised our assessment of the likelihood of prevailing on the technical merits of a certain position, and we recognized a tax benefit of $124 million. Additionally, in 2006, the IRS issued final regulations on Statutory Mergers and Consolidations, which impacted certain prior-period transactions, and we recorded a tax benefit of $217 million, reflecting the total impact of these regulations.

In 2005, we recorded an income tax charge of $1.7 billion, included in *Provision for taxes on income*, in connection with our decision to repatriate approximately $37 billion of foreign earnings in accordance with the *American Jobs Creation Act of 2004* (the Jobs Act). The Jobs Act created a temporary incentive for U.S. corporations to repatriate accumulated income earned abroad by providing an 85% dividend-received deduction for certain dividends from controlled foreign corporations, subject to various limitations and restrictions including qualified U.S. reinvestment of such earnings. In addition, in 2005, we recorded a tax benefit of $586 million related to the resolution of certain tax positions. . . .

Tax Rate Reconciliation
Reconciliation of the U.S. statutory income tax rate to our effective tax rate for continuing operations before the cumulative effect of a change in accounting principles follows:

	2007	2006	2005
U.S. statutory income tax rate	35.0%	35.0%	35.0%
Earnings taxed at other than U.S. statutory rate	(21.6)	(15.7)	(20.6)
Resolution of certain tax positions	—	(3.4)	(5.4)
Tax legislation impact	—	(1.7)	—
U.S. research tax credit and manufacturing deduction	(1.5)	(0.5)	(0.8)
Repatriation of foreign earnings	—	(1.0)	15.4
Acquired IPR&D	1.1	2.2	5.4
All other—net	(2.0)	0.4	0.4
Effective tax rate for income from continuing operations before cumulative effect of a change in accounting principles	11.0%	15.3%	29.4%

Exhibit 3.26 (*Continued*)

We operate manufacturing subsidiaries in Puerto Rico, Ireland, and Singapore. We benefit from Puerto Rican incentive grants that expire between 2017 and 2027. Under the grants, we are partially exempt from income, property and municipal taxes. Under Section 936 of the U.S. Internal Revenue Code, Pfizer was a "grandfathered" entity and was entitled to the benefits under such statute until September 30, 2006. In Ireland, we benefit from an incentive tax rate effective through 2010 on income from manufacturing operations. In Singapore, we benefit from incentive tax rates effective through 2031 on income from manufacturing operations.

The U.S. research tax credit was effective through December 31, 2007.

Source: Pfizer, Inc., annual report, December 2007.

Exhibit 3.27   Other income (expense) note—excerpts: Pfizer, Inc., years ended December 31 (in millions).

The components of Other (income)/deductions—net follow:

	2007	**2006**	**2005**
Interest income	$(1,496)	$(925)	$(740)
Interest expense	440	517	488
Interest expense capitalized	(43)	(29)	(17)
Net interest income[a]	(1,099)	(437)	(269)
Asset impairment charges[b]	—	320	1,159
Royalty income	(224)	(395)	(320)
Net gains on asset disposals[c]	(326)	(280)	(172)
Other, net	(110)	(112)	(1)
Other (income)/deductions—net	$(1,759)	$(904)	$ 397

[a]The increase in interest income in 2007 compared to 2006 is due primarily to higher net financial assets during 2007 compared to 2006, reflecting proceeds of $16.6 billion from the sale of our Consumer Healthcare business in late December 2006, and higher interest rates.
[b]In 2006, we recorded a charge of $320 million related to the impairment of our Depo-Provera intangible asset, for which amortization expense is included in *Amortization of intangible assets.* In 2005, we recorded charges totaling $1.2 billion, primarily related to the impairment of our Bextra intangible asset, for which amortization expense had previously been recorded in *Amortization of intangible assets.* . . .
[c]In 2007, includes a gain of $211 million related to the sale of a building in Korea. In 2006, gross realized gains were $8 million and gross realized losses were nil on sales of available-for-sale securities. In 2006, gross realized gains were $65 million and gross realized losses were $1 million on sales of available-for-sale securities. In 2005, gross realized gains were $171 million and gross realized losses were $14 million on sales of available-for-sale securities. . . .
Source: Pfizer, Inc., annual report, December 2007.

Exhibit 3.28   Management's discussion and analysis (excerpts from results of operations section): Pfizer, Inc., years ended December 31 (in millions).

Costs and Expenses

Cost of Sales

Cost of sales increased 47% in 2007 and increased 6% in 2006, while revenues were flat in 2007 and increased 2% in 2006. Cost of sales as a percentage of revenues increased in 2007 compared to 2006 and in 2006 compared to 2005.

Cost of sales in 2007, compared to 2006, increased as a result of:

- asset impairment charges, write-offs, and other exit costs associated with Exubera of $2.6 billion . . .;
- the unfavorable impact of foreign exchange on expenses;
- the impact of higher implementation costs associated with our cost-reduction initiatives of $700 million in 2007, compared to $392 million in 2006; and
- costs of $194 million for 2007, related to business transition activities associated with the sale of our Consumer Healthcare business, completed in December 2006,

partially offset by:

- savings related to our cost-reduction initiatives.

Cost of sales in 2006, compared to 2005, increased as a result of:

- the impact of higher implementation costs associated with our cost-reduction initiatives of $392 million in 2006, compared to $124 million in 2005;
- the timing of implementation of inventory-management initiatives;
- the unfavorable impact on expenses of foreign exchange; and
- charges related to certain inventory and manufacturing equipment write-downs,

partially offset by:

- changes in sales mix;
- savings related to our cost-reduction initiatives; and
- $73 million in write-offs of inventory and exit costs in 2005 related to suspension of sales and marketing of Bextra.

Selling, Informational and Administrative (SI&A) Expenses

SI&A expenses in 2007 were comparable to 2006, which reflects:

- savings related to our cost-reduction initiatives,

offset by:

- the unfavorable impact on expenses of foreign exchange;
- the impact of higher implementation costs associated with our cost-reduction initiatives of $334 million in 2007, compared to $243 million in 2006; and
- charges associated with Exubera of $85 million. . . .

Exhibit 3.28 *(Continued)*

SI&A expenses increased 2% in 2006, compared to 2005, which reflects:

- higher promotional investments in new product launches and in-line product promotional programs;
- expenses related to share-based payments; and
- the impact of higher implementation costs associated with our cost-reduction initiatives of $243 million in 2006, compared to $151 million in 2005,

partially offset by:

- the favorable impact on expenses of foreign exchange; and
- savings related to our cost-reduction initiatives.

Research and Development (R&D) Expenses

R&D expenses increased 6% in 2007, compared to 2006, which reflects:

- the impact of higher implementation costs associated with our cost-reduction initiatives of $416 million in 2007, compared to $176 million in 2006;
- an initial payment to BMS of $250 million and additional payments to BMS related to product development efforts, in connection with our collaboration to develop and commercialize apixaban, recorded in 2007;
- the unfavorable impact on expenses of foreign exchange;
- a one-time R&D milestone due to us from sanofi-aventis (approximately $118 million) recorded in 2006; and
- exit costs, such as contract termination costs, associated with Exubera of $100 million . . . ,

partially offset by:

- savings related to our cost-reduction initiatives.

R&D expenses increased 5% in 2006, compared to 2005, which reflects:

- the impact of higher implementation costs associated with our cost-reduction initiatives of $176 million in 2006, compared to $50 million in 2005;
- expenses related to share-based payments;
- timing considerations associated with the advancement of development programs for pipeline products; and
- higher payments for intellectual property rights . . . among other factors,

partially offset by:

- a one-time R&D milestone due to us from sanofi-aventis (approximately $118 million); and
- savings related to our cost-reduction initiatives.

R&D expenses also include payments for intellectual property rights of $603 million in 2007, $292 million in 2006 and $156 million in 2005. . . .

Acquisition-Related In-Process Research and Development Charges

The estimated value of acquisition-related IPR&D is expensed at the acquisition date. In 2007, we expensed $283 million of IPR&D, primarily related to our acquisitions of BioRexis and Embrex. In 2006, we expensed $835 million of IPR&D, primarily related

(continued)

Exhibit 3.28 *(Continued)*

to our acquisitions of Rinat and PowderMed. In 2005, we expensed $1.7 billion of IPR&D, primarily related to our acquisitions of Vicuron and Idun.

Cost-Reduction Initiatives

In connection with our cost-reduction initiatives, which were launched in early 2005 and broadened in October 2006, our management has performed a comprehensive review of our processes, organizations, systems and decision-making procedures in a company-wide effort to improve performance and efficiency. On January 22, 2007, we announced additional plans to change the way we run our businesses to meet the challenges of a changing business environment and to take advantage of the diverse opportunities in the marketplace. We are generating net cost reductions through site rationalization in R&D and manufacturing, streamlined organizational structures, sales force and staff function reductions, and increased outsourcing and procurement savings. . . .

The actions associated with the expanded cost-reduction initiatives include restructuring charges, such as asset impairments, exit costs and severance costs (including any related impacts to our benefit plans, including settlements and curtailments) and associated implementation costs, such as accelerated depreciation charges, primarily associated with plant network optimization efforts, and expenses associated with system and process standardization and the expansion of shared services worldwide. (See Notes to Consolidated Financial Statements—*Note 5. Cost-Reduction Initiatives.*). . . .

We incurred the following costs in connection with our cost-reduction initiatives:

	2007	2006	2005
Implementation costs[a]	$1,389	$ 788	$325
Restructuring charges[b]	2,523	1,296	438
Total costs related to our cost-reduction initiatives	$3,912	$2,084	$763

[a] For 2007, included in *Cost of sales* ($700 million), *Selling, informational and administrative expenses* ($334 million), *Research and development expenses* ($416 million) and in *Other (income)/deductions*—net ($61 million income). For 2006, included in *Cost of sales* ($392 million), *Selling, informational and administrative expenses* ($243 million), *Research and development expenses* ($176 million) and in *Other (income)/deductions*—net ($23 million income). For 2005, included in *Cost of sales* ($124 million), *Selling, informational and administrative expenses* ($151 million), and *Research and development expenses* ($50 million).
[b] Included in *Restructuring charges and acquisition-related costs.*

Through December 31, 2007, the restructuring charges primarily relate to our plant network optimization efforts and the restructuring of our worldwide marketing and research and development operations, and the implementation costs primarily relate to accelerated depreciation of certain assets, as well as system and process standardization and the expansion of shared services.

Exhibit 3.28 *(Continued)*

The components of restructuring charges associated with our cost-reduction initiatives follow:

	2007	2006	2005
Employee termination costs	$2,034	$ 809	$303
Asset impairments	260	368	122
Other	229	119	13
Total	$2,523	$1,296	$438

From the beginning of the cost-reduction initiatives in 2005 through December 31, 2007, *Employee termination costs* represent the expected reduction of the workforce by 20,800 employees, mainly in research, manufacturing and sales. As of December 31, 2007, approximately 13,000 of these employees have been formally terminated. *Employee termination costs* are recorded when the actions are probable and estimable and include accrued severance benefits, pension and postretirement benefits. *Asset impairments* primarily include charges to write down property, plant and equipment. *Other* primarily includes costs to exit certain activities.

Acquisition-Related Costs
We recorded in *Restructuring charges and acquisition-related costs* $11 million in 2007, $27 million in 2006 and $918 million in 2005, for acquisition-related costs. Amounts in 2005 were primarily related to our acquisition of Pharmacia on April 16, 2003 and included integration costs of $543 million and restructuring charges of $375 million. As of December 31, 2007, virtually all restructuring charges incurred have been utilized. Integration costs represent external, incremental costs directly related to an acquisition, including expenditures for consulting and systems integration. Restructuring charges can include severance, costs of vacating duplicative facilities, contract termination and other exit costs.

Other (Income)/Deductions—Net
In 2007, we recorded higher net interest income compared to 2006, due primarily to higher net financial assets during 2007 compared to 2006, reflecting proceeds of $16.6 billion from the sale of our Consumer Healthcare business in late December 2006, and higher interest rates. Also in 2007, we recorded a gain of $211 million related to the sale of a building in Korea. In 2006, we recorded a charge of $320 million related to the impairment of our Depo-Provera intangible asset. In 2005, we recorded charges of $1.2 billion primarily related to the impairment of our Bextra intangible asset. See also Notes to Consolidated Financial Statements—*Note 7. Other (Income)/Deductions—Net.*

Provision for Taxes on Income
Our overall effective tax rate for continuing operations was 11.0% in 2007, 15.3% in 2006 and 29.4% in 2005. The lower tax rate in 2007 is primarily due to the impact of charges associated with our decision to exit Exubera . . . , higher charges related to our cost-reduction initiatives in 2007, lower non-deductible charges for acquisition-related IPR&D, and the volume and geographic mix of product sales and restructuring charges in 2007 compared to 2006, partially offset by certain one-time tax benefits in 2006, all discussed below.

(continued)

Exhibit 3.28 *(Continued)*

The lower tax rate in 2006 compared to 2005 is primarily due to certain one-time tax benefits associated with favorable tax legislation and the resolution of certain tax positions, and a decrease in the 2005 estimated U.S. tax provision related to the repatriation of foreign earnings, all as discussed below, and the impact of the sale of our Consumer Healthcare business.

In the third quarter of 2006, we recorded a decrease to the 2005 estimated U.S. tax provision related to the repatriation of foreign earnings, due primarily to the receipt of information that raised our assessment of the likelihood of prevailing on the technical merits of a certain position, and we recognized a tax benefit of $124 million.

In the first quarter of 2006, we were notified by the Internal Revenue Service (IRS) Appeals Division that a resolution had been reached on the matter that we were in the process of appealing related to the tax deductibility of an acquisition-related breakup fee paid by the Warner-Lambert Company in 2000. As a result, in the first quarter of 2006, we recorded a tax benefit of approximately $441 million related to the resolution of this issue.

On January 23, 2006, the IRS issued final regulations on Statutory Mergers and Consolidations, which impacted certain prior-period transactions. In the first quarter of 2006, we recorded a tax benefit of $217 million, reflecting the total impact of these regulations.

In 2005, we recorded an income tax charge of $1.7 billion, included in *Provision for taxes on income*, in connection with our decision to repatriate approximately $37 billion of foreign earnings in accordance with the American Jobs Creation Act of 2004 (the Jobs Act). The Jobs Act created a temporary incentive for U.S. corporations to repatriate accumulated income earned abroad by providing an 85% dividend-received deduction for certain dividends from controlled foreign corporations in 2005. In addition, during 2005, we recorded a tax benefit of $586 million, primarily related to the resolution of certain tax positions.

Discontinued Operations—Net of Tax

... **The following amounts, primarily related to our former Consumer Healthcare business, have been segregated from continuing operations and included in *Discontinued operations—net of tax* in the consolidated statements of income:**

	2007	2006	2005
Revenues	$ —	$ 4,044	$3,948
Pretax income/loss	(5)	643	695
Benefit/(provision) for taxes on income	2	(210)	(244)
Income/loss from operations of discontinued businesses—net of tax	(3)	433	451
Pretax gains/(losses) on sales of discontinued businesses	(168)	10,243	77
Benefit/(provision) for taxes on gains	102	(2,363)	(30)
Gains/(losses) on sales of discontinued businesses—net of tax	(66)	7,880	47
Discontinued operations—net of tax	$(69)	$ 8,313	$ 498

Source: Pfizer, Inc., annual report, December 2007.

Exhibit 3.29   Summary of significant accounting policies note—excerpt: Pfizer, Inc., years ended December 31 (in millions).

Summary of Significant Accounting Policies

On January 1, 2006, we adopted the provisions of SFAS No. 123R, *Share-Based Payment*, as supplemented by the interpretation provided by SEC Staff Accounting Bulletin (SAB) No. 107, issued in March 2005. (SFAS 123R replaced SFAS 123, *Stock-Based Compensation*, issued in 1995.) We elected the modified prospective application transition method of adoption and, as such, prior-period financial statements were not restated for this change. Under this method, the fair value of all stock options granted or modified after adoption must be recognized in the consolidated statement of income. Total compensation cost related to nonvested awards not yet recognized, determined under the original provisions of SFAS 123, must also be recognized in the consolidated statement of income. The adoption of SFAS 123R primarily impacted our accounting for stock options (see *Note 16. Share-Based Payments*). Prior to January 1, 2006, we accounted for stock options under Accounting Principles Board Opinion (APB) No. 25, *Accounting for Stock Issued to Employees*, an elective accounting policy permitted by SFAS 123. Under this standard, since the exercise price of our stock options granted is set equal to the market price of Pfizer common stock on the date of the grant, we did not record any expense to the consolidated statement of income related to stock options, unless certain original grant date terms were subsequently modified. However, as required, we disclosed, in the Notes to Consolidated Financial Statements, the pro forma expense impact of the stock option grants as if we had applied the fair-value-based recognition provisions of SFAS 123.

As of December 31, 2005, we adopted the provisions of FASB Interpretation No. 47 (FIN 47), *Accounting for Conditional Asset Retirement Obligations (an interpretation of FASB Statement No. 143)*. FIN 47 clarifies that conditional obligations meet the definition of an asset retirement obligation in SFAS No. 143, *Accounting for Asset Retirement Obligations*, and therefore should be recognized if their fair value is reasonably estimable. As a result of adopting FIN 47, we recorded a non-cash pre-tax charge of $40 million ($23 million, net of tax). This charge was reported in *Cumulative effect of a change in accounting principles— net of tax* in the fourth quarter of 2005. In accordance with these standards, we record accruals for legal obligations associated with the retirement of tangible long-lived assets, including obligations under the doctrine of promissory estoppel and those that are conditional upon the occurrence of future events. We recognize these obligations using management's best estimate of fair value.

Source: Pfizer, Inc., annual report, December 2007.

Exhibit 3.30   Acquisitions note: Pfizer, Inc., years ended December 31 (in millions).

We are committed to capitalizing on new growth opportunities, a strategy that can include acquisitions of companies, products or technologies. During the three years ended December 31, 2007, 2006 and 2005, we acquired the following:

- In the first quarter of 2007, we acquired BioRexis Pharmaceutical Corp., (BioRexis) a privately held biopharmaceutical company with a number of diabetes candidates and a novel technology platform for developing new protein drug candidates, and Embrex, Inc., (Embrex) an animal health company that possesses a unique vaccine delivery system known as Inovoject that improves consistency and reliability by inoculating chicks while they are still in the egg. In connection with these and other smaller acquisitions, we recorded $283 million in *Acquisition-related in-process research and development charges.*
- In February 2006, we completed the acquisition of the sanofi-aventis worldwide rights, including patent rights and production technology, to manufacture and sell Exubera, an inhaled form of insulin, and the insulin-production business and facilities located in Frankfurt, Germany, previously jointly owned by Pfizer and sanofi-aventis, for approximately $1.4 billion (including transaction costs). Substantially all assets recorded in connection with this acquisition have now been written off. See *Note 4. Asset Impairment Charges and Other Costs Associated with Exiting Exubera.* Prior to the acquisition, in connection with our collaboration agreement with sanofi-aventis, we recorded a research and development milestone due to us from sanofi-aventis of $118 million ($71 million, after tax) in 2006 in Research and development expenses upon the approval of Exubera in January 2006 by the U.S. Food and Drug Administration (FDA).
- In December 2006, we completed the acquisition of PowderMed Ltd. (PowderMed), a U.K. company which specializes in the emerging science of DNA-based vaccines for the treatment of influenza and chronic viral diseases, and in May 2006, we completed the acquisition of Rinat Neurosciences Corp. (Rinat), a biologics company with several new central-nervous-system product candidates. In 2006, the aggregate cost of these and other smaller acquisitions was approximately $880 million (including transaction costs). In connection with those transactions, we recorded $835 million in *Acquisition-related in-process research and development charges.*
- In September 2005, we completed the acquisition of all of the outstanding shares of Vicuron Pharmaceuticals Inc. (Vicuron), a biopharmaceutical company focused on the development of novel anti-infectives, for approximately $1.9 billion in cash (including transaction costs). In connection with the acquisition, as part of our final purchase price allocation, we recorded $1.4 billion in *Acquisition-related in-process research and development charges. . . .*
- In April 2005, we completed the acquisition of Idun Pharmaceuticals Inc. (Idun), a biopharmaceutical company focused on the discovery and development of therapies to control apoptosis, and in August 2005, we completed the acquisition of Bioren Inc. (Bioren), which focuses on technology for optimizing antibodies. In 2005, the aggregate cost of these and other smaller acquisitions was approximately $340 million in cash (including transaction costs). In connection with these transactions, we recorded $262 million in *Acquisition-related in-process research and development charges.*

Source: Pfizer, Inc., annual report, December 2007.

Exhibit 3.31   Discontinued operations note: Pfizer, Inc., years ended December 31 (in millions).

We evaluate our businesses and product lines periodically for strategic fit within our operations. Recent activity includes:

- In the fourth quarter of 2006, we sold our Consumer Healthcare business for $16.6 billion, and recorded a gain of approximately $10.2 billion ($7.9 billion, net of tax) in *Gains on sales of discontinued operations—net of tax* in the consolidated statement of income for 2006. In 2007, we recorded a loss of approximately $70 million, after-tax, primarily related to the resolution of contingencies, such as purchase price adjustments and product warranty obligations, as well as pension settlements. This business was composed of:
  - substantially all of our former Consumer Healthcare segment;
  - other associated amounts, such as purchase-accounting impacts, acquisition-related costs and restructuring and implementation costs related to our cost-reduction initiatives that were previously reported in the Corporate/Other segment; and
  - certain manufacturing facility assets and liabilities, which were previously part of our Pharmaceutical or Corporate/Other segment but were included in the sale of our Consumer Healthcare business. The net impact to the Pharmaceutical segment was not significant.

The results of this business are included in *Income from discontinued operations—net of tax* for 2006 and 2005. . . .

We continued during 2007, and we will continue for a period of time, to generate cash flows and to report gross revenues, income and expense activity that are associated with our former Consumer Healthcare business, in continuing operations, although at a substantially reduced level. After the transfer of these activities, these cash flows and the income statement activity reported in continuing operations will be eliminated. The activities that give rise to these impacts are transitional in nature and generally result from agreements that ensure and facilitate the orderly transfer of business operations to the new owner. For example, we entered into a number of transition services agreements that allow the buyer sufficient time to prepare for the transfer of activities and to limit the risk of business disruption. The nature, magnitude and duration of the agreements vary depending on the specific circumstances of the service, location and/or business need. The agreements can include the following: manufacturing and product supply, logistics, customer service, support of financial processes, procurement, human resources, facilities management, data collection and information services. Most of these agreements extend for periods generally less than 24 months, but because of the inherent complexity of manufacturing processes and the risk of product flow disruption, the product supply agreements generally extend up to 36 months. Included in continuing operations for 2007 were the following amounts associated with these transition service agreements that will no longer occur after the full transfer of activities to the new owner: *Revenues* of $219 million; *Cost of Sales* of $194 million; *Selling, informational and administrative expenses* of $15 million; and *Other (income)/ deductions—net* of $16 million in income.

(continued)

Exhibit 3.31 *(Continued)*

None of these agreements confers upon us the ability to influence the operating and/or financial policies of the Consumer Healthcare business under its new ownership.

- In the third quarter of 2005, we sold the last of three European generic pharmaceutical businesses, which we had included in our Pharmaceutical segment, for 4.7 million euro (approximately $5.6 million). This business became a part of Pfizer in April 2003 in connection with our acquisition of Pharmacia. We recorded a loss of $3 million ($2 million, net of tax) in *Gains on sales of discontinued operations—net of tax* in the consolidated statement of income for 2005.

- In the first quarter of 2005, we sold the second of three European generic pharmaceutical businesses, which we had included in our Pharmaceutical segment, for 70 million euro (approximately $93 million). This business became a part of Pfizer in April 2003 in connection with our acquisition of Pharmacia. We recorded a gain of $57 million ($36 million, net of tax) in *Gains on sales of discontinued operations—net of tax* in the consolidated statement of income for 2005. In addition, we recorded an impairment charge of $9 million ($6 million, net of tax) related to the third European generic business in *Income from discontinued operations—net of tax* in the consolidated statement of income for 2005.

The following amounts, primarily related to our former Consumer Healthcare business, which was sold in December 2006 for $16.6 billion, have been segregated from continuing operations and included in *Discontinued operations—net of tax* in the consolidated statements of income:

	2007	2006	2005
Revenues	$ —	$ 4,044	$3,948
Pretax income/loss	(5)	643	695
Benefit/(provision) for taxes on income	2	(210)	(244)
Income/loss from operations of discontinued businesses—net of tax	(3)	433	451
Pretax gains/(losses) on sales of discontinued businesses	(168)	10,243	77
Benefit/(provision) for taxes on gains	102	(2,363)	(30)
Gains/(losses) on sales of discontinued businesses—net of tax	(66)	7,880	47
Discontinued operations—net of tax	$ (69)	$ 8,313	$ 498

Source: Pfizer, Inc., annual report, December 2007.

Exhibit 3.32   Asset impairment charges note: Pfizer, Inc., years ended December 31 (in millions).

In the third quarter of 2007, after an assessment of the financial performance of Exubera, an inhalable form of insulin for the treatment of diabetes, as well as its lack of acceptance by patients, physicians and payers, we decided to exit the product.

Our Exubera-related exit plans included working with physicians over a three-month period to transition patients to other treatment options, evaluating redeployment options for colleagues, working with our partners and vendors with respect to transition and exit activities, working with regulators on concluding outstanding clinical trials, implementing an extended transition program for those patients unable to transition to other medications within the three-month period, and exploring asset disposal or redeployment opportunities, as appropriate, among other activities.

Total pre-tax charges for 2007 were $2.8 billion, virtually all of which were recorded in the third quarter. The financial statement line items in which the various charges are recorded and related activity are as follows:

	Customer Returns— Revenues	Cost of Sales	Selling, Informational & Administrative Expenses	Research & Development Expenses	Total
Intangible asset impairment charges	$ —	$1,064	$41	$ —	$1,105
Inventory write-offs	—	661	—	—	661
Fixed assets impairment charges and other	—	451	—	3	454
Other exit costs	10	427	44	97	578
Total	$10	$2,603	$85	$100	$2,798

Source: Pfizer, Inc., annual report, December 2007.

Exhibit 3.33   Cost-reduction initiatives note—excerpts: Pfizer, Inc., years ended December 31 (in millions).

In the first quarter of 2005, we launched cost-reduction initiatives to increase efficiency and streamline decision-making across the company. These initiatives, announced in April 2005 and broadened in October 2006 and January 2007, follow the integration of Warner-Lambert and Pharmacia.

We incurred the following costs in connection with our cost-reduction initiatives:

	2007	2006	2005
Implementation costs[a]	$1,389	$ 788	$325
Restructuring charges[b]	2,523	1,296	438
Total costs related to our cost-reduction initiatives	$3,912	$2,084	$763

[a] For 2007, included in *Cost of sales* ($700 million), *Selling, informational and administrative expenses* ($334 million), *Research and development expenses* ($416 million) and in *Other (income)/deductions*—net ($61 million income). For 2006, included in *Cost of sales* ($392 million), *Selling, informational and administrative expenses* ($243 million), *Research and development expenses* ($176 million) and in *Other (income)/deductions—net* ($23 million income). For 2005, included in *Cost of sales* ($124 million), *Selling, informational and administrative expenses* ($151 million), and *Research and development expenses* ($50 million).
[b] Included in *Restructuring charges and acquisition-related costs.*
From the beginning of the cost-reduction initiatives in 2005, through December 31, 2007, the restructuring charges primarily relate to our plant network optimization efforts and the restructuring of our worldwide sales, marketing and research and development operations, while the implementation costs primarily relate to accelerated depreciation of certain assets, as well as system and process standardization and the expansion of shared services.

The components of restructuring charges associated with our cost-reduction initiatives follow:

	2007	2006	2005
Employee termination costs	$2,034	$ 809	$303
Asset impairments	260	368	122
Other	229	119	13
Total	$2,523	$1,296	$438

From the beginning of the cost-reduction initiatives in 2005 through December 31, 2007, *Employee termination costs* represent the expected reduction of the workforce by 20,800 employees, mainly in research, manufacturing and sales. As of December 31, 2007, approximately 13,000 of these employees have been formally terminated. *Employee termination costs* are recorded when the actions are probable and estimable and include accrued severance benefits, pension and postretirement benefits. *Asset impairments* primarily include charges to write down property, plant and equipment. *Other* primarily includes costs to exit certain activities.

Source: Pfizer, Inc., annual report, December 2007.

Exhibit 3.34   Acquisition-related costs note: Pfizer, Inc., years ended December 31 (in millions).

We recorded in *Restructuring charges and acquisition-related costs* $11 million in 2007, $27 million in 2006 and $918 million in 2005, for acquisition-related costs. Amounts in 2005 were primarily related to our acquisition of Pharmacia on April 16, 2003, and included integration costs of $543 million and restructuring charges of $375 million. As of December 31, 2007, virtually all restructuring charges incurred have been utilized.

Integration costs represent external, incremental costs directly related to an acquisition, including expenditures for consulting and systems integration. Restructuring charges can include severance, costs of vacating duplicative facilities, contract termination and other exit costs.

Source: Pfizer, Inc., annual report, December 2007.

Exhibit 3.35   Goodwill note—excerpt: Pfizer, Inc., years ended December 31 (in millions).

In 2007, we recorded charges of $1.1 billion in Cost of sales and Selling, informational and administrative expenses related to the impairment of Exubera (see Note 4. Asset Impairment Charges and Other Costs Associated with Exiting Exubera). In 2006, we recorded charges of $320 million in Other (income)/deductions—net related to the impairment of our Depo-Provera brand, a contraceptive injection (included in our Pharmaceutical segment). In 2005, we recorded an impairment charge of $1.1 billion in Other (income)/deductions—net related to the developed technology rights for Bextra, a selective COX-2 inhibitor (included in our Pharmaceutical segment), in connection with the decision to suspend sales of Bextra. In addition, in connection with the suspension, we recorded $5 million related to the write-off of machinery and equipment included in Other (income)/deductions—net; $73 million in write-offs of inventory and exit costs, included in Cost of sales; $8 million related to the costs of administering the suspension of sales, included in Selling, informational and administrative expenses; and $212 million for an estimate of customer returns, primarily included against Revenues.

Source: Pfizer, Inc., annual report, December 2007.

Exhibit 3.36   Share-based payment note—excerpt: Pfizer, Inc., year ended December 31, 2005 (in millions).

Transition Information
The following table shows the effect on results for 2005 as if we had applied the fair-value-based recognition provisions to measure stock-based compensation expense for the option grants:

Net income available to common shareholders used in the calculation of basic earnings per share:

As reported under U.S. GAAP	$8,079
Compensation expense—net of tax	(457)
Pro forma	$7,622

Source: Pfizer, Inc., annual report, December 2007.

Exhibit 3.37   Segment information note—excerpt: Pfizer, Inc., years ended December 31 (in millions).

Business Segments
We operate in the following business segments:

- **Pharmaceutical**
  The Pharmaceutical segment includes products that prevent and treat cardiovascular and metabolic diseases, central nervous system disorders, arthritis and pain, infectious and respiratory diseases, urogenital conditions, cancer, eye disease, endocrine disorders and allergies.
- **Animal Health**
  The Animal Health segment includes products that prevent and treat diseases in livestock and companion animals.

The following tables present segment, geographic and revenue information:

Segment	For/as of Year Ended Dec. 31		
	2007	**2006**	**2005**
Revenues			
Pharmaceutical	$44,424	$45,083	$44,269
Animal Health	2,639	2,311	2,206
Corporate/Other[a]	1,355	977	930
Total revenues	$48,418	$48,371	$47,405
Segment profit/(loss)[b]			
Pharmaceutical	$20,740	$21,615	$19,599
Animal Health	620	455	405
Corporate/Other[a][c]	(12,082)	(9,042)	(9,204)
Total profit/(loss)	$ 9,278	$13,028	$10,800

[a] *Corporate/Other* includes our gelatin capsules business, our contract manufacturing business and a bulk pharmaceutical chemicals business, and transition activity associated with our former Consumer Healthcare business (sold in December 2006). *Corporate/Other* under *Segment profit/(loss)* also includes interest income/(expense), corporate expenses (e.g., corporate administration costs), other income/(expense) (e.g., realized gains and losses attributable to our investments in debt and equity securities), certain performance-based and all share-based compensation expenses, significant impacts of purchase accounting for acquisitions, acquisition-related costs, intangible asset impairments and costs related to our cost-reduction initiatives.

[b] Segment profit/(loss) equals *Income from continuing operations before provision for taxes on income, minority interests and the cumulative effect of a change in accounting principles.* Certain costs, such as significant impacts of purchase accounting for acquisitions, acquisition-related costs and costs related to our cost-reduction initiatives and transition activity associated with our former Consumer Healthcare business, are included in *Corporate/Other* only. This methodology is utilized by management to evaluate our businesses.

[c] In 2007, *Corporate/Other* includes: i) restructuring charges and implementation costs associated with our cost-reduction initiatives of $3.9 billion; (ii) significant impacts of purchase accounting for acquisitions of $3.4 billion, including acquired in-process research and

Exhibit 3.37   *(Continued)*

development, intangible asset amortization and other charges; (iii) $2.8 billion of charges associated with Exubera. See *Note 4. Asset Impairment Charges and Other Costs Associated with Exiting Exubera;* (iv) net interest income of $1.1 billion; (v) all share-based compensation expense; (vii) gain on disposal of assets and other of $174 million; (vii) transition activity associated with our former Consumer Healthcare business of $26 million in income; and (viii) acquisition-related costs of $11 million.

In 2006, *Corporate/Other* includes: (i) significant impacts of purchase accounting for acquisitions of $4.1 billion, including acquired in-process research and development, intangible asset amortization and other charges; (ii) restructuring charges and implementation costs associated with our cost-reduction initiatives of $2.1 billion; (iii) all share-based compensation expense; (iv) net interest income of $437 million; (v) impairment of the Depo-Provera intangible asset of $320 million; (vi) gain on disposals of investments and other of $173 million; and (vii) a research and development milestone due to us from sanofi-aventis of approximately $118 million; and (viii) acquisition-related costs of $27 million.

In 2005, *Corporate/Other* includes: (i) significant impacts of purchase accounting for acquisitions of $4.9 billion, including acquired in-process research and development, intangible asset amortization and other charges; (ii) costs associated with the suspension of Bextra's sales and marketing of $1.2 billion; (iii) acquisition-related costs of $918 million; (iv) restructuring charges and implementation costs associated with our cost-reduction initiatives of $763 million; (v) net interest income of $269 million; (vi) all share-based compensation expense; and (vii) gain on disposals of investments and other of $134 million.

Source: Pfizer, Inc., annual report, December 2007.

The Pfizer Worksheet Analysis: Downloadable Tool 3.38

An enumeration of the nonrecurring items located in the Pfizer annual report is provided in the completed sustainable earnings base (SEB) worksheet found in Exhibit 3.38. Each of the nonrecurring items is recorded on the SEB worksheet. When an item is disclosed for the first, second, third, or fourth time, it is designated by a corresponding superscript in a summary of the search process provided in Exhibit 3.39. For purposes of illustration, all nonrecurring items have been recorded on the SEB worksheet without regard to their materiality. A materiality threshold could exclude a series of immaterial gains or losses that could, in combination, distort a firm's apparent profitability.

Without adjustment, Pfizer's income statement reports net income of $8,144 million, $19,337 million, and $8,085 million in 2007, 2006, and 2005, respectively, leaving the impression of a company with volatile earnings. However, the complete adjustment for nonrecurring items conveys a different message. After restatement, sustainable earnings amount to $13,627 million, $12,884 million, and $12,410 million in 2007, 2006, and 2005, respectively, indicating a stable sustainable earnings base with moderate growth. Similarly, reported profit margins of 16.8%, 40.0%, and 17.1% in 2007, 2006, and 2005, respectively, contrast with steadier adjusted profit margins of 28.1%, 26.6%, and 26.2%, in 2007, 2006, and 2005, respectively.

Clearly the number and magnitude of nonrecurring items identified in the Pfizer annual report caused its unanalyzed earnings data to be unreliable indicators of profit performance. Without the comprehensive identification of nonrecurring items and the

Exhibit 3.38 **Adjustment worksheet for sustainable earnings base: Pfizer, Inc., years ending December 31.**

	2007	2006	2005
Reported net income or (loss)	$ 8,144	$19,337	$ 8,085
Add			
Pretax LIFO liquidation losses			
Losses on sales of fixed assets			
Losses on sales of investments			
Losses on sales of other assets			
Restructuring charges (and implementation costs)	3,652	1,716	641
Investment write-downs			
Inventory write-downs	661		73
Other asset write-downs	1,559	688	1,286
Foreign currency losses			
Litigation charges			
Losses on patent infringement suits			
Exceptional bad-debt provisions			
Nonrecurring expense increases			
Temporary revenue reductions	10		212
Other: Acquisition-related costs	11	27	918
Other: Product exit costs	568		8
Other			
Subtotal	6,461	2,431	3,138
Multiply by			
(1 – combined federal, state tax rates)	84%	84%	84%
Tax-adjusted additions	5,427	2,042	2,636
Add			
After-tax LIFO liquidation losses			
Increases in deferred tax valuation allowances			
Other nonrecurring tax charges			1,114
Losses on discontinued operations	69		
Extraordinary losses			
Losses/cumulative-effect accounting changes			23
Other: Acquired in-process R&D	283	835	1,652
Other			
Other			
Subtotal	352	835	2,789
Total additions	$ 5,779	$ 2,877	$ 5,424

Exhibit 3.38 (*Continued*)

	2007	2006	2005
Deduct			
Pretax LIFO liquidation gains			
Gains on fixed asset sales	$ 318	$ 216	$ 15
Gains on sales of investments	8	64	157
Gains on sales of other assets			
Reversals of restructuring accruals			
Investment write-ups (trading account)			
Foreign currency gains			
Litigation revenues			
Gains on patent infringement suits			
Temporary expense decreases			
Temporary revenue increases			
Reversals of bad-debt allowances			
Other: Temporary income from discontinued ops	26		
Other			
Other			
Subtotal	352	280	172
Multiply by			
(1 – combined federal, state tax rates)	84%	84%	84%
Tax-adjusted deductions	296	235	144
After-tax LIFO liquidation gains			
Reductions in deferred tax valuation allowances			
Loss carryforward benefits from prior years			
Other nonrecurring tax benefits		782	
Gains on discontinued operations		8,313	498
Extraordinary gains			
Gains/cumulative-effect accounting changes			
Other: Stock option expense, pro forma			457
Other			
Other			
Subtotal	0	9,095	955
Total deductions	296	9,330	1,099
Sustainable earnings base	$13,627	$12,884	$12,410

development of the SEB worksheet, the company's three-year operating performance is virtually impossible to discern.

An efficient search sequence for identifying nonrecurring items was outlined in Exhibit 3.4.[38] While the recommended search sequence may not be equally effective in all cases, most of Pfizer's nonrecurring items could be located by implementing steps 1 to 6,

Exhibit 3.39 Summary of nonrecurring items search process: Pfizer, Inc.

Step and Search Location	Nonrecurring Item Revealed
1. Income statement	Restructuring charges (2005–2007)[1]
	Acquired in-process research and development (R&D) (2005–2007)[1]
	Discontinued operations (2005–2007)[1]
	Cumulative effect of accounting changes (2005)[1]
2. Statement of cash flows	Acquired in-process R&D (2005–2007)[2]
	Gains/losses on discontinued operations (2005–2007)[2]
	Gains on disposal of assets (2005–2007)[1]
	Intangible asset impairment charges (2005–2007)[1]
	Cumulative effect of accounting changes (2005)[2]
3. Inventory note	No nonrecurring items located
4. Income tax note	IRS audit settlement benefits (2005–2006)[1]
	Earnings repatriation charge (2005)[1]
	Acquired in-process R&D (2005–2007)[3]
5. Other income (expense) note	Gain on disposal of assets (2005–2007)[2]
	Gain on sale of available-for-sale securities (2005–2007)[1]
	Intangible asset impairment charges (2005–2007)[2]
6. MD&A	Restructuring and product exit charges (2005–2007)[2]
	Acquired in-process R&D (2005–2007)[4]
	Intangible asset impairment charges (2005–2007)[3]
	Discontinued operations (2005–2007)[3]
	Cumulative effect of accounting changes (2005)[3]
	IRS audit settlement benefits (2005–2006)[2]
7. Other notes revealing nonrecurring items:	
a. Significant accounting policies	Cumulative effect of accounting changes (2005)[4]
b. Acquisitions	Acquired in-process R&D (2005–2007)[5]
c. Discontinued operations	Income, gains/losses (2005–2007)[4]
	Temporary income from discontinued operations (2007)[1]
d. Asset impairment charges	Costs of exiting Exubera—details (2007)[2]
e. Cost reduction initiatives	Asset impairment and restructuring (2005–2007)[3]
f. Acquisition-related costs	Details by year (2005–2007)[1]
g. Goodwill and other intangibles	Costs of exiting Bextra—details (2005)[1]

Exhibit 3.39   Summary of nonrecurring items search process: Pfizer, Inc.

Step and Search Location	Nonrecurring Item Revealed
h. Share-based payment	Pro forma stock options expense (2005)[1]
i. Segment information	Restructuring and product exit charges (2005–2007)[3]
	Acquired in-process R&D (2005–2007)[6]
	Gain on disposal of assets (2005–2007)[3]
	Intangible asset impairment charges (2005–2007)[4]

Note: The superscripts 1, 2, 3 indicate the number of times the nonrecurring item was found. For instance, "Acquired in-process R&D" was found in the income statement (first location); in the statement of cash flows (second location); in the income tax note (third location); in MD&A (fourth location); in the acquisitions note (fifth location); and in the segment information note (sixth location).

a sequence that is relatively cost-effective. Although the other notes—step 7—provided details of some nonrecurring charges, the significant effects were already identified in the earlier steps.

Some Further Points on the Pfizer Worksheet

The construction of an SEB worksheet always requires the exercise of judgment. Materiality judgments are avoided by simply recording all nonrecurring items without regard to their materiality. However, the classification of items as nonrecurring, as well as on occasion their measurement, calls for varying degrees of judgment. Two examples of Pfizer items that required the exercise of judgment, in terms of either classification or measurement, are discussed next.

Acquired In-Process R&D

For a pharmaceutical firm like Pfizer, research and development—both internal and acquired—is a core component of operations. Consequently, some users of financial statements treat acquired in-process R&D as a component of R&D expense. Its irregularity, however, is a good reason to separate it from measures of sustainable earnings. Note that beginning in 2009, acquired in-process R&D will be capitalized as an identifiable intangible asset and will be expensed only when the R&D efforts are completed or abandoned.[39]

The Tax Rate Assumption

The tax rate used in the Pfizer worksheet was a combined (federal, state, and foreign) 16 percent. This is the three-year average effective tax rate for the company based on the recurring portions of the income tax provision, as disclosed in the income tax note in Exhibit 3.27. The tax rate scales the numbers in the worksheet to their after-tax amounts. The goal should be a rate that is a reasonable representation of this combined rate and reflects the effects of a company's geographic choices. Pfizer clearly enjoys tax benefits from its overseas operations.

Summary

An estimation of the sustainable portion of earnings should be the centerpiece of analyzing business earnings. This task has become a far greater challenge over the past decade as nonrecurring items have increased with corporate reorganizations and associated activities and with enhanced levels of disclosure. Some of the labels attached to these producers of nonrecurring items are restructuring, rightsizing, downsizing, reengineering, redeployment, repositioning, reorganizing, rationalizing, and realignment. The following are some key points to consider:

- An earnings series from which nonrecurring items have been purged is essential in order to both evaluate current trends in operating performance and make projections of future results.

- The identification and measurement of nonrecurring items will typically require the exercise of judgment.

- There are no agreed-upon definitions of nonrecurring items as part of GAAP. Moreover, various labels are used beyond the term *nonrecurring*, including special, unusual, non-operating, and noncore.

- It is common to treat items as nonrecurring even though they may appear with some frequency in the income statement. However, these items would usually be very irregular in terms of their amount as well as whether they are revenues and gains or expenses and losses.

- The key question to pose in making the nonrecurring judgment is: Will underlying trends in operating performance be obscured if the item remains in earnings?

- Some material nonrecurring items will be separately disclosed on the face of the income statement. However, a substantial number will be disclosed in other statements and locations. It is typically necessary to extend the search for nonrecurring items well beyond the income statement.

- In response to limitations on the time available for a whole range of important activities, an efficient and abbreviated search sequence is presented in this chapter and illustrated with a comprehensive case example. While a comprehensive review of the complete financial reporting is the gold standard, reliable information on sustainable earnings can typically be developed while employing only a subset of reported financial information.

Downloadable Resources for this chapter available at www.wiley.com/go/portablembainfinance

Exhibit 3.23: Adjustment Worksheet for Sustainable Earnings Base

Exhibit 3.38: Adjustment Worksheet for Sustainable Earnings Base, Pfizer, Inc.

Internet Links

www.fasb.org   This Web site provides updates on the agenda of the Financial Accounting Standards Board (FASB). It also includes both summaries and full text of FASB statements and other information related to standards setting.

www.freeedgar.com	This site provides a very convenient alternative source of SEC filings.
www.iasb.org	This site provides updates on the agenda of the IASB, as well as summaries and texts of pronouncements.
www.sec.gov	This site is a source for accessing companies' Securities and Exchange Commission filings. It also includes accounting and auditing enforcement releases of the SEC. These releases provide very useful examples of the actions sometimes taken by companies to misrepresent their financial performance or position.

Annual Reports Referenced in the Chapter

Abbott Laboratories (2007)

Adobe Systems, Inc. (2007)

Advanced Micro Devices, Inc. (2005)

AGCO, Inc. (2007)

Alliant Energy Corporation (2007)

Amazon.com (2005)

Archer Daniels Midland (2008)

Baxter International (2007)

Boston Scientific (2007)

Bristol-Myers Squibb Company (2007)

Campbell Soup Company (2008)

Cardinal Health, Inc. (2007)

Coca-Cola Enterprises, Inc. (2007)

Colgate-Palmolive Company (2007)

ConocoPhillips (2007)

Denny's Corporation (2007)

Dow Chemical Company (2007)

Eastman Kodak Company (2007)

eBay (2007)

E.I. du Pont de Nemours and Company (2007)

Electronic Arts (2007)

Eli Lilly & Company (2007)

EMC Corporation (2007)

FedEx Corporation (2007)

First Solar, Inc. (2007)

Hewlett-Packard (2007)

H.J. Heinz Company (2006)

Humana, Inc. (2006)

Interface, Inc. (2007)

Iron Mountain (2007)

Kimberly-Clark Corporation (2007)

Limited Brands, Inc. (2007)

Magma Design Automation, Inc. (2006)

McDonald's Corporation (2007)

Merck & Company (2007)

Monster Worldwide, Inc. (2006)

Motorola, Inc. (2007)

Navigant Consulting, Inc. (2006)

Netflix, Inc. (2004)

New York Times Company (2007)

Northrop Grumman Corporation (2005)

Northwest Airlines (2006)

Novartis, Inc. (2007)

Office Depot (2006)

Pacific Sunwear of California (2006)

Panera Bread Company (2007)

PepsiCo, Inc. (2007)

Pfizer, Inc. (2006)

Procter & Gamble Company (2007)

Southwest Airlines (2007)

Sprint Nextel Corporation (2007)

Starbucks Corporation (2006)

Tektronix, Inc. (2005)

TJX Companies (2007)

Under Armour (2007)

United Natural Foods (2007)

United States Steel (2005)

Walt Disney Company (2007)

Warner Music Group Corp. (2005)

Weyerhaeuser Company (2006)

Whole Foods Market (2007)

Winnebago Industries, Inc. (2007)

Wyeth (2007)

Yahoo! (2007)

Yum! Brands, Inc. (2007)

Notes

1. The American Institute of Certified Public Accountants' Special Committee on Financial Reporting, *Improving Business Reporting—A Customer Focus* (New York: AICPA, November 1993), 4.

2. Financial Accounting Standards Board, *Discussion Paper: Preliminary Views on Financial Statement Presentation* (Stamford, CT: FASB, October 2008).

3. U.S. Securities and Exchange Commission (SEC), *Final Rule: Conditions for Use of Non-GAAP Financial Measures*, Release No. 33-8176; 34-47226; FR-65; File No. S7-43-02, January 2003.

4. F. Heflin and C. Hsu, "The Impact of the SEC's Regulation of Non-GAAP Disclosures," *Journal of Accounting and Economics* 46 (2008), 349–365; A. Marques, "SEC Interventions and the Frequency and Usefulness of Non-GAAP Financial Measures," *Review of Accounting Studies* 11 (2006), 549–574.

5. D. Kieso, J. Weygandt, and T. Warfield, *Intermediate Accounting*, 11th ed. (Hoboken, NJ: John Wiley & Sons, 2004), 127.

6. Archer Daniels Midland, annual reports, June 2008 and June 2006.

7. Northwest Airlines Corporation, annual reports, December 2006 and December 2004.

8. Bristol-Myers Squibb Company, annual report, December 2007, Note 9.

9. Whole Foods Market, Inc., annual report, September 2007.

10. H. Choi, *Analysis and Valuation Implications of Persistence and Cash-Content Dimensions of Earnings Components Based on Extent of Analyst Following*, unpublished PhD thesis, Georgia Institute of Technology, October 1994, 80.

11. American Institute of Certified Public Accountants, *Accounting Trends and Techniques* (New York: AICPA, 2007), Table 3-2.

12. AICPA's Special Committee on Financial Reporting, *Improving Business Reporting—A Customer Focus* (New York: AICPA, November 1993), 4.

13. SFAS No. 144, *Accounting for the Impairment or Disposal of Long-Lived Assets* (Stamford, CT: FASB, 2001).

14. Accounting Principles Board Opinion No. 30, *Reporting the Results of Operations* (New York: AICPA, July 1973), para. 20.

15. AICPA, *Accounting Trends and Techniques* (New York: AICPA, 2007), Table 3-18.

16. Hampshire Group, Ltd., annual report, 2006, 19.

17. Procter & Gamble Company, annual report, June 2008, 63.

18. Netflix, Inc., annual report, 2004, F-14.

19. This statement needs some expansion. With the exception of barter transactions, almost all expenses involve a cash outflow at some point in time. In the case of depreciation, the cash outflow normally takes place when the depreciable assets are acquired. At that time, the cash outflow is classified as an *investing* cash outflow in the statement of cash flows. If the depreciation were not added back to net income in computing operating cash flow, then cash would appear to be reduced twice—once when the assets were purchased and a second time when depreciation is recorded and with it net income is reduced.

20. Securities and Exchange Commission, Regulation S-X, Rule 5-02.6 (Washington, DC: SEC).

21. SEC, Staff Accounting Bulletin No. 40 (Washington, DC: SEC).
22. Winnebago Industries, Inc., annual report, August 2007, Note 3.
23. PepsiCo, Inc., annual report, December 2007, Note 5.
24. Guidance in this area is found in SFAS No. 109, *Accounting for Income Taxes* (Norwalk, CT: FASB, February 1992).
25. SEC, Regulation S-K, Subpart 229.300, Item 303(a)(3)(i) (Washington, DC: SEC).
26. Conagra Foods, Inc., annual report, May 2008, 18.
27. A hedge of foreign currency exposure is achieved by creating an offsetting position to the financial statement exposure. The most common offsetting position is established by the use of a foreign currency derivative. These issues are discussed more fully in Chapter 15.
28. These alternative translation methods are discussed and illustrated in Chapter 15.
29. Hewlett-Packard Company, annual report, October 2007, 109.
30. E.I. du Pont de Nemours Company, annual report, December 2007, Note 25.
31. Bristol-Myers Squibb Company, annual report, December 2007, Note 24.
32. SFAS No. 130, *Reporting Comprehensive Income* (Norwalk, CT: FASB, June 1997).
33. Translation (remeasurement) gains and losses that result from the application of the temporal (remeasurement) method continue to be included in the income statement as part of conventional net income. Only translation adjustments that result from application of the all-current translation method are included in other comprehensive income. Some gains and losses for financial derivatives used as hedges are also included in other comprehensive income. SFAS No. 133, *Accounting for Derivative Instruments and Hedging Activities* (Norwalk, CT: FASB, November 1998).
34. SFAS No. 158, *Employers' Accounting for Defined Benefit and Other Postretirement Plans* (Norwalk, CT: FASB, September 2006).
35. The FASB-IASB proposal for a new income statement format would require the presentation of other comprehensive income with net income. Financial Accounting Standards Board, *Discussion Paper: Preliminary Views on Financial Statement Presentation* (Stamford, CT: FASB, October 2008).
36. An annual survey conducted by American Institute of Certified Public Accountants reveals the following pattern of adoption of the alternative reporting methods of SFAS No. 130, for 581 firms in 2006: (1) a combined statement of income and comprehensive income, 21 firms; (2) a separate statement of comprehensive income, 75 firms; and (3) reporting comprehensive income directly in shareholders' equity, 485 firms. AICPA, *Accounting Trends and Techniques* (New York: AICPA, 2007), Table 4-1.
37. The sustainable earnings base (SEB) worksheet template was developed by E. Comiskey and C. Mulford for earlier editions of this book.
38. This search sequence was developed by Eugene E. Comiskey and Charles W. Mulford, based on H. Choi, *Analysis and Valuation Implications of Persistence and Cash-Content Dimensions of Earnings Components Based on Extent of Analyst Following*, unpublished PhD thesis, Georgia Institute of Technology, October 1994.
39. SFAS No. 141R, *Business Combinations—Revised 2007* (Norwalk, CT: FASB, December 2007).

For Further Reading

Comiskey, E., and C. Mulford, *Guide to Financial Reporting and Analysis* (New York: John Wiley & Sons, 2000).

Revsine, L., D. Collins, B. Johnson, and F. Mittelstaedt, *Financial Reporting and Analysis*, 4th ed. (New York: McGraw-Hill/Irwin, 2008).

White, G., A. Sondhi, and D. Fried, *The Analysis and Use of Financial Statements*, 3rd ed. (New York: John Wiley & Sons, 2002).

Part II

Financial Management

Discounted Cash Flow

4

James A. Elfter

Time Value of Money

Saving with a goal in mind has been a part of most people's lives. Whether we are saving for a rainy day, saving to buy a stereo, a car, a house, a gift for someone special, or retirement, we set a goal and we strive to achieve the goal in a specific or fixed amount of time.

If I owe you a sum of money, would you rather receive it today or a year from today? The time value of money refers to what the value of a dollar amount is today (present value) versus what the value of that same dollar amount will be in X amount of time (future value). For example, what is the value of $10,000 today versus the value of $10,000 20 years ago, or 20 years in the future? Would $10,000 10 years ago have been enough money to buy a new car? Will $10,000 buy a car today? Will $10,000 buy you a car in 10 years?

Financial calculations for the time value of money can be done by algebra, by using compound interest tables, by using a financial calculator, or—most quickly and easily—by using Microsoft Excel®. Excel is the best number cruncher on this planet, and is used by financial professionals worldwide.

If you need some instruction in Excel—or a refresher—get started *now*. You will find links for Excel tutorials at the end of this chapter.

To see explanations and illustrations of using Excel for financial calculations involving the time value of money, check out the Web site for this chapter.

Further and more advanced uses of the time value of money will be found in Chapter 6, "Planning Capital Expenditure." To understand what we mean by time value of money, we will look at various measures used to determine the value of money over time.

Future Value

The future value of a dollar amount put into a savings account reflects what we expect the value of that dollar amount to be in a fixed amount of time, or how we expect the money to grow. Growth or, in the case of a savings account, the interest rate paid, is the amount that we expect to receive above the amount that we have deposited.

For example, on Billy's 10th birthday his aunt opens a savings account in his name and deposits $50 into that account. Over the years, Billy forgets that he has this bank account, and at the age of 20, he finds the passbook stuffed in the back of a drawer. When he

Exhibit 4.1   **How Billy's savings account grew.**

Year	1	2	3	4	5	6	7	8	9	10
Balance at beginning of year	$50.00	$52.50	$55.13	$57.88	$60.78	$63.81	$67.00	$70.36	$73.87	$77.57
Interest posted	2.50	2.63	2.76	2.89	3.04	3.19	3.35	3.52	3.69	3.88
Balance at year's end	$52.50	$55.13	$57.88	$60.78	$63.81	$67.00	$70.36	$73.87	$77.57	$81.44

opens the passbook, he remembers the birthday gift of $50 from his aunt. For Billy, this $50 is just the amount he needs to purchase a new pair of jeans.

Billy goes to the bank, presents the passbook, and requests to withdraw $50, assuming this will zero out his balance and close the account. After a few moments, the teller hands Billy the $50 he requested and returns his passbook. Before leaving the bank, Billy looks in his passbook and sees that he still has a balance of $31.44. It dawns on him that his account has earned interest on the initial amount of the savings. Let us analyze why Billy still has money in that account and how the $50 grew to a balance of $81.44. For this example, we will assume that the annual rate of interest that the bank paid over the 10 years remained fixed at 5%.

The initial balance was $50 with an annual interest rate of 5%. This means that at the end of the first year the balance was $50 + ($50 × 5%) or $50 + $2.50, which totals $52.50. The $2.50 is the amount earned from interest. Interest in this account is compound interest, which means that interest is earned on the original balance plus whatever interest has been added. Therefore, at the end of the second year, the amount on which interest was paid was the balance at the end of the first year, $52.50, which is the principal balance and the interest earned at the end of the first year. At the end of year 2, the balance was $52.50 + ($52.50 × 5%) or $52.50 + $2.63 in interest, which equals $55.13. Exhibit 4.1 provides us with the yearly balance details on how Billy's money grew over the 10-year period to the value of $81.44, which is the balance prior to withdrawing the money for the jeans.

The formula for calculating the future value is:

$$FV = PV \times (1 + I)^N \text{ (Formula 4a)}$$

We can use formula 4a to solve for any FV provided we know the other values.

FV = Unknown (future value or the value at the end of a time period)
PV = $50 (present value, the amount that was initially invested or deposited)
I = 5% (interest paid on the account)
N = 10 (number of time periods/years)

Substituting, we have:

$FV = \$50 \times (1 + .05)^{10}$, or $\$50 \times [(1.05) \times (1.05) \times (1.05) \times (1.05) \times (1.05) \times (1.05) \times (1.05) \times (1.05) \times (1.05) \times (1.05)] = \$81.44$, or $\$50 \times 1.62889 = \$81.44$

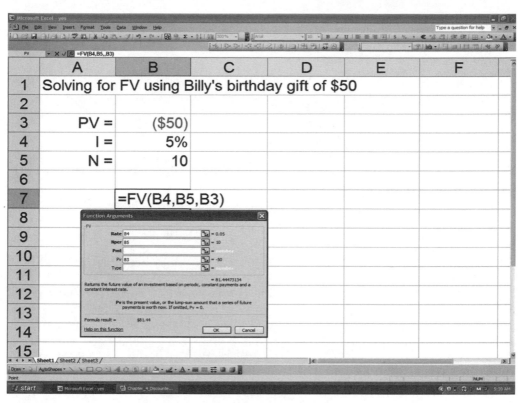

Exhibit 4.2   Solving for FV using Billy's birthday gift: Excel example 1.

To solve using Excel, open your Excel program and follow the directions given here. (See Exhibit 4.2.) If you have not installed the Excel Financial Add-Ins, please review the instructions posted in the Web site for this chapter.

- Enter the following values into cells B3, B4, and B5, respectively.

  B3 = −$50 (Note that this must be a negative value, as it is an outflow of cash.)

  B4 = 5%

  B5 = 10

- Enter the "=" sign into cell B7.
- Select "FV" from the functions box (may require you to use the drop-down menu to find FV).
- Enter the Rate value (select cell B4).
- Enter the Nper value (select cell B5).
- Skip the Pmt value or insert "0" (this is for a payment value made each period).
- Enter the PV value (select cell B3).
- Select "OK" in the function argument box.

The FV of the $50 calculated out to 10 years at 5% equals $81.44.

Additional FV Exercise

The following exercise illustrates solving for FV using algebra and using Excel.
Algebraic approach to finding the FV:

$$FV = \text{Future value (unknown)}$$
$$PV = \$6,000$$
$$I = 6\%$$
$$N = 5 \text{ years}$$

End of year 1	$6,000.00 will earn $6,000.00 × .06 = $360.00
FV or balance end of year 1, beginning of year 2	$6,000.00 + $360.00 = **$6,360.00**
End of year 2	$6,360.00 will earn $6,360.00 × .06 = $381.60
FV or balance end of year 2, beginning of year 3	$6,360.00 + $381.60 = **$6,741.60**
End of year 3	$6,741.60 will earn $6,741.60 × .06 = $404.50
FV or balance end of year 3, beginning of year 4	$6,741.60 + $404.50 = **$7,146.10**
End of year 4	$7,146.10 will earn $7,146.10 × .06 = $428.77
FV or balance end of year 4, beginning of year 5	$7,146.10 + $428.77 = **$7,574.86**
End of year 5	$7,574.86 will earn $7,574.86 × .06 = $454.49
FV or balance end of year 5	$7,574.86 + $454.49 = **$8,029.35**

The values in Exhibit 4.3 reflect the preceding calculations.
Here is a step-by-step Excel approach to finding the FV of $6,000 (see Exhibit 4.4).

- Enter the following values into cells C4, C5, and C6, respectively.

  C4 = −$6,000 (Note that this must be a negative value, as it is an outflow of cash.)
  C5 = 6%
  C6 = 5

- Now enter the "=" sign into cell B8.
- Now select "FV" from the functions box (may require you to use the drop-down menu to find FV).

Exhibit 4.3   Finding FV.

Time/Years	1	2	3	4	5
Present value (beginning of time period)	$6,000.00	$6,360.00	$6,741.60	$7,146.10	$7,574.86
Interest @ 6%	360.00	381.60	404.50	428.77	454.49
Future value	$6,360.00	$6,741.60	$7,146.10	$7,574.86	$8,029.35

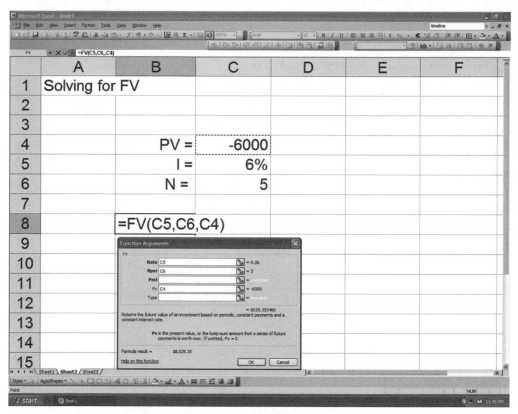

Exhibit 4.4   Solving for FV: Excel example 2.

- Now enter the Rate value (select cell C5).
- Now enter the Nper value (select cell C6).
- Skip the Pmt value or insert "0" (this is for a payment value made each period).
- Now enter the PV value (select cell C4).
- Now select "OK" in the function argument box.

The FV of our $6,000 calculated out to five years at 6% equals $8,029.35.

As you can see from the previous example, using Excel is quicker than using the algebraic approach.

To continue to illustrate solving FV calculations using Excel, we will use various present values.

$$FV = \text{Future value (unknown)}$$
$$PV = -\$8,000$$
$$PV = -\$9,000$$
$$PV = -\$10,000$$
$$PV = -\$15,000$$
$$PV = -\$20,000$$
$$I = 3.75\%$$
$$N = 3 \text{ years}$$

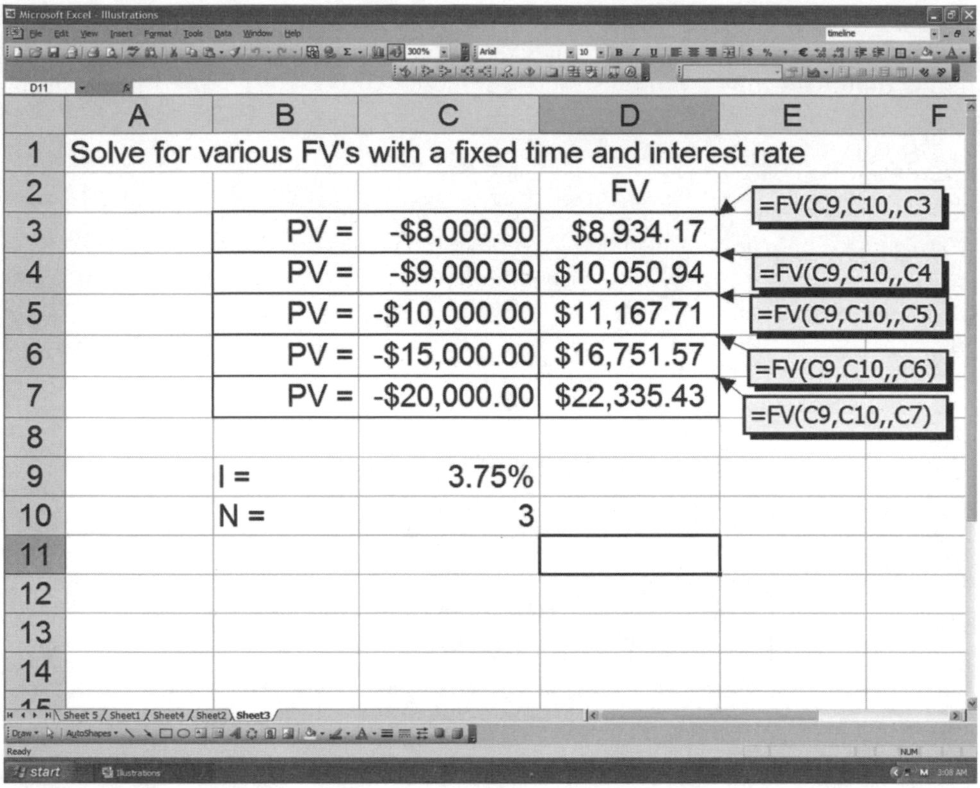

Exhibit 4.5 Solving for various FVs with a fixed time and interest rate: Excel example 3.

To solve for the various future values, follow the instructions in the previous problem and review the comments regarding the inputs into each cell as seen in Excel example 3 (Exhibit 4.5).

Present Value

One way to think of present value is to consider, "What is the amount that we need to invest or deposit today in order to have a specific amount in the future?" In solving for present value, we are asking this question; we must, however, know the amount we need at the end (FV), the interest rate (I), and the length of time (N). The formula for present value is:

$$PV = FV \div (1 + I)^N \text{ (Formula 4b)}$$

We previously solved for future value: $N = 10$ years, interest $(I) = 5\%$, and present value $(PV) = \$50$. Our result was \$81.44. We used formula 4a to solve for FV: $FV = PV \times (1 + I)^N$. Note the similarities in the two formulas. Using the rules of algebra, we change formula 4a to 4b and now solve for PV.

$$PV = \$81.44 \div (1 + .05)^{10}, \text{ or } \$81.44 \div [(1.05) \times (1.05) \times (1.05) \times (1.05) \times (1.05) \times (1.05) \times (1.05) \times (1.05) \times (1.05) \times (1.05)] \text{ or } \$81.44 \div 1.62889 = \$50.00$$

Note that the $50.00 was the initial amount deposited into Billy's account on his 10th birthday by his aunt. (When using financial calculators or Excel, the PV will result in a negative number; this represents the cash outflow or deposit required to result in a positive FV.)

PV Exercises

The following exercise illustrates solving for PV using algebra and Excel.

Find the PV, the amount we need to deposit today into a savings account that pays a fixed interest rate of 7% over the term of the deposit, which will result in a FV of $8,000 at the end of five years.

$$PV = \text{Present value (unknown)}$$
$$FV = \$8{,}000$$
$$I = 7\%$$
$$N = 5 \text{ years}$$

Using Formula 4b and substituting given values,

$$PV = FV \div (1 + I)^N$$
$$PV = \$8{,}000 \div (1.07)^5$$
$$PV = \$8{,}000 \div (1.07) \times (1.07) \times (1.07) \times (1.07) \times (1.07)$$
$$PV = \$8{,}000 \div 1.40255$$
$$PV = \$5{,}703.89$$

The values in Exhibit 4.6 reflect these calculations.

Here is a step-by-step Excel approach to finding the PV of $8,000 (see Exhibit 4.7).

- Enter the following values into cells C4, C5, and C6, respectively.

  C4 = $8,000 (Note that this not a negative value, as this is the FV.)

  C5 = 7%

  C6 = 5

- Now enter the "=" sign into cell B8.
- Now select "PV" from the functions box (may require you to use the drop-down menu to find PV).
- Now enter the Rate value (select cell C5).
- Now enter the Nper value (select cell C6).
- Skip the Pmt value, or insert "0" (this is for a payment value made each period).
- Now enter the FV value (select cell C4).
- Now select "OK" in the function argument box.

Exhibit 4.6   Finding PV.

Time/Years	1	2	3	4	5
Present value	$5,703.89	$6,103.00	$6,530.38	$6,987.51	$7,476.64
Interest @ 7%	399.27	427.22	457.13	489.13	523.36
Future value	$6,103.00	$6,530.38	$6,987.51	$7,476.64	$8,000.00

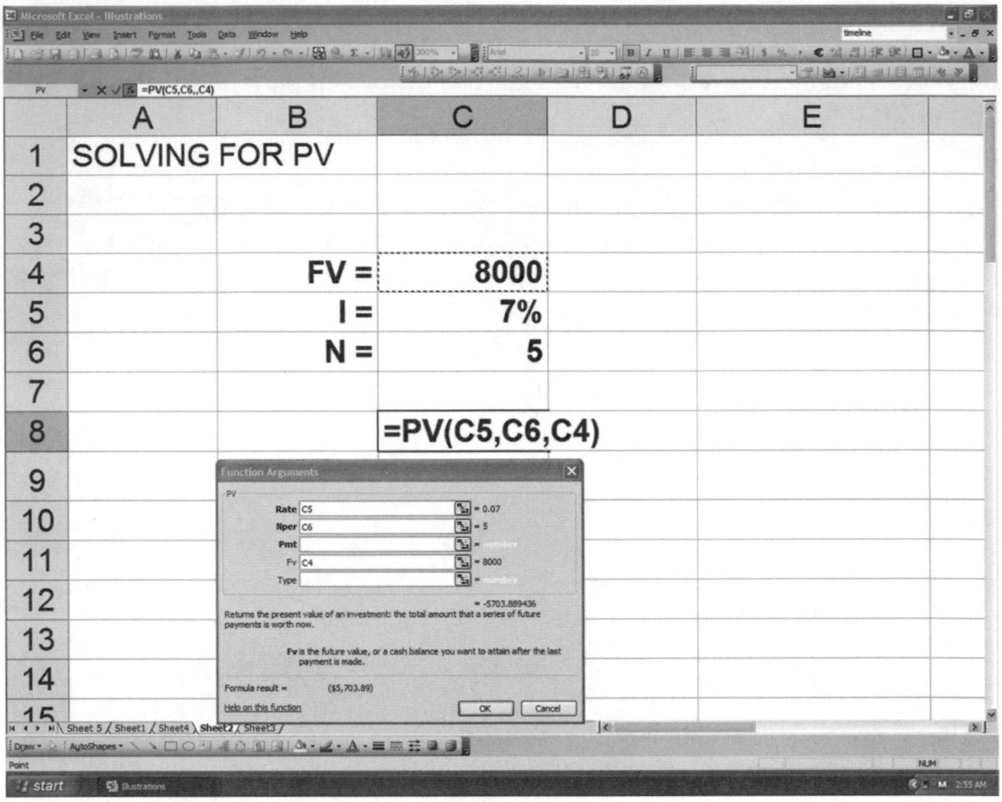

Exhibit 4.7 Solving for PV: Excel example 4.

The PV required to deposit today to produce a FV of $8,000 calculated out to five years at an interest rate of 7% equals −$5,703.89. (This is a cash outflow and requires a negative value using Excel.)

To continue to illustrate solving PV calculations using Excel, we will use various future values.

$$PV = \text{Present value (unknown)}$$
$$FV = \$8,000$$
$$FV = \$9,000$$
$$FV = \$10,000$$
$$FV = \$15,000$$
$$FV = \$20,000$$
$$I = 8\%$$
$$N = 3 \text{ years}$$

To solve for the various present values, follow the instructions in the previous PV exercise and review the comments regarding the inputs into each cell as seen in Excel example 5 (Exhibit 4.8).

Notice in Excel example 5 that the PVs are negative; this reflects that a cash outflow is required.

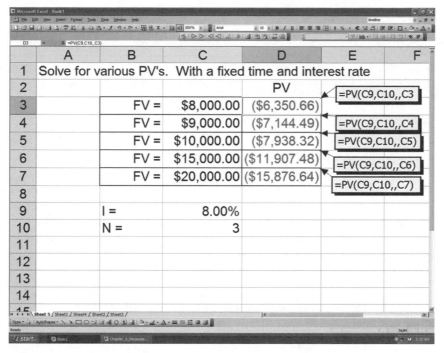

Exhibit 4.8   Solving for various PVs with a fixed time and interest rate: Excel example 5.

Annuities

While discussing present values and future values, we considered single payments at the beginning or at the end of a fixed time interval. Annuities differ, as they require or provide a cash flow (CF) or series of payments over a specific time period. The time period may be annually, quarterly, monthly, or even weekly.

Annuities meet three criteria: They (1) pay an equal amount, (2) at a specific time interval, (3) for a specific time period.

If we are placing money into an annuity, we need to consider in which type of annuity to invest. Two types of annuities are the ordinary annuity and the annuity due.

Ordinary Annuity

An ordinary annuity pays out at the end of the time interval. Most annuities fall into this category.

Consider the following two examples representing annuities that require payments of $500 per period over 10 periods.

For the ordinary annuity, we have the simple payment schedule shown in Exhibit 4.9.

Exhibit 4.9   Payments into an ordinary annuity.

Period	1	2	3	4	5	6	7	8	9	10
Payment	($500)	($500)	($500)	($500)	($500)	($500)	($500)	($500)	($500)	($500)

Exhibit 4.10   Payments into an annuity due.

Period	0	1	2	3	4	5	6	7	8	9	10
Payment	($500)	($500)	($500)	($500)	($500)	($500)	($500)	($500)	($500)	($500)	—

Annuity Due

An annuity due is one that pays at the beginning of the time interval. A good example of an annuity due would be paying into a savings account.

For the annuity due, we have the simple payment schedule shown in Exhibit 4.10.

Note that we have not considered the interest rate in the two examples, but confirm that these are annuities since they meet the three criteria: They (1) pay an equal amount, (2) at a specific time interval, (3) for a specific time period. Note also that each payment is a negative amount; this reflects payments made. As previously mentioned, the negative sign (indicated by parentheses) is important when using financial calculators, or Excel to solve for the present and future values of annuities.

Calculating the Future Value of an Ordinary Annuity

If we make payments into an annuity under the preceding two payment schedules, Exhibits 4.9 and 4.10, the FV of the annuity due will be higher than the FV of the ordinary annuity. The reason for this is that the first annuity due payment is made in period 0; therefore, it will begin to earn interest one period earlier than the ordinary annuity.

The algebraic formula for calculating the future value of annuity (FVA$_N$) of an ordinary annuity for our example is:

$$FVA_N = PMT(1 + I)^{N-1} + PMT(1 + I)^{N-2} + PMT(1 + I)^{N-3} + PMT(1 + I)^{N-4}$$
$$\cdots + PMT(1 + I)^{N-10} \text{ (Formula 4c)}$$

FVA_N = Future value of annuity at the end of a time period N

I = Interest = 7% (For this exercise, we will assume an interest rate of 7%.)

N = Number of periods = 10

PMT = $500

$FVA_{10} = \$500(1 + .07)^{10-1} + \$500(1 + .07)^{10-2} + \cdots + \$500(1 + .07)^{10-10}$

$FVA_{10} = \$500(1.07)^9 + \$500(1.07)^8 + \$500(1.07)^7 + \$500(1.07)^6 + \$500(1.07)^5$
$\qquad + \$500(1.07)^4 + \$500(1.07)^3 + \$500(1.07)^2 + \$500(1.07)^1 + \$500(1.07)^0$
$\qquad = \$6,908.22$

The values in Exhibit 4.11 reflect these calculations.

Exhibit 4.11   Future value of an ordinary annuity.

Period/ Years	1	2	3	4	5	6	7	8	9	10
Payment	($500)	($500)	($500)	($500)	($500)	($500)	($500)	($500)	($500)	($ 500)
FV	919	859	803	750	701	655	613	572	535	500
Interest	419	359	303	250	201	155	113	72	35	1,908
FVA$_N$										$6,908

Note that interest is compounded.

$$FVA_N = PMT \left[\frac{(1+I)^N - 1}{I} \right] \quad \text{(Formula 4c Simplified)}$$

Working with the simplified formula provides us the following:

$$FVA_N = \$500 \times \left[\frac{(1.07)^{10} - 1}{.07} \right] = \$500 \times \left(\frac{1.9672 - 1}{.07} \right) = \$500 \times \left(\frac{0.9672}{.07} \right)$$

$$= \$500 \times 13.816 = \$6,908$$

To understand the values presented in Exhibit 4.11, we see that the initial payment of $500 has a FV of $919. To verify this, we can use the formula for FV:

$$FV = PV \times (1+I)^N \quad \text{(Formula 4a)}$$

Substituting into the equation, we have the following:

$$PV = \$500$$
$$I = 7\%$$
$$N = 9 \,(\text{Payments are over a nine-year period})$$
$$FV = \$500 \times 1.07^9 = \$500 \times 1.838 = \$919$$

To confirm that the number of payments is correct, we look at the FV of the amount paid into the annuity in year 9. N in this case is 9; as mentioned, this is an ordinary annuity, which means that payments are made at the end of the time period. Therefore, the payment made at the end of year 9 receives interest for only one period. Substituting again into the FV formula 4a, we have $FV = PV \times (1+I)^N$.

Substituting into the equation, we have the following:

$$PV = \$500$$
$$I = 7\%$$
$$N = 1$$
$$FV = \$500 \times 1.07^1 = \$500 \times 1.07 = \$535$$
$$\text{or } \$500 + (500 \times .07) = \$500 + \$35 \text{ or } \$535$$

Let us now use Excel to calculate the FV of an ordinary annuity using the same values as before (see Exhibit 4.12).

Here is a step-by-step Excel approach to finding the FVA_N:

- Enter the following values into cells C4, C5, and C6, respectively:

  C4 = −$500

  C5 = 7%

  C6 = 10

- Now enter the "=" sign into cell C8.
- Now select "FV" from the functions box (may require you to use the drop-down menu to find FV).
- Now enter the Rate value (select cell C5).
- Now enter the Nper value (select cell C6).
- Now enter the Pmt value (select cell C4).

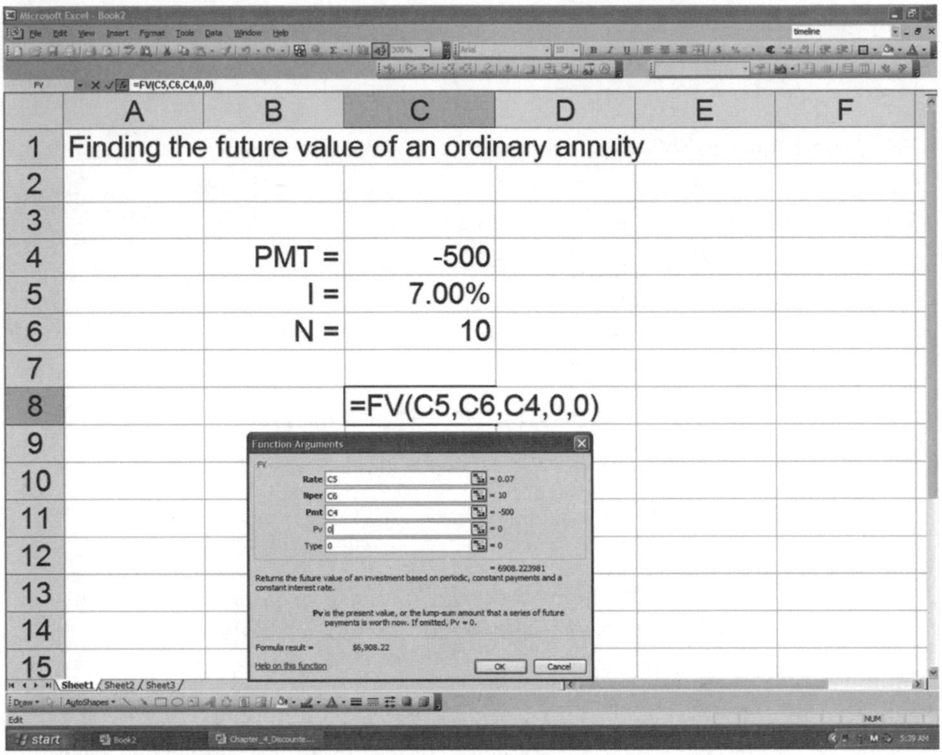

Exhibit 4.12 Finding the future value of an ordinary annuity: Excel example 6.

- Skip or enter a "0" for PV.
- Skip or enter a "0" for Type.
- Now select "OK" in the function argument box.

The FV of this ordinary annuity is $6,908.22.

We will use Excel to verify the future value of the $500 that was deposited into the annuity at the end of period 1. (See Exhibit 4.13.) As stated in Exhibit 4.11, this payment had a value of $919 at the end of the annuity. To determine the value of this individual payment:

- Enter the following values into cells C4, C5, and C6, respectively.

  C4 = −$500

  C5 = 7%

  C6 = 9 (The payment is made at the end of the period; therefore, the value of N = 9.)

- Now enter the "=" sign into cell C8.
- Now select "FV" from the functions box.
- Now enter the Rate value (select cell C5).
- Now enter the Nper value (select cell C6).
- Skip or enter a "0" for Pmt (we are only interested in the FV of a single payment).

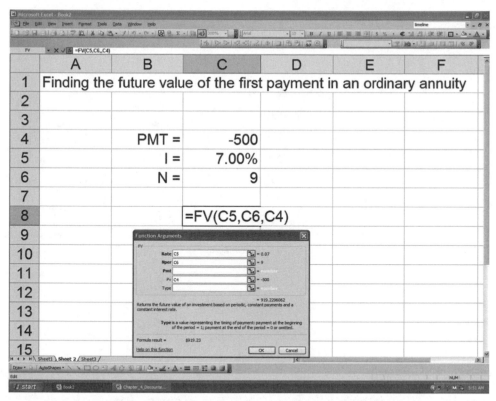

Exhibit 4.13   Finding the future value of the first payment in an ordinary annuity: Excel example 7.

- Now enter the PV value (select cell C4).
- Skip or enter a "0" for Type.
- Now select "OK" in the function argument box.

The FV of this first payment into the ordinary annuity is $919.23 at the end of the period, which confirms the future value of payment 1 in Exhibit 4.11.

Additional Exercise: Future Value of Annual Ordinary Annuity

To continue to illustrate solving FVA_N calculations using Excel, we will use various PMT values (see Exhibit 4.14).

$$FVA = \text{Future value of annuity (unknown)}$$
$$PMT = -\$350$$
$$PMT = -\$900$$
$$PMT = -\$1,000$$
$$PMT = -\$1,500$$
$$PMT = -\$2,000$$
$$I = 6\%$$
$$N = 5 \text{ years}$$

To solve for FVA_N, follow the instructions posted in reference to Excel example 6.

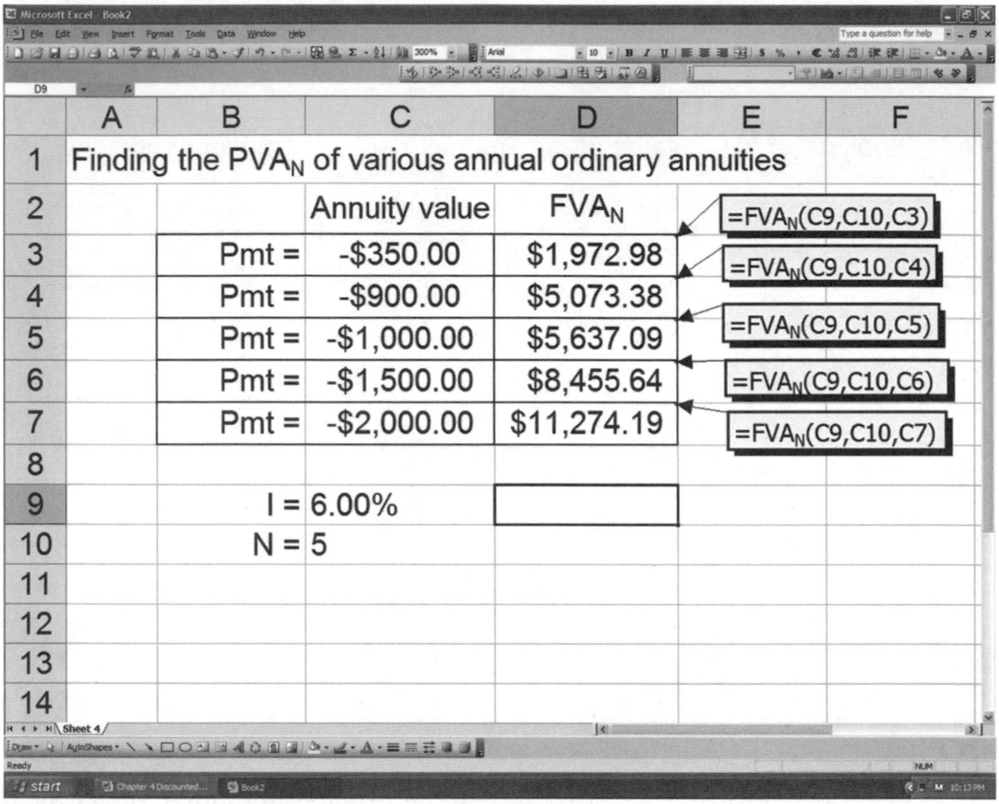

Exhibit 4.14   Finding the FVA$_N$ of various ordinary annuities: Excel example 8.

Additional Exercise: FVA$_N$

Determine the future value(s) of a 15-year, $2,000 ordinary annuity at various interest rates (see Exhibit 4.15).

$$Annuity = -\$2,000$$
$$N = 15$$
$$I = 0.5\%$$
$$I = 3.5\%$$
$$I = 6.5\%$$
$$I = 7.0\%$$
$$I = 9.5\%$$

To solve for *FVA$_N$*, follow the instructions posted in reference to Excel Example 6, but note that the cell addresses may differ.

Calculating the Present Value of an Ordinary Annuity

The algebraic formula for calculating the *PVA$_N$* is:

$$PVA_N = \frac{PMT}{(1+I)^1} + \frac{PMT}{(1+I)^2} + \frac{PMT}{(1+I)^3} + \cdots \frac{PMT}{(1+I)^N} \quad \text{(Formula 4d)}$$

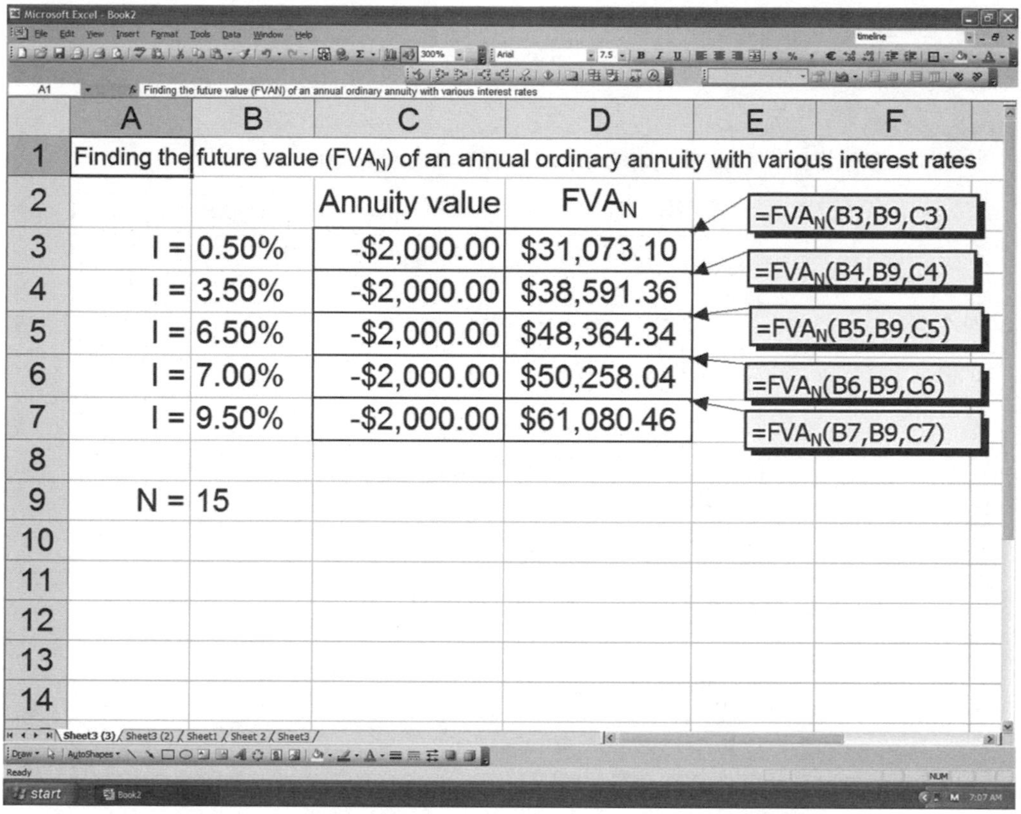

Exhibit 4.15 Finding the future value of an ordinary annuity: Excel example 9.

Note that deposits are discounted in the Exhibit 4.16 payment schedule.

We will forgo solving for PVA_N using the algebraic formula and instead use Excel to solve for PVA_N (see Exhibit 4.17).

$$PVA_N = \text{Present value of annuity at the end of a time period } N$$
$$I = \text{Interest} = 7\%$$
$$N = \text{Number of periods} = 10$$
$$PMT = \$500$$

Present value of the annuity = $3,511.79

Exhibit 4.16 Payment schedule for ordinary annuity.

Period	1	2	3	4	5	6	7	8	9	10
Payment	($500)	($500)	($500)	($500)	($500)	($500)	($500)	($500)	($500)	($ 500)
PV	467	437	408	381	356	333	311	291	272	254
PVA_N										$3,512

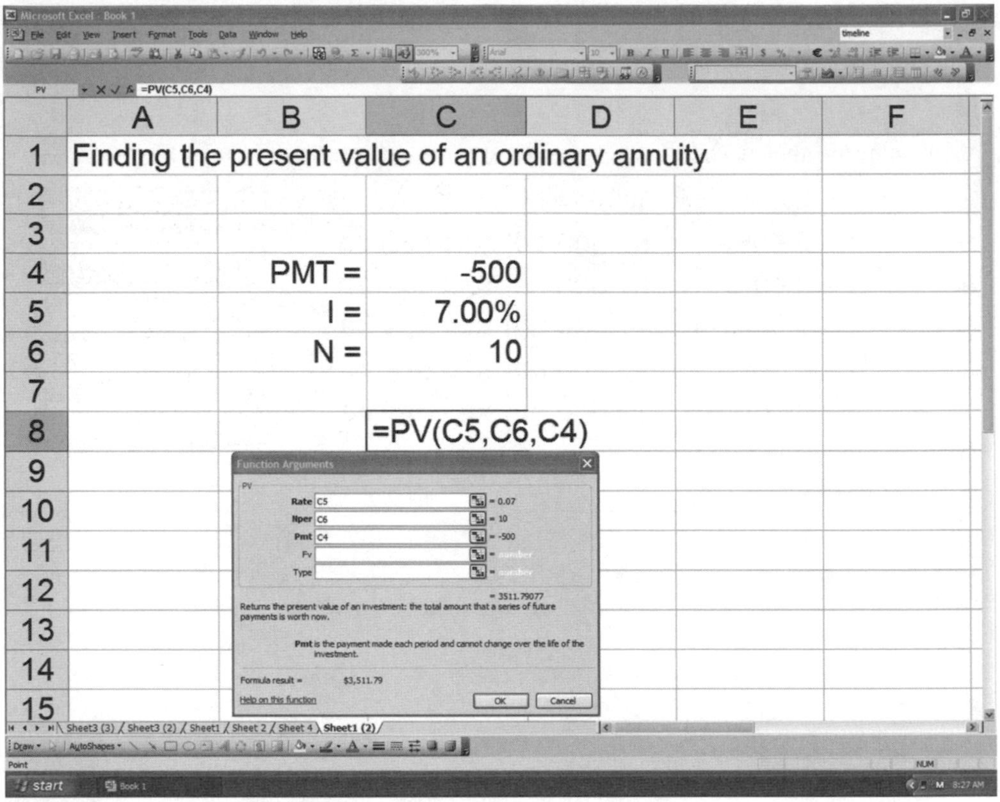

Exhibit 4.17   **Finding the present value of an ordinary annuity: Excel example 10.**

Additional Exercise Calculating PVA_N *Using Excel*

See Exhibit 4.18.

$$\text{Annuity} = \$2,000$$
$$N = 15$$
$$I = 0.5\%$$
$$I = 3.5\%$$
$$I = 6.5\%$$
$$I = 7.0\%$$
$$I = 9.5\%$$

Amortized Loans

Money borrowed from banks or other sources to purchase items such as factory machinery, inventory, personal residences, or automobiles is expected to be paid back over time. When the money is lent, an agreement is reached with the lender for the borrower to repay the loan, with interest, in a specified time. We generally agree to pay the lender back in equal installments, which may be weekly, bimonthly, monthly, or annually, over a specific period of time, and at a specific interest rate.

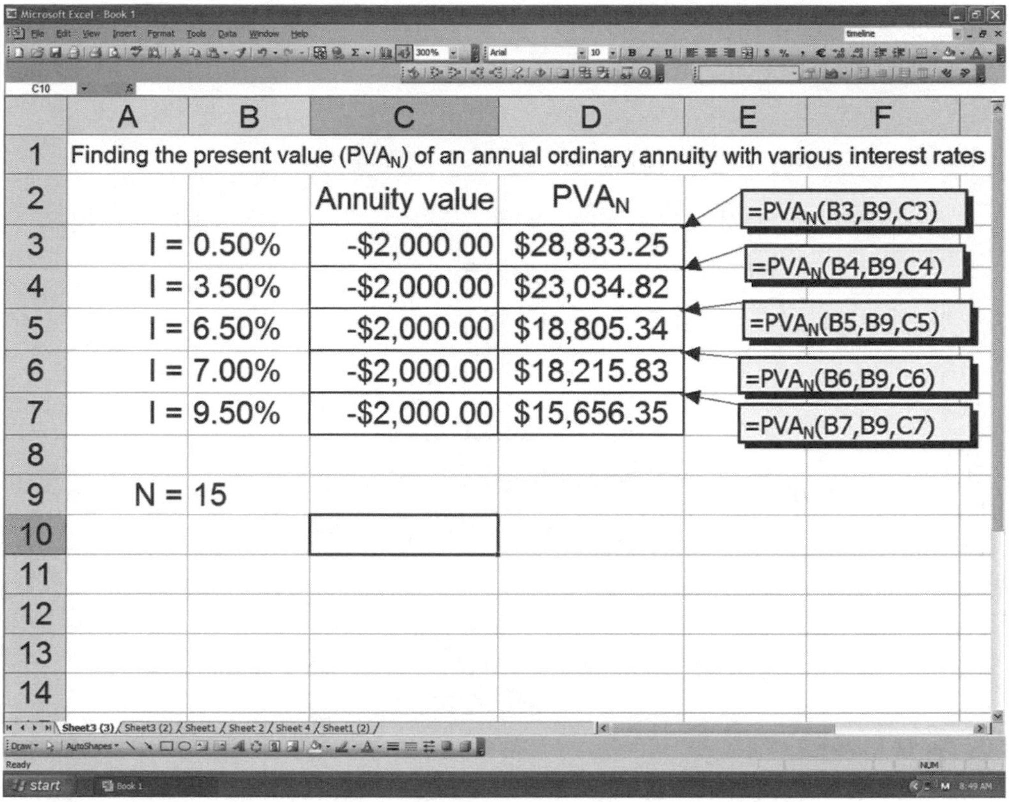

Exhibit 4.18   Finding the present value of an annual ordinary annuity with various interest rates: Excel example 11.

In this discussion on amortized loans, we will not cover any recent changes to the types of loans on offer. We will focus on loans repaid in equal installments over the life of the loan, with portions of the repayments applied toward the principal and interest, where the objective is to pay off the principal amount of the loan. *Amortize* is derived from the Latin *admortire*, to kill, which for this exercise is the result of paying off the loan. We will review the schedule and payment structures associated with amortizing loans.

Exercise on Amortized Loans

We need to borrow money to purchase a new machine for our production line. We are borrowing the entire cost of the machine, $200,000, for a period of 10 years, with an annual interest rate of 10%. To determine our annual repayments, we will use the Excel "PMT" function (see Exhibit 4.19). The first step is to determine what our annual payments will be; to do so we enter the known data:

- $PV = -\$200,000$ (note the minus sign). This is the cost of the machine, $200,000, entered into cell C4.
- $I = 10\%$. This is the annual interest rate, entered into cell C5.
- $N = 10$. The length of the loan is 10 years, entered into cell C6.

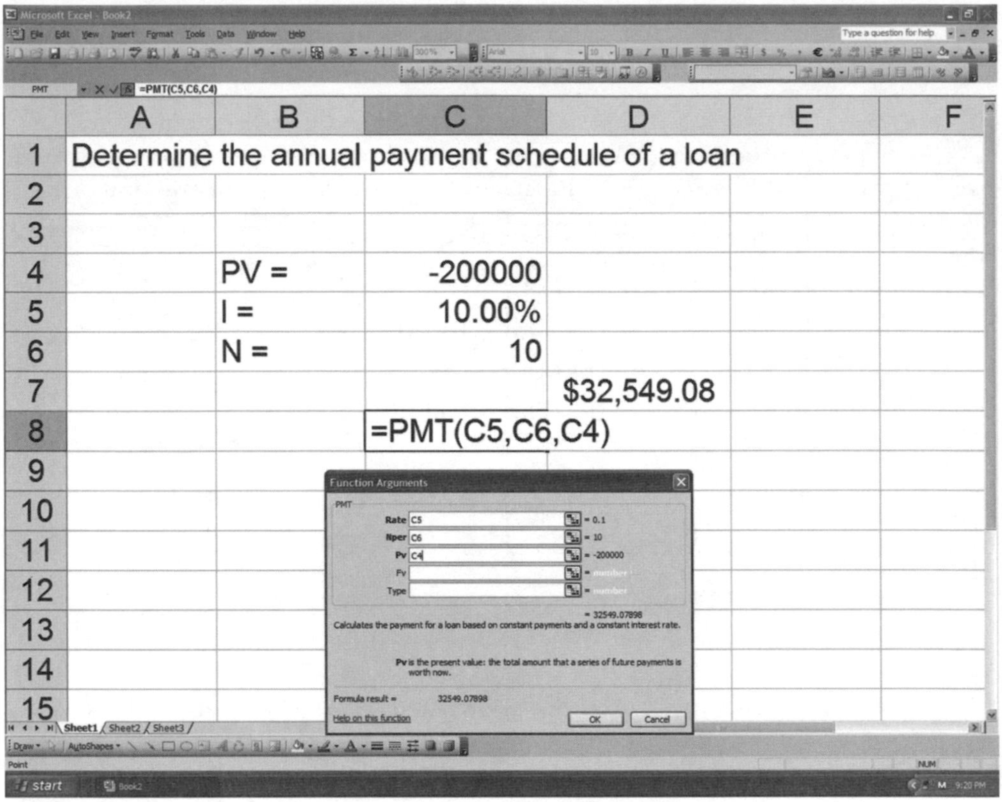

Exhibit 4.19   Determine the annual payment schedule of a loan: Excel example 12.

From the data we solve for "PMT," which provides a result of $32,549.08. This amount is due in annual installments for 10 years. A quick look at the payment schedule and number of payments tells us that this $200,000 machine will cost us $325,490.80 over the life of the loan (10 equal payments of $32,549.08).

To understand the distribution of the annual payments toward principal and interest, we will refer to the amortization schedule, Exhibit 4.20.

To create the table, we input the original loan amount of $200,000 into column B, the amount at the beginning of the year. The equal annual payments of $32,549 are posted in column C. We then determine the amount of interest due at the end of the first year by taking the beginning-of-the-year balance and multiplying it by the interest rate of 10%. For the first year, the result in an interest charge of $20,000, and the interest due is posted in column D. To determine the amount that is deducted from the principal amount of $200,000, we first subtract the interest from the payment amount. For year 1, this amount is $32,549 − $20,000 = $12,549. This amount is posted in column E. The balance at the end of year 1, which is also the balance at the beginning of year 2, is $200,000 − $12,549, or $187,451.

Exhibit 4.20 Amortization schedule.

A	B	C	D	E
Year	Amount at Beginning of Year	Payment	Interest	Toward Principal
1	$200,000	$ 32,549	$ 20,000	$ 12,549
2	187,451	32,549	18,745	13,804
3	173,647	32,549	17,365	15,184
4	158,463	32,549	15,846	16,703
5	141,760	32,549	14,176	18,373
6	123,387	32,549	12,339	20,210
7	103,177	32,549	10,318	22,231
8	80,945	32,549	8,094	24,455
9	56,490	32,549	5,649	26,900
10	29,590	32,549	2,959	29,590
Total	$ 0	$325,491	$125,491	$200,000

From Exhibit 4.20, we see that as the principal amount decreases, the amount put toward the principal increases, and the annual interest due decreases.

Additional Exercise on Amortizing Loans

When most consumers shop for home loans, they compare interest rates. For this exercise, we consider the same principal loan amount of $200,000 over 30 years, but with different interest rates of 4.89% and 5.25%. We will compare only single annual payments for this exercise. To review additional exercises, including a monthly payment schedule for this exercise, check out the Web site for this chapter. Using Excel, we determine our annual payments to be $12,847.61 at 4.89% and $13,383.39 at 5.25% (see Exhibit 4.21).

From the amortization schedule, Exhibit 4.22, we see that over the term of the loan, the higher interest rate costs the borrower more than $16,000 in additional interest payments.

If you are working with Excel online, you can find an excellent mortgage and loan amortization schedule by going to the "Type a question for help" box in Excel, enter "amortization", and then select the table that best suits your needs.

Irregular or Uneven Cash Flows

In earlier topics in this chapter, our discussions represented even cash flows, with calculations of future and present values of annuities. In discussing annuities, we stated that annuities must pay an equal amount, at a specific time interval, for a specific time period. An irregular cash flow means that cash flow varies over time. For example, banks adjust their interest rates on savings and variable-rate home loans, and companies adjust their annual stock dividends. All are examples of uneven cash flows.

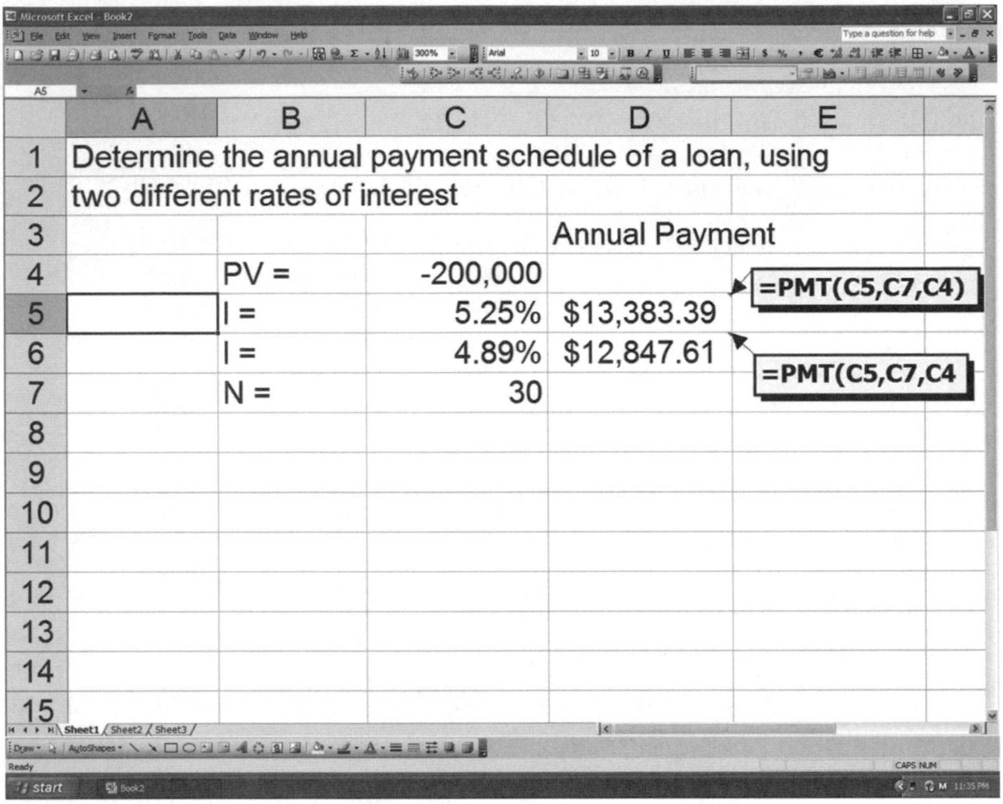

	A	B	C	D	E
1	Determine the annual payment schedule of a loan, using				
2	two different rates of interest				
3				Annual Payment	
4		PV =	-200,000		=PMT(C5,C7,C4)
5		I =	5.25%	$13,383.39	
6		I =	4.89%	$12,847.61	=PMT(C5,C7,C4
7		N =	30		
8					
9					
10					
11					
12					
13					
14					
15					

Exhibit 4.21 Determine the annual payment schedule of a loan: Excel example 13.

Uneven Cash Flow Exercise

In Exhibit 4.11, we calculated the FV of an annuity with regular cash flows. In Exhibit 4.16, we calculated the PV of the same annuity with regular cash flows. For this exercise, we are going to modify the cash flow in both of these examples to help us understand what occurs to the future and present values during uneven cash flows. We will keep the interest rate and time unchanged; however, we will change the payments to reflect uneven cash flows.

Exhibit 4.23 represents regular cash flows of $500 into an ordinary annuity over 10 periods at 7%, and the FV of the annuity.

Exhibit 4.24 has uneven cash flows in periods 4, 6, 7, and 8 compared to Exhibit 4.23. We see that the FVs of the uneven cash flows in periods *other* than 4, 6, 7, and 8 are unchanged. In the periods where the cash flow payments changed, we see that the FV *has increased or decreased*, depending on the difference in the value of the payment versus the original values in Exhibit 4.23; the final value at the end of the period has changed, too.

In calculating FV for an uneven cash flow, we are *unable* to use any Excel formulas and resort to calculating the individual FV of each payment. Exhibit 4.25 represents regular cash flows of $500 into an ordinary annuity over 10 periods at 7%, and the PV of the annuity.

Exhibit 4.22 Amortization schedule: equal principal, equal time length, different interest rates.

A	B	C	D	E	F	G	H	I
Year	Amount at Beginning of Year	Payment	Interest @ 4.89%	Toward Principal	Amount at Beginning of Year	Payment	Interest @ 5.25%	Toward Principal
1	$200,000	$12,848	$9,780	$3,068	$200,000	$13,383	$10,500	$2,883
2	196,932	12,848	9,630	3,218	197,117	13,383	10,349	3,035
3	193,715	12,848	9,473	3,375	194,082	13,383	10,189	3,194
4	190,340	12,848	9,308	3,540	190,888	13,383	10,022	3,362
5	186,800	12,848	9,135	3,713	187,526	13,383	9,845	3,538
6	183,087	12,848	8,953	3,895	183,988	13,383	9,659	3,724
7	179,192	12,848	8,762	4,085	180,264	13,383	9,464	3,920
8	175,107	12,848	8,563	4,285	176,344	13,383	9,258	4,125
9	170,822	12,848	8,353	4,494	172,219	13,383	9,041	4,342
10	166,328	12,848	8,133	4,714	167,877	13,383	8,814	4,570
11	161,613	12,848	7,903	4,945	163,307	13,383	8,574	4,810
12	156,669	12,848	7,661	5,187	158,497	13,383	8,321	5,062
13	151,482	12,848	7,407	5,440	153,435	13,383	8,055	5,328
14	146,042	12,848	7,141	5,706	148,107	13,383	7,776	5,608
15	140,336	12,848	6,862	5,985	142,499	13,383	7,481	5,902
16	34,351	12,848	6,570	6,278	136,597	13,383	7,171	6,212
17	128,073	12,848	6,263	6,585	130,385	13,383	6,845	6,538
18	121,488	12,848	5,941	6,907	123,847	13,383	6,502	6,881
19	114,581	12,848	5,603	7,245	116,965	13,383	6,141	7,243
20	107,337	12,848	5,249	7,599	109,723	13,383	5,760	7,623

(continued)

Exhibit 4.22 Amortization schedule: equal principal, equal time length, different interest rates. (*Continued*)

A	B	C	D	E	F	G	H	I
Year	Amount at Beginning of Year	Payment	Interest @ 4.89%	Toward Principal	Amount at Beginning of Year	Payment	Interest @ 5.25%	Toward Principal
21	99,738	12,848	4,877	7,970	102,100	13,383	5,360	8,023
22	91,767	12,848	4,487	8,360	94,076	13,383	4,939	8,444
23	83,407	12,848	4,079	8,769	85,632	13,383	4,496	8,888
24	74,638	12,848	3,650	9,198	76,744	13,383	4,029	9,354
25	65,440	12,848	3,200	9,648	67,390	13,383	3,538	9,845
26	55,793	12,848	2,728	10,119	57,545	13,383	3,021	10,362
27	45,673	12,848	2,233	10,614	47,182	13,383	2,477	10,906
28	35,059	12,848	1,714	11,133	36,276	13,383	1,904	11,479
29	23,926	12,848	1,170	11,678	24,797	13,383	1,302	12,082
30	12,248	12,848	599	12,249	12,716	13,383	668	12,716
Total	−$0.22	$385,428	$185,428	$200,000	−$0.23	$401,502	$201,501	$200,000

Exhibit 4.23   Regular cash flows with FV.

Period/ Years	1	2	3	4	5	6	7	8	9	10
Payment	($500)	($500)	($500)	($500)	($500)	($500)	($500)	($500)	($500)	($ 500)
FV	919	859	803	750	701	655	613	572	535	500
Interest	419	359	303	250	201	155	113	72	35	1,908
FVA_N										$6,908

Exhibit 4.24   Uneven cash flows with FV.

Period/ Years	1	2	3	4	5	6	7	8	9	10
Payment	($500)	($500)	($500)	($200)	($500)	($700)	($700)	($800)	($500)	($ 500)
FV	919	859	803	300	701	918	858	916	535	500
Interest	419	359	303	100	201	218	158	116	35	1,910
FVA_N										$7,309

Note: Values are compounded.

Exhibit 4.25   Regular cash flows with PV.

Period	1	2	3	4	5	6	7	8	9	10
Payment	($500)	($500)	($500)	($500)	($500)	($500)	($500)	($500)	($500)	($ 500)
PV	467	437	408	381	356	333	311	291	272	254
PVA_N										$3,512

Note: Values are discounted.

In Exhibit 4.26 the PVs of the uneven cash flows in periods other than 4, 6, 7, and 8 are *unchanged*. In the periods where the cash flow payments have changed, we see that the PV *has increased or decreased*, depending on the difference in the value of the payment versus the original values in Exhibit 4.25; also note that the final value at the end of the period has changed, too.

The NPV results of $3,715 in Exhibit 4.26 confirm our calculations in Excel example 14 (Exhibit 4.27) and confirm that we are able to calculate uneven cash flows using the NPV formula. When using Excel's NPV formula, we must keep in mind that the formula assumes that the first payment is made at the end of period 1.

Exhibit 4.26   Uneven cash flows with PV.

Period	1	2	3	4	5	6	7	8	9	10
Payment	($500)	($500)	($500)	($200)	($500)	($700)	($700)	($800)	($500)	($ 500)
PV	467	437	408	153	356	466	436	466	272	254
NPV										$3,715

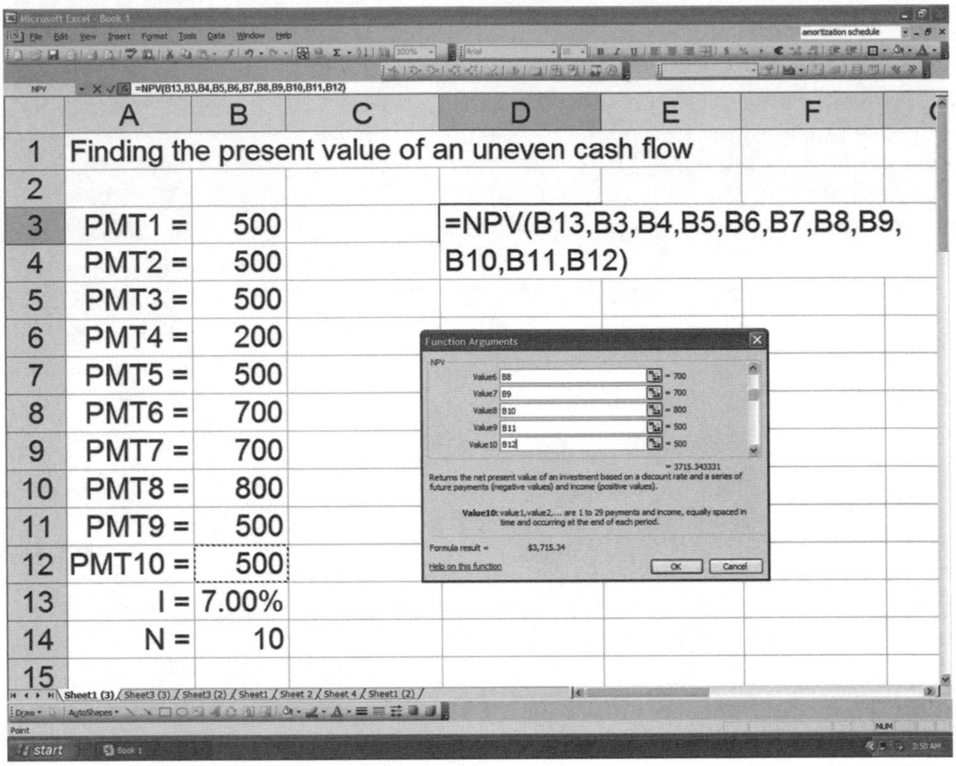

Exhibit 4.27   **Finding the present value of an uneven cash flow: Excel example 14.**

Summary

What is the value of a dollar today versus the value that the same exact dollar amount will have in two years? On January 2, 2009, we deposit $10,000 (*PV*) for two years (*N*) at 10% (*I*); we calculate our compounded interest and principal and determine that on January 2, 2011, the future value of our deposit will be $12,100 (*FV*). If we did not deposit or invest the $10,000 and allowed it to remain in a safe-deposit box, on January 2, 2011, we would have exactly $10,000.

When we calculate the value of the $10,000 in the safe-deposit box on January 2, 2011, we determine that its present value (*PV*) is only $8,264.46. If we discount the original $10,000 to $8,264.46 and invested it at 10% for two years, we calculate the future value (*FV*) of our $8,264.46 to be $10,000. When discussing the time value of money, we *assume that money invested or saved will earn interest*. Therefore, a known dollar amount today is worth more than that same dollar amount in the future.

Downloadable Resources for this chapter available at www.wiley.com/go/portablembainfinance

Discounted Cash Flow: Using Excel to Solve Financial Formulas

Discounted Cash Flow Web

Internet Links

www.usd.edu/trio/tut/excel/	Excel tutorial, review, and quizzes
http://archive.baarns.com/excel/free/ excelexp.asp#Functions	The Excel experience, learning and using Excel
www.youtube.com/watch?v= fM63moi1Qjo&feature=related	Time value of money
www.moneychimp.com/	Guides and tutorials on the basics of accounting, economics, and finance
http://web.utk.edu/~jwachowi/wacho_ world.html	A very large collection of useful links to Web sites on financial topics, techniques, and information
www.econlib.org/library/CEETitles.html	Short and easy-to-read articles on many different topics in economics
www.investopedia.com/?viewed=1	Articles, tutorials, and definitions
www.youtube.com/watch?v=2sXYobpdsUA	Video on net present value (NPV) and cash flow
www.youtube.com/watch?v=JOqEpxNGQjk	NPV using Excel
www.youtube.com/watch?v=KJIqK4nCo_ M&feature=related	Financial analysis using Excel
www.youtube.com/watch?v=VfjiWm VK2Z4&feature=related	Financial analysis using Excel
www.youtube.com/profile?user= SusanCrosson&view=videos	Good variety of online economic videos

For Further Reading

Brigham, Eugene F., and Joel F. Houston, *Fundamentals of Financial Management* (with Thomson ONE—Business School Edition), 12th ed. (Mason, OH: South-Western College Publishing, 2008).

Gallagher, Timothy J., and Joseph D. Andrew, *Financial Management: Principles & Practice*, 4th ed. (Freeload Press, 2007).

Hafer, Rik, and Speros Margetis, *A Student's Quick Guide to Understanding and Calculating Time Value of Money and Its Applications*, 1st ed. (Cengage Learning, 2005).

Van Horne, James C., and John M. Wachowicz, *Fundamentals of Financial Management*, 12th ed. (Upper Saddle River, NJ: Prentice-Hall, 2004).

5

Capital Structure

Craig A. Stephenson

Financial managers perform many tasks, and one of the most important of these tasks is raising capital to fund the internal investments of the firm. Businesses identify, analyze, and approve investment opportunities, and financial managers choose the most efficient way to fund these internal investments.

The decision criteria for efficient or inefficient funding of the firm's internal investments are based on the firm's cost of capital. If the firm raises capital in a manner that reduces or minimizes its cost of capital, then its financial managers have done well and raised capital efficiently. In contrast, if the firm raises capital in a manner that increases or does not minimize its cost of capital, then its financial managers have done poorly and not raised capital efficiently. Financial managers, therefore, regularly calculate and track their firm's cost of capital, so they can determine if the firm is being funded in an efficient manner.

Financial managers also use their firm's cost of capital as a critical input in the investment analysis process. Internal investment opportunities are identified, and the cash outflows and inflows of these opportunities are estimated. The cost of capital necessary to fund investment opportunities is used as a hurdle rate to determine whether the project is a good project or a poor project. If the cash inflows from the project produce a rate of return on the cash outflows greater than the cost of the capital invested in the project, then the project should be accepted. If the cash inflows from the project instead produce a rate of return on the cash outflows less than the cost of the capital invested in the project, then the project should be rejected.

Managing the firm's cost of capital requires that financial managers understand risk and return, and how to choose the right mix of debt finance and equity finance. This chapter works through these topics, using both financial theory and practice, so you will understand the factors that determine the cost of capital and the capital structure of the firm. Financial managers also need to understand how the firm's bonds and stocks are valued using discounted cash flow (DCF) methods, and the last sections of this chapter discuss and illustrate this process.

Risk and Return

The relationship between risk and return is one of the fundamental relationships in finance, because investors are risk averse, meaning they prefer less risk to greater risk. It is not true that investors are unwilling to invest in risky ventures or projects, but it is true

129

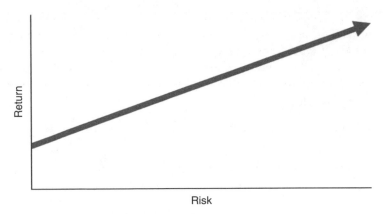

Exhibit 5.1   The relationship between risk and return.

that to entice investors to place their capital in riskier ventures or projects, they must expect to earn a higher rate of return. If you offer an investor two potential investments, one of lower risk and one of higher risk, and both projects have the same expected return, a rational investor will always choose the lower-risk investment. For investors to instead choose the higher-risk alternative, it must have a higher expected return. This higher expected return must be high enough, in fact, to entice the investor to select the higher-risk alternative. The relationship between risk and return is a positive one, as shown in Exhibit 5.1.

Investors who are risk averse will not invest in risky securities without greater expected returns. This also means that to earn greater expected returns investors must be willing to accept greater risk.

Measuring Returns

The periodic return earned by any investment is based on the value of the investment at the beginning of the period, any income received from the investment during the period, and the value of the investment at the end of the period. The rate of return earned over any period of time is called the holding period return and is calculated as:

$$\text{Holding Period Return} = \frac{\text{Income Received}}{\text{Beginning Value}} + \frac{\text{Ending Value} - \text{Beginning Value}}{\text{Beginning Value}}$$

This equation shows that investment returns have two components, income and capital gains. The first term in the equation is the income yield, calculated as the income received during the period divided by the initial investment. The second term in the equation is the capital gains yield, calculated as change in the value of the investment divided by the initial investment. If the beginning value of the investment was $10, the income received from the investment during the period was $1, and the ending value of the investment was $12, then the holding period return is:

$$\text{Holding Period Return} = \frac{\$1}{\$10} + \frac{\$12 - \$10}{\$10} = 0.10 + 0.20 = 0.30 = 30.0\%$$

In this example, the income yield was 0.10 or 10%, and the capital gains yield was 0.20 or 20%, producing a total holding period return of 0.30 or 30%.

This general formula works when measuring the holding period return for any period of time for any investment. For the more specific case of an investment in a share of stock (and we look at common stocks throughout this chapter), the income component is called the dividend yield, and the capital gains component is called the capital gains yield. The formula for holding period return on an investment in common stock is:

$$\text{Holding Period Return}_t = \frac{\text{Dividend}_t}{\text{Price}_{t-1}} + \frac{\text{Price}_t - \text{Price}_{t-1}}{\text{Price}_{t-1}}$$

where the holding period return earned during period t is based on the dividend received during period t, the stock price at the end of the prior period $t-1$, and the stock price at the end of period t.

Research on the common stock of the Walt Disney Company, a worldwide entertainment company with operations in media networks, parks and resorts, studio entertainment, and consumer products, shows Disney's stock price at the beginning of 2006 was $23.97 per share and at the end of 2006 was $34.27 per share, and its stock paid cash dividends per share of $0.31 in 2006. With these data, we are able to calculate the year 2006 holding period return to an investor in Disney's common stock as:

$$\text{Disney Return} = \frac{\$0.31}{\$23.97} + \frac{\$34.27 - \$23.97}{\$23.97} = 0.0129 + 0.4297 = 0.4426 = 44.26\%$$

During 2006 investors in Disney common stock were well rewarded, earning a dividend yield of 1.29% and a capital gains yield of 42.97%, which combine to produce a total return of 44.26%.

Many firms collect, analyze, and publish information about the returns earned by alternative investments. Ibbotson Associates, Inc., which publishes data showing, among other items, the average annual returns earned by different investments over different holding periods, is a well known and widely cited authority in this area. A selected group of average annual returns for the 80-year holding period from 1926 through 2005 is presented in Exhibit 5.2, which shows that investors in small company stocks earned the highest average returns over this 80-year holding period, and investors in U.S. Treasury bills earned the lowest average returns.

Exhibit 5.2   Average annual returns, 1926–2005.

Investment Series	Arithmetic Mean Return
Small company stocks	17.4%
Large company stocks	12.3
Long-term corporate bonds	6.2
Long-term U.S. government bonds	5.8
U.S. Treasury bills	3.8
Inflation	3.1

Source: Modified from *Stocks, Bonds, Bills, and Inflation: 2006 Yearbook,* Ibbotson Associates, Inc.

Exhibit 5.2 also reveals the positive relationship between risk and return, as small company stocks have the highest risk of the investment series shown in the table, and U.S. Treasury bills have the lowest risk.

Now that we have discussed how to measure investment returns, we will move on to measuring investment risk.

Measuring Risk

The risk of any investment is defined by the variability of the investment's returns. Investments with low variability of returns have lower risk, as their returns are more predictable. Investments with high variability of returns, in contrast, have higher risk, as their returns are less predictable. This variability can produce both better than predicted returns and worse than predicted returns, so we will measure variability of returns in both directions, upside and downside. We will begin our look at risk by considering the risk of a single asset held by itself and then move on to the case of a single asset held in a portfolio of assets.

Stand-alone risk is the risk associated with an investment in a single asset held alone. In this case, the investor has all of his or her wealth invested in this single asset and is entirely exposed to the variability of returns of this asset, so we measure stand-alone risk as the risk of this asset by itself. To do this we will look to the field of statistics, specifically the concept of standard deviation.

The standard deviation of returns for any investment, which is the square root of the variance of returns for the investment, measures the dispersion or variability of returns around the mean return for a period. A lower standard deviation of returns for an asset indicates a less variable and lower-risk investment, and a higher standard deviation of returns for an asset indicates a more variable and higher-risk investment.

Because of its predictive ability, standard deviation is particularly helpful in understanding the variability and risk of an asset's returns. For any data series that follows a standard normal distribution, the mean and standard deviation tell us how close or far the individual observations in the series will be from the mean. Exhibit 5.3 presents this relationship between the mean (μ) and standard deviation (σ) for any standard normal data series. This relationship, along with knowledge of the mean annual return and standard deviation of annual returns for any asset, allows us to predict the distribution of returns and therefore the variability and risk of the asset.

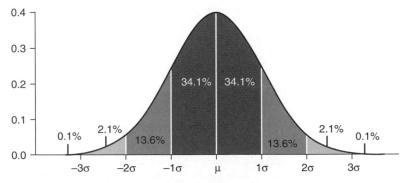

Exhibit 5.3   The normal distribution.

The region in black on both side of the mean, plus or minus one standard deviation, accounts for 68.2% of the observations, so if the mean annual return of an asset is 15% and the standard deviation of annual returns of the asset is 5%, then 68.2% of the asset's annual returns will be between 10% and 20%. The regions in dark gray and black on both sides of the mean, plus or minus two standard deviations, account for 95.4% of the observations, so for the same asset 95.4% of the annual returns will be between 5% and 25%. All three of the shaded regions on both sides of the mean, plus or minus three standard deviations, account for about 99.7% of the observations, so for the same asset 99.7% of the annual returns will be between 0% and 30%. This is the power of standard deviation in explaining the variability and risk of an asset. If the asset has a high standard deviation of annual returns, then the range of possible annual returns around the mean of the asset is very wide, and the asset is of higher risk. If the asset, in contrast, has a low standard deviation of annual returns, then the range of possible annual returns around the mean of the asset is very narrow, and the asset is of lower risk.

The standard deviation of returns for any asset is calculated in four steps:

1. Calculate the arithmetic mean return for the asset over some time period.
2. Subtract each individual return from the mean return to get the deviations.
3. Square each deviation, sum the deviations, and divide this sum by the number of observations minus 1, producing the variance.
4. Take the square root of the variance, which produces the standard deviation of returns for the asset.

The formula for standard deviation of returns is:

$$\sigma = \sqrt{\frac{\sum (R_i - \overline{R})^2}{n - 1}}$$

where σ is the standard deviation of returns, R_i is each individual return, $\overline{R}$ is the mean return, and n is the number of observed returns.

With a series of returns for any asset, the standard deviation of returns for the asset can be calculated with this formula. The Center for Research in Security Prices (CRSP) at the University of Chicago captures and reports returns for many investment securities, and CRSP data is frequently used by academics and practitioners when researching investment returns.

We will illustrate the calculation and interpretation of standard deviation of returns using common stock as the asset, specifically the common stock of the Walt Disney Company and IBM. The annual returns earned on the common stock of Disney and IBM, as captured and reported by CRSP, are shown in Exhibit 5.4.

Based on these 10 years of data, the mean annual return and standard deviation of annual returns for the common stock of Disney are 3.12% and 25.17%, respectively. For the common stock of IBM, the mean annual return is 12.54% and the standard deviation of annual returns is 32.43%. These results show the common stock of IBM has a higher standard deviation of annual returns than the common stock of Disney. Since standard deviation of returns is the appropriate measure of stand-alone risk, IBM's common stock is riskier than Disney's common stock for investors who choose to hold all of their wealth in a single asset. A stand-alone investment in IBM common stock is more variable and

Exhibit 5.4   Annual returns of Disney and IBM, 1998–2007.

Year	Disney Annual Returns	IBM Annual Returns
1998	−9.93%	77.05%
1999	−1.80	17.53
2000	−0.35	−20.73
2001	−27.67	42.95
2002	−20.27	−35.44
2003	44.33	20.40
2004	20.19	7.12
2005	−12.81	−15.82
2006	44.26	19.53
2007	−4.79	12.82

Source: Center for Research in Security Prices, Graduate School of Business of the University of Chicago.

volatile. In up years, IBM's stock performs better than Disney's stock, but in down years IBM's stock performs worse than Disney's stock. IBM's stock does have a higher mean annual return than Disney's stock, but IBM's stock is also riskier, reflecting the positive relationship between risk and return.

Portfolio Risk

Stand-alone risk is an important concept to understand, but it is also just the starting point in the study of risk and return, because investors usually do not hold all of their wealth in a single asset or stock. Investors typically hold a collection or portfolio of assets, so we need to examine risk in a portfolio context. Risk and return in a portfolio is very different from stand-alone risk and return due to diversification effects, which makes the risk of an asset when held in a portfolio lower than the risk of the asset alone. First we will examine the return of a portfolio, and then we will consider the risk of a portfolio.

Calculating the return of a portfolio of assets is quite simple, because the return of a portfolio is the weighted average of the return of the individual assets in the portfolio, with the weights determined by value. The formula for this calculation is

$$R_P = \sum_{i=1}^{n} W_i \times R_i$$

where R_P is the return of the portfolio, W_i is the weight by value of asset i, R_i is the return of asset i, and you sum these weighted returns for all n assets in the portfolio.

For example, if asset A is 50% of the value of the portfolio and has a return of 10%, asset B is 30% of the value of the portfolio and has a return of 15%, and asset C is 20% of the value of the portfolio and has a return of 18%, then the return of the portfolio is:

$$50\% \times 10\% + 30\% \times 15\% + 20\% \times 18\% = 5.0\% + 4.5\% + 3.6\% = 13.1\%$$

The return of any portfolio is the simple weighted average of the returns of the individual assets in the portfolio. As was true for the risk of an asset held alone, the correct measure of risk for a portfolio is the standard deviation of portfolio returns. The standard deviation of returns from a portfolio, however, is *not* the weighted average of the standard deviations of the individual assets in the portfolio. The reason this is true is due to the correlation between the assets in a portfolio, which results in the standard deviation of returns and therefore the risk of a portfolio, is lower than the standard deviation of returns and risk of the individual assets in the portfolio.

Correlation measures the joint variation between any two variables, which in finance means the extent to which asset values and returns move together. If two stocks have a correlation of +1.0, they are said to be perfectly positively correlated, and their values and returns always move in the same direction. Suppose asset A has a mean return of 6% per year, asset B has a mean return of 9% per year, and asset A and asset B are perfectly positively correlated. If asset A's annual return is higher than its mean return in a particular year, then asset B's annual return will also be higher than its mean return in the same year. Conversely, if asset A's annual return is lower than its mean return in a particular year, then asset B's annual return will also be lower than its mean return in the same year. If the assets in a portfolio are perfectly positively correlated, there is no risk reduction associated with holding the assets in a portfolio, because the individual asset returns always move together, in the same direction. In this unique and unrealistic situation, the standard deviation of the portfolio's returns actually is the weighted average of the standard deviation of returns of the individual assets in the portfolio, so risk is not reduced by holding assets in a portfolio.

In the opposite case, when two assets have a correlation of −1.0, they are said to be perfectly negatively correlated, and their value and returns always move in the exact opposite direction. Suppose asset Y has a mean return of 10% per year, asset Z has a mean return of 12% per year, and asset Y and asset Z are perfectly negatively correlated. If asset Y's annual return is higher than its mean return in a particular year, then asset Z's annual return will be lower than its mean return in the same year. Conversely, if asset Y's annual return is lower than its mean return in a particular year, then asset Z's annual return will be higher than its mean return in the same year. In this similarly unique and unrealistic situation, the standard deviation of the portfolio's returns will be significantly reduced, because the variability in the returns of the two assets offset each other. Any move by one asset above its mean return will be offset by a move by the other asset below its mean return, so the standard deviation, and risk, of the portfolio is greatly reduced.

In the real world of asset values and returns, we typically observe positive correlations between 0.5 and 0.7. This means most assets do move together, but this movement is not always in the same direction. This observed positive correlation, but much less than perfectly positive correlation, is due to unique factors that impact only individual assets, and common factors that impact many, and perhaps nearly all, assets. We will consider these factors in order.

There are many unique factors, also called diversifiable or nonsystematic factors, that impact only individual assets or particular stocks. Examples of such factors include the brilliance or folly of a company's managers, the success or failure of a large research and development initiative, consumer frenzy for or avoidance of a particular good or service, beneficial or harmful local weather, or accidents or strikes at a particular company. Since these unique factors by definition affect only individual companies, investors can diversify or reduce the risk associated with these factors by holding portfolios. In a portfolio, it is highly likely a few assets or stocks will experience poor returns due to unfavorable unique factors, but it's also highly likely a few assets or stocks will experience excellent returns due to their own unique factors. This reduces the volatility and standard deviation of returns and risk of the entire portfolio by offsetting the unique and poor returns of some of the assets or stocks in the portfolio with unique and good returns of some others of the assets or stocks in the portfolio. This is how holding a portfolio of assets reduces risk. As long as the components of the portfolio are not perfectly positively correlated, the standard deviation of returns (and risk) of the overall portfolio is less than the standard deviation of returns and risk of the individual assets held in the portfolio. The main point here is that unique or nonsystematic risks are diversified in a portfolio of assets, reducing this particular type of risk.

In spite of unique or diversifiable factors that differ across firms, asset or stock values and returns still tend to move up or down with general economic and financial market conditions. In good years, most investments earn good returns—not all investments, but certainly most. In poor years, most investments earn poor returns. There are common factors that drive economic conditions in favorable or unfavorable directions, and, not surprisingly, these common factors also impact the value and returns of most assets and stocks. Examples of common factors that impact economic conditions and asset returns include commodity prices, interest rates, foreign exchange rates, inflation, and consumer confidence, to name just a few. These common factors, called market, nondiversifiable, or systematic factors, cannot be eliminated by investing in portfolios, because the individual assets in the portfolio are all, or nearly all, affected by these factors. No matter how the portfolio is constructed or how many assets are in the portfolio, changes in these factors will affect the returns of most of the component assets in a similar manner, and will therefore affect the returns of the entire portfolio as well. Market or systematic risks are not diversified by holding a portfolio of assets, as this particular type of risk is not reduced.

We have seen that assets and stocks carry two different types of risk. Nonsystematic risks are unique to individual stocks, and as long as these stocks are held in a portfolio and have less than perfectly positive correlation, this type of risk is reduced. As the number of stocks in a portfolio increases, this risk gets smaller and smaller, and once the portfolio contains approximately 30 assets or stocks, the unique or nonsystematic risk is eliminated. Unique or nonsystematic risk, therefore, is irrelevant; it is not priced, and investors are not rewarded for holding it, because it can be easily eliminated.

Systematic or market risk, in contrast, which is created by factors common to all assets or stocks, cannot be diversified. This risk cannot be eliminated, no matter how many stocks are in a portfolio. Systematic or market risk, therefore, is relevant, it is priced, and investors expect to be rewarded for holding it. This logic is the basis of the capital asset pricing model (CAPM), which states that the appropriate measure of risk for any asset is that particular asset's contribution to the risk of a portfolio.

This measure of risk for any asset or stock in a portfolio is determined by the mathematics of the standard deviation of the portfolio. For example, if a portfolio contains two common stocks, stock A and stock B, the standard deviation of the portfolio is defined by a two-by-two variance/covariance matrix, which contains four statistical components: the variance of stock A, the variance of stock B, the covariance between stock A and stock B, and the covariance between stock B and stock A (which is identical to the covariance between stock A and stock B). In this portfolio of two stocks, there are two variance terms and two covariance terms, so in a small portfolio the variance of the individual stocks contributes significantly to the standard deviation of the portfolio.

If you have not encountered covariance in your studies, the covariance between any two stocks measures the extent to which the stocks move together and the volatility of these movements. Stocks with high covariance tend to have large movements frequently in the same direction, so placing stocks with high covariance together in a portfolio does not reduce the risk of the portfolio very much. Stocks with small covariance, in contrast, tend to have smaller movements less frequently in the same direction, so placing stocks with low covariance together in a portfolio reduces the risk of the portfolio much more.

If a portfolio contains five stocks it has five variance terms, one for each stock in the portfolio. With five stocks in the portfolio, the variance/covariance matrix is five by five, 25 terms in all. Since there are five variance terms, there are also 20 covariance terms, so the variance of the individual stocks contributes less to the standard deviation of the portfolio, and the covariance terms contribute more. If the portfolio contains 50 stocks, it has 50 variance terms, but the variance/covariance matrix is 50 by 50, 2,500 terms in all. Since there are 50 variance terms, there are also 2,450 covariance terms; now the variance terms contribute very little to the standard deviation of the portfolio, and the covariance terms dominate. In the limit, the variance of the individual stocks has zero effect on the standard deviation of the portfolio, as there are $1/N$ variance terms, and $(1 - 1/N)$ covariance terms, with N being the number of stocks in the portfolio. This allows us to conclude that in a portfolio of many different stocks, the variance of the individual stocks does not matter. The covariance between the stocks in the portfolio is what determines the standard deviation of returns and risk of the portfolio, and this covariance is based on the correlation between the stocks in the portfolio.

The appropriate measure of risk for any stock in a portfolio is its contribution to the risk of the overall portfolio, which we have seen is the covariance of returns between the stock and the other stocks in the portfolio. A stock with high covariance of returns with the other stocks in the portfolio has returns that are highly correlated with the returns of the other stocks and has a high standard deviation as well.

In nonstatistical language, this means a stock with a high covariance with the other stocks in the portfolio adds to the risk of the portfolio, because its returns move in the same direction as the returns of the other stocks, and these movements are large or volatile. If the portfolio increases in value because the majority of the component stocks are earning positive returns, then a high-covariance stock usually earns larger positive returns, further increasing the return of the overall portfolio. If the portfolio instead decreases in value because the majority of the component stocks are earning negative returns, then a high-covariance stock usually earns larger negative returns, further decreasing the return of the overall portfolio. This is how a high-covariance stock adds to the risk of the portfolio. In up years this type of stock is up more than the other stocks in the portfolio, pushing the portfolio up even more. In down years this same stock is down more than the other stocks in the portfolio, pushing the portfolio down even more.

A stock with low covariance of returns with the other stocks in the portfolio tends to move in a different direction than the other stocks in the portfolio, or these movements are not large or volatile. This type of stock does not increase in value as much as the other stocks in the portfolio in good years, and it does not decrease in value as much as the other stocks in the portfolio in poor years. A stock with a low covariance of returns, therefore, reduces the variability and standard deviation of returns and the risk of the portfolio.

Capital Asset Pricing Model

The capital asset pricing model (CAPM) developed the concept that the contribution of an individual stock to the risk of a portfolio is best measured by comparing the returns of the individual stock to the returns of the overall stock market. We have previously discussed how common factors, such as interest rates, foreign exchange rates, inflation, and consumer confidence, impact economic conditions and affect stock prices and returns. These common factors are the cause of market or systematic risk, which cannot be eliminated by diversification and is therefore relevant and priced.

If a particular stock is highly susceptible to market or systematic risk, during good economic conditions the stock will earn larger than average positive returns, and during poor economic conditions the stock will earn larger than average negative returns. This type of stock is risky to include in a portfolio, since it increases the standard deviation of returns of the portfolio by making good years even better and poor years even worse. Stocks that are not very susceptible to market or systematic risk, in contrast, are not risky when held in a portfolio. They do not go up much in good years, and they do not go down much in poor years, reducing the standard deviation of returns of the portfolio.

The CAPM measure of the risk of any stock when held in a portfolio is called a beta coefficient, and is calculated with this formula:

$$\beta_i = \frac{\text{Covariance}_{i,m}}{\text{Variance}_m}$$

This formula says the beta coefficient for any stock, i, is calculated as the covariance between the stock, i, and the overall stock market, m, divided by the variance of the overall stock market, m. Beta coefficients are published by many information sources, and they can be easily calculated with a time series of returns for an individual stock and the overall stock market. We will not go into the detail of how to calculate beta coefficients, but we will discuss in detail what a beta coefficient tells us about the risk of a stock when held in a portfolio.

The covariance of returns between a stock and the overall stock market is the multiplication of three terms; the correlation between the returns of the stock and the returns of the market, the standard deviation of returns of the stock, and the standard deviation of returns of the market. If the numerator in the beta calculation is larger than the denominator, it means the correlation between the stock and the market is high and the stock is highly volatile, having a large standard deviation of returns. This tells us the stock tends to move in the same direction as the overall market and these movements are of greater magnitude. From our previous discussion, this tells us the stock has greater than average risk when held in a portfolio, which results in a beta coefficient for the stock greater than 1.0.

If the numerator in the beta calculation is equal to the denominator, the covariance between the returns of the stock and the returns of the overall market is equal to the variance of returns of the overall market. This tells us the stock tends to move in the same direction as the overall market, and these movements are of the same magnitude.

Exhibit 5.5 Beta coefficients.

Company	Beta Coefficient
PepsiCo	0.60
IBM	0.85
Southwest Airlines	0.90
Disney	0.95
Boeing	1.00
Apple	1.10
JPMorgan Chase	1.20
Intel	1.20
Ford Motor	1.50
American Airlines	2.15

Source: Value Line Survey pages, Value Line Publishing, Inc., 2008.

A stock that behaves in this manner is exactly as volatile as the overall market, and it is therefore of average risk when held in a portfolio, which results in a beta coefficient of 1.0.

Finally, if the numerator in the beta calculation is less than the denominator, the covariance between the stock and the overall market is low—possibly because the returns of the stock and the returns of the market are not highly correlated, and possibly because the standard deviation of returns for the stock is low. In this case, the stock may or may not move in the same direction as the overall market, and if it does move in the same direction, these movements are of small magnitude. A stock with these characteristics has lower than average risk when held in a portfolio, as reflected in its beta coefficient of less than 1.0.

The beta coefficients published by a well-known source, Value Line, Inc., for several well-known firms, are listed in Exhibit 5.5.

These companies were chosen to show a wide range of beta coefficients. One company, Boeing, has a beta coefficient of 1.0, so it has the same amount of systematic risk as the stock market overall, making it an average risk stock when included in a portfolio. Four companies have beta coefficients less than 1.0, so these firms are all of lower than average risk when held in a portfolio. Five of the companies in the table, in contrast, have beta coefficients greater than 1.0, so these firms are all of higher than average risk when held in a portfolio. Again, market or systematic risk cannot be eliminated by diversification, so knowing a stock's beta coefficient tells you the amount of risk the stock contributes to a portfolio, which allows you to calculate the expected return on the stock, given its level of risk.

To summarize, the capital asset pricing model is based on the following logic:

- Unique or nonsystematic risk can be eliminated by diversification, so it is not relevant and not rewarded.
- Market or systematic risk cannot be eliminated and is therefore relevant and rewarded.

- The correct measure of market or systematic risk is beta, the covariance of the returns of the stock with the returns of the market, divided by the variance of the returns of the market, which indicates how exposed a stock is to market or systematic risk.

The CAPM Equation

The expected return of any stock is calculated as the expected risk-free return, plus an additional return based on the expected risk premium for investing in the market, times the beta coefficient of the stock. The CAPM equation for the expected return of any stock looks like this:

$$E(R_i) = R_f + [E(R_m) - R_f] \times \beta_i$$

The formula tells us that, to begin with, the expected return of any risky stock i—$E(R_i)$—must at least equal the return earned by investing in risk-free securities, R_f. No one would invest in a risky stock if its expected return was less than the risk-free rate of return. To entice investors to buy risky stocks instead of risk-free securities, there must be some positive expected premium, and the right side of the CAPM equation represents this premium. The term in the brackets is called the market risk premium, as it is the difference between the expected return on an investment in the overall stock market—$E(R_m)$—minus the risk-free rate of return, R_f. This market risk premium is the additional extra return above the risk-free return that an investor expects to earn by investing in the entire market of risky stocks. It is the expected additional return on the entire market of risky stocks, so if a company (and its stock) is of average market or systematic risk and has a beta coefficient of 1.0, like Boeing, this market risk premium equals the risk premium for the stock. In the case of the high-risk stocks shown in Exhibit 5.5, those with beta coefficients greater than 1.0, the market risk premium is not sufficient to attract investors. These stocks have more risk, so they require a larger risk premium. The size of this risk premium is the beta coefficient for the stock times the market risk premium. In the opposite case of the low-risk stocks with beta coefficients less than 1.0, this market risk premium is larger than necessary to attract investors. The risk premium for these stocks is calculated as the beta coefficient for the stock times the market risk premium, which produces a risk premium smaller than the market risk premium.

The CAPM equation for expected return is also called the security market line (SML). The graph of the SML is virtually identical to Exhibit 5.1 shown earlier in this chapter, except the horizontal axis for risk now has a more formal CAPM term, beta. The SML shown in Exhibit 5.6 reveals that a stock with a beta coefficient of zero has no systematic risk and no risk premium, and will earn the risk-free rate of return. A stock with a beta coefficient of 1.0 has the same amount of systematic risk as the overall market, has the same risk premium as the market, and has an expected return equal to the expected return of the market. Stocks with beta coefficients higher than 1.0 have expected returns greater than the expected return of the market, and stocks with beta coefficients lower than 1.0 have expected returns lower than the expected return of the market.

The CAPM advances the general concept of risk and return into a specific measure of risk and expected return, which can be estimated for any company and its stock. If you know the risk-free rate of return, the market risk premium, and the beta coefficient

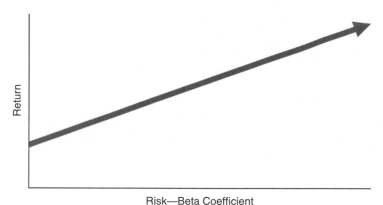

Exhibit 5.6   Security market line.

for a stock, you can calculate an investor's expected return from holding the stock. Beta coefficients for stocks can be obtained from many sources, and Exhibit 5.5 presented the Value Line beta coefficients for 10 well-known firms. To use the CAPM equation, we also need to know the risk-free rate of return, and the current yield to maturity of the 30-year U.S. Treasury bond is commonly used for this purpose, because U.S. Treasury bonds are presumed to be default risk free. The yield to maturity on U.S. Treasury bonds is reported on a daily, or minute-by-minute, basis by many information sources, and at the time this chapter was written, the yield to maturity of the 30-year U.S. Treasury bond was 4.20%.

The last bit of information required to calculate the expected return of a stock is the market risk premium, which is the difference between the expected return of the overall stock market and the risk-free rate of return. Unfortunately, the expected return of the overall market of risky stocks is not observable, so we cannot directly calculate the market risk premium. We instead use a proxy for this market risk premium based on available historical information about the returns earned by the market of risky stocks and risk-free U.S. Treasury bonds. This information was presented for large company stocks and U.S. Treasury bonds in Exhibit 5.2 earlier in the chapter, and these historic average annual returns for large company stocks and U.S. Treasury bonds for the 80-year period from 1926 to 2005 are presented in Exhibit 5.7.

From this information, we see, on average, over 80 years, an investment in the common stock of large companies returned 6.5% (12.3% − 5.8%) more than an investment in U.S. Treasury bonds. Stated in CAPM terms, the premium earned by investing in the market

Exhibit 5.7   Average annual returns, 1926–2005.

Investment Series	Arithmetic Mean Return
Large company stocks	12.3%
Long-term U.S. Treasury bonds	5.8

Source: Modified from *Stocks, Bonds, Bills, and Inflation: 2006 Yearbook*, Ibbotson Associates, Inc.

of risky stocks versus investing in risk-free securities was 6.5%. This is what we will use as the market risk premium in the CAPM equation, the difference between average annual returns earned by large company stocks and the average annual returns earned by U.S. Treasury bonds. We have a long time series of average annual returns earned by large company stocks and U.S. Treasury bonds, and we will use the difference between these two average returns as a proxy for the market risk premium.

With the risk-free rate of return, the beta coefficient for a stock, and the proxy for the market risk premium, the expected return of any stock can be calculated. For the Walt Disney Company the calculation is:

$$E(R_i) = R_f + [E(R_m) - R_f] \times \beta_i = 4.20\% + (6.5\%) \times 0.95 = 10.375\%$$

This is the CAPM expected return for Disney stock. For the other firms listed in Exhibit 5.5, their lower or higher beta coefficients result in lower or higher rates of expected return. For PepsiCo, this expected return is 8.10%; for Boeing, this expected return is 10.70%, which is also the expected return for the entire market of stocks since Boeing has a beta coefficient of 1.00; and for JPMorgan Chase, this expected return is 12.0%.

The last point to understand is that the CAPM expected return is also the required return for any common stock. Given the risk of the stock as reflected in its beta coefficient, the current risk-free rate of return, and the proxy market risk premium, investors must expect to earn the CAPM return; otherwise they will not invest in that stock. The capital asset pricing model, therefore, is widely used to determine the cost of equity capital for a company. The CAPM equation produces the return that investors must expect to earn if they are to hold the common stock of a company, which is the cost of equity capital for the company.

Cost of Capital

All companies calculate their cost of capital as a part of the investment analysis process. Capital is required to fund internal investment projects, and this capital has a cost. Once a company's cost of capital is known, this cost is used as the hurdle rate when evaluating investment projects. If a project earns a rate of return in excess of the cost of capital, it should be accepted. If a project earns a rate of return below the cost of capital, it should be rejected.

One more important point must be made here: We calculate the cost of capital provided to the firm by external investors, that is, long-term lenders and stockholders. These investors provide long-term capital to the firm, which is invested in long-lived projects, and they expect to earn an appropriate risk-adjusted return from their investment. This is why it is called the cost of *capital*. We omit sources of funds like accounts payable, wages payable, and taxes payable, for example, because they do not come from long-term lenders and stockholders. These are short-term sources of funds that do not carry an explicit cost and are typically created by the day-to-day operations of the firm. So remember to focus on the firm's long-term capital sources and the cost of these sources.

The cost of capital for a firm is the cost of its debt capital, plus the cost of its common and preferred equity capital, weighted by the relative amount of debt and common and preferred equity in the firm's capital structure. This is called the weighted average cost of capital (WACC) and is calculated with the following formula:

$$\text{WACC} = K_{\text{debt}} \times W_{\text{debt}} \times (1 - t) + K_{\text{common equity}} \times W_{\text{common equity}}$$
$$+ K_{\text{pref equity}} \times W_{\text{pref equity}}$$

This formula tells us the weighted average cost of capital for a firm is its current cost of debt capital (K_{debt}), times the relative weight of debt in the capital structure (W_{debt}), times 1 minus the corporate tax rate $(1 - t)$, plus its current cost of common equity capital ($K_{\text{common equity}}$), times the relative weight of common equity in the capital structure ($W_{\text{common equity}}$), plus its current cost of preferred equity capital ($K_{\text{pref equity}}$), times the relative weight of preferred equity in the capital structure ($W_{\text{pref equity}}$). Calculating a company's WACC is a mechanical process that requires determining the value of all the input variables in the formula and combining them into the WACC. We examine each input to the formula and the end result in the next section.

Cost of Debt and Equity Capital

We start with the first input variable in the equation, the firm's cost of debt. Specifically, we will use the interest rate the company would pay if it issued new debt capital right now. Recall that WACC is used as the hurdle rate for current internal investment projects, so we need to use the current cost of debt when calculating WACC. This cost of debt capital for any firm is the yield to maturity of its bonds currently traded in the financial markets. If the firm's bonds are being bought and sold in financial markets today at a price that yields, say, 8%, that tells us that 8% is the firm's current cost of debt. Investors are willing to buy and hold the company's bonds at an 8% yield, so this number is the firm's current cost of debt.

The yield to maturity for a company's traded bonds is reported by many financial information sources. Mergent BondViewer is an excellent source of information about corporate bonds, and at the time this chapter was written, Mergent reported that a long-term bond issued by the Walt Disney Company that matures in March 2032 was being traded with a yield to maturity of 6.96%. Since investors are willing to buy and hold Disney bonds at a 6.96% yield to maturity, this is Disney's current cost of debt capital. One warning is necessary when determining cost of debt capital. It is incorrect to use the coupon interest rate of a firm's bonds as the cost of debt, because that coupon interest rate was set when the bond was sold at some earlier date. In the case of this particular Disney bond, the coupon interest rate was set at 7% when the bond was issued in February 2002. Since Disney issued bonds with a 7% coupon interest rate and investors purchased these bonds, it is accurate to state that Disney's cost of debt was 7% when the bonds were issued. After the date of original issue, financial market conditions changed; in fact, they change every day, and bond yields change as well. Be sure to select the current yield to maturity of the company's traded bonds to determine its current cost of debt capital.

Interest paid by companies on borrowed capital is deductible for income tax purposes. If a firm's income tax rate is 40% and it pays $100 of tax deductible interest expense, taxable income is reduced by $100, which reduces income taxes by $40, leaving an after-tax interest expense of $60. This is why the cost of debt is multiplied by 1 minus the income tax rate when calculating WACC. The income tax rate for a company can be found in its income statement, and for Disney, its income tax rate averaged 36% during the three reporting years from fiscal year 2006 through fiscal year 2008. With an income tax rate of 36%, Disney's after-tax cost of debt is the current yield to maturity on its bonds, multiplied by 1 minus the income tax rate of 36%.

Through our previous discussion of risk and return and the capital asset pricing model, we have already determined that the cost of equity capital represented by Disney's common stock is 10.375%. Given Disney's beta coefficient of 0.95, a market risk premium of 6.5%, and the risk-free rate of return of 4.20%, the cost of equity capital provided by Disney common stockholders is 10.375%.

There is another category of equity capital, known as preferred stock, because it has preferences over common stockholders with respect to dividends and liquidation. This means preferred stockholders must receive their dividends before common stockholders are entitled to any dividend payments, and if the firm fails and is liquidated, preferred stockholders receive the par value of their shares before common stockholders receive any payments. Preferred stock dividends are stated as a dollar amount per share, so a share of preferred stock with a $50 par value and a $3 dividend per share earns a dividend yield of $3 ÷ $50 or 6.0% of par value.

The dividend per share for preferred stock is fixed through time, and, if the firm is liquidated, the preferred stockholders will receive par value at the most. These characteristics more closely describe debt securities or bonds, so preferred stock is often considered to be more like debt, but preferred stock differs from true debt because it has no maturity date; it has an infinite life and will pay its fixed dividend forever. Any asset or security that pays a fixed cash amount forever is called a perpetuity, and preferred stock with its infinite and fixed dividend fits this description precisely. The required return or cost of capital for preferred stock can therefore be calculated with the formula for a perpetuity, which is:

$$K_{\text{preferred stock}} = \frac{\text{Preferred Stock Dividend}}{\text{Current Price of Preferred Stock}}$$

So the cost of preferred stock is equal to the dividend yield at the current market price. If a share of preferred stock has a $3 dividend and a current market price of $40, then investors are willing to purchase the preferred stock at a return of $3 ÷ $40, which equals 0.075 or 7.5%; this is the required return and cost of capital for this share of preferred stock.

If a company has preferred stock outstanding, the cost of preferred stock as just calculated must be included when calculating the firm's cost of capital. For the majority of companies this is not necessary, as preferred stock is rarely observed in the capital structure of firms in the year 2008. Preferred stock has primarily been used in recent years as part of the early stage financing of start-up companies, where investors have received preferred stock convertible into shares of common stock, which they will convert into common stock if the company succeeds. If the company performs well and becomes a publicly owned company, or it is purchased by another firm, this preferred stock is converted into common stock and retired. If the company performs poorly and fails, the preferred stock disappears. Be aware, however, that preferred stock does exist in the capital structure of some companies, so be sure to look for it when examining the firm's balance sheet. If a company does have preferred stock outstanding, be sure to calculate the cost of this preferred stock and include it in the overall cost of capital for the firm.

Weight of Debt and Equity Capital

We have examined how to calculate a company's cost of debt and cost of common and preferred equity, but to determine its weighted average cost of capital we also need to know the relative proportions or weights of debt and common and preferred equity in its capital structure. The weight of debt in the capital structure is calculated as:

$$W_{debt} = \frac{\text{Long-Term Debt}}{\text{Long-Term Debt} + \text{Common Equity} + \text{Preferred Equity}}$$

This ratio is called the long-term debt to capitalization ratio, as the denominator is the total long-term capital of the firm, and the numerator is the firm's long-term debt. The weight of common equity in the firm's capital structure is calculated with the same formula, except common equity is the numerator:

$$W_{common\ equity} = \frac{\text{Common Equity}}{\text{Long-Term Debt} + \text{Common Equity} + \text{Preferred Equity}}$$

If the firm has preferred stock in its capital structure, the weight of preferred equity is calculated with preferred equity as the numerator:

$$W_{preferred\ equity} = \frac{\text{Preferred Equity}}{\text{Long-Term Debt} + \text{Common Equity} + \text{Preferred Equity}}$$

The values for a company's long-term debt and owners' equity can be found on its balance sheet, called book values, but we would prefer not to use them when calculating the relative weights of debt and equity capital. The reason for this preference is that the balance sheet captures and reports historical information about the financial position of the firm. The values shown on the balance sheet for long-term debt reflect the amount received when the debt was originally issued at some past date, less any amortized discount if the debt was issued for less than face value, or less any amortized premium if the debt was issued for more than face value.

The values shown on the balance sheet for common equity are the sum of the contributed capital received when the firm originally issued shares of common stock, plus any earnings from past operations retained in the firm, less any shares of common stock repurchased by the firm (called treasury stock). And if the firm has any shares of preferred stock outstanding, the values shown on the balance sheet for preferred equity are the amounts received when the preferred shares were originally issued, less any shares of preferred stock repurchased by the firm. These amounts are all based on events that occurred in the past.

Firms calculate their current cost of capital to determine their current hurdle rate for internal investment projects. Calculating the relative weights of debt and common and preferred equity in the capital structure using balance sheet book values, therefore, may not produce the current cost of capital. To do this, we instead want to calculate current weights of debt and equity in the firm's capital structure using current values, also called market values. The market value of common equity for any firm is the total current value of its shares of stock traded in the financial markets and is calculated as the current price per common share times the number of common shares currently outstanding, which is frequently called market capitalization, or "market cap" by the financial press.

The market value for preferred equity, if the firm has any outstanding, is calculated in the same manner: the current price per share of preferred stock times the number of preferred shares outstanding.

Ideally, the market value of debt for a firm is calculated in the same manner, multiplying the current price per bond times the number of bonds outstanding. Determining the firm's total market value of debt, however, is quite difficult because many firms have many different debt issues. It is not unusual for large corporations to have 10 or 20 (or more!) individual and unique bond issues, so to determine the total market value of debt for a company it is necessary to calculate the market value of each individual bond issue and then add up all the values to determine the total market value of debt. Calculating market value of debt is also made more difficult by two facts: (1) publicly owned bonds are traded infrequently compared to common stock, and their trades are not as widely reported, and (2) many bonds are privately held by institutional investors and are not publicly traded at all, so current prices for these bonds are not available.

The key point here is it is simple to determine market value of common and preferred equity; multiply the current price per share by the number of shares currently outstanding. Determining market value of debt is more troublesome, as the firm may have many different bond issues, and it can be difficult or impossible to find the current bond price for these different bond issues.

If you are able to determine the current market value of a company's debt, then use this value when calculating capital structure weights. Because of the difficulties in determining this number, financial analysts are often forced to use book values of debt as proxies for market values. This is not as problematic as it may sound, however, because as long as the company's bonds are being traded at a yield to maturity close to the coupon interest rate paid by the bonds, then the market value of the bonds will be very close to their book values. Again, in an ideal world, market values of long-term debt are used when calculating capital structure weights, but if these market values are not available, use book values of long-term debt as proxies.

Continuing with the Walt Disney Company to illustrate cost of capital, when this chapter was written, the most recent available balance sheet book value for long-term debt was $11.522 billion, for common equity this value was $32.323 billion, and Disney did not have any preferred stock outstanding. At the same time, the price per share of Disney common stock was $23.36 and Disney had 1.876 billion shares of common stock outstanding, which, when multiplied together, produces a market value of equity of $43.82336 billion.

With the above information about the value of Disney's long-term debt ($11.522 billion), common equity ($43.82336 billion), and preferred equity ($0), we can determine the relative weights of long-term debt, common equity, and preferred equity in Disney's capital structure:

$$W_{debt} = \frac{\$11,522,000,000}{\$11,522,000,000 + \$43,823,360,000 + \$0} = 0.2082 \ or \ 20.82\%$$

$$W_{common \ equity} = \frac{\$43,823,360,000}{\$11,522,000,000 + \$43,823,360,000 + \$0} = 0.7918 \ or \ 79.18\%$$

$$W_{preferred \ equity} = \frac{\$0}{\$11,522,000,000 + \$43,823,360,000 + \$0} = 0.0 \ or \ 0.0\%$$

Exhibit 5.8   Inputs for Disney's cost of capital (percents).

Cost of debt finance, K_{debt}	6.96%
Weight of debt finance, W_{debt}	20.82
Income tax rate, t	36.0
Cost of common equity, $K_{common\ equity}$	10.375
Weight of common equity, $W_{common\ equity}$	79.18
Cost of preferred equity, $K_{pref\ equity}$	0.0
Weight of preferred equity, $W_{pref\ equity}$	0.0

Based on these values of Disney's long-term debt and common and preferred equity, Disney's capital structure is 20.82% long-term debt, 79.18% common equity, and 0.0% preferred equity.

From our work we now have all the inputs necessary to calculate Disney's cost of capital, as presented in Exhibit 5.8. The complete cost of capital calculation for the Walt Disney Company is also shown in the cost of capital template included in the chapter materials. This template can be used to determine the cost of capital for any company.

When this information is input into the weighted average cost of capital formula, the result is:

$$\text{WACC} = K_{debt} \times W_{debt} \times (1 - t) + K_{common\ equity} \times W_{common\ equity}$$
$$+ K_{pref\ equity} \times W_{pref\ equity}$$
$$\text{WACC} = 6.96\% \times 20.82\% \times (1 - 36.0\%) + 10.375\% \times 79.18\%$$
$$+ 0.0\% \times 0.0\% = 9.14\%$$

The cost of capital for Disney, based on these inputs, is 9.14%. This means, on average, it costs Disney 9.14% to raise a dollar of long-term capital from external investors to fund investment projects. As discussed earlier in this chapter, all companies calculate their own cost of capital as a part of the investment analysis process. If an investment project is expected to earn a rate of return in excess of the firm's cost of capital, it should be accepted. If an investment project is expected to earn a rate of return less than the firm's cost of capital, it should be rejected. This is why a firm's cost of capital is often called the hurdle rate. If a project's expected return clears the hurdle rate it should be accepted, and if it fails to clear the hurdle rate, it should be rejected.

You will observe that a firm with a lower cost of capital or hurdle rate will be able to accept more projects than a firm with a higher cost of capital or hurdle rate. Financial managers are similarly aware of this fact, so they try to raise capital in a manner that minimizes the cost of capital. The relative mix of debt finance versus equity finance used when raising funds, which impacts cost of capital, is called the capital structure of a firm, and we discuss this topic in the next section.

Capital Structure Theory

One critical decision financial managers must make when raising funds for internal investment is the relative mix of debt and equity finance. We have seen in the previous section that this mix of debt and equity finance impacts the firm's cost of capital, as debt finance is less costly than equity finance. Recall that the cost of debt for the Walt Disney Company in November 2008 was 6.96% while the cost of common equity for Disney at the same time was 10.375%. This cost differential is driven by the nature of the claims by debt holders and equity holders on the cash flows of the firm. Debt is a contractual claim that takes priority in times of financial distress. Equity, in contrast, is a residual claim, meaning the cash flows available to stockholders are what are left over after the claims of debt holders, the contractual priority claimants, have been met. This makes debt finance safer for investors, and since debt is less risky to investors it has a lower required rate of return. This also makes equity finance riskier for investors, and since equity finance is more risky to investors, it has a higher required rate of return. Our previous work on the cost of capital for Disney reflects the lower risk and cost of debt finance, and the higher risk and cost of equity finance.

From the point of view of the firm, however, debt finance is actually more risky than equity finance. The reason is that debt finance creates contractual obligations that the firm must meet, specifically regular payments of interest and principal, which together are called debt service. When a firm uses debt finance it commits to paying its debt service, and if the firm cannot meet its debt service it will fall into financial distress and possibly bankruptcy. In contrast to debt finance, equity finance does not create contractual obligations that the firm must meet. Unlike payments of interest and principal, dividends are not legal obligations of the firm.

Debt finance is the lower-cost method for raising capital for the firm, but it also creates debt service, which increases firm risk, because missing its debt service can lead to dire consequences for the firm. Equity finance is the higher-cost method for raising capital for the firm, but equity finance does not create contractual obligations that the firm must meet, so equity finance is less risky for the firm. One of the theories of capital structure, called the trade-off theory, is based on this logic. Financial managers trade off the lower cost but higher risk of debt finance with the higher cost but lower risk of equity finance, possibly searching for an optimal mix. We will work through the entire development and logic of this theory in this section.

Any discussion of capital structure must begin with the work of Franco Modigliani and Merton Miller. Modigliani and Miller[1] (M&M) proved that in a world with perfect and frictionless capital markets, the value of any firm was independent of its capital structure, and was determined by discounting the expected cash flows from the firm at an interest rate appropriate to the risk of this cash flow stream. This is M&M's Proposition I, which states that the value of the levered firm, V_L, the firm with debt, is the same as the value of the unlevered firm, the firm without debt, V_U:

$$V_L = V_U$$

Effectively, M&M showed that the value of any firm comes from the cash-flow-generating ability of its assets, not from how it is financed. This result was dependent on several restrictive assumptions, including that identical information is available to all investors and managers; investors and managers have identical expectations from this information; there are no income taxes; companies and investors are able to borrow and lend at the riskless rate of interest; and bankruptcy is costless and can be entered and exited instantly. With these assumptions M&M showed with a mathematical proof and through an arbitrage argument that, given two firms of the same risk class and with the same expected cash flows, the value of the firms must be the same, no matter how the two firms are financed. This result also allowed M&M to state, under the restrictive assumptions, that the cost of capital for any firm is independent of its capital structure, which is often referred to as M&M's capital structure irrelevancy proposition.

But we have already seen that debt finance has a lower cost than equity finance. Doesn't this refute the M&M irrelevancy proposition? Wouldn't the use of more debt finance and less equity finance reduce the firm's overall cost of capital? Using these same assumptions, M&M proved that the firm's overall cost of capital does not change as more or less debt finance is used. Their Proposition II showed that the required return to equity holders is positively related to the use of debt finance, also called financial leverage, because the risk to equity holders increases with increasing financial leverage. It is true that debt finance is less costly and using relatively more debt finance means using a larger proportion of the lower-cost financing alternative. It is also true that using more debt finance increases the risk to equity holders, so the cost of equity increases. M&M's Proposition II on the cost of equity is expressed in the following formula:

$$k_S = k_O + \frac{B}{S} \times (k_O - k_B)$$

where k_S is the cost of equity, k_O is the cost of capital for an all-equity firm, k_B is the cost of debt, B is the value of the firm's debt, and S is the value of the firm's equity.

The formula shows that the cost of equity is a linear function of the firm's financial leverage. WACC is unaffected by financial leverage, even though you are adding cheaper debt finance, because the cost of equity increases to precisely offset it. M&M prove the two effects exactly offset each other, so the value of the firm and the WACC are not changed by the use of financial leverage.

It is important to understand how capital structure impacts firm value and cost of capital in the ideal world created by Modigliani and Miller's assumption of perfect and frictionless capital markets. In this world capital structure is irrelevant, as firm value and cost of capital are not affected by capital structure. We all know, however, that M&M's ideal world doesn't exist. There are market imperfections and frictions, particularly income taxes and costly bankruptcy. By peeling back these assumptions, we can see how and why capital structure can impact both firm value and cost of capital in the real world.

We will begin with income taxes, particularly the tax-deductible nature of interest expense. Deductible interest expense creates debt tax shields in any year equal to:

$$\tau_C \times k_B \times B$$

where τ_C is the corporate income tax rate, k_B is the cost of debt, and B is the amount borrowed.

As long as the firm is earning positive taxable income and paying income taxes, we can assume the yearly debt tax shield has the same risk as the interest on the amount borrowed, so k_B is also the appropriate discount rate for the yearly debt tax shields. Assuming the cash flows are a perpetuity, the present value of the debt tax shield is:

$$\frac{\tau_C \times k_B \times B}{k_B} = \tau_C \times B$$

This debt tax shield decreases the amount of cash flow paid to tax authorities and therefore increases the cash flow available to debt holders and equity holders. With more cash flow available for investors, total firm value increases by the present value of the debt tax shield. In a world with income taxes and tax-deductible interest expense, M&M's Proposition I changes to:

$$V_L = V_U + \tau_C B$$

where V_L is the value of the firm with financial leverage, V_U is the value of the firm without financial leverage, and $\tau_C B$ is the present value of the debt tax shield assuming perpetual cash flows.

M&M's Proposition I now shows that the value of the firm with financial leverage is equal to the value of the firm without financial leverage, plus the present value of the debt tax shield.

Income taxes and tax-deductible interest expense also change M&M's Proposition II. It is still true that increasing the use of debt finance (increasing financial leverage) increases the risk to equity holders and the cost of equity rises, but the Proposition II formula for cost of equity in this case now looks like this:

$$k_S = k_O + \frac{B}{S} \times (1 - \tau_C) \times (k_O - k_B)$$

The cost of equity is still a linear function of the firm's financial leverage, but the slope is not as steep. The increase in cost of equity, therefore, is not large enough to entirely offset the benefit from adding cheaper debt finance. In a world with income taxes and tax-deductible interest expense, an increase in the use of debt finance increases firm value and decreases the firm's overall cost of capital. If this were the only real-world condition that impacted firm value and cost of capital, the firm's optimal capital structure would be heavily weighted toward debt finance. In fact, clever financial managers would use as much debt finance as possible, as this would maximize firm value and minimize the firm's cost of capital.

We don't observe many firms whose capital structures consist of nearly all debt and hardly any equity, so there must be additional constraints or conditions that violate M&M's initial assumptions of perfect and frictionless markets. An obvious one is the assumption that bankruptcy is costless and can be entered and exited instantly. When firms are unlikely to meet their debt service, or they have actually failed to meet their debt service and defaulted on their debt obligations, they are said to be in financial distress, which imposes significant costs on the firm. These costs of financial distress include both direct bankruptcy costs, such as filing costs, court costs, and fees for lawyers and accountants, and indirect costs, such as reduced management and employee productivity due to time spent avoiding or managing bankruptcy, and lost sales when customers choose to do business with competitor firms that are not experiencing financial distress. The bankruptcy process is also long and involved, as illustrated by the 38 months between United Airlines' filing for Chapter 11 bankruptcy protection in December 2002 and February of 2006 when it emerged from bankruptcy.

Financial distress is both costly and lengthy in the real world. This is why financial managers do not select capital structures that are nearly all debt to maximize the value of the firm's debt tax shields. The greater the use of debt finance, the greater the firm's debt service, and the greater the likelihood of costly financial distress. The balance between valuable debt tax shields and the costs of financial distress is the basis of the trade-off theory of capital structure.

The trade-off theory holds that there is an optimal capital structure for any firm, and the firm's financial managers should maintain this optimal capital structure when funding the firm. This optimal capital structure occurs at the point where the increased debt tax shield benefits from additional borrowing are offset by the increased costs of financial distress from additional borrowing. The point where the benefit from $1 of additional borrowing is offset by the cost from $1 of additional borrowing is the firm's optimal capital structure, as at this point the value of the firm is maximized and the cost of capital of the firm is minimized. This optimal capital structure is often called the firm's target capital structure, as financial managers should select the amount of debt and equity finance necessary to maintain the firm at its optimal capital structure.

Another important theory of capital structure is the pecking order theory, which recognizes that two more of the initial M&M assumptions about perfect and frictionless markets are violated in the real world—namely, that identical information is available to all investors and managers, and investors and managers have identical expectations from this information. These assumptions are not accurate, because managers actually have asymmetric information; that is, compared to outside investors, they have superior information about the firm and know more about the firm's prospects and true value. Outside investors realize that managers know more than they do, so they draw conclusions about the firm's prospects and value based on the actions of informed managers.

Consider the situation where a firm's current stock price is $50 per share but its managers believe the stock's true value is $60 per share. In this case, the firm would never use equity finance and sell new shares of stock, because the firm's managers believe the stock is undervalued at its current market price. Compare this to the opposite situation where the firm's current stock price is $50 per share but its managers believe the stock's true value is $40 per share. In this case the firm would happily sell new shares of stock, since the firm's managers believe the stock is overvalued at its current market price.

In the real world asymmetric information exists; managers are better informed and act on their beliefs, and outside investors are aware of this fact. This means outside investors are always skeptical when a firm sells new shares of stock, and they react by reducing the price they are willing to pay for the newly offered shares. Outside investors, however, are less skeptical when a firm issues new debt securities, because debt holders have a contractual and priority claim on the cash flows of the firm. Debt finance and debt securities are safer to investors, and equity finance and shares of stock are riskier to investors. Investors, therefore, reduce the price they are willing to pay for newly issued shares relatively more, and they reduce the price they are willing to pay for new debt securities relatively less.

This logic is the basis of the pecking order theory of capital structure, which results in the following three-part pecking order when financing the firm:

1. Financial managers prefer to use internal financing first, because outside investors cannot undervalue your newly issued stock and bonds if you do not issue these securities.

2. If the firm's internal financing sources are exhausted, financial managers prefer to issue safer securities, as they are less likely to be undervalued by outside investors. That means financial managers will use debt finance and issue new debt securities next.

3. Financial managers will use equity finance and issue new shares of stock only when the firm's internal financing sources and debt capacity have been exhausted. Equity finance is the riskiest and most likely to be undervalued by outside investors, so financial managers will sell new shares of stock only when there is no other alternative.

Simply put, the pecking order theory tells us that financial managers finance the firm with internal sources, then issue safer debt securities, and, as a last resort, issue riskier equity securities.

The implications of the pecking order theory differ significantly from the trade-off theory of capital structure. The first implication is that there is no optimal or target capital structure. Each firm's capital structure is determined by its need to fund internal investments, and its internal sources of funds and debt capacity. Financial managers do not attempt to maintain an optimal capital structure. They instead fund projects in the order prescribed by the theory—internal sources, then safe securities, then risky securities. The next implication is that firms with large profits and cash flows from operations will use less debt. A profitable firm with operating cash inflows greater than the amount required to invest in its positive net present value projects will not need to use debt finance. The final implication is that worries about underpricing and other difficulties when issuing debt securities and selling shares of stock may motivate financial managers to carry financial slack. Building financial slack today, which means the firm accumulates excess cash and short-term investments, is a rational solution to possible underpricing and other difficulties when issuing securities tomorrow. Financial managers know they will be required to fund internal investments in the future, and by storing financial slack in the firm's balance sheet, they can quickly and easily fund these investments internally. There will be no need to issue securities of any type to fund the investments.

We have examined two theories of capital structure, the trade-off theory and the pecking order theory. Both are based on logical development and observations about the real world of business and economics, but they conflict in their primary predictions about capital structure. The trade-off theory holds that managers balance the benefits of debt tax shields with the costs of financial distress, and that each firm has an optimal or target capital structure. The pecking order theory believes that financial managers fund investments with internal funds first, then by issuing safer debt securities, and then by issuing riskier equity securities. The pecking order theory holds that financial managers do not pursue an optimal or target capital structure; the firm's capital structure results from the funds required to invest in good projects, along with the firm's internal sources of cash and its debt capacity. It is reasonable to ask which theory better explains capital structure in practice at real companies, and we look at that in the next section.

Capital Structure in Practice

Financial researchers have studied data from corporations over long time periods to determine whether any patterns or regularities exist in the capital structure of firms. Before we examine the results of these studies, let's look at some timely capital structure data for several well-known corporations. Exhibit 5.9 presents the capital structure at the time this chapter was written for 12 firms that can be classified into four broad categories; technology companies (Apple, Cisco, and Intel); consumer products companies (Colgate-Palmolive, Kraft Foods, and Procter & Gamble); manufacturers (Boeing,

Exhibit 5.9   Capital structure.

Company	Weight of Debt	Weight of Equity
Apple, Inc.	0.0%	100.0%
Cisco Systems, Inc.	5.9	94.1
Intel Corporation	1.8	98.2
Colgate-Palmolive Company	9.4	90.6
Kraft Foods, Inc.	30.3	69.7
Procter & Gamble Company	9.1	90.9
Boeing Company	20.0	80.0
Caterpillar, Inc.	37.8	62.2
United Technologies Corporation	13.7	86.3
Limited Brands, Inc.	40.9	59.1
Macy's, Inc.	67.1	32.9
Nordstrom, Inc.	40.4	59.6

Caterpillar, and United Technologies); and retailers (Limited Brands, Macy's, and Nordstrom). The numbers shown are debt and equity as a percent of total capitalization, using market value of equity for all companies.

Although there is some variability within categories, there are also easily observable differences between the four categories. As a group, the technology companies have the lowest debt percentages, the consumer products companies have higher debt percentages, the manufacturing companies have still higher debt percentages, and the retailers have the highest debt percentages. Upon examining these data you won't be surprised to learn that researchers have found strong industry effects in capital structure, with some industries using very little debt finance and other industries using much more debt finance. We next discuss some of the results obtained by research into capital structure, which will help to explain the industry effect shown in Exhibit 5.9.

Researchers have studied whether the investment opportunities available to a firm have an impact on the firm's capital structure. Companies with large investment opportunities are typically fast-growing firms in fast-growing and volatile industries, with industry beta coefficients well above 1.0, which also require large amounts of capital investment in risky new projects. Remember that debt finance creates debt service, and large amounts of debt and debt service can be dangerous for a fast-growing firm. Assume Company A has many good investment opportunities and a large amount of debt finance and debt service. In a strong economy, Company A has sufficient cash flow to pay its debt service and invest in all of its good projects, so all is well. In a weak economy, however, Company A has insufficient cash flow to pay its debt service and invest in all of its good projects. Since debt service is contractual, Company A is required to pay its debt service first, so the firm will be unable to invest in all of its good projects. If economic conditions worsen and Company A falls into financial distress and the market value of the firm's debt and equity falls significantly in value, the managers of Company A (who work for the stockholders) may consciously choose not to invest in good projects if the benefits of the projects flow only to the debt holders. These two effects combined are called the underinvestment problem, because in some instances the use of debt finance can cause the firm to underinvest, that is, not invest in all of its available good projects.

Compare this scenario to Company B, which has many good investment opportunities and little or no debt finance and debt service. With little or no debt service, Company B is much less likely to experience the underinvestment problem; in both strong and weak economies cash flow is more likely to be sufficient to fund all good investment opportunities, so Company B is more likely to be able to invest in all of its good projects. Recall that this underinvestment problem is especially troublesome for fast-growing firms in fast-growing and risky industries, which in Exhibit 5.9 best describes the three technology companies, Apple, Cisco, and Intel, which also have the lowest amount of debt finance. This result has been obtained consistently by financial researchers, so we can conclude that companies with large investment opportunities experiencing high growth rates in riskier industries tend to use significantly less debt finance in their capital structures.

Consistently profitable firms in lower-risk and slower-growth industries, in contrast, should use more debt in their capital structures. Companies with these characteristics have fewer investment opportunities, so the underinvestment problem created by the use of debt finance is not as troublesome. They are also in less volatile industries, with beta coefficients at or below 1.0, so their revenues, profits, and cash flows are more stable. These firms are also more likely to be consistent taxpayers, so they can take full advantage of debt tax shields. Since they are less risky and more stable, they will also have lower expected costs of financial distress, so the negative implications of debt finance are smaller. These predictions about capital structure are supported by financial research, which has found that companies with fewer investment opportunities and growth prospects in lower-risk industries use significantly more debt finance. The data in Exhibit 5.9, taken at a single point in time in November 2008, also somewhat support these findings in that the consumer products companies, which operate in a low-risk and slow-growth industry with fewer investment opportunities, have more debt finance than the technology companies. Of course, the companies with the highest debt percentages in Exhibit 5.9, the three retailers, are all in a slower-growth industry with fewer investment opportunities, but their beta coefficients are all above 1.0, so they also operate in a riskier industry. These particular three retailers, therefore, use more debt consistent with fewer growth opportunities, but inconsistent with their higher than average risk.

In conclusion, financial research has found several regularities in capital structure in real companies. Safe and consistently profitable firms with fewer growth opportunities should and do use more debt finance. Riskier companies in high-growth industries with large investment opportunities should and do use less debt finance. Variability around these predictions can be observed, but research has found these results to be both statistically and economically significant. These results are more consistent with the trade-off theory of capital structure, but some of the data shown in Exhibit 5.9 also supports the pecking order theory. The three technology firms with the lowest debt percentages in their capital structures have also been extremely profitable in recent years, so their internal sources of capital have been sufficient to fund their investment opportunities. At this time, financial research is unable to accept or reject either the trade-off theory or the pecking order theory with certainty, but we are able to observe regularities in capital structure practice, some of which are consistent with the theories.

This concludes the chapter's examination of risk and return, cost of capital, and capital structure. The final two sections of the chapter discuss and illustrate how to value bonds and stocks, the debt and equity financial instruments issued by companies when raising capital for internal investment.

Bond Valuation

The value of any financial instrument, also called the market price, is the present value of the cash flows from the instrument, discounted at the appropriate required return for the instrument. Recall that bonds make contractual payments to investors called debt service, consisting of periodic interest payments and repayment of the bond's face or par value when the bond matures. Bond valuation, therefore, requires knowledge of the interest and principal payments from the bond, the timing of these payments, and the required return of the bond. Since bonds are contractual, the amount and timing of the payments to investors are known, so once the required return of the bond is determined, the value of the bond can be calculated.

To illustrate the mechanics of bond valuation, let's create a hypothetical bond issued in the United States by the Breckenridge Company. The bond has a $100 face value, matures on October 15, 2023, and pays an annual coupon interest rate of 6.75%. Bonds issued in the United States typically pay interest twice a year—that is, semiannually—so investors who hold this bond receive coupon interest payments every year equal to 6.75% of the face value of the bond, but they actually receive one-half of this amount twice a year. With the $100 face value of the bond, this means bondholders receive coupon interest payments of $3.375 every six months for each bond they own, calculated as follows:

$$\$100.00 \times 0.0675 \div 2 = \$3.375$$

The maturity date of the bond is October 15, 2023, so these coupon interest payments are made every six months to the bondholders, every October 15 and April 15. On the maturity date, the bondholders will receive their last coupon interest payment of $3.375 for each bond they own, plus the $100 face value of the bond, and at this date the bond matures and is retired.

Assume it is December 17, 2008, and you would like to know the value or price of the bond on this day. (The date a bond is bought or sold is called the settlement date for the bond.) The last piece of information necessary to determine the bond's value is the market interest rate for this bond, also called the yield to maturity, as this is the required return for the bond. Assume the market interest rate for the Breckenridge Company bond on December 17, 2008, is 6.10%, which is used to determine the bond's value or price on the settlement date.

To summarize, the relevant information for the Breckenridge Company bond is:

Settlement date	December 17, 2008
Maturity date	October 15, 2023
Coupon interest rate	6.75%
Market interest rate	6.10%
Face value of the bond	$100
Coupon interest payments per year	2

With these inputs the Excel function PRICE can be used to determine the bond's value or price. An Excel template which can be used to calculate the price of any bond is included in the chapter materials, and this template was used to determine the price of the bond in this example. One final piece of information is necessary to use this template, and that is the basis day count to use in the calculation. Bonds are quoted and traded in the United States on a 30/360 basis, which means months and years are assumed to have 30 and 360 days, respectively. When using the PRICE function in Excel there are several options for the basis, and the template included in the chapter materials inputs zero as the basis, which tells Excel to calculate the bond price on a 30/360 basis.

With this information, the Excel template and PRICE function returns a bond price of 106.2727. This is the price of the bond as a percent of the face value, so to determine the price of the bond in dollars, multiply $100 by 106.2727%, which produces $106.2727. Given the bond's coupon interest and principal payments, the timing of these payments, the bond's $100 face value, and market interest rates on December 17, 2008, this is the price or value of the bond on that date.

The total price to purchase this bond on the settlement date will be higher, however, due to the interest accrued on the bond since the last coupon interest payment date. Recall the settlement date is December 17, 2008, and the coupon interest payment dates are every October 15 and April 15. Current bondholders who choose to sell the bond on December 17, 2008, must be paid for the interest accrued on their bond since the most recent coupon interest payment date of October 15, 2008, approximately two months in this case. The same template used to determine the bond price of $106.2727 uses Excel's COUPDAYBS function to determine that 62 is the number of days since the most recent coupon interest payment date, which is then used to calculate the accrued interest on the bond as follows:

$$\$100.00 \times 0.0675 \times \frac{62}{360} = \$1.162500$$

For the Breckenridge Company bond in this example, the accrued interest on the bond since October 15, 2008, is $1.1625, so the total price an investor would pay to purchase the bond on December 17, 2008, is the bond price of $106.2727 plus the accrued interest of $1.1625, for a total of $107.4352.

Using the specific information for the hypothetical bond issued by the Breckenridge Company and the Excel functions PRICE and COUPDAYBS in the template, we have determined the price of the bond as well as the accrued interest on the bond. Calculating the price and accrued interest of any bond is fairly simple due to the contractual nature of debt securities, particularly the known amount and timing of coupon interest and principal payments.

In the next section we will determine the value of common stock, which is significantly more difficult, due to the unknown amount and timing of cash flows to common stockholders, specifically dividends and capital gains. We will also calculate the value of preferred stock, which is simpler than common stock valuation, because preferred stock pays dividends that are fixed through time.

Equity Valuation

Determining the value of equity, particularly common stock, is more difficult than bond valuation. The reason for this is the nature of cash flows to equity holders. Recall that bonds are contractual obligations, and the interest and principal payments to bondholders are specified in the bonds' contracts. Common stockholders, in contrast, have a residual claim on the cash flows of the firm, so the cash payments to stockholders come from the variable cash flows generated by the company, less the contractual payments of interest and principal made to bondholders. This is what makes common equity valuation so difficult; the cash flows to equity holders are not known with certainty, and these cash flows last forever since in theory common stock has an infinite life. When calculating the value of common stock for any firm, it is first necessary to forecast the cash flows generated by the company and available to all investors. With these cash flows it is possible to determine the value of the firm to all investors, and after subtracting the amount owed to long-term debt holders the remainder is the value of the firm to common stockholders. Common equity valuation is a mechanical process with specific steps and processes, but during each step of the valuation process the financial analyst must use judgment because many of the inputs to equity valuation are forecasts or estimates. We work through a comprehensive example of common stock valuation for a hypothetical company in this section, using the equity valuation template that is included in the chapter materials.

The Hudson Hybrid Car Company designs and builds green cars using its own proprietary technology. Since we are valuing Hudson's common stock, we do not know the cash flows that Hudson will pay to its stockholders, but we do have detailed forecasts of Hudson's income statement and partial balance sheet accounts for the years 2009 through 2012, as well as Hudson's year 2008 actual results, which are presented in Exhibit 5.10.

Remember that the value of any asset is the discounted value of the cash flows from the asset, so to determine Hudson's value we merely need to discount the cash flows available to Hudson's investors. The obvious problem is that Hudson will design and build green cars for many years beyond the forecast horizon shown in Exhibit 5.10, so we need to find a way to value the cash flows generated by a company with a very long life. We will do this with the concept of terminal value, which can be applied to any asset that is growing at a constant and perpetual rate.

The data presented in Exhibit 5.10 show that Hudson is forecasting sales growth of 12.3% in year 2009 compared to the prior year. Since Hudson is a young company with excellent products, this fast growth rate is not surprising. Notice, however, that in each year after 2009 Hudson is forecasting a slower growth rate. In 2010 sales are forecast to increase by 11%; in 2011 the forecasted growth rate is 10%, and in 2012 sales are forecast to increase by 8%. This reduction in growth rate eventually occurs for all companies. As a firm grows and matures, its growth rate slows down; it's simply impossible for a company to grow very fast for very long. Once a company has reached the mature stage and is forecasting growth at a constant and perpetual rate, which means the same growth rate forever, we can apply the concept and formula for terminal value to determine the present value of the cash flows generated by the firm in all of its constant and perpetual growth years. For Hudson this change occurs in the years 2013 and beyond.

Hudson is growing quickly in the years 2009 to 2012, but in 2013 the company matures and achieves a constant and perpetual growth rate, which is forecast to be 6.5%. This means we must individually forecast the operations and cash flows of Hudson for each of the fast growth years, 2009 to 2012, but for the years 2013 and beyond we can apply the formula for terminal value to determine the value of the cash flows generated by the company in those years. The mechanics of equity valuation, therefore, are fairly simple. As long as the company is growing at a fast and unsustainable rate, you must forecast each

Exhibit 5.10   Hudson Hybrid Car Company financial results and forecasts, 2008–2012 (in thousands).

	Actual 2008	Forecast 2009	Forecast 2010	Forecast 2011	Forecast 2012
Operating revenues	$ 800,315	$ 898,754	$ 997,617	$1,097,379	$1,185,169
Operating costs— depreciation	630,907	710,344	790,416	869,458	939,015
Depreciation	47,086	52,736	58,379	64,217	69,354
Operating income (EBIT)	122,322	135,674	148,822	163,704	176,800
Interest expense	15,352	17,210	19,105	21,016	22,697
Income before income taxes	106,970	118,464	129,717	142,688	154,103
Income taxes	42,254	46,790	51,240	56,362	60,871
Net income	$ 64,716	$ 71,674	$ 78,477	$ 86,326	$ 93,232
Current assets	$ 108,854	$ 124,816	$ 141,955	$ 156,151	$ 168,643
Property, plant, and equipment at cost	1,309,522	1,433,732	1,562,412	1,718,653	1,856,145
Less allowance for depreciation	349,752	402,488	460,867	525,084	594,438
Net property, plant, and equipment	$ 959,770	$1,031,244	$1,101,545	$1,193,569	$1,261,707
Current liabilities	$ 173,964	$ 187,270	$ 200,047	$ 220,052	$ 237,656
Long-term debt	176,978	$ 198,398	$ 220,242	$ 242,273	$ 261,651
Common stock	77,434	$ 77,434	$ 77,434	$ 77,434	$ 77,434
Retained earnings	453,261	$ 524,935	$ 603,412	$ 689,738	$ 782,970
Total owners' equity	$ 530,695	$ 602,369	$ 680,846	$ 767,172	$ 860,404

year individually, but as soon as the company reaches a constant and perpetual growth rate, apply terminal value.

Any company like Hudson that is growing at a constant and perpetual rate is called a growing perpetuity, and the value of any growing perpetuity at year t, called V_t, with the growing perpetuity starting in year $t + 1$ with cash flow CF_{t+1}, a growth rate g, and discount rate k, can be calculated with the formula:

$$V_t = \frac{CF_{t+1}}{(k - g)}$$

When a company is a growing perpetuity we assume:

$$CF = EBIT \times (1 - t) + \text{Depreciation} - CAPX - \Delta NWC$$

where $EBIT$ is earnings before interest and taxes, t is the income tax rate, Depreciation is the firm's Depreciation expense, $CAPX$ is the firm's capital expenditures, and ΔNWC is the firm's change in net working capital (current assets less current liabilities).

Capital expenditures increase net assets, depreciation expense decreases net assets, and the change in net working capital changes net assets (NA), so:

$$(\text{Depreciation} - CAPX - \Delta NWC) = -\Delta NA = -g \times NA_{\text{prior year}}$$

Since the firm is growing through time, net assets increase, requiring an investment of cash; thus the negative sign in front of the growth rate, g. There is less cash flow available for investors, because cash must be invested in the firm to sustain firm growth. Net assets equal current assets minus current liabilities plus net property, plant, and equipment, so:

$$-g \times NA_{\text{prior year}} = -g \times (CA_{\text{prior year}} - CL_{\text{prior year}} + \text{Net } PP\&E_{\text{prior year}})$$

This implies that the terminal value for any firm at time t, with the first constant-growth cash flow at time $t + 1$, can be determined with this formula:

$$TV_t = \frac{[(1-t) \times EBIT_{t+1}] - (g \times NA_t)}{(k-g)}$$

where $EBIT_{t+1}$ equals EBIT in year t times 1 plus the growth rate, g.

This formula tells us that once any firm becomes a growing perpetuity in year $t + 1$, we can determine its value in year t once we have its income tax rate, earnings before interest and taxes in year t, constant growth rate, net assets in year t, and its discount rate. Our forecasts show Hudson Hybrid Car Company becomes a growing perpetuity in year 2013, so the formula can be applied to determine the value of the cash flows generated in the years 2013 and beyond, as of the year 2012. This is the benefit of terminal value; once a company becomes a growing perpetuity we can collapse the cash flows that are generated during the firm's constant and perpetual growth stage with one calculation.

We will now use the forecasted financial information presented in Exhibit 5.10, Hudson's constant and perpetual growth rate and cost of capital, and this terminal value formula to determine Hudson's total value to all investors. Once we have this figure, we will subtract the amount Hudson owes its long-term debt holders, and since common equity is a residual, Hudson's total value minus the amount owed long-term debt holders equals the value of Hudson's common equity. This result will be calculated using the stock valuation template included in the chapter materials.

The valuation template begins with Hudson's financial results for 2008 and forecasts for 2009 through 2012, as presented in Exhibit 5.10. The first thing that must be done with these data is calculate Hudson's net working capital, change in net working capital, and capital expenditures during the forecast period. The value of the company is calculated by discounting the cash flow generated by the company, and increases in working capital and capital expenditures require the investment of cash and therefore reduce the cash flow available to Hudson's investors, both debt and equity investors. These calculations are performed in the valuation template and are shown in Exhibit 5.11.

These calculations tell us that Hudson will invest $2,656,000 in net working capital, plus $124,210,000 in capital expenditures during 2009. These calculations are important because the total investment of $126,866,000 reduces the amount of cash flow available for Hudson's investors. These total investments, combined with the financial forecasts presented in Exhibit 5.10, along with Hudson's constant and perpetual growth rate of 6.5% for the years 2013 and beyond, almost provide sufficient information to determine the value of Hudson's equity. The last piece of information we need is Hudson's cost of

Exhibit 5.11   Hudson Hybrid Car Company working capital and capital expenditures, 2008–2012 (in thousands of $).

	Actual 2008	Forecast 2009	Forecast 2010	Forecast 2011	Forecast 2012
Net working capital (CA – CL)	–$65,110	–$ 62,454	–$ 58,092	–$ 63,901	–$ 69,013
Change in net working capital		2,656	4,362	–5,809	–5,112
Capital expenditures (Δ in PP&E at cost)		$124,210	$128,680	$156,241	$137,492

capital, which we will assume is 12.0%, and we will use this as the required return or discount rate for Hudson's cash flows to investors. Now we are able to calculate Hudson's cash flows available to investors, terminal value, discounted total firm value, and value of common equity. This calculation is performed in the valuation template and is presented in Exhibit 5.12.

This calculation of Hudson's value of equity follows the processes and steps discussed in this section. The cost of capital, income tax rate, and perpetual growth rate for Hudson are all used in determining firm value. EBIT times 1 minus the income tax rate is the after-tax earnings of the firm available to investors, and Hudson's free cash flow is

Exhibit 5.12   Hudson Hybrid Car Company calculation of value of equity, 2009–2012 (in thousands of $).

		Forecast 2009	Forecast 2010	Forecast 2011	Forecast 2012
Cost of capital	12.00%				
Income tax rate	39.50%				
Perpetual growth rate	6.50%				
EBIT		$135,674	$148,822	$163,704	$176,800
EBIT × (1 – t)		82,083	90,037	99,041	106,964
Depreciation expense		52,736	58,379	64,217	69,354
Change in net working capital		2,656	4,362	–5,809	–5,112
Capital expenditures		124,210	128,680	156,241	137,492
Free cash flow		7,953	15,374	12,826	43,938
+ Terminal value					661,665
= Total FCF		$ 7,953	$ 15,374	$ 12,826	$705,603
PV FCF @ WACC	$476,909				
– Long-term debt	176,978				
= Value of equity	$299,931				

this after-tax earnings plus depreciation expense, minus change in net working capital, and minus capital expenditures. The only complex calculation in Exhibit 5.12 is Hudson's terminal value of $661,665,000 in year 2012, which is based on Hudson's inputs and the terminal value formula:

$$TV_t = \frac{[(1-t) \times EBIT_{t+1}] - (g \times NA_t)}{k - g}$$

$$TV_{2012} = \frac{[(1 - 0.395) \times \$176,800 \times (1 + 0.065)] - (0.065 \times \$1,192,694)}{0.12 - 0.065}$$

$$TV_{2012} = \$661,665$$

Since Hudson becomes a constant and perpetual growth company in 2013, this value represents the value of Hudson's cash flows to investors during the years 2013 and beyond, as of 2012. Adding this terminal value as of 2012 to Hudson's yearly cash flows to investors produces total cash flows of $7,953,000 in 2009, $15,374,000 in 2010, $12,826,000 in 2011, and $705,603,000 in 2012. When these cash flows are discounted at Hudson's cost of capital, a total firm value of $476,909,000 results. This is the value of the company to all investors, based on the cash flows available to all investors.

Since long-term debt holders have a priority claim and common stockholders have a residual claim, to determine Hudson's value of common equity you must subtract the debt holders' current claim on the firm, or $176,978,000, from total firm value: $476,909,000 minus $176,978,000 equals $299,931,000, which is the value of Hudson's common equity.

The final step in determining the value of one share of Hudson's stock is to divide this value of common equity by the number of shares of common stock that Hudson has outstanding, so if Hudson has five million common shares outstanding, its stock value is $299,931,000 divided by 5,000,000, or $59.99 per share.

We have just discussed and illustrated the discounted cash flow (DCF) method of equity valuation. This method, and the valuation template included in the chapter materials, can be used to determine the value of any firm, with one modification. This modification is that terminal value cannot be calculated until the firm slows to a constant and perpetual growth rate. In the Hudson Hybrid Car Company example, this occurred in 2013, so four years (2009, 2010, 2011, and 2012) had to be individually forecast before using the terminal value formula. If a company is not expected to slow to a constant and perpetual growth rate until 2015, then two more years must be individually forecast before applying terminal value. If a company is already in a mature state and growing at a constant and perpetual rate, then terminal value can be applied immediately and there is no need to forecast any years individually.

It is also possible to calculate the value of equity for a company using the relative value method. This method is easier to use, as it involves taking some performance measure of a company and applying the price to performance measure from a comparable company. Continuing with the Hudson example, recall from Exhibit 5.10 that Hudson had net income of $64,716,000 in 2008. This was Hudson's sales revenues minus all expenses, including operating expenses, interest expenses paid to debt holders, and income tax expenses paid to governmental authorities, so it represents net income available to Hudson's common stockholders. Assume there is a publicly traded company, the Gracie Green Transit Company, which is comparable to Hudson. If Gracie's net income in 2008 was $221,976,000 and its total value of equity was $1,420,646,000, then Gracie's price-to-earnings ratio was $1,420,646,000 divided by $221,976,000, or 6.40 times earnings. If Hudson is a true and perfect peer to Gracie, then Hudson's total value of common equity through the relative value method is Hudson's 2008 net income times this same price-to-earnings ratio:

$$\$64,716,000 \times 6.40 = \$414,182,400$$

This relative value method can be used with many possible ratios, including price to cash flow and market price to book value, among others. The strength of the relative value method is its simplicity of use. Once you have identified a comparable firm you apply the price to performance ratio, and you have the value of equity for the target firm. This is also the weakness of the relative value method, because it applies the price ratio naively. If your target firm differs even a little from the comparable firm, and there are very few truly comparable firms in the world, then it's hard to have much confidence in the result. Alternatively, you could apply your personal judgment to the price to performance ratio, adjusting it up if you believe the target is a superior firm, and adjusting it down if you believe the target is an inferior firm, but this is highly subjective.

A good way to conclude this discussion of the relative value method is to be careful and thoughtful when using it, and be sure to also use the discounted cash flow valuation method and compare your results from both methods. Discounted cash flow valuation is the preferred method, but the relative value method can help a financial analyst better understand the company and support the result obtained by DCF valuation.

We conclude our work on equity valuation by calculating the value of preferred stock. Preferred stock is a perpetuity because it pays the same fixed cash dividend forever, so the formula for the value of a perpetuity can be used to determine the price of a share of preferred stock:

$$\text{Price}_{\text{preferred stock}} = \frac{\text{Preferred Stock Dividend}}{K_{\text{preferred stock}}}$$

The term in the denominator, $K_{\text{preferred stock}}$, is the current required rate of return for the preferred stock, so if a company's preferred stock pays a dividend of $4 per year and the required return of the preferred stock is 9%, then the value of the preferred stock is $4 divided by 0.09 or $44.44 per share. Since preferred dividends do not change over time and go on forever, the value of a share of preferred stock is calculated as this fixed dividend per share divided by the current required rate of return on the stock.

Conclusion

The topics discussed in this chapter, risk and return, cost of capital, capital structure, and valuation, are the bases of the tasks performed by financial managers. Businesses identify, analyze, and approve investment opportunities, and financial managers raise the capital necessary to fund these investment opportunities. Investors are willing to invest in companies and their projects, but only if the expected return from the investment is sufficient given its risk. Financial managers must understand this relationship between risk and return, so they can determine the cost of the capital provided to the business by investors.

Financial managers must also understand how capital structure decisions change cost of capital, because financing the firm in an efficient manner reduces the cost of capital and allows the firm to accept more investment projects. Reducing the cost of capital also reduces the discount rate on the cash flows available for investors, which increases total firm value and the value of equity.

It is important that financial managers have a good understanding and strong skills in all of the topics presented in this chapter, as they use them on a daily basis when performing their jobs.

Downloadable Resources for this chapter available at www.wiley.com/go/portablembainfinance

Capital Structure Problems and Solutions

Online Content

There are several files posted online to supplement the topics presented in the text of this chapter. The first file, "Chapter 5 Capital Structure Template for Cost of Capital," has an input template for the data items required to calculate cost of capital, and an output template which returns the firm's cost of capital. The second file, "Chapter 5 Capital Structure Template for Bond Pricing," has an input template for the data items required to determine a bond's price, and an output template that returns the price without accrued interest, the accrued interest, and the price including accrued interest. The third file, "Chapter 5 Capital Structure Template for Stock Valuation," presents the valuation of Hudson Hybrid Car Company's common stock; this file contains the financial data for Hudson, a box that calculates Hudson's investment in working capital and its capital expenditures, an input template for the data items required to calculate the value of Hudson's common stock, and an output template that returns the stock's value. The fourth file, "Chapter 5 Capital Structure Website," contains practice problems covering the topics presented in Chapter 5, along with their solutions. The final file, "Chapter 5 Capital Structure Crispy Dream Equity Valuation Solution Template," contains the solution template for the Crispy Dream Donuts valuation of a common equity problem contained in the "Chapter 5 Capital Structure Website" file.

Note

1. Franco Modigliani and Merton H. Miller, "The Cost of Capital, Corporation Finance, and the Theory of Investment," *American Economic Review* 48, no. 3 (June 1958): 261–297.

6

Planning Capital Expenditure

Steven P. Feinstein

A beer company is considering building a new brewery. An airline is deciding whether to add flights to its schedule. An engineer at a high-tech company has designed a new microchip and hopes to encourage the company to manufacture and sell it. A small college contemplates buying a new photocopy machine. A nonprofit museum is toying with the idea of installing an education center for children. Newlyweds dream of buying a house. A retailer considers building a Web site and selling on the Internet.

What do these projects have in common? All of them entail a commitment of capital and managerial effort that may or may not be justified by later performance. A common set of tools can be applied to assess these seemingly very different propositions. The financial analysis used to assess such projects is known as "capital budgeting." How should a limited supply of capital and managerial talent be allocated among an unlimited number of possible projects and corporate initiatives?

The Objective: Maximize Wealth

Capital budgeting decisions cut to the heart of the most fundamental questions in business. What is the purpose of the firm? Is it to create wealth for investors? To serve the needs of customers? To provide jobs for employees? To better the community? These questions are fodder for endless debate. Ultimately, however, project decisions have to be made, and so we must adopt a decision rule. The perspective of financial analysis is that capital investment belongs to the investors. The goal of the firm is to maximize investors' wealth. Other factors are important and should be considered, but this is the primary objective. In the case of nonprofit organizations, wealth and return on investment need not be measured in dollars and cents but rather can be measured in terms of benefits to society. But in the case of for-profit companies, wealth is monetary.

A project creates wealth if it generates cash flows over time that are worth more in present value terms than the initial setup cost. For example, suppose a brewery costs $10 million to build, but once built it generates a stream of cash flows that is worth $11 million. Building the brewery would create $1 million of new wealth. If there were no other proposed projects that would create more wealth than this, then the beer company would be well advised to build the new brewery.

This example illustrates the net present value (NPV) rule. Net present value is the difference between the setup cost of a project and the value of the project once it is set up. If that difference is positive, then the NPV is positive and the project creates wealth.

If a firm must choose from several proposed projects, the one with the highest NPV will create the most wealth, so it should be the one adopted. For example, suppose the beer company can either build the new brewery or, alternatively, introduce a new product—a light beer, for example. There is not enough managerial talent to oversee more than one new project, or maybe there are not enough funds to start both. Let us assume that both projects create wealth: The NPV of the new brewery is $1 million, and the NPV of the new-product project is $500,000. If it could, the beer company should undertake both projects; but since it has to choose, building the new brewery would be the right option because it has the higher NPV.

Computing NPV: Projecting Cash Flows

The first step in calculating a project's NPV is to forecast the project's future cash flows. Cash is king. It is cash flow, not profit, that investors really care about. If a company never generates cash flow, there can be no return to investors. Also, profit can be manipulated by discretionary accounting treatments such as depreciation method or inventory valuation. Regardless of accounting choices, however, cash flow either materializes or does not. For these reasons, cash flow is the most important variable to investors. A project's value derives from the cash flow it creates, and NPV is the value of the future cash flows net of the initial cash outflow.

We can illustrate the method for forecasting cash flows with an example. Let us continue to explore the brewery project. Suppose project engineers inform you that the construction costs for the brewery would be $8 million. The expected life of the new brewery is 10 years. The brewery will be depreciated to zero over its 10-year life using a straight-line depreciation schedule. Land for the brewery can be purchased for $1 million. Additional inventory to stock the new brewery would cost $1 million. The brewery would be fully operational within a year. If the project is undertaken, increased sales for the beer company would be $7 million per year. Cost of goods sold for this beer would be $2 million per year, and selling, administrative, and general expenses associated with the new brewery would be $1 million per year. Perhaps advertising would have to increase by $500,000 per year. After 10 years, the land can be sold for $1 million, or it can be used for another project. After 10 years the salvage value of the plant is expected to be $1.5 million. The increase in accounts receivable would exactly equal the increase in accounts payable, at $400,000, so these components of net working capital would offset one another and generate no net cash flow.

No one expects these forecasts to be perfect. Paraphrasing the famous words of physicist Niels Bohr (sometimes attributed to baseball player Yogi Berra), making predictions is very difficult, especially when they are about the future! However, when investors choose among various investments, they too must make predictions. As a financial analyst, you want the quality of your forecasts to be on a par with the quality of the forecasts made by investors. Essentially, the job of the financial analyst is to estimate how investors will value the project, because the value of the firm will rise if investors decide the new project creates wealth and will fall if investors conclude the project destroys wealth. If the investors have reason to believe that sales will be $7 million per year, then that would be the correct forecast to use in the capital budgeting analysis. Investors have to cope with uncertainty in their forecasts. Similarly, the financial analyst conducting a capital budgeting analysis must tolerate the same level of uncertainty.

Exhibit 6.1   Initial year cash flow for brewery project (thousands).

Construction	($8,000)
Land	(1,000)
Inventory	(1,000)
Accounts receivable	(400)
Accounts payable	400
Total cash flow	($10,000)

Note that cash flow projections require an integrated team effort across the entire firm. Operations and engineering personnel estimate the cost of building and operating the new plant. The human resources department contributes the labor data. Marketing people tell you what advertising budget is needed, and they forecast revenue. The accounting department estimates taxes, accounts payable, accounts receivable, and tabulates the financial data. The job of the financial analyst is to put the pieces together and recommend that the project be adopted or abandoned.

Initial Cash Outflow

The initial cash outflow required by the project is the sum of the construction cost ($8 million), the land cost ($1 million), and the required new inventory ($1 million). Thus, this project requires an investment of $10 million to launch. If accounts receivable did not equal accounts payable, then the new accounts receivable would add to the initial cash outflow, and the new accounts payable would be subtracted. These cash flows are tabulated in Exhibit 6.1.

Cash Flows in Later Years

We find cash flow in years 1 through 10 by applying the following formula:

> Cash Flow = Sales − Cost of Goods Sold
> − Selling, Administrative, and General Expenses
> − Advertising
> − Income Tax
> + Decrease in Inventory (or − Increase)
> + Decrease in Accounts Receivable (or − Increase)
> − Decrease in Accounts Payable (or + Increase)
> + Salvage
> − Windfall Tax on Salvage

Notice that we already have most of the data needed for the cash flow formula, but we are missing the forecasts for income tax and windfall tax. Before we can finalize the cash flow computation, we have to forecast taxes.

Income tax equals earnings before taxes (EBT) times the income tax rate. EBT is computed using the following formula:

Earnings before Taxes = Sales − Cost of Goods Sold
                           − Selling, Administrative, and General Expenses
                           − Advertising
                           − Depreciation

The formula for EBT is similar to the formula for cash flow, with a few important exceptions. The cash flow calculation does not subtract depreciation, whereas the EBT calculation does. This is because depreciation is not a cash flow; the firm never has to write a check payable to "depreciation." Depreciation does reduce taxable income, however, because the government allows this deduction for tax purposes. So depreciation influences cash flow via its impact on income tax, but it is not a cash flow itself. The greater the allowable depreciation is in a given year, the lower taxes will be, and the greater the resulting cash flow to the firm.

Treatment of Net Working Capital

Changes in inventory, accounts receivable, and accounts payable are included in the cash flow calculation but not in EBT. Changes in the components of working capital directly impact cash flow, but they are not deductible for tax purposes. When a firm buys inventory, it has essentially swapped one asset (cash) for another asset (inventory). Though this is a negative cash flow, it is not considered a deductible expenditure for tax purposes.

Similarly, a rise in accounts receivable means that cash that otherwise would have been in the company coffers is now owed to the company instead. Thus, an increase in accounts receivable effectively sucks cash out of the company and must be treated as a cash outflow. Increasing accounts payable has the opposite effect.

One way to gain perspective on the impact of accounts payable and accounts receivable on a company's cash flow is to think of them as adjustments to sales and cost of goods sold. If a company makes a sale but the customer has not yet paid, clearly there is no cash flow generated from the sale. Though the sales variable will increase, the increase in accounts receivable will exactly offset that increase in the cash flow computation. Similarly, if the company incurs expenses in the manufacture of the goods sold but has not yet paid its suppliers for the raw materials, the cost of goods sold will be offset by the increase in accounts payable.

Depreciation

According to a straight-line depreciation schedule, depreciation in each year is the initial cost of the plant or equipment divided by the number of years over which the asset will be depreciated. So, the $8 million plant depreciated over 10 years generates depreciation of $800,000 each year. Land is generally not depreciated. Straight-line depreciation is but one acceptable method for determining depreciation of plant and equipment. The tax authorities often sanction other methods and schedules.

Windfall Profit and Windfall Tax

In order to compute windfall profit and windfall tax, we must be able to track an asset's book value over its life. Book value is the initial value minus all previous depreciation. For example, the brewery initially has a book value of $8 million, but that value falls $800,000 per year due to depreciation. At the end of the first year, book value falls to $7.2 million. By the end of the second year, following another $800,000 of depreciation, the book value will be $6.4 million. By the end of the tenth year, when the brewery is fully depreciated, the book value will be zero.

Windfall profit is the difference between the salvage value and book value. We are told the beer company will be able to sell the old brewery for $1.5 million at the end of 10 years. By then, however, the book value of the brewery will be zero. Thus, the beer company will realize a windfall profit of $1.5 million. The government will want its share of that windfall profit. Multiplying the windfall profit by the tax rate determines the windfall tax. In this particular case, with a windfall profit of $1.5 million and a tax rate of 40%, the windfall tax would equal $600,000 (= $1.5 million × 40%).

Taxable Income and Income Tax

Exhibit 6.2 shows how taxable income and income tax are computed for the brewery example. Income tax equals EBT times the company's income tax rate. In each of the years 1 through 10, EBT is $2.7 million, so income tax is $1,080,000 (= $2.7 million × 40%).

Interest Expense

Notice that the calculation of taxable income and income tax in Exhibit 6.2 does not deduct any interest expense. This was not an oversight. Even if the company intends to finance the new project by selling bonds or borrowing from a bank, we should not deduct any anticipated interest expense from our taxable income, and we should not subtract interest payments in the cash flow computation. We will take the tax shield of debt financing into account later when we compute the company's cost of capital.

Exhibit 6.2   Income tax forecasts for brewery project (thousands).

	Years 1–10
Sales	$ 7,000
Cost of goods sold	(2,000)
Selling, administrative, and general expenses	(1,000)
Advertising	(500)
Depreciation	(800)
Earnings before taxes	$ 2,700
Income tax (40%)	($ 1,080)

Exhibit 6.3   Cash flow projections for brewery project (thousands).

Year	0	1–9	10
Construction	($ 8,000)		
Land	(1,000)		$ 1,000
Inventory	(1,000)		1,000
Account receivable	(400)		400
Accounts payable	400		(400)
Sales		$ 7,000	7,000
Cost of goods sold		(2,000)	(2,000)
Selling, administrative, and general expenses		(1,000)	(1,000)
Advertising		(500)	(500)
Income tax		(1,080)	(1,080)
Salvage			1,500
Windfall tax			(600)
Total cash flow	($10,000)	$ 2,420	$ 5,320

The reason for omitting interest expense at this stage cuts to the core of the purpose of capital budgeting. We are trying to forecast how much cash is required from investors to start this project and then how much cash this project will generate for the investors once the project is up and running. Interest expense is a distribution of cash to one class of investors—the debt holders. If we want the bottom line of our cash flow computation to reflect how much cash will be available to all investors, we must not subtract cash flow going to one class of investors before we get to that bottom line.

Putting the Pieces Together to Forecast Cash Flow

We now have all the puzzle pieces to construct our capital budgeting cash flow projection. These pieces and the resulting cash flow projection are presented in Exhibit 6.3. Cash flows in years 1 through 9 are forecast to be $2.42 million, and the cash flow in year 10 is expected to be $5.32 million. Year 10 has a greater cash flow because of the recovery of the inventory and the assumed sale of the land and plant.

Guiding Principles for Forecasting Cash Flows

The brewery example is one illustration of how cash flows are forecast. Every project is different, however, and the financial analyst must be keen to identify all sources of cash flow. The following three principles can serve as a guide: (1) focus on cash flow, not raw accounting data; (2) use expected values; and (3) focus on the incremental.

Principle No. 1: Focus on Cash Flow

Net present value (NPV) analysis focuses on cash flows—that is, actual cash payments and receipts flowing into or out of the firm. Recall that accounting profit is not the same thing as cash flow. Accounting profit often mixes variables whose timings differ. A sale made today may show up in today's profits, but since the cash receipt for the sale may be deferred, the corresponding cash flow takes place later. Since the cash flow is deferred, the true value of that sale to the firm is somewhat diminished.

By focusing on cash flows and when they occur, NPV reflects the true value of increased revenues and costs. Consequently, NPV analysis requires that accounting data be unraveled to reveal the underlying cash flows. That is why changes in net working capital must be accounted for and why depreciation does not show up directly.

Principle No. 2: Use Expected Values

There is always going to be some uncertainty over future cash flows. Future costs and revenues cannot be known for sure. The analyst must gather as much information as possible and assemble it to construct expected values of the input variables. Although expected values are not perfect, these best guesses have to be good enough. What is the alternative? The uncertainty in forecasting the inputs is accounted for in the discount rate that is later used to discount the expected cash flows.

Principle No. 3: Focus on the Incremental

NPV analysis is done in terms of incremental cash flows—that is, the change in cash flow generated by the decision to undertake the project. Incremental cash flow is the difference between what the cash flow would be with the project and what the firm's cash flow would be without the project. Any sales or savings that would have happened without the project and are unaffected by doing the project are irrelevant and should be ignored. Similarly, any costs that would have been incurred anyway are irrelevant. It is often difficult (yet nonetheless important) to focus on the incremental when calculating how cash flows are impacted by opportunity costs, sunk costs, and overhead. These troublesome areas will be elaborated on next.

Opportunity Costs

Opportunity costs are opportunities for cash inflows that must be sacrificed in order to undertake the project. No check is written to pay for opportunity costs, but they represent changes in the firm's cash flows caused by the project and must therefore be treated as actual costs of doing the project. For example, suppose the firm owns a parking lot, and a proposed project requires use of that land. Is the land free since the firm already owns it? No; if the project were not undertaken, then the company could sell or rent out the land. Use of the company's land is therefore not free. There is an opportunity cost. Money that could have been earned if the project were rejected will not be earned if the project is started. In order to reflect fully the incremental impact of the proposed project, the incremental cash flows used in NPV analysis must incorporate opportunity costs.

Sunk Costs

Sunk costs are expenses that have already been paid or have already been committed to. Past research and development is an example. Since sunk costs are not incremental to the proposed project, NPV analysis must ignore them. NPV analysis is always forward-looking. The past cannot be changed and so should not enter into the choice of a future course of action. If research was undertaken last year, the effects of that research might bear on future cash flows, but the cost of that research is already water under the bridge and so is not relevant in the decision to continue the project. The project decision must be made on the basis of whether the project increases or decreases wealth from the present into the future. The past is irrelevant.

Overhead

The treatment of overhead often gives project managers a headache. Overhead comprises expenditures made by the firm for resources that are shared by many projects or departments. Heat and maintenance for common facilities is an example. Management resources and shared support staff are other examples. Overhead represents resources required for the firm to provide an environment in which projects can be undertaken.

Different firms use different formulas for charging overhead expenses to various projects and departments. If overhead charges accurately reflect the shared resources used by a project, then they should be treated as incremental costs of operating the project. If the project were not undertaken, those shared resources would benefit another moneymaking project, or perhaps the firm could possibly cut some of the shared overhead expenditures. Thus, to the extent that overhead does represent resources used by the project, it should be included in calculating incremental cash flows. If, on the other hand, overhead expense is unaffected by the decision to undertake the new project, and no other proposed project could use those shared resources, then overhead should be ignored in the NPV analysis.

Sometimes the formulas used to calculate overhead for budgeting purposes are unrealistic and overcharge projects for their use of shared resources. If the financial analyst does not correct this unrepresentative allocation of costs, some worthwhile projects might incorrectly appear undesirable.

Computing NPV: The Time Value of Money

In deciding whether a project is worthwhile, one needs to know more than whether it will make money. One must also know *when* it will make money. Time is money! Project decisions involve cash flows spread out over several periods. As we shall see, cash flows in different periods are distinct products in the financial marketplace—as different as apples and oranges. To make decisions affecting many future periods, we must know how to convert the different periods' cash flows into a common currency.

The concept that future cash flows have a lower present value and the set of tools used to discount future cash flows to their present values are collectively known as time value of money (TVOM) analysis. I have always thought this to be a misnomer; the name should be the "money value of time." But there is no use bucking the trend, so we will adopt the standard nomenclature.

You probably already have an intuitive grasp of the fundamentals of TVOM analysis, as your likely answer to the following question illustrates: Would you rather have $100 today or $100 next year? Why?

The answer to this question is the essence of TVOM. You no doubt answered that you would rather have the money today. Money today is worth more than money to be delivered in the future. Even if there were perfect certainty that the future money would be received, we prefer to have money in hand today. There are many reasons for this. Having money in hand allows greater flexibility for planning. You might choose to spend it before the future money would be delivered. If you choose not to spend the money during the course of the year, you can earn interest on it by investing it. Understanding

TVOM allows you to quantify exactly how much more early cash flows are worth than deferred cash flows. An example will illuminate the concept.

Suppose you and a friend have dinner together in a restaurant. You order an inexpensive sandwich. Your friend orders a large steak, a bottle of wine, and several desserts. The bill arrives and your friend's share is $100. Unfortunately, your friend forgot his wallet and asks to borrow the $100 from you. You agree and pay. A year passes before your friend remembers to pay you back the money. "Here is the $100," he finally says one day. Such events test a friendship, especially if you had to carry a $100 balance on your credit card over the course of the year on which interest accrued at a rate of 18%. Is the $100 your friend is offering you now worth the same as the $100 he borrowed a year earlier? Actually, no, a $100 cash flow today is not worth $100 next year. The same nominal amount has different values depending on when it is paid. If the interest rate is 18%, a $100 cash flow today is worth $118 next year and is worth $139.24 the year after because of compound interest. The present value of $118 to be received next year is exactly $100 today. Your friend should pay you $118 if he borrowed $100 from you a year earlier.

The formula for converting a future value to a present value is:

$$PV = \frac{FV}{(1+r)^n}$$

where PV stands for present value, FV is future value, n is the number of periods in the future that the future cash flow is paid, and r is the appropriate interest rate or discount rate.

Discounting Cash Flows

Suppose in the brewery example that the appropriate discount rate for translating future values to present values is 20%. Recall that the brewery project is forecast to generate $2.42 million of cash in year 1. The present value of that cash flow, as of year 0, is $2,016,667, computed as follows:

$$PV = \frac{\$2,420,000}{(1.20)^1} = \$2,016,667$$

Similarly, the year 2 cash flow was forecast to be $2.42 million also. The present value of that second-year cash flow is only $1,680,556:

$$PV = \frac{\$2,420,000}{(1.20)^2} = \$1,680,556$$

The longer the time over which a cash flow is discounted, the lower is its present value. Exhibit 6.4 presents the forecasted cash flows and their discounted present values for the brewery project.

Exhibit 6.4   Discounted cash flows for brewery project (thousands).

Year	Cash Flow	Discounted Cash Flow
0	($10,000)	($10,000)
1	2,420	2,017
2	2,420	1,681
3	2,420	1,400
4	2,420	1,167
5	2,420	973
6	2,420	810
7	2,420	675
8	2,420	563
9	2,420	469
10	5,320	859

Summing the Discounted Cash Flows to Arrive at NPV

Finally, we can calculate the NPV. The NPV is the sum of all discounted cash flows, which in the brewery example equals $614,000. To understand precisely what this means, observe that the sum of the discounted cash flows from years 1 through 10 is $10,614,000. This means that the project generates future cash flows that are worth $10,614,000 today. The initial cost of the project is $10 million today. Thus, the project is worth $10,614,000 but costs only $10 million and therefore creates $614,000 of new wealth. The managers of the beer company would be well advised to adopt this project because it has a positive NPV and therefore creates wealth.

More NPV Examples

Consider two alternative projects, A and B. They both cost $1 million to set up. Project A returns $800,000 per year for two years starting one year after setup. Project B also returns $800,000 per year for two years, but the cash flows begin two years after setup. The firm uses a discount rate of 20%. Which is the better project, A or B?

Like project A, project C also costs $1 million to set up, and it will pay back $1,600,000. For both A and C, the firm will earn $800,000 per year for two years starting one year after setup. However, C costs $500,000 initially and the other $500,000 need only be paid at the termination of the project (it may be a cleanup cost, for example). Project A requires the initial outlay all at once at the outset. Which is the better project, A or C? Of projects A, B, and C, which project(s) should be undertaken?

We should make the project decision only after analyzing each project's NPV. Exhibit 6.5 tabulates each project's cash flows, discounted cash flows, and NPVs. The NPVs of projects A, B, and C, are, respectively, $222,222, −$151,235, and $375,000. Project C has the highest NPV. Therefore, if only one project can be selected, it should be project C. If than one project can be undertaken, then both A and C should be selected since they both have positive NPVs. Project B should be rejected since it has a negative NPV and would therefore destroy wealth.

Exhibit 6.5 Cash flows and discounted cash flows for three alternative projects (thousands).

Year	Project A Cash Flow	Project A Discounted Cash Flow	Project B Cash Flow	Project B Discounted Cash Flow	Project C Cash Flow	Project C Discounted Cash Flow
0	($1,000,000)	($1,000,000)	($1,000,000)	($1,000,000)	($500,000)	($500,000)
1	800,000	666,667	0	0	800,000	666,667
2	800,000	555,556	0	0	300,000	208,333
3	0	0	800,000	462,963	0	0
4	$ 0	0	$ 800,000	385,802	$ 0	0
NPV		$ 222,222		($ 151,235)		$375,000

It makes sense that project C should have the highest NPV, since its cash outflows are deferred relative to the other projects and its cash inflows are early. Project B, alternatively, has all costs up front, but its cash inflows are deferred.

Suppose a project has positive NPV, but the NPV is small, say, only a few hundred dollars. The firm should nevertheless undertake that project if there are no alternative projects with higher NPVs. The reason is that a firm's value is increased every time it undertakes a positive-NPV project. The firm's value increases by the amount of the project NPV. A small NPV, as long as it is positive, is net of all input costs and financing costs. So, even if the NPV is low, the project covers all its costs and provides additional returns. If accepting the small-NPV project does not preclude the undertaking of a higher-NPV project, then it is the best thing to do. A firm that rejects a positive-NPV project is rejecting wealth.

Of course, this does not mean a firm should jump headlong into any project that at the moment appears likely to provide positive NPV. Future potential projects should be considered as well, and they should be evaluated as potential alternatives. The projects, current or future, that have the highest NPVs should be the projects accepted. For maximum wealth-creation efficiency, the firm's managerial resources should be committed toward undertaking maximum-NPV projects.

Outsourcing and the Build/Buy Decision

Firms are often faced with the question of whether it is better to undertake a particular function internally or, alternatively, outsource the function to an external entity. For example, should an online retailer undertake the fulfillment process of packaging and shipping itself, or should it subcontract the job to an outside company? Similarly, firms are often faced with the dilemma of whether it is better to build enterprise software or other productive assets in-house, or alternatively buy such assets ready-made from outside vendors. While the issues of core competencies, strategic fit, and managerial capacity must also be considered when making such decisions, an NPV analysis can help organize the issues and can help point the firm toward the optimal path. The alternative with the highest NPV creates the most value for the company.

The Discount Rate

At what rate should cash flows be discounted to compute net present values? In most cases, the appropriate rate is the firm's cost of funds for the project. That is, if the firm secures financing for the project by borrowing from a bank, the after-tax interest rate should be used to discount cash flows. If the firm obtains funds by selling stock, then an equity financing rate should be applied. If the financing combines debt and equity, then the appropriate discount rate would be an average of the debt rate and the equity rate.

Cost of Debt Financing

The after-tax interest rate is the interest rate paid on a firm's debt less the impact of the tax break it gets from issuing debt. For example, suppose that a firm pays 10% interest on its debt and the firm's income tax rate is 40%. If the firm issues $100,000 of debt, then the annual interest expense will be $10,000 (10% × $100,000). But this $10,000 of interest expense is tax deductible, so the firm would save $4,000 in taxes (40% × the

$10,000 interest). Thus, net of the tax break, this firm would be paying $6,000 to service a $100,000 debt. Its after-tax interest rate is 6% ($6,000 ÷ $100,000 principal).

The formula for after-tax interest rate ($R_{D, \text{after-tax}}$) is:

$$R_{D, \text{after-tax}} = R_D(1 - \tau)$$

where R_D is the firm's pretax interest rate, and τ is the firm's income tax rate.

Borrowing from a bank or selling bonds to raise funds is known as "debt financing." Issuing stock to raise funds is known as "equity financing." Equity financing is an alternative to debt financing, but it is not free. When a firm sells equity, it sells ownership in the firm. The return earned by the new shareholders is a cost to the old shareholders. The rate of return earned by equity investors is found by adding dividends to the change in the stock price and then dividing by the initial stock price:

$$R_E = \frac{D + P_1 - P_0}{P_0}$$

where R_E is the return on the stock and also the cost of equity financing, D is the dollar amount of annual dividends per share paid by the firm to stockholders, P_0 is the stock price at the beginning of the year, and P_1 is the stock price at the end of the year.

For example, suppose the stock price is $100 per share at the beginning of the year and $112 at the end of the year, and the dividend is $8 per share. The stockholders would have earned a return of 20%, and this 20% is also the cost of equity financing:

$$R_E = \frac{\$8 + \$112 - \$100}{\$100} = 20\%$$

The capital asset pricing model (CAPM) is often used to estimate a firm's cost of equity financing. The idea behind the CAPM is that the rate of return demanded by equity investors will be a function of the risk of the equity, where risk is measured by a variable beta (β). According to the CAPM, β and cost of equity financing are related by the following equation:

$$R_E = R_F + \beta(R_M - R_F)$$

R_F is a risk-free interest rate, such as a Treasury bill rate, and R_M is the expected return for the stock market as a whole. For example, suppose the expected annual return to the overall stock market is 12%, and the Treasury bill rate is 4%. If a stock has a β of 2, then its cost of equity financing would be 20%, computed as follows:

$$R_E = 4\% + [2 \times (12\% - 4\%)] = 20\%$$

Analysts often use the Standard & Poor's 500 index stock portfolio as a proxy for the entire stock market when estimating the expected market return. The βs for publicly traded firms are available from a wide variety of sources, such as Bloomberg, Standard & Poor's, or the many companies that provide equity research reports. How β is computed and the theory behind the CAPM are beyond the scope of this chapter, but the textbooks listed in the bibliography to this chapter provide excellent coverage.

Weighted Average Cost of Capital

Most firms use a combination of both equity and debt financing to raise money for new projects. When financing comes from two sources, the appropriate discount rate is an average of the two financing rates. If most of the financing is debt, then debt should have greater weight in the average. Similarly, the weight given to equity should reflect how much of the financing is from equity. The resulting number, the weighted average cost of capital (WACC), reflects the firm's true cost of raising funds for the project:

$$WACC = W_E R_E + W_D[R_D(1 - \tau)]$$

where W_E is the proportion of the financing that is equity, W_D is the proportion of the financing that is debt, R_E is the cost of equity financing, R_D is the pretax cost of debt financing, and τ is the tax rate.

For example, suppose a firm acquires 70% of the funds needed for a project by selling stock. The remaining 30% of financing comes from borrowing. The cost of equity financing is 20%, the pretax cost of debt financing is 10%, and the tax rate is 40%. The weighted average cost of capital would then be 15.8%, computed as follows:

$$WACC = (0.7 \times 20\%) + 0.3[10\% \times (1 - 40\%)] = 15.8\%$$

This 15.8% rate should then be used for discounting the project cash flows.

Most often the choice of the discount rate is beyond the authority of the project manager. Top management will determine some threshold discount rate and dictate that it is the rate that must be used to assess all projects. When this is the policy, the rate is usually the firm's WACC with an additional margin added to compensate for the natural optimism of project proponents. A higher WACC makes NPV lower, and this biases management toward rejecting projects.

The Effects of Leverage

Leverage refers to the amount of debt financing used. The greater the ratio of debt to equity in the financing mix, the greater the leverage. The following example illustrates how leverage impacts the returns generated by a project. Suppose we have two companies that both manufacture scooters. One company is called NoDebt Inc., and the other is called SomeDebt Inc. As you might guess from its name, NoDebt never carries debt. SomeDebt is financed with equal parts debt and equity. Neither company knows whether the economy will be good or bad next year, but they can make projections contingent on the state of the economy. Exhibit 6.6 presents balance sheet and income statement data for the two companies for each possible business environment.

Each company has $1 million of assets. Therefore, the value of NoDebt's equity is $1 million, since debt plus equity must equal assets—the balance sheet equality. Since SomeDebt is financed with an equal mix of debt and equity, its debt must be worth $500,000, and its equity must also be worth $500,000. Aside from capital structure—that is, the mix of debt and equity used to finance the companies—the two firms are identical. In good times, both companies make $1 million in sales. In bad times, sales fall to $200,000. Cost of goods sold is always 50% of sales. Selling, administrative, and general

Exhibit 6.6   Performance of NoDebt Inc. and SomeDebt Inc.

	NoDebt, Inc. ($1,000s)		SomeDebt, Inc. ($1,000s)	
	Good Times	**Bad Times**	**Good Times**	**Bad Times**
Assets	$1,000	$1,000	$1,000	$1,000
Debt	0	0	500	500
Equity	1,000	1,000	500	500
Revenue	$1,000	$ 200	$1,000	$ 200
COGS	500	100	500	100
SAG	50	50	50	50
EBIT	450	50	450	50
Interest	0	0	50	50
EBT	450	50	400	0
Tax (40%)	180	20	160	0
Net earnings	$ 270	$ 30	$ 240	$ 0
ROA	45.0%	5.0%	45.0%	5.0%
ROE	27.0%	3.0%	48.0%	0.0%

expenses are a constant $50,000. For simplicity we assume there is no depreciation. Earnings before interest and taxes (EBIT) is thus $450,000 for both companies in good times, and $50,000 for both in bad times. So far, this example illustrates an important lesson about leverage: Leverage has no impact on EBIT. If we define return on assets (ROA) as EBIT divided by assets, leverage has no impact on ROA.[1]

If the pretax interest rate is 10%, however, then SomeDebt must pay $50,000 of interest on its outstanding $500,000 of debt, regardless of whether business is good or bad. NoDebt, of course, pays no interest. Because this is a standard income statement, not a capital budgeting cash flow computation, we must account for interest. EBT (earnings before taxes, which is the same thing as taxable income) for NoDebt is the same as its EBIT: $450,000 in good times and $50,000 in bad times. For SomeDebt, however, EBT will be $50,000 less in both states: $400,000 in good times and zero in bad times. Income tax is 40% of EBT, so it must be $180,000 for NoDebt in good times, $20,000 for NoDebt in bad times, $160,000 for SomeDebt in good times, and zero for SomeDebt in bad times. Here we see the second important lesson about leverage: Leverage reduces taxes.

Net earnings is EBT minus taxes. For NoDebt, net earnings is $270,000 in good times and $30,000 in bad times. For SomeDebt, net earnings is $240,000 in good times and zero in bad times. Return on equity (ROE) equals net earnings divided by equity. ROE is the profits earned by the equity investors as a function of their equity investment. If, as in this example, there is no depreciation, no changes in net working capital, and no capital expenditures, then net earnings would equal the cash flow received by equity investors, and ROE would be that year's cash return on their equity investment. Notice that ROE for NoDebt is 27% in good times and 3% in bad times. ROE for SomeDebt is much more volatile: 48% in good times and 0% in bad times. This is the third and most important lesson to be learned from this example: For the equity investors, leverage makes the good times better and the bad times worse. One student of mine, upon hearing this, exclaimed, "Leverage is a lot like beer!"

Because leverage increases the riskiness of the cash flows to equity investors, leverage increases the cost of equity capital. But for moderate amounts of leverage, the impact of the tax shield on the cost of debt financing overwhelms the rising cost of equity financing, and leverage reduces the WACC. Economists Franco Modigliani and Merton Miller were each awarded the Nobel Prize in economics (in 1985 and 1990, respectively) for work that included research on this very issue. Modigliani and Miller proved that in a world where there are no taxes and no bankruptcy costs the WACC is unaffected by leverage. What about the real world, in which taxes and bankruptcy exist? What we learn from their result, known as the Modigliani-Miller irrelevance theorem, is that as leverage is increased WACC falls because of the tax savings, but eventually WACC starts to rise again due to the rising probability of bankruptcy costs. The choice of debt versus equity financing must balance these countervailing concerns, and the optimal mix of debt and equity depends on the specific details of the proposed project.

Divisional versus Firm Cost of Capital

Suppose the beer company is thinking about opening a restaurant. The risk inherent in the restaurant business is much greater than the risk of the beer brewing business. Suppose the WACC for the brewery has historically been 20%, but the WACC for stand-alone restaurants is 30%. What discount rate should be used for the proposed restaurant project?

Considerable research, both theoretical and empirical, has been applied to this question, and the consensus is that the 30% restaurant WACC should be used. A discount rate must be appropriate for the risk and characteristics of the project, not the risk and characteristics of the parent company. The reason for this surprising result is that the volatility of the project's cash flows and their correlation with other risky cash flows are the paramount risk factors in determining cost of capital, not simply the likelihood of default on the company's obligations. The financial analyst should estimate the project's cost of capital as if it were a new restaurant company, not an extension of the beer company. The analyst should examine other restaurant companies to determine the appropriate β, cost of equity capital, cost of debt financing, financing mix, and WACC.

Other Decision Rules

Some firms do not use the NPV decision rule as the criterion for deciding whether a project should be accepted or rejected. At least three alternative decision rules are commonly used. As we shall see, however, the alternative rules are flawed. If the objective of the firm is to maximize investors' wealth, the alternative rules sometimes fail to identify projects that further this end and in fact sometimes lead to acceptance of projects that destroy wealth. We examine the payback period rule, the discounted payback rule, and the internal rate of return rule.

The Payback Period

The payback period rule stipulates that cash flows must completely repay the initial outlay prior to some cutoff payback period. For example, if the payback cutoff were three years, the payback rule would require that all projects return the initial outlay within three years. Projects that satisfy the rule would be accepted; projects that do not satisfy the rule would be rejected.

For example, suppose a project initially costs $100,000 to set up. Suppose the cash flows in the first three years are $34,000 each. The sum of the first three years' cash flows is $102,000. This is greater than the initial $100,000 outlay, so this project would be accepted under the payback period rule.

There are two major problems with the payback period rule. First, it does not take into account the time value of money. Second, it ignores what happens after the payback. Because of these two failings, the payback rule sometimes accepts projects that should be rejected and rejects projects that should be accepted. A project that costs $100,000 to set up and returns $34,000 for three years would have a negative NPV at a 10% discount rate, since the $102,000 in deferred cash flows is worth less than the initial $100,000 outlay. Yet the project would be adopted under the payback rule criterion.

Consider a project that costs $100,000 to set up, returns nothing for three years, and then returns $10 million in year 4. This project would have a positive NPV at any reasonable discount rate, yet would be rejected by the payback rule. The rejection stems from the fact that the payback rule is myopic; that is, it fails to take account of what happens after the payback period. Empirical studies have shown that, contrary to popular perceptions, stockholders do reward firms that take the longer-view, NPV approach to project analysis.

The Discounted Payback Period

An improved, though still flawed, variant of the payback period rule is the discounted payback period rule. The discounted payback rule stipulates that the discounted cash flows from a project over some payback horizon must exceed the initial outlay. If the horizon were three years, the rule would require that the discounted present value of a project's first three years of cash flows be greater than the initial outlay.

Although this rule explicitly takes into account the time value of money, it still ignores what might happen after the payback horizon. A project may be rejected even if the expected cash flows from the fourth year and beyond are very large, as might be the case in a research and development project. A project might be accepted even if there is a large cleanup cost that would have to be paid after the payback horizon. Although the rule incorporates the time value of money, it is still shortsighted.

One might conjecture that the payback and discounted payback rules are popular since they are easy to apply. Yet, this ease is paid for in lost opportunities for creating wealth and occasional misallocation of resources into wasteful projects.

Internal Rate of Return

A project's internal rate of return (IRR) is the interest rate that the project essentially pays out. It is the interest rate that a bank would have to pay so that the project's cash outflows would exactly finance its cash inflows. Instead of investing money in the project, one could invest money in a bank paying a rate of interest equal to the project's IRR and receive the same cash flows. One can think of the IRR as an interest rate that a project pays to its investors. For example, a project that costs $100,000 to set up but then returns $10,000 every year forever has an IRR of 10%. If a project costs $100,000 to set up and then ends the following year when it pays back $105,000, that project would have an IRR of 5%. The IRR is the rate of return generated by the project.

Most financial calculators and spreadsheet programs have functions that find IRR using cash flows supplied by the user. For example, consider a project that requires a cash outflow of $100 in year 0 and produces cash inflows of $40 for each of four years. To find the IRR using a financial calculator, one must specify that the present value equals –$100, annual payments equal +$40, and n, the number of years, equals 4. The present value and the annuity payments must have opposite signs in order to indicate to the calculator that the direction of cash flows has changed. The last step is to issue the instruction for the calculator to find the interest rate that makes these cash flows make sense. The answer is the IRR, which in this example is 21.9%. For the beer brewery cash flows specified in Exhibit 6.4, the IRR is 21.7%.

Most TVOM problems involve specifying an interest rate and some of the cash flows and then instructing the calculator to find the missing cash flow variable—either present value, future value, or annual payment. IRR calculations involve specifying all of the cash flows and instructing the calculator to find the missing interest rate.

The IRR also happens to be the discount rate at which the project's cash flows have an NPV of zero. This relationship can be used to verify that an IRR is correct. First, calculate NPV at a guessed IRR. If the resulting NPV is zero, the guessed IRR is in fact correct. If not, guess again. The IRR eventually can be found by trial and error.

For example, consider again the case in which the initial cash outflow is $100, followed by four annual cash inflows of $40. To use the trial and error method, one should calculate the NPV at a guessed discount rate. When we find the discount rate at which the NPV is zero, we will have identified the IRR. If we guess 10%, the NPV is $26.79. Apparently, the guessed discount rate is too low. A higher discount rate will give a lower NPV. So guess again, maybe 30% this time. At 30%, the NPV is –$13.35. Apparently, 30% is too high. The next guess should be lower. Following this algorithm, the IRR of 21.9% will eventually be located.

The IRR rule stipulates that a project should be accepted if its IRR is greater than some agreed-on threshold, and rejected otherwise. That is, to be accepted, a project must produce percentage returns higher than some company-mandated minimum. Often the minimum threshold is set equal to the firm's cost of capital. If the IRR beats the WACC, then the project is accepted. If the IRR is less than the WACC, the project is rejected.

For example, suppose a project costs $1,000 to set up, and then is expected to produce a one-time cash inflow of $1,100 one year later. The IRR of this project is 10%. If the company imposes a minimum threshold of 20%, this project will be rejected. If the company's threshold is 8%, this project will be accepted. We saw earlier that the brewery project IRR is 21.7%. If the agreed threshold is the brewery's 20% WACC, then the IRR rule would indicate that the project should be accepted.

The IRR rule is appealing in that it *usually* gives the same guidance as the NPV rule when the threshold equals the company's cost of capital. If a project's IRR exceeds the firm's cost of capital, the project must be creating wealth for the firm. The project would produce returns greater than the firm's financing costs, and the spread would be added wealth for the investors. Unfortunately, the IRR rule frequently breaks down and gives misleading advice.

The IRR rule suffers from two flaws. First, it ignores the relative sizes of alternative projects. For example, suppose a firm had to choose between two projects, each of which lasts one year. The first project costs $10,000 to set up but then pays back $16,000 one year later. The second project costs $100,000 to set up but pays back $120,000 one year later. Clearly, the IRR of the first project is 60%, and the IRR of the second project is 20%. On the basis of IRR, the first project seems to be superior. However, if the firm's cost of capital is 10%, the first project has an NPV of $4,454, whereas the second project has an NPV of $9,091. Clearly the second project creates more wealth. The first project has a higher rate of return but on a smaller investment. The second project's lower return on a larger scale is a better use of the firm's scarce managerial resources.

The second flaw in the IRR rule stems from the fact that a given project may have multiple IRRs. The IRR is not always a single, unique value. Consider a two-year project. Initially the project costs $1,000 to set up. In the first year it returns $3,000. In the second year there is a cleanup costing $2,000. It is easy to verify that 0% is one correct value for the firm's IRR: Discounting at 0% and adding up all the discounted cash flows gives an NPV of zero. Notice, however, that 100% is another correct value for the IRR: Discounting all cash flows at 100% per year also gives an NPV of zero. If the firm's cost of capital is 10%, should this project be accepted or rejected? Ten percent is greater than 0%, but less than 100%. Only by computing the NPV at the discount rate of 10% do we find out that this project has a positive NPV of $74 and so should be accepted. When a project has two or more IRRs, the analyst would have no way of knowing which was the correct one to use if he or she did not also compute the NPV and apply the NPV rule. If the analyst computed only the IRR of 100%, she or he would reject this valuable project.

It turns out that a project will have one IRR for every change in sign in its cash flows. If a project has an initial outlay and then subsequently all cash flows are positive inflows, there will be one unique IRR. If a project has an initial outlay, a string of positive inflows, and then a cleanup cost at the end, there will be two IRRs since the direction of cash flow changed twice. If there is an initial outlay, a positive inflow, another net outflow during a retooling year, followed by a positive inflow, the three sign changes would produce three different IRRs. The IRR rule would provide little guidance in such a scenario and could possibly lead to an incorrect judgment of the project's worth.

In situations where its two fatal flaws are not at issue, the IRR rule gives the same result as the NPV rule. If the project's cash flows change sign only once, there is no problem of multiple IRRs. If all competing projects are of the same magnitude or if there is only one project under consideration, the size issue will not be a problem, either. In such a situation, the firm would be justified in selecting the project on the basis of IRR.

One circumstance in which alternative projects are of equal size and cash flows change direction only once is in the analysis of alternative mortgage plans. These days, a person financing a home may choose from a multitude of mortgage plans. A variety of payment schedules are available, and some plans charge points in exchange for lower monthly payments. Since all mortgages considered by the home buyer finance the same house, the size issue is not a concern. Also, the typical home mortgage involves a cash inflow at the beginning and then only cash outflows over the period when the borrower must pay back the loan. Thus, there is only one sign change among the cash flows. Borrowers can thus compare mortgages on the basis of their IRRs. They should calculate the cash flows over the horizon during which they expect to pay back the mortgage, and should then choose the lowest-IRR mortgage from among those whose monthly payments are affordable. The annual percentage rate (APR) quoted by mortgage companies is the IRR of the mortgage calculated after factoring in points and origination fees and assuming the mortgage will not be prepaid.

Innovations in Capital Budgeting

While a general consensus has been reached that wealth maximization is the objective of optimal capital budgeting, the tools for measuring wealth creation and the indicators that business policy is succeeding at that goal continue to evolve. The fact that new paradigms are still being invented tells us that NPV is not the last word in capital budgeting. Analysts and investors are constantly looking for better tools for making long-range capital decisions. An approach known as Economic Value Added (EVA®) was introduced by the consulting firm Stern Stewart & Company, which owns the term as a registered trademark. Another advanced paradigm known as "real options" is complex but gaining traction.

Economic Value Added

Economic Value Added (EVA®) is an accounting metric that aims to capture how much wealth a company creates in a given year. EVA is the amount of invested capital multiplied by the spread between the company's return on invested capital and its cost of capital. EVA aims to measure wealth creation in a given year rather than over the life of a project. EVA's advocates advise managers to adopt projects that maximize EVA and manage projects so as to maximize EVA each year. Managers should monitor projects and make modifications, award incentives, and impose penalties to continuously boost EVA.

Real Options

The real options paradigm seeks to measure not only the value of a project's forecast cash flows but also the value of strategic flexibility that a project creates for a company. For example, suppose a company is contemplating an initiative to market its wares on the Internet. The forecast cash flows may be weak, but establishing a presence on the Internet may be valuable in that it wards off potential competition and creates opportunities that can later be exploited. The option to expand or the flexibility to later pursue a wide range of initiatives is captured using the real option paradigm, whereas the value of these options is usually missed completely in the standard NPV approach. The real options paradigm entails identifying the strategic options inherent in a proposed project and then valuing them using modern mathematical option-pricing formulas. If the value of a proposed project complete with its real options is greater than the cost of initiating the project, then the project should be given the go-ahead.

Summary and Conclusions

Capital budgeting is the process by which a firm chooses which projects to adopt and which to reject. It is an extremely important endeavor, because it ultimately shapes the firm and the economy as a whole. The fundamental principle underlying capital budgeting is that a firm should adopt the projects that create the most wealth. Net present value (NPV) measures how much wealth a project creates. NPV is computed by forecasting a project's cash flows, discounting those cash flows at the project's weighted average cost of capital (WACC), and then summing the discounted cash flows. The cost of capital used to discount the cash flows is a function of the riskiness of the project and the financing mix selected.

Measures such as payback period, discounted payback period, and internal rate of return (IRR) give rise to alternative project decision rules. These rules, however, are flawed and can potentially lead a company to adopt an inferior project or reject the optimal one. Economic value added (EVA) is a metric that helps managers choose among projects and then manage the projects once started. The real options paradigm is an innovation that aims to capture the value of strategic flexibility created by projects.

The tools of capital budgeting can be applied to large-scale corporate decisions, such as whether to build a new plant, but they can also be applied to smaller personal decisions, such as which home mortgage program to choose or whether to invest in new office equipment. Learning the language and tools of capital budgeting can help entrepreneurs better pitch their projects to investors or to the top executives at their own firms. Whether the decision is large or small, the fundamental principle is the same: A good project is one that is ultimately worth more than it costs to set up and thereby generates wealth.

Note

1. This is one definition of ROA; another definition is net earnings divided by total assets. Given the second definition, ROA would be affected by leverage.

For Further Reading

Amram, Martha, and Nalin Kulatilaka, *Real Options: Managing Strategic Investment in an Uncertain World* (Boston: Harvard Business School Press, 2000).

Bodie, Zvi, and Robert C. Merton, *Finance* (Upper Saddle River, NJ: Prentice Hall, 2000).

Brealey, Richard A., and Stewart C. Myers, *Principles of Corporate Finance* (New York: Irwin/McGraw-Hill, 2000).

Brigham, Eugene F., Michael C. Ehrhardt, and Louis C. Gapenski, *Financial Management: Theory and Practice* (New York: Dryden Press, 1999).

Dixit, Avinash K., and Robert S. Pindyck, "The Options Approach to Capital Investment," *Harvard Business Review* 73, no. 3 (May/June 1995): 105–115.

Emery, Douglas R., and John D. Finnerty, *Corporate Financial Management* (Upper Saddle River, NJ: Prentice Hall, 1997).

Higgins, Robert C., *Analysis for Financial Management* (New York: Irwin/McGraw-Hill, 2001).

Ross, Stephen A., Randolph W. Westerfield, and Jeffrey Jaffe, *Corporate Finance* (New York: Irwin/McGraw-Hill, 1999).

Trigeorgis, Lenos, *Real Options: Managerial Flexibility and Strategy in Resource Allocation* (Cambridge, MA: MIT Press, 1997).

7

Global Finance

Michael J. Riley

What does it matter that one invests, borrows, sells, or buys in foreign countries? Isn't it all the same?

Look at the following four case studies and two theories that can be at least a little helpful, and you will likely answer that this is understandable but risky. We start with a personal example, because many people can relate to complex subjects more easily on a personal level. The remaining examples are taken from real corporate situations and modified to disguise the companies.

Currency Exchange Rates: A Case of Individual Investing

Let's start with an example created to make a point. In May 2008, Rodney decided that rates on U.S. certificates of deposit (CDs) were too low and the time was right to invest in a bank in England. He expected to earn 4% on his money in six months (8% annually) and ended up with a loss. He discussed what went wrong with his dad.

Rodney: I can't understand what went wrong. I lost money and I thought it was a sure thing. I invested $10,000 in a six-month CD on May 31, 2008, that promised a 4% return.

Dad: The promised return of 4% for six months works out to be 8% per year. That was far above what CDs paid in the United States. Didn't you get the interest promised?

Rodney: I don't think so. My IRA statement said that my investment earned £202.45, which is 4%. Yet my statement also said that my account was worth only $8,087.95 on December 1, 2008. If that is true, what happened to the interest? How could I have lost that much on the currency exchange?

Dad: Let's take a look logically. The first thing is to create a time line that shows what you paid and what you got back. I always show cash outflow as negative and cash inflow as positive. That makes it simple to remember. When someone pays me, it is positive. When I have to pay someone else, it is negative.

We'll put months across the top and cash flows under the line (Exhibit 7.1). Your investment declined in value by 19.12% from $10,000 to $8,097.95.

Rodney: Okay, now I see that I lost 19.12% on my investment. That is a lot to lose on a sure thing in just six months. What went wrong?

Exhibit 7.1   Time line in dollars.

Month	0	1	2	3	4	5	6
Cash flow	($10,000)						$8,097.95

Dad: Before I answer that, did you check the history of the exchange rates between the dollar ($) and the pound (£)? The exchange rate is the amount of currency in one country that can be purchased by one unit of currency in another country. There is a small fee built in for the bank or dealer, but we will ignore that for our purposes.

Rodney: Yes, I looked on OANDA.com at www.oanda.com and found the history. Between January 1, 2007, and May 29, 2008, one U.S. dollar would buy an average of 0.50168 pounds. The range was from 0.47250 to 0.52130. When I moved my dollars to England, the bank gave me a rate of 0.50613 pounds per dollar. It seemed to be low-risk.

Dad: Of course there are other sites, like www.x-rates.com. Yahoo!, Google, and MSN also have currency converters. But I usually use OandA.com, too.

First of all, most currencies' exchange rates are quoted the way you just did: the amount of foreign currency that $1 would buy. But for pounds, people usually refer to the reverse: the number of dollars that it would take to buy one pound. Looking at it that way will make you consistent with the rest of the world. On May 31, 2008, that rate was 1.97578. It would cost $1.97578 to buy £1.00. So your $10,000 should have bought you about £5,061.29.

By December 1, the rate had changed to $1.53654 per £1.00. Your £5,061.29 before interest could be translated into dollars to get a worth of $7,776.88. You lost $2,223.12 or 22% of your initial investment just from the movement of currency. That is a 22% loss. Of course the interest that you earned lessened your loss.

Rodney: I feel terrible and very foolish.

Dad: If it makes you feel any better, you are not the first, nor will you be the last, to focus on the interest and lose sight of the principal. I'll tell you a story later about how the treasurer of a global company did the same and it cost the company hundreds of millions of dollars. He did not bother to do a time line. A time line is a very simple picture, but it can make a complex transaction much easier to understand. If you do it carefully, you will avoid a lot of problems.

Now, let's use that time line and see the cash flows in British pounds (Exhibit 7.2).

Now you can see the interest received in pounds. You did receive the promised 4% or £202.45. If you were in England, this would be a good return. Now let's put in the currency translation and we see that because of the change in currency exchange rates you lost $1,912.05 instead of gaining the $400 you had planned on (Exhibit 7.3).

Exhibit 7.2   Time line in pounds.

Month	0	1	2	3	4	5	6
Cash flow:							
Investment (principal)	(£5,061.29)						
Interest							£ 202.45
Return of principal							£5,061.29
Total							£5,263.74

Exhibit 7.3   Time line in dollars and pounds.

Month	0	1	2	3	4	5	6
Cash flow:							
Investment $	($10,000.00)						
Exchange rate, May 31, 2008	$1.97578 per £						
Investment £	(£5,061.29)						£5,061.29
Interest							£202.45
Principal plus interest							£5,263.74
Exchange rate, December 1, 2008							$1.53654 per £
Value in $							$8,087.95

Rodney: Okay, I see what happened, but how could I know that I would lose money?

Dad: Unfortunately, you can't know what will happen to currency exchange rates. There are theories that seem to work some of the time, but just like investors in the stock market, even the professionals get surprised from time to time.

Let me make the point about the time line. It is a simple device to make the complex seem easy. People who simply plug in formulas often make bad mistakes.

As an exercise, imagine the reverse situation. Assume that you were in England and decided to invest in a U.S. bank. Let's keep the initial investment the same. A 30-year-old teacher in London spends £5,061.29 to get $10,000 in U.S. dollars. He invests at only 2% interest and expects to end with $10,200. Why would he do that you may ask. One reason could be that he planned to take a Christmas vacation to Disney World and wanted to avoid any risk that his money would not cover his planned expenses.

By the way, this risk-avoidance measure can be used by almost anyone with the help of a bank. If you plan to make a purchase in another country, you can invest in anticipation of making the purchase. This avoids the risk of exchange rate movement. It also eliminates any gain from exchange rate movement. As you see, if your currency weakens, it buys less in a foreign country. If it strengthens, it buys more.

Let's assume that the vacation gets canceled and he decides to bring his investment dollars back to England. Now translate the investment to dollars at

Exhibit 7.4   Time line in pounds and dollars.

Month	0	1	2	3	4	5	6
Cash flow:							
Investment £	(£5,061.29)						
Exchange rate, May 31, 2008	$1.97578 per £						
Investment $	($10,000.00)						$10,000.00
Interest							$200.00
Principal plus interest							$10,200.00
Exchange rate, December 1, 2008							$1.53654 per £
Value in £							£6,638.29

$1.53654 per £1.00. You get £6,638.29. Divide by the original investment and get 131%. That is a 31% return. In both cases, the movement in the exchange rate is the major force behind the return that the investor receives. Currency moved against you and you lost 19%. The same movement earned a 31% return for the Londoner: £6,638.29 divided by £5,061.29 = 1.31 or 131%.

Let's do our time line again, but this time from the perspective of someone in London (Exhibit 7.4).

Rodney: Now I see what is happening. Exchange rate movement can make a big difference in the value of an investment even in a short period of time. Sometimes the rate is stable, and sometimes it moves a lot.

Dad: Right! You get it. By now you are beginning to see the disadvantage and perhaps the advantage of converting currency and investing in another country. Of course, things were not always this way. Most of the major countries operated with fixed exchange rates set by the Bretton Woods Agreement concluded in 1944. This functioned well for over 40 years. (By the way, Bretton Woods is a resort town in the shadow of Mount Washington in New Hampshire.) One advantage of fixed exchange rates is that they function as one currency. You do not have to worry about exchange rates in the United States—your dollar is the same in Maine as it is in Alaska, Texas, or even New York City.

Lesson: There can be significant risk for an investment due only to the potential change of exchange rates. There are periods of little movement and periods of strong movements.

One Currency: European Union and Eurozone

One reason many nations in Europe adopted the euro was to eliminate the risk and complexity of varying exchange rates. The euro avoids the need to change currency when you drive from Italy to France to Germany. It allows an investor in Ireland to invest in Austria without worrying about currency movements. You can see why this is an advantage, especially in small countries like Malta. Countries with the euro as their official currency are in the eurozone.

As a matter of fact, the following nations have adopted the euro as their official currency:

Austria	Germany	Malta
Belgium	Greece	Netherlands
Cyprus	Ireland	Portugal
Finland	Italy	Slovenia
France	Luxembourg	Spain

There are a number of countries in the European Union that share open borders and free trade but have not adopted the euro. As you know, Great Britain is one.

The countries in the European Union (EU) include the 15 eurozone countries and 12 other countries. This is a list of countries in the European Union:

Austria	Germany	Netherlands
Belgium	Greece	Poland
Bulgaria	Hungary	Portugal
Cyprus	Ireland	Romania
Czech Republic	Italy	Slovakia
Denmark	Latvia	Slovenia
Estonia	Lithuania	Spain
Finland	Luxembourg	Sweden
France	Malta	United Kingdom

There are about 300 million people in the nations that have officially adopted the euro and 500 million in the European Union (EU). The EU is designed to allow the free flow of goods, labor, services, and transit. In practice there are still some obstacles to the complete implementation of this concept.

You might notice that Switzerland is not on either list. That country has chosen to maintain its tradition of independence and neutrality.

Rodney: If there are such advantages, why don't all the countries in the EU adopt the euro?

Dad: Some countries have tried. They put the prospect to a vote and the people rejected the euro. Perhaps it is national pride. Other countries have leaders who are concerned about the promises made in the various countries' versions of Social Security. Unlike the United States, the population is declining in several countries and, just as here, the system is underfunded. Also, governments have different policies about taxing, spending, military expenditures, and international conflicts.

For now, take a look at the exchange rate between the dollar and the euro at the end of the month specified (Exhibit 7.5).

This is quite a large range. In December 2001 $1,000 would buy €1,289. By June 2008, it would take $2,036 to purchase the same amount of euros.

Let's do the math. Divide the euro amount by the exchange rate to get the dollar amount (Exhibit 7.6).

Exhibit 7.5   Amount of euros (€) purchased by one dollar ($).

Date	Exchange Rate	Date	Exchange Rate
12/98	0.857	6/04	0.828
6/99	0.969	12/04	0.733
12/99	0.996	6/05	0.829
6/00	1.051	12/05	0.844
12/00	1.062	6/06	0.797
6/01	1.178	12/06	0.758
12/01	1.289	6/07	0.742
6/02	1.009	12/07	0.679
12/02	0.954	6/08	0.633
6/03	0.875	12/08	0.710
12/03	0.797		

Source: FXHistory © 1997–2008 by OANDA Corporation.

Exhibit 7.6   Conversions between dollars and euros.

Date	Dollars	Exchange Rate	Euros
12/01	$1,000	€1.289	€1,289
6/08	$2,036	€0.633	€1,289

Lesson: One currency can eliminate some country risks, but the exchange rate risk still exists with other countries. Also, there may be added risks of different economic policies of countries within the European Union.

Currency Exchange Rates: A Case in China with Country Risk

Dad: Let's look at an investment from a business point of view.

Consider the following case: A multinational corporation needs to invest in many countries and for periods of many years. We will look at an investment in China. There is a long history, but we will look only at relatively recent background. I'll pick a period with interesting times. Let's assume that the initial investment was made on October 23, 1995.

China has been a special case because the government has taken steps to keep its currency stable compared to the U.S. dollar.

China is a manufacturing superpower. Assume that you are CFO of a small engine manufacturer, Small Co., looking to build a $100 million plant in China. Let's assume that your company requires a return of 10% on its investments in the United States and 16% on its investments in China. We will discuss the reasons for the 16% required return later in this section.

Before you invest, your (simplified) balance sheet might look like Exhibit 7.7.

We pick a date of October 23, 1995, for the investment, and your balance sheet looks like Exhibit 7.8 at the end of October:

Exhibit 7.7   Small Co. balance sheet, September 30, 1995 (in millions).

Assets		Liabilities and Equity	
Cash	$100	Debt	$ 0
Plant	0	Equity	100
Total	$100	Total	$100

Exhibit 7.8   Small Co. balance sheet, October 31, 1995 (in millions).

Assets		Liabilities and Equity	
Cash	$ 0	Debt	$ 0
Plant	100	Equity	100
Total	$100	Total	$100

Actually, the value of the investment will be in Chinese yuan renminbi (CNY), the currency of China. The accountants will convert that investment to dollars at the prevailing exchange rate at the end of each accounting period. If the $100 million were invested in China on October 31, 1995, it would buy CNY 831.490 million, and that would become the value of the plant. The exchange rate was CNY 8.31490 to one U.S. dollar on October 31, 1995. The balance sheet is important because public companies will report any gains or losses on investments on their income statements. So both the balance sheet and the income statement will change as a result of exchange rate movements. Of course, the major reason for this investment is to obtain goods for sale in the United States and in other countries at lower prices. Unlike Rodney's investment in England, the government of China had a policy to hold the exchange rate constant with the dollar. This effectively created one currency for China and the United States for 10 years. This was a huge advantage to companies doing business with China.

Look at the exchange rate of the yuan to the dollar in Exhibit 7.9.

As you can see, there has been a 10-year period of very stable exchange rates. Let's value your $100 million plant on December 31, 2004. Recall that the plant was actually valued at CNY 831.490 million on October 31, 1995. Assume no depreciation and no plant additions to allow us to see what happened because of exchange rates. We see that CNY 831.490 million divided by the December 31, 2004, exchange rate of 8.28650 converts to $100.34 million (Exhibit 7.10).

The change since 1995 is so small as to be insignificant. I'm sure Rodney wishes that his investment in England had had this stability. However, from 2005 onward, the yuan has strengthened against the dollar. The effect from a change in the rate from 8.3 to 6.9 has been to raise prices of Chinese goods by 20%, assuming that all else is equal. By now you should be able to tell what happened to the value of the investment. Since the yuan increased in value, the investment translated to dollars increased in value. Now let's convert the value of CNY 831.490 million as of December 31, 2008. The dollar amount becomes $121 million (Exhibit 7.11). Now we are seeing significant change, although it is helpful to the accounting statements.

Exhibit 7.9 Exchange rate: Number of Chinese yuan renminbi per U.S. dollar.

Date	Exchange Rate
10/31/1995	8.31490
12/31/1995	8.31740
12/31/1996	8.29820
12/31/1997	8.27960
12/31/1998	8.27890
12/31/1999	8.28033
12/31/2000	8.27823
12/31/2001	8.28670
12/31/2002	8.28710
12/31/2003	8.28670
12/31/2004	8.28650
12/31/2005	8.07338
12/31/2006	7.81750
12/31/2007	7.31410
12/31/2008	6.85419

Source: FXHistory © 1997–2008 by OANDA Corporation.

Exhibit 7.10 Small Co. balance sheet, December 31, 2004 (in millions).

Assets		Liabilities and Equity	
Cash	$ 0	Debt	$ 0
Plant	100.3	Equity	100.3
Total	$100.3	Total	$100.3

Exhibit 7.11 Small Co. balance sheet, December 31, 2008 (in millions).

Assets		Liabilities and Equity	
Cash	$ 0	Debt	$ 0
Plant	121	Equity	121
Total	$121	Total	$121

The negative side is that this same movement increased the cost of the engines that Small Co. was exporting from China and importing into the United States. Just as the assets rose in value by 21%, the cost of the engines also rose by this same 21%. If we look at a five-year history in January 2001 at OANDA.com, we would see the summary shown in Exhibit 7.12.

This table shows the success of the government of China in keeping the exchange rate stable. Of course, history can be a guide but not a guarantee of future events.

Exhibit 7.12   Summary of exchange rates: Chinese yuan per dollar.

Average (1,828 days)	8.28766
High	8.33550
Low	8.23710

Source: FXHistory © 1997–2008 by OANDA Corporation.

We could do a time line of cash flows if we had more information. For now let's make some points that do not require us to make a time line.

If Small Co. were importing the engines into the United States and buying them for $25 each, they would have been free of exchange rate risk for 10 of the past 13 years. The price of manufacturing the engines would still be subject to inflation in China. The cost of raw materials, parts, and labor might have risen, but there was no cost escalation from the exchange rate until relatively recently. By 2008, the price would have increased to $30 each even if there was zero inflation in China.

Of course, other risks remained. Someone else could have invented a better process, and this is business risk. The United States could have imposed a tariff or tax on engine imports. Unrest in China could have been a problem. Another company could have reverse engineered your engine and gone into competition with Small Co.

Dad: What risks do you see, Rodney?

Rodney: Well, for a start, the leadership in China has changed and it is possible that the new leadership could be hostile to exports.

Dad: Good thinking. Country risk is one of the first things to consider. If history is any guide, countries are more likely to seize the assets of companies than they are to stop exports. Also, some countries limit imports to favor local industry. Oil- and gas-rich nations have been known to limit exports in an effort to raise the price.

There are other country risks: There could be a war or rebellion and the assets could be destroyed. The government may refuse to allow the repatriation of profits earned in the country. International bodies may ask for import/export restrictions to protest pollution or treatment of political prisoners.

Intellectual property is valued more highly in some countries than in others. A company with a secret manufacturing process will want to consider carefully where to locate its manufacturing operations. Contracts may be more readily enforceable in some countries and may be easily abrogated in other countries.

Some people break country risk into repatriation risk and political risk.

The risk that a company or person will not be able to freely move money out of a country is repatriation risk. This has been a significant problem in various countries historically. Often it is the first thing people worry about in doing business in other countries.

Political risk comes from changes in the government or culture of a country and can take many forms, as described earlier.

Regardless of the category, the question is: What risk is imposed by doing business in another country? And, as we will see later, the follow-on question is: What can be done to lessen the risk?

Exhibit 7.13   Small Co.'s evaluation of risk for China venture.

Risk	Level	Required Return
Repatriation	Very low	1.0%
Political	Moderate	3.0
Exchange rate	Low	2.0
WACC		10.0%
Total required return		16.0%

Exchange rate risk has been lessened as a result of Chinese government policy. However, even government policy sometimes must give way to practical reality. Although the exchange rate between the United States and China was stable for 10 years, the price of engines in comparison with the world market would vary based on the exchange rates between the United States and other countries. Exchange rate risk arises from unexpected changes in the exchange rates. It can dramatically change the effective price of a purchase. Looking at the yuan, the effective price of purchases manufactured in China rose 20% from 2005 to 2008 just due to the currency exchange rate.

Dealing with risk is typically done in two ways. The first is to increase the required return necessary to make the investment, and we will discuss that now. The second is to look for other ways to lessen the risk.

Companies calculate a weighted average cost of capital (WACC) and use this as the discount rate or hurdle rate when estimating the returns for an investment. When looking at an investment in another country, they should make an explicit decision to raise the rate of return required to take into account the risks we discussed earlier. Careful analysis of the proposed country is necessary.

In our example we might use something like Exhibit 7.13.

Our numbers are not the result of any careful study. They are chosen to simply make an example of what might be found. Ultimately numbers like these are the result of judgment after looking at all available information. Each of these risks seems small, but the chance of something unforeseen happening over 10 or 15 years is often much larger than one would estimate. There are ways to simulate what might happen. In any case, it is always good to ask, "What can go wrong?" The answer can be surprising.

Risk Minimization

One way to eliminate the exchange rate risk associated with the balance sheet is to borrow all or almost all of the funds in local currency. If the currency weakens, the value of the assets will decline and so will the value of the liabilities. The reverse is also true. In our China example, Small Co. could have borrowed the CNY 831.490 million in China. Since the assets and the liabilities are equal, there would be no effect on the equity of the parent from translating the values in the balance sheet to dollars.

Many companies look to find places to manufacture with very favorable conditions. This serves to minimize the risk of adverse currency movements. These advantages might include a significant cost savings over manufacturing in the home country, tax savings, having a skilled and stable workforce, and a culture of hospitality toward the nation making the investment.

Exhibit 7.14   Index of Economic Freedom 2008.

Free	80–100
Mostly free	70–80
Moderately free	60–70
Mostly unfree	50–60
Repressed	0–50

Source: www.heritage.org/research/features/index/countries.cfm.

The use of local partners can be a third way to help minimize the risk. Their investment can spread the risk of currency and perhaps, more important, can lower political risk. Often the right local partner is better able to deal with emerging situations that could have an impact on the project.

Therefore, it is important to understand the culture of the country. In some countries, business practices differ from the United States. Just as we leave tips for waitstaff, in some parts of the world it is expected that companies make payments to government officials in order to do business. The Foreign Corrupt Practices Act of 1978 makes it illegal for a U.S. company to pay a bribe. The local partner can often advise how to avoid situations that would put the venture into an unlawful situation. In some cases, this may mean forgoing an investment in a country that otherwise seems to hold great potential.

There is a practical reason as well as a legal reason for avoiding payments to officials. These officials may be resented by the local citizens. If there is a change in the government, companies closely associated with the prior political leadership may be penalized. From time to time, there are news stories about attacks on American businesspeople and companies in countries in political turmoil.

It is possible to find information on country risk by looking to the Heritage Foundation's Index of Economic Freedom (www.heritage.org). The following information comes from the 2008 index:

China has an overall score of 52.8%, which ranks it 126th in the world. This score rates China "mostly unfree." The U.S. score is 80.6%, which ranks it 5th and rated "free." Dead last, ranked 157th, is North Korea with a score of 3.0%. Exhibit 7.14 shows the categories of economic freedom, which put China's score into perspective. Clearly China has a long way to go before it can be rated "free" or even "mostly free."

Useful information from the World Bank on the ease of doing business in many different countries can be found at www.doingbusiness.org/documents/Press_Releases_08/DB_08_Oveview_English.pdf.

Also see the Index of Economic Freedom at www.heritage.org/research/features/index/chapters/pdf/index2008_execsum.pdf.

Lesson from China case: Even though the Chinese government has been very favorable to business with its exchange rate policies and openness, there can be significant risks that should be considered. These risks add to the rate of return required on any investment.

Local Partner: Robinson Investment Case

The Robinson Company is a U.S. firm that found a new way to process high-end coffee for use in upscale restaurants. It is considering a joint venture with CCB, a Colombian firm that grows and processes coffee beans. Robinson has a patent for its new coffee-processing method, and this is motivating the company to expand beyond importing coffee. Robinson plans to invest $20 million in the proposed joint venture (JV) project, which will help to finance CCB's production using the newly patented process.

The Colombian government offers to guarantee that all profits, after tax, can be repatriated into U.S. dollars, and it will guarantee that the exchange rate will be the same for five years as it was on the day of the contract signing. Robinson and CCB have agreed that all profits will be divided equally between the two companies.

The plan is to locate a new facility in the Free Trade Zone, which will make the venture free of Colombian income taxes. Otherwise the corporate income tax rate of 35% would apply. There is a 7% tax on dividends from subsidiaries to parent companies that will apply.

Robinson also pays a U.S. corporate income tax of 35%.

Robinson is aware that there is some political instability. The Central Intelligence Agency (CIA)'s *World Factbook* has the following publicly available information:

> Colombia's economy has experienced positive growth over the past five years despite a serious armed conflict. In fact, 2007 is regarded by policy makers and the private sector as one of the best economic years in recent history, after 2005. The economy continues to improve in part because of austere government budgets, focused efforts to reduce public debt levels, an export-oriented growth strategy, improved domestic security, and high commodity prices. Ongoing economic problems facing President Uribe include reforming the pension system, reducing high unemployment, and funding new exploration to offset declining oil production. The government's economic reforms and democratic security strategy, coupled with increased investment, have engendered a growing sense of confidence in the economy. However, the business sector continues to be concerned about failure of the U.S. Congress to approve the signed FTA (Free Trade Agreement).

> *Source:* CIA, *World Factbook*, available at https://www.cia.gov/library/publications/the-world-factbook/geos/co.html#Issues

Robinson has a policy to focus on only the first five years of a venture for analysis purposes. Profits after the five-year period will be important, but the government guarantee will have expired.

The expected total profits resulting from the joint venture per year are as shown in Exhibit 7.15.

Robinson has an average cost of new medium-term debt of 6% and estimates its cost of equity at 10%. Its capital structure is 20% debt and 80% equity. It adds between two

Exhibit 7.15   Profits to joint venture of Robinson and CCB.

Year	Total Profits of Venture before Allocation
2008—Year 0	($20,000,000) Robinson investment
2009—Year 1	COP 90 billion (Colombian pesos)
2010—Year 2	COP 110 billion
2011—Year 3	COP 130 billion
2012—Year 4	COP 150 billion
2013—Year 5	COP 170 billion

and five percentage points to its weighted average cost of capital (WACC) when deriving its required rate of return on international joint ventures. Robinson plans to account for country and other risks within its cash flow estimates.

Robinson is mildly concerned about country risk because of the internal fighting in Colombia. Will the rebels overthrow the Colombian government? Robinson estimates that there is a 5% probability of this happening. If it does happen, Robinson expects to lose all profits from the joint venture beginning in year 3.

Let's do the analysis to see if this venture is worthwhile.

Step 1

Determine Robinson's cost of capital and required rate of return for the joint venture in Colombia.

We start with the cost of capital. Remember that the weighted average cost of capital is equal to the after-tax cost of debt multiplied by the weight of the debt in the capital structure plus the required return on equity multiplied by the weight of the equity in the capital structure. Exhibit 7.16 shows our numbers.

Now let's look at the required rate of return on the investment in Colombia. Since Robinson estimates the risk to be toward the high end of its range, it adds 4% to the WACC to get the required return: 8.78% plus 4% = 12.78%. The risk manager rounds this up to 13%.

Step 2

Determine the discrete probability distribution of the venture cash flows, calculate the net present value to Robinson for its share of this joint venture, and then calculate the expected net present value. First we calculate the investment in billions of Colombian pesos (COP): $20 million multiplied by an exchange rate of $1 to COP 2,212.64 equals COP 44,252 billion. We will assume straight-line depreciation over five years for U.S. tax purposes. (See Exhibit 7.17.)

Now let's take the net present value using the required return of 13% (Exhibit 7.18).

As you can see, we get $45 million positive NPV. If the project lasts only five years, the internal rate of return (IRR) can be computed using Excel as 57% for the case where all goes as expected.

Now let's assume that the rebels overthrow the government, a possible but unlikely event. In this case Robinson would receive only the cash flow from years 1 and 2. What we would see is shown in Exhibit 7.19.

Even without considering any tax break from writing off the investment, we see a positive NPV.

Exhibit 7.16   Calculation of weighted average cost of capital (WACC) for Robinson.

Capital	Pretax Cost	Tax Rate	After-Tax Cost	Capital Weights	Weighted Cost
Debt	6%	35%	3.9%	20%	0.78%
Equity			10%	80%	8.00%
WACC					8.78%

Exhibit 7.17 Time line of cash flows to CCB–Robinson venture.

Year	0 2008	1 2009	2 2010	3 2011	4 2012	5 2013	Total
JV cash flow time line (investment) or profits in COP billions	COP (44.25)	COP 90	COP 110	COP 130	COP 150	COP 170	COP 605.75
Robinson share in COP billions	COP (44.25)	COP 45	COP 55	COP 65	COP 75	COP 85	COP 280.75
7% Colombian dividend tax in billions		COP 3.15	COP 3.85	COP 4.55	COP 5.25	COP 5.95	COP 22.75
Robinson share after tax in COP		COP 41.85	COP 51.15	COP 60.45	COP 69.75	COP 79.05	COP 302.25
Convert to $ in millions	$20	$18.91	$23.12	$27.32	$31.52	$35.73	$136.60
Depreciation		$4.00	$4.00	$4.00	$4.00	$4.00	$20.00
Taxable income		$14.91	$19.12	$23.32	$27.52	$31.73	$116.60
U.S. tax		$5.22	$6.69	$8.16	$9.63	$11.10	$40.81
Cash flow to Robinson	($20.00)	$13.69	$16.43	$19.16	$21.89	$24.62	$95.79

Exhibit 7.18 Net present value of cash flows to Robinson (in millions).

Year	0	1	2	3	4	5	Total
Cash flow to Robinson	($20.00)	$13.69	$16.43	$19.16	$21.89	$24.62	$95.79
PV @ 13% NPV	($20.00)	$12.12	$12.86	$13.28	$13.43	$13.36	$45.05

Exhibit 7.19 Net present value of cash flows to Robinson, worst case (in millions).

Year	0	1	2	Total
Cash flow to Robinson	($20.00)	$13.69	$1643	$10.12
PV @ 13% NPV	($20.00)	$12.12	$12.86	$ 4.98

Exhibit 7.20 Calculation of expected net present value (in millions).

Probability (1)	NPV (2)	(1) × (2)
95%	$45	$42.75
5%	$ 5	$ 0.25
Total expected value		$43.00

In our analysis we have a 95% chance of obtaining an NPV of $45.05 million and a 5% chance of obtaining a NPV of $4.98 million. Let's round these numbers to $45 million and $5 million.

We can now calculate the expected value of $43 million (see Exhibit 7.20).

Based on the assumptions this project is acceptable. Even more, it has a very high return. The currency risk has been eliminated by the government guarantee. Perhaps the biggest risk comes from fluctuations in the world price for coffee.

There are some at Robinson who recommend that the company borrow the needed funds in Colombia. That way, if a new government seized the assets, the company could default on the loan. If the exchange rate guarantee were ended, the loan would offset the assets and thereby lessen or eliminate any accounting risk.

Lesson: We saw a venture with risk but also with exceptional returns. The company carefully considered the potential risks and looked for ways to lessen this risk. It performed the economic analysis in the same manner as it would for any project in the United States.

Unknown Rental Cars Borrowing Case: January 1, 1985

Dad: Rodney, let me tell you a true story about a major U.S. corporation. I'll change a few details and the name of the company. The case was told to me by someone who lived it. It was set way back in 1985, but the case is as relevant today as it was then. In many ways it is the same as your investment in the English CD.

It was December 1984 and Unknown Rental Cars needed to borrow $200 million to finance the purchase of an Unclear Airlines company. The assistant treasurer just made a recommendation about the choice between borrowing in the United States in U.S. dollars or in Japan in yen (¥ or JPY). The loan would begin on January 1, 1985, and end on December 31, 1989.

As background, Unknown owned Cheapy Hotels. It was buying Unclear Airlines from a major private equity firm that had purchased it out of bankruptcy. Unclear Airlines would generate about 50% of the total revenue and the remainder was to be evenly split between Unknown Rental Cars and Cheapy Hotels. All were worldwide service companies that generated revenue in many countries and currencies, mainly in the United States, Canada, Latin America, and Europe.

If the loan was in U.S. dollars in the United States, company policy required the use of a specific investment banker. This investment banking firm estimated terms of the United States loan as follows: The interest rate would be 11% per year paid semiannually in December and June for five years. The principal of $200 million would be repaid at the end of the five years. There would be a one-time underwriting fee of approximately 0.5% to be paid when the funds were received.

Exhibit 7.21   Amount of yen purchased by $1.

Average (732 days)	237.51027
High	250.45000
Low	222.70000

Source: FXHistory © 1997–2008 by OANDA Corporation.

A leading Japanese bank was expanding into the United States as it fulfilled its strategic objective of becoming a worldwide institution. It offered a loan with the interest and principal denominated in yen. The interest rate was 5%, and there were no up-front fees. Both the U.S. and the Japanese loans required interest payments to be paid in December and in June. The entire principal would be due in December 1989.

This seemed to be an easy choice. The assistant treasurer concluded that 5% was so much less than 11% that it would not matter what happened to exchange rates. The yen could double in value and the interest would still be less. If the yen strengthened to twice the current level, the effective interest rate would rise to 10%, and that was still less than 11%.

He believed that any further analysis would be a waste of time. His judgment told him that the Japanese yen loan was easily the better choice. Still, he looked at history to show his boss that he had considered what might happen. In the previous two years the dollar had strengthened against the yen. On December 31, 1982, the exchange rate was 234 yen to one dollar. By December 31, 1984, the rate had moved to 250 yen to the dollar. This meant that one dollar bought more yen. If the dollar continued to strengthen, each interest payment would be less than the previous one.

Looking at the history of exchange rates on OANDA.com, he found the statistics for the prior two years (Exhibit 7.21).

When the decision was made, the dollar was at the highest point of this range on December 31, 1984, at 250.45 yen to the dollar.

It was too much to hope that the dollar would continue to increase in value over the life of the loan, but that certainly was a possibility. In making his case, the assistant treasurer also compiled a table of data over the prior 10 years (Exhibit 7.22).

Exhibit 7.22   Amount of yen purchased by $1.

1975	305.060
1976	293.000
1977	239.980
1978	194.300
1979	240.550
1980	203.100
1981	219.800
1982	234.500
1983	231.700
1984	250.450

Source: FXHistory © 1997–2008 by OANDA Corporation.

Exhibit 7.23   Calculation of principal of yen loan to equal $200 million.

January 1, 1985	Borrow		¥50,000,000,000
	Convert to $	250 ¥/$	$200,000,000
June 30, 1985	Pay interest @ 2.5%		¥1,250,000,000
	Convert to $		$5,000,000

In his final presentation, he noted that even if the dollar weakened to its lowest point in that 10-year span of time, the effective interest would rise but not enough to make the interest payments uneconomical. His argument carried the day and the loan was made.

As you may guess, I am telling this story because disaster lay ahead. Let's do the math that the assistant treasurer did (Exhibit 7.23).

Borrow on January 1, 1985, at an exchange rate of 250 yen to the dollar. To get $200 million in U.S. dollars, you would need to borrow $200 million times 250 yen to the dollar. That works out to be ¥50 billion.

So now the question becomes, what rate do we assume for the conversion?

If we assume 250 ¥/$, then our interest paid will be the ¥1.25 billion divided by 250 or $5 million. If we assume that the rate will be 222.7 ¥/$, then the interest payment becomes ¥1.25 billion divided by 222.7 or $5.6 million.

Compare this to the loan in U.S. dollars, even forgetting about the fee, and this is far superior: $200 million borrowed at 11% per year requires interest payments of $22 million each year, or $11 million every six months. The savings is substantial.

The conclusion seemed clear. Even $5.6 million in interest was so far below the $11 million that there really was no choice.

Dad: So what was missing?

Rodney: What about the options and futures markets?

Dad: At the time they were showing that the dollar would weaken substantially against the yen. Still, that would not make the interest payment on the yen loan higher than the payment on the dollar loan.

   What caused your problem with the CD that you bought in London?

Rodney: Oh! The problem there was the effect of the exchange rate on the principal. The assistant treasurer focused on the interest payment and forgot about the principal.

Dad: Excellent. You are really thinking. You could have found the same answer listening to the accountants. They require that each company mark the asset or loan to its value at the end of the period.

   Let's assume that the assistant treasurer was correct and that the yen strengthened to 222.7 ¥/$. How much did the company pay in interest and how much did it owe at the end of the first year? Let's make a table (Exhibit 7.24).

   So if the assistant treasurer was right that the worst case was for the yen to strengthen to 222 ¥/$, then the company would report a loss of $14 million compared to the loan in dollars.

Exhibit 7.24 Correct analysis of loan assuming worst case of 222 ¥/$ (in millions).

Date	U.S. Loan		Exchange Rate	Japanese Loan Yen	Japanese Loan Dollars	Difference vs. Yen Loan
1/1/85	$200	Principal	250	¥50,000	$200	$ 0
6/30/85	($ 11)	Interest	222	(¥ 1,250)	($ 5.6)	+$ 5.4
12/31/85	($ 11)	Interest	222	(¥ 1,250)	($ 5.6)	+$ 5.4
12/31/85	($200)	Principal owed	222	(¥50,000)	($225.3)	−$25.3
1985 loss						−$14.5

The assistant treasurer missed the principal repayment because he did not make a cash flow time line. It was an easy mistake to make. Let's do a time line for him (Exhibit 7.25).

Looking quickly at this time line, we see that the amount of the principal payment dominates the interest charges. The effect of the exchange rate on the principal had the same kind of devastating effect on Unknown Rental Cars as it did on your CD in England. In both cases the effect was not expected. However, in the case of Unknown, this simple analysis of the worst case would have shown the problem. Unfortunately, the expected worst case was not as bad as reality.

You were in good company forgetting to consider the effect of foreign exchange movements on the principal. Let's jump ahead in time and look at the actual history for year-end exchange rates and what they imply for the principal repayment (Exhibit 7.26).

Exhibit 7.25 Cash flow time line for loan options (in millions).

Time	U.S. Loan		Japanese Loan
1/01/85	$200	Borrow	¥50,000
6/30/85	(11)	Interest	(1,250)
12/31/85	(11)	Interest	(1,250)
6/30/86	(11)	Interest	(1,250)
12/31/86	(11)	Interest	(1,250)
6/30/87	(11)	Interest	(1,250)
12/31/87	(11)	Interest	(1,250)
6/30/88	(11)	Interest	(1,250)
12/31/89	(11)	Interest	(1,250)
6/30/89	(11)	Interest	(1,250)
12/31/89	(11)	Interest	(1,250)
12/31/89	($200)	Repay loan	(¥50,000)

Exhibit 7.26   Actual yen-dollar exchange rates and effect of Japanese loan on liability in dollars (in millions).

Dec. 31	¥/$	Principal Amount	$ Value	Accounting Loss
Jan. 1984	250	¥50,000	$200	$0
1985	201.050	50,000	248.7	48.7 loss
1986	159.900	50,000	312.70	64.0 loss
1987	123.400	50,000	405.19	92.5 loss
1988	125.050	50,000	399.84	5.4 gain
1989	143.800	50,000	347.71	52.13 gain
Total				147.3 loss

As you can imagine, the presentation of financial statements to top management and the board at the end of 1985 was far from pleasant. The treasury department had saved $11 million in interest but lost almost $49 million in the exchange rate accounting.

The CEO was not pleased. The loan was repaid early so the company never saw the gains of 1988 and 1989.

Lesson: Borrowing in a foreign currency can generate similar risks to investing in assets or joint ventures. The history can be used as an indication, but the greatest risk comes from major moves in exchange rates that are not anticipated.

Theory: Interest Rate Parity

Interest rate parity theory says that over very long periods of time, the cost of money should equalize between countries after adjusting for exchange rate changes. Interest rates and changes in the value of the principal should be considered. In our examples, both the interest rate and the principal would change in terms of the home currency as a result of economic factors and exchange rate movement. Neither the Japanese loan nor the English CD actually worked out to be the same as the U.S. alternative. However, this theory would have led to more analysis if it had been considered.

If inflation is higher in one country than in another, we would expect the low-inflation country to have low interest rates. At the same time, we would expect the high-inflation country to have high interest rates. If investors in one country perceive that they can earn a higher return in another country, they will move their money and invest in the other country, just as Rodney did with the investment in England. The key is to correctly guess what will happen to exchange rates. Unfortunately, in many cases, there are large unexpected movements.

Money will flow toward the country with the greatest expected returns and that will put downward pressures on these returns. If the reverse happens and money flows to where the earned interest rates are lower, it is a signal that the market as a whole is expecting that currency to strengthen.

This theory is far from perfect, as disparities can exist for years. In part these are due to government policy about taxes, business and capital regulation, and the ease of moving money across international borders.

Just as major moves in the stock market are difficult or impossible to predict, exchange rates can vary dramatically and unexpectedly.

Theory: Purchasing Power Parity

Purchasing power parity tells us that, in general, things should cost the same in one country as they do in another.

When it is cheaper to buy durable goods or services in one country, there will be an incentive for businesses to shop for bargains there. People will tend to stop the purchase of local goods and services and instead look to that other country. At times, there can be an incentive to smuggle. Someone from the European Union may find that good-quality jeans sell for much less in the United States than they do in the major cities of Europe. If you need jeans and your business brings you to Indianapolis, you may purchase the jeans there. When you return to your home country, you are required to declare your purchases, and often this generates a duty or value-added tax.

The *Economist* magazine publishes the "Big Mac" index a couple of times each year. This table shows the price of a McDonald's Big Mac in a number of currencies and what those prices become when translated into U.S. dollars. The spread is quite large. There is a tendency for the prices to move toward each other, though, and it is just one indication of what may happen to future exchange rates. Still, the disparities have lasted many years.

Even within one country, the prices of goods and services will not be the same everywhere. For comparable quality, retail stores will reflect price differences based on local costs and taxes. Examples include the purchase of cigarettes in New York City versus an outlet in North Carolina, or the purchase of a flat panel TV at an upscale full-service retailer in San Francisco compared to a Wal-Mart in Venice, Florida.

One effect of the Internet is to allow consumers everywhere to compare prices and shop for bargains.

Dad: Rodney, if you decide to take a vacation in Europe, China, India, or any other country, it would be worth checking the Big Mac index to see how far your dollar will go. As you know by now, the exchange rates can vary enough that there have been good years for your vacation and bad years.

Futures and Options

It is possible to use contracts to reduce the risk of adverse movements in the exchange rates of foreign currencies. A company can enter into a contract to change a fixed amount of cash from one currency to another at a certain price at a point in the future. It is possible to purchase an option to either buy or sell currency at a specified price for a period of time. These tools allow companies flexibility but come at a cost. Generally, their use requires experience and knowledge of this highly complex field. They are beyond the scope of this chapter and may be a subject for future reading and research.

Summary

Global finance adds risk and return to corporations. The risks can be large if there is a major movement in exchange rates or if political risk materializes in the form of an expropriation of assets or a ban on repatriation of cash. Theory is of only moderate use, as practice often differs from what theory would predict. On the positive side, expanding business to other countries offers great rewards to the careful company.

Internet Links

www.oanda.com	Foreign exchange rates for current and historical ratios.
www.doingbusiness.org/documents/ Press_Releases_08/DB_08_Oveview_ English.pdf	Useful information from the World Bank on the ease of doing business in many different countries.
www.heritage.org/research/features/index/ countries.cfm	Heritage Foundation Index of Economic Freedom.
www.cia.gov/library/publications/ the- world-factbook/geos/co.html#Issues	CIA *World Factbook* contains country analysis of data and current facts.

For Further Reading

Gwartney, James, and Robert Lawson, *Economic Freedom of the World: 2007 Annual Report* (Washington, DC: Cato Institute, 2007). The leading index of global economic freedom.

Part III

Business Entities

8

Choosing a Business Form

Richard P. Mandel

The Consulting Firm

Jennifer, Jean, and George had earned their graduate business degrees together and had paid their dues in middle management positions in various large corporations. Despite their different employers, the three had maintained their friendships and were now ready to realize their dream of starting a consulting practice together. Their projections showed modest consulting revenue in the short term, offset by expenditures for supplies, an administrative assistant, subscriptions to various online services, computers, software, and similar necessities. Although each expected to clear no more than perhaps $45,000 for his or her efforts in their first year in business, they shared high hopes for future growth and success. Besides, it would be a great pleasure to run their own company and have sole charge of their respective fates.

The Software Entrepreneur

At approximately the same time that Jennifer, Jean, and George were hatching their plans for entrepreneurial independence, Phil was cashing a seven-figure check for his share of the proceeds from the sale of the computer software firm he had founded seven years before with four of his friends. Rather than rest on his laurels, however, Phil saw this as an opportunity to capitalize on a complex piece of software he had developed in college. Although Phil was convinced that there would be an extensive market for his software, there was still much development and testing to be done before it could be brought to market. In addition, there would have to be a significant marketing effort before the software was released. Phil anticipated that he would probably spend over $500,000 on programmers and salespeople before the first dollar of royalties would appear. But he was prepared to make that investment himself, in anticipation of retaining all the eventual profit.

The Hotel Venture

Bruce and Erika were not nearly as interested in high technology. Directly following their graduation from business school, they were planning to construct and operate a resort hotel near a popular ski area. They had chosen as their location a beautiful parcel of land in Colorado, owned by their third partner, Michael. Rich in ideas and enthusiasm, the three lacked funds. They were certain, however, that they could attract investors to their enterprise. The location, they were sure, would virtually sell itself.

The Purpose of This Chapter

Each of these three groups of entrepreneurs would soon be faced with what might well be the most important decision of the initial years of their businesses: which of the various legal business forms to choose for the operation of their enterprises. It is the purpose of this chapter to describe, compare, and contrast the most popular of these forms in the hope that the reader will then be able to make such choices intelligently and effectively. After discussing the various business forms, we will revisit our entrepreneurs and analyze their choices.

Business Forms

Two of the most popular business forms could be described as the default forms, because the law will deem a business to be operating under one of these forms unless it makes an affirmative choice otherwise. The first of these forms is the sole proprietorship. Unless the businessperson has actively chosen another form, the individual operating his or her own business is considered to be a sole proprietor. Two or more persons operating a business together are considered a partnership (or general partnership), unless they have elected otherwise. Both of these forms share the characteristic that for all intents and purposes they are not entities separate from their owners. Every act taken or obligation assumed as a sole proprietorship or partnership is an act taken or obligation assumed by the business owners as individuals.

Many of the rules applicable to the operation of partnerships are set forth in the Uniform Partnership Act, which has been adopted in one form or another by 49 states. That Act defines a partnership as "an association of two or more persons to carry on as co-owners a business for profit." Notice that the definition does not require that the individuals agree to be partners. Although most partnerships can point to an agreement among the partners (whether written or oral), the Act applies the rules of partnership to any group of two or more persons whose actions fulfill the definition. Thus, the U.S. Circuit Court of Appeals for the District of Columbia, in a rather extreme case, held, over the defendant's strenuous objections, that she was a partner in her husband's burglary "business" (for which she kept the books and upon whose proceeds she lived), even though she denied knowing what her husband was doing nights. As a result of this status, she was held personally liable for damages to the wife of a burglary victim her husband had murdered during a botched theft.

In contrast, a corporation is a legal entity separate from the legal identities of its owners, the shareholders. In the words used by James Thurber to describe a unicorn, the corporation is "a mythical beast," created by the state at the request of one or more business promoters upon the filing of a form and the payment of the requisite modest fee. Thereupon, in the eyes of the law, the corporation becomes for most purposes a "person" with its own federal identification number! Of course, one cannot see, hear, or touch a corporation, so it must interact with the rest of the world through its agents, the corporation's officers and employees.

Corporations come in different varieties. The so-called professional corporation is available in most states for persons conducting professional practices, such as doctors, lawyers, architects, psychiatric social workers, and the like. A subchapter S corporation is a corporation that is the same as a regular business corporation in all respects other than taxation. These variations are discussed later.

A fourth form of business organization is the limited partnership, which may best be described as a hybrid of the corporation and the general partnership. The limited partnership consists of one or more general partners—who manage the business, much in the same way as do the partners in a general partnership—and one or more limited partners, who are essentially silent investors with very little control over business operations. Like the general partnership, limited partnerships are governed in part by a statute, the Uniform Limited Partnership Act, which has also been adopted in one form or another by 49 states.

The limited liability company (LLC) is now available to entrepreneurs in all 50 states. The LLC is a separate legal entity owned by members who may, but need not, appoint one or more managers (who may, but need not, be members) to operate the business. Although it was initially necessary for there to be multiple members to form an LLC, all states now allow single-member LLCs. An LLC is formed by filing articles with the state government and paying the prescribed fee. The members then enter into an operating agreement setting forth their respective rights and obligations with respect to the business. Most states that have adopted the LLC have also authorized the limited liability partnership (LLP), which allows general partnerships to obtain limited liability for their partners by filing their intention to do so with the state. This form of business entity is normally used by professional associations that previously operated as general partnerships, such as law and accounting firms.

As will be discussed later, since the LLC affords its owners most of the benefits of the limited partnership without requiring that any owner be exposed to unlimited liability, the popularity of the limited partnership is definitely waning. It is currently used most often for certain sophisticated investment vehicles (such as hedge funds) and in complex family estate plans.

Comparison Factors

The usefulness of the five basic business forms could be compared on a virtually unlimited number of measures, but the most effective comparisons will likely result from employing the following eight factors:

1. *Complexity and cost of formation.* What steps must be taken before your business can exist in each of these forms?

2. *Barriers to operation across state lines.* What steps must be taken to expand your business to other states? What additional cost may be involved?

3. *Recognition as a legal entity.* Who does the law recognize as the operative entity? Who owns the assets of the business? Who can sue and be sued?

4. *Continuity of life.* Does the legal entity outlive the owner? This may be especially important if the business wishes to attract investors, or if the goal is an eventual sale of the business.

5. *Transferability of interest.* How does one go about selling or otherwise transferring one's ownership of the business?

6. *Control.* Who makes the decisions regarding the operation, financing, and eventual disposition of the business?

7. *Liability.* Who is responsible for the debts of the business? If the company cannot pay its creditors, must the owners satisfy these debts from their personal assets?

8. *Taxation.* How does the choice of business form determine the income tax payable on the profits of the business and the income of its owners?

Formation of Sole Proprietorships

Reflecting its status as the default form for the individual entrepreneur, the sole proprietorship requires no affirmative act for its formation. One operates a sole proprietorship because one has not chosen to operate in any of the other forms. The only exception to this rule arises in certain states when the owner chooses to use a name other than his or her own as the name of the business. In such event, the owner may be required to file a so-called d/b/a certificate with the local authorities, stating that the owner is "doing business as" someone other than himself or herself. This allows creditors and those otherwise injured by the operation of the business to determine who is legally responsible.

Formation of Partnerships

Similarly, a general partnership requires no special act for its formation other than a d/b/a certificate if a name other than that of the partners will be used. If two or more people act in a way that fits the definition set forth in the Uniform Partnership Act, they will find themselves involved in a partnership. However, it is strongly recommended that prospective partners consciously enter an agreement (preferably in writing) setting forth their understandings on the many issues that will arise in such an arrangement. Principal among these are the investments each will make in the business, the allocation and distribution of profits (and losses), the method of decision making (i.e., majority or unanimous vote), any obligations to perform services for the business, the relative compensation of the partners, and so on.

Regardless of the agreements that may exist among the partners, however, the partnership will be bound by the actions and agreements of each partner—as long as these actions are reasonably related to the partnership business, and even if they were not properly authorized by the other partners pursuant to the agreement. After all, third parties have no idea what the partners' internal agreement says and are in no way bound by it.

Formation of Corporations

In order to form a corporation, one must pay the appropriate fee and must complete and file with the state a corporate charter (otherwise known as a Certificate of Incorporation, Articles of Incorporation, or similar names in the various states). The fee is payable both at the outset and annually thereafter (often approximately $200). Promoters may form a corporation under the laws of whichever state they wish; they are not required to form the corporation under the laws of the state in which they intend to conduct most of their business.

This partly explains the popularity of the Delaware corporation. Delaware spent most of the preceding century competing with other states for corporation filing fees by repeatedly amending its corporate law to make it increasingly favorable to management. By now, the Delaware corporation has taken on an aura of sophistication, so that many promoters form their companies in Delaware just to appear to know what they are doing! In addition, it is often less expensive under Delaware law to authorize large numbers of shares for future issuance than it would be in other states. Nevertheless, the statutory advantages of Delaware apply mostly to corporations with many stockholders (such as those that are publicly traded, resulting in separation of management from stockholders) and will rarely be significant to small businesses such as those described at the beginning of this chapter. Also, formation in Delaware (or any state other than the site of the corporation's principal place of business) will subject the corporation to additional, unnecessary expense. It is, thus, usually advisable to incorporate in the company's home state.

The charter sets forth the corporation's name (which cannot be confusingly similar to the name of any other corporation operating in the state) as well as its principal address. The names of the initial directors and officers of the corporation are often listed. Most states also require a statement of corporate purpose. Years ago this purpose defined the permitted scope of the corporation's activities. A corporation that ventured beyond its purposes risked operating ultra vires, resulting in liability of its directors and officers to its stockholders and creditors. Today, virtually all states allow a corporation to define its purposes extremely broadly (e.g., "any activities that may be lawfully undertaken by a corporation in this state"), so that operation ultra vires is generally impossible. Still, directors are occasionally plagued by lawsuits brought by stockholders asserting that the diversion of corporate profits to charitable or community activities runs afoul of the dominant corporate purpose, which is to generate profits for stockholders. The debate over the responsibility of directors to corporate stakeholders (employees, suppliers, customers, neighbors, and so forth) currently rages in many forms, but is normally not a concern of the beginning entrepreneur. Issues of corporate governance are further discussed in Chapter 10.

Corporate charters also normally set forth the number and classes of equity securities that the corporation is authorized to issue. Here an analysis of a bit of jargon may be appropriate. The number of shares set forth in the charter is the number of shares authorized, that is, the number of shares that the directors may issue to stockholders at the directors' discretion. The number of shares issued is the number that the directors have in fact issued and is obviously either the same or smaller than the number authorized. In some cases, a corporation may have repurchased some of the shares previously issued by the directors. In that case, only the shares that remain in the hands of shareholders are outstanding (a number obviously either the same or lower than the number issued). Only the shares outstanding have voting rights, rights to receive dividends, and rights to receive distributions upon full or partial liquidation of the corporation. Normally, we would expect an entrepreneur to authorize the maximum number of shares allowable under the state's minimum incorporation fee (e.g., 275,000 shares for $275 in Massachusetts), and then issue only 10,000 or so, leaving the rest on the shelf for future financings, employee incentives, and so forth.

The charter also sets forth the par value of the authorized shares, another antiquated concept of interest mainly to accountants. The law requires only that the corporation not issue shares for less than the par value, but it can, and usually does, issue the shares for more. Thus, typical par values are $0.01 per share or even "no par value." Shares issued for less than par are watered stock, subjecting both the directors and holders of such stock to liability to other stockholders and creditors of the corporation.

Corporations also adopt bylaws that are not filed with the state but are available for inspection by stockholders. These are usually fairly standard documents, describing the internal governance of the corporation and setting forth such items as the officers' powers and notice periods for stockholders' meetings.

Formation of Limited Partnerships

As you might expect, given the limited partnership's hybrid nature, the law requires both a written agreement among the various general and limited partners and the filing of a Certificate of Limited Partnership with the state, along with the appropriate initial and annual fees. The agreement sets forth the partners' understanding of the items discussed earlier in the context of a general partnership. The certificate sets forth the name and address of the partnership, its purposes, and the names and addresses of its general partners. In many states, it is no longer necessary to reveal the names of the limited partners, just as the names of corporate stockholders do not appear on a corporation's publicly available incorporation documents.

Formation of Limited Liability Companies

The LLC is formed by filing a charter (e.g., a Certificate of Organization) with the state government and paying a fee (usually similar to that charged for the formation of a corporation). The charter normally sets forth the entity's name and address, its business purpose, and the names and addresses of its managers (or persons authorized to act for the entity vis-à-vis the state if no managers are appointed). The same broad description of the entity's business that is allowable for modern corporations is acceptable for LLCs. The members of the LLC are also required to enter into an operating agreement that sets forth their rights and obligations with regard to the business. These agreements are generally modeled after the agreements signed by the partners in a general or limited partnership.

Out-of-State Operation of Sole Proprietorships and Partnerships

Partly as a result of both the Commerce clause and Privileges and Immunities clause of the U.S. Constitution, states may not place limits or restrictions on the operations of out-of-state sole proprietors or general partnerships that are different from those placed on domestic businesses. Thus, a state cannot force registration of a general partnership simply because its principal office is located elsewhere, but it can require an out-of-state doctor to undergo the same licensing procedures it requires of its own residents.

Out-of-State Operation of Corporations, Limited Partnerships, and Limited Liability Companies

Things are different, however, with corporations, limited partnerships, and LLCs. As creations of the individual states, they are not automatically entitled to recognition elsewhere. All states require (and routinely grant) qualification as a foreign corporation, limited partnership, or LLC to nondomestic entities doing business within their borders. This procedure normally requires the completion of a form very similar to a corporate charter, limited partnership certificate, or LLC charter, and the payment of an initial and annual fee, similar in amount to the fees paid by domestic entities. This, incidentally, is one reason *not* to form a corporation in Delaware, if it will operate principally outside that state. Much litigation has occurred over what constitutes "doing business" within a state for the purpose of requiring qualification. Similar issues arise over the obligation to pay income tax, collect sales tax, or accept personal jurisdiction in the courts of a state. Generally these cases turn on the individualized facts of the particular situation, but courts generally look for offices or warehouses, company employees, widespread advertising, or negotiation and execution of contracts within the state.

Perhaps more interesting may be the penalty for failure to qualify. Most states will impose liability for back fees, taxes, interest, and penalties. More important, many states will bar a nonqualified foreign entity from access to its courts and, thus, from the ability to enforce obligations against its residents. In most of these cases, the entity can regain access to the courts merely by paying the state the back fees and penalties it owes, but in a few states access will then be granted only to enforce obligations incurred after qualification was achieved, leaving all prior obligations unenforceable.

Recognition of Sole Proprietorships as Legal Entities

By now it probably goes without saying that the law does not recognize a sole proprietorship as a legal entity separate from its owner. If Phil, our computer entrepreneur, were to choose this form, he would own all the company's assets; he would be the plaintiff in any suits it brought, and he would be the defendant in any suits brought against it. There would be no difference between Phil, the individual, and Phil, the business.

Recognition of Partnerships as Legal Entities

A general partnership raises more difficult issues. Although most states allow partnerships to bring suit, be sued, and own property in the partnership's name, this does not mean that the partnership exists, for most purposes, separately from its partners. As will be seen, especially in the areas of liability and taxation, partnerships are very much collections of individuals, not separate entities.

Ownership of partnership property is a particularly problematic area. All partners own an interest in the partnership, which entitles them to distributions of profit, much like stock in a corporation. This interest is the separate property of each partner, and is attachable by the individual creditors of a partner in the form of a "charging order." In many states, the assets of the partnership are owned in the name of the partnership and are treated, in terms of title, similarly to assets owned by a corporation.

However, in other states, the partners themselves jointly own the assets of the partnership. This form of ownership (similar to joint ownership of a family home by two spouses) is called tenancy in partnership. In those states, each partner may use partnership assets only for the benefit of the partnership's business, and such assets are exempt from attachment by the creditors of an individual partner, although not from the creditors of the partnership. Tenancy in partnership also implies that, in most cases of dissolution of a partnership, the ownership of partnership assets devolves to the remaining partners, to the exclusion of the partner who leaves in violation of the partnership agreement or dies. The former partner is left only with the right to a dissolution distribution in respect of his or her partnership interest.

Recognition of Corporations and Limited Liability Companies as Legal Entities

The corporation and LLC are our first full-fledged separate legal entities. Ownership of business assets is vested solely in the corporation or LLC, as separate legal entities. The corporation or LLC itself is plaintiff and defendant in suits and is the legally contracting party in all of its transactions. Stockholders and members own only their stock or membership interests and have no direct ownership rights in the business's assets.

Recognition of Limited Partnerships as Legal Entities

The limited partnership, continuing in its role as a hybrid, is a little of both partnership and corporation. Although in some states the partnership's property is owned in the name of the limited partnership and treated, for purposes of title, in the same way as property owned by a corporation, in other states the general partners own the partnership's property as tenants in partnership, operating in the same manner as partners in a general partnership. In those states, the limited partners have only their partnership interests and no direct ownership of the partnership's property. This is logically consistent with their roles as silent investors. If they directly owned partnership property, they would have to be consulted with regard to its use.

Continuity of Life

The issue of continuity of life is one that should concern most entrepreneurs, because it can affect their ability to sell the business as a unit when it comes time to cash in on their efforts as founders and promoters. The survival of the business as a whole, in the form of a separate entity, must be distinguished from the survival of the business's individual assets and liabilities.

Sole Proprietorships

Although a sole proprietorship does not survive the death of its owner, its individual assets and liabilities do. In Phil's case, for example, to the extent that these assets consist of the computer program, filing cabinets, and the like, they would all be inherited by Phil's heirs, who could then choose to continue the business or liquidate the assets as they pleased. Should they decide to continue the business, they would then have the same choices of business form that confront any entrepreneur. However, if Phil's major asset were a government license, qualification as an approved government supplier, or a contract with a software publisher, the ability of the heirs to carry on the business might be entirely dependent upon the assignability of these items. If the publishing contract is not assignable, Phil's death may terminate the business's major asset. If the business had operated as a corporation, Phil's death would likely have been irrelevant (other than to him and his loved ones); the corporation, not Phil, would have been party to the contract.

Partnerships

Consistent with the general partnership's status as a collection of individuals, not an entity separate from its owners, a partnership is deemed dissolved upon the death, incapacity, bankruptcy, resignation, or expulsion of a partner. This is true even if a partner's resignation violates the express terms of the partnership agreement. Those assets of the partnership that may be assigned devolve to those partners who are entitled to ownership. Those who thus retain ownership may continue the business as a new partnership, corporation, or LLC with the same or new partners and investors or may liquidate the assets at their discretion. The sole right of any partner who has forfeited direct ownership rights (e.g., by violating the partnership agreement) is to be paid a dissolution distribution, after the partnership's liabilities have been paid or provided for.

Corporations

Corporations, in contrast, normally enjoy perpetual life. Unless the charter contains a stated dissolution date (extremely rare), and as long as the corporation pays its annual fees to the state, it will go on until and unless it is voted out of existence by its stockholders. The death, incapacity, bankruptcy, resignation, or expulsion of any stockholder is entirely irrelevant to the corporation's existence. Such stockholder's stock continues to be held by the stockholder, is inherited by his or her heirs, or is auctioned by creditors as the circumstances demand, with no direct effect on the corporation.

Limited Partnerships

As you may have guessed, the hybrid nature of the limited partnership dictates that the death, incapacity, bankruptcy, resignation, or expulsion of a limited partner will have no effect on the existence of the limited partnership. The limited partner's partnership interest is passed in the same way as a stockholder's stock. However, the death, incapacity, bankruptcy, resignation, or expulsion of a general partner does automatically dissolve the partnership, in the same way as it would in the case of a general partnership. This can be extremely inconvenient if the limited partnership is conducting a far-flung enterprise with many limited partners. Thus, in most cases, the partners agree in advance in their limited partnership agreement that upon such a dissolution the limited partnership will continue under the management of a substitute general partner, chosen by those general partners who remain. In such a case, the entity continues until it is voted out of existence by its partners in accordance with their agreement or until the arrival of a termination date specified in its certificate.

Limited Liability Companies

Most states no longer impose dissolution on an LLC upon the occurrence of events similar to those that result in the dissolution of a limited partnership. Even those states that still do impose dissolution upon such events allow the remaining members to vote to continue the LLC's existence, notwithstanding an event of dissolution. Thus, as a practical matter, LLCs effectively have perpetual life in the same manner as corporations.

Transferability of Interest

To a large extent, transferability of an owner's interest in the business is similar to the continuity of life issue.

Sole Proprietorships

A sole proprietor has no interest to transfer because the proprietor and the business are one and the same, and thus the proprietor must be content to transfer each of the assets of the business individually—an administrative nightmare at best and possibly impractical in the case of nonassignable contracts, licenses, and government approvals.

Partnerships

To discuss transferability in the context of a general partnership, it is necessary to keep in mind the difference between ownership of partnership assets and ownership of an individual's partnership interest. A partner has no right to transfer partnership assets except as may be authorized by vote in accordance with the partnership agreement and in furtherance of the partnership business. However, a partner may transfer his or her partnership interest, or it may be attached by individual creditors pursuant to a charging order. This does not make the transferee a partner in the business, though, because partnerships can be created only by agreement of all parties. Rather, it sets up the rather awkward situation in which the original partner remains, but his or her economic interest is, at least temporarily, in the hands of another. In such cases, the law gives the remaining partners the right to dissolve the partnership by expelling the transferor partner.

Corporations

No such complications attend the transfer of one's interest in a corporation. Stockholders simply sell or transfer their shares of stock. Since stockholders (solely as stockholders) have no day to-day involvement in the operation of the business, the transferee becomes a full-fledged stockholder upon the transfer. This means that if Bruce, Erika, and Michael decide to operate as a corporation, each risks waking up one day to find that he or she has a new "partner" if one of the three has sold his or her shares. To protect themselves against this eventuality, most closely held corporations include restrictions on stock transfer in their charters, in their bylaws, or in stockholder agreements. These restrictions set forth some variation of a right of first refusal for either the corporation, the other stockholders, or both whenever a transfer is proposed. In addition, corporate stock, as well as most limited partnership interests and LLC membership interests, are securities under the federal and state securities laws, and because the securities of these entities will not initially be registered under any of these laws, their transfer is closely restricted by law.

Limited Partnerships

Just as with general partnerships, the partners of limited partnerships may transfer their partnership interests. The rules regarding the transfer of the interests of the general partners are similar to those governing general partnerships described earlier. Limited partners may usually transfer their interests (subject to securities laws restrictions) without fear of dissolution, but transferees normally do not become substituted limited partners without the consent of the general partners.

Limited Liability Companies

As previously mentioned, although a membership interest in an LLC may be freely transferable under applicable state law, most LLCs require the affirmative vote of at least a majority of the members or managers before a member's interest may be transferred. Furthermore, membership interests in an LLC will usually qualify as securities under relevant securities laws and will therefore be subject to the restrictions on transfer imposed by such laws.

Control

Simply put, control in the context of a business entity means the power to make decisions regarding all aspects of its operations. But the implications of control extend to many levels. These include control of the equity or value of the business, control over distribution of profits, control over day-to-day and long-term policy making, and control over distribution of cash flow. Each of these is different from the others, and control over each can be allocated differently among the owners and other principals of the entity. This can be seen as either complexity or flexibility, depending on one's perspective.

Sole Proprietorships

This complexity or flexibility doesn't extend to the sole proprietorship. In that business form, control over all these factors belongs exclusively to the sole proprietor. Nothing could be simpler or more straightforward.

Partnerships

Things are not so simple in the context of general partnerships. It is essential in understanding control in a partnership to appreciate the difference between the partners' relationships with each other (internal relationships) and the partnership's relations with third parties (external relationships).

Internally, the partnership agreement governs the decision-making process and sets forth the agreed division of equity, profits, and cash flows. Decisions made in the ordinary course of business are normally made by a majority vote of the partners, while major decisions, such as changing the character of the partnership's business, may require a unanimous vote. Some partnerships may weight the voting in proportion to each partner's partnership interest, while others delegate much of the decision-making power to an executive committee or a managing partner. In the absence of an agreement, the Uniform Partnership Act prescribes a vote of the majority of partners for most issues and unanimity for certain major decisions.

External relationships are largely governed by the law of agency; that is, each partner is treated as an agent of the partnership and, derivatively, of the other partners. (See Exhibit 8.1) Any action that a partner appears to have authority to take will be binding upon the partnership and the other partners, regardless of whether such action has been internally authorized.

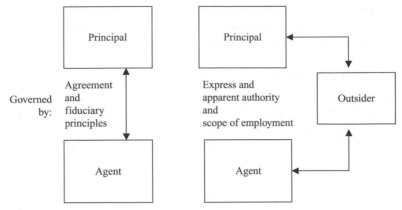

Exhibit 8.1   Principal and agent.

Thus, if Jennifer purchases a subscription to the *Harvard Business Review* for the partnership, and such an action is perceived to be within the ordinary course of the partnership's business, that obligation can be enforced against the partnership, even if Jean and George had voted against it. Such would not be the case, however, if Jennifer had signed a purchase and sale agreement for an office building in the name of the partnership, because reasonable third parties would be expected to know that such a purchase was not in the ordinary course of their business.

These rules extend to tort liability, as well. If Jean were to wrongfully induce a potential client to breach its consulting contract with a competitor, the partnership would be liable for interference with contractual relations, even if the other two partners were not aware of Jean's actions. Such might not be the case, however, if Jean decided to dynamite the competition's offices, because such an act could be judged to be outside the normal scope of her duties as a partner.

These obligations to third parties can even extend past the dissolution of the partnership if individual partners have not given adequate notice that they are no longer associated with the others. Thus, ex-partners can be held liable for legal fees incurred by former partners if they have not notified the partnership's counsel about leaving the firm.

It should also be noted that agency law reaches into the internal relationships of partners. The law imposes upon partners the same obligations of fiduciary loyalty, non-competition, and accountability as it does upon agents with respect to their principals.

Corporations

It is in the corporate form that the opportunities for flexibility and complexity probably reach their height. Many aspects of the corporate form have been designed specifically for the purpose of splitting off individual aspects of control and allocating them differently.

Stockholders

At its simplest, a corporation is controlled by its stockholders. Yet, except in those states that have specific (but rarely used) close corporation statutes governing corporations with very few stockholders, the decision-making function of stockholders is exercised only derivatively. Under most corporate statutes, a stockholder vote is required only with respect to four basic types of decisions: an amendment to the charter, a sale of the company, dissolution of the company, and election of the board of directors.

Charter amendments may sound significant, until one remembers what information is normally included in the charter. A name change, a change in purpose (given the broad purpose clauses now generally employed), and an increase in authorized shares (given the large amounts of stock normally left on the shelf) are neither frequent nor usually significant decisions. Certainly, a sale of the company is significant, but it normally can occur only after the recommendation of the board and will happen only once, if at all. The same can be said of the decision to dissolve. It is the board of directors that makes all the long-term policy decisions for the corporation. Thus the right to elect the board is significant, but indirectly so. Day-to-day operation of the corporation's business is accomplished by its officers, who are normally elected by the board, not the stockholders.

Even given the relative unimportance of voting power for stockholders, the corporation provides many opportunities to differentiate voting power from other aspects of control and allocate it differently. Assume Bruce and Erika (our hotel developers) were willing to give Michael a larger piece of the equity of their operation to reflect his contribution of the land, but wished to divide their voting rights equally. The three could authorize a class of nonvoting common stock and issue, for example, 1,000 shares of voting stock to each of themselves and an additional 1,000 shares of nonvoting stock to Michael. As a result, each would have one-third of the voting control, but Michael would have one-half of the equity interest.

Alternatively, Michael could be issued a block of preferred stock representing the value of the land. This would guarantee him a fair return on his investment before any dividends could be declared to the three of them as holders of the common stock. As a holder of preferred stock, Michael would also receive a liquidation preference upon dissolution or sale of the business in the amount of the value of his investment, but any additional value created by the efforts of the group would be reflected in the increasing value of the common shares.

The previous information illustrates how one can separate and allocate decision-making control differently from that of the equity in the business, as well as from the distribution of profits. Distribution of cash flow can, of course, be accomplished totally separately from the ownership of securities, through salaries based on the relative efforts of the parties, rent payments for assets leased to the entity by the principals, or interest on loans to the corporation.

Stockholders exercise what voting power they have at meetings of the stockholders, held at least annually but more frequently if necessary. Each stockholder of record, on a future date chosen by the party calling the meeting, is given a notice of the meeting containing the date, time, and purpose of the meeting. Such notice must be sent at least 7 to 10 days prior to the date of the meeting, depending on the individual state's corporate law, although the Securities and Exchange Commission requires as much as 40 days' notice for publicly traded corporations posting their proxy statements online. No action may be taken at a meeting unless a majority of voting shares is represented (known as a quorum). This results in the aggressive solicitation of proxy votes in most corporations with widespread stock ownership. Unless otherwise provided (as with the two-thirds vote of all shares required in most states for a sale or dissolution of the company), a resolution is carried by a majority vote of those shares represented at the meeting.

The preceding rules lead to the conclusion that the board of directors will be elected by the holders of a majority of the voting shares. Thus, in the earlier scenario, even though Bruce and Erika may have given Michael one-third of the voting shares of common stock, as long as they continue to vote together, Bruce and Erika will be able to elect the entire board. To prevent this result, prior to investing Michael could insist on a cumulative voting provision in the charter (under those states' corporate laws that allow it). Under this system, each share of stock is entitled to a number of votes equal to the number of directors to be elected. By using all one's votes to support a single candidate, individuals with a significant minority interest can guarantee themselves representation on the board.

More directly (and in states that do not allow cumulative voting), Michael could insist on two different classes of voting stock, differing only in voting rights. Bruce and Erika would each own 1,000 shares of class A and elect two directors. Michael, the sole owner of the 1,000 outstanding shares of class B stock, would elect a third director. Of course, the board also acts by majority, so Bruce and Erika's directors could dominate board decisions in any case, but at least Michael would have access to the deliberations.

In the absence of a meeting, stockholders may vote by unanimous written consent, where each stockholder indicates approval of a written resolution by signing it. This eliminates the need for a meeting and is very effective in corporations with only a few stockholders (such as our hotel operation). Unlike the rules governing stockholders' meetings, however, in some states unanimity is required to adopt resolutions by written consent. This apparently reflects the belief that minority stockholders are owed an opportunity to sway the majority with their arguments. A growing number of states, notably Delaware, permit written consents of a majority, apparently reacting to the dominance of proxy voting at most meetings of large corporations, where the most eloquent of minority arguments would fall on deaf ears (and proxy cards).

Directors

At the directors' level, absent a special provision in the corporation's charter, all decisions are made by majority vote. Typically, directors concentrate on long-term and significant decisions, leaving day-to-day management to the officers of the corporation. Decisions are made at regularly scheduled directors' meetings or at a special meeting if there is need to react to a specific situation. Under most corporate laws, no notice need be given for regular meetings and only very short notice need be given for special meetings (24 to 48 hours). The notice must be sent to all directors and must contain the date, time, and place of the meeting, but, unlike stockholders' notices, need not contain the purpose of the meeting. It is assumed that directors are much more involved in the business of the corporation and do not need to be warned about possible agenda items or given long notice periods.

At the meeting itself, no business can be conducted in the absence of a quorum, which, unless increased by a charter or bylaw provision, is a majority of the directors then in office. Reflecting recent advances in technology, many corporate statutes allow directors to attend meetings by conference call or teleconference, as long as all directors are able to hear and speak to each other at all times during the meeting. Individual telephone calls to each director will not suffice. Unlike stockholders, directors usually cannot vote by proxy, because each director owes to the corporation his or her individual judgment on items coming before the board. The board of directors can also act by written consent, but, even in Delaware, such consent must be unanimous, in recognition that the board is fundamentally a deliberative body.

Boards of directors, especially in publicly held corporations with larger boards, frequently delegate some of their powers to executive committees, or other committees formed for defined purposes. However, most corporate statutes prohibit boards from delegating certain fundamental powers, such as the declaration of dividends, the recommendation of charter amendments, or sale of the company. The executive committee can, however, be a powerful organizational tool to streamline board operations and increase efficiency and responsiveness.

Although directors are not agents of the corporation—they cannot bind the corporation to contract or tort liability through their individual actions—they are subject to many of the obligations of agents discussed in the context of partnerships, such as fiduciary loyalty. Directors are bound by the so-called corporate opportunity doctrine, which prohibits them from taking personal advantage of any business opportunity that may come their way, if the opportunity is such as would reasonably be expected to interest the corporation. In such an event, the director must disclose the opportunity to the corporation, which normally must consider it and vote not to take advantage before the director may act on his or her own behalf.

Unlike stockholders who, under most circumstances, can vote their shares totally in their own self-interest, directors must use their best business judgment and act in the corporation's best interest when making decisions for the corporation. At the very least, directors must keep informed regarding the corporation's operations, although they may in most circumstances rely on the input of experts hired by the corporation, such as its attorneys and accountants. Thus, when the widow of a corporation's founder accepted a seat on the board as a symbolic gesture of respect to her late husband, she found herself liable to minority stockholders for the misbehavior of her fellow board members. Nonparticipation in the misdeeds was not enough to exempt her from liability; she had failed to keep herself informed and exercise independent judgment. Furthermore, the standard of care for directors and the extent of their potential personal liability has been significantly raised in the context of publicly traded companies by recent statutes such as Sarbanes-Oxley.

Directors may also find themselves sued personally by minority stockholders or creditors of the corporation for declaration of dividends or other distributions to stockholders that render the corporation insolvent or for other decisions of the board that have injured the corporation. Notwithstanding such lawsuits, however, directors are not guarantors of the success of the corporation's endeavors; they are required only to have respected their obligation to be "loyal" to the corporation and to have used their best independent "business judgment" in making their decisions. When individual directors cannot be totally disinterested (such as the corporate opportunity issue or when the corporation is being asked to contract with a director or an entity in which a director has an interest), they are required to disclose their interest and are disqualified from voting. In many states, their presence will not even count for the maintenance of a quorum.

Apart from the question of the interested director, much of the modern debate on the role of the corporate director has focused around which constituencies directors may take into account when exercising their best business judgment. The traditional view has been that the directors' only concern is to maximize return on the investment of the stockholders. More recently, especially in the context of hostile takeovers, directors have been allowed to take into account the effect of their decisions on other constituencies, such as suppliers, neighboring communities, customers, and employees.

In an early case on this subject, the board of directors of the corporation that owned Wrigley Field and the Chicago Cubs baseball team was judged to have appropriately considered the effect on its neighbors and on the game of baseball in voting to forgo the extra revenue that it would probably have earned if it had installed lights for night games.

When the stockholders believe the directors have not been exercising their best independent business judgment in a particular instance, the normal procedure is to make a demand on the directors to correct the decision, either by reversing it or by reimbursing the corporation from their personal funds. Should the board refuse (as it most likely will), the stockholders then bring a derivative suit against the board on behalf of the corporation. They are, in effect, taking over the board's authority to decide whether such a suit should be brought in the corporation's name. The board's vote not to institute the suit is not likely to be upheld on the basis of the business judgment rule, since the board members are clearly interested in the outcome of the vote. As a result, the well-informed board will delegate the power to make such a decision to an independent litigation committee, usually composed of directors who were not involved in the original decision. The decision of such a committee is much more likely to be upheld in a court of law, although the decision is not immune from judicial review.

A more detailed discussion on the board of directors is contained in Chapter 10, "The Integrity of Financial Reporting."

Officers

The third level of decision making in the normal corporation is that of the officers, who take on the day-to-day operational responsibilities. Officers are elected by the board and consist, at a minimum, of a president, a treasurer, and a secretary or clerk (keeper of the corporate records). Many corporations elect additional officers such as vice presidents, assistant treasurers, CEOs, and the like.

Thus, the decision-making control of the corporation is exercised on three very different levels. Where each decision properly belongs may not be entirely obvious in every situation. The decision to go into a new line of business would normally be thought of as a board decision. Yet if by some chance the decision requires an amendment of the corporate charter, a vote of stockholders may be necessary. On the contrary, if the decision is merely to add a 12th variety of relish to the corporation's already varied line of condiments, the decision may be properly left to a vice president of marketing.

*   *   *

Often persons who have been exposed to the preceding analysis of the corporate-control function conclude that the corporate form is too complex for any but the largest and most complicated publicly held companies. This is a gross overreaction. For example, if Phil, our software entrepreneur, should decide that the corporate form is appropriate for his business, it is very likely that he will be the corporation's only stockholder. As such, he will elect himself the sole director and his board will then elect him as the president, treasurer, and secretary of the corporation. Joint meetings of the stockholders and directors of the corporation may be held in the shower adjacent to Phil's bathroom on alternate Monday mornings.

Limited Partnerships

As you might expect, the allocation of control in a limited partnership is reflective of its origin as a hybrid of the general partnership and the corporation. Simply put, virtually all management authority is vested in the general partners. The limited partners normally have little or no authority, analogous to minority stockholders in a corporation. Third parties cannot rely on any apparent authority of a limited partner, because a limited partner's name will not appear, as a general partner's name may, on the limited partnership's certificate on the public record.

General partners exercise their authority in the same way as they do in a general partnership. Voting control is allocated internally as set forth in the partnership agreement, but each general partner has the apparent authority to bind the partnership to unauthorized contracts and torts to the same extent as the partners in a general partnership.

Limited partners will normally have voting power over a very small list of fundamental business events, such as amending the partnership agreement and certificate, admitting new general partners, changes in the basic business purposes of the partnership, or dissolution. These are similar to the decisions that must be put to a stockholders' vote in a corporation. Revisions to the Uniform Limited Partnership Act, now accepted by many states, have widened the range of decisions in which a limited partner may participate without losing the protective limited liability of limited partners. However, this range is still determined by the language of the agreement and certificate for each individual partnership.

Limited Liability Companies

An LLC that chooses not to appoint managers is operated much like a general partnership. The operating agreement sets forth the percentages of membership interests required to authorize various types of actions on the LLC's behalf, with the percentage normally varying according to the importance of the action. As is the case for partners in general partnerships, the LLC members (in the absence of managers) are deemed to have apparent authority to bind the entity to contracts (regardless of whether they have been approved internally) and to expose the entity to tort liability for acts occurring within the scope of the entity's business.

An LLC that appoints managers is operated much like a limited partnership. The managers make most of the decisions on behalf of the entity, as do the general partners of a limited partnership. The members are treated much like limited partners and have voting rights only in rare circumstances involving very significant events. Apparent authority to act for the entity is reserved to the managers, as only their names appear on the Certificate of Organization.

Liability

Possibly the factor that most concerns the entrepreneur is personal liability. If the company encounters catastrophic tort liability, finds itself in breach of a significant contract, or just plain can't pay its bills, must the owner reach into his or her own personal assets to pay the remaining liability after the company's assets have been exhausted? If so, potential entrepreneurs may well believe that the risk of losing everything is not worth the possibility of success, and their innovative potential will be diminished or lost to society. Most entrepreneurs are willing to take significant risk, provided that the amount of that risk can be limited to the amount they have chosen to invest in the venture.

Sole Proprietorships

With the sole proprietorship, the owner has essentially traded off limitation of risk in favor of simplicity of operation. Since there is no difference between the entity and its owner, all the liabilities and obligations of the business are also liabilities and obligations of its owner. Thus, all the owner's personal assets are at risk. Failure of the business may well mean personal bankruptcy for the owner.

Partnerships

If possible, the result may be even worse within a general partnership. There, each owner is liable not only for personal mistakes, but also for those of the other partners. Each partner is jointly and severally liable for the debts of the partnership remaining after the partnership's assets have been exhausted. This means that a creditor may choose to sue any individual partner for 100% of any liability. The partner may have a right to sue the other partners for their share of the debt, as set forth in the partnership agreement, but that is of no concern to a third party. If the other partners are bankrupt or have fled the jurisdiction, the targeted partner may end up holding the entire bag.

If our three consultants operate as a partnership, Jennifer is not only 100% personally liable for any contracts she may enter into, but also 100% personally liable for any contracts entered into by either Jean or George. What's more, she is liable for those contracts, even if they were entered into in violation of the partnership agreement, because, as was demonstrated earlier, each partner has the apparent authority to bind the partnership to contracts in the ordinary course of the partnership's business, regardless of the partners' internal agreement. Worse, Jennifer is also 100% individually liable for any torts committed by either of her partners, as long as they were committed within the scope of the partnership's business. The only good news in all this is that neither the partnership nor Jennifer is liable for any debts or obligations of Jean or George incurred in their personal affairs. If George has incurred heavy gambling debts in Las Vegas, his creditors can affect the partnership only by obtaining a charging order against George's partnership interest.

Corporations

Thus we have the historical reason for the invention of the corporation. Unlike the sole proprietorship and the partnership, the corporation is recognized as a legal entity, separate from its owners. Its owners are thus not personally liable for its debts; they are granted limited liability. If the corporation's debts exhaust its assets, the stockholders have lost their investment, but they are not responsible for any further amounts. In practice, this may not be as attractive as it sounds, because sophisticated creditors such as the corporation's institutional lenders will likely demand personal guarantees from major stockholders. But the stockholders will normally escape personal liability for trade debt and, most important, for torts.

This major benefit of incorporation does not come without some cost. Creditors may, on occasion, be able to "pierce the corporate veil" and assert personal liability against stockholders, using any one of three major arguments. First, to claim limited liability behind the corporate shield, stockholders must have adequately capitalized the corporation at or near its inception. There is no magic formula with which to calculate the amount necessary to achieve adequate capitalization, but the stockholders normally will be expected to invest enough money or property and obtain enough liability insurance to offset the kinds and amounts of liabilities normally encountered by a business in their industry. Thus, the owner of a fleet of taxicabs did not escape liability by canceling his liability insurance and forming a separate corporation for each cab. The court deemed each such corporation inadequately capitalized, and, in a novel decision, pierced the corporate veil laterally, by combining all the corporations into one for purposes of liability.

It is necessary to capitalize only for those liabilities normally encountered by corporations in the industry. The word *normally* is key because it is obviously not necessary to have resources adequate to handle any circumstance, no matter how unforeseeable. Also, adequate capitalization is necessary only at the outset. A corporation does not expose its stockholders to personal liability by incurring substantial losses and ultimately dissipating its initial capitalization.

A second argument used by creditors to reach stockholders for personal liability is failure to respect the corporate form. This may occur in many ways. The stockholders may fail to indicate that they are doing business in the corporate form by leaving the words *Inc.* or *Corp.* off their business cards and stationery, thus giving the impression that they are operating as a partnership. They may mingle the corporate assets in personal bank accounts, or routinely use corporate assets for personal business. They may fail to respect corporate niceties such as holding annual meetings and filing the annual reports required by the state. After all, if the stockholders don't take the corporate form seriously, why should their creditors? They are entitled to adequate notice that they may not rely on the personal assets of the stockholders. Even Phil, the software entrepreneur who imagined earlier holding his stockholders' and directors' meetings in the shower, would be well advised to record the minutes of those meetings in a corporate record book.

A third argument arises from a common mistake made by entrepreneurs. Fearful of the expense involved in forming a corporation, they wait until they are sure that the business will get off the ground before they spring for the attorneys' and filing fees. In the meantime, they may enter into contracts on behalf of the corporation and perhaps even commit a tort or two. Once the corporation is formed, they may even remember to have it expressly accept all liabilities incurred by the promoters on its behalf. However, under simple agency law, one cannot act as an agent of a nonexistent principal. And a later assignment of one's liabilities to a newly formed corporation does not act to release the original obligor without the consent of the obligee. The best advice here is to form the corporation before incurring any liability on its behalf. Most entrepreneurs are surprised at how little it actually costs to get started.

Limited Partnerships

In the tradition of its hybrid nature, a limited partnership borrows some of its aspects from the corporation and some from the general partnership. In summary, each general partner has unlimited, joint and several, liability for the debts and obligations of the limited partnership after exhaustion of the partnership's assets. In this respect, the rules are identical to those governing the partners in a general partnership. Limited partners are treated as stockholders in a corporation. They have risked their investment, but their personal assets are exempt from the creditors of the partnership.

However, as you might expect, things aren't quite as simple as they may initially appear. In limited partnerships, it is rather common for limited partners to make their investments in the form of a cash down payment and an agreement to contribute the rest at a later time. This occurs partly for reasons of cash flow and partly for purposes of tax planning. This arrangement is much less common in corporations, because many corporate statutes do not permit it and because the tax advantages associated with this arrangement are generally not available in the corporate form. Should the limited partnership's business fail, limited partners will be expected, despite limited liability, to honor their commitments to make future contributions to capital.

In addition, it is fundamental to the status of limited partners that they have acquired limited liability in exchange for forgoing virtually all management authority over the business. The corollary to that rule is that limited partners who excessively involve themselves in management may forfeit limited liability and be treated, for the purposes of creditors, as general partners, with unlimited personal liability. Mitigating this somewhat harsh rule, revisions to the Uniform Limited Partnership Act have increased the categories of activities in which a limited partner may participate without crossing the line. Furthermore, and perhaps more fundamentally, in states that have adopted these revisions, the transgressing limited partner is now personally liable only to those creditors who were aware of the limited partner's activities and detrimentally relied on his or her apparent status as a general partner.

Limited Liability Companies

One of the major benefits of employing the LLC form of business entity is that it shields all members and managers from personal liability for the debts of the business. However, even though the LLC is relatively new on the legal scene, it is expected that most of the same doctrines that can result in piercing the corporate veil may be applied to the veil of the LLC as well. Furthermore, it can be expected that the managers of an LLC will be held to the same fiduciary standards as corporate directors and general partners of limited partnerships, resulting in their potential personal liability to the members.

Taxation

It is remarkable how many significant business decisions are made without first taking into account the tax consequences of the various options. Tax consequences should almost never be allowed to force entrepreneurs to take actions they otherwise would not have considered. But often tax considerations lead one to do what one wants in a different manner and to reap substantial savings as a consequence. Such is often the case in the organization of a business. The following discussion is confined to the federal income tax, the tax with the largest and most direct effect on organizational issues. Each entrepreneur would be well advised to consult a tax adviser regarding this tax as well as state income, estate, payroll, and other taxes to find out how they might impact a specific business.

Sole Proprietorships

Not surprisingly, given the factors already discussed, a sole proprietorship is not a separate taxable entity for federal income tax purposes. The taxable income and deductible expenses of the business are set forth on Schedule C of the entrepreneur's Form 1040, and the net profit (or loss) is carried back to page 1, where it is added to (or subtracted

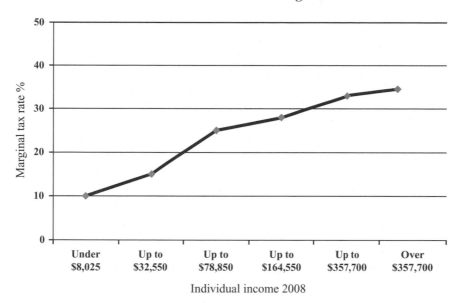

Exhibit 8.2   Individual federal income tax rates.

from) all the taxpayer's other income. The net effect of this is that the sole proprietor will pay tax on the income from this business at his or her highest marginal rate, which is determined by the amount of income received from this and other sources (see Exhibit 8.2).

In Phil's case, for example, if his software business netted $100,000 in a particular year, that amount would be added to the substantial interest and dividend income from his other investments, so that he would likely owe the Internal Revenue Service (IRS) $35,000 on this income. If Phil's business were run as a separate taxable corporation, the income generated from it would be taxed at the lowest levels of the tax rate structure, because it would not be added to any other income. For example, the first $50,000 of income would be taxed at only 15% and the next $25,000 at only 25% (see Exhibit 8.3).

This argument is turned on its head, however, if a business anticipates losses in the short term. Using Phil as an example, if his business operated at a $100,000 loss and as a separate taxable entity, the business would pay no tax in its first year and would be able to net its early losses against profits only in future years and only if it ever realized such profits. At best, the value of this tax benefit is reduced by the time value of money; at worst, the loss may never yield a tax benefit if the business never does better than break even. If Phil operated the business as a sole proprietorship, by contrast, the loss calculated on his Schedule C would be netted against the dividend and interest income generated by his investments, thus effectively rendering $100,000 of that income tax free. One can strongly argue, therefore, that the form in which one should operate one's business is dictated, in part, by the likelihood of its short-term success and the presence or absence of other income flowing to its owner.

Partnerships

Partnerships are also not separate taxable entities for the purposes of the federal income tax, although, in most cases, they are required to file informational tax returns with the

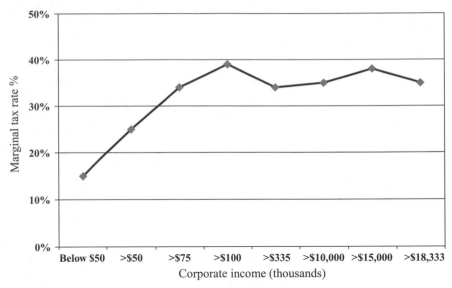

Exhibit 8.3   Corporate federal income tax rates.

IRS. Any profits generated by a partnership appear on the federal income tax returns of the partners, generally in proportions indicated by the underlying partnership agreement. Thus, as with sole proprietorships, this profit is taxed at the individual partner's highest marginal tax rate, and the lower rates for the initial income of a separate taxable entity are forgone. In addition, each partner is taxed upon his or her proportion of the income of the partnership, regardless of whether that income was actually distributed.

As an example, if Bruce and Erika, our hotel magnates, were to take $50,000 of a year's profits to add a deck to one of their properties, this expenditure would not lower the business's profits by that amount. As a capital expense it may be deducted over time only in the form of depreciation. Thus, assuming they were equal partners, even if Michael had objected to this expenditure, each of the three, including Michael, would be forced to pay a tax on $16,667 (minus that year's depreciation) despite having received no funds with which to make such a payment. The result would be the same in a sole proprietorship, but this rule is considered less of a problem since it can be expected that sole owners would manage cash flow in a way that would minimize this negative effect on themselves.

As with a sole proprietorship, this negative result becomes a positive one if the partnership is losing money. The losses appear on the partners' individual tax returns in the proportions set forth in the partnership agreement and render an equal amount of otherwise taxable income tax free. In addition, not all losses suffered by businesses result from the dreaded negative cash flow. As illustrated earlier in the case of the deck, the next year the hotel business might well break even or show a small profit on a cash flow basis, but the depreciation generated by the earlier addition of the deck might well result in a loss for tax purposes. Thus, with enough depreciation partners might have the double benefit of a tax-sheltering loss on their tax returns and ownership of a growing, profitable business. This is especially true regarding real estate, such as the hotel itself. While generating a substantial depreciation loss each year, the value of the building may well be increasing, yielding the partners a current tax-sheltering loss while at the same time generating a long-term capital gain a few years hence.

Corporations

Corporations are normally treated as separate entities for federal income tax purposes consistent with their treatment as separate entities for most other purposes. They have their own set of progressive tax rates, moving from 15% for the first $50,000 of income, through 25% for the next $25,000, and effectively 34% and 35% for amounts above that. There are also 5% and 3% additional taxes at higher levels of income to compensate for the lower rates in the lower brackets. Certain so-called personal service corporations have only a flat 35% rate at all levels of income. Also, losses currently generated by a corporation may be carried back as many as two years to generate a tax refund or carried forward as many as 20 years to shelter future income.

Although corporate rates may be attractive at lower levels of income, the common fear of using the corporate form is the potential for double taxation. Simply put, the corporation pays tax upon its profits and then distributes the remaining profit to its stockholders as nondeductible dividends. The stockholders then pay tax on the receipt of the dividends, thus amounting to two taxes on the same money. For a corporation in the 34% bracket given the current (2009) dividend tax rate of 15%, the net effect is a combined tax rate of approximately 44% with stockholders in the 28% bracket, the net effect is a combined tax rate of approximately 52.5%.

Yet double taxation is rarely a concern for the small business. Such businesses generally manage compensation to their employees, who are usually their shareholders, in such a way that there is rarely much, if any, corporate profit remaining at the end of the year. Since compensation (as opposed to dividends) is deductible, the only level of taxation incurred by such businesses is at the stockholder level.

Other opportunities for legitimate deductible payments to stockholders that have the effect of eliminating corporate profit include rental payments on assets leased by a stockholder to the corporation and interest on that portion of a stockholder's investment made in the form of debt.

Thus, the existence of the separate corporate entity with its own set of tax rates presents more of an opportunity for tax planning than a threat of double taxation. If the corporation intends to distribute all of its excess cash to its owners, it should manage compensation and other payments so as to show little profit and incur taxation only on the stockholder level. If the corporation intends to retain some of its earnings in the form of capital acquisitions (thus resulting in an unavoidable profit for tax purposes), it can take advantage of the lower corporate rates without subjecting its stockholders to taxation at their level. Contrast this to a partnership where the partners would be required to pay tax at their highest marginal rates on profits that they never received.

There are limits to the usefulness of these strategies. To begin with, one cannot pay salaries and bonuses to nonemployee stockholders who are not performing services for the corporation. Dividends may be the only way to give such stockholders a return on their investment. In addition, the Internal Revenue Service will not allow deductions for what it considers to be unreasonable compensation (measured by compensation paid to comparable employees in the same industry). Thus, a highly profitable corporation might find some of its excessive salaries to employee-stockholders recharacterized as nondeductible dividends. Last, even profits retained at the corporate level will eventually be indirectly taxed at the stockholder level as increased capital gains when the stockholders sell their shares.

For most start-up businesses, however, this corporate tax planning strategy will be useful, at least in the short term. In addition, entrepreneurs will find certain employee benefits are better offered in the corporate form because they are deductible to employers, but excluded from income only for employees. Since a sole proprietor or partner is not considered an employee, the value of benefits such as group life insurance and disability insurance policies may be taxable income to them but tax-free to the officers of a corporation.

Professional Corporations

There are two common variations of the corporate form. The first of these is the professional corporation. Taxation played a major part in its invention. Originally, limitations on the amounts of money that could be deducted as a contribution to a qualified retirement plan varied greatly, depending on whether the business maintaining the plan was a corporation, a partnership, or a sole proprietorship. The rules greatly favored the corporation. Partnerships and sole proprietorships were required to adopt Keogh or HR-10 plans with their substantially lower limits on deductibility. However, doctors, lawyers, architects, and other professionals, who often could afford large contributions to retirement plans, were not allowed to incorporate under applicable state laws. The states were offended by the notion that such professionals could be granted limited liability for the harms caused by their businesses.

Eventually, a compromise was struck and the so-called professional corporation was formed. Using that form, professionals could incorporate their businesses, thus qualifying for the higher retirement plan deductions but giving up any claim to limited liability. As time went by, however, the Internal Revenue Code was amended to eliminate most of the differences between the deductions available to Keogh plans and those available to corporate pension and profit-sharing plans. Today, professional corporations are subject to virtually all the same rules as other corporations, with the exception that most are classified as personal service corporations and therefore taxed at a flat 35% rate on undistributed profit.

As the tax incentive for forming professional corporations has decreased, many states, perhaps with an eye toward maintaining the flow of fees from these corporations, have greatly liberalized the availability of limited liability for these corporations. Today, in many states, professional corporations now afford their stockholders protection from normal trade credit as well as tort liability arising from the actions of their employees or other stockholders. Of course, even under the normal business corporation form, a stockholder is personally liable for torts arising from his or her own actions.

Subchapter S Corporations

The second common variation is the subchapter S corporation, named for the sections of the Internal Revenue Code that govern it. Although indistinguishable from the normal (or subchapter C) corporation in all other ways, including limited liability for its stockholders, the subchapter S corporation has affirmatively elected to be taxed similarly to a partnership. Thus, like the partnership, it is not a separate taxable entity and files only an informational return. Profits appear on the tax returns of its stockholders in proportion to shares of stock owned, regardless of whether those profits were distributed to the stockholders or retained for operations. Losses appear on the returns of the stockholders and may potentially be used to shelter other income.

Although the subchapter S corporation is often referred to as a "small business corporation," the size of the business has no bearing on whether this election is available. Any corporation that meets the following five tests may, but need not, elect to be taxed as a subchapter S corporation:

1. It must have 100 or fewer stockholders.
2. It may have only one class of stock (although variations in voting rights are acceptable).
3. All stockholders must be individuals (or certain trusts and nonprofits).
4. No stockholder may be a nonresident alien.
5. With certain exceptions, it may not own or be owned by another corporation.

The subchapter S corporation is particularly suited to resolving the problems presented by certain discrete situations. For example, if a corporation is concerned that its profits are likely to be too high to eliminate double taxation through compensation to its stockholders, the subchapter S election eliminates the worry over unreasonable compensation. Since there is no tax at the corporate level, it is not necessary to establish the right to a compensation deduction. Similarly, if a corporation has nonemployee stockholders who insist on current distributions of profit, the subchapter S election would allow declaration of dividends without the worry of double taxation. This would undoubtedly be attractive to most publicly traded corporations were it not for the 100-stockholder limitation mentioned earlier.

Many entrepreneurs have turned to the subchapter S election in order to eliminate the two layers of tax otherwise payable upon sale or dissolution of a corporation. The corporate tax otherwise payable upon the gain realized on the sale of corporate assets is eliminated by the use of the subchapter S election, as long as the election has been in effect for 10 years or, if less, since the corporation's inception. Finally, many entrepreneurs elect subchapter S status for their corporations if they expect to show losses in the short term. These losses can then be passed through to their individual tax returns to act as shelters for other income. When the corporation begins to show a profit, the election can be reversed.

Limited Partnerships

The tax treatment of limited partnerships is much the same as general partnerships. The profits and losses of the business are passed through to the partners in the proportions set forth in the partnership agreement. It must be emphasized that these profits and losses are passed through to all partners, including limited partners, even though one could argue that those profits and losses are derived entirely from the efforts of the general partners. It is this aspect of the limited partnership that made it the form of choice for tax-sheltered investments. The loss incurred by the business (much of which was independent of cash flow through depreciation and the like), could be passed through to the limited partners who, typically, had a considerable amount of other investment and compensation income to be sheltered.

Although the tax treatments of limited partnerships and subchapter S corporations are similar, there are some differences that drove the operators of tax shelters to use partnerships over the corporate form, even at the risk of some unlimited liability. First, although profits and losses must be allocated according to stock ownership in the subchapter S corporation, they are allocated by agreement in the limited partnership. Thus, in order to give the investors the high proportion of losses they demand, promoters did not necessarily have to give them an identically high proportion of the equity. The IRS will attack economically unrealistic allocations, but has issued regulations that, if followed, will protect most allocations. In addition, whereas the amount of loss the investor can use to shelter other income is limited to the investor's tax basis in both types of entities, the tax basis in subchapter S stock is essentially limited to direct investment in the corporation, while in a limited partnership it is augmented by certain types of debt incurred by the entity itself.

Both types of entities are afflicted by the operation of the passive loss rules, added by the Tax Reform Act of 1986 in the hope of eliminating the tax shelter. Thus, unless one materially participates in the operations of the entity (virtually impossible, by definition, for a limited partner), losses generated by those operations can normally be applied only against so-called passive income and not against active income (salaries and bonuses) or portfolio income (interest and dividends). Furthermore, owners of most tax pass-through real estate ventures are treated as subject to the passive loss rules, regardless of material participation.

Limited Liability Companies

Limited liability companies (LLCs) are taxed in a manner substantially identical to limited partnerships. This combination of limited liability for all members (without the necessity to construct the unwieldy, double-entity limited partnership with a corporate general partner) and a pass-through of all tax effects to the members' personal returns makes the LLC the ideal vehicle for whatever tax shelter activity remains after the imposition of the passive activity rules.

Technically, LLCs, limited partnerships, and all other unincorporated business entities may choose to be taxed either as partnerships or as taxable corporations. Recognizing that the vast majority of these entities are formed to take advantage of the opportunity to have taxable income or loss pass through to the owners, IRS regulations provide that these entities will be taxed as partnerships unless the entity affirmatively chooses to be taxed as a corporation. Most corporations have already achieved that level of comfort through the availability of the subchapter S election.

Although the LLC would seem to have the advantage of affording tax pass-through treatment without the limitations of the subchapter S corporation rules, there are some disadvantages as well. Since the nonelecting LLC is not a corporation, it is not eligible for certain provisions the Internal Revenue Code grants only to the corporate entity. Among those are the right to grant incentive stock options (ISOs) to employees and the right to take advantage of tax-free reorganizations when selling the company. LLCs must be converted to corporate entities well before relying on these provisions.

Choice of Entity

The sole proprietorship, partnership, corporation (including the professional corporation and subchapter S corporation), the limited partnership, and the LLC are the most commonly used business forms. Other forms exist, such as the so-called Massachusetts business trust in which the business is operated by trustees for the benefit of beneficiaries who hold transferable shares. But these are generally used for limited, specialized purposes. Armed with this knowledge and the comparative factors discussed previously, how should our budding entrepreneurs operate their businesses?

Consulting Firm

It will be obvious to Jennifer, Jean, and George that they can immediately eliminate the sole proprietorship and limited partnership as choices for their consulting business. The sole proprietorship, by definition, allows for only one owner and there does not seem to be any need for the passive, silent investors who would serve as limited partners. Certainly, no one of the three would be willing to sacrifice the control and participation necessary to achieve limited partnership status.

The corporation gives the consultants the benefit of limited liability, not for their own mistakes, but for the mistakes of each other and their employees. It also protects them from personal liability for trade debt. This protection, however, comes at the cost of additional complexity and expense, such as additional tax returns, annual reports to the state, and annual fees. Ease of transferability and enhanced continuity do not appear to be deciding factors, because a small consulting firm is often intensely personal and not likely to be transferable apart from its principals. Also, fear of double taxation does not appear to be a legitimate concern, since it is likely that the stockholders will be able to distribute any corporate profit to themselves in the form of compensation. In fact, to the extent that they may need to make some capital expenditures for computers and office furniture, the corporate form would afford them access to the lower corporate tax brackets for small amounts of income (unless they fell victim to characterization as a personal service corporation). Furthermore, if the consultants earn enough money to purchase various employee benefits, they will qualify as employees of the corporation and can exclude the value of such benefits from their taxable income, while the corporation deducts these amounts.

These positive aspects of choosing the corporate form argue strongly against making the subchapter S election. That election would eliminate the benefit of the low-end corporate tax bracket and put our consultants in the position of paying individual income tax on the capital purchases made. The election would also eliminate the opportunity to exclude the value of employee benefits from their personal income tax. The same problems argue against the choice of an LLC (or LLP) for this business.

The other possibility would be the general partnership. In essence, by choosing the partnership, the consultants would be trading away limited liability for less complexity. The partnership would not be a separate taxable entity and would not be required to file annual reports and pay annual fees. From a tax point of view, the partnership presents the same disadvantages as the subchapter S corporation and the LLC.

In summary, it appears that our consultants will be choosing between the subchapter C corporation and the partnership. The corporation adds complexity, but grants limited liability. And it certainly is not necessary for a business to be large in order to be incorporated. One might question, however, how much liability exposure a consulting firm is likely to face. In addition, although the corporation affords them the tax benefits associated with employee benefits and capital expenditures, it is not likely that our consultants will be able to afford much in the way of employee benefits and capital expenditures in the short term. Further, it is not likely that these consultants will have personal incomes placing them in tax brackets considerably higher than the corporation's. A strong case can be made for either the C corporation or the partnership in this situation. One can always incorporate the partnership in the future if the business grows to the point that some of the tax benefits become important.

It may also be interesting to speculate on the choice that would be made if our three consultants were lawyers or doctors. Then the choice would be between the partnership and the professional corporation. The comparisons would be the same with the exception that, as a personal service corporation, the professional corporation does not have the benefit of the low-end corporate tax brackets.

Software Entrepreneur

In Phil's case, he can easily eliminate the partnership and the limited partnership. Phil is clearly the sole owner of his enterprise and will not brook any other controlling persons. In addition, his plan to finance the enterprise with earnings from his previous business eliminates the need for limited partner investors. Almost as easily, Phil can eliminate the sole proprietorship, since it would seem highly undesirable to assume personal liability for whatever damage may be done by a product manufactured and distributed to thousands of potential plaintiffs. The corporation, therefore, appears to be Phil's obvious choice. It gives the benefit of limited liability, as well as the transferability and continuity essential to a business that seems likely to be an acquisition candidate in the future. Again the lack of size is not a factor in this choice. Phil will likely act as sole director, president, treasurer, and secretary.

There remains, however, the choice between subchapters C and S. As may well be obvious by now, Phil's corporation fits the most common profile of the subchapter S candidate. For the first year or more, the corporation will suffer serious losses as Phil pays programmers and marketers to develop and presell his product. Subchapter S allows Phil to show these losses on his personal tax return, where they will shelter his considerable investment income. The passive loss limitations will not affect Phil's use of these losses, since he is clearly a material participant in his venture.

Phil could achieve much the same results by choosing an LLC, rather than a subchapter S corporation. Since all states now allow single-member LLCs, there would be little to recommend one choice over the other. The single-member LLC eliminates the need to file a separate income tax return for the business. Phil might feel more comfortable with an S corporation, however, if he fears that suppliers, customers, and potential employees might be put off by the relative novelty of the LLC. This might especially be true if he has any plans to eventually go public, as the LLC has not gained wide acceptance in the public markets. An S corporation can then usually revoke its S election without undue negative tax effect. Beginning as an S corporation would also eliminate the need to reincorporate as a corporation prior to selling the business in a potentially tax-free transaction.

Hotel Venture

The hotel venture contemplated by Bruce, Erika, and Michael presents the opportunity for some creative planning. One problem they may encounter in making their decision is the inherent conflict presented by Michael's insistence upon recognition and reasonable return for his contribution of the land. Also, Bruce and Erika fear being unduly diluted by Michael's share in the face of their more than equal contribution to the ongoing work.

One might break this logjam by looking to one of the ways of separating cash flow from equity. Michael need not contribute the real estate to the business entity at all. Instead, the business could lease the land from Michael on a long-term (99-year) basis. This would give Michael his return, in the form of rent, without distorting the equity split among the three entrepreneurs. From a tax point of view, this plan also changes a nondepreciable asset (land) into deductible rent payments for the business. As their next move, the three may decide to form an entity to construct and own the hotel building, separate from the entity that manages the ongoing hotel business.

This plan would convert the hotel from a rather confusing real estate/operating venture into a pure real estate investment opportunity for potential investors. The hotel entity would receive enough revenue from the management entity to cover its cash flow and would generate tax losses through depreciation, interest, and real estate taxes. These short-term losses will eventually yield long-term capital gains when the hotel is sold, so this entity will attract investors looking for short-term losses and long-term capital appreciation. For the short-term losses to be attractive, however, they must be usable by the investors on their personal returns and not trapped at the business entity level.

All of these factors point inevitably to the use of either the limited partnership, LLC, or subchapter S corporation for the hotel building entity. All three choices allow the tax losses to pass through to the owners for use on their personal returns. Among these three choices, the limited partnership and LLC allow more flexibility in allocating losses to the investors, and away from Bruce, Erika, and Michael (who most likely do not need them), and they provide higher limits on the amounts of losses each investor may use.

In past years, our entrepreneurs would thus face the unenviable choice of either losing the tax advantages of the limited partnership to preserve the limited liability offered by the subchapter S corporation or preserving the tax advantages (and the ability to attract investors) by either accepting personal liability as general partners or attempting to adequately capitalize a corporate general partner. This choice is no longer necessary with the advent of the LLC, which solves the problem by offering the tax advantages of the limited partnership and the liability protection of the subchapter S corporation. However, the passive loss limitations will still have an impact on the usefulness of the losses for the members who do not have significant passive income, making this project (as is the case with most real estate investments in today's climate) more difficult to sell.

This leaves the entity that will operate the hotel business itself. The presence of our three principals immediately eliminates the sole proprietorship as a possibility. Because all the investment capital has already been raised for the real estate entity, there does not seem to be a need for further investors, thus eliminating the limited partnership as a possibility. The partnership seems inapplicable, since it is unlikely that any of the principals would wish to expose himself or herself to unlimited liability in such a consumer-oriented business.

Thus, the corporation and LLC, with their limited liability, continuity, and transferability, seem to be the obvious choices for this potentially growing and successful business. As with Phil, it becomes necessary to decide whether to make the subchapter S election or choose an LLC to achieve tax pass-through. This decision will be made on the basis of the parties' projections. Are there likely to be serious losses in the short term, which might be usable on their personal tax returns? Will there be a need for significant capital expenditures, thus indicating a need for the low-end corporate tax rates? Will the company offer a variety of employee benefits that our principals would wish to exclude from their taxable income? Is the company likely to generate more profit than can be distributed in the form of reasonable compensation, thus calling for the elimination of the corporate-level tax? If these factors seem to favor a tax pass-through entity, the principals will likely analyze the choice between subchapter S and LLC in a manner similar to Phil. In addition, they may find the LLC's lack of eligibility rules attractive in the short run should they ever consider the possibility of corporate or foreign investors, or creative divisions of equity.

Conclusion

These and the many other factors described in this chapter deserve careful consideration by the thousands of entrepreneurs forming businesses every month. After the basic decision to start a new business itself, the choice of the appropriate form for the business may well be the most significant decision facing the entrepreneur in the short run.

Internet Links

www.tannedfeet.com/choice_of_entity.htm   Entrepreneurs' Help Page

http://smallbusiness.findlaw.com/business-structures   FindLaw Small Business Center

www.llrx.com/features/llc.com   "The Limited Liability Company: The Importance of Choosing the Correct Business Vehicles," by Sarah Spear

Problems

Jake and Carolyn were convinced that their high-tech invention could revolutionize telecommunications. And apparently they were not too far off in that estimation, since they had gotten very positive early indications from a number of venture capital firms they had approached with the idea. Most of the venture capitalists had told Jake and Carolyn that they would be interested in making a substantial investment in a company to be formed to exploit the invention as soon as Jake and Carolyn had produced a working prototype. This would cost some money in design and engineering expenses, which Jake and Carolyn would pay with their own funds, but after that, all future development and marketing costs would be defrayed by the investors. What form of business entity should Jake and Carolyn choose for this business?

Acting upon their mutual love of cupcakes, Lauren and Claire were going into the bakery business together. Although neither of them had any capital to invest in the business, they were fortunate to have parents who were willing to lend money to the business on a favorable interest rate and repayment schedule. Lauren and Claire's projections showed that for at least the first 12 months of the business the costs of renting space and equipment and paying their employees would outpace their revenue, even with Lauren and Claire taking out virtually nothing for themselves. But they were convinced that the business would turn profitable after a year's time. What form of business entity should Lauren and Claire choose for their bakery?

For Further Reading

Bischoff, William, *Choosing the Right Business Entity: Tax Practitioner's Guide* (Gaithersburg, MD: Aspen Publishers, 2001).

Diamond, Michael R., *How to Incorporate: A Handbook for Entrepreneurs and Professionals* (Hoboken, NJ: John Wiley & Sons, 2007).

Mancuso, Anthony, *LLC or Corporation? How to Choose the Right Form for Your Business* (Berkeley, CA: Nolo, 2008).

Shenkman, Martin M., *Starting a Limited Liability Company* (Hoboken, NJ: John Wiley & Sons, 2003).

Spadaccini, Michael, *Business Structures: Forming a Corporation, LLC, Partnership or Sole Proprietorship* (Irvine, CA: Entrepreneur Press, 2007).

Steingold, Fred, *Legal Guide for Starting & Running a Small Business* (Berkeley, CA: Nolo, 2006).

Williamson, Harvey J., *Handbook on the Law of Small Business Enterprises* (Louisville, CO: Argyle Publishing Company, 2006).

9

Taxes and Business Decisions

Richard P. Mandel

It is not possible to fully describe the federal taxation system in the space of one book chapter. It may not even be realistic to attempt to describe federal taxation in a full volume. After all, a purchaser of the Internal Revenue Code can expect to carry home multiple volumes consisting of thousands of pages, ranging from Section 1 through Section 9833, if one includes the estate and gift tax and administrative provisions. And this does not even begin to address the myriad Regulations, Revenue Rulings, Revenue Procedures, Technical Advice Memoranda, Private Letter Rulings, court decisions, and other sources of federal tax law that have proliferated over the better part of the twentieth century and the early twenty-first century.

Fortunately, most people who enroll in a federal tax course during their progression toward an MBA have no intention of becoming professional tax advisers. An effective tax course, therefore, rather than attempting to impart encyclopedic knowledge of the tax code, instead presents taxation as another strategic management tool, available to managers or entrepreneurs in their quest to reach business goals in a more efficient and cost-effective manner. After completing such a course, the businessperson should always be conscious that failure to consider tax consequences when structuring a transaction may result in needless tax expense.

It is thus the purpose of this chapter to illustrate the necessity of taking taxation into account when structuring most business transactions, and of consulting tax professionals early in the process, not just when it is time to file the return. This will be attempted by describing various problems and opportunities encountered by a fictitious business owner as he progresses from early successes, through the acquisition of a related business, to intergenerational succession problems.

The Business

We first encounter our sample business when it has been turning a reasonable profit for the past few years under the wise stewardship of its founder and sole stockholder, Morris. The success of his wholesale horticultural supply business (Plant Supply, Inc.) has been a source of great satisfaction to Morris, as has the recent entry into the business of his daughter, Lisa. Morris paid Lisa's business school tuition, hoping to groom her to take over the family business, and his investment seems to be paying off as Lisa has become more and more valuable to her father. Morris (rightly or wrongly) does not feel the same way about his only other offspring, his son, Victor, the violinist, who appears to have no interest whatsoever in the business, except for its potential to subsidize his attempts to break into the concert world.

At this time, Morris is about to score another coup: Plant Supply has purchased a plastics molding business so it can fabricate its own trays, pots, and other planting containers instead of purchasing such items from others. Morris considers himself fortunate to secure the services of Brad (the plant manager of the molding company), because neither he nor Lisa knows very much about the molding business. He is confident that negotiations then under way will bring Brad aboard with a satisfactory compensation package. Thus, Morris can afford to turn his attention to the pleasant problem of distributing the wealth generated by his successful business.

Unreasonable Compensation

Most entrepreneurs long for the day when their most pressing problem is figuring out what to do with all the money their business is generating. Yet this very condition was now occupying Morris's mind. Brad did not present any problems in this context. His compensation package would be dealt with through ongoing negotiations and, of course, he was not family. But Morris was responsible for supporting his wife and two children. Despite what Morris perceived as the unproductive nature of Victor's pursuits, Morris was determined to maintain a standard of living for Victor befitting the son of a captain of industry. Of course, Lisa was also entitled to an affluent lifestyle, but surely she was additionally entitled to extra compensation for her long hours at work.

The simple and natural reaction to this set of circumstances would be to pay Lisa and Morris a reasonable salary for their work, and have the corporation pay the remaining distributable profit (after retaining whatever was necessary for operations) to Morris. Morris could then take care of his wife and Victor as he saw fit. Yet such a natural reaction would ignore serious tax complications.

The distribution to Morris beyond his reasonable salary would likely be characterized by the IRS as a dividend to the corporation's sole stockholder. Since dividends cannot be deducted by the corporation as an expense, both the corporation and Morris would pay tax on these monies (the well-known bugaboo of corporate double taxation). A dollar of profit could easily be reduced to as little as 43 cents of after-tax money in Morris's pocket (see Exhibit 9.1).

Knowing this, one might argue that the distribution to Morris should be characterized as a year-end bonus. Since compensation is tax deductible to the corporation, the corporate level of taxation would be removed. Unfortunately, Congress has long since limited the compensation deduction to a "reasonable" amount. The IRS judges the reasonableness of a payment by comparing it to the salaries paid to other employees performing

Exhibit 9.1   Double taxation.

$1.00	Earned
−0.34	Corporate tax at 34%
$0.66	Dividend
−0.10	Dividend tax at 15%
$0.56	Remains

similar services in similar businesses. It also examines whether such amount is paid as regular salary or as a year-end lump sum when profit levels are known. The scooping up by Morris of whatever money was not nailed down at the end of the year would surely come under attack by an IRS auditor. Why not, then, put Victor on the payroll directly, thus reducing the amount that Morris must take out of the company for his family? Again, such a payment would run afoul of the reasonableness standard. If Morris would come under attack despite his significant efforts for the company, imagine attempting to defend payments made to a so-called employee who expends no such efforts.

Subchapter S

The solution to the unreasonable compensation problem may lie in a relatively well-known tax strategy known as the subchapter S election. A corporation making this election remains a standard business corporation for all purposes other than taxation (retaining its ability to grant limited liability to its stockholders, for example). The corporation elects to forgo taxation at the corporate level and to be taxed similarly to a partnership. This means that a corporation that has elected subchapter S status will escape any taxation at the corporate level, but its stockholders will be taxed on their pro rata share of the corporation's profits, regardless of whether these profits are distributed to them. Under this election, Morris's corporation would pay no corporate tax, but Morris would pay income tax on all the corporation's profits, even those retained for operations.

This election is recommended in a number of circumstances. One example is the corporation that expects to incur losses, at least in its start-up phase. In the absence of a subchapter S election, such losses would simply collect at the corporate level, awaiting a time in the future when they could be carried forward to offset future profits (should there ever be any). If the election is made, the losses would pass through to the stockholders in the current year, and might offset other income of these stockholders, such as interest, dividends from investments, and salaries.

Another such circumstance is when a corporation expects to sell substantially all its assets sometime in the future in an acquisition transaction. Since the repeal of the so-called General Utilities doctrine, such a corporation would incur a substantial income tax on the difference between the value of its assets at the time of sale and their depreciated basis on the corporation's books, in addition to the capital gain tax incurred by its stockholders when the proceeds of such sale are distributed to them. The subchapter S election (if made early enough) again eliminates tax at the corporate level, leaving only the tax on the stockholders.

The circumstance most relevant to Morris is the corporation with too much profit to distribute as reasonable salary and bonuses. Instead of fighting the battle of reasonableness with the IRS, Morris could elect subchapter S status, thus rendering the controversy moot. It will not matter that the amount paid to him is too large to be anything but a nondeductible dividend, because it is no longer necessary to be concerned about the corporation's ability to deduct the expense. Not all corporations are eligible to elect subchapter S status. However, contrary to common misconception, eligibility has nothing to do with being a small business. In simplified form, to qualify for a subchapter S election, the corporation must have only one class of stock, held by 100 or fewer stockholders, all of whom must be individuals who are either U.S. citizens or resident aliens. Plant Supply qualifies on all these counts.

Alternatively, many companies have accomplished the same tax results, while avoiding the eligibility limitations of subchapter S, by operating as limited liability companies (LLCs).

Under subchapter S or as a LLC, Morris can pay himself and Lisa a reasonable salary and then take the rest of the money either as salary or as a dividend without fear of challenge. He can then distribute that additional money between Lisa and Victor, to support their individual lifestyles. Thus, it appears that the effective use of a strategic taxation tool has solved an otherwise costly problem.

Gift Tax

Unfortunately, like most tax strategies, the preceding solution may not be cost free. It is always necessary to consider whether the solution of one tax problem may create others, sometimes emanating from taxes other than the income tax. To begin with, Morris needs to be aware that under any strategy he adopts, the gifts of surplus cash he makes to his children may subject him to a federal gift tax. This gift tax supplements the federal estate tax, which imposes a tax on the transfer of assets from one generation to the next. Lifetime gifts to the next generation would, in the absence of a gift tax, frustrate estate tax policy. Fortunately, in order to accommodate the tendency of individuals to make gifts for reasons unrelated to estate planning, the gift tax exempts gifts by donors of up to $13,000 per year to each of their donees. That amount is adjusted for inflation as years go by. Furthermore, it is doubled if the donor's spouse consents to the use of his or her $13,000 allotment to cover the excess. Thus, Morris could distribute up to $26,000 in excess cash each year to each of his two children if his wife consented.

In addition, the federal gift tax does not take hold until the combined total of taxable lifetime gifts in excess of the annual exclusion exceeds $1 million (in 2009). Thus, Morris can exceed the annual $26,000 amount by quite a bit before the government will get its share.

These rules may suggest an alternative strategy to Morris under which he may transfer some portion of his stock to each of his children, and then have the corporation distribute dividends to him and to them directly each year. The gift tax would be implicated to the extent of the value of the stock in the year it is given, but from then on no gifts would be necessary. Such strategy, in fact, describes a fourth circumstance in which the subchapter S election is recommended: when the company wishes to distribute profits to nonemployee stockholders for whom salary or bonus in any amount would be considered excessive. In such a case, like that of Victor, the owner of the company can choose subchapter S status for it, make a gift to the nonemployee of stock, and adopt a policy of distributing annual dividends from profits, thus avoiding any challenge to a corporate deduction based on unreasonable compensation.

Making the Subchapter S Election

Before Morris rushes off to make his election, however, he should be aware of a few additional complications. Congress has historically been aware of the potential for corporations to avoid corporate-level taxation on profits and capital gains earned prior to the subchapter S election, but not realized until afterward. Thus, for example, if Morris's corporation has been accounting for its inventory on a last in, first out (LIFO) basis, in an inflationary era (such as virtually any time during the past 50 years) taxable profits have been depressed by the use of higher-cost inventory as the basis for calculation. Earlier lower-cost inventory has been left on the shelf (from an accounting point of view), waiting for later sales. However, if those later sales will now come during a time when the corporation is avoiding tax under subchapter S, those higher taxable profits will never be taxed at the corporate level. Thus, for the year just preceding the election, the tax code requires recalculation of the corporation's profits on a first in, first out (FIFO) inventory basis to capture the amount that was postponed. If Morris has been using the LIFO method, his subchapter S election will carry some cost.

Similarly, if Morris's corporation has been reporting to the IRS on a cash accounting basis, it has been recognizing income only when collected, regardless of when a sale was actually made. The subchapter S election, therefore, affords the possibility that many sales made near the end of the final year of corporate taxation will never be taxed at the corporate level, because these receivables will not be collected until after the election is in effect. As a result, the IRS requires all accounts receivable of a cash-basis taxpayer to be taxed as if collected in the last year of corporate taxation, thus adding to the cost of Morris's subchapter S conversion.

Of course, the greatest source of untapped corporate tax potential lies in corporate assets that have appreciated in value while the corporation was subject to corporate tax, but are not sold by the corporation until after the subchapter S election is in place. In the worst nightmares of the IRS, corporations that are about to sell all their assets in a corporate acquisition first elect subchapter S treatment and then immediately sell out, avoiding millions of dollars of tax liability.

Fortunately for the IRS, Congress has addressed this problem by imposing taxation at the corporate level of all so-called built-in gain realized by a converted S corporation within the first 10 years after its conversion. Built-in gain is the untaxed appreciation that existed at the time of the subchapter S election. It is taxed not only upon a sale of all the corporation's assets, but anytime the corporation disposes of an asset it owned at the time of its election. This makes it advisable to have an appraisal done for all the corporation's assets as of the first day of subchapter S status, so that there is some objective basis for the calculation of built-in gain upon sale somewhere down the line. This appraisal will further deplete Morris's coffers if he adopts the subchapter S strategy. However, despite these complications, it is still likely that Morris will find the subchapter S election to be an attractive solution to his family and compensation problems.

Just in case Morris is thinking in this direction, converting his corporation to an LLC has even more dire tax consequences. Such a transaction is treated, for tax purposes, as a dissolution of the corporation and the formation, by its shareholders, of the LLC by contribution of the dissolved corporation's assets and liabilities to the new entity. This will cause the immediate recognition of all built-in gain at the corporate level in addition to capital gain for the shareholders as their shares are constructively redeemed.

Pass-Through Entity

Consider how a subchapter S corporation might operate were the corporation to experience a period during which it was not so successful. Subchapter S corporations (as well as most LLCs, partnerships, and limited partnerships) are known as pass-through entities, because they pass through their tax attributes to their owners. This not only operates to pass through profits to the tax returns of the owners (whether or not accompanied by cash), but also results in the pass-through of losses. As discussed earlier, these losses can then be used by the owners to offset income from other sources rather than having the losses frozen at the corporate level waiting for future profit.

The Internal Revenue Code, not surprisingly, places limits on the amount of loss that can be passed through to an owner's tax return. In a subchapter S corporation, the amount of loss is limited by a stockholder's basis in his or her investment in the corporation. Basis includes the amount invested as equity plus any amount the stockholder has advanced to the corporation as loans. As the corporation operates, the basis is raised by the stockholder's pro rata share of any profit made by the corporation and lowered by the pro rata share of loss and any distributions received.

These rules might turn Morris's traditional financing strategy on its head the next time he sits down with the corporation's bank loan officer to negotiate an extension of the corporation's financing. In the past, Morris has always attempted to induce the loan officer to lend directly to the corporation. This way Morris hoped to escape personal liability for the loan (although in the beginning he was forced to give the bank a personal guarantee). In addition, the corporation could pay back the bank directly, getting a tax deduction for the interest. If the loan were made to Morris, he would have to turn the money over to the corporation and then depend on the corporation to generate enough profit so it could distribute monies to him to cover his personal debt service. He might try to characterize those distributions to him as repayment of a loan he made to the corporation, but, given the amount he had already advanced to the corporation in its earlier years, the IRS would probably object to the debt-to-equity ratio and recharacterize the payment as a nondeductible dividend fully taxable to Morris. We have already discussed why Morris would prefer to avoid characterizing the payment as additional compensation: His level of compensation was already at the outer edge of reasonableness.

Under the subchapter S election, however, Morris no longer has to be concerned about characterizing cash flow from the corporation to himself in a manner that would be deductible by the corporation. Moreover, if the loan is made to the corporation, it does not increase Morris's basis in his investment (even if he has given a personal guarantee). This limits his ability to pass losses through to his return. Thus, the subchapter S election may result in the unseemly spectacle of Morris begging his banker to lend the corporation's money directly to him, so that he might in turn advance the money to the corporation and increase his basis. This would not be necessary in an LLC, since most loans advanced to this form of business entity increase the basis of its owners.

Passive Losses

No discussion of pass-through entities should proceed without at least touching on what may have been the most creative set of changes made to the Internal Revenue Code in recent times. Prior to 1987, an entire industry had arisen to create and market business enterprises whose main purpose was to generate losses to pass through to their wealthy investors/owners. These losses, it was hoped, would normally be generated by depreciation, amortization, and depletion. These would be mere paper losses, incurred while the business itself was breaking even or possibly generating positive cash flow. They would be followed some years in the future by a healthy long-term capital gain. Thus, an investor with high taxable income could be offered short-term pass-through tax losses with a nice long-term gain waiting in the wings. In those days, long-term capital gain was taxed at only 40% of the rate of ordinary income, so the tax was not only deferred, but also substantially reduced. These businesses were known as tax shelters.

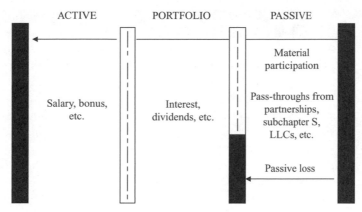

Exhibit 9.2   Passive activity losses.

The Tax Reform Act of 1986 substantially reduced the effectiveness of the tax shelter by classifying taxable income and loss into three major categories: active, portfolio, and passive. Active income consists mainly of wages, salaries, and bonuses; portfolio income is mainly interest and dividends; while passive income and loss consist of distributions from the so-called "pass-through" entities, such as LLCs, limited partnerships, and subchapter S corporations. In their most simple terms, the passive activity loss rules add to the limits set by the above described basis limitations (and the similar so-called "at-risk rules"), making it impossible to use passive losses to offset active or portfolio income. Thus, tax shelter losses can no longer be used to shelter salaries or investment proceeds; they must wait for the taxpayer's passive activities to generate the anticipated end-of-the-line gains, or be used when the taxpayer disposes of a passive activity in a taxable transaction (see Exhibit 9.2).

Fortunately for Morris, the passive activity loss rules are unlikely to affect his thinking for at least two reasons. First, the Internal Revenue Code defines a passive activity as the conduct of any trade or business "in which the taxpayer does not materially participate." Material participation is further defined in a series of tax code sections and Regulations (which mock the concept of tax simplification, but let Morris off the hook) to include any taxpayer who participates in the business for more than 500 hours per year. Morris is clearly materially participating in his business, despite his status as a stockholder of a subchapter S corporation, and thus the passive loss rules do not apply to him. The second reason Morris is not concerned is that he does not anticipate any losses from this business; historically, it has been very profitable. Therefore, let us depart from this detour into unprofitability and consider Morris's acquisition of the plastics plant.

Acquisition

Morris might well believe that the hard part of accomplishing a successful acquisition is locating an appropriate target and integrating it into his existing operation. Yet, once again, he would be well advised to pay some attention to the various tax strategies and results available to him when structuring the acquisition transaction.

To begin with, Morris has a number of ways to acquire the target business. Simply put, these choices boil down to either acquiring the stock of the owners of the business,

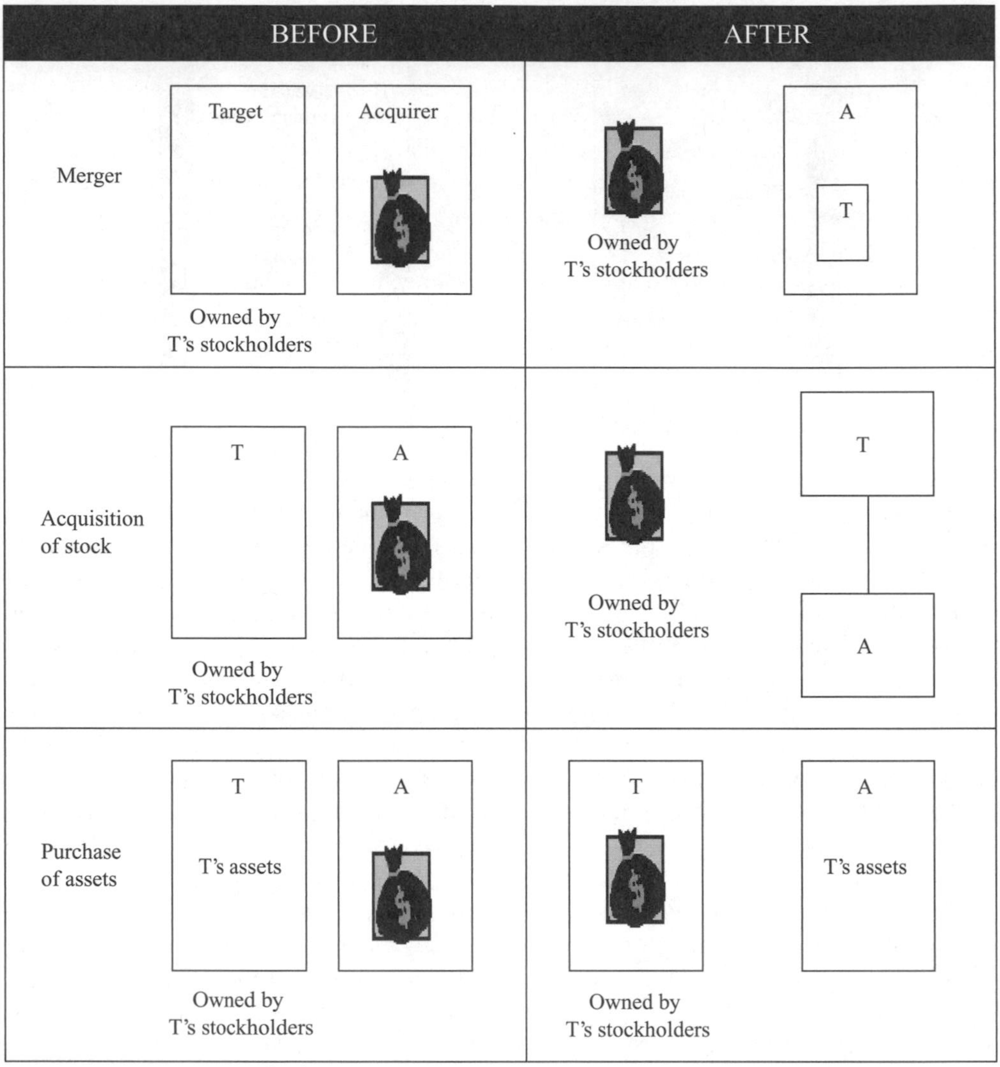

BEFORE	AFTER
Merger Target Acquirer Owned by T's stockholders	Owned by T's stockholders A (T)
Acquisition of stock T A Owned by T's stockholders	Owned by T's stockholders T — A
Purchase of assets T (T's assets) A Owned by T's stockholders	T (T's assets) A (T's assets) Owned by T's stockholders

Exhibit 9.3   Acquisition strategies.

merging the target corporation into Plant Supply, or purchasing the assets and liabilities of the target (see Exhibit 9.3). The choice of method will depend on a number of factors, many of which are not tax-related. For example, acquisition by merger will force Plant Supply to acquire all the liabilities of the target, even those that neither it nor the target knows about. Acquisition of the stock of the target by Plant Supply will also result in acquisition of all liabilities, but isolates them in a separate corporation, which becomes a subsidiary. (The same result would be achieved by merging the target into a newly formed subsidiary of Plant Supply—the so-called triangular merger.) Acquisition of the assets and liabilities normally results in exposure to only the liabilities Morris chooses to acquire and is thus an attractive choice for the acquirer.

Yet tax factors normally play a large part in structuring an acquisition. For example, if the target corporation has a history of losses and thus boasts a tax-loss carryforward,

Morris may wish to apply such losses to its future profitable operations. This would be impossible if he acquired the assets and liabilities of the target for cash, since the target corporation would still exist after the transaction, keeping its tax characteristics to itself. Cash mergers are treated as asset acquisitions for tax purposes. However, if the acquirer obtains the stock of the target, the acquirer has taken control of the taxable entity itself, thus obtaining its tax characteristics for future use. This result inspired a lively traffic in tax-loss carryforwards in years past, where failed corporations were marketed to profitable corporations seeking tax relief.

Congress has put a damper on such activity by limiting the use of a tax-loss carryforward in each of the years following an ownership change of more than 50% of a company's stock. The amount of that limit is the product of the value of the business at acquisition (normally its selling price) times an interest rate linked to the market for federal Treasury obligations. This amount of tax-loss carryforward is available each year until the losses expire (15 to 20 years after they were incurred). Since a corporation with significant losses would normally be valued at a relatively low amount, the yearly available loss is likely to be relatively trivial.

Acquisition of the corporation's assets and liabilities for cash or through a cash merger eliminates any use by the acquirer of the target's tax-loss carryforward, leaving it available for use by the target's shell. This may be quite useful to the target, because, as discussed earlier, if it has not elected subchapter S status for the past 10 years (or for the full term of its existence, if shorter), it is likely to have incurred a significant gain upon the sale of its assets. This gain would be taxable at the corporate level before the remaining portion of the purchase price could be distributed to the target's shareholders (where it will be taxed again).

The acquirer may have lost any carryforwards otherwise available, but it does obtain the right to carry the acquired assets on its books at the price paid (rather than the amount carried on the target's books). This is an attractive proposition because the owner of assets used in business may deduct an annual amount corresponding to the depreciation of those assets, subject only to the requirement that it lower the basis of those assets by an equal amount. The amount of depreciation available corresponds to the purchase price of the asset. This is even more attractive, because Congress has adopted available depreciation schedules that normally exceed the rate at which assets actually depreciate. Thus, these assets likely have a low basis in the hands of the target (resulting in even more taxable gain to the target upon sale). If the acquirer were forced to begin its depreciation at the point at which the target left off (as in a purchase of stock), little depreciation would likely result. All things being equal (and especially if the target has enough tax-loss carryforward to absorb any conceivable gain), Morris would likely wish to structure his acquisition as an asset purchase and allocate all the purchase price among the depreciable assets acquired.

This last point is significant because Congress does not recognize all assets as depreciable. An asset will generally be depreciable only if it has a demonstrable useful life. Assets that will last forever or whose lifetimes are not predictable are not depreciable, and the price paid for them will not result in future tax deductions. The most obvious example of this type of asset is land. Unlike buildings, land has an unlimited useful life and is not depreciable. This has spawned some very creative approaches, including one enterprising individual who purchased a plot of land containing a deep depression that he intended to use as a garbage dump. The taxpayer allocated a significant amount of his purchase price to the depression and took depreciation deductions as the hole filled up.

Congress has recognized that the aforementioned rules give acquirers incentive to allocate most of their purchase price to depreciable assets like buildings and equipment and very little of the price to nondepreciable assets such as land. Additional opportunities for this include allocating high prices to acquired inventory so that it generates little taxable profit when sold. This practice has been limited by legislation requiring the acquirer to allocate the purchase price in accordance with the fair market value of the individual assets, applying the rest to goodwill (which may be depreciated over 15 years).

Although this legislation will limit Morris's options significantly, if he chooses to proceed with an asset purchase, he should not overlook the opportunity to divert some of the purchase price to consulting contracts for the previous owners. Such payments will be deductible by Plant Supply over the life of the agreements and are, therefore, just as useful as depreciation. However, the taxability of such payments to the previous owners cannot be absorbed by the target's tax-loss carryforward. And the amount of such deductions will be limited by the now-familiar unreasonable compensation doctrine. Payments for agreements not to compete are treated as a form of goodwill and are deductible over 15 years regardless of the length of such agreements.

Executive Compensation

Brad's compensation package raises a number of interesting tax issues that may not be readily apparent but deserve careful consideration in crafting an offer to him. Any offer of compensation to an executive of his caliber will include, at the very least, a significant salary and bonus package. These will not normally raise any sophisticated tax problems; the corporation will deduct these payments, and Brad will be required to include them in his taxable income. The IRS is not likely to challenge the deductibility of even a very generous salary, since Brad is not a stockholder or family member and thus there is little likelihood of an attempt to disguise a dividend.

Business Expenses

However, even in the area of salary, there are opportunities for the use of tax strategies. For example, Brad's duties may include the entertainment of clients or travel to suppliers and other business destinations. It is conceivable that Brad could be expected to fund these activities out of his own pocket on the theory that such amounts have been figured into his salary. Such a procedure avoids the need for the bookkeeping associated with expense accounts. If his salary reflects these expectations, Brad may not mind declaring the extra amount as taxable income, since he will be entitled to an offsetting deduction for these business expenses.

Unfortunately, however, Brad would be in for an unpleasant surprise under these circumstances. First of all, these expenses may not all be deductible in full. Meals and entertainment expenses are deductible, if at all, only to the extent they are not "lavish and extravagant" and even then they are deductible only for a portion of the amount expended. In addition, Brad's business expenses as an employee are considered miscellaneous deductions; they are deductible only to the extent that they and other similarly classified deductions exceed 2% of Brad's adjusted gross income. Thus, if Brad's adjusted gross income is $150,000, the first $3,000 of miscellaneous deductions will not be deductible.

Moreover, as itemized deductions, these deductions are valuable only to the extent that they along with all other itemized deductions available to Brad exceed the standard deduction, an amount Congress allows each taxpayer to deduct if all itemized deductions are forgone. Furthermore, itemized deductions that survive the aforementioned cuts are further limited for taxpayers whose incomes are over $159,950 (the 2008 inflation-adjusted amount). The deductibility of Brad's business expenses is, therefore, greatly in doubt.

Knowing all this, Brad would be well advised to request that Morris revise his compensation package. Brad should request a cut in pay by the amount of his anticipated business expenses, along with a commitment that the corporation will reimburse him for such expenses or pay them directly. In that case, Brad will be in the same economic position, since his salary is lowered only by the amount he would have spent anyway. In fact, his economic position is enhanced, since he pays no taxes on the salary he does not receive, as well as escaping from the limitations on deductibility described earlier.

The corporation pays out no more money this way than it would have if the entire amount were salary. Taxwise, the corporation is only slightly worse off, since the amount it would have previously deducted as salary can now still be deducted as ordinary and necessary business expenses (with the sole exception of the limit on meals and entertainment). In fact, were Brad's salary below the Social Security contribution limit (FICA), both Brad and the corporation would be better off, because what was formerly salary (and thus subject to additional 7.65% contributions to FICA by both employer and employee) would now be merely business expenses and exempt from FICA.

Before Brad and Morris adopt this strategy, however, they should be aware that in recent years Congress has turned a sympathetic ear to the frustration the IRS has expressed about expense accounts. Legislation has conditioned the exclusion of amounts paid to an employee as expense reimbursements upon the submission by the employee to the employer of reliable documentation of such expenses. Brad should get into the habit of keeping a diary of such expenses for tax purposes.

Deferred Compensation

Often, high-level executives negotiate salaries and bonuses that far exceed their current needs. In such a case, the executive might consider deferring some of that compensation until future years. Brad may feel, for example, that he would be well advised to provide for a steady income during his retirement years, derived from his earnings while an executive of Plant Supply. He may be concerned that he would simply waste the excess compensation and may consider a deferred package as a form of forced savings. Or he may wish to defer receipt of the excess money to a time (such as retirement) when he believes he will be in a lower tax bracket. This latter consideration was more common when the federal income tax law encompassed a large number of tax brackets and the highest rates were as high as 70%.

Whatever Brad's reasons for considering a deferral of some of his salary, he should be aware that deferred compensation packages are generally classified as one of two varieties for federal income tax purposes. The first such category is the qualified deferred compensation plan, such as the pension, profit-sharing, or stock bonus plan. All these plans share a number of characteristics. First and foremost, they afford taxpayers the best of all possible worlds by granting the employer a deduction for monies contributed to the plan each year, allowing those contributions to be invested and to earn additional monies without the payment of current taxes, and taxing the employee only upon withdrawal of funds in the future. However, in order to qualify for such favorable treatment, these plans must conform to a bewildering array of conditions imposed by both the Internal Revenue Code and the Employee Retirement Income Security Act (ERISA). Among these requirements is the necessity to treat all employees of the corporation on a nondiscriminatory basis with respect to the plan, thus rendering qualified plans a poor technique for supplementing a compensation package for a highly paid executive.

The second category is nonqualified plans. These come in as many varieties as there are employees with imaginations, but they all share the same disfavored tax treatment. The employer is entitled to its deduction only when the employee pays tax on the money, and if money is contributed to such a plan the earnings are taxed currently. Thus, if Morris were to design a plan under which the corporation receives a current deduction for its contributions, Brad will pay tax now on money he will not receive until the future. Since this is the exact opposite of what Brad (and most employees) have in mind, Brad will most likely have to settle for his employer's unfunded promise to pay him the deferred amount in the future.

Assuming Brad is interested in deferring some of his compensation, he and Morris might well devise a plan that gives them as much flexibility as possible. For example, Morris might agree that the day before the end of each pay period, Brad could notify the corporation of the amount of salary, if any, he wishes to defer for that period. Any amount thus deferred would be carried on the books of the corporation as a liability to be paid, per their agreement, with interest, after Brad's retirement. Unfortunately, such an arrangement would be frustrated by the "constructive receipt" doctrine. Using this potent weapon, the IRS will impose tax (allowing a corresponding employer deduction) upon any compensation that Brad, the employee, has earned and might have chosen to receive, regardless of whether he so chooses. The taxpayer may not turn his back upon income otherwise unconditionally available to him. Further, under the recently enacted Section 409A of the Internal Revenue Code, the IRS has been given additional weapons to use against optional deferral schemes.

Taking the constructive receipt theory to its logical conclusion, one might argue that deferred compensation is taxable to the employee because he might have received it if he had simply negotiated a different compensation package. After all, the impetus for deferral in this case comes exclusively from Brad; Morris would have been happy to pay the full amount when earned. But the constructive receipt doctrine does not have that extensive a reach. The IRS can tax only monies the taxpayer was legally entitled to receive, not monies he might have received if he had negotiated differently.

Frankly, however, if Brad is convinced of the advisability of deferring a portion of his compensation, he is likely to be less concerned about the irrevocability of such election as about ensuring that the money will be available to him when it is eventually due. Thus, a mere unfunded promise to pay in the future may result in years of nightmares over a possible declaration of bankruptcy by his employer. Again, left to their own devices, Brad and Morris might well devise a plan under which Morris contributes the deferred compensation to a trust for Brad's benefit, payable to its beneficiary upon his retirement. Yet such an arrangement would be disastrous to Brad, since the IRS would currently assess income tax to Brad using the much criticized "economic benefit" doctrine.

Under this theory, monies irrevocably set aside for Brad grant him an economic benefit (presumably by improving his net worth or otherwise improving his creditworthiness) upon which he must pay tax.

If Brad were aware of this risk, he might choose another method to protect his eventual payout by requiring the corporation to secure its promise to pay with such devices as a letter of credit or a mortgage or security interest in its assets. All of these devices, however, have been successfully taxed by the IRS under the self-same economic benefit doctrine. Very few devices have survived this attack. However, the personal guarantee of Morris himself (merely another unsecured promise) would not be considered an economic benefit by the IRS.

Another successful strategy is the so-called rabbi trust, a device first used by a rabbi who feared his deferred compensation might be revoked by a future hostile congregation. This device works similarly to the trust described earlier except that Brad would not be the only beneficiary of the money contributed. Under the terms of the trust, were the corporation to experience financial reverses, the trust property would be available to the corporation's creditors. Since the monies are thus not irrevocably committed to Brad, the economic benefit doctrine is not invoked. This device does not protect Brad from the scenario of his bankruptcy nightmares, but it does protect him from a corporate change of heart regarding his eventual payout. From Morris's point of view, he may not object to contributing to a rabbi trust, since he was willing to pay all the money to Brad as salary, but he should be aware that since Brad escapes current taxation, the corporation will not receive a deduction for these expenses until the money is paid out of the trust in the future.

Interest-Free Loans

As a further enticement to agree to work for the new ownership of the plastics plant, Morris might additionally offer to lend Brad a significant amount of money to be used, for example, to purchase a new home or acquire an investment portfolio. Significant up-front money is often part of an executive compensation package. While this money could be paid as a bonus, Morris might well want some future repayment (perhaps as a way to encourage Brad to stay in his new position). Brad might wish to avoid the income tax bite on such a bonus so he can retain the full amount of the payment for his preferred use. Morris and Brad might agree to an interest rate well below the market or even no interest at all, to further entice Brad to take his new position. Economically, this would give Brad free use of the money for a period of time during which it could earn him additional income with no offsetting expense. In a sense, he would be receiving his salary in advance while not paying any income tax until he earned it. Morris might well formalize the arrangement by reserving a right to offset loan repayments against future salary. The term of the loan might even be accelerated should Brad leave the corporation's employ.

Under current tax law, however, despite the fact that little or no interest passes between Brad and the corporation, the IRS deems full market interest payments to have been made and further deems that said amount is returned to Brad by his employer. Thus, each year, Brad is deemed to have made an interest payment to the corporation for which he is entitled to no deduction. Then, when the corporation is deemed to have returned the money to him, he realizes additional compensation upon which he must pay tax. The corporation realizes additional interest income but gets a compensating deduction for additional compensation paid (assuming it is not excessive when added to Brad's other compensation). (See Exhibit 9.4.)

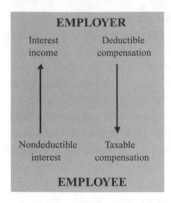 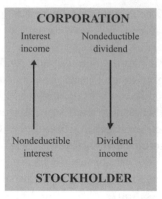 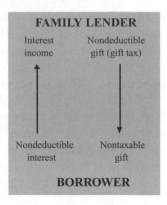

Exhibit 9.4   Taxable interest.

Moreover, the IRS has not reserved this treatment for employers and employees only. The same treatment is given to loans between corporations and their shareholders and loans between family members. In the latter situation, although there is no interest deduction for the borrower, the deemed return of the interest is a gift and is thus excluded from income. The lender receives interest income and has no compensating deduction for the return gift. In fact, if the interest amount is large enough, he may have incurred an additional gift tax on the returned interest. The amount of income created for the lender, however, is limited to the borrower's investment income, except in very large loans. In the corporation/stockholder situation, the lender incurs interest income and has no compensating deduction, as its deemed return of the interest is characterized as a dividend. Thus the IRS gets increased tax from both parties unless the corporation has selected subchapter S.

All may not be lost in this situation, however. Brad's additional income tax arises from the fact that there is no deduction allowable for interest paid on unsecured personal loans. Interest is deductible, however, in limited amounts on loans secured by a mortgage on the taxpayer's principal or secondary residence. If Brad grants Plant Supply a mortgage on his home to secure the repayment of his no- or low-interest loan, his deemed payment of market interest may become deductible mortgage interest and may thus offset his additional deemed compensation from the imaginary return of this interest. Before jumping into this transaction, however, Brad will have to consider the limited utility of itemized deductions described earlier, as well as certain limits on the deductibility of mortgage interest.

Sharing the Equity

If Brad is as sophisticated and valuable an executive employee as Morris believes he is, Brad is likely to ask for more than just a compensation package, deferred or otherwise. Such a prospective employee often demands a piece of the action—a share in the equity of the business—so that he may directly share in the growth and success he expects to create. Morris may even welcome such a demand because an equity share (if not so large as to threaten Morris's control) may serve as a form of golden handcuffs, giving Brad additional reason to stay with the company for the long term.

Assuming Morris is receptive to the idea, there are a number of different ways to grant Brad a share of the business. The most direct way would be to grant him shares of the corporation's stock. These could be given to Brad without charge, for a discount from fair market value, or for their full value, depending on the type of incentive Morris wishes to design. In addition, given the privately held nature of Morris's corporation, the shares will probably carry restrictions, designed to keep the shares from ending up in the hands of persons who are not associated with the company. Thus, the corporation will retain the right to repurchase the shares should Brad ever leave the corporation's employ or wish to sell or transfer the shares to a third party. Finally, in order to encourage Brad to stay with the company, the corporation will probably reserve the right to repurchase the shares from Brad at cost should Brad's employment end before a specified time. As an example, all the shares (called restricted stock) would be subject to forfeiture at cost (regardless of their then actual value) should Brad leave before one year; two-thirds would be forfeited if he left before two years, and one-third if he left before three years. The shares not forfeited (called vested shares) would be purchased by the corporation at their full value should Brad ever leave or attempt to sell them.

One step back from restricted stock is the stock option. This is a right granted to the employee to purchase a particular number of shares for a fixed price over a defined period of time. Because the employee's purchase price of the stock does not change, the employee has effectively been given the ability to share in whatever growth the company experiences during the life of the option, without paying for the privilege. If the stock increases in value, the employee will exercise the option near the end of the option term. If the stock value does not grow, the employee will allow the option to expire, having lost nothing. The stock option is a handy device when employees object to paying for their piece of the action (after all, they are expecting compensation, not expense), but the employer objects to giving them stock whose current value represents growth from the period before the employees' arrival. The exercise price can be more than, equal to, or less than the fair market value of the stock at the time of the grant, depending on the extent of the incentive the employer wishes to give. Also, the exercisability of the option will likely vest in stages over time.

Often, however, the founding entrepreneur cannot bring himself or herself to give an employee a current or potential portion of the corporation's stock. Although the block of stock going to the employee is too small to have any effect on the founder's control over the company, the objection may be psychological and impossible to overcome. Or, in the case of a subchapter S corporation operating in numerous different states, the employee may not want to have to file state income tax returns in all those jurisdictions. The founder seeks a device that can grant the employee a growth potential similar to that granted by stock ownership, but without the stock. Such devices are often referred to as phantom stock or stock appreciation rights (SARs). In a phantom stock plan, employees are promised that they may, at any time during a defined period so long as they remain employed by the corporation, demand payment equal to the then value of a certain number of shares of the corporation's stock. As the corporation grows, so does the amount available to the employees, just as would be the case if they actually owned some stock. SARs are very similar, except that the amount available to the employee is limited to the growth, if any, that the given number of shares has experienced since the date of grant.

Tax Effects of Phantom Stock and SARs

Having described these devices to Morris and Brad, it is, of course, important to discuss their varying tax impacts upon employer and employee. If Brad has been paying attention, he might immediately object to the phantom stock and SARs as vulnerable to the constructive receipt rule. After all, if he may claim the current value of these devices at any time he chooses, might not the IRS insist that he include each year's growth in his taxable income as if he had claimed it? Although the corporation's accountants will require that these devices be accounted for in that way on the corporation's financial statements, the IRS has failed in its attempts to require inclusion of these amounts in taxable income, because the monies are not unconditionally available to the taxpayer. In order to receive the money, one must give up any right to continue to share in the growth represented by one's phantom stock or SAR. If the right is not exercisable without cost, the income is not constructively received.

However, there is another good reason for Brad to object to phantom stock and SARs from a tax point of view. Unlike stock and stock options, both of which represent a recognized form of intangible capital asset, phantom stock and SARs are really no different from a mere promise by the corporation to pay a bonus based on a certain formula. Since these devices are not recognized as capital assets, they are not eligible to be taxed as long-term capital gains when redeemed. This difference is quite meaningful, as the maximum tax rates on ordinary income and long-term capital gains in 2008 are 35% and 15%, respectively. Thus, Brad may have good reason to reject phantom stock and SARs and insist upon the real thing.

Taxability of Stock Options

If Morris and Brad resolve their negotiations through the use of stock options, careful tax analysis is again necessary. The Code treats stock options in three different ways, depending upon the circumstances, and some of these circumstances are well within the control of the parties (see Exhibit 9.5).

If a stock option has a "readily ascertainable value," the IRS will expect the employee to include in his or her taxable income the difference between the value of the option and the amount paid for it (the amount paid is normally zero). Measured in that way,

Exhibit 9.5   Taxation of stock options.

		Grant	Exercise	Sale
Readily ascertainable value	Employee Employer	Tax of value Deduction	No tax No deduction	Capital gain No deduction
No readily ascertainable value	Employee Employer	No tax No deduction	Tax on spread Deduction	Capital gain No deduction
ISO	Employee Employer	No tax No deduction	No tax No deduction	Capital gain No deduction

the value of an option might be quite small, especially if the exercise price is close or equal to the then fair market value of the underlying stock. After all, the value of a right to buy $10 of stock for $10 is only the speculative value of having that right when the underlying value has increased. That amount is then taxed as ordinary compensation income, and the employer receives a compensating deduction for compensation paid. When the employee exercises the option, the tax code imposes no tax, nor does the employer receive any further deduction. Finally, should the employee sell the stock, the difference between the price received and the total of the previously taxed income and the amounts paid for the option and the stock is included in the employee's income as capital gain. No deduction is then granted to the employer, as the employee's decision to sell the stock is not deemed to be related to the employer's compensation policy.

This taxation scenario is normally quite attractive to employees, because they are taxed on a rather small amount at first, escape tax entirely upon exercise, and then pay tax on the growth at a time when they have realized cash with which to pay the tax at a lower long-term capital gain rate. Although the employer receives little benefit, it has cost the employer nothing in hard assets, so any benefit would be a windfall.

Because this tax scenario is seen as very favorable to the employee, the IRS has been loath to allow it in most cases. Generally, the IRS will not recognize an option as having a readily ascertainable value unless the option is traded on a recognized exchange. Short of that, a case has occasionally been made when the underlying stock is publicly traded. But the IRS has drawn the line at options on privately held stock and at all options that are not themselves transferable. Since Morris's corporation is privately held and since he will not tolerate Brad's reserving the right to transfer the option to a third party, there is no chance of Brad's taking advantage of this beneficial tax treatment.

The second tax scenario attaches to stock options that do not have a readily ascertainable value. Since, by definition, one cannot include their value in income on the date of grant (it is unknown), the Internal Revenue Code allows the grant to escape taxation. However, upon exercise, the taxpayer must include in income the difference between the then fair market value of the stock purchased and the total paid for the option and stock. When the purchased stock is later sold, the further growth is taxed at the applicable rate for capital gain. The employer receives a compensation deduction at the time of exercise and no deduction at the time of sale. Although the employee receives a deferral of taxation from grant to exercise in this scenario, this method of taxation is generally seen as less advantageous to the employee, since a larger amount of income is exposed to ordinary income rates, and this taxation occurs at a time when the taxpayer has still not received any cash from the transaction with which to pay the tax.

Recognizing the harshness of this result, Congress invented a third taxation scenario, which attaches to incentive stock options (ISOs). The recipient of such an option escapes tax upon grant of the option and again upon exercise. Upon sale of the underlying stock, the employee includes in taxable income the difference between the price received and the total paid for the stock and option, and pays tax upon that amount at long-term capital gain rates. This scenario is extremely attractive to the employee, who defers all tax until the last moment and pays at a lower rate. Under this scenario, the employer receives no deduction at all, but since the transaction costs the employer nothing, that is normally not a major concern. Lest you believe that ISOs are the perfect compensation device, however, be aware that although the employee escapes income taxation upon exercise of the option, said exercise may be deemed taxable under the alternative minimum tax (described later in this chapter).

The tax code imposes many conditions upon the grant of an incentive stock option. Among these are that the options must be granted pursuant to a written plan setting forth the maximum number of shares available and the class of employees eligible; only employees are eligible recipients; the options cannot be transferable; no more than $100,000 of underlying stock may be initially exercisable in any one year by any one employee; the exercise price of the options must be no less than the fair market value of the stock upon the date of grant; and the options must expire substantially simultaneously with the termination of the employee's employment. Perhaps most important, the underlying stock may not be sold by the employee prior to the expiration of two years from the option grant date or one year from the exercise date, whichever is later.

This latter requirement has led to what was probably an unexpected consequence. Assume that Plant Supply has granted an incentive stock option to Brad. Assume further that Brad has recently exercised the option and has plans to sell the stock he received. It may occur to Brad that by waiting a year to resell, he will be risking the vagaries of the market for a tax savings that cannot exceed 20% (the difference between the maximum income tax rate of 35% and the maximum capital gain rate of 15%). By selling early, Brad will lose the chance to treat the option as an incentive stock option, but will pay, at worst, only a marginally higher amount of tax at a time when he does have the money to pay it. Furthermore, by disqualifying the options, he will be giving his employer a tax deduction at the time of exercise. An enterprising employee might go so far as to offer to sell early in exchange for a split of the employer's tax savings.

Tax Impact on Restricted Stock

The taxation of restricted stock is not markedly different from the taxation of nonqualified stock options without a readily ascertainable value (see Exhibit 9.6). Restricted stock is defined as stock that is subject to a condition that affects its value to the holder and that will lapse upon the happening of an event or the passage of time. The Internal Revenue Code refers to this as "a substantial risk of forfeiture." Since the value of the stock to the employee is initially speculative, the receipt of the stock is not considered a taxable event. In other words, since Brad may have to forfeit whatever increased value his stock may acquire if he leaves the employ of the corporation prior to the agreed time, Congress has allowed him not to pay the tax until he knows for certain whether he will be able to retain that value. When the stock is no longer restricted (when it vests), the tax is payable. Of course, Congress is not being entirely altruistic in this case; the amount taxed when the stock vests is not the difference between what the employee pays for it and its value when first received by the employee, but the difference between the employee's cost and its value at the vesting date. If the value of the stock has increased, as everyone involved has hoped, the IRS receives a windfall. The employer receives a compensating deduction at the time of taxation, and further growth between the vesting date and the date of sale is taxed upon sale at appropriate capital gain rates. No deduction is then available to the employer.

Recognizing that allowing the employee to pay a higher tax at a later time is not an unmixed blessing, Congress has provided that an employee who receives restricted stock may, nonetheless, elect to pay ordinary income tax on the difference between its value at grant and the amount paid for it, if the employee files notice of that election within

Exhibit 9.6 Restricted stock tax impact.

		Grant	Restriction Removed	Sale
Restricted stock	Employee	No tax	Tax based on current value	Capital gain
	Employer	No deduction	deduction	No deduction
Restricted stock	Employee	Tax based on value without restriction	No tax	Capital gain
83(b) Election	Employer	deduction	No deduction	No deduction

30 days of the grant date—the so-called 83(b) election. Thus, employees can choose for themselves which gamble to accept.

This scenario can result in disaster for the unaware employee. Assume that Morris and Brad resolve their differences by allowing Brad to have an equity stake in the corporation, if he is willing to pay for it. Thus, Brad purchases 5% of the corporation for its full value on the date he joins the corporation, say, $5 per share. Since this arrangement still provides incentive in the form of a share of growth, Morris insists that Brad sell the stock back to the corporation for $5 per share should he leave the corporation before he has been employed for three years. Brad correctly believes that since he has bought $5 shares for $5, he has no taxable income, and reports nothing on his income tax return that year.

Brad has failed to realize that despite his paying full price, he has received restricted stock. As a result, Congress has done him the favor of imposing no tax until the restrictions lapse. Three years from now, when the shares may have tripled in value and have finally vested, Brad will discover to his horror that he must include $10 per share in his taxable income for that year ($15 value minus $5 initially paid). Despite the fact that he had no income to declare in the year of grant, Brad must elect to include that nullity in his taxable income for that year by filing such an election with the IRS within 30 days of his purchase of the stock.

In situations in which there is little difference between the value of stock and the amount an employee will pay for it (e.g., in start-up companies when stock has little initial value), a grant of restricted stock accompanied by an 83(b) election may be preferable to the grant of an ISO, since it avoids the alternative minimum tax, which may be imposed upon exercise of an ISO.

Vacation Home

Morris has much reason to congratulate himself on successfully acquiring the plastics molding operation as well as securing the services of Brad through an effective executive compensation package. In fact, the only real disappointment for Morris is that the closing of the deal is scheduled to take place during the week in which he normally takes his annual vacation.

Some years ago, Morris purchased a country home for use by his wife and himself as a weekend getaway and vacation spot. With the press of business, however, Morris and his wife have not been able to use the home except on occasional weekends and for his two-week summer vacation each year. Morris always takes the same two weeks for his vacation so he can indulge his love of golf. Each year, during those two weeks, the professional golfers come to town for their annual tournament. Hotels are always booked far in advance, and Morris feels lucky to be able to walk from his home to the first tee and enjoy seeing his favorite sport played by some of the world's best.

Some of Morris's friends have suggested that Morris rent his place during the weeks that he and his wife don't use it. Even if such rentals would not generate much cash during these off-season periods, the income might allow Morris to deduct some of the expenses of keeping the home, such as real estate taxes, mortgage payments, maintenance, and depreciation. Morris can see the benefit in that, since the latter two expenses are deductible only in a business context. Although taxes and mortgage interest are deductible as personal expenses (assuming, in the case of mortgage interest, that Morris is deducting such payments only with respect to this and his principal residence and no other home), the previously mentioned limits on the use of itemized deductions make the usefulness of these deductions questionable.

However, in addition to the inconvenience of renting out one's vacation home, Morris has discovered a few unfortunate tax rules that have dissuaded him from following his friends' advice. First of all, the rental of a home is treated by the tax code in a fashion similar to the conduct of a business. Thus, Morris would generate deductions only to the extent that his expenses exceeded his rental income. In addition, to the extent he could generate such a loss, the rental of real estate is deemed to be a passive activity under the Internal Revenue Code, regardless of how much effort one puts into the process. Thus, in the absence of any relief provision, these losses would be deductible only against other passive income and would not be usable against salary, bonus, or investment income.

Such a relief provision does exist, however, for rental activities in which the taxpayer is actively involved. In such a case, the taxpayer may deduct up to $25,000 of losses against active or portfolio income, unless total income (before any such deduction) exceeds $100,000. The amount of loss that may be used by such taxpayer, free of the passive activity limitations, is then lowered by $1 for every $2 of additional income, disappearing entirely at $150,000. Given his success in business, the usefulness of rental losses in the absence of passive income seems problematic to Morris, at best.

Another tax rule appears to Morris to limit the usefulness of losses even further. Under the Internal Revenue Code, a parcel of real estate falls into one of three categories: personal use, rental use, or mixed use. A personal use property is one that is rented 14 days or less in a year and otherwise used by the taxpayer and family. No expenses are deductible for such a facility except taxes and mortgage interest. A rental use property is used by the taxpayer and family for less than 15 days (or 10% of the number of rental days) and otherwise offered for rental. All the expenses of such an activity are deductible, subject to the passive loss limitations. A mixed use facility is one that falls within neither of the other two categories.

If Morris were to engage in a serious rental effort of his property, his occasional weekend use, combined with his two-week stay around the golf tournament, would surely result in his home falling into the mixed use category. This would negatively impact him in two ways. The expenses that are deductible only for a rental facility (such as maintenance and depreciation) would be deductible only on a pro rata basis for the total number of rental days. Worse yet, the expenses of the rental business would be deductible only to the extent of the income, not beyond. Expenses that would be deductible anyway (taxes and mortgage interest) are counted first in this calculation, and only then are the remaining expenses allowed. The result of all this is that it would be impossible for Morris to generate a deductible loss, even if it were possible to use such a loss in the face of the passive loss limitations.

Naturally, therefore, Morris has long since decided not to bother with attempting to rent his country getaway when he and his wife are unable to use it. However, the scheduling of the closing this year presents a unique tax opportunity of which he may be unaware. In a rare stroke of fairness, the Internal Revenue Code, while denying any deduction of not otherwise deductible expenses in connection with a home rented for 14 days or less, reciprocates by allowing taxpayers to exclude any rental income should they take advantage of the 14-day rental window. Normally, such an opportunity is of limited utility, but with the tournament coming to town and the hotels full, Morris is in a position to make a killing by renting his home to a golfer or spectator during this time at inflated rental rates. All that rental income would be entirely tax-free. Just be sure the tenants don't stay beyond two weeks.

Like-Kind Exchanges

Having acquired the desired new business and secured the services of the individual he needs to run it, Morris turns his attention to consolidating his two operations so that they might function more efficiently. After some time, he realizes that the factory building acquired with the plastics business is not contributing to increased efficiency because of its age and, more important, because of its distance from Morris's home office. Morris finds a more modern facility near his main location that can accommodate both operations and allow him to eliminate some amount of duplicative management.

Naturally, Morris puts the molding facility on the market and plans to purchase the new facility with the proceeds of the old one plus some additional capital. Such a strategy will result in a tax upon the sale of the older facility, equal to the difference between the sale price and Plant Supply's basis in the building. If Morris purchased the molding company by merging or purchasing its assets for cash, then the capital gain to be taxed here may be minimal, because it would consist only of the growth in value since this purchase plus any amount depreciated after the acquisition. If, however, Morris acquired the molding company through a purchase of stock, his basis will be the old company's preacquisition basis, and the capital gain may be considerable. Either way, it would surely be desirable to avoid taxation on this capital gain.

The tax code affords Morris the opportunity to avoid this taxation if, instead of selling his old facility and buying a new one, he can arrange a trade of the old for the new so that no cash falls into his hands. Under Section 1031 of the Internal Revenue Code, if properties of like kind used in a trade or business are exchanged, no taxable event has occurred. The gain on the disposition of the older facility is merely deferred until the eventual disposition of the newer facility. This is accomplished by calculating the basis in the newer facility, starting with its fair market value on the date of acquisition, and subtracting from that amount the gain not recognized upon the sale of the older facility. That process builds the unrecognized gain into the basis of the newer building so that it will be recognized (along with any future gain) upon its later sale. There has been considerable confusion and debate over what constitutes like-kind property outside of real estate, but there is no doubt that a trade of real estate used in business for other real estate to be used in business will qualify under Section 1031.

Although undoubtedly attracted by this possibility, Morris would quickly point out that such an exchange would be extremely rare since it is highly unlikely that he would be able to find a new facility that is worth exactly the same amount as his old facility, and thus any such exchange will have to involve a payment of cash as well as an exchange of buildings. Fortunately, however, Section 1031 recognizes that reality by providing that the exchange is still nontaxable to Morris so long as he does not receive any non-like-kind property (e.g., cash). Such non-like-kind property received is known as boot, and will include, besides cash, any liability of Morris's (such as his mortgage debt) assumed by the exchange partner. The facility he is purchasing is more expensive than the one he is selling, so Morris will have to add some cash, not receive it. Thus, the transaction does not involve the receipt of boot and still qualifies for tax deferral. Moreover, even if Morris did receive boot in the transaction, he would recognize gain only to the extent of the boot received, so he might still be in a position to defer a portion of the gain involved. Of course, if he received more boot than the gain in the transaction, he would recognize only the amount of the gain, not the full amount of the boot.

But Morris has an even more compelling, practical objection to this plan. How often will the person who wants to purchase your facility own the exact facility you wish to purchase? Not very often, he would surmise. In fact, the proposed buyer of his old facility is totally unrelated to the current owner of the facility Morris wishes to buy. How then can one structure this as an exchange of the two parcels of real estate? It would seem, therefore, that a taxable sale of the one, followed by a purchase of the other, will be necessary in almost every case.

Practitioners have, however, devised a technique to overcome this problem, known as the three-corner exchange. In a nutshell, the transaction is structured by having the proposed buyer of Morris's old facility use his purchase money (plus some additional money contributed by Morris) to acquire the facility Morris wants to buy, instead of giving that money to Morris. Having thus acquired the new facility, he then trades it to Morris for Morris's old facility. When the dust settles, everyone is in the same position they would have occupied in the absence of an exchange. The former owner of the new facility has his cash; the proposed buyer of Morris's old facility now owns that facility and has spent only the amount he had proposed to spend; and Morris has traded the old facility plus some cash for the new one. The only party adversely affected is the IRS, which now must wait to tax the gain in Morris's old facility until he sells the new one.

This technique appears so attractive that when practitioners first began to use it, they attempted to employ the technique even when the seller of the old facility had not yet found a new facility to buy. They merely had the buyer of the old facility place the purchase price in escrow and promise to use it to buy a new facility for the old owner as soon as he picked one out. More often, these delayed exchanges are conducted through an independent third-party intermediary, who keeps the cash out of the seller's hands until the new facility is found. Congress has since limited the use of these delayed like-kind exchanges by requiring the seller of the old facility to identify the new facility to be purchased within 45 days of the transfer of the old one and by further requiring that the exchange be completed within six months of the first transfer.

Dividends

Some time after Morris engineered the acquisition of the molding facility, the hiring of Brad to run it, and the consolidation of his company's operations through the like-kind exchange, Plant Supply is running smoothly and profitably enough for Morris's thoughts to turn to retirement. Morris intends to have a comfortable retirement funded by the fruits of his lifelong efforts on behalf of the company, so it is not unreasonable for him to consider funding his retirement through dividends on what would still be his considerable holdings of the company's stock. Although Brad already holds some stock and Morris expects that Lisa and Victor will hold some at that time, he still expects to have a majority position and thus sufficient control of the board of directors to ensure such distributions.

Morris also knows enough about tax law, however, to understand that such distributions would cause considerable havoc from a tax viewpoint. We have already discussed how characterizing such distributions as salary or bonus would avoid double taxation, but with Morris no longer working for the company such characterization would be unreasonable. These payments would be deemed dividends on his stock. They would be nondeductible to the corporation (if it were not a subchapter S corporation at the time) and would be fully taxable to him. But Morris has another idea. He will embark on a strategy of turning in small amounts of his stock on a regular basis in exchange for the stock's value. Although not a perfect solution, the distributions to him will no longer be dividends but payments in redemption of stock. Thus, they will be taxable only to the extent they exceed his basis in the stock, and even then, only at long-term capital gain rates (not as ordinary income). Best of all, if such redemptions are small enough, he will retain his control over the company for as long as he retains more than 50% of its outstanding stock.

However, the benefits of this type of plan have attracted the attention of Congress and the IRS over the years. If an individual can draw monies out of a corporation without affecting the control he or she asserts through the ownership of stock, is the person really redeeming his stock or simply engaging in a disguised dividend? Congress has answered this question with a series of Internal Revenue Code sections purporting to define a redemption.

Substantially Disproportionate Distributions

Most relevant to Morris is Section 302(b)(2), which provides that a distribution in respect of stock is a redemption (and thus taxable as capital gain after subtraction of basis) only if it is substantially disproportionate. This is further defined by requiring that the stockholder hold, after the distribution, less than half of the total combined voting power of all classes of stock, and less than 80% of the percentage of the company's total stock that the stockholder owned prior to the distribution.

Thus, if Morris intended to redeem five shares of the company's stock at a time when he owned 85 of the company's 100 outstanding shares, he would be required to report the entire distribution as a dividend. His percentage of ownership would still be 50% or more (80 out of 95 shares, or 84%), which in itself dooms the transaction. In addition, his percentage of ownership will still be more than 80% of his percentage before the distribution (dropping only from 85% to 84%, or 99% of the before percentage).

To qualify, Morris would have to redeem 71 shares, since only that amount would drop his control percentage below 50% (14 of 29 or 48%). And since his percentage of control would have dropped from 85% to 48%, he would retain only 56% of the percentage he previously had (less than 80%).

Yet even such a draconian sell-off as thus described would not be sufficient for the tax code. Congress has taken the position that the stock ownership of persons other than oneself must be taken into account in determining one's control of a corporation. Under these so-called attribution rules, a stockholder is deemed to control stock owned not only by himself or herself but also by his or her spouse, children, grandchildren, and parents. Furthermore, stock owned by partnerships, estates, trusts, and corporations affiliated with the stockholder may also be attributed to that stockholder. Thus, assuming that Lisa and Victor owned 10 of the remaining 15 shares of stock (with Brad owning the rest), Morris begins with 95% of the control and can qualify for a stock redemption only by selling all of his shares to the corporation.

Complete Termination of Interest

Carried to its logical conclusion, even a complete redemption would not qualify for favorable tax treatment, since Lisa's and Victor's shares would still be attributed to Morris, leaving him in control of 67 percent of the corporation's stock. Fortunately, however, Code Section 302(b)(3) provides for a distribution to be treated as a redemption if the stockholder's interest in the corporation is completely terminated. The attribution rules still apply under this section, but they may be waived if the stockholder files a written agreement with the IRS requesting such a waiver. In such an agreement, Morris would be required to divest himself of any relationship with the corporation other than as a creditor and agree not to acquire any interest in the corporation for a period of 10 years.

In addition to the two safe harbors described in Sections 302(b)(2) and (3), the Internal Revenue Code, in Section 302(b)(1), grants redemption treatment to distributions which are "not essentially equivalent to a dividend." Unlike the previous two sections, however, the Code does not spell out a mechanical test for this concept, leaving it to the facts and circumstances of the case. Given the obvious purpose of this transaction to transfer corporate assets to a stockholder on favorable terms, it is unlikely that the IRS under this section would recognize any explanation other than that of a dividend.

Thus, Morris's plan to turn in his stock and receive a tax-favored distribution for his retirement will not work out as planned unless he allows the redemption of all his stock; resigns as a director, officer, employee, consultant, and so forth; and agrees to stay away for a period of 10 years. He may, however, accept a promissory note for all or part of the redemption proceeds and thereby become a creditor of the corporation. Worse yet, if Lisa obtains her shares from Morris within the 10 years preceding his retirement, even this plan will not work unless the IRS can be persuaded that her acquisition of the shares was for reasons other than tax avoidance. It may be advisable to be sure she acquires her shares from the corporation rather than from Morris, although one can expect, given the extent of Morris's control over the corporation, that the IRS would fail to appreciate the difference.

Employee Stock Ownership Plans

Although Morris should be relatively happy with the knowledge that he may be able to arrange a complete redemption of his stock to fund his retirement and avoid being taxed as if he had received a dividend, he may still believe that the tax and economic effects of such a redemption are not ideal. Following such a plan to its logical conclusion, the

Exhibit 9.7 Corporate redemption versus ESOP purchase.

Corporate Redemption	ESOP Purchase
Only interest deductible	Principal and interest deductible
Capital gain	Gain deferred if proceeds rolled over

corporation would borrow the money to pay for Morris's stock. Its repayments would be deductible only to the extent of the interest. At the same time, Morris would be paying a substantial capital gain tax to the government. Before settling for this result, Morris might well wish to explore ways to increase the corporation's deduction and decrease his own tax liability.

Such a result can be achieved through the use of an employee stock ownership plan (ESOP), a form of qualified deferred compensation plan, as discussed earlier in the context of Brad's compensation package. Such a plan consists of a trust to which the corporation makes deductible contributions of either shares of its own stock or cash to be used to purchase such stock. Contributions are divided among the accounts of the corporation's employees (normally in proportion to their compensation for that year), and distributions are made to the employees at their retirement or earlier separation from the company (if the plan so allows). ESOPs have been seen as a relatively noncontroversial way for U.S. employees to gain more control over their employers, and they have been granted a number of tax advantages not available to other qualified plans, such as pension or profit-sharing plans. One advantage is illustrated by the fact that a corporation can manufacture a deduction out of thin air by issuing new stock to a plan (at no cost to the corporation) and deducting the fair market value of the shares.

A number of attractive tax benefits would flow from Morris's willingness to sell his shares to an ESOP established by his corporation rather than to the corporation itself. Yet, before he could appreciate those benefits, Morris would have to be satisfied that some obvious objections would not make such a transaction inadvisable (see Exhibit 9.7).

To begin with, the ESOP will have to borrow the money in the same way the corporation would; yet the ESOP has no credit record or assets to pledge as collateral. This is normally overcome, however, by the corporation's giving the lender a secured guarantee of the ESOP's obligation. Thus, the corporation ends up in the same economic position it would have enjoyed under a direct redemption.

Morris might also object to the amount of control an ESOP might give to lower-level employees of Plant Supply. After all, his intent is to leave the corporation under the control of Lisa and Brad, but qualified plans must be operated on a nondiscriminatory basis. This objection can be addressed in a number of ways. First, the allocation of shares in proportion to compensation, along with standard vesting and forfeiture provisions, will tilt these allocations toward highly compensated, long-term employees, such as Lisa and Brad. Second, the shares are not allocated to the employees' accounts until they are paid for. While the lender is still being paid, an amount proportional to the remaining balance of the loan would be controlled by the plan trustees (chosen by management). Third, even after shares are allocated to employee accounts, in a closely held company, employees are allowed to vote those shares only on questions that require a two-thirds vote of the stockholders, such as a sale or merger of the corporation. On all other more routine questions (such as election of the board), the trustees still vote the shares. Fourth, upon employees' retirement and before distribution of their shares, a closely held corporation must offer to buy back the distributed shares at fair market value. As a practical matter, most employees will accept such an offer rather than move into retirement with illiquid, closely held company stock.

If Morris accepts these arguments and opts for an ESOP buyout, the following benefits accrue. Rather than being able to deduct only the interest portion of its payments to the lender, the corporation may now contribute the full amount of such payment to the plan as a fully deductible contribution to a qualified plan. The plan then forwards it to the lender as a payment of its obligation.

Furthermore, the Internal Revenue Code allows an individual who sells stock of a corporation to the corporation's ESOP to defer paying any tax on the proceeds of such sale if the proceeds are rolled over into purchases of securities. No tax is then paid until the purchased securities are ultimately resold. Thus, if Morris takes the money received from the ESOP and invests it in the stock market, he pays no tax until and unless he sells any of these securities, and then only on those sold. In fact, if Morris purchases such securities and holds them until his death, his estate will likely receive a step-up in basis for such securities and thus avoid income tax on the proceeds of his company stock entirely.

Estate Planning

Should Morris rebel at the thought of retiring from the company, his thoughts may naturally turn to the tax consequences of his remaining employed by the company in some capacity until his death. Morris's lifelong efforts have made him a rather wealthy man, and he knows that the government will be looking to reap a rather large harvest from those efforts upon his death. He would no doubt be rather disheartened to learn that after a $3.5 million exemption (in 2009), the federal government will receive up to 48% of the excess upon his death. Proper estate planning can double the amount of that grace amount by using the exemptions of both Morris and his wife, but the amount above $7 million appears to be at significant risk, and that risk will likely increase when Congress turns its attention to years following 2009.

Redemptions to Pay Death Taxes and Administrative Expenses

Since much of the money to fund this estate tax liability would come from redemption of company stock, if Morris had not previously cashed it in, Morris might well fear the combined effect of dividend treatment and estate taxation. Of course, if Morris's estate turned in all his stock for redemption at death, dividend treatment would appear to have been avoided and redemption treatment under Section 302(b)(3) would appear to be available, since this would amount to a complete termination of his interest in the company, and death would appear to have cut off Morris's relationship with the company rather convincingly. However, if the effect of Morris's death on the company, or other circumstances, made a wholesale redemption inadvisable or impossible, Morris's estate could be faced with paying both ordinary income and estate tax rates on the full amount of the proceeds.

Fortunately for those faced with this problem, Code Section 303 allows capital gain treatment for a stock redemption if the proceeds of the redemption do not exceed the amount necessary to pay the estate's taxes and those further expenses allowable as administrative expenses on the estate's tax return. To qualify for this treatment, the company's stock must equal or exceed 35% of the value of the estate's total assets. Since Morris's holdings of company stock will most likely exceed 35% of his total assets, if his estate finds itself in this uncomfortable position it will at least be able to account for this distribution as a stock redemption instead of a dividend. This is much more important than it may first appear, and much more important than it would have been were Morris still alive. The effect is to allow payment at long-term capital gain rates (rather than ordinary income tax rates), for only the amount received in excess of the taxpayer's basis in the stock (rather than the entire amount of the distribution). Given that the death of the taxpayer increases his basis to the value at date of death, the effect of Section 303 is to eliminate all but that amount of gain occurring after death, thus eliminating virtually all income tax on the distribution. However, unless Congress acts, this step-up of basis will be significantly less generous for taxpayers dying after 2009.

Assuring sufficient liquidity to pay taxes due upon death is one thing; controlling the amount of tax actually due is another. Valuation of a majority interest in a closely held corporation is far from an exact science, and the last thing an entrepreneur wishes is to have his or her spouse and other heirs engage in a valuation controversy with the IRS after the entrepreneur's death. As a result, a number of techniques have evolved over the years that may have the effect of lowering the value of the stock to be included in the estate, or at least making such value more certain for planning purposes.

Family Limited Partnerships

One such technique that has recently gained in popularity is the so-called family limited partnership. This strategy allows individuals to decrease the size of their taxable estates through gifts to their intended beneficiaries both faster and at less tax cost than would otherwise be possible, while at the same time retaining effective control over the assets given away. Were Morris interested in implementing this strategy, he would form a limited partnership, designating himself as the general partner and retaining all but a minimal amount of the limited partnership interests for himself. He would then transfer to the partnership a significant portion of his assets, such as stock in the company, real estate, or marketable securities. Even though he would have transferred these interests out of his name, he would be assured of continued control over these assets in his role as general partner. The general partner of a limited partnership exercises all management functions; limited partners sacrifice all control in exchange for limited liability.

Morris would then embark on a course of gifting portions of the limited partnership interests to Lisa, Victor, and perhaps even Brad. You will remember that Morris and his wife can combine to give no more than $26,000 to each beneficiary each calendar year before eating into their lifetime $1 million gift tax exemption. The advantage of the family limited partnership, besides retaining control over the assets given away, is that the amounts that may be given each year are effectively increased. For example, were Morris and his wife to give $26,000 of marketable securities to Lisa in any given year, that would use up their entire annual gift tax exclusion. However, were they instead to give Lisa a portion of the limited partnership interest to which those marketable securities had been contributed, it can be argued that the gift should be valued at a much lower amount. After all, while there was a ready market for the securities, there is no market for the limited partnership interests; and while Lisa would have had control over the securities if they had been given to her, she has no control of them through her limited partnership interest. These discounts for lack of marketability and control can be substantial, freeing up more room under the annual exclusion for further gifting. In proper circumstances, one might use this technique when owning a rapidly appreciating asset (such as a pre-IPO stock) to give away more than $26,000 in a year, using up all or part of the lifetime exclusion, to remove the asset from your estate at a discount from its present value, rather than having to pay estate tax in the future on a highly inflated value.

The IRS has challenged these arrangements when there was no apparent business purpose other than tax savings, or when the transfer occurred just before the death of the transferor. And you can expect the IRS to challenge an overly aggressive valuation discount. But if Morris is careful in his valuations, he might find this arrangement attractive, asserting the business purpose of centralizing management while facilitating the grant of equity incentives to his executive employees.

Buy-Sell Agreements

Short of establishing a family limited partnership, Morris might be interested in a more traditional arrangement requiring the corporation or its stockholders to purchase whatever stock he may still hold at his death. Such an arrangement can be helpful with regard to both of Morris's estate-planning goals: setting a value for his stock that would not be challenged by the IRS and assuring sufficient liquidity to pay whatever estate taxes may ultimately be owed.

There are two basic variations of these agreements. Under the most common, Morris would agree with the corporation that it would redeem his shares upon his death for a price derived from an agreed formula. The second variation would require one or more of the other stockholders of the corporation (e.g., Lisa) to make such a purchase. In both cases, in order for the IRS to respect the valuation placed on the shares, Morris will need to agree that he will not dispose of the shares during his lifetime without first offering them to the other party to his agreement at the formula price. Under such an arrangement, the shares will never be worth more to Morris than the formula price, so it can be argued that whatever higher price the IRS may calculate is irrelevant to him and his estate.

This argument had led stockholders in the past to agree to formulas that artificially depressed the value of their shares when the parties succeeding to power in the corporation were also the main beneficiaries of the stockholders' estates. Since any value forgone would end up in the hands of the intended beneficiary anyway, only the tax collector would be hurt. Although the IRS had long challenged this practice, this strategy has been put to a formal end by legislation requiring that the formula used result in a close approximation to fair market value.

Which of the two variations of the buy-sell agreement should Morris choose? If we assume for the moment that Morris owns 80 of the 100 outstanding shares and Lisa and Brad each own 10, a corporate redemption agreement leaves Lisa and Brad each owning half of the 20 outstanding shares remaining. If, however, Morris chooses a cross-purchase agreement with Lisa and Brad, each would purchase 40 of his shares upon his death, leaving them as owners of 50 shares each. Both agreements leave the corporation owned by Lisa and Brad in equal shares, so there does not appear to be any difference between them (see Exhibit 9.8).

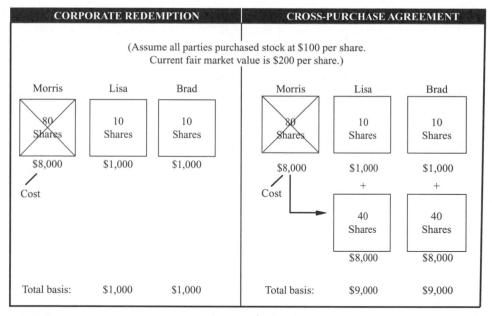

Exhibit 9.8   Corporate redemption versus cross-purchase agreement.

Once again, however, significant differences lie slightly below the surface. To begin with, many such agreements are funded by the purchase of a life insurance policy upon the life of the stockholder involved. If the corporation were to purchase this policy, the premiums would be nondeductible, resulting in additional taxable profit for the corporation. In a subchapter S corporation, such profit would pass through to the stockholders in proportion to their shares of stock in the corporation. In a C corporation, the additional profit would result in additional corporate tax. If, instead, Lisa and Brad bought policies covering their halves of the obligation to Morris's estate, they would be paying the premiums with after-tax dollars. Thus, a redemption agreement will cause Morris to share in the cost of the arrangement, whereas a cross-purchase agreement puts the entire onus on Lisa and Brad. This burden can, of course, be rationalized by arguing that they will ultimately reap the benefit of the arrangement by succeeding to the ownership of the corporation. Or their compensation could be adjusted to cover the additional cost.

If the corporation is not an S corporation, however, there is an additional consideration that must not be overlooked. Upon Morris's death, the receipt of the insurance proceeds by the beneficiary of the life insurance will be excluded from taxable income. However, a C corporation (other than certain small businesses) is also subject to the alternative minimum tax. Simply described, that tax guards against individuals and profitable corporations paying little or no tax by overuse of certain deductions and tax credits otherwise available. To calculate the tax, the taxpayer adds to its otherwise taxable income, certain so-called tax preferences and then subtracts from that amount an exemption amount ($40,000 for most corporations). The result is taxed at 20% for corporations (26% and 28% for individuals). If that tax amount exceeds the income tax otherwise payable, the higher amount is paid. The result of this is additional tax for those taxpayers with substantial tax preferences.

Among those tax preferences for C corporations is a concept known as adjusted current earnings. This concept adds as a tax preference three-quarters of the difference between the corporation's earnings for financial reporting purposes and the earnings otherwise reportable for tax purposes. A major source of such a difference would be the receipt of nontaxable income. And the receipt of life insurance proceeds is just such an event. Therefore, the receipt of a life insurance payout of sufficient size will ultimately be taxed, at least in part, to a C corporation, whereas it would be completely tax-free to an S corporation or the remaining stockholders.

An additional factor pointing to the stockholder cross-purchase agreement rather than a corporate redemption is the effect this choice would have on the taxability of a later sale of the corporation after Morris's death. If the corporation were to redeem Morris's stock, Lisa and Brad would each own one-half of the corporation through their ownership of 10 shares each. If they then sold the company, they would be subject to tax on capital gain measured by the difference between the proceeds of the sale and their original basis in their shares. However, if Lisa and Brad purchased Morris's stock at his death, they would each own one-half of the corporation through their ownership of 50 shares each. Upon a later sale of the company, their capital gain would be measured by the difference between the sale proceeds and their original basis in their shares plus the amount paid for Morris's shares. Every dollar paid to Morris lowers the taxable income received upon later sale. In a redemption agreement, these dollars are lost.

Spin-Offs and Split-Ups

Morris's pleasant reverie caused by thoughts of well-funded retirement strategies and clever estate plans is brought to a sudden halt a mere two years after the acquisition of the molding operation, when it becomes clear that the internecine jealousies between Brad and Lisa are becoming unmanageable. Ruefully, Morris concedes that it is not unforeseeable that the manager of a significant part of his business would resent the presence of a rival who would be perceived as having attained her present position simply by dint of her relationship to the owner. This jealousy is, of course, inflamed by the thought that Lisa might succeed to Morris's stock upon his death and become Brad's boss.

After some months of attempting to mediate the many disputes between Lisa and Brad, which are merely symptoms of this underlying disease, Morris comes to the conclusion that the corporation cannot survive with both of them vying for power and influence. He determines that the only workable solution would be to break the two businesses apart once again, leaving the two rivals in charge of their individual empires, with no future binding ties.

Experienced in corporate transactions by this time, Morris gives the problem some thought and devises two alternate scenarios to accomplish his goal. Both scenarios begin with the establishment of a subsidiary corporation, wholly owned by the currently existing company. The assets, liabilities, and all other attributes of the molding operation would then be transferred to this new subsidiary in exchange for its stock. At that point in the first scenario (known as a spin-off), the parent corporation would declare a dividend of all such stock to its current stockholders. Thus, Morris, Lisa, and Brad would own the former subsidiary in the same proportions in which they own the parent. Morris, as the majority owner of the new corporation, could then give further shares to Brad, enter into a buy-sell agreement with him, or sell him some shares. In any case, upon Morris's death, Brad would succeed to unquestioned leadership in this corporation. Lisa would stay as a minority stockholder, or, if she wished, sell her shares to Morris while he was alive. Lisa would gain control of the former parent corporation upon Morris's death.

In the second scenario (known as a split-off), after the formation of the subsidiary, Brad would sell his shares of Plant Supply to that parent corporation in exchange for stock affording him control of the subsidiary. Lisa would remain the only minority stockholder of the parent corporation (Brad's interest having been removed) and would succeed to full ownership upon Morris's death through one of the mechanisms discussed earlier.

Unfortunately, when Morris brought his ideas to his professional advisers, he was faced with serious tax objections. The IRS would likely take the position that the distribution of the subsidiary's stock to Plant Supply's stockholders in the first scenario was a taxable dividend to the extent of Plant Supply's earnings and profits at the time of the distribution. This would be less of a concern if his corporation were operating as an S corporation, although even then, he would have to be concerned about undistributed earnings and profits dating from before the S election. And in the second scenario, Brad's sale of his Plant Supply stock to the parent in exchange for stock in the subsidiary would be treated as a taxable sale or exchange of his stock.

Fortunately, however, recognizing that not all transactions of this type are entered into to disguise the declaration of a dividend, the Internal Revenue Code does allow spin-offs and split-offs to take place tax-free, under the limited circumstances described in Section 355. These circumstances track the scenarios concocted by Morris, but are limited to circumstances in which both the parent and the subsidiary will be conducting an active trade or business after the transaction. Moreover, each trade or business must have been conducted for a period exceeding five years prior to the distribution and cannot have been acquired in a taxable transaction during such time. Since Morris's corporation acquired the molding business only two years previously and such transaction was not tax-free, the benefits of Section 355 are not available now. Short of another solution, it would appear that Morris will have to live with the bickering of Brad and Lisa for another three years.

Sale of the Corporation

Fortunately for Morris, another solution is not long in coming. Within months of the failure of his proposal to split up the company, Morris is approached by the president of a company in a related field who is interested in purchasing Plant Supply. Such a transaction is very intriguing to Morris. He has worked very hard for many years and would not be averse to an early retirement. A purchase such as this would relieve him of all his concerns over adequate liquidity for his estate and strategies for funding his retirement. He could take care of both Lisa and Victor with the cash he would receive, and both Lisa and Brad would be free to deal with the acquirer about remaining employed and collecting on their equity.

However, Morris knows better than to get too excited over this prospect before consulting with his tax advisers. And his hesitance turns out to be justified. Unless a deal is appropriately structured, Morris is staring at a significant tax bite, at both the corporate and the stockholder levels.

Morris knows from his experience with the molding plant that a corporate acquisition can be structured in three basic ways: a merger, a sale of stock, or a purchase of assets.

In a merger, the target corporation disappears into the acquirer by operation of law, and the former stockholders of the target receive consideration from the acquirer. In the sale of stock, the stockholders sell their shares directly to the acquiring corporation. In a sale of assets, the target sells its assets (and most of its liabilities) to the acquirer, and the proceeds of the sale are then distributed to the target's stockholders through the liquidation of the target. A major theme of all three of these scenarios involves the acquirer forming a subsidiary corporation to act as the acquirer in the transaction.

In each case, the difference between the proceeds received by the target's stockholders and their basis in the target's stock would be taxable as capital gain. Morris is further informed that this tax at the stockholder level could be avoided if these transactions qualified under the complex rules that define tax-free reorganizations. In each case, one of the requirements would be that the target stockholders receive largely stock of the acquirer rather than cash. Since the acquirer in this case is closely held and there is no market for its stock, Morris is determined to insist on cash. He thus accepts the idea of paying tax at the stockholder level.

Morris is quite surprised, however, to learn that he might also be exposed to corporate tax on the growth in the corporation's assets over its basis in them if they are deemed to have been sold as a result of the acquisition transaction. He is further disappointed when reminded that even subchapter S corporations recognize all built-in gain that existed at the time of their subchapter S election if their assets are sold within 10 years after their change of tax status.

As a result of the previous considerations, Morris is determined not to structure the sale of his corporation as a sale of its assets and liabilities, to avoid any tax on the corporate level. He is also determined not to structure it as a sale of stock by the target stockholders, because he is not entirely sure Brad can be trusted to sell his shares. If he could structure the transaction at the corporate level, he would not need Brad's minority vote to accomplish it. Thus, after intensive negotiations, he is pleased that the acquiring corporation has agreed to structure the acquisition as a merger between Plant Supply and a subsidiary of the acquirer (to be formed for the purpose of the transaction). All stockholders of Plant Supply will receive a cash down payment and a five-year promissory note from the parent acquirer in exchange for their stock.

Yet even this careful preparation and negotiation leaves Morris, Lisa, and Brad in jeopardy of unexpected tax exposure. To begin with, if the transaction remains as nego-tiated, the IRS will take the position that the assets of the target corporation have been sold to the acquirer, thus triggering tax at the corporate level. In addition, the target's stockholders may have to recognize, as proceeds of the sale of their stock, both the cash and the fair market value of the promissory notes in the year of the transaction, even though they will receive payments on the notes over a period of five years. Fortunately, the latter exposure could always be eliminated by having Plant Supply adopt a plan of liquidation and complete the transaction within 12 months of its adoption.

As for the risk of double taxation, a small adjustment to the negotiated transaction can cure most of these problems. Through an example of corporate magic known as the reverse triangular merger, the newly formed subsidiary of the acquirer may disappear into Morris's target corporation, but the target's stockholders can still be jettisoned for cash, leaving the acquirer as the parent (see Exhibit 9.9). In such a transaction, the assets of the target have not been sold; they remain owned by the original corporation. Only the target's stockholders have changed. In effect, the parties have sold stock without the

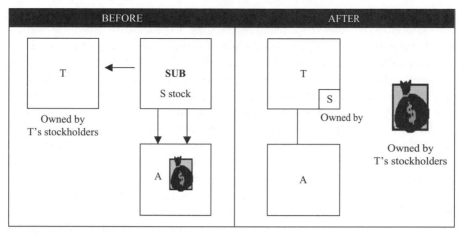

Exhibit 9.9   Reverse triangular merger.

necessity of getting Brad's approval. Because the assets have not changed hands, there is no tax at the corporate level. In addition, since the target corporation has not liquidated, no plan of liquidation is required, and the target stockholders may elect installment treatment and pay tax on the notes when payment is received, just as if they had sold their shares directly.

Conclusion

Perhaps no taxpayers will encounter quite as many cataclysmic tax decisions in as short a time as did Morris and Plant Supply. Yet Morris's experience serves to illustrate that tax issues lurk in almost every major business decision made by a corporation's management. Many transactions can be structured to avoid unnecessary tax expense if proper attention is paid to tax implications. To be unaware of these issues is to play the game without knowing the rules.

Internet Links

http://smallbusiness.findlaw.com/ small-business-taxes/	FindLaw for Business
http://pwc.com	PricewaterhouseCoopers, *Tax Management in Companies*
www.smsmallbiz.com/taxes	Taxes

Problems

Assume that a limited liability company passes through to a taxpayer more loss that she can use due to the fact that she is not materially participating in the business in that year. Assume further that in the following year she ramps up her activities in the business and is now deemed to be materially participating. Can she now use the unused previous-year losses against active and portfolio income?

A taxpayer is the founder and CEO of a corporation owned by himself and his daughter. Getting close to retirement, the taxpayer arranges for the corporation to buy back all his stock. In order to avoid taxation as a dividend, he takes advantage of the waiver of family attribution rules by filing the required agreement to end any participation in the corporation for 10 years. However, his daughter requests that his expertise remain available and asks that he enter into a consulting agreement with the corporation. Can he do that without jeopardizing the tax treatment of his redemption payments?

A taxpayer is a doctor who practices through a C corporation of which she is the sole stockholder. All the corporation's revenue comes from fees for medical services, and all the services are rendered by the taxpayer. After paying expenses, she distributes all the corporation's revenue to herself. The corporation deducts all those distributions, and the doctor treats them as taxable compensation. In the past few years, her medical practice has generated a very high level of income. Imagine her surprise when the IRS takes the position that her distributions in those years were unreasonable compensation, recharacterizing them as dividends and subjecting them to double taxation. Is the IRS correct?

For Further Reading

Daily, Frederick W., *Tax Savvy for Small Business*, 12th ed. (Berkeley, CA: Nolo, 2008).

Gevurtz, Franklin A., *Business Planning* (New York: Foundation Press, 2008).

Karayan, John E., *Strategic Business Tax Planning* (Hoboken, NJ: John Wiley & Sons, 2007).

Scholes, Myron S., *Taxes and Business Strategy* (Upper Saddle River, NJ: Prentice Hall, 2008).

10

The Integrity of Financial Reporting

Les Livingstone

Introduction

Until the late 1990s, only a few occasional scandals disturbed the calm scene of U.S. corporate financial reporting. Certainly, there had been major corporate frauds and audit failures over the years, such as:

- McKesson & Robbins (1940).
- BarChris Construction (1968).
- Continental Vending (1969).
- National Student Marketing (1975).
- Equity Funding (1978).
- The savings and loan debacle of the early 1990s.

But these scandals were isolated events, and, on the whole, the CPA profession retained the trust of the investment community. Investors had faith in the accuracy of the financial statements of our largest corporations because they carried the blue-chip imprimatur of one or another of the well-known and respected Big Five auditing firms.[1]

In the late 1990s U.S. stock markets soared to new highs on optimistic expectations. Few observers would have predicted the coming financial scandals that were soon to afflict U.S. financial markets. The symptom of trouble ahead was the increasing number of restatements of previously issued audited financial statements by U.S. corporations. A restatement is required when it is found that information in the previously issued financial statement has been materially misstated. By law, the previously issued financial statement must be withdrawn, and the restated financial statement must be issued.

The restatement of financial statements does not necessarily indicate that there was fraud or that the audit failed. For example, when a corporate merger takes place, the previous audited financial statements of the acquiring and acquired corporations must be withdrawn and replaced by merged financial statements of the new union, just as if the corporations had merged two years earlier. Otherwise there would be no merged financial statements for past years to compare with the postmerger audited financial statements. Further, no audit is absolutely guaranteed to detect material error or fraud. The auditor is not an insurer, and provides reasonable (but not absolute) assurance that the financial statements are free of material misstatement. An audit that is thorough enough to absolutely guarantee the absence of material misstatement would be prohibitively expensive. Therefore the occasional restatement is not necessarily a smoking gun that points to audit failure. But when restatements happen more than occasionally, they create suspicion. Coincidence can stretch only so far.

Restatements of Previously Published Financial Statements

Probably the best indicator of possible accounting and auditing failure is when a corporation restates its previously issued financial statements. Restatements are required by law when material misstatements are found to have occurred in previously issued financial statements. These restatements are sometimes claimed to have been necessary due to acquisitions (which is legitimate, but infrequent) or errors or misinterpretation of generally accepted accounting principles (GAAP) (also infrequent).

Excuses of this latter kind should be viewed with skepticism. In the case of public companies, the materially misstated financial statements had been produced by the professional accountants inside corporations, and had been audited by the outside independent auditors. It seems very unlikely that material misstatements would not be detected by either the inside professional accountants or the outside independent auditors. A suspicion is that the material misstatements were not accidental, but rather deliberate. In other words, one suspects fraud.

It is an acute embarrassment to a corporation, and to its outside auditors, when the financial statements that had received approval have to be restated. Corporations and their auditors have every incentive to avoid this embarrassment by getting the financial statements right the first time around. Naturally everything of a material nature would be very carefully checked to ensure that it is correct and in compliance with GAAP. One would think that restatements would very seldom be required if audits were thorough. One would also think that restatements could be a sign that the auditors had failed.

So restatements are a red flag, and raise a suspicion of fraud. That is why restatements are considered an indicator of accounting and auditing failures. And that is why there are studies published every year about restatements. In past years, restatements were rare. In recent years, they have become more frequent. In 2006, 1,300 U.S. public companies restated their financial statements.

The *Wall Street Journal* of December 23, 2006, reported a study of companies that restated their 1998 and 1999 financial statements. The study found that 47% of the CEOs of these restating companies were gone within two years of the restatements. This was twice the turnover of CEOs of similar companies in the same industries that had no restatements. Clearly, restatements are an embarrassing symptom of lax financial controls and/or fraud.

In 2002 the U.S. General Accounting (now Accountability) Office (GAO) made a study of restatements by publicly listed companies and reported:

> The number of financial statement restatements identified each year rose from 92 in 1997 to 225 in 2001. The proportion of listed companies on NYSE, AMEX, and NASDAQ identified as restating their financial reports tripled from less than 0.89 percent in 1997 to about 2.5 percent in 2001 and may reach almost 3 percent by the end of 2002. From January 1997 through June 2002, about 10 percent of all listed companies announced at least one

restatement. . . . The 689 publicly traded companies we identified that announced financial statement restatements between January 1997 and March 2002 lost billions of dollars in market capitalization in the days around the initial restatement announcement.[2]

There were an alarming number of restatements in the late 1990s and early 2000s, often accompanied by accounting scandals involving huge sums. Some examples are:

- **Adelphia** filed Chapter 11 bankruptcy in June 2002. This cable TV operator and several related individuals were sued in July 2002 by the Securities and Exchange Commission (SEC) and charged with one of the most extensive financial frauds ever to take place in a public company: fraudulently excluding from its mid-1999 to end of 2001 annual and quarterly financial statements over $2 billion in debt, caused by systematically recording those liabilities on the books of unconsolidated affiliates, which violated GAAP. The Rigas family, who founded Adelphia, received $3.1 billion in off-balance-sheet loans backed by Adelphia. Three Rigas family members were arrested on allegations of fraud. Adelphia sued its independent auditor[3] for malpractice.

- **Baptist Foundation of Arizona** was an audit client of Arthur Andersen, which paid $217 million to settle lawsuits alleging malpractice in the Baptist Foundation audit.

- **Enron Corporation** filed Chapter 11 bankruptcy in December 2001, setting a record for the largest corporate bankruptcy up to that time. Enron announced restatements that reduced reported net income by a total of $586 million and increased reported debt by $2.6 billion for 1997 to 2001. Enron's auditor, Arthur Andersen, was charged with obstruction of justice through destruction of audit work papers, and was no longer permitted to audit public companies in the United States. Andersen offered $750 million to settle civil lawsuits filed against that firm, which was turned down. Soon after that Andersen collapsed.

- **Qwest Communications** admitted inflating reported sales by $1.16 billion in its financial statements, and restated results for 2000 to 2002.

- **Rite Aid Corporation** announced restatements that reduced reported retained earnings by a total of $1.6 billion due to overstated net income for 1998 and 1999. Rite Aid did not restate 1996 and 1997 financial statements because it would require "unreasonable cost and expense," but reported that the financial data for 1996 and 1997 should not be relied on. Rite Aid's auditor, KPMG, resigned in November 1999 and withdrew its audit reports for 1997 to 1999, stating that it was unable to continue to rely on management's representations (a polite way of saying that the auditors no longer could trust what management told them).

- **Sunbeam Corporation** filed Chapter 11 bankruptcy in February 2001. Sunbeam announced restatements that improved the reported 1996 net loss by $20 million, reduced reported 1997 net income by $71 million, and increased reported 1998 net income by $10 million. This strange pattern resulted from Sunbeam's creation of improper reserves in 1996, which were used to inflate 1997 reported income and give the false impression of a rapid turnaround. Sunbeam's auditor, Arthur Andersen, and other Sunbeam parties (including ex-CEO "Chainsaw" Al Dunlap) were sued, and settled in 2002 for $141 million, the largest portion of which was paid by Arthur Andersen.

- **Tyco International** lost more than 75% of its market value. All of its directors resigned, and its three most senior executives were accused of looting the company by taking hundreds of millions of dollars in secret, unauthorized, and improper low-interest loans from 1996 through June 2002.

- **Waste Management, Inc.** restatements reduced reported net income for 1992 through the first quarter of 1999 by more than $1.1 billion. Its auditor, Arthur Andersen, had issued clean audit opinions for those financial statements. Waste Management paid out $220 million to settle some, but not all, of the lawsuits filed against it.

- **WorldCom** was accused of overstating income by $9 billion (mainly in 2000), and it provided founder Bernard Ebbers $400 million in off-the-books loans. Two former WorldCom executives were arrested on allegations of fraud. WorldCom has superseded Enron as the largest-ever corporate bankruptcy. WorldCom's auditor? Arthur Andersen.

As a result of these accounting scandals, the once-immaculate reputation of the certified public accountant (CPA) profession has been severely tarnished. In fact, the media constantly refer to the "accounting industry" rather than the "accounting profession." In the past, CPAs were stereotyped as passive, boring, and unimaginative, but unquestionably honest. That is probably still true for the vast majority of CPAs. But a significant minority of CPAs has shown unsuspected imagination, aggression, and an absence of ethics.

Asleep at the Switch

There is plenty of blame from the corporate scandals for the abject failures of all the gatekeepers responsible for safeguarding the integrity of large corporations, namely:

- Boards of directors.
- Audit committees of the boards of directors.
- Regulators, such as the SEC.
- Bond rating agencies.
- Major institutional stockholders such as pension funds and mutual funds.
- Professional associations such as the American Institute of Certified Public Accountants.
- Independent audit firms.

Every one of these gatekeepers has failed to perform its duty in one corporate fraud after another. But no failure has been as abject as that of the audit watchdogs that have turned out to be lapdogs. They have seriously eroded the credibility of audited financial statements and impaired the efficient functioning of the securities markets. They have been derelict in their duty to investors, employees, creditors, and the public. How is the lost trust in auditors going to be restored?

The Remedies

In 2002 the U.S. Congress passed the Sarbanes-Oxley Act (sometimes referred to as SOX) in response to the flood of corporate frauds. The main provisions of SOX[4] are:

- The self-regulation of independent auditors was replaced by the creation of the Public Company Accounting Oversight Board (PCAOB), which is under the jurisdiction of the SEC.

- Generally accepted auditing standards (GAAS) for public companies were transferred from the private sector to the PCAOB under the oversight of the SEC.

- Independent auditing firms are no longer permitted to provide certain management consulting services to their audit clients.[5]

- The CEO and CFO of each U.S. public company must certify that the company's financial statements fairly present and disclose its operations and financial condition.

- Directors and officers of U.S. public companies are prohibited from fraudulently influencing, coercing, or manipulating the independent auditors.

- If financial statements are restated due to "material noncompliance" with financial reporting requirements, the CEO and CFO must disgorge any bonus or other incentive-based or equity-based compensation received during the 12 months following the issue of the noncompliant financial statements.

- It is a felony to knowingly destroy or create documents to impede any federal investigation, and auditors are required to maintain "all audit or review work papers" for five years.

How effective will these provisions be in preventing future Enrons and WorldComs? No doubt potential perpetrators of large-scale corporate fraud (including rogue accountants) will be chastened for the next few years by the punishments meted out to recent offenders. But memories may quickly recede, and the chastening effect may fade all too soon.

It seems that SOX does as much as any law can do to create compliance with the rules of financial reporting. Certainly SOX gets to key issues like fraud by CEOs and CFOs, audit failures, and ineffective audit committees. SOX erases classic defenses by corporate officers accused of fraud, such as:

- "How was I to know? I'm not an accountant or a lawyer."
- "I trusted the auditors."
- "The lawyers said it was okay."

SOX strengthens existing law and significantly increases penalties for violations, including imprisonment. Also it takes self-regulation out of the hands of the accounting profession and makes auditors the first and only U.S. profession to be regulated by the federal government.

SOX does have a major weakness—namely, feeble encouragement and feeble protection for whistle-blowers, who are put into the hands of the Occupational Safety and Health Administration (OSHA), a federal agency sadly lacking in knowledge, experience, and skill in corporate finance and financial markets.

While SOX does about as much as any law can do regarding financial reporting, it cannot assure the validity of financial statements. And from an economic perspective, SOX has several main flaws:

- It creates substantial government interference in free financial markets, and economics tells us that government interference in free markets is usually expensive and often counterproductive.

- SOX adds significantly to the SEC bureaucracy, which has a very unimpressive past record of reducing financial fraud relating to the securities markets.

- It focuses on penalties for noncompliance, but offers few, if any, positive incentives to improve the validity of financial reporting. It seems blind to the importance of incentives in economics and unaware of the power of self-interest and Adam Smith's "invisible hand."

SOX contains little or no thinking outside the box. For example, with regard to internal control:

- Since enactment of the Foreign Corrupt Practices Act (FCPA) of 1978, public companies have been required by law to create and maintain adequate systems of internal control. Regrettably, the FCPA simply mandated systems of internal control, but failed to make these systems subject to a cost-benefit test—which would have made more sense. For example, we could design an accounting system that could keep track of every paper clip, every postage stamp, and every eraser. But we don't go that far, because so precise a system would be incredibly expensive to create and maintain, and it clearly flunks the cost-benefit test.

- SOX added the requirement for both the top management and the auditors of all public companies to report on the adequacy of the corporate internal control systems. Again, no provision was made for a cost-benefit test—which would have made more sense.

- To prove that they are meeting this requirement, and to protect against legal liability, top managements have spent large amounts of corporate funds on reviewing, documenting, and adding improvements to internal control systems—regardless of cost-benefit analysis.

- But internal control system weaknesses were not a factor in any of the major financial reporting scandals. In Enron and all the other major financial frauds, top management simply overrode or bypassed the corporate control systems when they perpetrated their huge financial frauds.

- It is well-known that a corrupt top management can always defeat internal controls by means of overriding, subverting, or bypassing any inconvenient internal control provisions. The *Journal of Accountancy* reported, "According to a 1999 COSO research project, at least 83% of 200 financial statement frauds were engineered by the CEO, CFO or both. These control frauds are most often accomplished by upper management by overriding existing internal controls."[6]

- An important study about top management overrides of internal control can be found at www.aicpa.org/audcommctr/download/achilles_heel.pdf.

- Here is a short summary of the introduction to this study:

  Even though internal controls over financial reporting may seem well-designed and effective, they can be overridden by top management. Many financial statement frauds have been committed by intentional senior management override of internal controls. Top management override of internal controls is the Achilles' heel of fraud prevention. Management is primarily responsible for the design, implementation, and maintenance of internal controls. Therefore, the entity is always exposed to the hazard of management override of controls. When the opportunity to override internal controls is combined with powerful incentives to meet accounting objectives, top management may engage in fraudulent financial reporting. Thus, otherwise effective internal controls cannot be relied upon to prevent, detect, or deter fraudulent financial reporting perpetrated by top management.

- So it makes little economic sense for SOX to require companies to make significant expenditures to upgrade their internal controls, when the best internal controls on the planet would not have prevented the major financial reporting scandals. Even a control system on steroids can be overridden or bypassed by a corrupt top management.

- Very few employees will risk their jobs to defy a top management that is overriding or bypassing internal controls.

- The major financial frauds were not due to weak controls. They were due to corrupt top management overriding or bypassing internal controls by bullying or bribing lower-level employees.

Conclusion: The SOX requirement for top management and the auditors of public companies to report on internal controls would have done nothing to head off top management fraud before SOX was enacted. It is very doubtful if it will be effective after SOX has been enacted. The recent financial scandals have shown us:

- The dominance of powerful CEOs over weak boards of directors, as evidenced by breathtakingly high CEO compensation.

- The vulnerabilities of internal controls when top management is corrupt.

- The ineffectiveness of audit committees.

- The reluctance of auditors to stand up to corporate crooks and to risk being fired from large and lucrative audit engagements.

- The passivity of large stockholders, such as pension funds, mutual funds, and institutional investors like insurance companies and investment houses, which could have major influence but choose not to use it.

- The ineptness of government regulators.

In view of these considerations, it appears that some more enterprising approaches are needed to improve the validity of financial reporting. Maybe we should think outside the box, and use some carrots in addition to the sticks. Here are a few ideas:

- Fraudulent financial reporting inflates the financial statements, making them look better than they really should look. That should attract the attention of corporate raiders and takeover artists. But laws designed to prevent takeovers and unfriendly mergers have handicapped corporate raiders and takeover artists. For example, the Williams Act requires any investor who acquires 5% or more of a company's stock to file a report with the SEC. That alerts the target to the takeover threat, and gives it time to create defenses against takeovers, such as poison pills. It also causes the stock price of the takeover target to rise in anticipation of an offer by the raider to buy a controlling interest in the stock at a premium price.

If laws that protect incumbent management, like the Williams Act, were repealed, a corrupt incumbent management would have less incentive to fake the financial statements to make them look better than they really should look. It would also have the effect of reducing excessive top management compensation, because corporate raiders would see the opportunity to launch a takeover in order to cut excessive top management compensation; this would raise profits and thus increase the stock price, giving the raider a capital gain over the price it paid for acquiring its stock.

- Conceivably, the outside auditors should no longer be hired by the corporations that they audit. As long as auditors are hired and fired by their audit clients, they cannot be truly independent. They don't want to bite the hand that feeds them. Instead, it may be advisable to increase the independence of auditors by having them hired by:

  - The major stock exchanges, like the New York Stock Exchange or NASDAQ, to audit listed companies. That would create competition between stock exchanges to attract listed companies and investors in listed securities by assuring the integrity of reported financial information. And companies would compete to be listed on an exchange known for honest financial reporting.

  - Insurance companies that sell directors and officers insurance against negligence to corporations. These insurance companies would require auditors to be truly independent and diligent, because that would reduce insurance claims for negligence by directors and officers.

- If the auditors are not employed by the major stock exchanges or insurance companies, as just suggested, there is an alternative method to protect auditors from being fired for standing up to a corrupt top management. That method would be to require a shareholder resolution with a 75% majority in order to replace an independent audit firm.

- Boards of directors could be strengthened by requiring:

  - Separate individuals to be CEO and chair of the board of directors. One person should not hold both offices; that concentrates too much power in one individual.

  - No more staggered terms of office for directors. That is a defense against takeovers, and takeovers are a good way to replace top management that is serving its own selfish interests rather than the interests of stockholders. All directors should stand for election at the same time.

  - Individual shareholders should nominate candidates for directorships—no more voting for or against one official slate of directors.

  - Cumulative voting for election of directors; that would allow any stockholder to use all of his or her director votes for or against any single director.

It's Not Just the Private Sector

In viewing financial improprieties, we should understand that the problems go beyond corporations. There are serious problems in the public sector as well as the private sector. For example, here are some financial issues relating to our federal government.

- The federal government made at least $37 billion in overpayments in 2005. Current estimates are between $40 billion and $100 billion in annual overpayments.

- The Heritage Foundation reports:

  Federal spending has reached $22,000 per household, in constant dollars, for the first time since World War II. "Discretionary" spending voted on each year by Congress has jumped 49 percent in just three years, and entitlement spending nears 11 percent of gross domestic product (GDP) for the first time ever. Furthermore, the upcoming retirement of the baby boomers will put an enormous strain on Social Security, Medicare, and Medicaid and sharply increase spending. It is imperative for lawmakers to get the nation's finances in order immediately by restructuring entitlement programs and reducing federal spending. Putting off the difficult decisions until the federal budget's condition deteriorates further will result in much harsher and more expensive policy choices.[7]

Summary and Conclusions

Clearly ethics, the rule of law, and property rights have great importance in financial reporting. But this statement needs to be elaborated as follows:

- The laws have to be based on sound economics in order to be cost-effective and efficient. SOX seems to be cost-effective and efficient in several ways, but the SOX provisions on whistle-blowers and internal control face serious doubts about being cost-effective and efficient.

- The proportion of stocks held by individual persons has greatly declined, and the proportion of stocks held by institutions such as mutual funds, pension funds, and hedge funds has greatly increased. As a result, the property rights of individuals in stocks have become diluted, so the vigilance of stock-owning individuals over top management has been eroded. Now the financial institutions do less to scrutinize the performance of top management and do more to pursue their own profit from money management fees. This dilution of individual property rights also dilutes economic efficiency, because people tend to be more careful with their own money than with other people's money.

- The relationship between corporate owners and managers used to be one of principal (owner) and agent (manager). Now it is one of principal (owner), agent (financial institution), and subagent (manager). The new relationship is more distant, more remote, more bureaucratic, and more inefficient. The previously efficient ownership society has become the less efficient agency society.

- If laws that handicap corporate raiders were repealed, more stock would end up in the hands of individuals, and less in the possession of financial institutions. That would slow down the dilution of individual property rights that also dilutes economic efficiency.

- But one thing has not changed. Our economy and our society are as dependent on ethical behavior as they ever were. On the one hand, ethics cannot be forced upon the unwilling. On the other hand, unethical behavior can be punished and deterred with greater force. That is the main accomplishment of SOX.

Downloadable Resources for this chapter available at www.wiley.com/go/portablembainfinance

The Integrity of Financial Accounting: Sarbanes-Oxley and Fraudulent Financial Reporting

Information about the Sarbanes-Oxley Act and Corporate Governance and Financial Reporting

Ethics and the Golden Rule

Internet Links

www.soxlaw.com/	SOX requirements
www.pcaobus.org/	Web site of the Public Companies Accounting Oversight Board
www.iccwbo.org/corporate-governance/	For helpful information on corporate governance
www.cato.org/events/friedman.html	"The Social Responsibilities of Corporations," a cogent view by Nobel Prize–winning economist Milton Friedman
http://securities.stanford.edu/news-archive/2008/20080826_Headline108080_Writer.html	"Sarbanes-Oxley Requirements Have Made Financial Statements More Confusing"
www.aicpa.org/audcommctr/download/achilles_heel.pdf	Top management overrides of internal control
www.aicpa.org/PUBS/jofa/jun2004/mccarthy.htm	Impact of SOX
www.ethicsline.com/sox.asp	Ethics and SOX
www.heritage.org/Research/Budget/bg1733.cfm	"How to Get Federal Spending under Control," by Brian M. Riedl, Heritage Foundation Backgrounder No. 1733, March 10, 2004

Notes

1. Arthur Andersen, Deloitte & Touche, Ernst & Young, KPMG, and Pricewaterhouse-Coopers.
2. GAO Report to the U.S. Senate Committee on Banking, Housing, and Urban Affairs, October 4, 2002.

3. Deloitte & Touche.
4. Some of the Sarbanes-Oxley provisions are not new, but simply reiterate and codify existing laws.
5. For example, in 2000 Enron paid Arthur Andersen $25 million for audit work and another $27 million for consulting services. Also in 2000, Sprint paid Ernst & Young $2.5 million in audit fees plus $63.8 million for other services, General Electric paid KPMG $23.9 million for audit fees plus $79.7 million for other services, and JPMorgan Chase paid PricewaterhouseCoopers $21.3 million for audit work plus $84.2 million for other services.
6. From the *Journal of Accountancy*, official journal of the American Institute of Certified Public Accountants, January 2007, 33.
7. See www.heritage.org/Research/features/issues/pdfs/Budget.pdf.

For Further Reading

Anand, Sanjay, *Sarbanes-Oxley Guide for Finance and Information Technology Professionals* (Hoboken, NJ: John Wiley & Sons, 2006).

Jackson, Pegg M., *Nonprofit Strategic Planning: Leveraging Sarbanes-Oxley Best Practices* (Hoboken, NJ: John Wiley & Sons, 2007).

Livingstone, Les, *A Practical Framework for Ethical Decision-Making* (Freeload Press, 2007). A free e-book download after you register at www.textbookmedia.com/.

Ramos, Michael J., *How to Comply with Sarbanes-Oxley Section 404: Assessing the Effectiveness of Internal Control* (Hoboken, NJ: John Wiley & Sons, 2008).

Part IV

Management Accounting

11

Forecasts and Budgeting

Robert F. Halsey

The Concept of Budgeting

Budgets serve a critical role in managing any business, from the smallest sole proprietor to the largest multinational corporation. Businesses cannot operate effectively without estimating the financial implications of their strategic plans and monitoring their progress throughout the year. During preparation, budgets require managers to make resource allocation decisions and, as a result, to reaffirm their core operating strategy by requiring each business unit to justify its part of the overall business plan. During the subsequent year, variances of actual results from expectations serve to direct management to the areas that may deserve a greater allocation of capital and those that may need adjustments to retain their viability.

A *budget* is a comprehensive, formal plan, expressed in quantitative terms, describing the expected operations of an organization over some future time period. As you can see, the characteristics of a budget are that it deals with a *specific entity*, covers a *specific future time period*, and is expressed in *quantitative terms*.

This chapter describes the essential features of a budget and includes a comprehensive example of the preparation of a monthly budget for a small business. Although the focus of the chapter is on budgeting from a business perspective, many of the principles can be applied to an individual's personal financial planning.

Functions of Budgeting

Planning and control are the two basic functions of budgeting. *Planning* encompasses the entire process of preparing the budget, from initial strategic direction through preparation of expected financial results. Planning is the process that most people think of when the term *budgeting* is mentioned. The majority of the time and effort devoted to budgeting is expended in the planning stage. Careful planning provides the framework for the second function of budgeting, control.

Control is the comparison of actual results with budgeted data, evaluation of the differences, and then the taking of corrective actions when necessary. The comparison of budget and actual data can occur only after a period is over and actual accounting data are available. For example, April manufacturing cost data are necessary to compare with the April production budget to measure the difference between planned and actual results for the month of April. The comparison of actual results with budget expectations is called performance reporting. The budget acts as a gauge against which managers compare actual financial results.

Reasons for Budgeting

Budgeting is a time-consuming and costly process. Managers and employees are asked to contribute information and time in preparing the budget and in responding to performance reports and other control-phase budgeting activities. Is it all worth it? Do firms get their money's worth from their budgeting systems?

The answer to those questions cannot be generalized for all firms. Some firms receive far more value than others do for the dollars they spend on budgeting. Budgets do, however, provide a wealth of value for many firms that effectively operate their budgeting systems. I now discuss some of the reasons for investing in formal budgeting systems. In the next section of this chapter I discuss issues that contribute to effective budgeting.

Budgets offer a variety of benefits to organizations, including these seven:

1. Requiring periodic planning.
2. Fostering coordination, cooperation, and communication.
3. Forcing quantification of proposals.
4. Providing a framework for performance evaluation.
5. Creating an awareness of business costs.
6. Satisfying legal and contractual requirements.
7. Orienting a firm's activities toward organizational goals.

Periodic Planning

Virtually all organizations require some planning to ensure efficient and effective use of scarce resources. Some people are compulsive planners who continuously update plans that have already been made and plan for new activities and functions. At the other extreme are people who do not like to plan at all and, therefore, find little or no time to get involved in the planning process. The budgeting process closes the gap between these two extremes by creating a formal planning framework that provides specific, uniform periodic deadlines for each phase of the planning process. People who are not attuned to the planning process must still meet budget deadlines. Of course, planning does not guarantee success. People must execute the plans, but budgeting is an important prerequisite to the accomplishment of many activities.

Coordination, Cooperation, and Communication

Planning by individual managers does not ensure an optimum plan for the entire organization. The budgeting process, however, provides a vehicle for the exchange of ideas and objectives among people in the various organizational segments. The budget review process and other budget communication networks should minimize redundant and counterproductive programs by the time the final budget is approved.

Quantification

Because we live in a world of limited resources, virtually all individuals and organizations must ration their resources. The rationing process is easier for some than for others.

Each person and each organization must compare the costs and benefits of each potential project or activity and choose those that result in the most appropriate resource allocation decisions.

Measuring costs and benefits requires some degree of quantification. Profit-oriented firms measure costs and benefits using monetary metrics. This task is not always an easy one, however. For example, an advertising campaign may generate increased sales and improve company image, but it is difficult to quantify precisely the additional revenue caused by a particular advertising campaign, and it is even more difficult to quantify the impact on the company's image. In not-for-profit organizations such as government agencies, quantification of benefits can be even more difficult. For example, how does one quantify the monetary benefits of better police protection, more music programs at the city park, or better fire protection, and how should the benefits be evaluated in allocating resources to each activity? Despite the difficulties, resource allocation decisions necessitate some reasonable quantification of the costs and benefits of the various projects under consideration.

Performance Evaluation

Budgets can serve as means for measuring one's performance. Managerial effectiveness in each budgeting entity is appraised by comparing actual results with budgeted projections. Most managers want to know what is expected of them so that they may monitor their own performance. Budgets help to provide that type of information. Of course, managers can also be evaluated on other criteria, but it is valuable to have some quantifiable measure.

Cost Awareness

Accountants and financial managers are concerned daily about the cost implications of decisions and activities, but many other managers are not. Production supervisors focus on output, marketing managers on sales, and so forth. It is easy for people to overlook costs and cost-benefit relationships. At budgeting time, however, all managers with budget responsibility must convert their plans for projects and activities to costs and benefits. This cost awareness provides a common ground for communication among the various functional areas of the organization.

Legal and Contractual Requirements

Some organizations are required to budget. Local police departments, for example, cannot ignore budgeting even if it seems too much trouble, and the National Park Service would soon be out of funds if its management decided not to submit a budget this year. Some firms commit themselves to budgeting requirements when signing loan agreements or other operating agreements. For example, a bank may require a firm to submit an annual operating budget and monthly cash budgets throughout the life of a bank loan.

Goal Orientation

Resources should be allocated to projects and activities in accordance with organizational goals and objectives. Logical as this may sound, it is sometimes difficult to relate general organizational goals to specific projects or activities. Many general goals are not operational, meaning that it is difficult to determine the impact of specific projects on the achievement of the general goals of the organization. For example, three organizational goals may be stated as follows:

1. Earn a satisfactory profit.
2. Maintain sufficient funds for liquidity.
3. Provide high-quality products for customers.

These goals, which use subjective terms such as *satisfactory*, *sufficient*, and *high-quality*, are not tangible goals. The goals stated here may be interpreted differently by each manager. To be effective, goals must be more specific and provide clear direction for managers. For example, these same three goals can be made operational as follows:

1. Provide a minimum return on gross assets invested of 18%.
2. Maintain a minimum current ratio of 2:1 and a minimum quick ratio of 1.2:1.
3. Products must receive at least an 80% approval rating on customer satisfaction surveys.

Effective Budgeting

For firms to use budgets as effective tools:

- Budgets should be goal-oriented so that they help a firm accomplish its goals and objectives.
- Budgets must be realistic plans of action rather than wishful thinking.
- Participative budgeting should be utilized to instill a sense of cooperation and team play.
- The control phase of budgeting must be used effectively to provide a framework for evaluating performance and improving the budget-planning stage activities.
- Budgets should not be used as an excuse for denying appropriate employee resource requests.
- The budgeting process should be used by management as an excellent vehicle for modifying the behavior of employees to achieve company goals.

Goal Orientation

Some firms have more resources than others, but no firm seems to have all of the resources it needs to accomplish all of its goals. Consequently, budgets should provide a means by which resources are utilized for projects, activities, and business units in accordance with the goals and objectives of the organization. As logical as this may sound, it is sometimes difficult to relate general, organizational goals to specific projects or activities. Many general goals are not operational, meaning that it is difficult to determine the impact of specific projects on the achievement of the general goals of the organization.

A logical first step toward effective budgeting, then, is to formalize the goals of the organization. Starting at the top, general organizational goals should be as specific as possible, carefully established, and put in writing. Next, each major unit of the organization should develop more specific operational goals. The process should continue down the organizational structure to the lowest level of budget responsibility. This goal development process requires management at all levels to resolve difficult issues, but it also results in a budgeting framework that is much more likely to be effective. Even individuals need to understand their goals and objectives as they prepare budgets for their own activities.

Realistic Plan

Budgeting is not wishful thinking; rather it is a process designed to optimize the use of scarce resources in accordance with the goals of the company. Many firms have budget plans that call for sales growth, higher profits, and improved market share. To be effective, however, such plans must be based on specific executable plans, and on available resources and management talent that the company can bring to bear in accomplishing the budget plan. If the management of a firm wants to improve its level of operations, there must be a clearly defined path between the two points that the firm is able to travel.

The process begins with an analysis of the market and preparation of a strengths, weaknesses, opportunities, and threats (SWOT) analysis. Utilizing this background information, the company develops its overall strategy, together with the operational tactics required to achieve it. The financial impact of this strategy is then assessed in the preparation of the budget. If the financial results are unfavorable, strategies and tactics must be revisited until an acceptable outcome is achieved. Once the budget is finalized, strategies are implemented and the company's operations are subsequently monitored throughout the year in the control phase, as discussed later. Exhibit 11.1 presents an iterative model that embodies these concepts.

Participative Budgeting

The concept of building budgets up from the bottom with the input from all employees and managers affected by the budget is called participative budgeting. Most behavioral experts believe that individuals work harder to achieve objectives that they have played a part in creating. Applied to budgeting, this concept states that employees will strive harder to achieve performance levels defined by budgets if they have had a role in

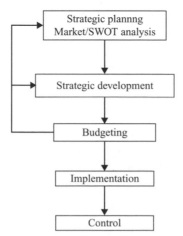

Exhibit 11.1   Comprehensive budgeting process.

Exhibit 11.2   Budget variance report.

	Budgeted	Actual	Variance
Revenues	$ 800,000	$ 780,000	$(20,000)U
Expenses	(500,000)	(470,000)	30,000 F
Profit	$ 300,000	$ 310,000	$ 10,000 F

creating the budget. By contrast, budgets imposed by top-level management may get little support from employees.

Control Phase of Budgeting

The first and most time-consuming phase of budgeting is the planning process. The control phase of budgeting, however, may be when firms get the most value from their budgeting activities. Exhibit 11.2 is a budget-performance report for first quarter of the year. The difference between the budgeted amount and the actual amount is called a budget variance. Budget variances are reported for both revenues and costs separately. In this case, revenues were $20,000 under budget and are, therefore, considered as an unfavorable budget variance (U). Expenses, however, were $30,000 less than expected, a favorable budget variance (F). The net result is a favorable profit budget variance of $10,000.

Each category is then separately analyzed to uncover the source of the variance. Although revenues in total are lower than expected, management is interested in the actual product lines causing this variance. Further analysis might reveal, for example, that all of the product lines are performing satisfactorily except for one that is performing more poorly than expected. On the expense side, a favorable budget variance may be due to positive effects of management's actions to operate the company more efficiently; or, positive variances may be due to the reduction of costs necessary for long-term performance to achieve short-term gains, such as a reduction in maintenance of machinery, research and development, advertising, and so forth.

Management must thoroughly investigate the causes for budget discrepancies so that corrective action can be taken. Are markets as a whole performing better or worse than expected? Is the company's marketing support adequate? Has the competitive landscape changed? Are cost variances the result of management's actions in response to competitive pressures or rather due to inadequate control? The answers to these questions may suggest changes in the company's strategic and tactical plans to compensate for the variances.

When actual prices and quantities are compared with expected prices and quantities, an additional level of analysis can be conducted.

Exhibit 11.3 illustrates a more in-depth level of price and quantity variance analysis. During the month, the firm realizes a positive variance of $6,000 relating to the cost of aluminum required for the production of its products.

This $6,000 variance can then be further decomposed into a price variance and a quantity variance. The price variance is $21,000 favorable due to the lower than expected purchase price for aluminum. It is computed by multiplying the price variance per unit ($3 − $2.80) by the actual pounds utilized (105,000). The quantity variance of $15,000

Exhibit 11.3 Price and quantity variance analysis.

	Budgeted	Actual	Variance
Production level in units	20,000	20,000	0
Lbs. aluminum/unit	5	5.25	0.25 U
Aluminum cost/lb.	$3	$2.80	$0.20 F
Total lbs. aluminum	100,000	105,000	5,000 U
Total material cost	$300,000	$294,000	$6,000 F
Price variance	($3 – $2.80) × 105,000 =	$21,000 F	
Quantity variance	(105,000 – 100,000) × $3 =	$15,000 U	
	Total net variance	$6,000 F	

unfavorable is a result of lower efficiency in the production process, which led to more material usage than had been expected. This variance is computed by multiplying the quantity variance (105,000 − 100,000) by the expected price ($3). This analysis reveals that the manufacturing process was less efficient than planned, in that it utilized more material to produce its products. This inefficiency was more than offset, however, by lower prices for direct materials than had been forecast. The price variance, therefore, masks the production inefficiency, and this would not be revealed without the additional level of analysis.

Comparing actual results with the budget, adjusting plans when necessary, and evaluating the performance of managers are essential elements of budget control. Many people, however, find the control phase difficult. When business results are less than expected, it may be painful to evaluate the results. For some it is much easier to look ahead to future time periods when they hope things will be better. But, frequently, plans for future success can be made realistically only when management learns from its past mistakes. The control phase of budgeting provides much of that learning process. Firms must be willing to evaluate performance carefully, adjusting plans and performance to stay on track toward achieving goals and objectives.

Many companies have intricate budget performance reporting systems in place, but the firms achieve little control from their use. In order to provide effective control, a business must use the system as an integral part of the reward system of the company. That is, employees must understand that budget performance reports are a component of their performance evaluation. There should be a relationship between budget performance and rewards such as pay raises, bonuses, and promotions.

Generally it is easy to determine whether a company's budget performance reporting system is working effectively. If discussions with managers yield comments such as "If we fail to achieve the budget, we just add more to it next period," it is likely that the budget control process is not effective. If, by contrast, employees state, "If we are over our budget by more than 2%, we will be called on the carpet and forced to explain the problem," then one knows the control process is having an impact.

Improper Use of Budgets

Sometimes managers use budgets as scapegoats for unpopular decisions. For example, rather than telling a department head that his or her budget request for three additional employees was not convincing when compared with all of the other budget requests, the vice president says, "The budget just would not allow any new employees this year." In another case, the director of the marketing department has requested travel funds to send all of his staff to an overseas education program. The vice president believes the program is a waste of money. Instead of giving the marketing director his opinion, the vice president says, "We would really like to send your staff to the program, but the budget is just too tight this year." The truth in this situation is that the trip is not a good use of business resources, regardless of the condition of the budget. The marketing director is left with the impression that the real problem is the state of the budget, when in fact the benefits of his travel proposal did not outweigh the cost. Management should be careful not to undermine the budgeting process by assigning adverse characteristics to it.

Behavioral Issues in Budgeting

Many of the internal accounting reports prepared in business are intended to influence managers and employees to behave in a particular way. For example, many manufacturing cost reports are designed to make employees aware of costs with the intent of controlling or keeping costs at some desired or acceptable level. Similarly, reports that compare the performance of one division with the performance of others are used to evaluate the performance of division managers and encourage better results for each division.

Budgets and budget performance reports are among the more useful internal accounting reports used by businesses to influence employee performance in a positive manner. Budget control is based on the concept that managers are held responsible for activities they manage. Performance reports reflect the degree of achievement of plans as embodied in the budget. To minimize adverse behavioral problems, care should be taken to develop and administer budgets appropriately. Budgets should not be used as a hammer to demand unattainable performance from employees. The best safeguard against unrealistic budgets is participative budgeting.

Developing a Budget

Budgets are useful, and in most cases they are essential to the success of virtually all organizations, whether they are for-profit companies or not-for-profit organizations. The larger and more complex the organization, the more time, energy, and resources must be used in preparing and using the budget.

The Structure of Budgets

Regardless of the size or type of organization, however, most budgets can be divided into two categories: the operating budget and the financial budget. The operating budget consists of plans for all of those activities that make up the normal operations of the firm. For a manufacturing business, the operating budget includes plans for sales, production, marketing, distribution, administration, and any other activities that the firm carries on in its normal course of business. For a merchandising firm, the operating budget includes plans for sales, merchandise purchases, marketing, distribution, advertising, personnel, administration, and any other normal activities of the merchandising firm. The financial budget includes all of the plans for financing the activities described in the operating

Exhibit 11.4   A manufacturing firm's master budget.

Operating Budget
- Sales budget
- Budget of ending inventories
- Production budget
  - Materials budget
  - Direct labor budget
  - Manufacturing overhead budget
- Administrative expense budget
- Budgeted non-operating items
- Budgeted net income

Financial Budget
- Capital expenditure budget
- Budgeted statement of financial position (balance sheet)
- Budgeted statement of cash flows

---

budget plus any plans for major new projects such as a new production plant or plant expansions. Both the operating and financial budgets are described later in more detail.

The Master Budget

The master budget is the total budget package for an organization; it is the end product of the budget preparation process. The master budget consists of all the individual budgets for each part of the organization combined into one overall budget. The exact composition of the master budget depends on the type and size of the business. However, all master budgets represent the organization's overall plan for a specific budget period. Exhibit 11.4 lists the common components of a master budget for a manufacturing business.

The components of the master budget form the firm's detailed operating plan for the coming year. As noted earlier, the master budget is divided into the operating budget and the financial budget. The operating budget includes revenues, product costs, operating expenses, and other components of the income statement. The financial budget includes the budgeted balance sheet, capital expenditure budget, and other budgets used in financial management. A large part of the financial budget is determined by the operating budget and the beginning balance sheet.

Exhibit 11.5 is a simplified budget for C&G's Gift Shop. It is prepared on a monthly basis. The numbers after the following subheadings refer to the applicable lines in the budget.

Sales Budget (1–3)

The sales budget or revenue budget is the first budget to be prepared. It is usually the most important budget because so many other budgets are directly related to sales and are therefore largely derived from the sales budget. Inventory budgets, production budgets, personnel budgets, marketing budgets, administrative budgets, and other budget areas are all affected significantly by the level of overall sales volume expected.

Exhibit 11.5 C&G's Gift Shop: 2009 master budget.

	Assumptions	Nov-PY	Dec-PY	Jan	Feb	Mar	Apr	May	Jun	Jul	Aug	Sep	Oct	Nov	Dec
1 Total Sales—Units	5,000	5,000	6,430	3,680	3,530	2,760	2,630	2,580	2,600	2,650	2,780	2,990	4,370	5,220	7,200
2 Selling Price	100	100	100	100	100	100	100	100	100	100	100	100	100	100	100
3 TOTAL GROSS SALES		500,000	643,000	368,000	353,000	276,000	263,000	258,000	260,000	265,000	278,000	299,000	437,000	522,000	720,000
4 TOTAL COST OF SALES	65%	325,000	417,950	239,200	229,450	179,400	170,950	167,700	169,000	172,250	180,700	194,350	284,050	339,300	468,000
5 GROSS MARGIN	35%	175,000	225,050	128,800	123,550	96,600	92,050	90,300	91,000	92,750	97,300	104,650	152,950	182,700	252,000
6															
7 Selling Expense	15%	75,000	96,450	55,200	52,950	41,400	39,450	38,700	39,000	39,750	41,700	44,850	65,550	78,300	108,000
8 Administration (fixed)	23,000	23,000	23,000	23,000	23,000	23,000	23,000	23,000	23,000	23,000	23,000	23,000	23,000	23,000	23,000
9 Administration (variable)	10%	50,000	64,300	36,800	35,300	27,600	26,300	25,800	26,000	26,500	27,800	29,900	43,700	52,200	72,000
10 Depreciation Expense	15 yr sl amort	3,472	3,472	3,472	3,472	3,472	3,472	3,472	3,472	3,472	3,472	3,472	3,472	3,472	3,472
11 TOTAL OPERATING EXPENSE		151,472	187,222	118,472	114,722	95,472	92,222	90,972	91,472	92,722	95,972	101,222	135,722	156,972	206,472
12															
13 OPERATING PROFIT		23,528	37,828	10,328	8,828	1,128	-172	-672	-472	28	1,328	3,428	17,228	25,728	45,528
14 Interest Income		0	0	0	0	354	675	874	932	953	952	921	855	401	0
15 Interest Expense		-1,956	-2,872	-1,989	-441	0	0	0	0	0	0	0	0	0	-80
16 PROFIT BEFORE TAX		21,572	34,956	8,339	8,387	1,482	503	202	460	981	2,280	4,349	18,083	26,129	45,448
17 Taxes @ 35%		7,550	12,235	2,918	2,936	519	176	71	161	343	798	1,522	6,329	9,145	15,907
18 PROFIT AFTER TAX		14,022	22,721	5,420	5,452	963	327	132	299	637	1,482	2,827	11,754	16,984	29,541
19 Cumulative Profit				5,420	10,872	11,835	12,162	12,294	12,593	13,231	14,713	17,540	29,294	46,278	75,819
20 BALANCE SHEET															
21 Cash			25,000	25,000	95,836	160,060	199,895	211,494	215,548	215,369	209,279	196,033	105,282	25,000	25,000
22 Accounts and Interest Receivable	65%, 30/35%, 60 Next month sales		637,000	412,050	300,800	218,904	179,275	169,924	170,232	175,953	190,702	216,221	361,505	494,351	721,700
23 Inventory			239,200	229,450	179,400	170,950	167,700	169,000	172,250	180,700	194,350	284,050	339,300	468,000	274,300
24 TOTAL CURRENT ASSETS			901,200	666,500	576,036	549,914	546,871	550,419	558,031	572,022	594,331	696,304	806,087	987,351	1,021,000
25															
26 Property, Plant, & Equipment (Gross)	15 yr sl amort		625,000	625,000	625,000	625,000	625,000	625,000	625,000	625,000	625,000	625,000	625,000	625,000	625,000
27 Accumulated Depreciation			-41,667	-45,139	-48,611	-52,083	-55,555	-59,027	-62,499	-65,971	-69,443	-72,915	-76,387	-79,859	-83,331
28 Property, Plant, & Equipment (Net)			583,333	579,861	576,389	572,917	569,445	565,973	562,501	559,029	555,557	552,085	548,613	545,141	541,669
29															
30 TOTAL ASSETS			1,484,533	1,246,361	1,152,425	1,122,831	1,116,316	1,116,392	1,120,532	1,131,051	1,149,888	1,248,389	1,354,700	1,532,492	1,562,669

	Assumptions	Nov-PY	Dec-PY	Jan	Feb	Mar	Apr	May	Jun	Jul	Aug	Sep	Oct	Nov	Dec
31															
32 Bank Loan (Line of Credit)			198,949	44,056	0	0	0	0	0	0	0	0	0	8,042	146,036
33 Accounts Payable			239,200	229,450	179,400	170,950	167,700	169,000	172,250	180,700	194,350	284,050	339,300	468,000	274,300
34 Accrued Expenses			198,857	119,908	114,626	92,519	88,926	87,571	88,161	89,593	93,298	99,272	138,579	162,645	218,987
35 TOTAL CURRENT LIABILITIES			637,006	393,414	294,026	263,469	256,626	256,571	260,411	270,293	287,648	383,322	477,879	638,687	639,323
36															
37 Common Stock			800,000	800,000	800,000	800,000	800,000	800,000	800,000	800,000	800,000	800,000	800,000	800,000	800,000
38 Retained Earnings			47,527	52,947	58,399	59,362	59,689	59,821	60,120	60,758	62,240	65,067	76,821	93,805	123,346
39 TOTAL SHAREHOLDERS' EQUITY			847,527	852,947	858,399	859,362	859,689	859,821	860,120	860,758	862,240	865,067	876,821	893,805	923,346
40															
41 TOTAL LIAB. + SH. EQUITY	1,484,533		1,246,361	1,152,425	1,122,831	1,116,316	1,116,392	1,120,532	1,131,051	1,149,888	1,248,389	1,354,700	1,532,492	1,562,669	
42 STATEMENT OF CASH FLOWS (INDIRECT METHOD)															
43 Net Income				5,420	5,452	963	327	132	299	637	1,482	2,827	11,754	16,984	29,541
44 Depreciation				3,472	3,472	3,472	3,472	3,472	3,472	3,472	3,472	3,472	3,472	3,472	3,472
45 Change in current assets (other than cash)				234,700	161,300	90,346	42,879	8,051	−3,558	−14,170	−28,399	−115,220	−200,534	−261,546	−33,649
46 Change in current liabilities (other than notes payable)				−88,699	−55,332	−30,557	−6,843	−55	3,840	9,882	17,355	95,674	94,557	152,766	−137,358
47 Net cash flow from operations				154,893	114,892	64,224	39,835	11,599	4,054	−179	−6,091	−13,246	−90,751	−88,324	−137,994
48															
49 Net cash flow from investing activities				0	0	0	0	0	0	0	0	0	0	0	0
50															
51 Net cash flow from financing activities				−154,893	−44,056	0	0	0	0	0	0	0	0	8,042	137,994
52															
53 Net change in cash				0	70,836	64,224	39,835	11,599	4,054	−179	−6,091	−13,246	−90,751	−80,282	0
54 Beginning cash				0	25,000	95,836	160,060	199,895	211,494	215,548	215,369	209,279	196,033	105,282	25,000
55 Ending cash				25,000	95,836	160,060	199,895	211,494	215,548	215,369	209,279	196,033	105,282	25,000	25,000

For C&G's Gift Shop, expected sales in units are reported on line 1. Note that the business is highly seasonal, with most of the sales and profits realized during the months of November and December. To keep the budget simple, we assume an average sales price of $100 per unit. In practice, however, the business would forecast unit sales by individual product lines.

Budgeted Cost of Goods Sold (4)

C&G assumes a cost of goods sold of 65% of sales revenues. This results in a gross profit of 35%. For a retail company, cost of goods sold represents the purchase cost of inventories sold during the period. It is computed as:

$$\text{Cost of Goods Sold} = \text{Beginning Inventory} + \text{Purchases during Period} - \text{Ending Inventory}$$

where all inventories and purchases are computed at the purchase price to the company.

For a manufacturing company, cost of goods sold is computed similarly, but in place of purchases we have the cost of the raw materials of the goods manufactured, together with the labor and overhead incurred in the manufacturing process. Beginning and ending inventories consist of raw materials, work in process, and finished goods.

Administrative Expense Budget (7–10)

The expected administrative costs for an organization are presented in the administrative expense budget. The administrative expense budget may contain many fixed costs, some of which may be avoidable if subsequent operations indicate that some cost cuts are necessary. These avoidable costs, sometimes called discretionary fixed costs, include such items as research and development, employee education and training programs, and portions of the personnel budget. Fixed costs that cannot be avoided during the period are called committed fixed costs. Mortgage payments, bond interest payments, and property taxes are classified as committed costs. Variable administrative costs may include some personnel costs, a portion of the utility costs, computer service bureau costs, and supplies costs.

For C&G's Gift Shop, selling expenses are budgeted at 15% of sales. These are variable costs since they change in proportion to the change in sales. You might think of these as commissions paid to the sales personnel as a percent of the sales made during the period. The fixed portion of administration expense is budgeted at $23,000 per month. These expenses might be rent, salaries of administrative personnel, and so forth. The administrative expense also contains a variable component, budgeted at 10% of sales. Finally, depreciation is computed on a straight-line basis over 15 years and is a fixed expense, budgeted at $3,472 per month.

Budgeted Income Statement (3–18)

The budgeted income statement shows the expected revenues and expenses from operations during the budget period. Budgeted income is a key figure in the firm's profit plan and reflects a majority of the firm's commitment of talent, time, and resources for the period.

A firm may have budgeted non-operating items such as interest on investments or gains or losses on the sale of fixed assets. Usually they are relatively small, although in large firms the dollar amounts can be sizable. If non-operating items are expected, they should be included in the firm's budgeted income statement. Income taxes are levied on actual, not budgeted, net income, but the budget plan should include expected taxes; therefore, the last figure in the budgeted income statement is budgeted after-tax net income.

Non-operating items in C&G's income statement include interest income and interest expense. Amounts borrowed carry an interest rate of 12% (1% per month), and cash in excess of the $25,000 required for daily transactions is invested in marketable securities earning an investment return of 6% per annum (0.5% per month). Finally, taxes are levied at the rate of 35% on pretax income.

The Financial Budget

The financial budget presents the plans for financing the operating activities of the firm. The financial budget is made up of the budgeted balance sheet and the budgeted statement of cash flows, each of which provides essential financial information.

Budgeted Balance Sheet (20–41)

The budgeted balance sheet is derived from the budgeted balance sheet at the beginning of the budget period and the expected changes in the account balances reflected in the operating budget, capital expenditure budget, and cash budget. It is necessary to use a budgeted balance sheet for the beginning of the period because the new budget is prepared before the previous accounting period has ended. When the budgeted balance sheet for the coming accounting period is prepared, there may be several months left in the current accounting period.

The budgeted balance sheet is more than a collection of residual balances resulting from other budget estimates. Undesirable projected balances and account relationships may cause management to change the operating plan. For instance, if a lending institution requires a firm to maintain a certain relationship between current assets and current liabilities, the budget must reflect these requirements. If it does not, the operating plan must be changed until the agreed requirements are met.

Budgeted Accounts Receivable (22)

Budgeted accounts receivable are a function of expected sales on open account and the period of time that the receivables are expected to be outstanding. For C&G's Gift Shop, all sales are assumed to be on open account to other businesses. The company expects that 65% of the sales during the period will be collected in the following month, and 35% will be collected in the next month. For this exercise, we have assumed that all of the accounts are collectible. If not, the company would have to build in a provision for uncollectible accounts that would reduce expected collections and be reflected in the income statement as bad debt expense.

Budget of Ending Inventories (23)

Inventories comprise a major portion of the current assets of many manufacturing firms. Separate decisions about inventory levels must be made for raw materials, work in process, and finished goods. Raw material scarcities, management's attitude about inventory levels, inventory carrying costs, inventory ordering costs, and other variables may all affect inventory-level decisions.

C&G's Gift Shop has a policy to maintain inventory levels on hand equal to the next month's expected cost of goods sold.

Capital Expenditure Budget (26)

The capital expenditure budget is one of the budget components that make up the financial budget. Each of the budget components has its own unique contribution to make toward the effective planning and control of business operations. Some budget components, however, are particularly crucial in the effective management of businesses. The cash budget and the capital expenditure budget are two of the most important.

Capital budgeting is the process of identifying, evaluating, planning, and financing major investment projects of an organization. Decisions to expand production facilities, acquire new production machinery, buy a new computer, or remodel the office building are all examples of capital expenditure decisions. Capital budgeting decisions made now determine to a large degree how successful an organization will be in achieving its goals and objectives in the years ahead. Capital budgeting plays an important role in the long-range success of many organizations because of several characteristics that differentiate it from most other elements of the master budget.

First, most capital budgeting projects require relatively large commitments of resources. Major projects, such as plant expansion or equipment replacement, may involve resource outlays in excess of annual net income. Relatively insignificant purchases are not treated as capital budgeting projects even if the items purchased have long lives. For example, the purchase of 100 calculators at $15 each for use in the office would be treated as a period expense by most firms, even though the calculators may have a useful life of several years.

Second, most capital expenditure decisions are long-term commitments. The projects last more than a year, and many extending over 5, 10, or even 20 years. The longer the life of the project, the more difficult it is to predict revenues, expenses, and cost savings. Capital budgeting decisions are long-term policy decisions and should reflect clearly an organization's policies on growth, marketing, industry share, social responsibility, and other goals.

For purposes of this exercise, we have assumed that C&G's Gift Shop will not incur any capital expenditures in the upcoming year. As a result, line 26, property, plant, and equipment, remains constant. Net PP&E (line 28), however, is reduced each period by the addition of depreciation expense to accumulated depreciation.

Budgeted Accounts Payable (33)

Accounts payable represent amounts owed to other businesses for the purchase of goods and services. These are usually non-interest-bearing. We have assumed that all of the inventories are purchased on open account and that the terms of credit require payment in full in the following month. As a result, accounts payable are equal to the cost of inventories in this example.

Budgeted Accrued Expenses (34)

Expenses are recognized in the income statement when incurred, regardless of the period in which they are paid. For this example, we assume that all of the operating expenses incurred and recognized during the month are paid in the following month. These expenses include selling expenses, administrative expenses other than depreciation, interest expense, and taxes.

Bank Loan (Line of Credit) (32)

Businesses require cash to cover the portion of inventories and accounts receivable that are not financed by trade accounts payable and accrued expenses. This need is very pronounced in seasonal businesses. For example, C&G's Gift Shop must purchase inventories one month in advance of sales. And when these inventories are sold, 65% of the proceeds are collected in the subsequent month and 35% in the month thereafter. As a result, C&G has a considerable amount of cash invested in the business that is not recouped for at least two months.

Typically, short-term cash needs, such as the needs of seasonal businesses, are met with a bank line of credit that allows the company to borrow funds up to a predetermined maximum amount and to repay those loans at a later date. In this case, funds are borrowed to finance the purchase of inventories, and these amounts are repaid when the receivables are collected.

Stockholders' Equity (37–39)

No sales of common stock are budgeted. Since no dividends are projected, retained earnings (line 38) increase by the amount of profit for the month.

Cash Budget

Of all the components of the master budget, none is more important than the cash budget. Of the two major goals of most profit-seeking firms—to earn a satisfactory profit and to remain liquid—liquidity is the more important. Many companies lose money for years, but with adequate financing they are able to remain in business until they can become profitable. In contrast, firms that cannot remain liquid are unable to pay their bills as they come due. In such cases, creditors can, and often do, force them out of business. Even government and not-for-profit organizations such as churches and charities must pay their bills and other obligations on time.

Meeting cash obligations as they come due is not as simple as it may appear. Profitability and liquidity do not necessarily go hand in hand. Some firms experience their most critical liquidity problems when they go from a break-even position to profitability. At that time, growing receivables, increased inventories, and growing capacity requirements may create cash shortages.

The cash budget is a very useful tool in cash management. Managers estimate all expected cash flows for the budget period. The typical starting point is cash from operations, which is net income adjusted for noncash items, such as depreciation, and required investment in net working capital (accounts receivable and inventories, less accounts payable). All non-operating cash items are also included. Purchase of land and equipment, sales of bonds and common stock, and the acquisition of treasury stock are a few examples of non-operating items affecting the cash budget. The net income figure for an accounting period usually is very different from the cash flow for the period because of non-operating cash flow items or changes in working capital.

Often, cash budgets are prepared much more frequently than other budgets. For example, a company may prepare quarterly budgets for all of its operating budget components such as sales and production, and also for its other financial budget components such as capital expenditures. For its cash budget, however, the firm prepares weekly budgets to ensure that it has cash available to meet its obligations each week and that any excess cash is properly invested. In companies with very critical cash problems, even daily cash budgets may be necessary to meet management's information requirements. The frequency of cash budgets depends on management's planning needs and the potential for cash management problems.

Cash management is intended to optimize cash balances; this means having enough cash to meet liquidity needs and not having so much cash that profitability is sacrificed. Excess cash should be invested in earning assets and should not be allowed to lie idly in the cash account. Cash budgeting is useful in dealing with both types of cash problems.

Budgeted Statement of Cash Flows—Indirect Method (42–55)

The final element of the master budget package is the statement of cash flows. The increased emphasis by management in recent years on cash and the sources and uses of cash have made this an ever more useful management tool. This statement is usually prepared from data in the budgeted income statement and changes between the estimated balance sheet at the beginning of the budget period and the budgeted balance sheet at the end of the budget period.

The statement of cash flows consists of three sections: net cash flows from operations, net cash flows from investing activities, and net cash flows from financing activities. Net cash flows from operations are equal to net income plus depreciation expense and plus or minus changes in current assets (other than cash) and current liabilities (other than bank loans). Increases (or decreases) in current assets are treated as cash outflows (or inflows) and increases (or decreases) in current liabilities are treated as cash inflows (or outflows).

Net cash flows from investing activities consist of changes in long-term assets. Since we do not project any capital expenditures, net cash flows from investing activities are equal to zero in all months.

Net cash flows from financing activities consist of changes in borrowed funds (short-term and long-term), changes in other long-term liabilities, changes in common stock, and dividends paid. The only activities of a financing nature in this example are increases (or decreases) in bank loans outstanding. The bank line of credit is the buffer that keeps assets equal to liabilities and stockholders' equity. As assets grow with increases in inventories and accounts receivable, bank loans increase as well to finance this growth. As the inventories are sold and the receivables are collected during slower periods, the excess cash is used to repay the amounts borrowed. Banks typically require that the line of credit be paid in full at some point during the year. Any excess funds generated after repayment of the bank loans are invested in short-term marketable securities until they are required again to finance seasonal growth in assets.

Forecasting

Sales budgets are influenced by a wide variety of factors, including general economic conditions, pricing decisions, competitor actions, industry conditions, and marketing programs. Often the sales budget starts with individual sales representatives or sales managers predicting sales in their particular areas. The basic sales data are aggregated to arrive at a raw sales forecast that is then modified to reflect many of the variables mentioned previously. The resulting sales budget is expressed in dollars and must include sufficient detail on product mix and sales patterns to provide the information necessary for making decisions about changes in inventory levels and production quantities.

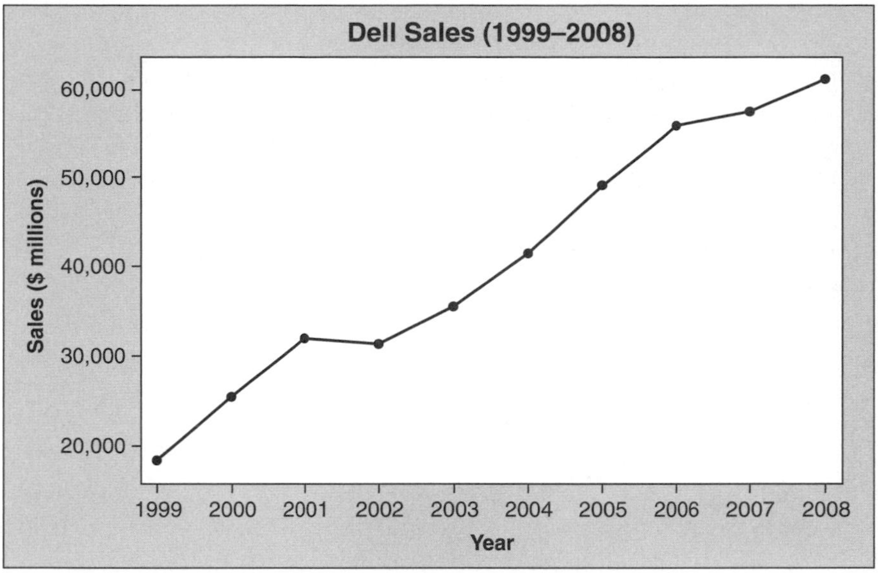

Exhibit 11.7   Dell, Inc. annual sales, 1999–2008.

In addition to the input from sales personnel, companies frequently also utilize a number of statistical techniques to estimate future sales. For example, Exhibit 11.7 is a graph of the Dell, Inc.'s annual sales from 1999 to 2008.

Sales appear to demonstrate a pronounced upward trend. How would one forecast sales for the next three years? Projecting from the most recent sales level might understate the estimates if the last year was unusually low, say, due to the effects of a business downturn or new product introductions by competitors. Another alternative is to attempt to estimate the underlying trend in annual sales. Exhibit 11.8 presents such a graph.

In Exhibit 11.8, a statistical technique called regression analysis has been used to estimate a trend line for Dell's annual sales. This line was estimated with a statistical software package called *Minitab*, but the analysis is also available in Microsoft Excel and many other programs. The equation for the trend line is $Sales_t = \$14,330 + (\$4,796 \times t)$. This equation states that the sales for the first forecast year are equal to $\$14,330 + (\$4,796 \times 11)$ (since our data ended at year 10), or \$67,086 million. Our forecasts for years 2 and 3 extend linearly with a continuation of the same slope that was estimated in the trend line fit through the data.

A potential problem with fitting a trend line through the data with regression analysis is that each observation is treated the same way. That is, we are not weighting the information contained in the latest set of observations more heavily than those that occurred eight years ago. Other statistical techniques, such as exponential smoothing, are available to address this concern. Exhibit 11.9 presents the same annual sales data with a trend line that has been exponentially smoothed.

Notice how the estimated trend line reacts to changes in the annual sales. This technique weights recent observations more heavily than those in the distant past. The result is a trend line whose slope changes over time to reflect changes in sales growth. Projections for the next three years, then, begin with the last estimate of the underlying trend and at the most recent slope indicated by the data. For example, the estimate

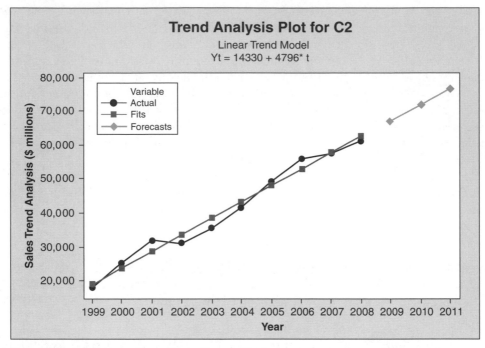

Exhibit 11.8   **Trend analysis for Dell, Inc. annual sales, 1999–2011.**

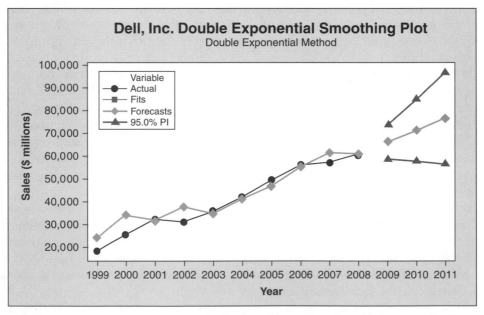

Exhibit 11.9   **Double exponential smoothing of Dell, Inc.'s annual sales, 1999–2011.**

of Dell's sales for the next year is $66,241.7 million, somewhat lower than the $67,086 million estimated for the next year's sales using the trend line. This reduction weights the more recent downward trend more heavily, thus dampening the forecast.

Many other statistical techniques can also be brought to bear on this problem. These provide an objective estimate of future sales from the data itself. Their advantage is that they are not prone to biases in the form of either wishful thinking or undue pessimism. Their drawback is that they cannot take into account all of the variables witnessed by sales personnel and, therefore, do not have as much of a feel for the market. Companies must utilize a variety of inputs into the projection process, and they derive some level of comfort when several different approaches yield similar results.

The projection process is a critical part of the budgeting process. It follows from the SWOT analysis and the resulting strategic and tactical plans. Once these are formulated, sales projections and the subsequent budgeting process just outlined provide an evaluation of the effectiveness of the business plan.

Fixed Budgets versus Flexible Budgets

Many organizations operate in an environment where they can predict with great accuracy the volume of business they will experience during the upcoming budget period. In such cases, budgets prepared for a single level of activity typically are very useful in planning and controlling business activities. Budgets prepared for a single level of activity are called fixed budgets.

Organizations that have trouble predicting accurately the volume of activity they will experience during the budget period often find that a budget prepared for only one level of activity is not very helpful in planning and controlling their business activities. These organizations can operate better with a budget prepared for several levels of activity and covering a range of possible levels of activity. This type of budget is called a flexible budget.

Fixed Budgets

A fixed budget, sometimes called a *static budget*, contains budget data for only one specific volume of activity. Because fixed budgets use only one volume of activity in determining all budgeted data, the fact that some costs are fixed and some costs are variable has no impact on the budgeted figures. The budget data used in preparing the budget for the planning phase of the process are also used in budget performance reports during the control phase of the budget process regardless of whether the volume of activity is actually achieved.

The planning and control framework provided by a budgeting system is an essential element of effective management. In many organizations, fixed budgets are tools that offer managers the ability to plan and control operations and to evaluate performance. If, however, the actual volume of activity achieved by a firm is sufficiently different from the volume of activity planned in the fixed budget, the fixed budget may be a very poor measure on which to base the performance measurement of employees.

Flexible Budgets

A flexible budget, also called a *dynamic budget*, is prepared for more than one level of activity. For example, a firm may prepare budgets for 10,000, 11,000, and 12,000 units of production. The purpose of preparing budgets for multiple activity levels is to provide managers with information about a range of activity in case the actual volume of activity differs from the expected level. Managers continue to rely heavily on the budget based on the expected level of activity for planning material acquisitions, labor needs, and other resource requirements, but the flexible budget provides additional information useful in modifying plans if operating data indicate that some other level of activity will occur. When performance reports are prepared, actual results are compared with a budget based specifically on the level of activity actually achieved.

Actual activity may differ significantly from budgeted activity because of an unexpected strike, cancellation of a large order, an unexpected new contract, or other factors. In a business that frequently experiences variations in its volume of activity, a flexible budget may be more useful than a fixed budget. Flexible budgets provide managers with more useful information for planning and a better basis for comparing performance when activity levels fluctuate than is available from a fixed budget.

The Profit Plan

The term *profit plan* is sometimes used to refer to a master budget. Profit plan probably best describes the operating part of the master budget of a profit-oriented firm. However, it can be argued that the entire master budget of profit-oriented firms is the total profit plan for the firm. The operating budget shows details of budgeted net income, but the financial budgets, such as cash and capital expenditure budgets, are also an integral part of the overall profit planning of the firm.

Naturally, the term *profit plan* is not suitable for public-sector firms. Organizations such as a fire department do not generate a net income. For public-sector organizations, *master budget* is the more logical term for the total budget package. Because we are concerned with both public- and private-sector organizations, we use *master budget* predominantly. However, be aware of *profit plan*, because it is used occasionally in practice.

The Budget Review Process

The budget plan determines the allocation of resources within the organization. Typically, the resources available are less than the demand for the resources. Consequently, there should be some systematic process for evaluating all proposals relating to the budget. The process of systematically evaluating budge proposals is referred to as the budget review process.

In the early planning stages, budget review may not be a formal process. Sometimes a few people (or even a single individual) may make the budgeting decisions. For example, production-line supervisors may determine resource allocations within their departments. Next, a plant budget committee may evaluate budget proposals for all production supervisors. The budget proposals for the entire plant go to a division budget committee, and the final budget review is made by a budget committee of the controller and corporate vice presidents.

The budget review process varies among organizations. Even within a single firm, different budget review processes may be used in various segments of the firm and at various levels of responsibility. However, the basic review process is fairly standard.

Accountants and financial managers participate in the preparation and implementation of the budget, but all business managers, including marketing managers, production supervisors, purchasing officers, and other nonfinancial managers are interested in developing budgets for their particular part of the business. In addition, each functional manager must be keenly interested in selling his or her budget to higher-level management. Selling the budget means convincing the budget review committee that a particular budget proposal should be accepted. For some managers, selling the budget is the single most important activity in their job, because if they fail at this task, even a tremendous management effort cannot obtain desired results.

With such an awesome description of the importance of selling the budget, one might conclude that it is an exceedingly difficult process. Not so! Actually, the process requires a mixture of logic and diligence. There is no precise formula for success, but some common suggestions are to:

- Know your audience.
- Make a professional presentation.
- Quantify the material.
- Avoid surprises.
- Set priorities.

Know Your Audience

A large part of the budget selling strategy may be determined by the nature of the budget review audience, whether it is one person or a group of people. Information that may prove essential to the successful budget approval effort includes:

- Strategies that have succeeded or failed in the past.
- Pet peeves or special likes of review members.
- A variety of other committee characteristics.

Make a Professional Presentation

Not all managers approach the budgeting process with the same level of enthusiasm. By the time budget review arrives, some managers just want to get it over with. Such an attitude can easily show during the budget review process. Review committees may interpret it as disdain for one's job and one's management function in general. Often the result is unfavorable action on the budget proposals under review.

A professional presentation includes:

- Enthusiasm and polish.
- A neat, concise, and understandable budget proposal.
- Ample supporting documentation.
- A willingness and ability to answer relevant questions.

Quantify the Material

Because most resource allocation decisions are in some way affected by their cost-benefit relationships, it is necessary to quantify both the costs and benefits of virtually all budget proposals. Cost estimation is seldom easy, but it is usually far easier than the measurement of benefits. Even in the private sector, benefits are not always easy to measure in terms of the corporate goals of profitability and liquidity. In the not-for-profit sector, benefit measurement is even more difficult. For example, how does one measure the benefits of 20 new park rangers, 10 new police cars, or a decorative fountain in the city park? Obviously the quantification process would be different for each of these, and direct comparisons could be inconclusive. Yet, such comparisons may be necessary in arriving at final budget allocations.

It is easy to dismiss the value of quantification when the resulting numbers are hard to compare with other budget proposals, or the numbers are hard to verify. Nevertheless, some quantitative support typically is better than mere general statements about the desirability of the budget proposal. Budget salesmanship should be approached with the same ingenuity that is found in the external marketing effort. If certain budget proposals have benefits that are difficult to quantify directly, various types of statistics might support the projects in an indirect way. For example, if a police department wants to justify 10 new police officers, it might offer supporting statistics on rising population in the community, rising crime rates, or relatively low per-capita police cost ratios. Although none of the suggested statistics measures direct benefits, they may be more useful in swaying a budget review committee than a vague statement about the value of more officers. Statistics that are not direct measures of benefits can be used widely in both the public and private sectors when supporting budget proposals.

Avoid Surprises

Avoid surprises to the review committee as well as surprises to those who present the budget. New proposals and information are hard to sell to a budget review committee and should be introduced and developed long before the final review process.

Surprises to managers presenting the budgets most often occur during the questioning process or when a budget proposal is more detailed than prior budgets. To minimize this problem, budget presentations should be carefully rehearsed. The rehearsal might include a realistic or even pessimistic mock review committee. The mock review should ask pointed and difficult questions. Sometimes knowing the answer to a relatively immaterial question is enough to secure a favorable opinion.

Set Priorities

Few managers receive a totally favorable response to all budget requests. In a world of limited resources, wants exceed available resources, and managers should be prepared for a budget allocation that is somewhat different from the initial request. Typically, all proposed budget items are not equally desirable. Some projects and activities are essential; others are highly desirable. Some would be nice, but are really not essential.

Priority systems established by the managers of each budgeting entity before the review process starts aid in structuring the budget proposal so that important items are funded first. Setting priorities avoids embarrassing questions and last-minute decision crises that affect the quality of a professional presentation.

Recent Trends

The budgeting process provides a mechanism for planning, allocating resources, and performance evaluation that has endured, largely unchanged, for decades.[1] Despite its longevity, managers have expressed frustration with the budgetary process on a number of levels:

- *Fixed targets do not take into account the myriad of events that can affect outcomes.* The flexible budget discussed earlier estimates the impact on the profitability of differing levels of production and sales. Although a useful exercise, it does not address the more fundamental types of shocks that can render an existing business plan obsolete.

- *Financial incentives may not build motivation and commitment.* Budgets tend to elicit temporary compliance, but may not create a lasting commitment to value creation. Further, the basis for reward tends to be localized rather than across the entire organization.

- *Centralized resource allocation may not be effective.* Using the budgetary process for capital allocation removes the resource allocation process farther from the customer for which the capital investment is intended. Further, the resource allocation process is largely risk averse, focusing on more certain returns and short-term in nature.

- *Segments of the business cannot be viewed in isolation.* Businesses are highly integrated, and a budgetary process that is too localized can lead to conflicts, as cutbacks in one area may adversely affect another area's ability to achieve its goals.

- *Focus on financial metrics may not lead to discovery of root causes.* Financial metrics reflect outcomes. The focus, however, must be on the root causes of those outcomes. Managers may be motivated to manage what the company measures rather than the underlying business dynamics.

The Alternative to Budgets

The budgetary process serves a useful function in organizations, and suggested alternatives do not typically include the substitution of another process for the budgetary process. Rather, they tend to focus on cultural changes to augment the budgetary process. Some suggestions include the following:

- *Primary focus on the customer.* Companies succeed when they find ways of satisfying customer needs profitably. They must manage the entire production and delivery system, rather than focus on its components, to make sure that the entire organization is focused on the satisfaction of customer needs.

- *Companies should focus on relative success.* Static benchmarks tend to lead to a short-term focus and reversion to old habits once the objective is achieved or thought to be unachievable. Developing a culture of continual improvement may result in more long-lasting changes. Change, then, continues long after the benchmarks have been achieved.

- *Planning need not revolve around a calendar.* Annual monitoring is the cornerstone of financial reporting, and budgets are typically geared to this annual cycle. Businesses, however, are fluid. They operate on cycles that may not be annual in nature. Nor does the cycle of one business unit necessarily correspond to that of another. The planning process needs to take these inherent differences into account.

- *Companies must decentralize decision making.* Good decisions are made at all levels of an organization, and generally the closer the decision maker is to the customer, the better the decision.

Bill Gates, the founder of Microsoft, once described the organization as a web of relationships rather than a machine with distinct parts. The biological nervous system gives you the information that you need to trigger your reflexes so that you can react quickly to an external stimulus. In addition, it blocks out unimportant information that might distract you from reacting appropriately. Information systems for companies need to embrace those qualities: quickly provide only the needed information to those who need it so that they can make appropriate decisions to respond. Those who think beyond budgets embrace this type of thinking.

Internet Link

www.bbrt.org   CAM-I Beyond Budgeting Round Table

Note

1. This discussion draws upon the ideas of Jeremy Hope and Robin Fraser, "Beyond Budgeting: Questions and Answers," Beyond Budgeting Round Table, October 2001.

For Further Reading

Brownell, P., "Participation in the Budgeting Process: When It Works and When It Doesn't," *Journal of Accounting Literature* 1 (1982): 124–153.

Carruth, Paul J., and Thurrel O. McClendon, "How Supervisors React to Meeting the Budget Pressure," *Management Accounting* (November 1984): 50.

Chandler, John S., and Thomas N. Trone, "Bottom Up Budgeting and Control," *Management Accounting* (February 1982): 37.

Chandler, Susan, "Lands' End Looks for Terra Firma," *BusinessWeek*, July 8, 1996, 130–131.

Collins, Frank, Paul Munter, and Don W. Finn, "The Budgeting Games People Play," *Accounting Review* (January 1987): 29.

Geurts, Michael D., and Thomas A. Buchman, "Accounting for Shocks in Forecasts," *Management Accounting* (April 1981): 21.

Hofstede, G. H., *The Game of Budget Control* (New York: Barnes & Noble, 1968).

Hope, Jeremy, and Robin Fraser, "Beyond Budgeting: Questions and Answers," Beyond Budgeting Round Table, October 2001.

Leitch, Robert A., John B. Barrack, and Sue H. McKinley, "Controlling Your Cash Resources," *Management Accounting* (October 1980): 58.

Merchant, Kenneth A., "The Design of the Corporate Budgeting System: Influences on Managerial Behavior and Performance," *Accounting Review* (October 1981): 813.

Merchant, Kenneth A., and J. Manzoni, "The Achievability of Budget Targets in Profit Centers: A Field Study," *Accounting Review* 64, no. 3 (July 1989): 539–558.

Merewitz, Leonard, and Stephen H. Sosnick, *The Budget's New Clothes* (Chicago: Markham Publishing, 1973).

Penne, Mark, "Accounting Systems, Participation in Budgeting, and Performance Evaluation," *Accounting Review* 65, no. 2 (April 1990): 303–314.

Rechfield, John F., "What Working for a Japanese Company Taught Me," *Harvard Business Review* (November–December 1990): 168–169.

Taylor, William, "Message and Muscle: An Interview with Swatch Titan Nicolas Hayek," *Harvard Business Review* (March–April 1993): 110.

"Tenneco CEO Mike Walsh's Fight of His Life," *BusinessWeek*, September 20, 1993, 62.

Trapani, Cosmo S., "Six Critical Areas in the Budgeting Process," *Management Accounting* (November 1982): 52.

Wildavsky, Aaron, *The Politics of the Budgetary Process*, 2nd ed. (Boston: Little, Brown, 1974).

Cost Structure Analysis, Profit Planning, and Value Creation

William C. Lawler

In the highly volatile markets of today's economy, detailed profit planning is the foundation for long-term value creation. It is the basis for efficient resource allocation within a firm and the root of all strategic plans. This, however, is only a necessary condition, and by itself is not sufficient for the goal of value creation. One also must be able to identify the economic logic embedded in the strategic plan of competitors. Running a business is like playing a game of chess; in order to win one must be able to anticipate the moves of the competitor. And in order to achieve this insight, the first step is to discern the cost structure of that competitor.

Economic literature defines *cost structure* as the relative portion of a firm's costs that are fixed as opposed to variable. The definitions of *fixed* and *variable* are very precise. A fixed cost does not vary *in total* with changes in output, whereas a variable cost *in total* will change in a manner proportionate with changes in volume.[1] A term that is often used in describing this structure is *degree of operating leverage*. A firm with relatively high fixed costs is said to have high operating leverage. This implies that a firm has a choice in creating operating leverage; one could build a large infrastructure and lock oneself into high fixed cost for a period of time, or one could create a more variable cost structure. An example of this would be when a firm creates a strategic alliance with a supplier rather than building a vertically integrated value chain. In this case, as output increases, costs from sourcing would increase in a relative manner. That is, they would be variable in nature. If the firm were to have built the infrastructure, the costs would have been fixed.

Although this discussion can easily describe a manufacturing environment, it is also relevant for a service business. Throughout this chapter we will use the generic term *output*, which can describe a tangible unit of production or the more intangible unit of service. Finally, profit planning and the analysis of cost structure assume some type of relevant range since it is clear that if a firm were to double output, its fixed infrastructure costs would most certainly increase and variable costs per unit would be impacted by scale factors.[2]

History is overflowing with examples of the importance of cost structure analysis in strategic planning. In the early 1980s the U.S. airline industry was deregulated. Given a set number of routes flown every day, which then required a fleet of planes and salaried employees, this industry, at the time, had one of the highest operating leverage factors of any industry. Almost all of its costs were fixed. The more financially sound competitors cut prices, fully aware of the short-term impact on their profits. But they also realized that those less financially sound carriers would not be able to sustain the losses due to lack of coverage of the fixed cost burden. Airlines such as Braniff and Eastern soon fell into bankruptcy. Ten years later Sun Microsystems did much the same thing in the computer industry. At that time, Hewlett-Packard, IBM, and Digital Equipment Corporation all had vertically integrated infrastructures, which produced proprietary designed systems sold at premium prices. Andy Bechtolsheim, one of the three founders of Sun and the technology leader, realized that with the advances in technology, a competitive system now could be assembled from low-cost, readily available components at a fraction of the traditional cost. Sun built its business model on an open platform and priced aggressively. Management argued it was "better positioned to deal with low margins than IBM or DEC, who've got to financially feed layer upon layer of bureaucracy."[3] In approximately 10 years, this initiative restructured the industry from proprietary technology players with vertically integrated infrastructures and correspondingly high operating leverage to open players with minimal infrastructure and radically different cost structures. And in today's business environment, all one has to do is follow the debate on outsourcing to understand the continued impact of cost structure on business models.

This chapter starts with a discussion of how one can estimate the cost structure of competitors given publicly available information and the pitfalls that can lead one to improper results. Given this information, we then discuss what are considered best practices for managing cost structure in today's business environment. We conclude with how this analysis can be used internally by product managers who have much better cost data available to them.

Estimating Cost Structure from Publicly Available Information

Company X is a well-known U.S. technology firm with quarterly financial results as shown in Exhibit 12.1. This format is common for publicly traded companies and is based on the functional nature of costs. First, costs of producing and delivering the product (cost of sales) are matched against the revenues generated from sale of the products to arrive at a gross profit number. Next, the operating expenses associated with research and development, marketing and sales, and corporate administration (e.g., legal, accounting, and corporate management) are deducted to arrive at operating profit. For those analysts involved in developing competitive intelligence (and financial analysts), this is the line that is the focus of attention. It represents the profit from the primary function of the company—the results from the normal, recurring activities that then can be extrapolated into the future. From operating profit, taxable income is arrived at by compiling the results of other activities that are not the primary focus of the business. Common items such as interest income on investments of excess cash that will be needed in the future, interest expense on debt instruments, and losses from restructuring are included in the "Other" account for Company X. As stated earlier, these are not the primary focus of the business, are often nonrecurring and therefore cannot be extrapolated into the future, and are of little interest to analysts.[4] Deducting income tax then yields the net income for the period. The quarterly numbers of Company X reflect the seasonal pattern of demand for this business, with sales peaking in quarter 2 and 3 and then falling off in quarter 4 and 1. As is evident, operating profit follows the same pattern. For any company traded on any stock exchange in the world, information such as this must be reported on a periodic

Exhibit 12.1 Company X—Quarterly Income Statements (costs reported by function).

	Qrt 1	Qrt 2	Qrt 3	Qrt 4	Fiscal Year
	($ millions)				
Net sales	$253.7	$288.7	$299.5	$260.4	$1,102.3
Cost of sales	140.3	151.5	155.2	141.8	588.8
Gross profit	$113.4	$137.2	$144.3	$118.6	$ 513.5
R&D	49.3	52.4	52.2	50.4	204.3
Selling, general, & adm.	63.0	62.8	62.9	62.2	250.9
Total operating expenses	$112.3	$115.2	$115.1	$112.6	$ 455.2
Operating profit	$ 1.1	$ 22.0	$ 29.2	$ 6.0	$ 58.3
Other	(7.5)	8.6	10.8	9.1	21.0
Income before tax	$ (6.4)	$ 30.6	$ 40.0	$ 15.1	$ 79.3
Income tax	1.4	3.5	4.7	(2.2)	7.4
Net income	$ (7.8)	$ 27.1	$ 35.3	$ 17.3	$ 71.9

basis. Formats will differ, but as a general rule financial information is reported with a focus on the functional nature of the cost item, as shown in Exhibit 12.1.

As stated earlier, analysts focus the majority of their attention on forecasting operating profit for the future. Those involved with the strategic planning process of a competitor would be building scenarios of Company X. Perhaps Company X has excess facilities and could increase output by 10% but this might require more aggressive pricing. Operationally this may make sense but would this move increase operating profits and create value for its investors? Is it possible to calculate what the lower price point would be to justify the increase in output? How about if changing its marketing messaging could garner more market share?

Questions such as these abound in the area of competitive intelligence, but the first step is reformatting the data to reflect the cost structure of the company of interest. As reported in Exhibit 12.1, one cannot extrapolate income numbers given a change in sales volume. What would happen if Company X were to increase sales volume by 10%? Would cost of sales increase by the same amount? It would, but only if this cost element was totally variable, which is highly improbable! So the challenge becomes: How can we estimate the cost structure of the various cost line items for Company X in order to run the scenarios?

The process is relatively straightforward. Cost of sales mostly likely is comprised of a fixed and a variable element. From quarter 1 to quarter 2 as net sales increased by $35.0 million ($253.7 → $288.7), cost of sales increased $11.2 million ($140.3 → $151.5). This implies that the variable cost element is 32% of net sales ($11.2 ÷ $35.0 = 0.32). And if we assume that this is true, then we can estimate the fixed cost element since total cost of sales = variable cost of sales + fixed cost of sales. Using either quarterly numbers:

$$\text{Qrt } 1 \rightarrow \$140.3 = 32\% \times \$253.7 + \text{Fixed Cost of Sales}$$

Solving yields $140.3 = $81.2 + Fixed Cost of Sales, and Fixed Cost of Sales = $140.3 − $81.2 = $59.1.

$$\text{Qrt } 2 \rightarrow \$151.5 = 32\% \times \$288.7 + \text{Fixed Cost of Sales}$$

Solving yields $151.5 = $92.4 + Fixed Cost of Sales, and *Fixed Cost of Sales* = $151.5 – $92.4 = $59.1.

The result of this analysis of the cost of sales line item for the first two quarters of data is therefore:

$$\text{Cost of Sales} = 32\% \times \text{Net Sales Variable} + \$59.1 \text{ Fixed}$$

But how reliable is this analysis? With quarterly reports, one has four quarters of data, so we can apply the same analytic technique to each of the succeeding quarters to test for consistency and then test the result on the overall fiscal year total. Exhibit 12.2 contains the results.

Exhibit 12.2   Cost Behavior Analyses.

	($ millions)			
	Qrt 1 to 2	Qrt 2 to 3	Qrt 3 to 4	Fiscal Year
Change in sales, Qrt X to Qrt X + 1	$35.0	$10.8	$(39.1)	
Change in cost of sales, Qrt X to Qrt X + 1	11.2	3.7	(13.4)	
Implied variable cost of sales percentage	32.0%	34.3%	34.3%	
Implied fixed cost	$59.1	$52.6	$ 52.6	
Estimated variable cost for year @ 34%				$374.8
Estimated fixed cost ~ 4 × $54				$216.0
				$590.8
Error		0.34% = [($590.8 – $588.8)/$588.8]		

Interestingly the numbers for quarters 3 and 4 are a bit different than our first analysis but are exactly the same and are still quite close to what was arrived at using quarter 1 and 2 figures.[5] Given this result, one could feel very confident that cost of sales for Company X is somewhere close to 34% of net sales variable and approximately $54 million per quarter fixed. It should be understood that we are estimating the future and we do not expect to be correct to a decimal point. Using this estimate, we would have forecast cost of sales at $591.8 for the entire year if told that net sales would be $1,102.3 → $1,102.3 × 34% + $216.0 ($54 × 4 quarters). Given that the actual total was $588.8, an error of 0.34% is more than acceptable [($590.8 – $588.8)/$588.8] for this type of analysis.

Unfortunately, using the same technique for the operating expenses (R&D and selling, general, and administrative) does not work. Cost of sales is often called an "discretionary" cost, which means that it is the result of an infrastructure built to support a long-term strategic plan. Operating expenses are more often discretionary costs that are set by management's judgment based on the revenue estimate for the coming fiscal year that would have to support them. They are more short-term in nature and fixed for the period. From the cost data in Exhibit 12.1 it looks like Company X set the R&D spend at about

$50 million in the two lean quarters (quarters 1 and 4) and a bit above $52 million in the other quarters. Selling, general, and administrative looks more like a constant $63 million a quarter (or a bit under, to be exact).

Having now generated this cost structure information, is it possible to run forecasts for the scenarios mentioned earlier?

Company X could increase output by 10% by utilizing excess facilities but would probably have to be more aggressive in pricing to accomplish this or spend more on the marketing and sales promotion.[6]

To facilitate these types of analyses, it is helpful to reformat the income statement in a manner that now emphasizes the cost behavior of the firm rather than the functional nature of its costs. Exhibit 12.3 illustrates this by reformatting the fiscal year results for Company X, the first column showing the dollar amounts and the second the percentages based on sales for variable costs. net sales less variable cost of sales yields a number that is often called "contribution."[7] On a percentage basis, it reflects that for every dollar of incremental revenue, variable costs would increase by 34 cents, resulting in a net contribution of 66 cents. The term *contribution* is literal since this 66 cents contributes to a sum that must cover the fixed costs for the period as well as any profit that is needed to satisfy investors.

It also should be clear why the fixed cost elements are not shown as a percentage. This information would be at best meaningless, and at worst misleading, since these percentages would only be for a sales volume of $1,102. These costs are fixed, so the percentage of sales amounts would change as sales change. Note that in this format only the variable costs of sales are considered product-related costs and all the fixed cost are now termed period costs since they are more related to a period of time than a level of output. Also note that regardless of how the data are formatted, the operating profit is still the same (except of the minimal error of our estimates); all that is changed is the financial data now conveyed in a manner that facilitates scenario analysis.

Now turning to the scenarios, Exhibit 12.4 demonstrates how the contribution format facilitates forecasting. The first two columns show the base case from the past fiscal year, and the next four columns reflect the results of the price-cut scenario to increase volume split into two stages. The first two columns show the results of a 10% increase in volume under the current pricing scheme. The large increase in operating profit should not be surprising since the fixed costs have already been covered, and the 10% volume increase is utilizing idle facilities, so no additional infrastructure is needed. For any increase in sales dollars, 66% would drop through to the bottom line for a 10% increase in sales or $110; about $73 ($110 × 66%) would drop to the operating profit line, increasing it from $56 to $128.

But this volume increase might necessitate a corresponding 10% price decrease. The next two columns reflect the second stage of the scenario. Net sales would now be $1,091.3 ($1,102.3 × 110% × 90%) since a 10% price decrease would drop the first-stage forecasted sales of $1,212 by $121. And since the price has been changed, the 34% variable cost factor has to be adjusted. The easiest way is as follows: Since there is still the 10% volume increase, the variable costs of $412 from column 3 would remain the same but now these units would be sold for less, $1,091 versus $1,212, thereby increasing the variable cost percentage to 37.8% ($412.1/$1,091.3). Fixed costs would again remain the same, resulting in a drastic cut in operating profit. The conclusion of this scenario: It is highly unlikely that the top management of Company X would increase volume by dropping prices by this amount.

Exhibit 12.3 Company X—Quarterly Income Statements (costs reported by behavior).

($ millions)

	Qrt 1		Qrt 2		Qrt 3		Qrt 4		Fiscal Year	
Net sales	$253.7	100.0%	$288.7	100.0%	$299.5	100.0%	$260.4	100.0%	$1,102.3	100.0%
Cost of sales: variable	86.3	34.0%	98.2	34.0%	101.8	34.0%	88.5	34.0%	374.8	34.0%
Contribution	$167.4	66.0%	$190.5	66.0%	$197.7	66.0%	$171.9	66.0%	$ 727.5	66.0%
Fixed costs:										
Cost of sales	54.0		54.0		54.0		54.0		216.0	
R&D	50.0		52.0		52.0		50.0		204.0	
Selling, general, & adm.	63.0		63.0		63.0		63.0		252.0	
Total operating expenses	$167.0		$169.0		$169.0		$167.0		$ 672.0	
Operating profit	$ 0.4		$ 21.5		$ 28.7		$ 4.9		$ 55.5	
Other	(7.5)		8.6		10.8		9.1		21.0	
Income before tax	$ (7.1)		$ 30.2		$ 39.5		$ 14.0		$ 76.5	
Income tax	1.4		3.5		4.7		(2.2)		7.4	
Net income	$ (8.5)		$ 26.7		$ 34.8		$ 16.2		$ 69.1	

Exhibit 12.4   Scenario analysis.

($ millions)

	Base Past Fiscal Year		Scenario 1.2 10% Volume Increase		Scenario 1.2 10% Volume Inc. 10% Price Dec.		Scenario 2 10% Volume Increase	
Net sales	$1,102.3	100.0%	$1,212.5	100.0%	$1,091.3	100.0%	$1,212.5	100.0%
Cost of sales: variable	374.8	34.0%	412.3	34.0%	412.3	37.8%	412.3	34.0%
Contribution	$ 727.5	66.0%	$ 800.3	66.0%	679.0	62.2%	$ 800.3	66.0%
Fixed period costs:								
Fixed cost of sales	216.0	N/A	216.0	N/A	216.0	N/A	216.0	N/A
R&D	204.0	N/A	204.0	N/A	204.0	N/A	204.0	N/A
Selling, general, & adm.	252.0	N/A	252.0	N/A	252.0	N/A	324.8	N/A
Total fixed costs	$ 672.0	N/A	$ 672.0	N/A	$ 672.0	N/A	$ 744.8	N/A
Operating profit	$ 55.5	N/A	$ 128.3	N/A	$ 7.0	N/A	$ 55.5	N/A

323

Scenario 2 might be a volume increase driven by more aggressive marketing and sales expenditures rather than a price decrease. Sales would then be $1,212 and the last two columns show this result by solving for the maximum spend in the selling, general, and administrative discretionary fixed expense to drive a 10% volume increase, keeping prices constant. The $325 figure in the box shows that Company X could increase its budget in this area by 29% [($324.8 − $252.0)/$252.0] and still maintain its operating profit of $55.5.

These scenarios are rather simplistic but do demonstrate the power of developing this type of information on competitors. In a relatively short set of analyses, given the identification of the cost structure and the contribution format, it becomes clear that in this situation, scenario 2 is the much more probable one. Generalizing this, one can easily run multiple scenarios in a short period of time. Unfortunately, companies take great pains to make it difficult for this type of cost structure analysis to be done on their publicly available financial statements. The next section of this chapter discusses the pitfalls that can commonly occur when trying to decipher this information from Security and Exchange Commission (SEC) filings.

Pitfalls

Although this analytic technique can be very powerful, it is rife with assumptions. One must use this methodology carefully, because ceteris paribus exists only in textbooks.

Price and Variable Cost Changes

The scenario analysis discussed earlier illustrates a situation where a change in pricing required an adjustment in the estimated variable cost percentage. Since the dollar amount of variable cost per unit is assumed to remain relatively constant, a decrease in price of the unit would make the variable cost higher on a percentage basis. Likewise, variable cost factors are subject to market pressures. In 2008, petroleum cost indexes increased over 100%. One must constantly monitor trends and make the requisite adjustments to the variable cost percentage.

Product Mix

The earlier analysis of Company X over the four quarters assumed a constant product mix. Few companies, if any, offer only a single product. Company X has a service offering and two products groups, one high-end and the other midrange. Each of the three has a different cost structure, which implies that the calculated cost structure, 34% of sales variable and fixed costs of $672 annually, is correct if and only if the mix remains constant. The 10K SEC filing does report the service revenue separately at $165 million for the year and that it was relatively constant at 15% of total revenues for each of the four quarters. In addition, a close read of the annual report discloses that this service is mostly break/fix and totally outsourced, which means that the cost of service, reported at 45% of service revenue, is predominantly variable in nature. In addition, an industry report by an investment house estimates the ratio of high-end to midrange at 40:60 for the period, yielding sales estimates of $375 [40% × ($1,102 − $165)] and $562 [60% × ($1,102 − $165)], respectively. The variable costs for the two product classes, however, are not reported, but a competitor familiar with the products should be able to estimate them with some degree of accuracy.

Exhibit 12.5 illustrates the analysis. The known factors are the service data (columns 1 and 2) and the annual data that was calculated earlier (columns 7 and 8). In addition, the high-end and midrange revenue figures are estimated with some degree of confidence given the investment house report. What is necessary is to plug in estimates for the variable costs of these two offerings knowing that the total variable costs of all three offerings must be close to our annual estimate, $374.8. A competitor with a good sense of the market would probably have little trouble arriving at the figures in the boxes, 26% and 36%, which then yield a total variable cost for the mix very close to the $374.8 figure in column 7.

Assume that competitive pressures are commoditizing the market, driving the high-end to midrange mix from 40:60 to 1:2, and Company X is responding to this potential drop in profitability by aggressively driving its service business with a stated goal of increasing it to 25% of total revenue (that is, overall sales would remain about the same at $1.1 billion but now with services and high-end each at 25%, or $275 million, and midrange at the other 50%, or $550 million).

What would be the new estimated variable cost percentage, assuming pricing remains constant? Exhibit 12.6 demonstrates the impact on the variable cost element of the cost structure. The management of Company X seems to be planning well for this loss of value position. By driving the higher-contribution service business, if the 25% goal is attained, the cost structure would remain relatively the same, allowing Company X to maintain profitability at the same revenue level even with the negative shift of the product business. Unfortunately, sales mixes are always evolving, requiring constant vigilance of cost structure assumptions of competitors.

Data Reporting Format

In order to be thorough, one needs to read the footnotes that accompany the financial statements of the company under review. Often nonrecurring events such as write-offs of obsolete inventory are contained in the cost of sales figure. In this case, Company X did report a $15 million inventory charge in quarter 1 that was buried in the cost of sales number. This was pulled out of the "cost of sales" account and transferred to the "Other" account in order to once again focus only on the recurring nature of the costs. If this adjustment had not been made, the results for the quarter 1 to quarter 2 analysis would have shown an increase in sales of $35 million and a decrease in cost of sales of $4 million, clearly a result that makes no sense. Only in the footnotes was this revealed, which in turn led to the required adjustment which then yielded a meaningful result.

Relevant Range Assumption

So far the examples used to illustrate how cost structure analysis is employed in a competitive setting have assumed that (1) Company X had idle facilities sufficient to support a 10% increase in output and (2) a mix change would have no impact on facility requirements. Often this is not the case. The cost analysis discussed in the preceding pages of this chapter was applicable only for the current output capacity of Company X. If Company X were to grow beyond this, a new estimate would have to be calculated. Additional scale factors might drive variable costs down and would certainly increase fixed costs. Different industries have different inherent relevant ranges.

Exhibit 12.5 Company X—Product Mix Analysis.

($ millions)

	Service Revenue as Reported		High-End 40% of Nonservice Revenue		Midrange 60% of Nonservice Revenue		Base Past Fiscal Year	
Net sales	$165.3	100.0%	$374.8	100.0%	$562.2	100.0%	$1,102.3	100.0%
Cost of sales: variable	74.4	45.0%	97.4	26.0%	202.4	36.0% >	374.8	34.0%
Contribution	$ 90.9	55.0%	$277.3	74.0%	$359.8	64.0%	$ 727.5	66.0%
Fixed period costs:								
Fixed cost of sales							216.0	N/A
R&D							204.0	
Selling, general, & adm.							252.0	N/A
Total fixed costs							$ 672.0	N/A
Operating profit							$ 55.5	N/A

326

Exhibit 12.6   Variable cost element of the cost structure.

	Service	High-End	Midrange	Total
Old mix:				
Revenue dollars	$165	$375	$562	$1,102
Revenue percentage	15%	34%	51%	100%
Variable cost %	45%	26%	36%	
Weighted variable cost %	6.7%	8.8%	18.4%	34.0%
New mix:				
Revenue dollars	$275	$275	$550	$1,100
Revenue percentage	25%	25%	50%	100%
Variable cost %	45%	26%	36%	
Weighted variable cost %	11.3%	6.5%	18.0%	35.8%

*High-end is 40% of nonservice revenue → 40% × 85% = 34%; midrange → 60% × 85% = 51%.

Exhibit 12.7 illustrates the extremes. On the left is the large relevant range of a semiconductor company such as Intel or Texas Instruments where output is measured in millions of logic chips and a change in relevant range might require an investment in the area of $3 billion. On the right might be a consulting firm where output is measured in billable hours and senior associates are brought on in increments of 2,000 annual billable hours at a cost much less than that of a chip fabricator. When doing this type of competitive analysis, one must be aware of the size of the relevant range and be ready to adjust estimates accordingly.

The statement of cash flows provides a window into this area. By carefully comparing the depreciation expense for the period to the corresponding investment in plant, property, and equipment, one can monitor movement within and outside the relevant range. As demonstrated in the left-hand side of Exhibit 12.7, changes in relevant range are chunky. Texas Instruments investing in a new fabrication plant would be evidenced by an investment in plant, property, and equipment account much larger than the depreciation charge for the period.

Exhibit 12.8 shows the relevant portion of the statement of cash flows for Company X. Over the past three years, total investment in plant infrastructure of $128 million ($53.17 + $38.32 + $36.75) reflects the depreciation charges $130 million ($40.68 +

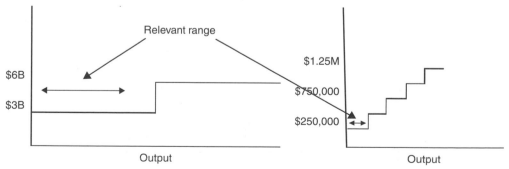

Exhibit 12.7   Relevant Range Extremes.

Exhibit 12.8   Company X—Cash Flow Data.

	Current Year	Prior Years	
Cash flows from operating activities:			
Profit before tax	$ 71.90	$ 68.40	$ 64.50
Adjustments to reconcile net income (loss) to net cash provided by operating activities:			
Depreciation and amortization	40.68	45.58	44.41
Other items	(5.05)	(5.47)	(4.67)
	107.53	108.51	104.24
Changes in operating assets and liabilities, net of effects of purchased businesses:			
Short-term receivables	2.30	(8.24)	(9.51)
Inventories	(4.20)	(3.54)	(6.51)
Increase in short-term liabilities	(3.25)	2.26	0.76
Cash generated from operations	$ 102.38	$ 98.99	$ 87.46
Cash flows from investing activities:			
Purchases of property, plant, and equipment, net	$ (53.17)	$(38.32)	$(36.75)
Net acquisition of subsidiary, net of cash	(1.61)	—	—
Change in available-for-sale investments	20.58	(4.46)	(14.74)
Other, net	(0.13)	7.08	17.73
Net cash used in investing activities	$ (34.33)	$(35.70)	$(33.76)

$45.58 + $44.41), which indicates that this would be an ideal time period for this type of analysis—assuming all other factors constant. If there were a significant plant investment, then a new analysis would have to be compiled once there was adequate data to establish the impact of the changed cost structure. During the interim time period, the only way to estimate the new cost structure would be conjecture given what information could be found on the investment. At a minimum, three to four quarters of data would be needed.

Variable Cost as a Function of Output

Most experienced managers understand that costs do not vary only with output. In the services industry, the quantity of new business often drives costs. One spends a good deal of resources on first-time clients learning their industry and the uniqueness of their business practices, but follow-on business is much more efficient. In manufacturing, any experienced production manager would say that cost is a function of the size of the run as well as the quantity of output. Small lot sizes are almost always at the root of unfavorable cost variances. In all industries these front-end setups are a major driver of costs and can account for as much as 40% of variable costs. Most firms are aware of this and try to minimize these, but in industries where they are prevalent they may require some focused thought on how to adjust the analysis.

Profit Planning from an Internal Perspective

When done from an internal perspective, profit planning is often called cost-volume-profit (CVP) analysis. It is much less complex and more straightforward since both cost structures and profit targets are known. Rather than discussing it in the abstract, it is easier to demonstrate how this tool is used.

Returning to Company X, assume that it is true; management is targeting growth of the service revenue at 25% of total revenue due to market research it has compiled. Although the customer service revenue is indeed profitable as currently configured, management has found that growth is constrained by product sales, since service revenue is sold only as an add-on warranty to product sales. But market feedback has shown that customers could be using the product technology of Company X much more effectively to drive their own revenue growth. On a test basis, Company X has provided a targeted set of customers with more professionally oriented services. The result was that these customers were willing to pay high premiums in line with the additional revenues these services provided them—in essence, a price based on the value that these services created for the customers. The downside of this, however, is that the third party Company X uses to provide the basic break/fix warranty services is not skilled enough to provide these professional services. Company X would have to build a global service infrastructure to develop this business. After much analysis of the two alternatives—status quo, which means providing just the basic warranty services through the third party, or building the global professional services business—Company X chooses the second. Given the data shown next, do you agree with the decision? Before turning to Exhibit 12.9, run the numbers yourself to see what decision you would support.

- *Status quo:* Company X can expect the service revenue to remain relatively constant at $165 million per year and it might even drop a bit given the mix change moving more to the midrange product offering, which has a lower service component. The third-party costs were estimated correctly earlier at 45% of service revenue, but there also is a fixed component of $15 million annually associated with this business representing global spare parts warehousing and administrative expenses. These costs are not expected to change appreciably in the future.

- *Build the professional business:* Company X expects sales to increase to 25% of total revenues, and this initiative would offset the impact of the change in mix from the high-end product to the lower-priced midrange offering. Initially, Company X would build and staff four regional offices to cover the world, increasing fixed costs by an estimated $150 million per year. Once in place, the office would provide both service offerings (the original $165 million of warranty work) and the planned additional $110 million of professional services (i.e., total service would now be 25% of $1,100 million or $275 million). The third-party contract would be terminated, and it is estimated that Company X could provide each of these offerings internally at variable costs of 25% and 20%, respectively.

The status quo analysis in Exhibit 12.9 is straightforward. The cost structure is given, as is the service volume, so it takes little effort to arrive at the expected profit level of $75.8 million. The second scenario is a bit more complex. First, how was the variable cost of 23% calculated? Given that the service revenue components were $165 million

Exhibit 12.9 Service Scenarios.

CVP Methodology → Sales = Variable Costs + Fixed Costs + Profit

Service Scenarios

Status quo:

CVP → Sales = Variable Costs + Fixed Costs + Profit
$165 = 45\% \times \$165 + \$15 + Profit$
$Profit = \$165 - (45\% \times \$165) - \$15$
$Profit = \$165(1 - 45\%) - \$15$
$Profit = \$165(55\%) - \$15 = \$75.8$

Build global infrastructure:

CVP → Sales = Variable Costs + Fixed Costs + Profit
$275 = 23\% \times \$275 + \$150 + Profit$
$Profit = \$275 - (23\% \times \$275) - \$150$
$Profit = \$275(1 - 23\%) - \$150$
$Profit = \$275(77\%) - \$150 = \$61.8$

for warranty and an incremental $110 million for the planned professional services, the planned services mix is 60:40 (60% of $275 = $165). This implies that the weighted average variable cost for this mix of services is 60% warranty at 25% and 40% professional services at 20% → $60\% \times 25\% + 40\% \times 20\% = 23\%$. Once this is understood, the rest of the analysis follows the same pattern as the first scenario, with the result being an expected profit of $61.8 million.

If scenario 2 yields a lower profit, why does the management team choose it? The short answer is growth. How much growth in the service revenue would be necessary for scenario 2 to be more profitable, and could the current four regional offices handle this increase? To answer the first question it is easier to use a shortcut equation than to do the analysis longhand as illustrated in Exhibit 12.9. Following the analysis in the exhibit, the last equation in either scenario in words is: Profit equals contribution margin less fixed costs. In these cases, we knew the cost structure and the output levels, and we simply solved for the resulting profit. In the question above, we now know the target profit of $75.8 in the first scenario and the cost structure of the second scenario and now must solve for the level of output required. This can be done by rearranging the equation to what is known as the classic CVP equation:

Contribution Margin × Quantity of Output = Fixed Cost + Target Profit

and therefore:

Quantity of Output = (Fixed Cost + Target Profit)/Contribution

To solve for what level of service revenue would be necessary to match the same profit level as scenario 1:

Service Revenue = ($150 million + $75.8 million)/77%
Service Revenue = $293 million

This states that service revenue would have to increase by only approximately 7% for scenario 2 to be as profitable. This should not be a surprise since for every additional dollar of revenue, 77 cents drops through to the bottom line. Seven percent of $275 million is approximately $18 million in incremental revenue, and at 77% contribution margin this equals the difference in scenario profits (77% × $18 = $14 → $75.8 – $61.8).

This short example displays many aspects of CVP as a profit planning tool. First, one can use the longhand version as shown in Exhibit 12.9—Sales = Variable Costs + Fixed Costs + Profit—or the shortened version—Required Output to Reach a Targeted Level of Profit = (Fixed Costs + Target Profit)/Contribution—where output can be solved in units using the contribution margin per unit in the denominator or in dollars using the contribution percentage, as illustrated earlier. When one becomes experienced with this tool, it is very easy to use the shortened version; but when starting off, the longer version is less prone to error. In addition to the format of the calculations, this example also shows when this is used most effectively. CVP analysis is a simple, back-of-the-envelope method for doing first-pass analysis. Should Exhibit 12.9 be the only analysis done? Clearly, a more lengthy and in-depth discounted cash flow analysis would follow before an investment decision of this magnitude would be undertaken. But CVP allows one easily to identify the alternatives that should be scrutinized in more detail—it is a front-end time-saving analytic tool for profit planning. And last, this example shows that this type of analysis almost automatically leads to follow-on scenarios. Yes, scenario 2 is not as profitable, but once given transparency into the cost structures of each alternative, it is simple to see that scenario 2 is the better one if there is any growth at all in this scenario. Using the relevant range discussion from earlier in the chapter, the global infrastructure could easily accommodate $350 million in service offerings before any additional investments would have to be made. Once again, at 77% drop-through this could lead to a large additional profit pool.

Pricing in CVP Analysis

Cost-volume-profit (CVP) analysis is often erroneously used to set prices. The "P" in CVP does not stand for "price"; it stands for "profit." A rule to remember is the following: There is no such thing as cost-based pricing. Prices are market driven. If a firm finds itself in a competitive marketplace where competition among rivals is based on delivering comparable value to customers at the lowest cost, the market sets the price. As Adam Smith wrote centuries ago, only the most efficient will survive. To use CVP analysis in this situation, one starts with estimates of the market-driven price and then calculates the profitability given probable unit demand and the current cost structure. If the forecast profit is not sufficient to satisfy investors, one must then focus on reducing costs, not raising prices.

Incumbent firm behavior in the U.S. health care industry after deregulation in the 1980s is a perfect example of incorrect use of this technique. New entrants into the lower-cost, more profitable segments of this industry—for example, the walk-in clinics that sprang up in metropolitan areas—gave patients (and insurance providers) a lower-cost option than traditional hospitals for minor health care procedures. Large hospitals responded to this loss of segment revenue by spreading their costs (mostly fixed) over their remaining health care offerings and raising prices. With those higher prices, the clinics were able to offer lower-cost alternatives for more complex procedures. With the loss of these revenues, the hospitals responded in the same manner. This doom loop led to the closing of many such institutions. The proper move for the hospitals should have been to pare expenses on the noncompetitive offerings.

For firms that compete by differentiating themselves from rivals by offering additional value to customers at comparable cost, pricing should be based on value to the customer and not cost. Microsoft certainly does not price its products on the costs to develop and deliver them. Bill Gates long ago understood the value of having the industry-standard PC operating system and has priced Microsoft's offerings accordingly. The key here, of course, is that the additional value must exceed the costs to create it. CVP analysis in this situation is basically no different than in the Company X example. Only here, one starts with estimates of the *value-based* price and then calculates the profitability given probable unit demand and the current cost structure. If the forecast profit is not sufficient to satisfy investors, one must then focus on reducing costs or increasing the willingness of consumers to pay more, not simply on raising prices.

Predatory Pricing

In recent years a legal battle raged between two of the nation's largest tobacco companies.[8] The Brooke Group Inc. (previously known as Liggett Group Inc.) accused Brown & Williamson Tobacco Corporation of predatory pricing in the wholesale cigarette market. At trial in federal court, the jury decided that Brown & Williamson had indeed engaged in predatory pricing against Brooke. The jury awarded damages of $150 million to be paid to Brooke by Brown & Williamson. However, the presiding judge threw out this verdict. Brooke then filed an appeal, and the case continued.

Predatory pricing cases are not unusual, and damage awards as large as $150 million are not unheard of. Predatory pricing, as the name implies, is a tactic where the predator company slashes prices in order to force its competitors to follow suit. The purpose is to wage a price war and inflict upon the competition losses of such severity that they will be driven out of business. After destroying the competition, the predator company will be free to raise prices so that it can recover the losses it sustained in the price war and also rake in profits that will greatly exceed normal earnings at the competitive level. This final result is harmful to competition, and therefore predatory pricing has been made unlawful.

In order to determine whether a firm has engaged in predatory pricing, the courts need a test that will supply the correct answer. One of the usual tests is whether there is a sustained pattern of pricing below average variable cost. If the answer is yes, this indicates predatory pricing. Let us examine the logic underlying this widely used test.

First, recall that contribution is the margin between selling price and variable cost. Contribution goes toward paying fixed costs and providing a profit. Now, if price is less than variable cost, contribution is negative. In that case, the firm cannot fully cover its fixed costs, and certainly it will suffer losses. Therefore, it makes no sense for the firm to charge a price that is below variable cost unless the firm is engaging in predatory pricing in order to destroy competing firms. That is why pricing below variable cost is considered to be consistent with predatory pricing.

We should bear in mind that the variable cost used in the test is that of the alleged predator, not of the alleged victim. The reason is that the alleged predator may be an efficient low-cost producer, whereas the alleged victim may be an inefficient high-cost producer. Therefore, a price below the alleged victim's variable cost may be above that of the alleged predator, in which case it could be a legitimate price and simply a reflection of the superior efficiency of the alleged predator. The antitrust laws are designed to protect competition, but not competitors (especially those competitors who are inefficient).

Of course, this is only one indicator of predatory pricing, and all of the relevant evidence must be considered. It is also appropriate to note that there should be a pattern of sustained pricing below variable cost. Prices that are slashed only sporadically or occasionally are probably legitimate business tactics, such as loss-leader pricing to attract customers or clearance sales to get rid of obsolete goods.

Predatory pricing is an important topic and has been the subject of major lawsuits in a wide variety of industries. Because it is a common test for predatory pricing, variable cost is also a very important topic that all successful businesspeople will benefit from thoroughly understanding.

Predatory pricing is usually thought of in a regional sense, or perhaps on a national scale. But it can also occur on an international basis. In that case, it is known as dumping.

Dumping

If a foreign company is the predator, there is no inherent difference in the tactics or the goal of predatory pricing. Pricing below variable cost would still remain a valid test. However, U.S. law imposes a stricter test on foreign than on domestic companies. The legal test for dumping does not involve variable cost. Rather, it focuses on whether the foreign company is selling its product here at a price less than the price in its home market.

Dumping is simply predatory pricing by a foreign company. So the logic that supported using variable cost as a test for predatory pricing would also support using the same test for dumping. But the test actually used is the domestic selling price (usually higher than variable cost). This test makes it easier to prove dumping than to prove predatory pricing. It favors the domestic firms and is harder on the foreign company. This may be a matter of politics as well as one of economics.

Perhaps the best-known cases of dumping have involved the textile and steel industries. Another recent case of dumping concerned Japanese auto companies accused by U.S. competitors of dumping minivans in this country. Also, the Japanese makers of flat screens for laptop computers (active matrix liquid crystal displays) were alleged to have sold their products in the United States at prices below those in the home market.

It is not always easy to ascertain the home market selling price. Even if there are list prices or catalog prices in the home market, there may be discounts or rebates that are difficult to detect. Therefore, instead of using the home market selling price as the test, the production cost may be used. This is reasonable, because the production cost is likely to be below the home market selling price. Therefore a dumping price below production cost is virtually certain to also be below the home market selling price. But production cost includes both fixed and variable costs and is therefore above variable cost. Also, it may be arguable as to what should be included in production cost. For example, some may include interest expense on money borrowed to purchase manufacturing material inventories. Others may believe that interest is not part of production cost.

If it is determined that dumping has indeed taken place, then the U.S. International Trade Commission (ITC) will impose an import duty on the foreign product involved. This duty will be sufficiently high to boost the U.S. selling price up to the same level as the home market price.

Dumping has a large potential impact on businesses and industries in our economy. By extension, production cost is also a subject that successful businesspeople will find profitable to understand.

Notes

1. Note that *on a unit basis* fixed costs will decline as output increases, but variable costs are assumed to be relatively static. This can be confusing, so when discussing cost structure ensure that all discussants have the same orientation.
2. This is where accountants deviate from the economics. Within this relevant range, accounting assumes that the variable cost per unit remains constant, whereas economists assume scale and scope factors will impact the per-unit variable cost rate. As long as the relevant range estimate is relatively narrow, the accounting assumptions will not cause material error.
3. *Computerworld*, July 7, 1990.
4. If they were material they would be scrutinized, but for Company X they comprise less that 3% of sales.
5. Those who want to test their understanding of this technique should use the data in Exhibit 12.1 to verify Exhibit 12.2 results.
6. As long as Company X utilizes excess facilities, the cost structure will not change. If the 10% increase necessitated an additional build-out of infrastructure, the fixed costs would increase.
7. In Europe this term is often called drop-through.
8. The final two sections of this chapter were written by John Leslie Livingstone for earlier editions of this book. They are reproduced here in their entirety.

13

Activity-Based Costing

William C. Lawler

Leaving government agencies and not-for-profit organizations aside, the accounting profession can be divided into two camps, financial and managerial. Each has an important role in creating an economic environment where commerce can thrive. The former has the responsibility of developing and reporting financial information for external users such as current and potential investors to aid in the macroeconomic process of efficient allocation of capital. The latter, the managerial camp, has the task of providing information to internal managers to aid in their quest to create investor return, a more microeconomic process focused on providing relevant and timely cost information to drive optimized performance. This chapter focuses on the challenge of how one builds such a relevant management accounting system.

In 1987 Harvard Business School Press published an interesting research study on U.S. economic history by H. Thomas Johnson and Robert S. Kaplan entitled *Relevance Lost: The Rise and Fall of Management Accounting*. Johnson and Kaplan found that in the late 1800s through the early 1900s, as a result of work by business analysts such as Frederick Taylor, Alexander Church, and J. Maurice Clark, leading U.S. firms developed relatively sophisticated management accounting systems that were instrumental in the overall emergence of the post–industrial revolution American manufacturing sector. Carnegie Steel, both Ford and General Motors, and many of the railroads had sophisticated systems that produced daily reports connecting input factors to outputs, enabling management to optimize their systems. Management accounting was the dominant sector within the accounting profession.

Over time, two factors reversed this dominance, and the result had a negative influence on American competitiveness in the emerging global business environment. First, business processes became more complex as consumers demanded an expanded mix of product choices. Henry Ford was famous for his statement "You can have any color you want as long as it is black"; but that era ended with Alfred P. Sloan at General Motors indeed offering choice of not only color but also body style and other features. The process of developing relevant cost information where joint resources now produced this expanding mix of outputs required much more detail within these cost systems. At the same time, the rise of capital markets in the 1920s and the regulations that followed in the 1930s led to the increasing importance of financial information. But corporate annual reports required only that costs be reported in the aggregate, such as total cost of goods sold and sales, marketing, and administrative expenses. The focus on detailed cost information for the expanding mix of products needed to satisfy consumer demand became less important. By the late 1940s, further development of management accounting systems had all but ended.

The increasing operational complexity driven by consumer demand for more choice drove increased costs. As stated earlier, financial accounting systems did not require detailed accounting for this increased complexity, and management accounting systems were not modified to capture this complexity. As a result, the costs were simply aggregated and charged to products based on factors readily available within the financial systems. For example, overhead was aggregated in total for a production floor and then allocated based on labor hours, labor dollars, or some similar method. This overhead was spread like peanut butter over the product mix with no logical basis, and, as the overhead component of production cost increased during this time period, so, too, did the error. Interestingly, this, however, had minimal impact on U.S. business success for the next two decades, as evidenced by a comment from a Continental Can division manager: "Does it hinder our ability to compete? Probably not, because we're no dumber than our competition."[1]

But the post–World War II emergence of Japanese and European competition ended this era of unawareness. Unfettered by legacy infrastructures, the rebuilding of their business systems allowed these competitors to invest in both new technology and new thinking. By the 1970s, American industry had lost dominance in key industries such as steel, automobiles, and electronics.

Johnson and Kaplan argued that one major reason for this decline in competitiveness was the lack of relevant internal cost information needed to compete on this global stage. Poor management accounting systems did, in fact, hinder U.S. firms' ability to compete. The authors then called for a rebuilding of management accounting systems based on the work of the early pioneers such as Church and Clark. In the ensuing years, many manuscripts were written detailing best practices in constructing internal management information systems that traced costs to outputs on a more logical or causal basis. This body of work became known as activity-based accounting (ABC), and this chapter discusses both the positive and the negative aspects of this movement.

Basics of Activity-Based Systems

It is perhaps easiest to first review how an ABC system is built and then reflect on the process. A relatively simple example is used here to illustrate.

Company Z was an entrepreneurial venture focused on Web merchandising. A number of executives experienced in this area formed the company to provide back-room operations to aspiring Web merchants. Processes such as credit verification, fulfillment, and delivery tracking were a constant headache to those selling online, especially if they did not have scale to provide these services in an efficient manner. By building a hosted network, the entrepreneurs reasoned that they could attract many of these merchants and build a revenue stream by providing an on-demand product, back-room transaction processing. They crafted the following customer value proposition:

> Join our network and get all these services seamlessly provided with state-of-the-art applications run by highly trained IT professionals. We will convert a difficult-to-manage fixed infrastructure cost into a totally scalable variable one since you pay only on a per-transaction basis. With us as your partner, you can spend your creative energies where your investors expect.

It was not surprising that, given the massive growth in Web commerce, first-round financing from venture capitalists (VCs) focused on proving the value proposition was oversubscribed. In 12 months, Company Z was back for second-round money to scale the business. In that time period the start-up had signed 10 merchants to contracts, built a smaller-scale system, and had 8 of the 10 merchants up and running on it. But what the new firm did not have was a concise explanation of the underlying economic model. The VC community did understand how one invested in bricks-and-mortar businesses but needed a clear understanding of the evolving Web commerce arena. Company Z was told to build this economic model if it wanted more funding.

A consultant was brought in to aid the firm. By talking with all involved in the business it established that Company Z had three high-level processes that led to value creation. First, it had to capture customers, defined as attaining a signed contract for transaction processing. Then it had to load these customers onto the network, enabling them to process all their back-room operations through Company Z systems. Only then could Company Z make money on the final process, transaction processing. Each process involved activities that required substantial time and resources. The key to building the economic model was to identify the resulting value and cost elements of these activities, because, ultimately, if the value did not exceed the costs, there was no business model.

The capture process had three activities: customer identification, customer qualification, and customer sale. To accomplish the first, Company Z advertised in trade publications, and employees attended trade shows where they demonstrated their system to identify leads (i.e., potential customers). These leads were then qualified through an outside third party that prepared a short one-page summary of each lead's credit history, revenue size, and growth rate. From these outside reports, target customers were identified and a direct sales process followed. Over the past 12 months, 1,200 leads were generated, of which 80 were targeted and 10 ultimately signed contracts.

The first two activities were relatively homogeneous in accomplishing the end goal. Essentially, equal amounts of effort and resources were expended first to identify each customer and then to qualify. As a result, these could be aggregated and then averaged without any material error in the calculation. The sale activity, however, proved very different. It required visits to the customer site to demonstrate the relative cost of the current internal customer system compared to that of Company Z. For customers that were knowledgeable about the cost of their back rooms, this process went relatively smoothly and the sale became dependent on a CEO-to-CEO discussion of the long-term viability of Company Z. No firm wanted to outsource these critical operations, no matter what degree of pain they caused, if it did not have confidence in the service provider. For the customers that were not so aware of their costs—and unfortunately most of the 10 signed so far (7 out of 10) fell into this category—sales were much more difficult to close. The analysis showed that this group required more than twice the effort, and the close rate was far lower.

Unfortunately, the financial reporting system did not support this analysis. In it, costs were organized by function (e.g., sales and marketing, technicians, travel and entertainment, administration, etc.), and it took more than a month searching through travel reports, service procurement reports, and the like to arrive at an estimate of what those activities cost. The job was made even more complex by the yield factor. Of the 80 leads that were qualified, only 10 were brought to signed contracts, with the other 70 having fallen out of the process either due to their choice or by the decision of Company Z.

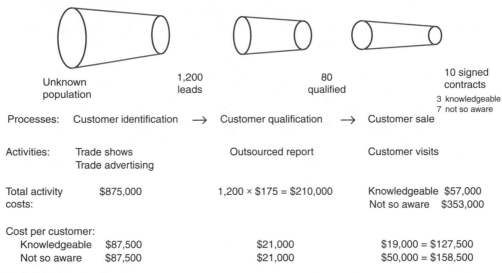

Processes:	Customer identification	→	Customer qualification	→	Customer sale
	Unknown population	1,200 leads	80 qualified	10 signed contracts 3 knowledgeable 7 not so aware	

Activities: Trade shows   Outsourced report   Customer visits
              Trade advertising

Total activity costs: $875,000   1,200 × $175 = $210,000   Knowledgeable $57,000
                                                    Not so aware $353,000

Cost per customer:
   Knowledgeable $87,500 $21,000 $19,000 = $127,500
   Not so aware $87,500 $21,000 $50,000 = $158,500

Exhibit 13.1   Cost to capture a customer.

It was possible to estimate the cost of the 10 signed contracts, but it was far too time-consuming to detail the effort wasted on those dropped individually. Exhibit 13.1 shows the final results.

Company executives were amazed at this outcome. They did know a great deal of money was spent on this process since this was a radically new business service requiring a great deal of customer contact, but the magnitude of the final acquisition cost numbers for the two customer groupings in Exhibit 13.1—$127,500 and $158,500—caused them to rethink their customer capture process. There was no doubt that it could be done in a more efficient manner.

The costs for the second process, loading 8 of the 10 customers signed to contracts onto the network, as shown in Exhibit 13.2, only added to this new focus on efficiency. The first two activities, an outsourced business process review that cost $4,000 apiece for a total of $32,000 (8 customers loaded × $4,000) and the approximately $5,000 internal system design cost that was relatively routine, were expected. The implementation and

Exhibit 13.2   Customer loading cost summary.

Activity		Total Cost
Business process review—outsourced		$ 32,000
System design		$ 40,000
Implementation and Certification		
Knowledgeable	$ 18,000	
Not so aware	$123,000	$141,000
		$213,000
Cost per customer:		
Knowledgeable		$ 15,000
Not so aware		$ 33,600

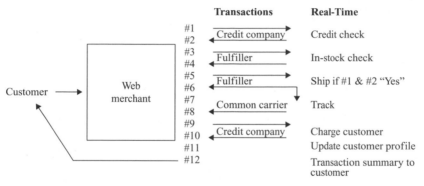

Exhibit 13.3   E-commerce transaction detail.

certification activity was once again a surprise. The 3 knowledgeable customers loaded in the first year had internal IT professionals that made this step simple and relatively inexpensive—$6,000 each—but for the 5 not so aware, Company Z had to do all the work once again, making this customer segment much more costly at $24,600. To spend at a minimum about $140,000 on getting a single customer (a knowledgeable customer cost $127,500 to get to signed contract and another $15,000 to load onto the network) to the revenue-producing stage of their business was a challenge. Research showed, however, that customers were willing to pay about 10 cents per individual transaction processed (e.g., a request for a credit check or the receiving of the credit check), which resulted in about $1.20 per item sold, so maybe this front-end investment could be recouped over time (see Exhibit 13.3 for back-room transaction details for every item sold).

The final step was to understand the costs associated with transaction processing to see if, in fact, there was a viable business model. The network had to be running 24 hours 365 days a year, and to staff it required nine technicians working in shifts of two at a total annual fully loaded cost of approximately $750,000. The total costs of the IT infrastructure amounted to another $1.35 million annually for depreciation and amortization, utilities, and facility expenses, yielding a total overall cost of running the network of $2.1 million per year. At the time the eight customers that were on the network were averaging in total 20,000 transactions per day or 7.3 million for a year. Given the costs of $2.1 million, this resulted in a cost of about $0.29 per transaction.

It was costing Company Z far more to process a transaction than the customer's willingness to pay—29 cents versus the 10 cents per transaction given earlier. Upon further analysis, it became evident what the root cause of this problem was. As Exhibit 13.4 illustrates, the IT infrastructure was poorly utilized. On one hand, approximately one-third was now idle—the difference between peak demand and capacity—but this was only a short-term issue since the other two contracts that had been signed but were not yet on the system would probably move the system toward full demand. Basically, one-third of the network may be idle currently but this would soon be marketable. The key problem was the volatility in the system—at the present time peak demand was 80,000 transactions per day, but the average was only 20,000. In essence, 50% of the network (the difference between peak and current average demand over total capacity) was not currently marketable due to the buffer needed to meet peak demand when it occurred. The distribution of costs as a function of volatility is shown in Exhibit 13.5, highlighting

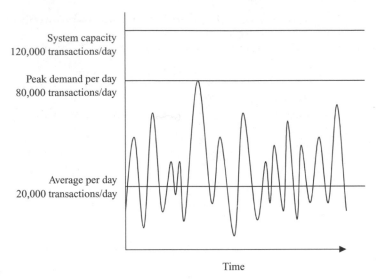

Exhibit 13.4   **Transaction processing demand.**

Exhibit 13.5   **Transaction processing detail.**

		Total Annual Capacity		
	Productive Capacity	Idle Marketable	Idle Nonmarketable	Total
Transactions	7,300,000	21,900,000	14,600,000	43,800,000
	365 × 20k	365 × 60k	365 × 40k	365 × 120k
	16.7%	50.0%	33.3%	100.0%

		Total Annualized Costs		
	Value-Add Portion	Idle Marketable	Idle Nonmarketable	Total
Personnel	$125,000	$ 375,000	$250,000	$ 750,000
H/W & S/W	225,000	675,000	450,000	1,350,000
	$350,000	$1,050,000	$700,000	$2,100,000

that $1.05 million, half the network cost, was currently idle but marketable if volatility could be solved.

This drove the customer identification process to focus on those companies with low variation in demand. Companies such as Flowers Are Us, Godiva Chocolates, and the like, with high peak demands for only short periods, were eliminated from the target group. In addition, Company Z was experimenting with offering off-peak pricing and batching rather than offering only real-time processing. Mathematically, it was easy to solve for the amount of volatility that could justify a business model, but it was much more challenging to build a customer base to match this targeted volatility. As Exhibit 13.6

Exhibit 13.6 Transaction processing detail with and without volatility.

Scenario # 1—No Volatility Yields a Cost of $0.048 per Transaction

		Total Annual Capacity		
	Productive Capacity	Idle Marketable	Idle Nonmarketable	Total
Transactions	43,800,000	—	—	43,800,000
	365 × 120k	365 × 0k	365 × 0k	365 × 120k
	100.0%	0.0%	0.0%	100.0%

		Total Annualized Costs		
	Value-Add Portion	Idle Marketable	Idle Nonmarketable	Total
Personnel	$ 750,000	$—	$—	$ 750,000
H/W & S/W	1,350,000	—	—	1,350,000
	$2,100,000	$—	$—	$2,100,000

Scenario # 2—Volatility That Yields a Cost of $0.065 per Transaction

		Total Annual Capacity		
	Productive Capacity	Idle Marketable	Idle Nonmarketable	Total
Transactions	32,302,500	11,497,500	—	43,800,000
	365 × 88.5k	365 × 31.5k	365 × 0k	365 × 120k
	73.8%	26.3%	0.0%	100.0%

		Total Annualized Costs		
	Value-Add Portion	Idle Marketable	Idle Nonmarketable	Total
Personnel	$ 553,125	$196,875	$—	$ 750,000
H/W & S/W	995,625	354,375	—	1,350,000
	$1,548,750	$551,250	$—	$2,100,000

illustrates, if all volatility was eliminated, the cost per transaction would fall to $0.048 ($2.1 million in annual costs spread over 120,000 transactions × 365 days). This, of course, would be impossible, but Company Z targeted a volume of 88,500 thousand transactions per day, which was equivalent to a productivity factor of about 75% or, stated another way, a spread between peak and average demand of about 25%. At this level, the cost per transaction would be $0.065, yielding a reasonably high 35% gross margin for this type of high-volume business ($0.10 − $0.065)/($0.10).

To summarize the analysis, the business model for Company Z was relatively straight-forward: Capture customers and then recoup these costs and build a profit flow through transaction processing. What was enticing was that once these customers were loaded onto the network, they were actually captured, since the switching costs for them would be high. If Company Z could deliver the service as promised, it would have loyal customers as long as the price remained in the target range. Its revised business plan reflected a targeted cost to capture and load of $60,000, a volatility factor of 25%, and a resulting gross profit per transaction of $0.035 (target price of 10 cents less the costs to process the transaction). If these were met, it would need to process only 1.7 transactions for a customer to recoup the front-end acquisition cost (1.7 million × $0.035 margin ≅ $60,000), and at 12 transactions per item sold, this amounted to a bit over 40,000 items to break even. Company Z did get second-round financing once this business model was presented along with the actions it was taking to (1) lower the costs of customer acquisition, (2) target that segment of the market that would drive volatility from the network, and (3) move from real-time processing to other methods that would also address the volatility issue.

Reflections

The preceding example provides a number of key lessons for building an ABC system. First and foremost, building the system requires an intimate knowledge of the operations. This is why more and more accountants are being moved from corporate headquarters to the regional business that they are supposed to support. Operations require resources; resources support activities; and it is only through a hands-on knowledge of how the activities consume the resources that one can understand the underlying cost model. The first step in building the ABC system is a high-level mapping of the processes and the activities that they entail.

When building these systems, the overriding criterion is the cost-benefit ratio. If total accuracy was desired for Company Z, one could examine the costs in minute detail and build a cost report for every customer targeted. This, however, would have been extremely time consuming and costly. As was discussed, a simple segmentation of "knowledgeable" versus "not so aware" was probably sufficient to provide actionable cost information with an acceptable level of accuracy. Getting the right balance of accuracy versus cost is a difficult decision to make and often a function of the level of competition in the marketplace.[2]

Microeconomics is based on the short-run assumption that all costs either are fixed or vary with units of output. The Company Z example shows that this is not true and demonstrates that costs are much more complex and can vary with many factors. For example, the cost to capture and load a customer varies with the knowledge of that customer, with the less aware customer segment costing 35% more ($127,500 + $15,000 v. $158,500 + $33,600). Exhibit 13.7 demonstrates the depth of analysis that was required at the activity level to support this conclusion. For a knowledgeable customer, a salesperson and a technician would spend three days on the road, typically one for travel and the other two at the client site demonstrating the system. A second trip by the salesperson was typically necessary to close the sale, as well as a call from the CEO of Company Z to discuss and authenticate the company's capabilities. This call required a bit of preparation work on the client for the CEO prepared by the sales rep. Salary costs, travel, and lodging were estimated from travel reports. A like analysis supports the third activity for the customer loading process, implementation and certification, which together with the

Exhibit 13.7 Cost of a customer sale.

Knowledgeable Customer	Days	Salary/ Day	Total Salary	Travel	Lodging	
3-day 1st trip:						
Salesperson	3	$ 650	$1,950	$1,000	$825	$ 3,775
Technician	3	550	1,650	1,000	825	3,475
2-day 2nd trip:						
Salesperson	2	650	1,300	1,000	550	2,850
CEO call:						
Salesperson	0.5	650	325	0	0	325
CEO	0.5	2,040	1,020	0	0	1,020
						$ 11,445

Not So Aware Customer	Days	Salary/ Day	Total Salary	Travel	Lodging	
2-day 1st trip						
Salesperson	2	$ 650	$1,300	$1,000	$ 550	$ 2,850
5-day 2nd trip						
Salesperson	5	650	3,250	1,000	1,375	5,625
Technician	5	550	2,750	1,000	1,375	5,125
2-day 3rd trip						
Salesperson	2	650	1,300	1,000	550	2,850
CEO trip						
CEO	2	2,040	4,080	1,000	550	5,630
						$ 22,080

Total: 3 knowledgeable customers @ $11,445 + 7 not so aware @ $22,080 = $188,895

data in Exhibit 13.7 revealed the higher costs for the unaware customers. In general, an ABC analysis reveals four types of costs:

1. Those that truly vary with output, which, in the case of Company Z, if output is defined as transactions processed, there are none.

2. Those that vary with the number of setups or batches, which in this example equates to the front-end costs of capturing and loading a customer. In some instances, these costs can be uniform, as for instance the $175 paid for the customer qualification or the $5,000 system design, which were the same for all potential customers. In other cases, such as the two segments of customers, one must seek more information, as discussed in Exhibit 13.7.

3. Those that vary at the product level. In the discussion earlier, Company Z had only one product, a transaction, but it is far more common to have a diverse mix of products, and this requires a careful analysis of which expenses can be traced to product-level activities. For instance, in the semiconductor industry, this may entail clean room facilities required for some products.

4. Those that are traced to capacity decisions for infrastructure investments (discussed next).

Capacity costs are probably the most difficult to deal with conceptually but also the most important, especially with advances in technology driving these costs upward. Most managers simply take the period capacity cost and divide by the units of output.[3] As shown in Exhibits 13.5 and 13.6, this can be extremely misleading. To better manage an infrastructure cost, one must take into consideration the capacity of that infrastructure.[4]

As is evident from the previous discussion, ABC systems require a different format for aggregating costs. Financial accounting reports costs by function, which is close to worthless for internal decision making. The Company Z analysis focused on identifying the activities that consumed resources, thereby creating costs. The next step would be to aggregate these costs by activity, as shown in Exhibit 13.8. For example, the activity "customer identification" aggregates costs from the following line items in the financial ledger: sales expense, marketing expense, technical support, travel, and administration expense. See Exhibit 13.8.

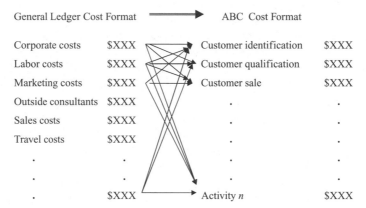

Exhibit 13.8   Activity-based costing process.

Having identified the appropriate level of activities and the resources that support them, building ABC systems is done in two steps. First, costs are pooled for each activity; then the underlying causal driver for each pool is identified and used to attach or trace these costs to the unit of analysis. Cost pools that are more variable in nature have usage drivers. For example, Company Z incurred $32,000 in total cost for the business process review activity supporting the customer loading process (see Exhibit 13.2). This was a variable cost for the eight reviews outsourced, and since they were all the same in intensity of resources, the driver is simply "a review"—one would cost $4,000, two would cost $8,000, and so on. For those that differ in intensity, such as the customer sale activity, shown in Exhibit 13.7, a driver that reflected the intensity, in this case "knowledgeable" versus "not so aware," was used—still a variable cost but with different drivers. Those cost pools that are more fixed should have drivers reflecting their causal factor, capacity, and not usage. The previous discussion around Exhibits 13.5 and 13.6 reflects the danger of using a usage driver for a fixed cost pool. Idle costs were buried in the initial calculation of the $0.29 per transaction, indicating the absence of a viable business model. It was only when these idle costs were identified and a capacity cost was derived that the potential business model emerged.

The purpose of ABC analysis is not costing but rather to make the economics of the underlying business model transparent. Once this is accomplished, one automatically seeks to optimize the model; that is, ABC leads to what is called activity-based management (ABM). As such, ABC analysis is more a journey than a destination. By making the economics transparent, ABM then seeks to optimize the business model. Note that in the Company Z example, once executives understood that the costs they saw simply as period-related sales and marketing costs were attached to the causal factor, capturing a customer, they immediately began to seek other ways of managing this process. Likewise, when the data on the capacity costs were presented, they quickly identified the root cause, volatility, and shifted their focus to the customer segment that had a steadier demand flow. These seems very simple on the face of it, but until the ABC analysis revealed the underlying costs, business in year 2 was being transacted much as was done in the first year. As discussed throughout this chapter, financial reporting simply does not provide data in a format that supports such analysis and decision making.

What an ABC Systems Is and Is Not

As with any new management development, consulting firms quickly built ABC practices and software companies wrote applications. Unfortunately, many of these new entrants did not fully appreciate the tool and did more harm than good. Most sold ABC as a better way to organize data, which it was, but for the inventory valuation function within financial reporting rather than as a support tool for management decision making. They were focused on the dominant part of the accounting profession, financial reporting. Large firms attempted to replace parts of their legacy financial systems with ABC modules with disastrous results. Rather than poor application, ABC as an overall business tool carried the brunt of the blame.

A large abrasives firm with a complex mix of offerings, from standard sandpaper to high-tech grinding wheels, that installed an ABC system provides a telling example of this. The system as designed had over 6,000 activity cost pools and almost that many drivers. Costs reports for product managers ran multiple pages showing the allocations from the many pools, with drivers abbreviated to three letters, most undecipherable. The consultants who designed and installed the system were long gone, and the reports were so complex that even the internal personnel who worked on the project could not explain them. As a result, the reports were ignored—managers favored no information (or gut assumptions) over these reports. Over time, processes changed and new technology was introduced, but no one was experienced enough to adapt the system. As a result, the system became obsolete. Within three years, the large, multimillion-dollar project was scrapped. Any further mention of ABC systems within the company was deemed "career limiting."

At the same time, this firm was rebuilding its distribution channel infrastructure, moving away from a predominantly direct method where its own salespeople sold all products in the mix to all customers to a more indirect system. The top 100 key accounts were identified and assigned key account managers, while the rest were designated for placement with outside third-party distributors and value-added resellers (VARs). An analysis showed that this change would save four to five percentage points on the sales and marketing line of the financial report. Nine months into this, the targeted cost had actually increased.

A consultant was brought in to analyze the situation and make recommendations for restructuring the distribution system. The first step was a detailed mapping of the indirect channel architecture and the resources that supported it. On a sampling basis, the consultant identified and studied both the distributor and VAR relationships. The results were interesting.

First, the indirect channel third parties could be put into three classifications, or buckets. There were those that were called one-stop shops. They sold everything from toilet paper to sandpaper. The second sold only abrasives, carried the full line from low end to high end, and had extensive contacts within the manufacturing sector. The third group were more focused players who had deep technical knowledge of the high-end segment of the abrasives market. They often worked as consultants with their manufacturing clients recommending which abrasive technologies would fit their needs.

In addition, the resources dedicated to these three buckets followed a Noah's Ark approach. When approaching a new client or trying to expand the mix for an existing client, it was typical for a technical field salesperson from the company to accompany the indirect partner. In many instances, this two-by-two approach led to redundant resources focused on the client and additional non-value-added costs. Not only was the company paying the distributor its commission, but it was also incurring the cost for the salesperson. But this did not happen in all instances. Often, the full-line distributor from the second bucket did not have the expertise to present the higher-end technologies and needed the technical support. Different circumstances dictated different approaches.

The final report from the consultant recommended the following five steps:

1. Divide the indirect channel partners into the three classifications as just discussed.
2. For each of these, map the activities necessary to satisfy the end customer, regardless of who provides them—third party or company.
3. Identify the company resources that support each of these activities (e.g., technical field sales, internal sales, etc.).
4. Derive the costs for each of these activities.
5. Offer a sliding commission schedule that reflects the activity costs from step 4.

It became clear that the one-stop shops were merely order takers that dedicated few resources to building the business. Abrasive products were a necessary element for their portfolios of products, and their primary focus was on building the overall volume from a client since this drove their revenues. They needed the abrasives line as much as the company needed this indirect channel, and a lower commission might be acceptable.

The full-line group was a bit different. Their primary focus was on abrasive products, and their revenue line was dependent on building volume in this arena only. With the higher-end offerings, they often needed technical assistance and did see the value of this. To build volume in this area, they would be willing to adjust the commission in recognition of the effort of the technical field salesperson; they basically saw it as a payment for services rendered.

The high-end group were mostly VARs who needed little technical assistance but who dedicated a good amount of resources in building their businesses. To compensate them for the sales they generated, a much higher commission structure was necessary.

The company was very happy with this report and implemented it with little change. There was some push-back from those who wound up with lower commissions, but the logic of the changes when communicated often was accepted. On the high end, sales increased markedly and within two quarters the overall costs for channel management were moving in the right direction.

It should be clear that the basis of this analysis was ABC. If, however, the consultant had called it such, the job would have been lost. This discussion represents the bad and the good of ABC systems. It can be argued that ABC was never developed as a better model for inventory costing within a financial reporting system. It is best used as a process analysis tool to add transparency in the area of value creation. As in the earlier Company Z example, once the costs of the indirect distribution activities for the abrasives company became apparent, the obvious next step was to reengineer the system to capture the value embedded in the system.

Activity-Based Costing → Activity-Based Management → Strategic Cost Management

An interesting reflection on the two examples discussed so far might be: Why are the companies examining their costs systems after the fact? Would not the insights gained from the analyses have been of more value in the planning process—before the fact rather than after the fact? Shank and Govindarajan argued exactly this point and called for a change in context in management accounting systems. Rather than focusing only on the internal scorekeeping and problem-solving arena, they urged a more strategic view, noting that "what we do starts with our consensus about why we do it."[5] They called this strategic cost management (SCM) and defined it as the development of cost information systems for strategic planning. This required three changes in mind-set:

1. A more expansive view for cost analysis is needed. Since many costs are influenced by decisions made by either upstream or downstream partners, one must move from the internal company perspective to the value system level. The abrasives example discussed earlier is a micro-example of this where the costs were a function of the distribution of activities between the channel partner and the firm, but, again, it was done after the fact. In developing the strategic plan for implementing the indirect channel, much of the same analysis could have been done *ex ante*. It has been rumored that Coca-Cola management has mapped its entire value system from a customer putting money into a vending machine for a can of Coke all the way back to the sugar beet farmer and aluminum smelter. Like the small distribution example, once understood, Coca-Cola managers can then optimize the entire value system rather than the individual pieces.

2. One size does not fit all. A firm pursuing a cost leadership strategy would need a management accounting system that drove efficiency, since pricing is controlled by market conditions. Quite the opposite, one pursuing a differentiation strategy would need to focus more on customer willingness to pay, costs to differentiate, and value-based pricing. In the SCM world, management accounting systems are designed to fit the strategy.

3. In the strategic planning stage, all costs are variable and are dependent on both the strategy's formulation and its implementation. In the formulation stage, cost drivers now are based on decisions concerning scale (how big), scope (where to play in the value system), technology (how to play), and complexity (how broad a product offering). At implementation, execution factors such as capacity utilization, product design, and employee involvement come to the forefront. In essence, costs are now driven by strategic choice and the ability to execute.

The entry of Airborne Express into the express mail delivery industry is an excellent example of the proper use of SCM. A structural analysis of this industry quickly identifies it as not very attractive. It has high entry barriers, little ability to differentiate, intense competition from two large entrenched companies (UPS and FedEx), and powerful customers. This competition focused on cost leadership, and both major players were far along the experience curve. Yet Airborne was able to enter, capture about 20% of the market, and do it profitability. How did it accomplish this?

In developing its entry strategy, Airborne precisely structured its operations to minimize costs. First, it assured itself of scale and minimized complexity by targeting a narrow band of high-volume customers in a limited number of locations. This customer segment had to meet two other criteria besides high volume—business-to-business and low volatility of demand. It purposely ignored the residential customer, who created high variability in demand for UPS and FedEx. This target customer population also allowed Airborne to minimize its technology investment in relation to those two competitors. An analysis of the most important executional cost driver, capacity utilization, reveals the wisdom of Airborne's structural choices.

The largest cost item for this industry is transportation. Airborne had 175 planes and over 13,000 trucks. For the planes, by targeting that segment of the population with low variability in demand, it was able to fly its planes at an average of 80% of capacity, substantially higher than the industry average of 67%. Since all competitors used basically the same type of plane, Airborne calculated its relative cost of capacity as follows:

At full capacity, the cost per package delivered by plane = $$\$\$/\text{Cap}$$, where $$\$\$$$ is the total cost of the flight (basically fixed) and Cap the number of packages at full capacity.

If Airborne attains 80% of capacity, its cost per package = $$\$\$/(80\%)\text{Cap}$$, which can be rewritten as $$1/80\% \times \$\$/\text{Cap}$$, which equals $$1.25 \ \$\$/\text{Cap}$$.

At 67% of capacity, a competitor's cost per package = $$\$\$/(67\%)\text{Cap}$$, which can be rewritten as $$1/67\% \times \$\$/\text{Cap}$$, yielding $$1.50 \ \$\$/\text{Cap}$$.

In summary, by computing the ratio of Airborne's air delivery cost to its competitors' costs, the impact of this lower-volatility strategic target on cost per package can be calculated: $$1.25 \ \$\$/\text{Cap} \div 1.50 \ \$\$/\text{Cap} = 83\%$$. In an industry that competes based on cost leadership, Airborne has a 17% cost advantage in the air delivery cost. An analysis of the truck utilization factor shows an even larger advantage, given that drivers make fewer stops due to the narrowly defined customer characteristics and pick up more at each stop. Although this cost advantage may seem small, assuming that Airborne passes on, say, half this advantage in the form of lower prices to the targeted customers and keeps the rest, any services purchasing manager whose performance is based on attainment of budget would jump at an 8% drop in price of a high-volume delivery cost.

A short but precise definition of strategy is to do something different that others cannot imitate. Is Airborne's cost advantage sustainable? Can FedEx or UPS easily copy? A thorough analysis would reveal that before Airborne's entry, this high-volume, low-volatility customer segment was subsidizing the other customers. In response, both the competitors could match Airborne's price in this segment, but this would mean that if they wish to maintain profitability they would have to raise prices to the other more volatile customers while providing them the same level of service. Those firms that have found themselves in this situation realize how hard this is to accomplish.

A noteworthy epilogue to this story is that approximately 10 years prior to Airborne's entry into this market, FedEx did much the same thing to UPS. At that time UPS dominated package delivery but did not recognize express as a separate segment. FedEx targeted this segment with a value proposition based on uniqueness of service and low cost, successfully capturing a large and profitable portion of UPS's business. In the "Reflections" section of this chapter I stated that defining the right level of detail for an ABC system is based on a cost-benefit criterion, which, in turn, is a function of the competitiveness of an industry. In hindsight, should FedEx have understood the cost structure of the segment Airborne targeted and acted accordingly, thereby closing the door before Airborne entered? Maybe the cost for this level of detail was deemed greater than the benefit. Hindsight being 20/20, there is no doubt that FedEx and/or UPS now wish they had built this level of detail into their cost systems. The lesson here is that one cannot ignore the competitive forces in an industry. SCM systems must be constantly monitored to ensure that they produce the requisite level of detail as industries evolve.

Lessons from Japan

By the early 1990s a number of researchers began studying Japanese management cost systems. They hypothesized that the recent dominance of these firms in such industries as automobiles, steel, and electronics might be due to better management cost information. Their findings were to the contrary. If anything, Japanese cost systems had more "peanut buttering" of overhead costs than their U.S. counterparts.

A closer study, however, revealed something else. Many Japanese firms understood that reporting costs after the fact was of little value and dedicated few resources to these systems. Instead, well-developed SCM systems were an integral part of the product development process. Early in this process, market research established price ranges, and return on investment (ROI) criteria were applied to the asset intensity for the planned production infrastructure to calculate necessary profits. The difference between the expected price and the required return established a target cost for the development process, which was then cascaded down through the various components. Project managers at every level were expected to meet this target. All project managers were schooled in target costing and value engineering disciplines to aid in this process, and this permeated down through the development organization. For instance, new project managers at Toyota might start at a minor component such as a brake caliper; if successful, they would graduate to a brake assembly, and on up until ultimately responsible for a new car model. No product was released to production without first meeting its target cost, and once in production these targets were monitored closely.

From a U.S. accounting perspective, the detail and rigor embedded in the system was eye-opening but also somewhat disconcerting since the engineering function actually had responsibility for this finely tuned SCM system. When asked where they found the insight for such a finely tuned system, Toyota management provided references to systems developed in Detroit in the early 1950s.

Summary

Activity-based costing is a powerful management tool when used properly. It is not a narrow product costing methodology but, rather, a key element of any process management analysis. By making the economics of a business model transparent, it is the necessary first step of any planning initiative whether it be the reengineering of a flawed process or the creation of a new strategic plan. The design of ABC systems is based on a simple paradigm: Costs are a function of activities that consume resources that have been acquired to execute a strategy. Only when this is understood at the value system level can one effectively lead an organization.

Notes

1. "Accounting Bores You? Wake Up," *Fortune*, October 12, 1987, 44.
2. This will be discussed further in the final section of this chapter.
3. If there is a mix of units, then equivalent units are often used, such as the semiconductor industry using the number of layers to define an equivalent unit (e.g., an equivalent unit might be a chip with five layers, so a more complex chip with, say, 10 layers would be the equivalent of two chips).
4. This will be discussed in more detail later in the chapter.
5. John Shank and Vijay Govindarajan, "Strategic Cost Management: New Wine, or Just New Bottles?" *Journal of Management Accounting Research* (Fall 1989): 47–65.

Part V

Planning and Strategy

14

Business Planning

Andrew Zacharakis

How This Chapter Fits in a Typical MBA Curriculum

Business planning is often central to teaching entrepreneurship.[1] Entrepreneurship is an iterative cycle between *thinking* and *acting*. If would-be entrepreneurs only *think* and never *act* on that thinking, then they are what I affectionately term "cocktail entrepreneurs." For any new business or invention that comes around, cocktail entrepreneurs will regale you with tales about how they thought of this idea first and how the company that ultimately launched it stole their idea or some other reason why the entrepreneur didn't *act*. In reality, "cocktail entrepreneurs" are missing a key component to entrepreneurial success—the ability to *act* on their ideas. Likewise, entrepreneurs who *act* without *thinking* are apt to make more mistakes, and those mistakes are often much more costly than the less serious missteps of entrepreneurs who are active *thinkers*. Thus, entrepreneurship is an iterative balance between *thinking* and *acting*.

Within most MBA programs, there is a course that is focused on business planning, because it is a means to gain deep learning about the opportunity that you wish to pursue. While most MBA courses focus on producing a formal finished product that the entrepreneur can share with investors or other stakeholders, it is the process that is important. As I tell my students, I don't care whether they produce an actual written document or just accumulate numerous computer files on areas of importance. But following a formal process can help ensure that you don't miss any important gaps in your planning process. As General Dwight D. Eisenhower famously stated, "In preparing for battle I have always found that plans are useless, but planning is indispensable."[2]

Who Uses This Material in the Real World

Business planning is widely used throughout the business world. Entrepreneurs use business planning to launch nascent ventures, and managers throughout existing organizations use business planning on a regular basis as they anticipate their companies' next moves. Large Fortune 500 companies also see the benefits of business planning. For example, Bert DuMars, vice president of e-business and interactive marketing at Newell Rubbermaid, was tasked with integrating social media marketing into well-established products, such as the Sharpie pen. "This is a new area for us and heavy investing (whether dollars, personnel or both) without understanding how, when and why our consumers would like to engage with us is risky and dangerous for our brands."[3] For Newell Rubbermaid, it would be considered reckless to pursue a new opportunity without the benefit of thoughtful evaluation that is achieved through a well-prepared business plan.

The Story of Your Business

The purpose of business planning is to tell a story: the story of your business. Thorough business planning can establish that there is an opportunity worth exploiting and should then describe the details of how this will be accomplished. During the dot-com boom of the late 1990s, many entrepreneurs and venture capitalists questioned the importance of business planning. Typical of this hyper-start-up phase are stories like that of James Walker, who generated financing on a 10-day-old company based on "a bunch of bullet points on a piece of paper." He stated, "It has to happen quick in the hyper-competitive wireless-Internet-technology world. There's a revolution every year and a half now."[4] The implication was simple: Business planning took time—time that entrepreneurs didn't have.

April 2000 was a sobering wake-up call for investors and entrepreneurs who had invested in the dot-com boom of the late 1990s. Previously, many entrepreneurs believed that all that was needed to find investors and go public were a few PowerPoint slides and a good idea. The NASDAQ crash in April dispelled those beliefs as people came to realize that the majority of these businesses never had the potential to produce profits. Today, investors have learned from this lesson and demand well-researched market opportunities and solid business planning. Entrepreneurs also have learned the various benefits of a well-researched plan.

There is a common misperception that business planning is primarily used for raising capital. Although a good business plan assists in raising capital, the primary purpose of the process is to help entrepreneurs gain a deeper understanding of the opportunity they are envisioning. Many would-be entrepreneurs doggedly pursue ideas that will never be profitable because they lack deep understanding of the business model. The relatively little time spent developing a sound business plan can save thousands or even millions of dollars that might be wasted in a wild goose chase. For example, if a person makes $100,000 per year, spending 200 hours on a business planning process equates to a $10,000 investment in time spent ($50/hour × 200 hours). However, launching a flawed business concept can quickly accelerate into millions in spent capital. Most entrepreneurial ventures raise enough money to survive two years, even if the business will ultimately fail. Assuming the only expense is the time value of the lead entrepreneur, a two-year investment equates to $200,000, not to mention the lost opportunity cost and the likelihood that employees were hired and paid and other expenses were incurred. So do yourself a favor and spend the time and money up front.

The business planning *process* helps entrepreneurs shape their original vision into a better opportunity by raising critical questions, researching answers for those questions, and then answering them. For example, one question that every entrepreneur needs to answer is: "What is the customer's pain?" Conversations with customers and other trusted advisers assist in better targeting the product offering to what customers need and want. This pre-start-up work saves untold effort and money that an entrepreneur might spend trying to reshape the product after the business has been launched. While all businesses adjust their offerings based on customer feedback, business planning helps the entrepreneur to anticipate some of these adjustments in advance of the initial launch.

Perhaps the greatest benefit of business planning is that it allows the entrepreneur to articulate the business opportunity to various stakeholders in the most effective manner. The plan provides the background so the entrepreneur can communicate the upside potential and attract equity investment. The business plan provides the validation needed to convince potential employees to leave their current jobs for the uncertain future of a new venture. It is also the instrument that can secure a strategic partner or key customer or supplier. In short, business planning provides entrepreneurs with the deep understanding they need to answer the critical questions that various stakeholders will ask. Completing a well-founded business plan gives the entrepreneur credibility in the eyes of various stakeholders.

Types of Plans

A business plan can take a number of forms depending on its purpose. Each form requires the same level of effort and leads to the same conclusions, but the final document is crafted differently depending on who uses it and when they use it. For instance, when you are introducing your concept to potential investors, you might send them a short, concise summary plan. As their interest grows and they want to more fully investigate the concept, they may ask for a more detailed plan. Although commonly associated with raising capital, a business plan serves so much more than the needs of potential investors. Employees, strategic partners, financiers, and board members all may find use in a well-developed business plan. Most important, the entrepreneurs themselves gain immeasurably from the business planning process as it allows them not only to run the company better, but also to clearly articulate their story to stakeholders who may never read the plan. Different consumers of the business plan require different presentations of the work.

If outside capital is needed, a business plan geared toward equity investors or debt providers typically is 25 to 40 pages long. Entrepreneurs need to recognize that professional equity investors, such as venture capitalists, and professional debt providers, such as bankers, will not read the entire plan from front to back. That being the case, the entrepreneur needs to produce the plan in a format that facilitates spot reading. We will investigate the major sections that comprise business plans throughout this chapter. My general rule of thumb is that "less is more." For instance, I've seen more plans receive venture funding that were closer to 25 pages than 40 pages.

A second type of business plan, the operational plan, is primarily for the entrepreneur and his or her team to guide the development, launch, and initial growth of the venture. There really is no length specification for this type of plan; however, it is common for these plans to exceed 80 pages. The basic organizational format of the two types of plans is the same; however, the level of detail tends to be much greater in an operational plan. The creation of this document is where the entrepreneur really gains the deep understanding so important in discerning how to build and run the business. Since this document is typically for internal use only, it may not be published per se, but it might exist virtually on various computer files.

The last type of plan is called a dehydrated business plan or expanded executive summary. This type is considerably shorter than the previous two, typically no more than 10 pages. The purpose of this plan is to provide an initial conception of the business. As such, it can be used to test initial reaction to the entrepreneur's idea. It is a document that the entrepreneur can share with confidants and receive feedback before investing significant time and effort on a longer business planning process.

After entrepreneurs complete the business planning process, I encourage them to come back and rewrite the dehydrated plan. This expanded executive summary can be used to attract attention. For instance, entrepreneurs may send it to investors whom they have recently met to spur interest and a meeting. It is usually better to send an expanded executive summary than a full business plan, as investors will be more apt to read the shorter version. If they are interested, they will call the entrepreneur in for a meeting. If the meeting goes well, the investor often then asks for the full business plan.

From Glimmer to Action: The Process

Perhaps the hardest part of business planning is getting started. Compiling the data, shaping it into an articulate story, and producing a finished product can be a daunting task. That being the case, the best way to attack business planning is in steps. First, write a short (less than five pages) summary of your current vision. This provides a road map for you and others to follow as you complete the rest of the planning process. Second, start attacking major sections of the planning process. Although each section interacts and influences every other section, it is often easiest for entrepreneurs to write the product/service description first. This is usually the most concrete component of the entrepreneur's vision. Keep in mind, however, that business planning isn't purely a sequential process. You will be skipping around, filling in different parts of the plan simultaneously or in whatever order makes the most sense in your mind. Finally, after completing a first draft of all the major sections, it is time to come back and rewrite a shorter, more concise executive summary. Not too surprisingly, the new executive summary will be quite different from the original summary because of all the learning and reshaping that the business planning process facilitates.

Wisdom is in realizing that the business plan is a living document. Although your first draft will be polished, most business plans are obsolete the day they come off the presses. That means that entrepreneurs are continuously updating and revising their business plan. Each major revision should be kept and filed, and occasionally looked back upon for the lessons you have learned. Remember, the importance of the business plan isn't the final product, but the learning that is gleaned from writing the story line of your vision. It articulates what you see in your mind and crystallizes that vision for you and your team. It also provides a history, a photo album if you will, of the birth, growth, and maturity of your business. Although daunting, business planning can be exciting and creative, especially if you are working on it with your founding team. So now let us dig in and examine how to effectively conduct the business planning process.

The Story Model

One of the major goals of business planning is to attract various stakeholders and convince them of the potential of your business. Therefore, you need to keep in mind how these stakeholders will interpret your plan. The guiding principle is that you are writing a story. All good stories have a theme, a unifying thread that ties the setting, characters, and plot together. If you think about the most successful businesses in the United States, they all have well-publicized themes. When you hear these taglines, you instantly gain insight into the business (see Exhibit 14.1). For example, when you hear the tagline "Absolutely,

Exhibit 14.1   Taglines.

Nike	Just do it.
FedEx	Absolutely, positively has to be there overnight.
McDonald's	We love to see you smile.
Cisco Systems	Discover all that's possible on the Internet.
Microsoft	Where do you want to go today?
Apple	Think different.
BMW	The ultimate driving machine.
GE	We bring good things to life.
United Airlines	Fly the friendly skies.
American Express	Don't leave home without it.

positively has to be there overnight," most people connect that to FedEx and package delivery. In addition, most people think of reliability—the quality that is associated with FedEx. Similarly, "Just do it." is intricately linked to Nike and the image of athletic proficiency. A tagline is a sentence, or even a fragment of a sentence, that summarizes the pure essence of your business. It is the theme that every sentence, paragraph, page, and diagram within your business plan should adhere to, the unifying idea of your story. A useful tip is to put your tagline in a footer that runs on the bottom of every page. As you are writing, if the section doesn't build on, explain, or otherwise directly relate to the tagline, it most likely isn't a necessary component to the business plan. Rigorous adherence to the tagline facilitates writing a concise and coherent business plan.

The key to the story model is capturing the reader's attention. The tagline is the foundation, but in writing the plan you want to create a number of visual catch points. Too many business plans are text-laden, dense manifestos. Only the most diligent reader will wade through all that text. Help the reader by highlighting different key points throughout the plan. How do you create these catch points? Some effective techniques include extensive use of headings and subheadings, strategically placed bullet-point lists, diagrams, charts, and the use of sidebars.[5] The point is to make the document not only content rich, but visually attractive.

Now, let's take a look at the major sections of the plan (see Exhibit 14.2). Keep in mind that although there are variations, most plans have these components. It is important to keep your plan as close to this format as possible, because many stakeholders are accustomed to the format and it facilitates spot reading. If you are seeking venture capital, for instance, you want to facilitate quick perusal because venture capitalists often spend as little as five minutes on a plan before rejecting it or putting it aside for further attention. A venture capitalist who becomes frustrated with an unfamiliar format is more likely to reject it rather than try to pull out the pertinent information. Even if you aren't seeking venture capital, the standard structure is easy for other investors to follow and understand. Furthermore, the sections highlighted provide a road map for questions that you need to consider as you prepare to launch your business.

The Business Plan

We will progress through the sections in the order that they typically appear, but keep in mind that you can work on the sections in any order that you wish.

Exhibit 14.2   Business plan outline.

I.	Cover
II.	Executive Summary
III.	Table of Contents
IV.	Industry, Customer, and Competitor Analysis
V.	Company and Product Description
VI.	Marketing Plan
VII.	Operations Plan
VIII.	Development Plan
IX.	Team
X.	Critical Risks
XI.	Offering
XII.	Financial Plan
XIII.	Appendixes

The Cover

The cover of the plan should include the following information: company name, tagline, contact person and address, phone, fax, e-mail address, date, disclaimer, and copy number (see Exhibit 14.3). Most of the information is self-explanatory, but a few things should be pointed out. First, the contact person for a new venture should be the president or another founding team member. I have seen some business plans that failed to have the contact person's name, e-mail address, and phone number on the cover. Imagine the frustration of an excited potential investor who can't find out how to contact the entrepreneur to gain more information. More often than not, that plan will end up in the rejected pile. Second, business plans should have a disclaimer along these lines:

> This business plan has been submitted on a confidential basis solely to selected, highly qualified investors. The recipient should not reproduce this plan, nor distribute it to others without permission. Please return this copy if you do not wish to invest in the company.

Controlling distribution is particularly important when seeking investment, especially if you do not want to violate Regulation D of the Securities and Exchange Commission, which specifies that you may solicit only qualified investors (high-net-worth and high-income individuals).

The cover should also have a line specifying the copy number. For example, you will often see on one of the bottom corners of the cover a line that says something like "Copy 1 of 5 copies." Entrepreneurs should keep a log of who has copies so that they can control for unexpected distribution.

Finally, the cover should be eye-catching. If you have a product or prototype, a picture of it can draw the reader in. Likewise, a catchy tagline draws attention and encourages the reader to look further.

Executive Summary

This section is the most important part of the business plan. If you don't capture readers' attention in the executive summary, it is unlikely that they will read any other parts of the plan. This is just like a book's jacket notes. Most likely, readers will buy the book only

THE HISTORY SHOPPE™

Making history come to life.

Matthew J. Feczko
13333 Washington Street Suite 33
Wellesley, MA 02481
mfellows@historyshoppe.com

Dated: December 4, 2008

The components of this business plan have been submitted on a confidential basis. It may not be reproduced, stored, or copied in any form. By accepting delivery of this plan, the recipient agrees to maintain its confidentiality and return it upon request. Do not copy, fax, reproduce, or distribute without permission.

Copy **3 of 5**   Distributed to: Zacharakis

Exhibit 14.3   Cover of The History Shoppe business plan.

if they are impressed with the notes on the jacket flaps. Therefore, you want to hit them with the most compelling aspects of your business opportunity right up front.

Hook the Reader

That means having the first sentence or paragraph highlight the potential of the opportunity. "The current market for widgets is $50 million, growing at an annual rate of

20%. Moreover, the emergence of mobile applications is likely to accelerate this market's growth. Company XYZ is positioned to capture this wave with its proprietary technology: the secret formula VOOM." This creates the right tone. The first sentence emphasizes that the potential opportunity is huge and that company XYZ has some competitive advantage that enables it to become a big player in this market. Yet, I have read too many plans that start with "Company XYZ, incorporated in the state of Delaware, will develop and sell widgets." Ho-hum. That does not excite me. I don't really care, at this point, that the business is incorporated or that it is a Delaware corporation (aren't they all?). Capture my attention immediately or risk losing me altogether.

Common subsections within the executive summary include:

- Description of Opportunity.
- Business Concept.
- Industry Overview.
- Target Market.
- Competitive Advantage.
- Business Model and Economics.
- Team and Offering.
- Financial Snapshot.

Remember that since this is an executive summary all of these components are covered in the body of the plan. As such, we will explore them in greater detail as we progress through the sections. Keep it brief here.

Because the executive summary is the most important part of the finished plan, it should be written after you have gained your deep learning by going through all of the other sections. Don't confuse the executive summary included in the plan with the expanded executive summary that I suggested you write as the very first step of the business plan process. Again, the two summaries are likely to be significantly different, as the later summary incorporates all the deep learning that you have gained throughout the process. Don't recycle your initial summary. Rewrite it entirely based on the hard work you have done going through the business planning process.

Table of Contents

Continuing the theme of making the document easy to read, a detailed table of contents is critical. It should include major sections, subsections, exhibits, and appendixes. The table provides the reader a road map to your plan (see Exhibit 14.4).

Industry, Customer, and Competitor Analysis

The first major section of the business planning process creates a platform that answers the question of why your product/service is needed. Too many entrepreneurs lead with a detailed description of the product/service, but it is more effective to illustrate the gap in the marketplace that you're filling. Remember, people will know what your product is from the executive summary so there is no need to lead with it here. Get them excited about the opportunity. To do that, focus on the industry, the customers, and the competition.

Exhibit 14.4   Sample table of contents.

Industry

The goal of this section is to illustrate the opportunity and how you are going to capture that opportunity. Before you can develop your plot and illustrate a theme, you need to provide a setting or context for your story. A useful framework for visualizing the opportunity is Timmons's Model of Opportunity Recognition.[6] Using the "3 Ms" helps quantify an idea and assess how strong an opportunity the idea is.

First, examine *M*arket demand. If the market is growing at 20% or better, the opportunity is more exciting. Second, we look at *M*arket size and structure. A market that is currently $50 million with $1 billion potential is attractive. This often is the case in emerging markets, those that appear poised for rapid growth and have the potential to change how we live and work. For example, the PC, disk drive, and computer hardware markets of the 1980s were very hot. Many new companies were born and rode the wave of the emerging technology, including Apple, Microsoft, and Intel. In the 1990s, it was anything dealing with the Internet. eBay, Google, and Facebook have leveraged the Internet and changed the way we live. Today, we are seeing important trends in energy and environment that have created a clean technology boom. According to the 2008 *Clean Energy Trends* report, revenue from clean technologies grew 40% from $55 billion in 2006 to $77 billion in 2007 and is projected to grow to $255 billion by 2017.[7]

Another market structure that tends to have promise is a fragmented market where small, dispersed competitors compete on a regional basis. Many of the big names in retail revolutionized fragmented markets. For instance, category killers such as Wal-Mart, Staples, and Home Depot consolidated fragmented markets by providing quality products at lower prices. These firms replaced the dispersed regional and local discount office supply and hardware stores.

The final *M* is *M*argin analysis. Do firms in the industry enjoy high gross margins (revenues minus cost of goods sold) of 40% or greater? Higher margins allow for higher returns, which again lead to greater potential businesses.

The 3 *M*s help distinguish opportunities and therefore should be highlighted as early as possible in your plan. Describe your overall industry in terms of revenues, growth, and pertinent future trends. Within this section, avoid discussing your concept—the proposed product or service you will offer. Instead, use dispassionate, arm's-length analysis of the industry with the goal of highlighting a space or gap that is underserved. How is the industry segmented currently, and how will it be segmented in the future? After identifying the relevant industry segments, identify the segment that your product will target. Again, what are the important trends that will shape the segment in the future?

Customer

Once the plan has defined the market space it plans to enter, the target customer needs to be examined in detail. The entrepreneur needs to define who the customer is by using demographic and psychographic information. The better the entrepreneur can define the specific customers, the more apt the new company is to deliver a product that the customer truly wants. Although you may argue that everyone who is hungry is a restaurant's customer, such a vague definition makes it hard to market to the core customer. As a middle-aged man with a family, I have different eating habits than I did in my twenties. I frequent different types of establishments and expect certain kinds of foods within a certain price range. Entrepreneurs need to understand who their core customer is so that they can create a product that the core customer wants and then market a message to which the core customer responds.

A venture capitalist recently told me that the most impressive entrepreneur is the one who comes into his office and not only identifies who the customer is in terms of demographics and psychographics, but can also name who that customer is by address, phone number, and e-mail address. When you understand who your customers are, you can assess what compels them to buy; how your company can sell to them (direct sales, retail, Internet, direct mail, etc.); how much it is going to cost to acquire and retain that customer; and so forth. For example, Best Buy has profiled a variety of customers, which serves as an aid to help employees to better understand their customers' needs. "Buzz" is a young urban male who might be interested in video games, whereas "Barry" is an upscale suburban client who wants premium products that are packaged as a total solution.[8] A schedule inserted into the text describing customers in terms of the basic parameters can be very powerful. It communicates a lot of data quickly.

Competition

The competition analysis follows directly from the customer analysis. Specifically, you have previously identified your market segment, described what the customer looks like, and stated what the customer wants. The key factor leading to competitive analysis is what the customer wants in a particular product. These product attributes form a basis of comparison against your direct and indirect competitors. A competitive profile matrix not only creates a powerful visual catch point, it conveys information regarding your competitive advantage and also the basis for your company's strategy (see Exhibit 14.5).

The competitive profile matrix should lead the section and be followed by text describing the analysis and its implications. In Exhibit 14.5, the entrepreneur rates each competitor (or competitor type) on various key success factors using a five-point scale

Exhibit 14.5 The History Shoppe (THS) competitive profile matrix.

	THS	Big Box	Amazon	THC Web Site	Museum Stores	Specialty Web Sites
History book selection	2	3	1	3	4	3
Display of artifacts	1	5	5	5	3	5
History-related gift items	1	5	4	2	1	2
Videos/DVDs	1	4	3	3	5	2
Price	3	2	1	2	3	3
Atmosphere	1	2	5	5	4	5
Employee knowledge	1	4	5	5	2	5
Ease to shop specific item	2	2	1	1	3	4
Ease to browse	1	2	3	3	2	4

Exhibit 14.6   Sample sources for information on public/private companies.

Infotrac   Index/abstracts of journals, general business and finance magazines, market overviews, and profiles of public and private firms.

Dow Jones Interactive   Searchable index of articles from over 3,000 newspapers.

Lexis/Nexis   Searchable index of articles.

Dun's Principal International Business   International business directory.

Dun's One Million Dollar Premium   Database of public and private firms with revenues greater than $1 million or more than eight employees.

Hoover's Online   Profiles of private and public firms with links to Web Sites, etc.

Corp Tech   Profiles of high-technology firms.

Bridge Information Services   Detailed financial information on 1.4 million international securities that can be manipulated in tables and graphs.

RDS Bizsuite   Linked databases providing data and full-text searching on firms.

Bloomberg   Detailed financial data and analyst reports.

(with 1 being strong on the attribute and 5 being weak). The entrepreneur has also listed his concept, The History Shoppe (THS), in the matrix. We can see that THS expects to do well on most attributes, except for price. The rationale is that customers are willing to pay a bit more for the added benefit of the THS concept. Up to this point in his business plan, the entrepreneur has been setting the platform to introduce his concept by using dispassionate analysis of the industry, customer, and competition. By including THS in the matrix, he is foreshadowing the company section.

Finding information about your competition can be easy if the competitor company is public, harder if it is private, and very difficult if it is operating in stealth mode (it hasn't yet announced itself to the world). Most libraries have access to databases that contain a wealth of information about publicly traded companies (see Exhibit 14.6 for some sample sources), but privately held companies or those stealth ventures represent a greater challenge.

The best way for savvy entrepreneurs to gather competitor information is through their network and via trade shows. Who should be in the entrepreneur's network? First and foremost are the customers the entrepreneur hopes to sell to in the near future. Just as you are (or should be) talking to your potential customers, your existing competition is interacting with the customers every day, and your customers are likely to be aware of the stealth competition that is on the horizon.

Although many entrepreneurs are fearful (verging on the brink of paranoia) that valuable information will fall into the wrong hands and lead to new competition that invalidates the current venture, the reality is that entrepreneurs who operate in a vacuum (meaning they don't talk to customers or show up to trade shows, etc.) fail far more often than those who are talking to everybody they can. Take the risk. Talking allows entrepreneurs to get valuable feedback that enables them to reshape their offering prior to launching a product that may or may not be accepted by the marketplace. So, network

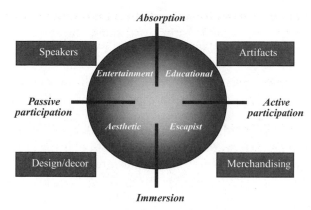

Exhibit 14.7   The History Shoppe's customer value proposition.

not only to find out about your competition, but also to improve your own venture concept.

Company and Product Description

Completing the dispassionate analysis described in the previous section lays the foundation for describing your company and concept. In one paragraph, identify the company name, state where it is incorporated, and provide a brief overview of the concept for the company. This section should also highlight what the company has achieved to date—what milestones you have accomplished that show progress.

More space should be used to communicate the product. Again, graphic representations are visually powerful (see Exhibit 14.7). Highlight how your product fits into the customer value proposition. What is incorporated into your product and what added value do you deliver to the customer? Which of the customer's unmet wants and needs are fulfilled by your offering? The History Shoppe uses retailing research by Pine and Gilmore[9] that identify the attributes customers desire in experiential shopping. As shown in Exhibit 14.7, The History Shoppe then illustrates how it meets the needs of the customer in each quadrant (it will have guest speakers, display historical artifacts, and sell books and historical merchandise, all in a pleasing atmosphere). The diagram captures The History Shoppe's customer value proposition and explains why THS believes its customers will pay a bit more for its books than they would at Barnes & Noble.

This section should clearly and forcefully identify your venture's competitive advantage. Based on your competitive analysis, why is your product better, cheaper, faster than what customers currently have access to? Your advantage may be a function of proprietary technology, patents, distribution, and so on. In fact, the most powerful competitive advantages are derived from a bundle of factors, because this makes them more difficult to copy. The History Shoppe, for example, plans on bundling products, museumlike atmosphere, and educated sales personnel (history buffs) with locations near historic sites. Achieving a good fit among all the items in this bundle is what will set your business apart.

Entrepreneurs also need to identify their market entry and growth strategies. Since most new ventures are resource constrained, especially in terms of available capital, it is crucial that the lead entrepreneur establish the most effective way to enter the market. Based on analysis in the market and customer sections, entrepreneurs need to identify their primary target audience (PTA). Focusing on a particular niche or subset of the overall market allows new ventures to effectively utilize scarce resources to reach those customers and prove the viability of their concept.

The business plan should also sell the entrepreneur's vision for growth, because that indicates the true potential for the business. Thus, a paragraph or two should be devoted to the firm's growth strategy. If the venture achieves success in its entry strategy, it will either generate internal cash flow that can be used to fuel the growth strategy or be attractive enough to get further equity financing at improved valuations. The growth strategy should talk about the secondary and tertiary target audiences that the firm will pursue. For example, The History Shoppe plans on building a flagship store in Lexington, Massachusetts (birthplace of the Revolutionary War), and then expanding to other states with strong customer demographics and important historic sites. Other industries might show growth strategies along other dimensions. For instance, technology companies might shift from selling to users who want the best performance (early adopters) to users who want ease of use (mainstream market).

Marketing Plan

Up to this point we have described your company's potential to successfully enter and grow in a market place. Now we need to devise the strategy that will allow the company to reach its potential. The primary components of this section include a description of the target market strategy, the product/service strategy, pricing strategy, distribution strategy, advertising and promotion, sales strategy, and sales and marketing forecasts. Let's take a look at each of these subsections in turn.

Target Market Strategy

Every marketing plan needs some guiding principles. Based on the knowledge gleaned from the customer analysis, entrepreneurs need to target and position their product accordingly. For instance, product strategies often fall on a continuum with the endpoints being rational purchase and emotional purchase. As an example, when I buy a new car, the rational purchase might be a low-cost, reliable car such as the Ford Focus. However, there is an emotional element as well. I want the car to be an extension of my personality. So, based on my economic means and self-perception, I might buy a BMW or an Audi because of the emotional benefits I derive from it. Within every product space, there is room for products measured at different points along this continuum. You may also find other dimensions that define continuums upon which you can classify your marketplace. These tools help entrepreneurs decide where their product fits (or where they would like to position it). Your target market strategy determines the other aspects of the marketing plan.

Product/Service Strategy

Building from the target market strategy, this section of the plan describes how your product is differentiated from the competition. Discuss why the customer will switch to your product and how you will retain customers so that they don't switch back to your competition in the future. Using the attributes defined in your customer profile matrix, a product attributes map is a powerful visual to show how your firm compares

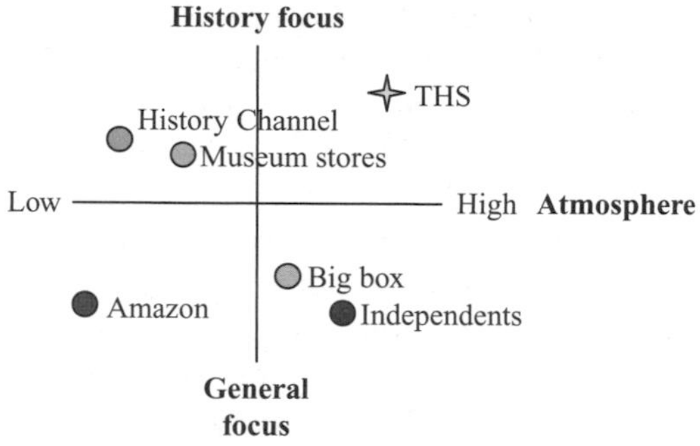

Exhibit 14.8 Competitive map for The History Shoppe.

to the competition. It is best to focus on the two most important attributes, putting one on the x-axis and the other on the y-axis. The map should show that you are clearly distinguishable from your competition on desirable attributes.

Exhibit 14.8 shows the competitive map for The History Shoppe. The two attributes upon which it evaluates competitors are atmosphere (is this a place that people will linger?) and focus (broad topic focus or specialized focus). As you can see from Exhibit 14.8, The History Shoppe (THS) plans to have a high level of history specialization and atmosphere, placing it in the upper right quadrant. The competitor map identifies how THS plans on distinguishing itself from the competition. THS believes that history specialization and atmosphere will attract history buffs and entice them to return time and again.

This section should also address how you will service the customer. What type of technical support will you provide? Will you offer warranties? What kind of product upgrades will be available and when? It is important to detail all these efforts, as they must all be accounted for in the pricing of the product. Many times, entrepreneurs underestimate the costs of these services, which leads to a drain on cash and ultimately to bankruptcy.

Pricing Strategy

Determining how to price your product is always difficult. The two primary approaches can be defined as a "cost-plus" approach and as a "market demand" approach. I advise entrepreneurs to avoid cost-plus pricing for a number of reasons. First, it is difficult to accurately determine your actual cost, especially if this is a new venture with a limited history. New ventures consistently underestimate the true cost of developing their products. For example, how much did it really cost to write that software? The cost would include salaries and burden, computer and other assets, overhead contribution, and so on. Since most entrepreneurs underestimate these costs, there is a tendency to underprice the product. Often, I hear entrepreneurs claim that they are offering a low price so that they can penetrate and gain market share rapidly. The problems with a low price are that it may be difficult to raise the price later; it can send a signal of lower quality; demand at that price may overwhelm your ability to produce the product in sufficient volume; and it may unnecessarily strain cash flow.

Therefore, the better method is to canvass the market and determine an appropriate price based on what the competition is currently offering and how your product is positioned. If you are offering a low-cost value product, price below market rates. Price above market rates if your product is of better quality and possesses many features (the more common case).

Distribution Strategy

This section identifies how you will reach the customer. A company's distribution strategy is more than an operational detail. It can define a company's fortune as much as or more than the company's product. Much of the cost of delivering a product is tied up in its distribution. For example, the e-commerce boom of the late 1990s assumed that the growth in Internet usage and purchases would create new demand for pure Internet companies. Yet the distribution strategy for many of these firms did not make sense. Pets.com and other online pet supply firms were based on a strategy where the pet owner would log on, order the product from the site, and then receive delivery via UPS or the U.S. Postal Service. In theory this works, except that the price the market would bear for this product didn't cover the exorbitant shipping costs of a 40-pound bag of dog food.

It is wise to examine how the customer currently acquires the product. If I buy my dog food at Wal-Mart, then you should probably use primarily traditional retail outlets to sell me a new brand of dog food.

This is not to say that entrepreneurs might not develop a multichannel distribution strategy, but if they want to achieve maximum growth, at some point they will have to use common distribution techniques or reeducate the customer on a new buying process (which can be very expensive). If you determine that Wal-Mart is the best distribution channel, the next question becomes whether you can access it. As a new start-up in the dog food industry, it may be difficult to get shelf space at Wal-Mart. That may suggest an entry strategy of boutique pet stores to build brand recognition. The key here is to identify appropriate channels and then assess how costly it is to access them.

Advertising and Promotion

Communicating effectively to your customer requires advertising and promotion. Resource-constrained entrepreneurs need to carefully select the appropriate strategies. What avenues most effectively reach your primary target audience (PTA)? If you can identify your PTA by names, then direct mail may be more effective than mass media blitzes. Try to utilize grassroots techniques such as public relations efforts geared toward mainstream media. Sheri Poe, founder of Ryka shoes, geared toward women, appeared on *The Oprah Winfrey Show* touting shoes for women, designed by women. The response was overwhelming. In fact, she was so besieged by demand that she couldn't supply enough shoes.

Referring again to the dot-com boom of the late 1990s, the soon-to-be-defunct Computer.com made a classic mistake in its attempt to build brand recognition. It blew over half of the venture capital it had raised on a series of expensive Super Bowl ads for the January 2000 event (it spent $3 million of $5.8 million raised on three Super Bowl ads).[10]

As you develop a multipronged advertising and promotion strategy, create detailed schedules that show which avenues you will pursue and the associated costs (see Exhibits 14.9a and 14.9b). These types of schedules serve many purposes, including

Exhibit 14.9a   Advertising schedule.

Promotional Tools	Budget over 1 Year
Print advertising	$ 5,000
Direct mail	3,000
In-store promotions	2,000
Tour group outreach	1,000
Public relations	1,000
Total	$12,000

Exhibit 14.9b   Magazine advertisement schedule: Budget for year 1.

Publication	Circulation	Ad Price for Quarter Page	Total
Lexington Minuteman newspaper	7,886	$ 500	$4,000
Boston magazine	1,400,000	$1,000	$1,000

providing accurate cost estimates that will help in assessing how much capital you need to raise. These schedules also build credibility in the eyes of potential investors, as they show that you understand the nuances of your industry.

Sales Strategy

This section provides the backbone that supports all of the aforementioned endeavors. Specifically, it illustrates what kind and level of human capital you will devote to the effort. How many salespeople, customer support personnel, and so on do you need? Will these people be internal to the organization or outsourced? If they are internal, will there be a designated sales force or will different members of the company serve in a sales capacity at different times? Again, this section builds credibility if the entrepreneur demonstrates an understanding of how the business should operate.

Sales and Marketing Forecasts

Gauging the impact of these efforts is difficult. Nonetheless, to build a compelling story, entrepreneurs need to show projections of revenues well into the future. How do you derive these numbers? There are two methods: the comparable method and the buildup method. After detailed investigation of the industry and market, entrepreneurs know the competitive players and have a good understanding of their history. The comparable method models sales forecasts after what other companies have achieved, adjusting for age of company, variances in product attributes, support services such as advertising and promotion, and so on. In essence, the entrepreneur monitors a number of comparable competitors and then explains why his or her business varies from those models.

In the buildup method, the entrepreneur identifies all the revenue sources and then estimates how much of that revenue type the company can generate per day, or some other small time period. For example, The History Shoppe generates revenues from books and artifacts. The entrepreneur would estimate the average sales price for each category, and then might estimate the number of people to come through the store on a daily basis and what percentage would purchase each revenue source. Those estimates can then be aggregated into larger blocks of time (months, quarters, or years) to generate rough estimates, which might be further adjusted based on seasonality in the retail industry.

The buildup technique is an imprecise method for the new start-up with limited operating history, but it is critically important to assess the viability of the opportunity. It is so important, in fact, that I advise entrepreneurs to use both the comparable and buildup techniques to assess how well they converge. If the two methods are widely divergent, go back through and try to determine why. The deep knowledge you gain of your business model will greatly help you articulate the opportunity to stakeholders, as well as manage the business when it is launched. Chapter 11, "Forecasts and Budgeting," provides more detail on how to derive these estimates.

The one thing we know for certain is that these forecasts will never be 100% accurate, but the question is the degree of error. Detailed investigation of comparable companies reduces that error. Triangulating the comparable results with the buildup method reduces that error further. The smaller the error, the less likely the company will run out of cash. Rigorous estimates also build credibility with your investors.

Operations Plan

The key in the operations section is to address how operations will add value to your customers. The section details the production cycle, allowing the entrepreneur to gauge the impact on working capital. For instance, when does the company pay for inputs? How long does it take to produce the product? When does the customer buy the product and, more important, when does the customer pay for the product? The time from the beginning of this process until the product is paid for will drain cash flow and has implications for financing. Counterintuitively, many rapidly growing new companies run out of cash even though they have increasing sales and substantial operating profit, because they fail to properly finance the time cash is tied up in the procurement, production, sales, and receivables cycle.

Operations Strategy

The first subsection provides a strategy overview. How does your business win/compare on the dimensions of cost, quality, timeliness, and flexibility? The emphasis should be on those aspects that provide your venture with a comparative advantage.

It is also appropriate to discuss geographic location of production facilities and how this enhances the firm's competitive advantage. Discuss available labor, local regulations, transportation, infrastructure, proximity to suppliers, and so on. The section should also provide a description of the facilities, how the facilities will be acquired (bought or leased), and how future growth will be handled (e.g., renting an adjoining building). As with all sections detailing strategy, it is imperative that you support your plans with actual data.

Scope of Operations

What is the production process for your product or service? A diagram of the operations flow facilitates the decision as to which production aspects to keep in-house and which to outsource (see Exhibit 14.10a). Considering that cash flow is king and

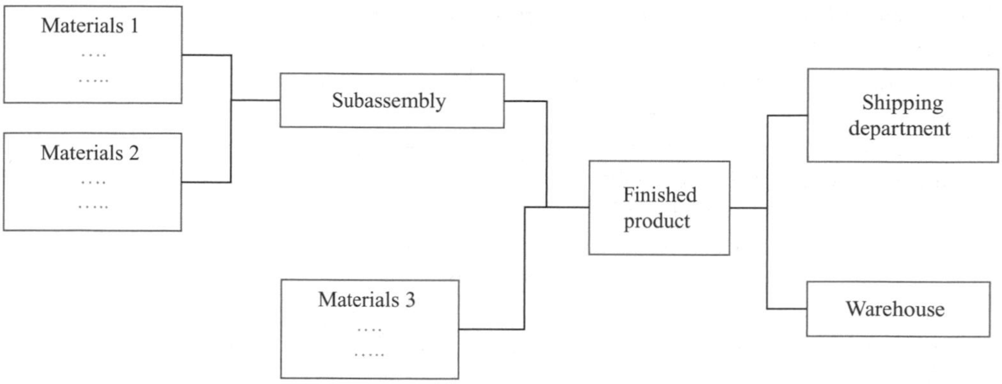

(a)

Exhibit 14.10a   Operations flow.

Source: Adapted from Professor Bob Eng, Babson College.

that resource-constrained new ventures typically should minimize fixed expenses on production facilities, the general rule is to outsource as much production as possible. However, there is a major caveat to that rule. Your venture should control aspects of production that are central to your competitive advantage. Thus, if you are producing a new component with hardwired proprietary technology—let's say a voice recognition security door entry—it is wise to internally produce that hardwired component. The locking mechanism, however, can be outsourced to your specifications. Outsourcing the aspects that aren't proprietary reduces fixed cost for production equipment and facility expenditures, which means that you don't have to raise as much money and give up as much equity.

The scope of operations should also discuss partnerships with vendors, suppliers, and partners. Again, the diagram should illustrate the supplier and vendor relationships by category (or by name if the list isn't too long and you have already identified your suppliers). The diagram helps you visualize the various relationships and strategies to better manage or eliminate them. The operations diagram also helps entrepreneurs to identify personnel needs. For example, the diagram provides an indication of how many production workers might be needed depending on the hours of operations, number of shifts, and so forth.

Ongoing Operations

This section builds on the scope of operations by providing details on day-to-day activities. For example, how many units will be produced in a day, and what kinds of inputs are necessary? An operating cycle overview diagram graphically illustrates the impact of production on cash flow (see Exhibit 14.10b). As entrepreneurs complete this detail, they can start to establish performance parameters, which will help monitor and modify the production process in the future. If this is an operational business plan, the level of detail may include specific job descriptions, but for the typical business plan, this level of detail would be much more than an investor, for example, would need or want to see in the initial evaluation phase.

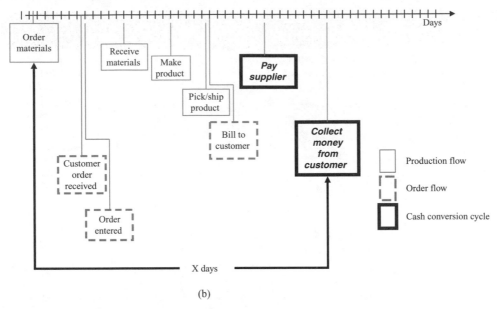

(b)

Exhibit 14.10b Operating cycle overview.

Source: Adapted from Professor Bob Eng, Babson College.

Development Plan

The development plan highlights the development strategy and also provides a detailed development time line. Many new ventures will require a significant level of effort and time to launch the product or service. This is the prologue of your story. For example, new software or hardware products often require months of development. Discuss what types of features you will develop and tie them to the firm's competitive advantage. This section should also talk about patent, trademark, or copyright efforts, if applicable.

Development Strategy

What work remains to be completed? What factors need to come together for development to be successful? What risks does the firm face? For example, software development is notorious for taking longer and costing more than most companies originally imagined. Detailing the necessary work and what is required for the work to be considered successful helps entrepreneurs understand and manage the risks involved. After you have laid out these details, a development time line is assembled.

Development Time Line

A development time line is a schedule that highlights major milestones and can be used to monitor progress and make changes. Exhibit 14.11 details the steps The History Shoppe needs to take prior to opening its doors. The time line helps entrepreneurs track major events and schedule activities to best execute on those events. It is also a good idea to show what has already transpired as of the writing of the business plan. Illustrate which development milestones you have already achieved. It is also helpful to assign names to the tasks. Who is responsible for ensuring that the milestone is met? As the old adage says, time is money. For every day your product is in development and not on the market, you

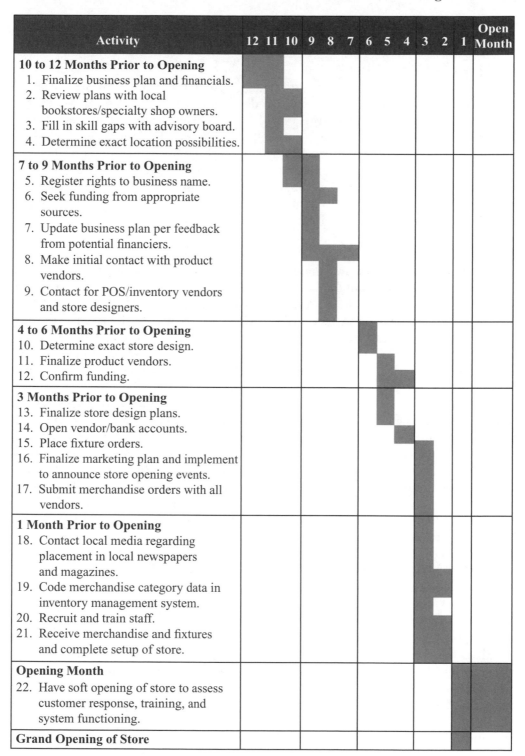

Activity	12	11	10	9	8	7	6	5	4	3	2	1	Open Month
10 to 12 Months Prior to Opening													
1. Finalize business plan and financials.													
2. Review plans with local bookstores/specialty shop owners.													
3. Fill in skill gaps with advisory board.													
4. Determine exact location possibilities.													
7 to 9 Months Prior to Opening													
5. Register rights to business name.													
6. Seek funding from appropriate sources.													
7. Update business plan per feedback from potential financiers.													
8. Make initial contact with product vendors.													
9. Contact for POS/inventory vendors and store designers.													
4 to 6 Months Prior to Opening													
10. Determine exact store design.													
11. Finalize product vendors.													
12. Confirm funding.													
3 Months Prior to Opening													
13. Finalize store design plans.													
14. Open vendor/bank accounts.													
15. Place fixture orders.													
16. Finalize marketing plan and implement to announce store opening events.													
17. Submit merchandise orders with all vendors.													
1 Month Prior to Opening													
18. Contact local media regarding placement in local newspapers and magazines.													
19. Code merchandise category data in inventory management system.													
20. Recruit and train staff.													
21. Receive merchandise and fixtures and complete setup of store.													
Opening Month													
22. Have soft opening of store to assess customer response, training, and system functioning.													
Grand Opening of Store													

Exhibit 14.11   Month-to-month activities.

lose a day's worth of sales. So work hard to meet those deadlines, especially in industries where speed to market is critical.

Team

Georges Doriot, the father of venture capital and founder of American Research and Development Corporation (the first modern-day venture capital firm), said that he would rather "back an 'A' entrepreneur with a 'B' idea than a 'B' entrepreneur with an 'A' idea." The team section of the business plan is often the section that professional investors read after the executive summary. This section is also critically important to the lead entrepreneur. It depicts the members responsible for key activities and conveys why they are exceptionally skilled to execute on those responsibilities. The section also helps the entrepreneur consider how well this group of individuals will work together. It is well established that ventures started by strong teams tend to succeed at a greater rate.

Team Bios and Roles

Every story needs a cast of characters. The best place to start is by identifying the key team members and their titles. Often, the lead entrepreneur assumes a CEO role. However, if you are young and have limited business experience, it is usually more productive to state that the company will seek a qualified CEO as it grows. In these cases, the lead entrepreneur may assume a chief technology officer role (if you develop the technology) or vice president of business development. However, don't let these options confine you. The key is to convince investors that you have assembled the best team possible and that your team can execute on the brilliant concept you are proposing.

A simple, relatively flat organization chart is often useful to visualize what roles you have filled and what gaps remain. It also provides a road map for reading the bios that follow. The bios should demonstrate records of success; if you have previously started a business (even if it failed), highlight the company's accomplishments. If you have no previous entrepreneurial experience, discuss your achievements within your last job. For example, bios often contain a description of the number of people the entrepreneur previously managed and, more important, a measure of economic success, such as growing division sales by 20+%. The bio should demonstrate your leadership capabilities. To complement this description, resumes are often included as an appendix.

Advisory Boards, Board of Directors, Strategic Partners, External Members

To enhance the team's credentials, many entrepreneurs find that they are more attractive to investors if they have strong advisory boards. In building an advisory board, identify individuals with relevant experience within your industry. Industry experts provide legitimacy to your new business as well as strong technical advice. Other advisory board members may bring other skills, such as financial, legal, or management expertise. Thus, it is common to see lawyers, professors, and accountants who can assist the venture's growth on advisory boards. Moreover, if your firm has a strategic supplier and/or key customer, it may make sense to invite them onto your advisory board. Typically, these individuals are remunerated with a small equity stake and compensation for any organized meetings.

By law, most organization types require a board of directors. This is different from an advisory board (although these members can also provide needed expertise). The board's primary role is to oversee the company on behalf of the investors. Therefore, the business plan needs to briefly describe the size of the board, its role within the organization, and any current board members. Most major investors, such as venture capitalists, will require one or more board seats. Usually, the lead entrepreneur and one or more inside company members (e.g., chief financial officers, vice presidents, etc.) will also have board seats.

Strategic partners may not necessarily be on your advisory board or your board of directors, but they still provide credibility to your venture. In such cases, it makes sense to highlight their involvement in your company's success. It is also common to list external team members, such as the law firm and the accounting firm that your venture uses. The key in this section is to demonstrate that your firm can successfully execute the concept. A strong team provides the foundation that conveys your venture will implement the opportunity successfully.

Compensation and Ownership

A capstone to the team section should be a table containing key team members by role, compensation, and ownership equity. A brief description of the table should explain why the compensation is appropriate. Many entrepreneurs choose not to pay themselves in the early months. Although this strategy conserves cash flow, it would misrepresent the individual's worth to the organization. Therefore, the table should contain what salary the employee is due, and then, if deemed necessary, that salary can be deferred until a time when cash flow is strong. Another column that can be powerful shows what the person's current or most recent compensation is/was and what he or she will be paid in the new company. I am most impressed when I see highly qualified entrepreneurs taking a smaller salary than at their previous job. Doing so suggests that the entrepreneur really believes in the upside payoff the company's growth will generate. Of course, the entrepreneur plans on increasing this salary as the venture grows and starts to thrive. Therefore, the description of the schedule should underscore the plan to increase salaries in the future. It is a good idea to hold stock aside for future key hires and also establish a stock option pool for lower-level but critical employees, such as software engineers. Again, the plan should discuss such provisions.

Critical Risks

Every new venture faces a number of risks that may threaten its survival. Although the business plan, to this point, is creating a story of success, there are a number of threats that readers will identify and recognize. The plan needs to acknowledge these potential risks; otherwise, investors will believe that the entrepreneur is naive or untrustworthy, and they may possibly withhold investment. How should you present these critical risks without scaring your investors? Identify each risk and then state your contingency plan (see Exhibit 14.12). Critical risks are critical assumptions, factors that need to happen if your venture is to succeed as currently planned. The critical assumptions vary from one company to another, but some common categories are: market interest and growth potential, competitor actions and retaliation, time and cost of development, operating expenses, and availability and timing of financing.

Market Interest and Growth Potential

The biggest risk any new venture faces is that once the product is developed, no one will buy it. Although there are a number of things that can be done to minimize this

Exhibit 14.12 Sample critical risk.

Highly Competitive Industry

The book and DVD industries are highly competitive across many different channels, including superstores, independent bookstores, Internet retailers, book clubs, and specialty stores. Many of these competitors have been in business for years, have developed significant brand recognition and loyal customers, and possess substantial resources to promote their products. We believe the THS concept is in a unique position with its offering of a complete selection of historical merchandise across several product categories and its superior shopping environment. However, unexpected increases in local competition, including Internet competition, alternative delivery methods for books and video, or unanticipated margin pressures caused by irrational pricing by competitors, could have a materially adverse effect on the company's financial results and growth plans. THS can modify its product offerings, initiate additional marketing activities, and add an Internet site if the retail store isn't generating enough sales.

---

risk, such as market research, focus groups, and beta sites, it is difficult to gauge overall demand and growth of that demand until your product hits the market. This risk must be stated, but countered with the tactics and contingencies the company will undertake. For example, sales risk can be reduced by an effective advertising and marketing plan or identifying not only a primary target customer but also secondary and tertiary target customers that the company will seek if the primary customer proves less interested.

Competitor Actions and Retaliation

Having the opportunity to work with entrepreneurs and student entrepreneurs over the years, I have always been struck by the firmly held belief that direct competition either didn't exist or that it was sleepy and slow to react. I caution against using it as a key assumption of your venture's success. Most entrepreneurs passionately believe that they are offering something new and wonderful that is clearly different from what is currently being offered. They go on to state that existing competition won't attack their niche in the near future. The risk that this assessment is wrong should be acknowledged. One counter to this threat is for the venture to have room in its gross margins and cash available to withstand and fight back against such attacks. You should also identify some strategies to protect and reposition yourself should an attack occur.

Time and Cost to Development

As mentioned in the development plan section, many factors can delay and add to the expense of developing your product. The business plan should identify the factors that may hinder development. For instance, as the popularity of mobile device applications grows, there will be an increased demand for software engineers who are skilled in mobile application development. That leads to the risk of not being able to hire and retain the most qualified professionals. One way to counter the problem might be to outsource some development to the underemployed engineers in India. Compensation, equity participation, flexible hours, and other benefits that the firm could offer might also minimize the risk.

Operating Expenses

Operating expenses have a way of growing beyond expectations. Sales and administration, marketing, and interest expenses are some of the areas that the entrepreneur needs to monitor and manage. The business plan should highlight how these expenses were forecast (comparable companies and detailed analysis), but also talk about contingencies such as slowing the hiring of support personnel, especially if development or other key tasks take longer than expected.

Availability and Timing of Financing

I can't stress enough how important cash flow is to the survival and flourishing of a new venture. One major risk that most new ventures face is that they will have difficulty obtaining needed financing, both equity and debt. If the current business plan is meant to attract investors and is successful, that isn't a near-term risk, but most ventures will need multiple rounds of financing. If the firm fails to make progress (or meet key milestones), it may not be able to secure additional rounds of financing on favorable terms. A contingency to this risk is to identify alternative sources that are viable or strategies to slow the burn rate.[11]

There are a number of other risks that might apply to your business. Acknowledge them and discuss how you can overcome them. Doing so generates confidence in your investors and helps you anticipate corrective actions that you may need to take.

Offering

Based upon the entrepreneur's vision and estimates of the capital required to achieve it, the entrepreneur can develop a "sources and uses of funds" schedule (see Exhibit 14.13). The sources section details how much capital the entrepreneur needs and the types of financing such as equity investment and debt infusions. The uses section details how the money will be spent. Typically, the entrepreneur should secure enough financing to last 12 to 18 months. An entrepreneur who takes more capital than needed has to give up more equity. If the entrepreneur takes less capital than needed, it may mean that the entrepreneur runs out of cash before reaching milestones that equate to higher valuations.

Financial Plan

If the proceeding plan is your verbal description of the opportunity and how you will execute it, the financial plan is the mathematical equivalent. The growth in revenues speaks to the upside of your opportunity. The expenses illustrate what you need to execute on that opportunity. Cash flow statements serve as an early warning system to potential problems (or critical risks), and the balance sheet enables monitoring and adjustment of the venture's progress. That being said, generating realistic financials is one of the most intimidating hurdles that many entrepreneurs face. Chapter 11, "Forecasts and Budgeting," goes into detail on how to construct your pro forma financials.

This section of the plan should include a description of the key drivers that impact your revenues and costs so that the reader can follow your pro forma financials. I typically break the description down into four main sections. First, the "Overview" paragraph briefly introduces the business model. For example, The History Shoppe might highlight that the projections are based on one store in year 1, growing to three stores by year 5. This helps the reader understand the growth in revenues. The overview might

Exhibit 14.13　Sources and uses of funds.

Sources of Funds			Uses of Funds		
Founder	$ 50,000		Inventory	$94,541	
			Computers, software, and office		
Friends/family	$200,000		equipment	20,000	
			Leasehold		
		$250,000	improvements	30,000	
			Furniture and fixtures	51,000	
			Opening costs	17,000	
					$212,541
			Working capital/ Contingencies	$37,459	
					$ 37,459
Total sources		$250,000	Total uses		$250,000

then reiterate the main sources of revenues and any other information that gives a sense of the numbers behind the concept.

The first subsection should discuss the income statement. Talk about the factors that drive revenue, such as store traffic, percentage of store visitors that buy, average ticket price, and so forth. It is also important to talk about seasonality and other factors that might cause uneven sales growth. Then, discuss the expense categories, paying attention to cost of goods sold and major operating expense categories, such as rent, interest expense, and so forth. Based on your description, the reader should be able to look at and understand the actual financials. The key focus here is to help the reader follow your financials; you don't need to provide the level of detail that accountants might if they were auditing your company.

The next subsection should discuss the cash flow statement. Here, you focus on major infusions of cash, such as equity investments and loan disbursements. It is also good to describe the nature of your accounts receivable and payable. How long, for instance, will it be before your receivables convert to cash? If you are spending money on leasehold improvements, plant and equipment, and other items that can be depreciated, you should mention them here. Typically, the discussion of the cash flow statement is quite a bit shorter than the discussion of the income statement.

The final subsection discusses the balance sheet. Here you would talk about major asset categories, such as amount of inventory on hand and any liabilities that aren't clear from the previous discussion.

Appendixes

The appendixes can include anything and everything that you think adds further validation to your concept, but doesn't fit or is too large to insert in the main parts of the plan. Common inclusions would be one-page resumes of key team members, articles that feature your venture, technical specifications, and so on. As a general rule, I try to put all exhibits discussed within the written part of the plan on the same page that the exhibit is discussed. This facilitates reading, as the reader doesn't have to keep flipping back to the end of the plan to look at an exhibit. However, some exhibits are very large (such as the store layout of The History Shoppe). In such cases, it is acceptable to put large exhibits in the appendix.

Conclusion

The business plan is more than just a document; it is a process, a story. Although the finished product is often a written plan, the deep thinking and fact-based analysis that goes into that document provide the entrepreneur with keen insight needed to marshal resources and direct growth. The whole process can induce pain, but it almost always maximizes revenue and minimizes costs, as it allows the entrepreneur to better anticipate instead of react. Business planning also provides talking points so that entrepreneurs can get feedback from a number of experts, including investors, vendors, and customers. Think of business planning as one of your first steps on the journey to entrepreneurial success.

Other Resources

A number of resources exist for those seeking help to write business plans. There are numerous software packages, but I find that generally the templates are too confining. The text boxes asking for information drive writers into a dull, dispassionate tone. The best way to learn about business plans is by digging out the supporting data, writing sections as you feel compelled to, and circulating drafts among your mentors and advisers. Nonetheless, I have provided links to some business planning software sites. I also firmly believe that the entrepreneur should read as many other articles, chapters, and books about writing business plans as possible. You will want to assimilate different perspectives so that you can find your own personal voice.

Internet Links

Business Plan Preparation Sites

www.bplans.com/

www.pasware.com/

www.brs-inc.com/

www.jian.com/

Other Great Sites

http://www.entreworld.org/ www.entrepreneurship.org/	The Kauffman Foundation offers a comprehensive site providing a variety of information for entrepreneurs and links to other helpful sites.
http://www.bizmove.com/ www.bizmove.com/	The Small Business Knowledge Base is a comprehensive, free resource of small business information packed with dozens of guides and worksheets.

http://www.babson.edu/ www3.babson.edu/ESHIP/eship .cfm	The Babson College entrepreneurship site links to different resources of interest to those studying and practicing entrepreneurship.
http://www.nbia.org/www.nbia.org/	National Business Incubation Association: Business incubators nurture young firms, helping them to survive and grow during the start-up period when they are most vulnerable.
http://www.nfibonline.com/ www.nfibonline.com/	The National Federation of Independent Business (NFIB) is the largest advocacy organization representing small and independent businesses in Washington, D.C., and all 50 state capitals—a great resource.
http://www.score.org/online/ www.score.org/online/	SCORE is a national nonprofit association and a resource partner with the U.S. Small Business Administration, with 11,500 volunteer members and 389 chapters throughout the United States.
http://www.morebusiness.com/ www.morebusiness.com/	This site, updated daily, is a comprehensive business resource center providing entrepreneurs with information on start-up, running the business, templates, and more.
www.entrepreneur.com	*Entrepreneur* magazine publishes stories on entrepreneurship, management, and opportunities.

Notes

1. Special thanks to Matt Feczko, Michael DiPietro, Dan Goodman, Henry McGovern, and R. Gabriel Shih for their assistance in writing this chapter.
2. The Quotations Page, www.quotationspage.com/quote/36892.html (accessed December 18, 2008).
3. J. Leggio, "How Newell Rubbermaid Uses Social Media," Fortune 500 Series, ZDNet, http://blogs.zdnet.com/feeds/?p=346&page=1 (accessed December 18, 2008).
4. P. Thomas, "Rewriting the Rules: A New Generation of Entrepreneurs Find Themselves in the Perfect Time and Place to Chart Their Own Course," *Wall Street Journal*, May 22, 2000, R4.
5. A running sidebar is a visual device that is positioned down the right-hand side of the page that periodically highlights some of the key points in the plan. Don't overload the sidebar, but one or two items per page can draw attention to highlights that maintain reader interest.
6. J. Timmons and S. Spinelli, *New Venture Creation*, 8th ed. (New York: McGraw-Hill/Irwin, 2008).
7. J. Makower, R. Pernick, and C. Wilder, *Clean Energy Trends 2008* (San Francisco: Clean Edge, 2008).

8. M. Marco, "Leaks: Best Buy's Internal Customer Profiling Document," The Consumerist, March 18, 2008, http://consumerist.com/368894/leaks-best-buys-internal-customer-profiling-document (accessed December 19, 2008).

9. B. J. Pine and J. H. Gilmore, *The Experience Economy: Work Is Theatre and Every Business a Stage* (Boston: Harvard Business School Press, 1999).

10. O. Sacirbey, "Private Companies Temper IPO Talk," *IPO Reporter*, December 18, 2000.

11. Burn rate is how much more cash the company is expending each month than earning in revenue.

For Further Reading

Bhide, A., "The Questions Every Entrepreneur Should Ask," *Harvard Business Review* (November/December 1996): 120–130.

Bygrave, W., and A. Zacharakis, *Entrepreneurship* (Hoboken, NJ: John Wiley & Sons, 2008).

Kim, C., and R. Mauborgne, *Blue Ocean Strategy: How to Create Uncontested Market Space and Make the Competition Irrelevant* (Boston: Harvard Business School Press, 2005).

Timmons, J., A. Zacharakis, and S. Spinelli, *Business Plans That Work* (New York: McGraw-Hill, 2004).

15

Financial Management of Risks

Steven P. Feinstein

For better or worse, the business environment is fraught with risks. Uncertainty is a fact of life. Profits are never certain, input and output prices change, competitors emerge and disappear, customers' tastes constantly evolve, technological progress creates instability, the economy may be volatile, and interest rates, foreign currency values, and asset prices fluctuate. Nonetheless, managers must continue to make decisions. Businesses must cope with risk in order to operate. Managers and firms are often evaluated on overall performance, even though performance may be affected by risky factors beyond their control. The goal of risk management is to maximize the value of the firm by reducing the negative potential impact of forces beyond the control of management.

There are essentially four basic approaches to risk management: risk avoidance, risk retention, loss prevention and control, and risk transfer.[1] Suppose after a firm has analyzed a risky business venture and weighed both the costs and benefits of exposure to risk, management chooses not to embark on the project. They determine that the potential rewards are not worth the risks. Such a strategy would be an example of risk avoidance. *Risk avoidance* means choosing not to engage in a risky activity because of the risks. Choosing not to fly in a commercial airliner because of the risk that the plane might crash is an example of risk avoidance.

Risk retention is another simple strategy, in which the firm chooses to engage in the project and do nothing about the identified risks. After weighing the costs and benefits, the firm chooses to proceed. It is the "damn the torpedoes" approach to risk management. For many firms, risk retention is the optimal strategy for all risks. Investors expect the company's stock to be risky, and they do not reward managers for reducing risks. Investors cope with business risks by diversifying their holdings within their portfolios, and so they do not want business managers to devote resources to managing risks within the firm.

Loss prevention and control involves embarking on a risky project, yet taking steps to reduce the likelihood and severity of any losses potentially resulting from uncontrollable factors. In the flying example, loss prevention and control would be the response of the airline passenger who chooses to fly, but also selects the safest airline, listens to the preflight safety instructions, sits near the emergency exit, and perhaps brings his or her own parachute. The passenger in this example has no control over how many airplanes crash in a given year, but he or she takes steps to make sure not to be on one of them, and if so, to be a survivor.

Risk transfer involves shifting the negative consequences of a risky factor to another person, firm, or party. For example, buying flight insurance shifts some of the negative financial consequences of a crash to an insurance company and away from the passenger's family. Should the airplane crash, the insurance company suffers a financial loss, and the passenger's family is financially compensated. Forcing foreign customers to pay for finished goods in your home currency rather than in their local currency is another example of risk transfer, whereby you transfer the risk of currency fluctuations to your foreign customers. If the value of the foreign currency drops, the customers must still pay you an agreed-upon number of dollars, for example, even though it costs them more to do so in terms of their home currency.

No one risk management approach is ideal for all situations. Sometimes risk avoidance is optimal; sometimes risk retention is the desired strategy. Recent developments in the financial marketplace, however, have made risk transfer much more feasible than in the past. More and more often now, especially when financial risks are involved, it is the most desirable alternative.

In recent years there has been revolutionary change in the financial marketplace. The very same marketplace that traditionally facilitated the transfer of funds from investors to firms has brought forth numerous derivative instruments that facilitate the transfer of risk. Just as the financial marketplace has been innovative in engineering various types of investment contracts, such as stocks, bonds, preferred stock, and convertible bonds, the financial marketplace now engineers risk transfer instruments, such as forwards, futures, options, swaps, and a multitude of variants of these derivatives.

Reading stories about derivatives in the popular press might lead one to believe that derivative instruments are dangerous and destabilizing—evil creatures that emerged from the dark recesses of the financial marketplace. *Time* magazine once introduced a cover story about derivatives with a caption "High-tech supernerds are playing dangerous games with your money."[2] The use of derivatives has been implicated in many of the financial calamities over the past two decades: the bankruptcy of Lehman Brothers, the demise of Bear Stearns, the collapse of Barings Bank, and devastating losses suffered by Procter & Gamble, Metallgesellschaft, Askin Capital Management, Orange County (California), Union Bank of Switzerland, and Long-Term Capital Management. In each of the cases, vast sums of money quickly vanished, and derivatives seemed to be to blame.

What Went Wrong: Case Studies of Derivatives Debacles

Derivatives were not solely responsible for the financial calamities of the 1990s and 2000s. Greed, speculation, and probably incompetence were. But just as derivatives facilitate risk management, they facilitate greed and accelerate the consequences of speculation and incompetence. For example, consider the following case histories and then draw your own conclusions.

Barings Bank

On February 26, 1995, Baring PLC, Britain's oldest merchant bank and one of the most venerable financial institutions in the world, collapsed. Did this failure follow years of poor management and bad investments? Hardly. All of the bank's $615 million of capital had been wiped out in less than four months by one employee halfway around the world from London. It seems that a Barings derivatives trader named Nicholas Leeson, stationed in Singapore, had taken huge positions in futures and options on Japanese stocks. Leeson's job was supposed to be index arbitrage, meaning that he was supposed to take low-risk positions exploiting discrepancies between the prices of futures contracts traded in both Singapore and Osaka. Leeson's job was to buy whichever contract was cheaper and sell the one that was more dear. The difference would be profit for Barings. When he was long in Japanese stock futures in Osaka, he was supposed to be short in Japanese stock futures in Singapore, and vice versa. Such positions are inherently hedged. If the Singapore futures lost money, the Japanese futures would make money, so little money, if any, could be lost.

Apparently, Leeson grew impatient taking hedged positions. He began to take unhedged bets, selling both call options and put options on Japanese stocks. Such a strategy, consisting of writing call options and writing put options, is called a straddle. If the underlying stock price stays the same or does not move much, the writer keeps all the option premium and profits handsomely. If, in contrast, the underlying stock price either rises or falls substantially, the writer is vulnerable to large losses. Leeson bet and lost. Japanese stocks plummeted, and the straddles became a huge liability. Like a panicked gambler, Leeson tried to win back his losses by going long in Japanese stock futures. This position was a stark naked speculative bet. Leeson lost again. Japanese stocks continued to fall. Leeson lost more than $1 billion, and Barings had lost all of its capital. The bank was put into receivership.

Procter & Gamble

Procter & Gamble, the well-known manufacturer of soap and household products, had a long history of negotiating low interest rates to finance operations. Toward this end, Procter & Gamble entered an interest rate swap with Bankers Trust in November 1993. The swap agreement was far from plain-vanilla. It most certainly fit the description of an exotic derivative. The swap's cash flows were determined by a formula that involved short-term, medium-term, and long-term interest rates. Essentially, the deal would allow Procter & Gamble to reduce its financing rate by 0.4% on $200 million of debt if interest rates remained stable until May 1994. If, however, interest rates spiked upward, or if the spread between 5-year and 30-year rates narrowed, Procter & Gamble would lose money and have to pay a higher rate on its debt.

Even in the rarefied world of derivatives, one cannot expect something for nothing. In order to achieve a cheaper financing rate, Procter & Gamble had to give up or sell something. In this case, implicit in the swap, the company sold interest rate insurance. The swap contained an embedded option, sold by Procter & Gamble. If the interest rate environment remained calm, Procter & Gamble would keep a modest premium, thereby lowering its financing costs. If interest rates became turbulent, Procter & Gamble would have to make big payments. Most economists in 1993 were forecasting calm, so the bet seemed safe. But it was a bet, nevertheless. This was not a hedge; this was speculation. And Procter & Gamble lost.

The Federal Reserve unexpectedly raised interest rates on February 4, 1994. Procter & Gamble suddenly found itself with a $100 million loss. Rather than lower its financing rate by 0.4%, it would have to pay an additional 14%!

Instead of licking its wounds and retiring from swaps, Procter & Gamble went back for more—with prodding, of course, from Bankers Trust. As losses mounted on the first deal, Procter & Gamble entered a second swap, this one tied to German interest rates. German medium-term interest rates are remarkably stable, so this bet seemed even safer than the first one. Guess what happened. Another $50 million of losses mounted before

Procter & Gamble finally liquidated its positions. Losses totaled $157 million. Procter & Gamble sued Bankers Trust, alleging deception, mispricing, and violation of fiduciary responsibilities. Procter & Gamble claimed that it did not fully understand the risks of the swap agreements, nor how to calculate their value. Bankers Trust settled with Procter & Gamble, just as it settled with Gibson Greeting Cards, Air Products and Chemicals, and other companies that lost money in similar swaps.

Metallgesellschaft

Experts are still divided over what went wrong in the case of Metallgesellschaft, one of Germany's largest industrial concerns. This much is certain: In 1993, Metallgesellschaft had assets of $10 billion, sales exceeding $16 billion, and equity capital of $50 million. By the end of the year, this industrial giant was nearly bankrupt, having lost $1.3 billion in oil futures.

What makes the Metallgesellschaft case so intriguing is that the company seemed to be using derivatives for all the right reasons. An American subsidiary of Metallgesellschaft, MG Refining and Marketing (MGRM), had embarked on an ingenious marketing plan. The subsidiary was in the business of selling gasoline and heating oil to distributors and retailers. To promote sales, the company offered contracts that would lock in prices for a period of 10 years. A variety of different contract types was offered, and the contracts had various provisions, deferments, and contingencies built in, but the important feature was a long-term price cap. The contracts were essentially forwards. The forward contracts were very popular, and MGRM was quite successful at selling them.

MGRM understood that the forward contracts subjected the company to oil price risk. MGRM now had a short position in oil. If oil prices rose, the company would experience losses, as it would have to buy oil at higher prices and sell it at the lower contracted prices to the customers. To offset this risk, MGRM went long in exchange-traded oil futures. The long position in futures should have hedged the short position in forwards. Unfortunately, things did not work out so nicely.

Oil prices fell in 1993. As oil prices fell, Metallgesellschaft lost money on its long futures, and had to make cash payments as the futures were marked to market. The forwards, however, provided little immediate cash, and their appreciation in value would not be fully realized until they matured in 10 years. Thus, Metallgesellschaft was caught in a cash crunch. Some economists argue that if Metallgesellschaft had held on to its positions and continued to make margin payments the strategy would have worked eventually. But time ran out. The parent company took control over the subsidiary and liquidated its positions, thereby realizing a loss of $1.3 billion.

Other economists argue that Metallgesellschaft was not an innocent victim of unforeseeable circumstances. They argue that MGRM had designed the entire marketing and hedging strategy just so it could profit by speculating that historical patterns in oil prices would persist. Traditionally, oil futures prices are lower than spot prices, so the general trend in oil futures prices is upward as the contracts near expiration. MGRM's hedging plan was to repeatedly buy short-term oil futures, holding them until just before expiration, at which point they would roll over into new short-term futures. If the historical pattern had repeated itself, MGRM would have profited many times from the rollover strategy. It has been alleged that the futures was the planned source of profits, while the forward contracts with customers was the hedge against oil prices dropping.

Regardless of MGRM management's intent, the case teaches at least two lessons. First, it is important to consider cash flow and timing when constructing a hedge position. Second, when a hedge is working effectively, it will appear to be losing money when the position it is designed to offset is showing profits. Accounting for hedges should not be independent of the position being hedged.

Askin Capital Management

Between February and April 1994, David Askin lost all $600 million that he managed on behalf of the investors in his Granite Hedge Funds. Imagine the surprise of the investors. Not only had they earned over 22% the previous year, but the fund was invested in mortgage-backed securities—instruments guaranteed by the U.S. government not to default. The lesson from the Askin experience is that in the age of derivatives, investments with innocuous names might not be as safe and secure as they sound.

The particular type of mortgage-backed securities that Askin purchased were collateralized mortgage obligations (CMOs), which are bonds whose cash flows to investors are determined by a formula. The formula is a function of mortgage interest rates and also of the prepayment behavior of home buyers. Since the cash flow to CMOs is a function of some other economic variable, interest rates in this case, these instruments are categorized as derivatives. Some CMOs rise in value as interest rates rise, whereas others fall. Askin's CMOs were very sensitive to interest rates. His portfolio rose in value as interest rates fell in 1993. When interest rates began to rise again in February 1994, his portfolio suffered. Interest rate increases alone, however, were not the sole cause of Askin's losses. As interest rates rose and CMO prices fell, CMO investors everywhere got scared and sold. CMO prices were doubly battered as the demand dried up. It was a classic panic. Prices fell far more than the theoretical pricing models predicted. Eventually, calm returned to the market, investors trickled back, and prices rebounded. But it was too late for Askin. He had bought on margin, and his creditors had liquidated his fund at the market's bottom.

Orange County, California

Robert Citron, treasurer of Orange County, California, in 1994, fell into the same trap that snared Procter & Gamble and David Askin. He speculated that interest rates would remain low. The best economic forecasts at the time supported this outlook. Derivatives allowed speculators to bet on the most likely scenario. Small bets provided modest returns, and big bets promised sizable returns. What these speculators did was akin to selling earthquake insurance in New York City. The likelihood of an earthquake there is very small, so insurers would almost certainly get to keep the modest premiums without having to pay out any claims. If an earthquake did hit New York, however, the losses to the insurers would be enormous.

Citron bet and lost. The earthquake that toppled his portfolio was the series of unexpected interest rate hikes beginning in February 1994. Citron had borrowed against the bonds Orange County owned, and he invested the proceeds in derivative bonds called inverse floaters, whose cash flow formulas made them extra sensitive to interest rate increases. Citron lost about $2 billion of the $7.7 billion he managed, and Orange County filed for bankruptcy in December 1994.

Union Bank of Switzerland

What happened at Union Bank of Switzerland (UBS) in 1997 would be funny if it weren't so sad. Imagine a bakery that sells cakes and cookies for less than the cost of the ingredients. Business would no doubt be brisk, but eventually the bakers would discover that they were not turning a profit. This is essentially what happened to UBS. UBS manufactured and sold derivatives to corporate customers. Unfortunately, there was an error in its pricing model, and the bank was selling the derivatives for too low a price. By the time it found the mistake, it had managed to lose over $200 million. Swiss banking officials concluded that losses sustained by the Global Equity Derivatives Business arm of UBS amounted to 625 million Swiss francs (about $428 million), but these losses stemmed not only from the pricing model error, but also from unlucky trading, an unexpected change in British tax laws, and market volatility. Some speculate that these losses forced the merger of UBS with Swiss Bank Corporation, a merger that was arranged exactly when the derivatives losses were discovered.

Long-Term Capital Management

The most surprising of the derivatives debacles is the saga of Long-Term Capital Management (LTCM). LTCM was a company founded by John Meriwether, and joined by Myron Scholes and Robert Merton. Meriwether had a reputation for being one of the savviest traders on Wall Street. Scholes and Merton are Nobel Prize laureates, famous for inventing the Black-Scholes option pricing model.[3] Unlike the folks at Procter & Gamble, these individuals cannot plead ignorance. They were without a doubt among the smartest players in the financial marketplace. Paradoxically, it may have been their intellectual superiority that did them in. Their overconfidence engendered a false sense of security that seduced investors, lenders, and the portfolio managers themselves into taking enormous positions. The story of LTCM is a classic Greek tragedy set on modern Wall Street.

LTCM was organized as a hedge fund. A hedge fund is a limited partnership that, in exchange for limiting the number and type of investors who can buy in, is not required to register with the Securities and Exchange Commission, and is not bound by the same regulations and reporting standards imposed on traditional mutual funds. Investors must be rich. A hedge fund can accept investments from no more than 500 investors who each have net worth of at least $5 million, or no more than 99 investors if they each have net worth of at least $1 million. A hedge fund is essentially a private investment club, unfettered by the rules designed to protect the general public.

Ironically, hedge funds are generally unhedged. Most hedge funds speculate, aiming to capture profits by taking risks. LTCM was a little different, and for it the moniker "hedge fund" appeared to fit. Capitalizing on its brainpower, LTCM sought to exploit market inefficiencies. That is, with an understanding of what the prices of various financial instruments *should* be, LTCM would identify instruments that were priced too high or too low. Once such an opportunity was identified, the fund managers would buy or sell accordingly, hedging long positions with matching shorts. As the prices in the financial marketplace tended toward the fair equilibrium dictated by the financial models, the prices of the assets held long would rise, and the prices of the instruments sold short would fall, thereby delivering to LTCM a handsome profit. LTCM's deals were generally not naked speculation, but hedged exploitation of arbitrage opportunities. With price risk thought to be hedged out, LTCM and its investors felt comfortable borrowing heavily to lever up the impact of the trades on profits. The creditors, banks, and brokerages mostly happily obliged.

LTCM opened its doors in 1994 with an initial equity investment of $150 million from the founding partners and an investment pool of $1.25 billion in client accounts. Success was immediate and pronounced. The hedge fund thrived in the tumultuous market of the mid-1990s. Apparently, as some of the institutions described earlier lost fortunes during this period, it was LTCM that managed to be on the receiving end. The fund booked a 28% return in 1994, a whopping 59% in 1995, followed by another 57% return in 1996. Word of this success spread, and new investors were clamoring to get into LTCM.[4]

LTCM could be picky when it came to choosing investors. This was not a fund for your typical dentist or millionaire next door. Former students of mine who have gone on to jobs at some of the world's largest banks and investment companies have confided to me that their firms subcontracted sizable portions of their portfolios to LTCM. By the end of 1995, bolstered by reinvested profits and by newly invested funds, LTCM managed $3.6 billion of invested funds. However, the portfolio was levered 28 to 1. For every $1 a client invested, the fund was able to borrow $28 from banks and brokerage houses. Consequently, LTCM managed positions worth over $100 billion. Moreover, because of the natural leverage inherent in the derivatives they bought, these positions were comparable to investments of a much larger magnitude, estimated to be in the $650 billion range.

By 1997, however, when the fund's capital base peaked at $7 billion, managers realized that profitable arbitrage opportunities were growing scarce. The easy pickings of the early days were over. The partners began to intentionally shrink the fund by returning money to investors, essentially forcing them out. Performance was sound in 1997, a 25% return, but with the payout of capital, the fund's capital base fell to $4.7 billion.

Things unraveled disastrously in 1998. Each of LTCM's major investment strategies failed. Based on sophisticated models and historical data, LTCM gambled that (1) stock market volatility would stay the same or fall, (2) swap spreads—a variable used to determine who pays whom how much in interest rate swaps—would narrow, (3) the spread of the interest rate on medium-term bonds over long-term bonds would flatten out, (4) the credit spread—the interest rate differential between risky bonds and high-grade bonds—would narrow, and (5) calm would return to the financial markets of Russia and other emerging markets. However, in each case the opposite happened. Equity volatility increased. Swap spreads widened. The yield curve retained its hump. Credit spreads grew. Emerging markets deteriorated.

Though LTCM had spread its bets over a wide variety of positions, the hedge fund seemed to gain no diversification benefit. Everything went wrong at once. Recent research has shown that diversification does not protect speculative positions when markets behave erratically. Markets tend to go awry in tandem.

In August 1998 alone, the fund suffered losses of $1.9 billion. Losses for the year so far were 52%. Fund managers were confident that their strategies were sound and that time would both prove them right and reward their prescience. But time is not a friend to a levered fund losing money. Banks and brokerages itched for their loans back. How ironic it was that Long-Term Capital Management faced a short-term liquidity crunch.

Leverage amplified LTCM's remaining $2.28 billion of equity into managed assets of $125 billion. If the market continued to move against its positions, LTCM would be wiped out in short order, and that is essentially what happened. On September 10, LTCM lost $145 million. The next day, it lost $120 million. The following three trading days brought losses of $55 million, $87 million, and $122 million, respectively. On one day alone, Monday, September 21, 1998, LTCM lost $553 million. By now traders at other firms could guess what LTCM's positions were, and by anticipating what LTCM would eventually have to sell, they could gauge which securities were good bets to short. This selling pressure added to LTCM's losses and woes.

At this point, in September 1998, any of several banks could bankrupt LTCM by calling in its loans. The Federal Reserve, which is the central bank of the United States and is responsible for guaranteeing the stability of the American banking system, monitored the predicament. Though LTCM's equity was shrinking precipitously, on account of its borrowed funds and the inherent leverage of its derivatives positions, the notional principal of its positions was about $1.4 trillion. To put this quantity into perspective, the gross national product of the United States was about $8.8 trillion in 1998. Total bank assets in the United States stood at $4.3 trillion. It was feared that if LTCM went bankrupt, it would probably default on its derivatives positions, triggering a domino effect of defaults and bankruptcies throughout the world's financial markets. It was decided that LTCM was too big too fail.

The Federal Reserve orchestrated a plan for LTCM's creditors to buy the hedge fund's portfolio. Each of 14 banks ponied up money in exchange for a slice of the portfolio. The $3.65 billion paid by the bank syndicate for the portfolio was clearly greater than the value of the portfolio by then, but this infusion of capital prevented defaults that would have cost the banks much more. The money was used to pay off debts and shore up the trading accounts so that existing positions would perform without default. Very little was left over for the original partners, who were required to run the fund until it was ultimately liquidated in 1999. The bottom line is that LTCM had lost $4.5 billion since the start of 1998. These losses included the personal fortunes amassed so quickly by the founding partners, which totaled $1.9 billion at one point but were completely wiped out by the end.

The Casualties of Credit Default Swaps

Many factors contributed to the financial market meltdown of 2008 and 2009, and further research is required to arrive at a full understanding of all the causes. However, the early analysis points to derivative instruments known as credit default swaps as being partly responsible. Credit default swaps are essentially private insurance contracts linked to the credit status of a third party's outstanding debt. For example, a bank and an investor may enter into a credit default swap tied to the credit performance of XYZ, Inc.'s corporate bonds. If XYZ defaults on the bonds, under the terms of the credit default swap the bank would have to pay some specified amount of money to the investor. In this case, the bank is acting like an insurance company, and the investor is buying insurance on XYZ's bonds.

Financial engineers designed a wide variety of credit derivatives to accommodate the particular needs of various investors, issuers, and speculators. For example, some credit derivative structures were designed to pay off when the credit rating of the underlying bond is downgraded even if no default occurs.

Many credit default swaps were linked to mortgage bonds, which are bonds backed by pools of mortgages rather than issued against the cash flows earned by corporations. Credit default swaps were used to enhance the credit ratings of bonds issued against risky mortgage pools—that is, pools of subprime mortgages. In theory, a pool of low-rated mortgages coupled with the insurance of a credit default swap should be just as safe as a pool of high-rated mortgages. If the subprime mortgage bond defaults, the payment from the credit default swap would make up the loss.

An investor who wished to invest in a pool of subprime mortgages but did not want to bear the default risk inherent in subprime mortgages would seek to enter a credit default swap as an insurance guarantee. Financial institutions were willing to offer the insurance in exchange for the premiums they expected to receive.

What went wrong in recent years in the markets for subprime mortgages and credit default swaps is still a matter of some debate. Apparently, while credit default swaps were used to shift risk around, the aggregate level of risk in the mortgage market was not well understood. Derivatives can spread risk around, but they cannot eliminate it. Also, while some institutions apparently gauged the risk embedded in subprime mortgages assuming normal real estate market conditions, they failed to consider what would happen if the entire real estate sector declined severely. The earthquake insurance example described earlier is again apt. A property insurance company can probably handle losses from a fire that damages one or several insured homes, but would have difficulty satisfying its obligations if a natural disaster devastated an entire city. Similarly, the parties bearing subprime mortgage risk could probably have handled sporadic mortgage defaults, but a downturn in real estate values nationwide, as did happen starting in mid-2006, was another matter altogether.

So, how did credit default swaps impact the venerable investment banks Lehman Brothers and Bear Stearns? Were credit default swaps responsible for the Lehman bankruptcy and the Bear Stearns collapse? These questions are still being investigated and litigated, and the verdict is not yet in. However, it seems that the crises at Lehman and Bear Stearns were precipitated by their *investments* in subprime mortgages, not their insurance of those mortgages via credit default swaps. Both Lehman and Bear Stearns were major players in the business of selling bonds backed by subprime mortgages. Those banks held on to the risky mortgage bonds they could not sell, so they were not only issuers of risky mortgage bonds, but also heavy investors. When the real estate and mortgage bond markets crashed, the value of their investments declined, wiping out the banks' equity. One might argue on the one hand that the banks suffered from not engaging enough in credit default swaps. They needed protection for their risky investments. On the other hand, the advent of credit default swaps helped make the subprime mortgage bond market possible, fed the speculative frenzy during which the market grew dangerously big, and brought down the banks when the speculative bubble popped.

When Bear Stearns was in trouble, the federal government feared that credit default swaps would create a domino effect, as credit derivatives now linked the fortunes of financial institutions throughout the system. Because of credit default swaps, a default at one bank would create financial obligations at other banks. One bank failure could precipitate many. Acting on this concern, the federal government orchestrated a rescue of Bear Stearns. Surprisingly, however, Lehman Brothers, which found itself in a similar situation as Bear Stearns, was allowed to fail.

Because the credit default swap market is largely unregulated, no one knows for sure how much money was transferred to settle the credit default swaps linked to Lehman Brothers' bonds. Some estimate the amount at $6 billion, whereas others estimate over

$100 billion. Similarly, there is not enough transparency in the system to determine to what extent losses from the Lehman failure, spread via credit default swaps, contributed to the subsequent collapses of numerous other investment banks, commercial banks, and investment funds in 2008 and 2009.

Moral of the Story

The lesson from these case studies should now be obvious. Risk management is not the art of picking good bets. Bets, no matter how good, are speculation. Speculation increases risk and subjects corporations, investors, and even municipalities to potential losses. Derivatives are powerful tools to shed risk, but they can also be used to take on risk. The root causes of the debacles described in these cases are greed, speculation, and in some cases incompetence, not derivatives. But just as derivatives facilitate risk management, they facilitate greed and speculation. Anything that can be done with derivatives can be done more slowly the old-fashioned way with positions in traditional financial instruments. Speculators have always managed to lose large sums. With the aid of derivatives they now can lose larger sums faster.

Superior intellect and sophistication cannot protect the speculator. As the Long-Term Capital Management story illustrates, when you are smarter than the market, you can go broke waiting for the market to wise up.

Government regulation is not the answer, either. The benefits of regulation must be weighed against the costs. Derivatives, properly used, are too important in the modern financial marketplace to be severely restricted. Abuse by a few does not warrant constraints on all users. A better solution to prevent repetition of the past debacles is full information disclosure by firms, portfolio managers, and municipalities. Investors and citizens should demand to know how derivatives are being used when their money is at stake. Better information and oversight provide the most promising approach to prevent misuse of derivatives while retaining the benefits.

Derivatives can be dangerous, but they can also be tremendously useful. Dynamite is an appropriate analogy. Misused, it is destructive; handled with care, it is a powerful and constructive tool.

Derivatives are tools that facilitate the transfer of risk. Interest rate derivatives enable managers to shed business exposure to interest rate fluctuations, for example. But when one party sheds risk, another party necessarily must take on that very exposure. And therein lies the danger of derivatives. The same instrument that serves as a hedge to one firm might be a destabilizing speculative instrument to another. Without a proper understanding of derivatives, a manager who intends to reduce risk might inadvertently increase it. This chapter aims to provide the reader with a basic understanding of derivatives so that they can be used appropriately to manage financial risks. This understanding should help the reader avoid the common pitfalls that have proved disastrous to less informed managers.

Size of the Derivatives Market and Widespread Use

A derivative is a financial instrument whose value or contingent cash flows depend on the value of some other underlying asset. For example, the value of a stock option depends on the value of the underlying stock. Derivatives as a class comprise forwards, futures, options, and swaps. Numerous hybrid instruments combining the features of these basic building blocks have also been engineered. The first thing the interested manager must understand about derivatives is that the business in these instruments is now huge and their use is pervasive. Since the initiation of trading in the first stock index futures contract in December 1982—the Standard & Poor's 500 futures contract—the daily volume of stock index futures has grown so that it now rivals the daily volume in all trading on the New York Stock Exchange. (Volume of futures is measured in terms of *notional principal*, which is a measure of exposure.)

Similarly, the swaps market has revolutionized banking and finance. The notional principal of outstanding swaps today is greater than the sum total of all assets in banks worldwide. The Bank for International Settlements reports that the sum total of all assets in banks around the world was approximately $39 trillion in June 2008. At that same time, according to the same source, the notional principal of outstanding swaps was over $680 trillion. Measured this way, the swaps business is now far bigger than traditional banking.

The volume of the derivatives market reflects how widespread derivatives use has become in business. Almost all major corporations now use them in one form or another. Some use derivatives to hedge commodity price risks. Some use them to speculate on price movements. Some firms reduce their exposures to volatile interest rates and foreign exchange. Other firms take on exposures via derivatives in order to potentially increase profits. Some firms use derivatives to secure cheaper financing. Many corporations use derivatives to reduce the transaction costs associated with managing a pension fund, borrowing money, or budgeting cash. Some firms implement derivatives strategies to reduce their tax burdens. Many companies offer stock options, a derivative, as employee compensation. Some investment funds enhance returns by replacing traditional portfolios with what are called synthetic portfolios—portfolios composed in part of derivatives. Some investment funds buy derivatives that act as insurance contracts, protecting portfolio value. Since their emergence in the early 1980s, derivatives have touched every aspect of corporate finance, banking, the investments industry, and, arguably, business in general.

The Instruments

The major derivative instruments are forwards, futures, options, and swaps. Also available today are hybrid instruments, exotics, and structured or engineered instruments. The hybrids, exotics, and engineered instruments are contracts that combine features of the basic building blocks: the options, futures, forwards, and swaps. Consequently, familiarity with the basic building blocks goes a long way toward understanding the whole mélange of derivative instruments available today. We begin with forwards.

Forwards

Imagine the following nearly idyllic scenario. It is late summer. You are a wheat farmer in Kansas. The hard work of sowing and tending your acreage is about to pay off. You expect a bumper crop this year, and the harvest is just a few weeks away. The weather is expected to remain favorable. The crops have been sprayed to protect them from pests. In fact, you may even have purchased crop insurance to protect against crop damage.

Still, you cannot relax. One major uncertainty is keeping you awake at night. You figure that if you are expecting a bumper crop, the likelihood that your neighbors are also expecting a bumper crop is high. If the market is flooded with wheat, prices will plummet. If prices drop, you will receive little revenue for your harvest, and perhaps you will show a loss for the year. A worst-case scenario might be that prices fall so low that you cannot make the mortgage payments on your land or loan payments for the machinery you bought. You very well might lose the farm—and through no fault of your own. You farmed well, but if prices fall, you will fail nevertheless.

Meanwhile, at the same time, another group of businesspeople is feeling similar anxiety. A baked goods company has recently built a new cookie bakery. The company identified its market niche as a provider of inexpensive, mass-produced, medium-quality cookies. The project analysis that led to the go-ahead for the new bakery assumed that wheat prices would stay fixed at their current levels. If wheat prices should rise, it is altogether possible that the firm will not be able to sell its cookies for a profit. The new bakery will appear to be a failure.

In these scenarios, both the farmer and the bakers are exposed to wheat price risk. The farmer worries that wheat prices will fall. The bakers worry that prices will rise. A forward contract is the obvious solution for both parties.

The farmer and the bakers can negotiate a deferred wheat transaction. The farmer will deliver wheat to the bakers one month from now for a price currently agreed upon. Such a contract for a deferred transaction is a forward contract. A forward contract specifies an underlying asset to be delivered, a price to be paid, and the date of delivery. The specified transaction price is called the forward price. The party that will be selling wheat (farmer) is known as the short party; the party that will be buying wheat (bakers) is known as the long party. In the jargon of the derivatives market, the long party is said to buy the forward, and the short party sells the forward. Note, however, that when the deal is initially struck, no money changes hands and no one has yet bought or sold anything. The buyer and seller have agreed to a deferred transaction.

Notice that the wheat forward reduces risk for both the farmer and the bakers. In this transaction, both parties are hedgers; that is, they are using the forward to reduce risk. Forward contracts are over-the-counter instruments, meaning that they are negotiated between two parties and custom-tailored, rather than traded on exchanges.

Suppose after one month, when the forward expires and the wheat is delivered, the current, or spot, price of wheat has risen dramatically. The farmer, on the one hand, may have some regret that he entered into the contract. Had he not sold the forward, he would have been able to receive more for his wheat by selling on the spot market. He may feel like a loser. The bakers, on the other hand, will feel like winners. By contracting forward they insulated themselves from the rising wheat price. When spot prices rise, the long party wins while the short party loses. A little reflection, however, will convince the farmer that although he lost some money relative to what he could have gotten on the spot market, going short in the forward was indeed a worthwhile strategy. He had peace of mind over the one month. He was guaranteed a fair price, and he did not have to fear losing the farm. Though there was an opportunity loss, he benefited by shedding risk. The farmer probably never regrets that he has not collected on his life insurance, either. He similarly should not regret that the forward contract represents an opportunity loss. He would be well advised to go short again next year.

The wheat forward contract can be used by speculators as well as hedgers. An agent who anticipates a rise in wheat prices can profit from that foresight by going long in the forward contract. By going long in the contract, the speculator agrees to buy wheat at the fixed forward price. Upon expiration of the contract, the speculator takes delivery of the wheat, pays the forward price, and then sells the wheat on the spot market for the higher spot price. The profit is the difference between the spot and forward prices. Of course, if the speculator's forecast is wrong, and the wheat price falls, the speculator would suffer losses equal to the difference between the forward price and the spot price. For example, suppose the initial spot price is $3 per bushel, and the forward price is $3.50 per bushel. If the spot price upon expiration is $4.50 per bushel, the long speculator would earn a profit of $1 per bushel. The profit is the terminal spot of $4.50 minus the $3.50 initial forward price. If, alternatively, the terminal spot price is $3.25, the speculator would *lose* 25 cents per bushel—that is, $3.25 minus $3.50. Notice that the $3 initial spot price is irrelevant in both cases.

Speculators play important roles in the derivatives markets. First, speculators provide liquidity. If farmers wish to short forward contracts but there are no bakers around who want to go long, speculators will step in and offer to take the long side when the forward price is bid down low enough. Similarly, they will take the short side when the forward price is bid up high enough. Speculators also bring information to the marketplace. The existence of derivatives contracts and the promise of speculative profits make it worthwhile for speculators to devote resources to forecasting weather conditions, crop yields, and other factors that impact prices. Their forecasts are made known to the public as they buy or sell futures and forwards.

Futures

Futures contracts are closely related to forward contracts. Like forwards, futures are contracts that spell out deferred transactions. The long party commits to buying some underlying asset, and the short party commits to sell. The differences between futures and forwards are mainly technical and logistical. Forward contracts are custom-tailored, over-the-counter agreements, struck between two parties via negotiation. Futures, alternatively, are standardized contracts that are traded on exchanges between parties who probably do not know each other. The exact quantity, quality, and delivery location can be negotiated in a forward contract, but in a futures contract the terms are dictated by the exchange. Because of their standardization and how they are traded, futures are very liquid, and their associated transaction costs are very low.

Another feature differentiating futures from forwards is the process of marking to market. All day and every day, futures traders meet in trading pits at the exchanges and cry out orders to buy and sell futures on behalf of clients. The forces of supply and demand determine whether futures prices rise or fall. Marking to market is the process by which at the end of each day losers pay winners an amount equal to the movement of the futures price that day. For example, if the wheat futures price at Monday's close is $4.00 per bushel and the price rises to $4.10 by the close on Tuesday, the short party must pay the long party 10 cents per bushel after trading ends on Tuesday. If the price has fallen 10 cents, then long would pay short 10 cents per bushel. Both long and short parties have trading accounts at the exchange clearinghouse, and the transfer of funds is automatic. The purpose of marking to market is to reduce the chance of default by a party who has lost substantially on a futures position. When futures are marked to market, the greatest possible loss due to a default would be an amount equal to one day's price movement.

As mentioned, futures are marked to market every day. When the contract expires, the last marking to market is based on the spot price. For example, suppose two days prior to expiration the futures price is $4.10 per bushel. On the second to last day the futures price has risen to $4.30. Short pays long 20 cents per bushel. Suppose at the end of the next day, the last day of trading, the spot price is recorded at $4.55. The last mark-to-market payment is from short to long for 25 cents per bushel, equal to the difference between the spot price upon expiration and the previous day's futures price.

Upon expiration, the futures contract might stipulate that the short party now deliver to the long party the specified quantity of wheat. The long party must now pay the short party the *spot price* for this wheat. Yes, the spot price, not the original futures price! The difference between the terminal spot price and the original futures price has already been paid via marking to market. A numerical example will make the mechanics of futures clearer and show how similar futures are to forwards.

Suppose with five days remaining until expiration, the wheat futures price is $4.00 per bushel. A baker buys a futures contract in order to lock in a purchase price of $4.00. Suppose the futures prices on the next four days are $4.10, $3.90, $4.00, and $4.25. The spot price on the fifth day, the expiration day, is $4.30. Given those price movements, short pays the long baker 10 cents the first day. The long baker pays short 20 cents on the second day. On the third day, short pays long 10 cents, followed by a payment from short to long of 25 cents on the fourth day, and a payment from short to long of 5 cents on the last day. On net, over those five days, short has paid long 30 cents. When long now pays the spot price of $4.30 to short for delivery of the wheat, long indeed is paying $4.00 per bushel, net of the 30 cents profit on the futures contract. Recall that $4.00 was the original futures price. Thus, the futures contract did effectively lock in a fixed purchase price for the wheat.

A contract that stipulates a spot transaction in which the underlying commodity is actually delivered at expiration is called a "physical delivery" contract. Many futures contracts do not stipulate such a final spot transaction with actual delivery of the underlying asset. After the last marking to market, the game is over—no assets are delivered. Contracts that stipulate no terminal spot transaction are called "cash settled." It should make little difference to traders whether a contract is cash settled or physical delivery. A cash settled contract can be turned into a physical delivery deal simply by choosing to make a spot transaction at the end. Likewise, a physical delivery contract can be turned into a cash settled deal either by making an offsetting spot transaction at the end or by exiting the futures contract just before it expires.

Examples of the Use of Forwards and Futures in Risk Management

A wide variety of underlying assets is covered by futures and forwards contracts these days. For example, exchange-traded futures contracts are available on stocks, bonds, interest rates, foreign currencies, oil, gasoline, grains, livestock, metals, cocoa, coffee, sugar, and even orange juice. Consequently, these instruments are versatile risk management tools in a wide variety of situations. The most actively traded futures, however, are those that cover financial risks. Consider the following examples.

A Foreign Currency Hedge

Suppose an American electronics manufacturer has just delivered a large shipment of finished products to a customer in France. The French buyer has agreed to pay 1 million euros in exactly 30 days. The manufacturer is worried that the euro may be devalued relative to the American dollar during that interval. If the euro is devalued, the dollar value of the promised payment will fall and the American manufacturer will suffer losses. The American manufacturer can shed this foreign currency exposure by going short in a euro forward contract or a euro future. The contract will specify a quantity of euros to be exchanged for dollars at a fixed exchange rate 30 days in the future. The contract locks in the terms at which the deferred euro revenue can be converted to dollars. No matter what happens to the euro-dollar exchange rate, the American manufacturer now knows exactly how many dollars it will receive.

A Short-Term Interest Rate Hedge

Suppose a manufacturer of automotive parts has just delivered a shipment of finished products to a client. Business has been growing, and the company has approved plans to expand capacity next year. The manufacturer expects to receive payment from the customer in 60 days, but will need to use those funds for the planned capital expenditure 90 days after that. The plan is to invest the revenue in three-month Treasury bills as soon as the revenue is received. Interest rates are currently high. Managers worry that by the time the receivables are collected from the customer, however, interest rates will fall, resulting in less interest earned on the invested funds. The company can hedge against this risk by buying a Treasury bill futures contract that essentially locks in the price and yield of Treasury bills to be purchased 60 days hence.

Longer-Term Interest Rate Hedge

A manufacturer of speed boats notices that when interest rates rise, sales fall, and the value of the firm's stock gets battered. The correlation is easy to understand. Customers buy boats on credit, and so when rates rise, the boats effectively become more expensive to buy. In order to insulate the company's fortunes from the vicissitudes of interest rates, the company could enter a contract that pays money when rates rise. A short position in a Treasury bond futures contract would pay off when rates rise and could thus be a desirable hedge. Each time the futures contract expires, the company can roll over into a new contract. The size of the position in the futures should be geared to the fluctuation in sales resulting from changes in interest rates. The Treasury bond hedge can reduce the volatility in the firm's net income, as well as the volatility of the firm's equity value.

Synthetic Cash

A company's pension fund is invested primarily in the stocks of the Standard & Poor's 500 index. The pension fund manager worries that there may be a downturn in the stock market sometime over the next six months. She considers selling all of the stock and investing the funds in Treasury bills. An alternative hedge strategy that will save considerable transaction costs would be to short S&P 500 futures contracts. By establishing a short futures position, she locks in the price at which the stocks will be sold six months hence. The fund is now insulated from any fluctuations in stock prices. Since the fund is now essentially risk free, it will earn the risk-free interest rate. Selling futures while holding the underlying spot instrument is a strategy known as "synthetic cash." The strategy essentially turns stock into cash. The fund performs as if it were invested in Treasury bills.

Synthetic Stock

A company's pension fund is invested primarily in Treasury bills. The stock market has been rising rapidly in recent weeks, and the pension fund manager wishes to participate in the boom. One strategy would be to sell the T-bills and invest the proceeds in equities. A more economical strategy would be to leave the value parked in T-bills, and gain exposure to the stock market by going long in stock futures. When the market rises, the futures will pay off. Should the market fall, the fund will suffer losses. The fund will thus behave as if it were invested in stocks. Ergo the name "synthetic stock."

Market Timing

A manager wishes to be exposed to the stock market when he anticipates a market rise, and be out of stocks and into T-bills when he anticipates a drop. Buying and selling stocks to achieve this purpose is very expensive in terms of commissions, but entering and exiting the market via futures is very cheap. The manager should keep all his funds invested in T-bills. When he feels the market will rise, he should go long in stock index futures, such as S&P 500 futures. When he feels the market will drop, he should sell those futures, unwinding the position. If, alternatively, he wished to assemble a diversified portfolio such as the S&P 500 the old-fashioned way—a portfolio consisting of actual stocks and no derivatives—he would have to buy each of the 500 stock issues while selling his Treasury bills. This positioning would involve 501 separate transactions. Turning the actual stock portfolio back into T-bills would similarly require 501 transactions. Turning T-bills effectively into stocks via long futures contracts, however, involves just one futures trade. Unwinding the futures position would also be just a single trade. Market timing is much more economically executed with futures contracts than with actual equity trades.

A Cross-Hedge

A manufacturer of plastic water pistols wishes to hedge against increases in raw plastic pellet prices. Unfortunately, there are no futures contracts covering plastics prices. There is, however, a contract on oil prices, and the price of plastic is highly correlated with the price of oil. By going long in an oil contract, the manufacturer will be paid money when oil prices rise, which is also likely to be when plastics prices rise. Hedging an exposure with a contract tied to a correlated underlying instrument is called a cross-hedge.

A Common Pitfall

The ease with which futures facilitate hedging may coax managers to occasionally take speculative positions. A photographic film manufacturer, for example, might become experienced and comfortable hedging silver prices by going long in silver futures. Managers at the firm might come to believe that no one is better able to forecast silver prices than they are. A time may come when they wholeheartedly believe that silver prices will fall. Not only might they choose not to enter a long silver futures hedge at this time, but they may choose to go short in silver futures so as to capitalize on the falling price. If silver prices fall, not only will they benefit from a cheaper raw input, but the short silver futures will pay off as well. The danger here is that the manufacturer has lost sight of the fact that it is in the film manufacturing business, not the business of speculating on commodity prices. Although silver prices might be expected to fall, there is always the possibility that they will rise instead. The probability of a rise might be small, but the consequences would be catastrophic. Not only will the firm's raw material price rise, but the firm will suffer additionally as it loses on the futures contract. The lesson here is that firms should stay clearly focused on what their business line is and what role the use of futures plays in their business. Futures use should generally be authorized only for hedging and not for speculation. Auditing systems should be in place to oversee that futures are used appropriately.

Futures and Forwards Summary

As these examples illustrate, futures and forwards are useful tools for hedging a wide variety of business and financial risks. Futures and forward contracts essentially commit the two parties to a deferred transaction. No money changes hands initially. As prices subsequently change, however, one party wins at the other's expense. Futures and forwards thus enable businesses to shed or take on exposure to changing prices. When used to offset an exposure the firm faces naturally, futures and forwards reduce risk.

Options

Options are another breed of derivatives. They share some similarities with futures and forwards, but they also differ in many important respects. Like futures and forwards, option prices are a function of the value of an underlying asset; thus they satisfy the definition of derivative. Unlike futures and forwards, however, options are assets that must be paid for initially. Recall that no money changes hands initially as parties enter into forwards and futures. Options, though, are an asset that have to be bought for a price at the outset.

There are two kinds of options, call and puts.

Call Options

A call option is an asset that gives the owner the right but not the obligation to buy some other underlying asset for a set price, on or up to a set date. For example, consider a call option on Disney stock that gives the owner the right to purchase one share of Disney stock for $30 per share, on or up to next June 15. (Actually, options are usually sold in blocks covering 100 shares. For expository purposes, however, we will describe an option on only a single share.) The underlying asset would be one share of Disney stock. The prespecified price, known as the "strike price," would be $30 per share. The expiration date would be June 15. The Disney option might cost $3 initially.

If on the expiration date, June 15, the market price of Disney stock stood at $35, the call option owner would exercise the option and buy a share of Disney stock for $30. The new share owner could then turn around and sell the share for $35 in the marketplace, realizing a terminal payoff from the option of $5. The terminal payoff is $5, so the profit net of the $3 initial option price is $2.

Suppose, alternatively, that the market price of Disney stock on June 15 were $29. It would not be profitable to exercise the call option and thereby purchase for $30 what is elsewhere available for $29. In such a case, the option owner would choose not to exercise, and the call would expire worthless. It is the right not to execute the transaction that is the major difference between options and forwards. The long party in a forward contract must buy the goods upon expiration whether it is advantageous to do so or not. By contrast, call option owners do not have to buy the underlying asset if they choose not to. At expiration, a call option should be exercised if and only if the market price exceeds the strike price. When the market price is above the strike price, the call option is said to be "in the money." When the market price is less than the strike price, the call is "out of the money." When the market price equals the strike price, the option is "at the money." An option that is out of the money, or even at the money, at expiration will expire unexercised and worthless.

An option's payoff is defined as the maximum amount of money the option owner would receive at expiration, if she totally liquidated her position. If the option expires out of the money, the payoff is zero. If the option expires in the money, the payoff is the amount of money received from exercising the call option and then selling the stock in the open market. For example, if the strike price is $30 and the terminal stock price is $20, the payoff would be zero, since the option would be out of the money and should not be exercised. If the terminal stock price were $40, the payoff would be $10, since the option should be exercised, allowing the owner to buy the stock for $30, and then sell that stock for $40 in the open market. Mathematically, the payoff is the maximum of zero or the stock price minus the strike price.

The payoff ignores the initial price that was paid for the option. Payoff treats the initial price as a sunk cost, and measures only what the option owner might subsequently receive. The payoff minus the initial price is known as the option profit. The option payoff is the same for all owners of the option, regardless of what they each initially paid for it. Profit, however, depends on what was initially paid and therefore differs from one investor to another.

A payoff diagram is a valuable analytical device for understanding options. A payoff diagram graphs the payoff of an option as a function of the underlying asset's spot price at expiration. Exhibit 15.1 depicts the payoff diagram for the Disney call option with a strike price of $40. The payoff diagram is a picture of the option. It tells you when you will receive money and when you will not. It helps to visualize how the contract will perform, and whether the option is appropriate for any particular application.

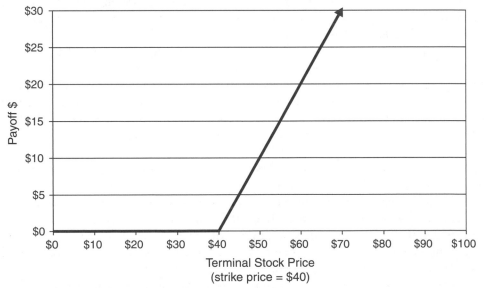

Exhibit 15.1   Call option payoff diagram.

The payoff diagram is flat and equal to zero in the entire range where the option is out of the money—that is, where the stock price is less than the strike price. This means that someone who buys an option might lose his entire investment in that option. You may pay $3 for the option and lose 100% of that $3 by the expiration date. On the brighter side, the payoff diagram confirms that the most you can lose in an option is the initial premium, the $3 you paid for it. Unlike futures or forwards, an option will never call upon you to make additional payments at a later date. Initially, you pay for the option, perhaps $3. From then on you can only receive cash inflows.

Note that the payoff diagram begins to rise at the point where the stock price equals the strike price. The payoff is dollar for dollar greater than zero for every dollar that the stock price exceeds the strike price. Thus we see that a call option rises in value as the underlying asset rises in price. For this reason, some people refer to call options as bullish instruments.

Hedging with a Call Option

Consider the trucking company whose rates are regulated, yet costs fluctuate with market prices. The chief raw material purchased by the company is diesel fuel. If fuel prices rise, the trucking company will suffer losses, and may in fact be put out of business. As we saw earlier, the company can guarantee a fixed price for fuel by going long in a future or a forward. Another strategy would be to buy a diesel fuel call option contract. The strike price of the call option would lock in the *highest* price that the company will have to pay for fuel. If fuel prices should drop below the strike price, the company would be under no obligation to exercise the option. It would simply buy fuel at the low market price. If, however, fuel prices rise above the strike price, the company would exercise the option and buy fuel at the relatively low strike price.

The added flexibility of the option over the futures strategy comes at a cost. When the company buys the call option, it must pay a price or "premium." The call option is essentially an oil price insurance contract for the firm, insuring that fuel prices will not exceed the strike price. If fuel prices remain low, below the strike price, the company will not collect on this insurance policy, and the initial premium, which paid for the insurance, will be lost.

Pricing Options

At this point the reader may wonder how the initial price of an option is determined. Option pricing is no trivial exercise, and a thorough treatment of option pricing is beyond the scope of this chapter. Some basic principles, however, can be explained here. First, an option's intrinsic value prior to expiration is equal to its payoff. That is, if an option is out of the money, its intrinsic value is zero. If a call option is in the money, for example if the strike price is $40 and the current stock price is $50, then the intrinsic value equals the stock price minus the strike price, $10.

The value of an option, however, exceeds its intrinsic value. An out-of-the-money option is worth more than zero, and the in-the-money option described earlier is worth more than $10. This extra value is due to the fact that the downside losses are capped off, but the upside potential is unlimited. As long as there is still time remaining in the option's life, it is possible that an out-of-the-money option can go in the money. An in-the-money option can go further in the money, and has more upside potential than downside.

A call option's value is a function of the underlying stock price, the strike price, the amount of time remaining to expiration, the interest rate, the stock's dividend rate, and the volatility of the underlying asset price. As the underlying stock price rises, so will the call option's value. Holding the other variables constant, a call option's value will be greater when there is a higher stock price, lower strike price, longer time to expiration, higher interest rate, lower dividend rate, and more volatility in the underlying asset. Researchers have succeeded in formalizing an equation that prices options as a function of these input variables. The formula is known as the Black-Scholes option pricing formula. It is widely available on programmed computer software and in many options theory textbooks.

A Written Call Option

In the case of life insurance or automobile insurance, when the insured party collects, another party must pay. It is a zero-sum game. So it is with options. The party that sells the option is liable for the future payoff. "Writing" an option and shorting an option are synonymous with selling an option. The payoff diagram for a written call option position is the mirror image of the long or bought call option position. As shown in Exhibit 15.2, the x-axis is the reflecting surface.

Note that once the call option writer has received the initial premium, all subsequent cash flows will be outflows. The best the writer can hope for is that the call will expire out of the money. Note that the potential liability of the written option position is unlimited. Notice as well that the amount of money the buyer of the option might receive at expiration is the exact amount that writer will have to pay. Thus, when the media report that a particular company has lost millions of dollars in options, the reader should realize that this means some other party has made millions. The newspapers tend to focus on the losers.

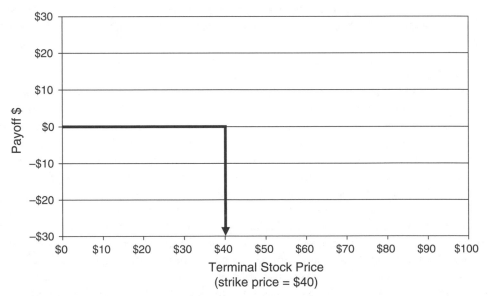

Exhibit 15.2   Payoff diagram for a written call option position.

Strategies Using Written Call Options

Why would anybody wish to sell a call option if doing so subjects them to the possibility of unlimited future liabilities? One answer is that speculators sometimes deem the risks worthwhile in light of the expected reward. They may be confident that the underlying asset price will not rise and the option will expire worthless.

Written call options can also be used to hedge in certain circumstances. Consider oil-exporting nations such as Mexico and Venezuela. When oil prices are low, they are hungry for funds, funds that are much needed for national development projects. When oil prices are high, they have plenty of excess revenue. A reasonable strategy would be to sell high-strike-price oil call options when oil prices are low. The country thus receives premiums when funds are most needed, and incurs a liability that needs to be paid only when funds are most plentiful. The oil call options help to smooth the flow of funds into the country. Abken and Feinstein, in their 1994 paper "Covered Call Options: A Proposal to Ease Less Developed Country Debt," elaborate on the use of written call options in such a setting.

Warrants

Warrants are call options that are sold by the company whose stock is the underlying asset. If Microsoft pays its executive with Microsoft call options, those options would be called warrants. When the warrants are exercised, the total outstanding supply of Microsoft stock would rise. Warrants are valuable, even if they are not yet in the money. Clearly they must be worth something; otherwise, executives would not want them and would give them away! Offering warrants as compensation to executives is not free for the firm's shareholders. Stories abound nowadays of young Internet executives who became fabulously wealthy when they exercised warrants paid to them as part of their employment compensation.

Put Options

The second type of option is a put. A put option is a contract that gives the owner the right but not the obligation to *sell* some underlying asset for a prespecified price, on or up to a given date. Consider a put option on Exxon stock. Suppose the strike price is $100 and the expiration date is December 15. The put option owner has the right, but not the obligation, to sell a share of Exxon stock for $100, on or up to December 15. If the market price of Exxon is above $100, for example $120, the put option owner would not exercise. Why should he force someone to pay $100 for the stock? He can make more money by selling the stock in the open market. Thus, a put option is out of the money if the stock price is *above* the strike price. If the stock price is below the strike price, however, then the put option is in the money. If the market price of Exxon is $80 on December 15, the owner of the put can reap a $20 payoff. To realize this payoff, he would buy the Exxon stock in the marketplace for $80, and then turn around and sell it for $100 by exercising the put option. Thus, a put option is in the money when the stock price is below the strike price. A put option's payoff at expiration, and its intrinsic value prior to expiration, is the strike price minus the stock price, or zero, whichever is greater.

Exhibit 15.3 presents the payoff diagram for a put option. Should the stock price fall to zero, the put option's payoff would be equal to the strike price. At that point the put option owner would have the right to sell a worthless stock for $100. From that point, the put option payoff falls one dollar for each dollar that the stock price rises. The payoff

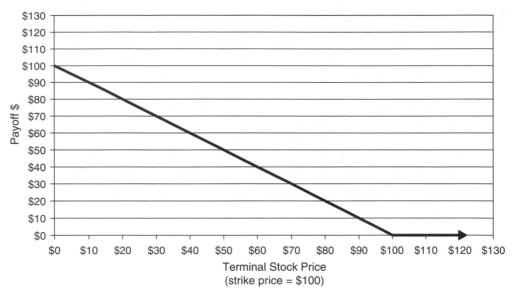

Exhibit 15.3   Put option payoff diagram.

reaches zero when the stock price equals the strike price, and then remains at zero no matter how much higher the stock price goes. As is the case with call options, the put option cannot fall in value below zero. Once the put option premium is paid, the owner is never called upon to make another payment. Any subsequent cash flow is positive. It is altogether possible, however, for the buyer of the put option to lose the entire premium, so one should not think that buying a put option is a safe investment.

Notice that the put option payoff rises as the stock price falls. For this reason, puts are thought of as bearish instruments—instruments that are more profitable the further the underlying asset falls in value. Because of this negative relationship with the underlying asset, puts can be good hedging instruments for someone who owns the underlying asset.

Like the call option's payoff diagram, the put's payoff diagram is kinked; that is, there is an elbow at the strike price. A kinked payoff diagram is the hallmark of an option. If a payoff diagram has no kink, then the instrument depicted is not an option.

The payoff diagram for a written put option position is the mirror image of the purchased put's payoff diagram. Such a payoff diagram is shown in Exhibit 15.4. The possible payoff reaped by the buyer of the put option is exactly equal to the possible outflow paid by the writer. Put options, too, are a zero-sum game. Notice that whereas the writer of a call option has unlimited potential liability, the writer of a put option has a potential liability limited to the strike price. Furthermore, notice that a long put option payoff looks nothing like that of a short call option. Similarly, notice that a long call option payoff is not the same as that of a short put. Both long puts and short calls are bearish positions, just as both short puts and long calls are bullish positions, but each of these four positions is unique in the direction, size, and timing of cash flows. Long calls and long puts have to be paid for up front, and then receive a subsequent positive payoff depending on what happens to the underlying stock. Short calls and short puts receive all of their cash inflows up front and then become potential liabilities.

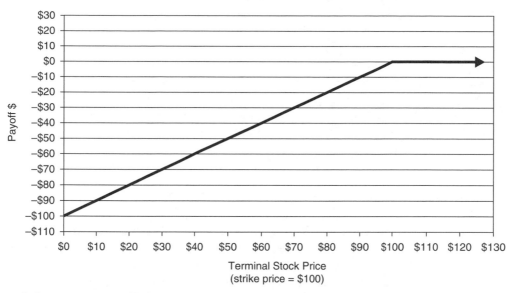

Exhibit 15.4   Payoff diagram for a written put option position.

A Protective Put Strategy

A put option can be thought of as price insurance for someone who owns the underlying asset. For example, suppose you are a pension fund manager, and you hold hundreds of shares of Exxon stock. You hold the stock because you believe the stock will rise in value. You worry, however, that if the stock price does fall, losses could be so great that the fund would be unable to meet the needs of the retirees. An effective hedging strategy would be to buy Exxon put options. You would choose the strike price to be at a level that would guarantee the solvency of the fund. If Exxon stock falls below the strike price of the put options, the put options will pay off the difference between the new lower market price and the strike price. If Exxon stock rises, the put options would expire out of the money. The insurance would not pay off, but you would reap the high return of the rising stock. This strategy is known as buying a protective put. It is essentially portfolio insurance. The strategy allows for the upside appreciation of the portfolio, yet sets a floor below which the value of the portfolio cannot fall.

A protective put strategy can also be implemented by producers who face the risk of their products' prices falling. For example, cattle ranchers can buy put options on cattle, thereby fixing the lowest price at which they will be able to sell their herd.

Swaps

The third category of derivative we examine is swaps. A swap is an agreement between two parties to exchange cash flows over a period of time. The size and direction of the cash flows are determined by an agreed-upon formula spelled out in the swap agreement—a formula that is contingent on the performance of other underlying instruments. Due to this contingency on other underlying assets, swaps are considered derivatives.

One easy type of swap to understand is the equity swap. Suppose Back Bay Investment Management owns a large block of Standard & Poor's 500 stocks. Suppose another firm,

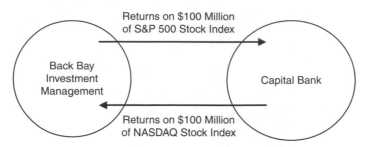

Exhibit 15.5   Equity swap.

Capital Bank, owns a large block of NASDAQ stocks. Back Bay would like to diversify into NASDAQ stocks, and simultaneously Capital Bank would like to diversify into S&P 500 stocks. The old-fashioned way of achieving the desired objectives would be for each party to sell the stocks they do not want and reinvest the proceeds in the stocks they do want. Such an approach is very expensive in terms of commissions. A much cheaper alternative is for each party to keep its own portfolio intact, and arrange between themselves an equity swap.

The swap agreement might dictate the following terms. For every percentage point that the NASDAQ stock index rises over the course of the year, Capital Bank will pay Back Bay Investment Management $1 million. Simultaneously, for every percentage point that the S&P 500 rises over the course of the year, Back Bay will pay Capital Bank $1 million. Thus, if the NASDAQ index rises 15% and the S&P 500 rises 11%, there will be a net payment of $4 million from Capital Bank to Back Bay. If in the following year the NASDAQ index rises 23% and the S&P 500 rises 29%, Back Bay will pay Capital Bank $6 million on net. The equity swap is illustrated in Exhibit 15.5.

In this equity swap, the notional principal is $100 million; that is, the payments equal a base of $100 million times the indexes' respective returns. The net effect of the swap is to essentially convert $100 million of Back Bay's Standard & Poor's stocks into $100 million of NASDAQ stocks. Simultaneously, $100 million of Capital Bank's NASDAQ stocks will now perform as if they were $100 million of Standard & Poor's 500 stocks. Both sides keep their assets parked where they were, but they swap exposures on the notional principal.

Some arithmetic will prove the point that Back Bay's portfolio will now perform as if it were invested in NASDAQ stocks instead of S&P stocks. If Back Bay did in fact own $100 million of NASDAQ stocks, by the end of the first year, after the 15% rise in NASDAQ stocks, this portfolio would have grown to be worth $115 million. But Back Bay owns $100 million of S&P stocks, and has a position in an equity swap. The $100 million of S&P stocks grows to $111 million after the 11% S&P rise in the first year. The swap, however, pays Back Bay $4 million at the end of the first year. Thus, at the end of the first year, Back Bay does have $115 million in total portfolio value. The total value of Capital Bank's portfolio at the end of the first year will be $111 million, just as if it had invested $100 million in S&P stocks.

Since the notional principal remains fixed at $100 million, the swap will continue to convert $100 million of Back Bay's S&P stocks into $100 million of NASDAQ stocks, and vice versa for Capital Bank. Total portfolio performance in subsequent years depends on how the swap proceeds are reinvested by each party.

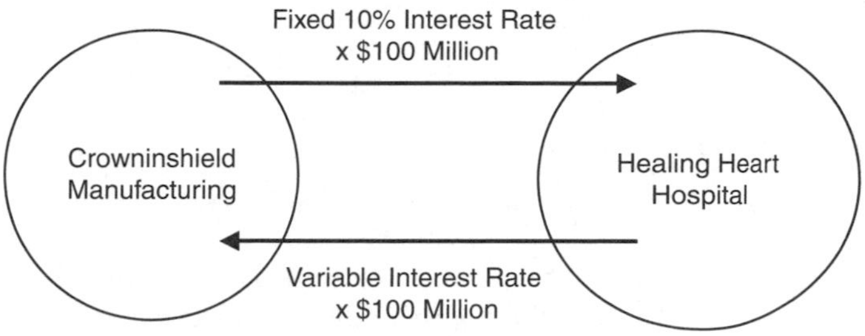

Exhibit 15.6   Interest rate swap.

Interest Rate Swaps

The most common type of swap is an interest rate swap. The typical or plain-vanilla interest rate swap is a "fixed for floating" swap, whereby cash flows depend on the movement of variable interest rates. For example, consider two firms Crowninshield Manufacturing (C) and Healing Heart Hospital (H). The swap agreement might specify that C pays H a fixed 10% per year on a notional principal of $100 million, and H pays to C the prime rate, as quoted in the *Wall Street Journal*, times $100 million. Settlement might be once per year. The prime rate quoted at the beginning of each year will determine the cash flow paid at the end. Thus, if at first the prime rate is 12%, H will pay C $2 million at the end of the first year. If by the end of the first year the prime rate has fallen to 7%, at the end of the second year C will pay H $3 million. And so the swap continues for a specified number of years. H will benefit if rates fall; C will benefit if rates rise. This interest rate swap is depicted in Exhibit 15.6.

Examples of Hedging Interest Rate Exposure with a Swap

The Keating Computer Company assembles and markets computer hardware systems. In the past several years Keating Computer has been one of the fastest-growing computer hardware companies. It borrowed extensively to finance this growth. Currently on the books is a very large long-term variable-rate loan. Also on the books is a sizable amount of short-term debt. The managers of Keating Computer have observed that they are dangerously exposed to interest rate risk. If rates should rise, they will have to pay more in debt service on the variable-rate loan, and they will face higher interest rates when they roll over their short-term debt. The company is currently profitable, but they worry that rising interest rates can wipe out that profit. Since the company is planning an equity offering in coming years, management is very concerned about the prospect of reporting any losses over the near term.

One solution to Keating Computer's problem would be to refinance at fixed interest rates. The transaction costs of refinancing, however, are sizable, and the rates currently offered on long-term debt are not favorable. Entering an interest rate swap is a better hedging strategy. The company should enter as the fixed rate payer, which means it would be the variable rate receiver. As interest rates rise, the company will make money on the swap, offsetting the higher payments it must make on its own debt. Since swaps are over-the-counter instruments, the company can tailor the terms of the swap so that the hedge will be in force for the exact number of years needed. Moreover, the notional principal can be tailored so that the money received when rates rise is closely matched to the new higher debt service obligations.

Another Example

Kayman Savings and Loan holds most of its assets in the form of long-term mortgages, mortgage-backed securities, and 30-year Treasury bonds. The liabilities of Kayman Savings are mostly short-term certificates of deposit. Kayman has also sold some short-term commercial paper of its own. Stephen Kayman, the president of Kayman Savings, suddenly realizes that the institution is in the same precarious predicament as that of many savings and loans (S&Ls) that went bust in the 1980s. Long-term fixed-income instruments are more sensitive to interest rates than short-term instruments. When interest rates rise, both long-term and short-term instruments fall in value, but the long-term instruments fall much more. Consequently, if interest rates should rise, the market value of the S&L's assets will fall further than the market value of its liabilities. When this happens, the S&L's equity will be wiped out. The bank will be bankrupt. Even if government auditors do not shut down the S&L, the institution will experience cash flow problems. The relatively low fixed-interest revenue from the long-term assets will not be enough to keep up with the rising interest expenses of the short-term liabilities. What can Kayman do to protect against the risk of rising interest rates?

The predicament faced by Kayman Savings is known as a "duration gap." The duration of the assets is greater than the duration of the liabilities. As rates rise, equity vanishes. Kayman Savings needs a hedge that will pay off when rates rise. Entering an interest rate swap as the fixed payer can close the duration gap. The swap will grow in value as rates rise, offsetting the equity losses. Again, the size, timing, and other terms of the interest rate swap can be tailored to meet the particular needs of Kayman Savings.

How to Choose the Appropriate Hedge

We have now examined forwards, futures, call options, put options, and swaps. We have observed how these instruments can be used to hedge in a wide variety of risky scenarios. How does one choose which of these instruments to use in a particular situation? When is a future better than a forward? When should an option be used instead of a future? Should interest rate exposure be hedged with bond futures or with swaps? The following steps will provide some guidance.

The first task in implementing a hedge strategy is to identify the natural exposures that the firm faces. Does the firm gain or lose when interest rates rise? Does it gain or lose as the dollar appreciates? Is a falling wheat price good news or bad news for the company? What about oil prices and stock prices? How about foreign stock and bond prices? Is the company exposed, and if so, which direction causes a loss?

Clearly the answers to these questions vary from firm to firm. The bakers benefited from falling wheat prices while the farmer suffered. Rising interest rates might hurt a firm that has variable-rate debt, but might help a pension fund that is about to invest in bonds. A rising dollar benefits American importers but hurts American exporters. The first step in risk management is to identify the exposures.

Once the exposures are identified, one should narrow the search for an appropriate hedge to the set of derivatives that compensate the firm when the adverse scenario is realized. For example, an airline that purchases jet fuel will see higher costs when the price of oil rises. The airline should look for derivatives that pay off when oil prices rise. Thus, the airline should consider a long position in an oil futures contract, or a long oil forward, or an oil call option. A bank that suffers losses when interest rates rise should consider a short position in a bond future or forward, bond put options, or the fixed-payer side of an interest rate swap. An exporter that expects to receive Mexican pesos might wish to go short in peso futures or forwards, or buy peso puts.

The next step is to choose from among futures, forwards, options, and swaps. This is perhaps the trickiest part of the analysis. To guide the selection, it is helpful to categorize the risks and the instruments as either symmetric or asymmetric. Futures, forwards, and swaps are symmetric hedging instruments, in that they pay off money if prices move in one direction, but incur losses if prices move in the opposite direction. Options, by contrast, are asymmetric hedging instruments. They pay off money if prices move in one direction, yet result in no cash outflows if prices should move the other way. A symmetric risk is one in which the firm is hurt if underlying prices move one way but benefits if prices move in the opposite direction. An asymmetric risk is one in which the firm is hurt if prices move in one direction, but the firm does not benefit appreciably if the price moves in the other direction. For example, a firm that exports to Japan and receives payment in yen benefits when the value of the yen rises, but is hurt when the yen falls in value. This foreign exchange risk is thus symmetric. The symmetric foreign exchange risk can be eliminated almost completely with a symmetric instrument such as a future or forward, not an option.

A portfolio manager invested in stocks also faces a symmetric risk. The portfolio benefits if stock prices rise, and loses money if stock prices fall. The portfolio manager, however, might wish to modify the exposure in an asymmetric way, insuring against losses on the downside while maintaining the potential for upside appreciation. An asymmetric instrument, a put option, would be the appropriate hedge instrument in this case, since an asymmetric instrument converts a symmetric risk into an asymmetric exposure.

An automobile leasing company is an example of a commercial venture that faces an asymmetric risk. If interest rates rise, the firm's interest expenses rise. If the firm tries to offset these higher costs by charging higher prices to customers, the firm would lose business. However, if interest rates fall, buying an automobile on credit becomes a more attractive substitute for leasing unless the leasing company also lowers its prices. Thus, the leasing company suffers when rates rise, but does not benefit when rates fall. An asymmetric hedge such as a bond put option would be the best choice of instrument in this case. The bond put option will pay off when rates rise, but will not require a cash outflow when rates fall.

The key to choosing between symmetric and asymmetric instruments is to first identify the nature of the risk that is faced, and then choose the type of instrument that will modify the risk appropriately. A symmetric risk can best be eliminated with a symmetric instrument. An asymmetric risk can best be eliminated with an asymmetric instrument. A symmetric risk can be turned into an asymmetric exposure with an asymmetric instrument.

Finally, the last step is to choose whether the instruments should be of the exchange-traded or over-the-counter variety. Forwards and swaps are over-the-counter instruments; futures are exchange-traded instruments. Options are generally exchange-traded, but they can also be bought over the counter. Exchange-traded instruments are standardized, and are thus liquid and entail low transaction costs. But since they are standardized, they may not perfectly suit the risk exposure the firm wishes to hedge. Over-the-counter instruments can be custom tailored, but they are therefore less liquid and more expensive in terms of transaction costs. The firm must weigh the costs and benefits of liquidity, differences in transaction costs, and custom fit. The correct choice depends on the particular hedging situation.

A couple of examples will illustrate the process of putting all the factors together to pick the best-suited hedge. An American manufacturing firm owns a production facility in Canada. Rent and wages are paid in Canadian dollars. Consequently, if the Canadian dollar rises in value, the wages and rent translated into American dollars would become more expensive. If the Canadian dollar falls, the expenses in terms of American dollars decline. Thus, the exposure is symmetric. If the firm wishes to completely eliminate the exposure, a symmetric instrument is called for, ruling out options.

The firm should go long in Canadian dollar futures or forwards, since either of these instruments will provide positive cash flows when the Canadian dollar is rising. An exchange-traded Canadian dollar futures contract is available. The commission on the forward is greater than the commission on the futures, but the futures contract covers slightly more Canadian dollars than the firm wishes to hedge, and the timing does not exactly correspond to the timing of wage and rent payments. An over-the-counter forward contract could be constructed so that cash flows are synchronized with wage and rent payments. After weighing the two alternatives, the managers decide that the benefit from lower commissions on the futures contract outweighs the disadvantage of the futures' slight mismatch in the hedge. They go long in Canadian dollar futures.

The same manufacturing firm has many customers in Venezuela. If the Venezuelan currency (the bolivar) falls in value, the American dollar value of the revenue will fall. If the Venezuelan currency rises in value, the dollar revenue will rise. Thus, the risk is symmetric, and so the list of hedging candidates is narrowed to futures and forwards. The firm benefits from a rise in the bolivar, and loses when the bolivar falls. Thus, the firm should go short in bolivar futures or forwards, so that a cash flow will be received if the bolivar falls. No bolivar futures contracts are available on exchanges, so the firm must go short in over-the-counter Venezuelan bolivar forwards.

A producer of copper wire purchases large amounts of copper as a raw material. When copper prices rise, the firm must either absorb the higher expenses or raise the price of copper wire. Raising the price of wire, however, causes customers to cut back on purchases, causing the firm to be stuck with unsold inventory. When copper prices fall, alternatively, competitors lower their prices, so the firm must also lower its price in order to sell its output. Consequently, the firm's profits suffer when copper prices rise, but profits do not increase when copper prices fall. Management would like to increase production capacity, but it is difficult to forecast how much the firm can sell, given recent copper price fluctuations. With current levels of raw copper inventory, management believes that raw copper prices can rise as much as 10% without significantly impacting the firm's bottom line. What is the appropriate hedge?

Clearly, the firm faces an asymmetric risk. The firm is hurt when copper prices rise, but does not benefit when the price falls. An option will best mitigate the risk. Since the firm is hurt when copper prices rise, a call option that pays off when copper prices rise is the best choice. Since the firm can tolerate a 10% rise in copper prices without suffering significant losses, an out-of-the-money copper call option that begins to pay off only when copper prices rise more than 10% is ideal. Exchange-traded copper call options exist, so, due to their greater liquidity and low transaction costs, they would be the best choice.

A cellular communications firm has sold a six-year variable-rate bond whose interest payments are tied to the London Interbank Offered Rate (LIBOR). When LIBOR rises, so too do the company's interest payments. When LIBOR falls, the firm's interest payments fall. The company's interest payments are due twice a year, on the last days of February and August. The firm raised $160 million this way. With competition holding cellular telephone rates down, the executives worry that an increase in interest rates can wipe out all profits. What is the appropriate hedge instrument?

The interest rate exposure is symmetric, ruling out options. The firm needs an instrument that will pay it money when interest rates rise. Thus, the firm should go short in either bond futures or forwards, or the firm should be the fixed-rate payer in an interest rate swap. Since the cash flows that the firm is trying to hedge do not conform to those of any exchange-traded futures contract, the correct choice is narrowed to the over-the-counter instruments—a forward or a swap. The firm must hedge 12 interest rate payments, two per year for six years. Forwards are generally constructed to provide one payment only. Swaps are designed to hedge multiple payments over longer terms. Thus, entering a six-year interest rate swap as the fixed payer is the ideal hedge in this situation.

Summary and Final Recommendations

This chapter has presented the basics of risk management using derivatives. By separating an asset's value from its exposure, derivatives allow firms to exchange exposures without exchanging the underlying assets. It is much more economical to transfer exposures rather than assets, and thus derivatives have greatly facilitated risk management. Derivatives are indeed powerful risk management tools, but in the wrong hands they can be dangerous and destructive. It is essential that managers fully understand how much and under what conditions derivatives will provide positive cash flows or require cash outflows. If it is not absolutely clear when and how much the cash flows will be, do not enter the contract. Managers should strive to identify the nature, magnitude, and size of their risk exposures. They can then match those exposures with countervailing positions in derivatives. Managers should never forget that their job is to preserve value by reducing risk. The temptation to speculate should be avoided. Don't be greedy.

Notes

1. Zvi Bodie and Robert C. Merton, *Financial Economics*, 2nd ed. (Upper Saddle River, NJ: Prentice Hall, 2009) deserve credit for this perspective on risk management techniques.
2. *Time*, April 11, 1994.
3. Fischer Black, who co-invented the model, passed away prior to recognition from the Nobel committee.
4. All data referring to equity positions, assets under management, exposure, and profits and losses in this section come from Roger Lowenstein, *When Genius Failed: The Rise and Fall of Long-Term Capital Management* (New York: Random House, 2000).

For Further Reading

Abken, Peter, and Steven Feinstein, "Covered Call Options: A Proposal to Ease Less Developed Country Debt," in *Financial Derivatives: New Instruments and Their Uses* (Atlanta: Federal Reserve Bank of Atlanta, 1994).

Bernstein, Peter, *Against the Gods: The Remarkable Story of Risk* (New York: John Wiley & Sons, 1998).

Bodie, Zvi, and Robert C. Merton, *Financial Economics* (Upper Saddle River, NJ: Prentice Hall, 2009).

Chance, Don M., *An Introduction to Derivatives* (New York: Dryden Press, 1998).

Chew, Lillian, *Managing Derivative Risks: The Use and Abuse of Leverage* (New York: John Wiley & Sons, 1996).

Daigler, Robert T., *Financial Futures and Options Markets: Concepts and Strategies* (New York: HarperCollins, 1994).

Dunbar, Nicholas, *Inventing Money: The Story of Long-Term Capital Management and the Legends Behind It* (New York: John Wiley & Sons, 2001).

Fraser, Andrew, "Top Banks Plan Bailout for Fund," Associated Press, September 24, 1998.

16

Business Valuation

Michael A. Crain

It has been said that estimating the value of a private business is similar to analyzing securities of public companies. The theories are similar and not overly complex on the surface. There are even Web sites that say they can value a private firm. But like so many things in the business world, the devil is in the details. The valuation of a closely held business depends on many variables. While valuation theory does not seem overly complex, the accuracy is only as good as the variables that go into it. The valuation of private firms is often complicated by the quantity and quality of information and the way private firms are operated. Unlike public companies, private firms often do not have complete and accurate information available. Dollar for dollar, the time to value most profitable private firms is out of proportion to the analysis of public company securities. This is shown in the following case study, which illustrates valuation theory and types of information that are used.

* * *

For the past 20 years, Bob has owned and operated a manufacturing business that has grown significantly since it started. Bob is 60 years of age, and his children do not appear capable of taking over the company. He is thinking about the future of the firm at a time when he would like to slow down. One of his options is selling his business. Bob's company, Acme Manufacturing, Inc., makes certain types of adhesives and sealants and has revenues of approximately $50 million. It has six plants throughout the country. Bob owns 100% of the firm's common stock. He does not know what the business is worth, nor does he know how its value would be determined. Bob asked his accountant about valuing the business. The accountant recommends that Bob hire someone who specializes in business valuations. After interviewing several candidates, Bob hires Victoria to value his firm. The valuation date is December 31, 2008, and the standard of value is fair market value. Victoria explains the valuation process and the scope of her work.

Three Approaches to Value

Victoria tells Bob that the value of a firm is usually estimated by considering three approaches:

1. Income approach.
2. Market approach.
3. Asset (or cost) approach.

413

The income approach estimates a value by using a method to convert expected future economic benefits, such as cash flows, into a present single amount. This approach is based on the concept that the value of an asset—such as a stock or a business—is all of its expected future benefits expressed in present-value dollars. (A simple example of present value is that a dollar to be received a year from now is worth perhaps 95 cents today.)

Next, the market approach is a way of estimating a value by observing the prices of identical or similar assets. For instance, real estate appraisals using the market approach often rely on the sales prices of comparable properties. In business valuation, it is sometimes possible to observe prices of similar firms that have been sold.

The asset approach is a way of estimating value based on the individual values of the firm's assets less its liabilities. The firm's balance sheet serves as a starting point. This approach requires that all of the assets be identified—even if they do not appear on the balance sheet. Often, a balance sheet does not include assets that the firm has created through internal activity, such as goodwill and other intangible assets. Once all the firm's assets and liabilities have been identified, each item is valued.

Different Types of Buyers

Victoria explains to Bob that buyers have different motives for buying businesses. They may be willing to pay different prices for the same business depending on their motive. Most buyer motives can be grouped into these categories:

- *Financial buyers*. These buyers are mostly motivated to earn a reasonable return on their investment. Financial buyers often have a wide range of investment options, because they seek financial returns on whatever sort of investment they make. Furthermore, financial buyers are also often focused on an exit strategy to sell their investment in the future. Finally, those sorts of buyers usually pay fair market value (defined later).

- *Strategic/investment buyers*. These buyers probably already know the firm or already operate in its industry. Therefore, the number of potential strategic buyers of a firm is usually smaller than the number of financial buyers. A strategic buyer is often looking to integrate its operations with the target firm. Most of these sorts of buyers will pay a higher price that reflects business synergies that are not available to financial buyers. This price is called investment value, which is different than the concept of fair market value.

The smallest of businesses—sometimes called mom-and-pop businesses—often have two other types of buyers with different motives: lifestyle buyers and those seeking employment. A lifestyle buyer wants to buy a business that provides a desired lifestyle (e.g., a motel in the mountains or a business that complements a hobby). Another type of buyer of small businesses is motivated to provide employment for the buyer and/or family members.

After explaining the different types of buyers to Bob, Victoria discusses how they apply to Acme. Obviously, Bob would like to obtain the highest price possible if he sold his business. Neither Bob nor Victoria, however, has any way to foresee who that buyer may be or that buyer's strategic motives for buying Acme. Therefore, Victoria is going to estimate what a financial buyer would likely pay—the firm's fair market value. Practically, determining the fair market value will help Bob set a minimum target price to accept when selling Acme. But if Bob can find a strategic buyer who would pay a higher price, he would, of course, prefer to do that.

Bob asks Victoria to explain fair market value and how it differs from investment value. She tells him that *fair market value* is commonly defined as "the price, expressed in terms of cash equivalents, at which property would change hands between a hypothetical willing and able buyer and a hypothetical willing and able seller, acting at arm's length in an open and unrestricted market, when neither is under compulsion to buy or sell and when both have reasonable knowledge of the relevant facts."[1] The idea of fair market value is what the market of buyers and sellers would agree on as a price. Alternatively, *investment value* is the price a specific buyer would pay based on that buyer's needs and expectations. It often reflects a higher price than fair market value because of unique synergies between the buyer and target firm. But, as discussed earlier, investment value requires some idea of a specific buyer.

An Overview of the Business Valuation Process

Victoria explains to Bob that a thorough business valuation is both a quantitative and a qualitative process involving an analysis of many factors, such as risk and investment return. A valuation is more than simply analyzing the firm's historical financial statements or its financial forecast. Valuations that give the most reliable results analyze qualitative factors such as technology changes, competition, and customers. In addition, other factors are also often analyzed, such as macroenvironment factors like the firm's industry and the national and local economies. A business valuation will often include the following areas:

- Analysis of the company.
- Industry analysis.
- Economic analysis.
- Analysis of the firm's financial statements.
- Application of valuation methods.
- Application of any needed valuation adjustments.

A large part of valuing a firm is analyzing the *investment risk* of buying and owning a business. After the sale, the buyer bears the risk that the expected economic benefits may not materialize in the future. Of course, there is no guarantee of actually receiving the forecasted earnings. A key concept in finance is the relationship between risk and reward in making any investment. Rational people make investment decisions by weighing the risk of an investment against the expected rewards. For instance, a certificate of deposit from a bank that is guaranteed against default may have a rate of return (interest) of 5%. This investment has virtually no risk. But over the long run, investments in large and small public company stocks have historically earned an average of 10% to 12% and 15% to 20% per year, respectively. These three types of investments illustrate the relationship between risk and reward. Buying large company stocks instead of certificates of deposit carries more risk, and the market has rewarded the investors with a higher return. Furthermore, small company stocks are usually more risky than large company stocks, and they have historically rewarded investors with even higher returns. This idea flows to business valuation. A large part of the analysis looks at the risk of an investment in a firm and compares it to the risks of other types of investments. Next, the relative rewards to an investor are considered.

Victoria further explains that valuation concepts are founded in several economic principles. The first is the principle of alternatives, which states that each person has alternatives to completing a particular transaction. In the preceding example, someone has options of investing funds in a bank certificate of deposit, large company stocks, or small company stocks. Investing in a private firm is yet another alternative.

The second economic principle in valuation is the principle of substitution. It states that the value of something tends to be determined by the cost of acquiring an equally desirable substitute. For instance, someone who is selling a home will likely set the asking price based on recent sales prices of other houses in the neighborhood. If the asking price is significantly higher than prices of other houses in the area, it is unlikely that anyone will buy that home. Rather, they would buy a home in the same neighborhood for less money. Likewise, a potential buyer of a business is not likely to pay significantly more than the price for a similar firm or other similar investment.

In business valuation, we must remember that buyers have other ways to invest their money, and they will generally not pay significantly more for a business than the price of comparable investments. Thus, a business valuation will usually benchmark a profitable private firm against other investments. This process involves an analysis of the risk of those other investments as well as of the risk of the business being valued.

Industry Analysis

Acme operates in the adhesive and sealant industry. The U.S. government's Standard Industrial Classification (SIC) for this industry is number 2891. Victoria researches this industry and finds that the segment consists of approximately 1,100 U.S. establishments primarily engaged in manufacturing industrial and household adhesives, glues, caulking compounds, sealants, linoleum, tile, and rubber cements. The annual sales in this industry segment are $16.9 billion, and the industry employs roughly 36,000 people. The industry has grown at an average annual compound rate of 6.7% over the past 10 years. Victoria finds that this industry segment is a large growing global segment. However, the U.S. portion is highly fragmented, and a significant majority of the industry participants are small and regional companies. It is expected that the industry will consolidate as companies seek to enhance operating efficiencies in new product development, sales and marketing, distribution, production, and administrative overhead.

From her analysis, Victoria concludes that the industry outlook is positive in revenues and earnings, but it is moderated by the high degree of competition from numerous smaller firms selling similar products.

The Fundamental Position of the Firm

During Victoria's interviews with the firm's managers, she discovers that Bob founded Acme 20 years ago, and its history has been one of relative success. It started in a small garage and grew by expanding the number of products and its customer base. Over the years, Acme acquired new facilities, not only in its hometown but in other cities as well. The firm's growth was primarily funded by reinvesting its profits and with long-term financing when purchasing real estate. During the past five years, Acme's sales increased from $33 million to $50 million. Acme expects to expand its manufacturing capacity by adding equipment to the existing locations.

Victoria's analysis reveals that Acme has competition from many firms, and many of them are small, private companies. She also finds that Acme's customers are retail distributors of its products, and the firm does not have any significant customer concentration. In general, customer relationships have historically been long-term.

Acme has several trademarks and products that are widely known to the public, as is Acme's name. Victoria also finds that the risk of product obsolescence or replacements by new products is a minimal risk to Acme.

Acme has had research and development activities, and those costs have ranged from $250,000 to $500,000 per year over the past five years. Management does not expect any significant product developments in the near future.

Victoria's financial analysis includes looking at Acme's dividend-paying capacity. Because the company is private, she asks for information about compensation paid to family members and perquisites. Victoria finds that officers' compensation, shareholder distributions, and perquisites over the past five years have been as follows:

Year	Officers' Compensation, Perquisites, and Shareholder Distributions (in millions)
2008	$7.7
2007	5.5
2006	8.2
2005	6.3
2004	6.5

Private firms are often operated to minimize taxable income and therefore taxes. In contrast, public companies are usually operated to maximize earnings for their shareholders and to increase share prices.

When valuing a firm, a financial analysis should make adjustments so that revenues and expenses are normalized. In this case, Victoria analyzes the amount of wages the family members have taken from the firm and compares that amount with lower market wages of other people employed in similar positions. The difference between the two amounts is a form of Acme's profits flowing out of the firm as wages instead of dividends. Victoria's analysis strives to identify the firm's total earnings, even though they are different from what is reported on the income statement.

In addition, Acme has about 240 employees at its six locations. The top three individuals in management are family members, including Bob. Should the company be sold, it is unlikely that the three family members would remain working there.

Summary of Positive and Negative Fundamental Factors

As a result of Victoria's analysis, she identifies the following key positive and negative factors of the firm.

Positive

- Acme has been in existence for 20 years.
- Acme has a long-term history of growing sales and profits.

- Acme owns several trademarks for products that are well known.
- Acme has diversification in the number of its manufacturing locations.
- Acme's industry outlook is moderately positive.
- The demand for Acme's products is expected to continue.

Negative
- Acme is highly dependent on the three family members who hold the top management positions.
- Acme's products face a high degree of competition.

Financial Statement Analysis

An analysis of a firm's historical financial statements is usually needed—unless it is a start-up business—as the past is often a basis to forecast future earnings. If a firm has had high growth in recent years, that might indicate future growth potential. If past earnings have been volatile, this might be a signal of risk for a buyer. While an analysis of the financial statements is important, valuation does not stop with only looking at the firm's past performance. The goal of an analysis is estimating the firm's future earnings since that is what a buyer is looking to receive.

Balance Sheet Analysis

Victoria prepares Exhibit 16.1, which is a summary of Acme's historical balance sheets in condensed form for the most recent five years.

She finds that total assets grew an average of 15% per year over the five years and a similar amount in the most recent year. The current assets consist mostly of accounts receivable and inventory. Moreover, fixed assets mostly consist of land, buildings, improvements, machinery and equipment, factory construction in progress, and transportation equipment. As of the most recent year-end, Acme's depreciable fixed assets were amortized to 48% of their original costs.

The most recent year reflects unamortized intangible assets, consisting mostly of goodwill that is related to Acme's purchase of a plant.

Current liabilities consist of accounts payable and the amounts due within the next year on promissory notes and capital leases.

Acme is moderately leveraged from borrowings. During the past five years, Acme's interest-bearing debt—both current and noncurrent portions—increased from $6.6 million to $10.4 million. Debt consists of real estate mortgage notes, term loans, a revolving line of credit, and obligations under capital leases.

Over the past five years, the shareholders' equity increased from $6.7 million to $11.4 million. Shareholders' equity decreased slightly as a percentage of total liabilities and equity over the past five years.

Income Statement Analysis

Victoria also prepares Exhibit 16.2, which is a summary of Acme's historical income statements in condensed form for the past five years. She also prepares Exhibit 16.3, which is a graph of Acme's annual revenues for the previous five years. It illustrates the

Exhibit 16.1 Acme Manufacturing, Inc.: Summary of condensed balance sheets, 2004–2008.

	($ millions)					Growth Rates	
	2008	**2007**	**2006**	**2005**	**2004**	**2004–2008**	**2007–2008**
Assets							
Current assets	$11.69	$11.56	$12.37	$ 9.43	$ 9.17	6.3%	1.1%
Fixed assets, net	13.87	10.36	9.37	7.65	6.79	19.5	33.9
Other assets	3.17	3.00	3.25	1.12	0.62	50.4	5.5
Total assets	$28.72	$24.92	$24.98	$18.20	$16.58	14.7%	15.3%
Liabilities and Equity							
Current liabilities	$11.50	$6.41	$ 8.78	$ 4.34	$ 4.94	23.5%	79.4%
Long-term liabilities	5.83	7.26	7.78	4.85	4.96	4.1	−19.7
Total liabilities	17.33	13.67	16.56	9.19	9.90	15.0%	26.8%
Equity	11.39	11.25	8.42	9.01	6.69	14.2	1.3
Total liabilities and equity	$28.72	$24.92	$24.98	$18.20	$16.58	14.7%	15.3%

Common Size

	2008	**2007**	**2006**	**2005**	**2004**
Assets					
Current assets	40.7%	46.4%	49.5%	51.8%	55.3%
Fixed assets, net	48.3	41.6	37.5	42.0	41.0
Other assets	11.0	12.0	13.0	6.1	3.7
Total assets	100.0%	100.0%	100.0%	100.0%	100.0%
Liabilities and Equity					
Current liabilities	40.1%	25.7%	35.1%	23.9%	29.8%
Long-term liabilities	20.3	29.1	31.2	26.6	29.9
Total liabilities	60.3	54.9	66.3	50.5	59.7
Equity	39.7	45.1	33.7	49.5	40.3
Total liabilities and equity	100.0%	100.0%	100.0%	100.0%	100.0%

419

Exhibit 16.2   Acme Manufacturing, Inc.: Summary of condensed income statements, 2004–2008.

	($ millions)					Growth Rates	
	2008	2007	2006	2005	2004	2004–2008	2007–2008
Revenues	$ 50.29	$ 48.59	$ 40.85	$ 37.94	$ 33.02	11.1%	3.5%
Cost of goods sold	34.80	33.95	28.45	25.25	22.63	11.4	2.5
Gross profit	15.49	14.64	12.39	12.69	10.39	10.5	5.7
Operating expenses	5.95	5.58	4.34	3.72	3.31	15.8	6.7
Officers' compensation	3.38	2.86	3.53	3.03	2.23	11.1	18.4
Operating EBITDA	6.15	6.20	4.52	5.94	4.86	6.0	–0.9
Depreciation and amortization	0.31	0.22	0.10	0.05	0.07	44.9	42.3
Operating income (EBIT)	5.84	5.99	4.42	5.89	4.79	5.1	–2.5
Miscellaneous (income)	(0.30)	(0.25)	(0.19)	(0.18)	(0.12)	26.1	17.1
Interest expense	0.84	0.74	0.55	0.47	0.59	9.0	12.6
Pretax income	5.29	5.49	4.06	5.60	4.31	5.3	–3.6
Less: Income taxes*	—	—	—	—	—	N/A	N/A
Net income	$ 5.29	$ 5.49	$ 4.06	$ 5.60	$ 4.31	5.3%	–3.6%

	Common Size				
	2008	2007	2006	2005	2004
Revenues	100.0%	100.0%	100.0%	100.0%	100.0%
Cost of goods sold	69.2	69.9	69.6	66.6	68.5
Gross profit	30.8	30.1	30.3	33.4	31.5
Operating expenses	11.8	11.5	10.6	9.8	10.0
Officers' compensation	6.7	5.9	8.6	8.0	6.8
Operating EBITDA	12.2	12.8	11.1	15.7	14.7
Depreciation and amortization	0.6	0.5	0.2	0.1	0.2
Operating income (EBIT)	11.6	12.3	10.8	15.5	14.5
Miscellaneous (income)	–0.6	–0.5	–0.5	–0.5	–0.4
Interest expense	1.7	1.5	1.3	1.2	1.8
Pretax income	10.5	11.3	9.9	14.8	13.1
Less: Income taxes*	0.0	0.0	0.0	0.0	0.0
Net income	10.5%	11.3%	9.9%	14.8%	13.1%

*Acme is an S corporation for tax purposes, and taxable income is passed through to the shareholder. Thus, the corporation does not pay income taxes.

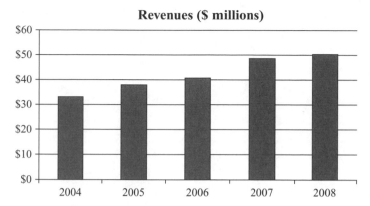

Exhibit 16.3   Acme Manufacturing, Inc.: Revenue growth, 2004–2008.

revenues from Exhibit 16.2 and more clearly shows a trend in revenue growth. The firm had a compounded annual growth rate in revenues of 11.1% during the previous five years and 3.5% for the most recent year. Acme's revenue growth rate over the past five years was substantially higher than the 5.6% revenue growth reported by the chemical products industry.

Cost of goods sold as a percentage of revenues were in a range of 66.6% to 69.9% over the past five years. Operating expenses, exclusive of officers' compensation, varied between 9.8% and 11.8%, with an upward trend.

Acme reported consistent profitability during the past five years. In 2004, income before officers' compensation and taxes was $6.5 million ($4.31 + $2.23). For 2008, it increased to $8.7 million ($5.29 + $3.38).

Ratio Analysis

Victoria also prepares Exhibit 16.4, which summarizes financial operating ratios of Acme for the past five years.

Liquidity ratios show Acme's ability to meet current obligations as they come due. The current ratio decreased from 1.9 to 1.0 during the five-year period. Working capital also decreased from $4.2 million to $190,000 during the same five-year period. These statistics indicate that the firm has a greater risk in not being able to pay its bills.

Activity ratios reveal how effectively a firm's managers are utilizing its assets. The average number of days in Acme's accounts receivable was similar over the past five years, at around 50 days. The average number of days that inventory remained at the plant before being sold decreased from 58 days to 47 days. The average number of days of accounts payable was fairly similar over the five-year period, at around 48 days.

Coverage ratios indicate a firm's ability to pay its debt. The number of times interest was earned, as measured by earnings before interest and taxes (EBIT) divided by interest expense, decreased from 8 to 7 times.

Leverage ratios generally indicate a firm's vulnerability to business downturns. Firms with high leverage have more risk to downturns than those with less debt. Acme's debt

Exhibit 16.4   Acme Manufacturing, Inc.: Ratio analysis, 2004–2008.

	2008	2007	2006	2005	2004
Liquidity Ratios:					
Current ratio	1.0	1.8	1.4	2.2	1.9
Quick ratio	0.6	1.1	0.9	1.3	1.1
Activity ratios:					
Revenue/accounts receivable	7.3	7.5	7.0	7.8	7.2
Days' receivable	49.8	48.6	52.4	46.9	50.4
COS/inventory	7.8	7.6	6.4	7.2	6.3
Days' inventory	46.6	47.8	57.2	50.5	58.1
COS/payables	7.6	9.4	4.9	7.4	7.6
Days' payables	47.7	39	73.9	49.2	48
Revenue/working capital	274.2	9.4	11.4	7.5	7.8
Coverage/leverage ratios:					
EBIT/interest	7.3	8.4	8.4	13	8.3
Fixed assets/tangible worth	1.5	1.1	1.5	0.9	1.0
Debt/tangible worth	1.8	1.5	2.6	1.0	1.5
Profitability & operating ratios:					
EBT/tangible worth	55.4%	58.8%	63.4%	62.8%	65.5%
EBT/total assets	18.4%	22.1%	16.2%	30.8%	26.0%
Revenue/fixed assets	3.6	4.7	4.4	5	4.9
Revenue/total assets	1.8	2	1.6	2.1	2

to tangible worth increased in the past five years from 1.5 to 1.8. Fixed assets to tangible worth increased from 1.0 to 1.5.

Profitability ratios reflect the returns earned by Acme and assist in evaluating manager performance. Acme has been consistently profitable in each of the past five years. The earnings before taxes to tangible worth fluctuated between 55% and 66%. Officers' compensation ranged from $2.2 million to $3.5 million during the five years and was $3.4 million in the most recent year.

Comparison to Industry Averages

Victoria also compares Acme's key financial ratios to peer companies. The main differences between Acme and other firms of similar size in the same industry are as follows:

- Acme's liquidity is much less than that of other firms in the group. Similar companies have a ratio of 1.6, whereas Acme has a current ratio of 1.0. This is likely to be due to Acme having a large part of its debt due within 12 months instead of long-term financing.

- The average number of days in accounts payable for Acme is 48 days, which is much higher than the peer group's average of 32 days. This is probably due to the firm taking longer to pay for raw materials and inventory because of its low working capital.

- The times interest earned measure for Acme is much higher than its peer group's average. The firm had a measure of 7.3 as compared to its peers at 4.0. This is likely to be due to Acme having a higher profit margin than its peers.

- Acme is much more leveraged that its peer group. Its measure of debt to tangible worth is 1.8, compared to its peers at 1.2. Furthermore, the firm's measure of fixed assets to tangible worth is 1.5, compared to its peers at 0.5. Acme has a higher amount of fixed assets compared to its tangible worth.

- Acme is more profitable than its peers. The measure of earnings before taxes to total assets is 18%, compared to its peers at 12%. In addition, Acme's earnings before taxes to tangible worth is 55%, compared to its peers at 22%. This is due to Acme's profit margin of 11%, compared to its peers at 5%.

The purpose of this part of Victoria's analysis is to evaluate the risk factors of owning this business as compared to an investment in the average peer company. As previously discussed in this chapter, investors have options of where to place their capital and rational investors require a higher reward—in the form of returns—for investments with higher risks.

Valuation Methods

Victoria tells Bob that Acme's shares of common stock are private securities and there is no liquid market for their sale. Furthermore, no obvious firms can easily be found that would serve as price benchmarks to value Acme. Next, in her analysis, Victoria considers all relevant valuation approaches and ultimately relies on two ways to estimate the value of Acme's common stock—the market approach and the income approach. She rejects the asset approach because the premise of value is a going concern and the company has no intention to liquidate its assets. In addition, the asset approach does not clearly reflect the value of this firm arising from its earnings potential.

Debt-Free Analysis

Victoria further explains to Bob that there are two ways to value the shares of a private firm using the income approach. The first way is the *direct equity methodology*. Using this approach, a firm's net cash flow drives the value of its stock. This methodology either *capitalizes* the net cash flow for one year or calculates the present value of a series of future cash flows.

The second way is the *debt-free methodology* (sometimes called the invested capital methodology). How much or how little a firm is leveraged can have a significant impact on the value of its stock. If a firm has too little leverage or too much leverage compared to an ideal blend of debt and equity capital, the direct equity methodology may result in a distorted valuation of the firm; therefore, the debt-free method should be used instead to value the firm.

A firm's *invested capital* represents all of its sources of capital to fund the business—capital from investors (equity) and creditors (debt). When we say the value of a business or a business enterprise, it has a different meaning from the value of the firm's equity. This concept is illustrated in the accompanying diagram.

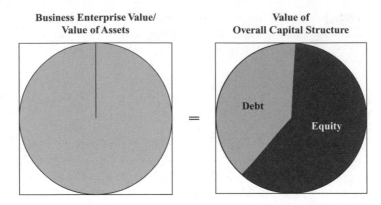

When we talk about the value of a business enterprise, we are usually referring to the value of the firm without thinking about its debt. (This idea is similar to talking about the value of a house. The mortgage loan does not affect the home's value.) The *business enterprise value* is represented by the left-hand graph. This amount is equal to the values of the firm's equity and debt. After subtracting the value of the debt from the business enterprise value, the resulting amount is the value of the firm's equity. We might want to know the business enterprise value in a sale transaction because many sales are structured to transfer only a firm's assets to the buyer, and it is up to the buyer to raise capital from investors and/or borrow from lenders. (In an asset sale, the *seller* would be responsible for paying off the firm's existing debt, usually upon receipt of the sales proceeds.)

We usually think about the debt-free methodology in two steps. First, determine the business enterprise value based on the firm's cash flow. But this level of cash flow should be *before* any principal and interest payments on the firm's debt. Second, if the firm's equity is being valued, then subtract the value of the firm's debt from the business enterprise value.

Alternatively, the direct equity methodology values a firm's equity by using the net cash flow *after* the firm makes payments on its debt. The result of this method is the value of the firm's equity.

The direct equity and debt-free methodologies are summarized as follows:

Debt-Free Methodology	Direct Equity Methodology
1. Estimate net cash flow to the firm available to all holders of the company's invested capital.	1. Estimate net cash flow to equity holders.
2. Apply to the discount rate or capitalization rate on a weighted average cost of capital basis.	2. Apply to the discount rate or capitalization rate on a cost of equity basis.
3. The result is the value of the firm.	3. The result is the value of the company's equity.
4. Subtract value of debt to arrive at the value of the company's equity.	

Cost of Capital

Bob asks Victoria to explain the concept of cost of capital. She says that when a business manager or prospective buyer of a firm is raising capital, debt capital is less expensive than equity capital. Debt capital is monies borrowed from lenders, such as banks, to fund a business. The lender expects a return on its investment in the form of interest. In financial terms, interest expense on debt is called the firm's *cost of debt*. Therefore, a firm pays interest—or a cost of debt—that is based on lending rates in the capital markets. Acme's current cost of debt is 9% per year. However, since Acme can take a tax deduction for its interest expense, its after-tax cost of debt capital is 5.4% based on a 9% borrowing rate less 40% of that amount in reduced taxes: $5.4\% = 9\% \times (1 - 40\%)$. So, for every $100 Acme pays in interest expense to the bank, its income tax obligation is lowered by $40 because interest is a business expense that lowers the firm's taxable income. Thus, in this example, Acme's after-tax interest expense is $60 ($100 paid to the bank minus $40 in reduced taxes).

In order for a firm to raise equity capital by selling stock to investors, it needs to offer an incentive: the hope of earning a fair reward for making an investment. For stocks, those rewards come in the form of dividends or capital gains, or both. Collectively, these rewards are an investor's return on investment. As previously discussed, stocks of large U.S. public companies have created average historical returns of 10% to 12% per year over the long run. Small public company stocks in the United States have had average historical annual returns of 15% to 20% over the long run. Since private firms are usually riskier than most small public companies, private firms must offer a rate of return to their shareholders higher than the returns of less risky stocks of small public firms.

When raising capital by a stock offering, investors can get a higher rate of return if the stock price is lower. In other words, a lower stock price results in a lower investment for the person buying the shares. Holding the expected future returns to investors constant, their return on investment is higher when buying the shares at a low price and, conversely, their return on investment is lower if they pay a high price for the shares.

Let's say that a private firm is raising capital by selling stock. The returns a firm gives its stockholders are called the firm's *cost of equity*. In other words, to raise new equity capital, the firm needs to work to reward those new investors. Those rewards are the firm's cost of equity.

Furthermore, a firm has both a cost of debt capital and a cost of equity capital, and these two costs differ. Combined, these costs are called a firm's *cost of capital*. The cost of debt is less than the cost of equity. Lenders demand a lower rate of return than investors because lenders are in a less risky position since they normally get paid before investors. Moreover, a firm's managers can maximize the returns to its shareholders by using a blend of debt financing (less expensive) and equity capital (more expensive). When managers get capital from lenders, the firm does not issue as much stock and, therefore, the firm's profits are divided among fewer shares. Say that a prospective buyer of a firm must raise $10 million to acquire a target company. If it raised the entire $10 million from the sale of stock, it would need to offer those shareholders a rate of return of, say, 20% per year on average. Alternatively, it could raise a portion of the $10 million by borrowing from a bank at, say, an after-tax interest cost of 5%. In this example, the cost of debt is significantly less than the cost of equity. If the buyer borrows $5 million from the bank and raises another $5 million through the sale of stock, its overall cost of capital is much lower than if the full amount was raised from the sale of stock. The following tables compare the cost of capital in two situations:

Blended Capital Structure of Debt and Equity

Type of Capital	Amount (in millions)	%	Cost of Capital	Weighted Average Cost of Capital
Debt	$ 5	50%	5% (after-tax)	2.5%
Equity	5	50	20%	10.0
Debt and equity	$10	100%	N/A	12.5%

No Debt in Capital Structure

Type of Capital	Amount (in millions)	%	Cost of Capital
Equity	$10	100%	20%

This example illustrates that with the prudent blending of debt and equity capital, managers can decrease the firm's total cost of capital from 20% to 12.5%. This has the effect of increasing the current shareholders' rate of return. It also has a positive effect on the firm's stock price.

The relevance of all of this to valuing a business is that if the goal is to value a firm's shares—rather than the business enterprise value—and the firm does not already have the good blend of debt and equity capital, a valuation may produce a wrong result unless the debt-free methodology is used. When valuing stock, the direct equity methodology does not take into account a firm's *optimal* blend of debt and equity—unless the business already happens to have it. Consequently, the result of the valuation of a firm's shares using the direct equity methodology may result in an incorrect value because the firm's cost of capital is misestimated. However, if the firm already has a good blend of capital, the direct equity method produces a reasonable estimate of the stock's value and is a simpler methodology.

Victoria's analysis shows that Acme does not have the ideal capital structure. Therefore, she concludes that a debt-free methodology is necessary to properly value Acme's shares. This methodology first estimates Acme's cash flows before paying its debt. This level of cash flows will be higher than a firm's net cash flows, which has reductions for principal and interest payments to the firm's lenders. Using this higher level of cash flows produces a higher value. Conceptually, this higher level of cash flows and value is shared between investors *and* lenders. This concept was illustrated in the graphic earlier in this chapter. Once Acme's business enterprise value is estimated, then the value of its debt capital is subtracted, resulting in the value of Acme's equity.

Victoria summarizes these ideas for Bob. The debt-free methodology first estimates Acme's business enterprise value. If Bob were to sell Acme in an asset sale, he would be interested in this value. But if the transaction were structured as a sale of all of Acme's stock, Bob would want to know the value of the shares. In this case, the value of

Acme's debt capital would be subtracted from its business enterprise value, which would produce an estimate of the value of Acme's shares. Victoria tells Bob that although the debt-free methodology is more complex than the direct equity methodology, it is needed to value Acme's shares since the firm does not have the optimal capital structure of debt and equity.

Adjustments to Earnings for Valuation Purposes

As discussed earlier, financial statements of private firms sometimes do not show the true profitability. Victoria tells Bob that adjustments to the financial statements are sometimes needed for a valuation analysis.

These adjustments fall into two areas. The first type removes unusual or nonrecurring items. These sorts of adjustments remove the effect of past events that are not expected to occur again, such as operations that have been closed, legal costs to defend an extraordinary lawsuit, or a nonrecurring capital gain from the sale of an asset. A buyer of a firm would not expect these items to occur in the future and, therefore, they are not relevant to the analysis.

The second type of adjustment is economic. These include adjustments to costs on the financial statements that are not shown at their market values, such as officers' wages being paid at an above-market amount, the firm's rent expense being paid to a related party at an amount different from market rent, or a shareholder's extra perquisites being expensed by the business for tax purposes. In addition, some private firms fail to report all of their revenues in order to improperly lower their taxes, and any unreported sales would be an adjustment. Furthermore, expenses related to non-operating assets (e.g., a ski condominium owned by the firm but used only for nonbusiness reasons) would also be eliminated. Many adjustments of the second type arise from activities between the firm and related parties.

Once these adjustments are made to the historical income statements, they represent what the firm would have earned if revenues, related-party transactions, and so forth were properly recorded and if unusual or nonrecurring events had not occurred. Those adjusted earnings are a historical benchmark for estimating the firm's future earnings and cash flows.

For Acme, Victoria determines that the amount of officers' wages paid to Bob and his family were more than the wages the firm would have paid to nonfamily employees in the same job positions. Thus, officers' wage expense on the historical income statements are reduced to the amount of market wages, and therefore the firm's earnings increase. In addition, Bob personally owns the property where the factories are located, leases the properties to the firm, and collects rents. Victoria finds that Acme is paying rents to Bob that exceed market rents, so she reduces the firm's rent expense. As reflected in Exhibit 16.2, Acme has elected to be treated as an S corporation for U.S. income tax purposes. Thus, Acme does not pay income taxes since the income is reported on Bob's personal income tax return. As a result, Bob—rather than Acme—pays the income taxes on the firm's profits, and Acme's income statements do not show an expense for income taxes. Victoria believes the most likely buyer of Acme would be a large corporation that would not be able to maintain Acme's S corporation tax status. The buyer would be a corporation that pays income taxes. Therefore, Victoria makes an economic adjustment to Acme's income statements to include an expense for income taxes. This adjustment is made because the after-tax income is what a typical buyer of Acme expects to earn. That buyer would use Acme's after-tax income—what it would receive as its return on investment—in estimating a price it would pay to buy the firm.

Once Victoria determines Acme's true historical profitability, she now applies the valuation methodologies.

Income Approach: Discounted Cash Flow Method

As discussed earlier, the income approach is based on the concept that the value of an asset today represents its expected future benefits discounted to a present value. Victoria uses the discounted cash flow (DCF) methodology in her analysis. This method forecasts Acme's cash flows for several years—often five years—into the future and discounts them to a present value. In addition, this method assumes that Acme will be sold at some point in the future and the owner will receive sales proceeds at that time. That estimated future sales price—called the *residual value* or terminal value—is also discounted back to a present value. Next, the sum of the present values of future cash flows and the present value of the residual value are added together to estimate the value of Acme. This concept is summarized as follows:

Discounted Cash Flow Valuation Method (Simplified)

     Annual future cash flows, discounted to a present value

+   Future residual value, discounted to a present value

=   Value (today)

As discussed earlier, cash flows may be after-debt costs (called the net cash flow to equity holders) or on a debt-free basis (called the net cash flow to the firm). The formulas for these two levels of cash flows are shown next. The use of either level of cash flow can be used in a DCF model.

Net Cash Flow to Equity Holders

     After-tax net income

+   Depreciation and amortization and other noncash expenses

−   Capital expenditures

−   Increases (or + decreases) in working capital requirements

+   Increases (or − decreases) in long-term debt

=   Net cash flow to equity holders

Net Cash Flow to the Firm

     After-tax net income

+   Depreciation and amortization and other noncash expenses

−   Capital expenditures

−   Increases (or + decreases) in working capital requirements

+   Interest expense × (1 − tax rate)

=   Net cash flow to the firm

Application of DCF Model

Level of Cash Flows	Type of Discount Rate
Net cash flow to equity holders	Cost of equity capital
Net cash flow to the firm	Weighted average cost of capital

An error when using the income approach is mismatching the level of cash flows and the type of discount rate. The net cash flow to equity holders represents the return to investors. Thus, the discount rate for this level of cash flows is the firm's cost of equity capital. Alternatively, the net cash flow to the firm is the return the firm generates to pay the investors and lenders. For this level of cash flows, the DCF model should use the firm's weighted average cost of capital as the discount rate.

In summary, it is very important to think about the level of cash flows in the valuation model and match it with the proper type of discount rate.

Forecasted Financial Statements

Acme's managers have prepared a financial forecast and discuss it with Victoria. The forecasts are presented in Exhibits 16.5, 16.6, and 16.7. Key assumptions in the forecasts include:

- Sales would grow 12% in 2009 and 2010, 11% in 2011 and 2012, and 10% in 2013.
- Costs of goods sold are 69% of sales.
- Operating expenses (exclusive of officers' wages) are 12% of sales.
- Officers' wages (at market amounts) are 3.1% of sales.
- The 2009 capital expenditures are $2.8 million and increase thereafter 5% per year.
- The firm needs a minimum cash balance of $200,000.
- The dividend payout ratio (the amount of cash flows actually distributed to shareholders; the remainder is reinvested in the firm) ranges from 55% to 65% per year.

Residual Value

The DCF valuation methodology assumes that the firm will be sold in the future and the shareholders will receive the proceeds at that time. Victoria assumes Acme will be sold five years in the future on December 31, 2013. (Five years is common among analysts for mature firms. Start-up firms, however, may require financial forecasts for a longer period until the firm's earnings growth rate becomes stable.) The value of a firm at that time is called the residual value, as discussed earlier. The residual value of Acme is estimated from its forecasted net cash flows in 2013 and then by estimating the cash flows for the following year, 2014. The model assumes that the firm will be sold at the end of 2013, its earnings growth rate is stable on average, and a hypothetical new owner would expect to receive the amount of 2014 cash flows reflected in the model.

Next, a price multiple is applied to Acme's estimated 2014 net cash flow in order to estimate the firm's residual value at December 31, 2013. The multiple is based on a

Exhibit 16.5 Acme Manufacturing, Inc.: Forecasted income statements, 2009–2013.

	($ millions)					
	Pro Forma	**2009**	**2010**	**2011**	**2012**	**2013**
Revenue	$50.29	$56.32	$63.08	$70.02	$77.72	$85.50
Cost of goods sold	34.58	38.86	43.53	48.32	53.63	58.99
Gross profit	15.70	17.46	19.56	21.71	24.09	26.50
Operating expenses	5.95	6.76	7.57	8.40	9.33	10.26
Officers' wages	1.54	1.75	1.96	2.17	2.41	2.65
Depreciation & amortization	1.00	0.88	1.01	1.14	1.28	1.43
Interest expense	0.84	1.04	1.10	1.14	1.21	1.28
Operating profit	6.37	7.03	7.92	8.85	9.87	10.88
Other expenses/(income)	(0.30)	(0.21)	(0.21)	(0.21)	(0.21)	(0.21)
Income before taxes	6.66	7.24	8.13	9.06	10.08	11.09
Income taxes	2.67	2.90	3.25	3.63	4.03	4.44
Adjusted net income	$ 4.00	$ 4.34	$ 4.88	$ 5.44	$ 6.05	$ 6.65

	Common Size					
	Pro Forma	**2009**	**2010**	**2011**	**2012**	**2013**
Revenue	100.0%	100.0%	100.0%	100.0%	100.0%	100.0%
Cost of goods sold	68.8	69.0	69.0	69.0	69.0	69.0
Gross profit	31.2	31.0	31.0	31.0	31.0	31.0
Operating expenses	11.8	12.0	12.0	12.0	12.0	12.0
Officers' wages	3.1	3.1	3.1	3.1	3.1	3.1
Depreciation & amortization	2.0	1.6	1.6	1.6	1.6	1.7
Interest expense	1.7	1.8	1.7	1.6	1.6	1.5
Operating profit	12.7	12.5	12.6	12.6	12.7	12.7
Other expenses/(income)	−0.6	−0.4	−0.3	−0.3	−0.3	−0.2
Income before taxes	13.2	12.9	12.9	12.9	13.0	13.0
Income taxes	5.3	5.1	5.2	5.2	5.2	5.2
Adjusted net income	8.0%	7.7%	7.7%	7.8%	7.8%	7.8%

formula: the reciprocal of the firm's weighted average cost of capital less its estimated sustainable long-term earnings growth rate. This formula is:

Discount Rate − Sustainable Long-Term Earnings Growth Rate = Capitalization Rate

1 ÷ Capitalization Rate = Price Multiple

Discount Rate for the Valuation Model

As discussed earlier, since Acme is being valued using a debt-free methodology, Victoria uses the *weighted average cost of capital* (WACC) as the discount rate in her valuation

Exhibit 16.6 Acme Manufacturing, Inc.: Forecasted net cash flows to the firm, 2009–2013.

	($ millions)				
	2009	**2010**	**2011**	**2012**	**2013**
Forecasted after-tax income	$ 4.35	$ 4.88	$ 5.44	$ 6.05	$ 6.65
Forecasted interest expense	1.04	1.10	1.14	1.21	1.28
Tax shield of interest expense	(0.42)	(0.44)	(0.45)	(0.48)	(0.51)
Common stock dividend adjustment	(0.30)	(0.26)	—	—	—
Forecasted depreciation/ amortization	0.88	1.01	1.14	1.29	1.43
After-tax gross cash flow to the firm	5.55	6.28	7.26	8.06	8.86
± Decrease/increase in working capital (excluding interest-bearing ST debt)	(0.54)	(0.63)	(0.65)	(0.72)	(0.73)
± Decrease/increase in investments	(2.80)	(2.94)	(3.09)	(3.24)	(3.40)
± Decrease/increase in other assets	(0.13)	(0.15)	(0.16)	(0.18)	(0.20)
± Increase/decrease in other liabilities	—	—	—	—	—
Cash available for financing	2.08	2.57	3.37	3.92	4.53
− Preferred stock dividends	—	—	—	—	—
Net cash flow	2.08	2.57	3.37	3.92	4.53
+ Beginning cash balance	0.04	0.20	0.20	0.20	0.20
Preliminary cash available	2.12	2.77	3.57	4.12	4.73
− Minimum required cash balance	(0.20)	(0.20)	(0.20)	(0.20)	(0.20)
Net cash flow to the firm	$ 1.92	$ 2.57	$ 3.37	$ 3.92	$ 4.53

model. WACC uses both the firm's cost of debt and cost of equity and weights them based on the firm's ideal capital structure. Each element of Acme's weighted average cost of capital is discussed in the following sections.

Cost of Equity

As discussed earlier in this chapter, investors have many choices to invest their funds, and a rational investor expects to receive a higher rate of return when an investment is riskier than alternatives. In estimating Acme's cost of equity capital, Victoria uses the modified capital asset pricing model (CAPM), which is defined as:

$$\text{Cost of Equity} = \text{Risk-Free Rate} + (\text{Equity Risk Premium} \times \text{Beta})$$
$$+ \text{Premium for Size Risk} + \text{Premium for Risks Unique to Firm}$$

Investments in private firms are widely considered to be long-term rather than short-term investments. Accordingly, the *risk-free rate*, the first part of the modified CAPM, is based on the 20-year U.S. Treasury bond yield. U.S. Treasuries are considered risk-free

Exhibit 16.7   Acme Manufacturing, Inc.: Forecasted balance sheets, 2009–2013.

	($ millions)					
	Adjusted 2008	2009	2010	2011	2012	2013
Cash	$ 0.04	$ 0.20	$ 0.20	$ 0.23	$ 0.24	$ 0.40
Accounts receivable	6.87	7.69	8.61	9.55	10.61	11.67
Inventory	4.45	4.98	5.58	6.19	6.88	7.56
Other current assets	0.34	0.38	0.42	0.47	0.52	0.57
Total current assets	11.69	13.24	14.81	16.44	18.24	20.20
Fixed assets	14.34	17.14	20.08	23.16	26.40	29.80
Accumulated depreciation	(2.94)	(3.82)	(4.83)	(5.97)	(7.26)	(8.69)
Net fixed assets	11.40	13.32	15.25	17.19	19.15	21.12
Other assets	1.33	1.47	1.61	1.77	1.95	2.15
Total assets	$24.42	$28.03	$31.67	$35.41	$39.34	$43.46
Accounts payable	$ 4.55	$ 5.12	$ 5.74	$ 6.37	$ 7.07	$ 7.77
Notes payable	—	0.30	0.26	—	—	—
Current portion LTD	4.58	3.28	3.45	3.63	3.85	4.07
Other current liabilities	2.37	2.66	2.97	3.30	3.66	4.03
Total current liabilities	11.50	11.35	12.42	13.29	14.58	15.87
Long-term debt	5.83	7.65	8.04	8.46	8.98	9.49
Total liabilities	17.33	19.00	20.46	21.75	23.57	25.36
Equity	7.09	9.03	11.21	13.66	15.77	18.10
Total liabilities & equity	$24.42	$28.03	$31.67	$35.41	$39.34	$43.46

investments because they have virtually no default risk. Victoria finds the yield on the 20-year Treasury bonds is 6.4%, which is a proxy for the risk-free rate in the modified CAPM.

Victoria explains that the second part of the modified CAPM is the *equity risk premium*. This is the extra return investors require above a risk-free rate to invest in risky stocks. A common benchmark for the equity risk premium is the returns of the S&P 500 stock index. Several researchers and commercial data providers have analyzed historical equity risk premiums. For instance, Morningstar's Ibbotson Associates performs annual empirical studies of the historical equity risk premium going back to 1926. Since investors in private firms have long investment horizons, business valuation theory uses an equity risk premium with a long-term perspective. Based on her research, Victoria believes a reasonable estimate of Acme's equity risk premium is 8.1% above the risk-free rate.

The modified CAPM uses the sensitivity of a firm's stock price to swings in the broader market. Beta is a measure of the relationship between the returns on an individual stock to returns of the overall market. A proxy for the market is often a stock index such as the S&P 500 index. Moreover, the prices of some stocks tend to rise and fall faster than the overall market. When a stock's beta is greater than 1.0, its returns tend to be more volatile than those of the market. Alternatively, a stock with a beta below 1.0 tends to be less volatile than overall market returns. In summary, beta measures a stock's volatility relative to the overall market. If a stock has a beta greater than 1.0, its returns are more volatile and, therefore, it is riskier than the overall market. If beta is less than 1.0, its returns are less volatile, and it is less risky than the market.

One can obtain beta measurements of public stocks from free Web sites like Yahoo! Finance or MSN Money and from proprietary financial sources like Bloomberg. But how does one get the beta of a private firm to apply the modified CAPM? One way is to use the average beta of public firms that are in the same industry as a proxy.

Victoria's analysis finds that the average beta of public firms in Acme's industry is 0.99. She believes this average is a reasonable proxy for Acme's beta for use in the modified CAPM. Furthermore, she estimates Acme's equity risk premium is 8.0% (the general equity risk premium of 8.1% multiplied by the average industry beta of 0.99).

Victoria tells Bob that the capital asset pricing model widely used by analysts and portfolio managers assumes a stock's unsystematic risks can be eliminated by portfolio diversification. But owners of private firms often do not (or cannot) diversify their portfolios and therefore do not avoid the unsystematic risks of an investment. Business valuation theory has modified the common CAPM to add a premium for unsystematic risks of a private firm investment. Acme's unsystematic risks are discussed shortly.

Research has shown that the returns of small public company stocks are higher than those of large public company stocks over the long run. Many argue that these higher returns occur because smaller firms are riskier than larger ones. Historical data from Morningstar's Ibbotson Associates shows that the smallest 20% of public firms have produced an extra 2% to 4% return above the returns of companies in the S&P 500 index over the long run. Business valuation theory adopts this idea and adds a premium in the modified CAPM for the extra risk from a private firm's smaller size relative to S&P 500 companies. Based on her research, Victoria adds a premium of 2.2% to Acme's cost of equity for the risks associated with its size.

Finally, differences between Acme and small public firms are analyzed. Victoria has identified Acme's features that are positive and negative risk factors (these factors were discussed earlier in this chapter). After reviewing her analysis, she determines that Acme is slightly more risky than small public firms. In Victoria's judgment, she adds a 2% premium to Acme's cost of equity.

In summary, Victoria estimates Acme's cost of equity using the modified CAPM, as shown in Exhibit 16.8.

Exhibit 16.8 Acme Manufacturing, Inc.: Cost of equity.

Risk-free rate		6.4%
Overall equity risk premium	8.1%	
Multiply by beta	0.99	
Acme's equity risk premium		8.0%
Risk premium for small size		2.2%
Risk premium for Acme's features		2.0%
Estimate of Acme's cost of equity		18.6%

Exhibit 16.9   Acme Manufacturing, Inc.: Cost of debt.

Acme's borrowing rate	9.0%
Multiply by the tax effect (1 – tax rate of 40%)	60%
Acme's after-tax cost of debt	5.4%

Cost of Debt

Victoria analyzes Acme's audited financial statements—including the footnotes—and interviews management on the firm's current borrowing rates for its long-term financing. Based on her analysis, she estimates the firm's current borrowing rate is 9%. Since interest is a business expense that reduces tax income, the effective interest rate is less than 9%. Victoria finds that Acme has a 40% tax rate. Therefore, she finds Acme's after-tax cost of debt is 5.4%, as presented in Exhibit 16.9.

Weighted Average Cost of Capital

Victoria estimates that Acme's optimal capital structure is 40% debt and 60% equity. She bases her findings on the average capital structures of public firms in the same industry as Acme and then considers that Acme does not have the same access to equity capital as do public firms.

Based on this weighting between debt and equity, Victoria estimates Acme's weighted average cost of capital at 13.3%. The calculation is presented in Exhibit 16.10.

Discounted Cash Flow Calculation

As discussed earlier, Acme's forecasted net cash flows for 2009 to 2013 are discounted to a present value as of the December 31, 2008, valuation date. The discount rate Victoria uses is Acme's weighted average cost of capital of 13.3%. In addition, Acme's residual value as of December 31, 2013, is discounted to a present value using the same discount rate.

Victoria prepares Exhibit 16.11, which shows the discounting of the cash flows for the five-year period and the discounting of the residual value. Her calculations assume that the annual cash flows are earned equally during each year. Therefore, the present value calculation for the annual cash flows uses the middle of each year—June 30—for the discounting computations. For instance, the first forecasted year (2009) is discounted one-half year—rather than one full year—to the valuation date of December 31, 2008.

Exhibit 16.10   Acme Manufacturing, Inc.: Weighted cost of capital.

Cost of equity (above)	18.6%	
Equity weighting (above)	60%	
		11.1%
Cost of debt (above)	5.4%	
Debt weighting (above)	40%	
		2.2%
Acme's weighted average cost of capital		13.3%

Exhibit 16.11   Acme Manufacturing, Inc.: DCF method of valuation as of December 31, 2008.

Forecast Year	(Exhibit 16.6) Forecasted Cash Flows	WACC	Present Value
2009	$1,921,000	13.3%	$ 1,804,731
2010	2,565,000	13.3	2,126,878
2011	3,367,000	13.3	2,464,157
2012	3,917,000	13.3	2,530,165
2013	4,533,000	13.3	2,584,349
Residual value (see below)		13.3%	30,591,919
Business enterprise value			42,102,198
Less: Debt capital			(10,411,554)
Value of equity			$ 31,690,644
Value of equity (rounded)			$ 31,700,000

Residual Value at December 31, 2013		
2013 forecasted cash flow		$ 4,533,000
Estimated sustainable growth rate		1.05
2014 forecasted cash flow		4,759,650
Price multiple		
WACC (discount rate)	13.3%	
Less: Sustainable growth rate	−5.0	
Capitalization rate	8.3%	
Multiple (reciprocal of capitalization rate)		12
Residual value at December 31, 2013		$ 57,115,800
Present value of residual value		$ 30,591,919

The residual value is based on the expected net cash flow to the firm in the last year of the forecast in 2013 of $4.533 million. Victoria estimates Acme's *long-term sustainable* earnings growth rate is 5% per year on average. Therefore, she estimates the cash flow for 2014 at $4.760 million ($4.533 million × 1.05). She applies a price multiple of 12 to this cash flow. The calculation for the multiple is presented in Exhibit 16.11. Therefore, Acme's future residual value as of December 31, 2013, is estimated as $57.1 million. Next, Victoria calculates the present value as of December 31, 2008, of the residual value as $30.6 million.

The present values of the five years of cash flows are added together along with the present value of the residual value. The sum of the present values represents Acme's business enterprise value of $42.1 million. Next, Acme's interest bearing debt of $10.4 million is subtracted, resulting in $31.7 million for the value of Acme's common stock as of December 31, 2008.

Next, Victoria considers whether valuation adjustments should be made to the $31.7 million value. If Acme were sold, it would probably take months or even longer to sell. The process of selling private firms is much different than selling marketable securities that generally have an active market. Unlike marketable securities like public stocks and bonds, the market for private firms is thin and often requires a team of professional advisers to verify the firm's information, perform valuations, draft legal documents, and so forth. Since the discounted cash flow model Victoria used relies on a discount rate developed from marketable securities, Victoria will make a valuation discount from the $31.7 million for Acme's lack of liquidity.

In summary, the discounted cash flow methodology determines the value of Acme's stock, which represents all of the owner's expected future benefits discounted to a present value. The DCF method forecasts Acme's cash flows into the future and discounts them to their present value. Furthermore, this method assumes that an owner will sell the firm in the future and receive that sales price. That estimated future sales price—the residual value—is also discounted back to a present value. The present values of the future cash flows and the present value of the residual value are added together. Depending on the circumstances, an analysis could estimate either a firm's business enterprise value or the value of its stock. In this case, Victoria estimates the value of Acme's stock.

Market Approach: Publicly Traded Guideline Companies Method

Bob asks Victoria to explain the market approach of valuation. She says it is a general way of estimating a value by comparing an asset to identical or similar assets that have sold where the prices can be observed. For instance, if Bob owned 100 shares of Microsoft stock, his stock could be easily valued by observing prices of Microsoft shares in recent sales transactions. Similarly, a real estate appraiser will often value a property by observing the prices of comparable properties that have recently been sold. But the sales of private firms are less frequent and data about the sales are often private, making the task more challenging.

In a business valuation, the market approach might be applied by observing the prices of any prior sales of the firm's stock, sales of private or public firms, or the share prices of public firms traded on a stock exchange. In the latter two cases, careful analysis should be done to evaluate whether those other firms provide a reliable pricing benchmark. Other firms that are used as benchmarks are sometimes called guideline companies or comparables. The American Society of Appraisers describes guideline public companies as those firms that provide:

> a reasonable basis for comparison to the investment characteristics of the company . . . being valued. Ideal guideline companies are in the same industry as the subject company; however, if there is insufficient market evidence available in that industry, it may be necessary to select other companies having an underlying similarity to the subject company in terms of relevant investment characteristics such as markets, products, growth, cyclical variability, and other relevant factors.[2]

In Acme's case, there have never been any prior sales of its stock. Furthermore, Victoria is unable to find any sales of entire guideline companies where good data are available. She is, however, able to identify five public firms whose shares are actively traded that might serve as pricing benchmarks.

Having identified these public firms through online searches, Victoria then analyzes those firms to evaluate whether their stock prices are reliable pricing benchmarks. She analyzes each firm's financial statements, growth rates, margins, returns on assets and equity, and financial ratios. Next, she calculates several price multiples of those public firms such as:

- Market value of invested capital to sales.
- Market value of invested capital to earnings before interest, taxes, depreciation, and amortization (EBITDA).
- Market value of invested capital to earnings before interest and taxes (EBIT).
- Market value of equity to pretax income.
- Market value of equity to net income.
- Market value of equity to cash flow.
- Market value of equity to book value.

Based on her analysis of those firms and comparing them to Acme, Victoria finds that several types of price multiples are more consistently correlated than others. She believes four of these multiples provide a good basis for pricing benchmarks. Those multiples are: market value of invested capital to sales, market value of invested capital to EBITDA, market value of invested capital to EBIT, and market value of equity to pretax income. For these multiples, the median price multiples of the five public firms are:

	Median Price Multiple
Market value of invested capital to sales	0.54
Market value of invested capital to EBITDA	5.80
Market value of invested capital to EBIT	7.26
Market value of equity to pretax income	6.72

Next, Victoria applies these median multiples to Acme. See Exhibit 16.12 for her calculations. This analysis shows a value of Acme's equity at December 31, 2008, of $35.2 million (rounded).

Reconciliation of Valuation Methods

The overall results of Victoria's analysis before any valuation adjustments are:

Method	Value
Income approach	$31.7 million
Market approach	35.2 million
Average	$33.5 million

Victoria believes both approaches are equally reliable. Therefore, she weights them equally and calculates the average of $33.5 million.

Exhibit 16.12 Acme Manufacturing, Inc.: Publicly traded guideline companies method of valuation.

| | | | Acme ($ millions) | | | | |
Price Multiple	Median Multiple of Guidelines	Pro Forma Amounts[*]	Market Value of Invested Capital	Less: Debt	Market Value of equity	Weight	Weighted Average
Market value of invested capital to sales	0.54	Sales $50.29	$27.16	$10.41	$16.75	25%	$ 4.19
Market value of invested capital to EBITDA	5.80	EBITDA 8.21	47.62	10.41	37.21	25	9.30
Market value of invested capital to EBIT	7.26	EBIT 7.21	52.34	10.41	41.93	25	10.48
Market value of equity to pretax income	6.72	Pretax inc. 6.66	N/A	N/A	44.76	25	11.19
Value of equity							$35.16

[*] See Exhibit 16.5 pro forma amounts for 2008 after valuation adjustments were made.

Adjustment for Illiquidity

As previously discussed, when shares of a *public* firm are sold, the seller will usually receive the proceeds in just a few days. These sorts of investments are liquid and can be quickly converted to cash because they are mostly traded in active markets. But Acme's shares—like those of most private firms—are relatively illiquid. In most cases, an owner of these sorts of shares cannot quickly sell them. It may take months—if not longer—to sell these types of investments. Since people prefer to own assets that are liquid over assets that are not, research shows that people will pay more for liquid assets. Conversely, people pay less for illiquid assets.

Victoria believes that she needs to make a valuation adjustment to consider Acme's illiquidity since she used valuation methods that have not already considered illiquidity. Recall that Victoria used rates of returns from publicly traded securities in developing Acme's cost of equity for the income approach. Furthermore, she used price multiples of publicly traded shares when she applied the market approach. Victoria believes that the values that result from these two approaches represent amounts as if Acme's shares were liquid. Therefore, she makes a downward adjustment from the $33.5 million value developed from her analysis.

Victoria discusses this concept with Bob. She tells him the closest empirical evidence to quantify this sort of adjustment comes from studies of prices of restricted stocks and studies of share prices just prior to initial public offerings. In the first type, the studies compare stock prices of public firms that are freely traded in markets to the prices of stocks whose shares have some sort of legal restriction preventing their sale in public stock exchanges. The second type of study compares stock prices of firms before and after the firms went public through an initial public offering. In each type of study, the two share prices were different. Researchers and analysts believe this evidence shows that investors demand a lower price for shares that are relatively illiquid. From those studies, the observed differences in prices produce a range of valuation discounts that are often attributed to illiquidity. The price differences from these types of studies show valuation adjustments from the liquid prices of around 35% to 45% on average. In other words, these studies suggest that illiquid stocks typically sell for 35% to 45% less than liquid stocks.

Since this research studied shares with *minority* equity positions in public firms instead of controlling positions, Victoria believes that a valuation adjustment for all of Acme's shares should be smaller because she is not valuing a minority position in the firm. Based on her analysis and judgment, she believes a 10% downward adjustment to the $33.5 million value is needed to account for Acme's relative illiquidity.

Valuation Conclusion for Acme

Victoria has now completed her valuation analysis. She estimates the fair market value of Acme's shares is $30.2 million ($33.5 million less 10% valuation adjustment for illiquidity).

Valuing Minority Interests

The Acme case study estimated the value of all of the shares in the firm. Had Bob owned, say, only 25% of the shares and wanted only those shares valued, Victoria would need to do some further work. The financial characteristics of a block of shares that has legal rights to *control* the operations and policies of a firm are different from the characteristics of a noncontrolling, minority block of shares. With only a 25% interest in Acme, Bob would no longer have the legal right to control the firm. He would have only a small voice. Furthermore, if Bob sold his shares to someone, that person would not be able to control the firm, either (unless the person already owned shares).

People generally prefer to have control over something than not have control. Research shows that controlling positions in firms sell for higher prices than noncontrolling positions, all other things being equal. For instance, a 51% ownership in a firm would normally sell for much more than a 49% interest—more than what is explained by the small difference in percentage. One can reason that a 51% position sells for a higher price because it provides control over the firm whereas a 49% position does not.

An equity position of less than 50% of the shares in a firm is called a *minority interest*. In many cases, owners of minority interests in private firms do not have much influence or control over the firm's operations and policies. Alternatively, an equity position of more than 50% is a *controlling interest* in a firm that generally has power over how the business operates, distributes its profits, and so forth.

Owning a stock position that has the legal rights to control the firm is more desirable, and investors usually pay more for that privilege over minority stock positions. In a business valuation analysis, this idea leads to two types of valuation adjustments. The first sort of adjustment accounts for differences in value due to the inability to control or influence the firm. The second type of valuation adjustment accounts for the difference in value arising from illiquidity of the minority shares—which are even more illiquid than Bob's 100% stock interest in the case study. Both of these types of adjustments are often applied when valuing noncontrolling, minority equity interests in a private firm.

Furthermore, when both adjustments are made, they can be large—perhaps 50% or more from the equivalent value of a controlling stock interest, all other things being equal. One can reason that this discount might be so large because noncontrolling interests in most private firms are difficult to sell and have few legal rights other than getting their portion of whatever the managers decide to distribute to shareholders. These features make buying this sort of investment not very desirable in most cases.

Business Valuation Standards

Individuals who specialize in business valuation often follow published professional standards when doing their work. Those guidelines usually cover what one should do in a business valuation analysis and what should be in a valuation report. In North America, business valuation standards have been published by several organizations, including the American Institute of Certified Public Accountants, American Society of Appraisers, The Appraisal Foundation, Canadian Institute of Chartered Business Valuators, Institute of Business Appraisers, and National Association of Certified Valuation Analysts.

Value Engineering

Just as the CEO of a public firm tries to enhance the value of the shares, managers of a private firm can work to increase the value of the firm. Some factors can have a large effect on the value of a private firm. Managers can focus on these factors to possibly increase the firm's value in the future. Some of the factors are obvious, while some are not. The factors include the following:

- Decrease expenses (doing so increases cash flows).
- Increase revenues (increases cash flows).
- Significantly increase the earnings growth rate (may increase earnings forecasts, and lower the capitalization rate due to the growth factor).
- Eliminate the owners' nonbusiness expenses and perquisites (increases cash flows and lowers a buyer's risk of inaccurate financial information).
- Report all revenue on the financial statements and tax return (increases cash flows).
- Develop a team of qualified managers for the possibility that the current owner(s) may leave the firm upon a sale (lowers buyer's risk of earnings volatility and other uncertainties).
- Plan for the current owner-managers to continue working for the firm under new ownership for a fixed period (lowers buyer's risk of earnings volatility and loss of customers, employees, and vendors).
- Have the firm's annual financial statements audited or reviewed by a certified public accountant (a chartered accountant in some countries), and improve interim financial reporting (lowers buyer's risk of inaccurate financial information).
- Develop a list of possible strategic buyers (search for buyers willing to pay a higher price for unique synergies between the buyer and the target firm).
- Decrease dependency on major customers and vendors (lowers buyer's risk of earnings volatility in the event of the loss of a key customer or vendor).
- Develop and organize business data that would be needed by potential buyers (lowers buyer's risk of perceptions of potential earnings volatility without having such knowledge).
- Improve any current financial statistics or ratios that are poor (lowers buyers financial risk).

Public firms report their earnings and performance at least quarterly, and the share prices often react quickly. Values of private firms usually react more slowly to changes. Thus, managers of private firms may need to start working on value improvements one to two years before selling a firm.

Summary

The fair market value of a private firm is essentially an estimate of the price that a willing buyer would pay and a willing seller would accept. Buyers have different motives for buying a business. Financial buyers look for a return on their investment. Strategic buyers often look to integrate their firm with the target firm for strategic reasons. Theoretically, financial buyers pay fair market value, whereas strategic buyers often pay a higher price that reflects synergies.

Although it seems possible to quickly value a private firm by simply plugging numbers into a discounted cash flow model or applying a price multiple to the firm's historical earnings, the question remains whether the resulting value is indeed reliable. Many variables go into a valuation analysis, and those variables often require lots of work to develop. Most private firms have much less information readily available than public firms have. A business valuation analysis is *both* a quantitative *and* a qualitative process that is mostly focused on evaluating investment risk and investment return. It is largely an assessment of the risks an investor is taking on by acquiring and owning the firm. In addition, a valuation analysis often attempts to forecast the earnings an investor can expect to receive in the future as a return on investment.

* * *

Author's Note: This chapter is not intended to be a complete discussion of business valuation. It is meant to illustrate many of the fundamental ideas of business valuation and their application through examples. The proper application of valuation theory in practice depends on the specific facts and circumstances of the business or business interest being valued.

Internet Links

www.aicpa.org/fvs	American Institute of Certified Public Accountants
www.bvappraisers.org	American Society of Appraisers
www.appraisalfoundation.org	Appraisal Foundation
www.bvresources.com	Business Valuation Resources
www.cicbv.ca	Canadian Institute of Chartered Business Valuators
www.cfainstitute.org	CFA Institute
www.instbusapp.org	Institute of Business Appraisers
www.ibbotson.com	Morningstar's Ibbotson Associates
www.nacva.com	National Association of Certified Valuation Analysts

Notes

1. *International Glossary of Business Valuation Terms*, jointly published by the American Institute of Certified Public Accountants, American Society of Appraisers, Canadian Institute of Chartered Business Valuators, Institute of Business Appraisers, and National Association of Certified Valuation Analysts. Further terminology from this jointly published glossary is included in the Glossary at the end of this book.
2. American Society of Appraisers, *Statements on ASA Business Valuation Standards*, SBVS-1 Guideline Public Company Method, revised July 2008.

For Further Reading

Damodaran, Aswath. *Investment Valuation*, 2nd ed. (New York: John Wiley & Sons, 2002).

Hitchner, James R., ed., *Financial Valuation: Applications and Models*, 2nd ed. (Hoboken, NJ: John Wiley & Sons, 2006).

Koller, Tim, Marc Goedhart, and David Wessels, *Valuation: Measuring and Managing the Value of Companies*, 4th ed. (Hoboken, NJ: John Wiley & Sons, 2005).

Morningstar, *Ibbotson Stocks, Bonds, Bills, and Inflation Valuation Yearbook* (Chicago: Morningstar, published annually).

Pratt, Shannon P., and Roger J. Grabowski, *Cost of Capital: Applications and Examples* (Hoboken, NJ: John Wiley & Sons, 2008).

Pratt, Shannon P., and Alina V. Niculita, *Valuing a Business*, 5th ed. (New York: McGraw-Hill, 2007).

Trugman, Gary R., *Understanding Business Valuation: A Practical Guide to Valuing Small to Medium Sized Businesses*, 3rd ed. (New York: American Institute of Certified Public Accountants, 2008).

17

Profitable Growth by Acquisition

Richard T. Bliss

The subject of this chapter is growth by acquisition, and few other business transactions receive more scrutiny in both the popular and the academic presses. There are several reasons for this. One is the sweeping nature of the deals, which typically result in major upheaval and job losses up to the highest levels of the organization. A second is the sheer magnitude of the deals—the merger in 2000 between Time-Warner and America Online (AOL), worth more than $150 billion, exceeds the 2007 gross domestic products (GDPs) of 80% of the world's nations! Third, the products involved are known to billions of people around the world. Budweiser, M&M's, The *Wall Street Journal*, and Porsche are just a few of the world-renowned brand names involved in recent mergers and acquisitions (M&A) transactions. Finally, the personalities and plots in M&A deals are worthy of any novelist or Hollywood scriptwriter. The 1988 leveraged buyout of RJR Nabisco—at that time the largest deal ever at $25 billion—was the subject of a *New York Times* best seller and a popular film, both called *Barbarians at the Gate.* In the ensuing two decades, there have been numerous other best-selling books and movies based on real and fictional M&A deals.

In spite of this publicity and the huge amounts of money involved, it is important to remember that M&A transactions are similar to any other corporate investment; that is, they involve uncertainty and the fundamental trade-off between risk and return. To lose sight of this simple fact or to succumb to the emotion and frenetic pace of M&A deal-making activities is a sure path to an unsuccessful result. The goal of this chapter is to identify the potential pitfalls you may face and to create a road map for a successful corporate M&A strategy. We review the historical evidence and discuss some of the characteristics of both unsuccessful and successful deals. The importance of value creation is highlighted, and we present simple analytical tools that can be used to evaluate the potential of any merger or acquisition. Practical aspects of initiating and structuring M&A transactions are presented and the issues critical to the successful implementation of a new acquisition are briefly described. It is important to understand that there are many legal and financial intricacies involved in most M&A transactions. Our objective here is not to explain each of these in detail, as there are professional accountants, lawyers, and consultants available for that. Instead, we hope to provide valuable and concise information for busy financial managers so that they can design and implement an effective M&A strategy.

Definitions and Background

Before examining the historical evidence on acquisitions, we need to define some terminology. An *acquisition* is one form of a *takeover*, which is loosely defined as the transfer of control of a firm from one group of shareholders to another. In this context, control comes with the ability to elect a majority of the board of directors. The firm seeking control is called the *bidder* and the one that surrenders control the *target*. Other forms of takeovers include *proxy contests* and *going private*. We will briefly discuss going-private transactions, which have increased with the recent surge in private equity deals, but the focus of this chapter is takeover via acquisition.

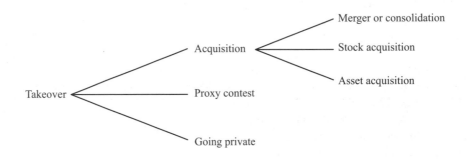

As we can see, acquisitions may occur in several ways. In a *merger*, the target is absorbed by the bidder and the target's original shareholders receive shares of the bidder. In a *consolidation*, the firms involved become parts of an entirely new firm, with the bidder usually retaining control of the new entity. All original shareholders hold shares in the new firm after the deal. The two transactions have different implications for shareholders, as the following examples make clear.

Example 1 There has recently been a wave of takeover activity in the stuffed animal industry. Griffin's Giraffes Inc. (GGI) has agreed to merge with Hayley's Hippos Inc. (HHI). GGI offers one of its shares for three shares of HHI. When the transaction is completed, HHI shares will no longer exist. The original HHI stockholders own GGI shares equal in number to one-third of their original HHI holdings. GGI's original shareholders are unaffected by the transaction, except to have their ownership stake diluted by the newly issued shares.

Example 2 Kristen's Kangaroos Inc. (KKI) wishes to take over the operations of Michael's Manatees Inc. (MMI) and Brandon's Baboons Inc. (BBI). Rather than giving its shares to the owners of MMI and BBI, KKI decides to establish a new firm, Safari Ventures Inc. (SVI). After this consolidation, shareholders of the three original companies (KKI, MMI, and BBI) will hold shares in the new firm (SVI), with KKI having the controlling interest. The three original firms cease to exist.

Another method of acquisition involves the direct purchase of shares, either with cash, shares of the acquirer, or some combination of the two. These *stock acquisitions* may be negotiated with the managers of the target firm or by appealing directly to its shareholders, often via a newspaper advertisement. The latter transaction is called a *tender offer*, which typically occurs after negotiations with the target firm's management have failed.

	SIRIUS SATELLITE RADIO	XM SATELLITE RADiO
Founded	1990	1988
First satellite launched	July 2000	March 2001
First broadcast	February 2002	September 2001
Subscribers (millions)	6.0	7.6
Channels	130	More than 170
Average revenue per subscriber	$11.01/month	$11.41/month
Revenue (millions)	$637	$933
Profit (loss) (millions)	$(1,105)	$(719)
Employees	772	860
Biggest star	Howard Stern	Oprah Winfrey

Exhibit 17.1   The Sirius/XM merger.

Source: Company filings, www.fundinguniverse.com. All data as of year-end 2006.

Finally, an acquisition can be effected by the purchase of the target's assets. *Asset acquisitions* are sometimes done to escape the liabilities (real or contingent) of the target firm or to avoid having to negotiate with minority shareholders. The downside is that the legal process of transferring assets may be expensive.

Acquisitions can be categorized based on the level of economic activity involved according to the following:

- *Horizontal:* The target and bidder in a *horizontal merger* are involved in the same type of business activity and industry. These mergers typically result in market consolidation (i.e., more market share for the combined firm). Because of this, the proposed merger is subject to extra antitrust scrutiny. The 2008 merger of Sirius and XM—the two main satellite radio providers—is an example of a horizontal merger (see Exhibit 17.1). Because the combined entity would have a near-monopoly market share in the United States, the Justice Department demanded caps on price increases before approving the deal.

- *Vertical:* A *vertical merger* involves firms that are at different levels of the supply chain in the same industry. For example, the 1984 merger between Texaco and Getty was prompted by the former's desire to secure Getty's drilling operations and oil fields to complement Texaco's strengths in refining, distribution, and marketing.

- *Conglomerate:* In a *conglomerate merger*, the target and bidder firms are not related. These were popular in the 1960s and 1970s, but are rare today. An auto manufacturer acquiring an ice cream producer would be an example.

In the typical *going private* transaction, all of a public company's outstanding shares are purchased on the open market and the company becomes a private entity. Many of these deals are initiated by private equity (PE) firms, often in conjunction with a management team, and they typically involve high levels of debt.[1] PE buyers usually have a four- to seven-year time horizon and look to exit their investments either by finding a strategic purchaser or returning the business to public ownership.

Armed with a basic understanding of the types of acquisitions and how they occur, we now turn our attention to the track record of M&A transactions. Be forewarned that it is spotty at best and that many practitioners, analysts, and academics believe that the odds are stacked against acquirers. We do not say this to dissuade anyone from pursuing an acquisition strategy, but rather to highlight the fact that without careful planning, there is little chance of success.

Recent Trends and the Performance Record of Mergers and Acquisitions

After recovering from the market meltdown at the start of the decade, global M&A activity reached an all-time high in 2007, before declining significantly in both the number and dollar value of M&A transactions with the financial crisis of 2008 (see Exhibit 17.2). Exhibit 17.3 lists the 10 largest M&A transactions since 2000.

The upturn in M&A activity in 2004 coincided with an increased role for private equity firms. After accounting for less than 3% of M&A volume between 1996 and 2003, PE deals surged to almost one-quarter of all M&A activity in the second quarter of 2007 (see Exhibit 17.4). This jump was due in part to the ready availability of cheap debt, a critical component of most highly leveraged PE transactions. Exhibit 17.4 also shows the predictable impact of the 2007–2008 credit crunch on PE deals.

The historical volume of deal making might lead one to assume that mergers and acquisitions are an easy way for corporate managers to create value for their shareholders.

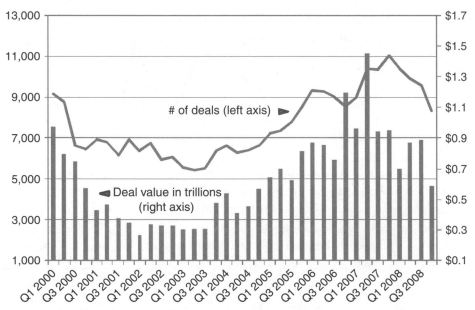

Exhibit 17.2   Global M&A activity, 2000–2008.

Source: Wall Street Journal, January 2, 2009; data from Dealogic.

Rank	Year	Country	Bidder	Target	Country	Price
1	2000	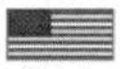	America Online Inc.	Time-Warner Inc.	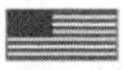	$164.8
2	2007	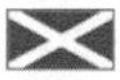	Royal Bank of Scotland	ABN Amro Holdings		$ 95.6
3	2000	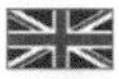	Glaxo Wellcome	SmithKline Beecham	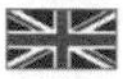	$ 76.0
4	2004		Royal Dutch	Shell Transport	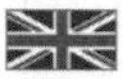	$ 74.4
5	2006	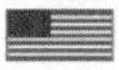	AT&T	BellSouth Corporation	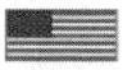	$ 72.7
6	2001	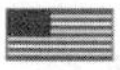	Comcast	AT&T Broadband	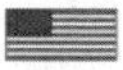	$ 72.0
7	2004		Sanofi-Synthelabo SA	Aventis SA		$ 60.2
8	2002	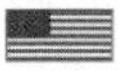	Pfizer	Pharmacia Corporation	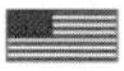	$ 59.5
9	2004	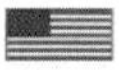	JPMorgan Chase	Bank One Corporation	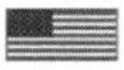	$ 58.8
10	2005	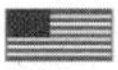	Procter & Gamble	Gillette	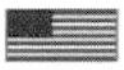	$ 54.9

Exhibit 17.3   Largest M&A deals, 2000–2008.

Source: http://watchmojo.com/web/blog/index.php/2008/01/09/largest-internet-ma-deals-of-all-time/, January 12, 2009.

To assess this, we now examine the empirical evidence on mergers and acquisitions. Let's begin with the wealth of academic studies that analyze M&A performance.[2]

M&A activity has been the focus of volumes of academic research over the past 40 years. The evidence is mixed, but we can draw several clear conclusions from the data. We break our discussion into two pieces: short-term and long-term M&A performance.

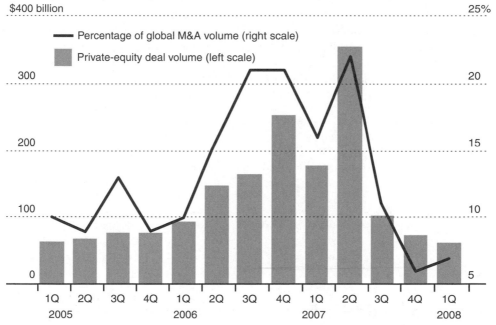

Exhibit 17.4   Private equity activity.

Source:

The short-term is a narrow window—typically three to five days—around the merger announcement. Long-term studies examine postmerger performance two to five years after the transaction is completed.

We can offer three unambiguous conclusions about the short-term financial impact of M&A transactions:

1. Shareholders of the target firms do very well, with average premiums between 20% and 40%, depending on the return window and time period.[3]

2. Returns to bidders have fallen over time as the market for corporate control becomes more competitive; recent evidence finds bidder returns indistinguishable from zero or even slightly negative.

3. The combined return of the target and the bidder (i.e., the measure of overall value creation) was slightly positive.

However, these results are highly variable depending on the specific samples and time periods analyzed. The findings on the long-term performance of mergers and acquisitions are not any more consistent or encouraging. Agrawal et al. (1992) report that "shareholders of acquiring firms experience a wealth loss of about 10% over the five years following the merger completion." Other studies' conclusions range from underperformance to findings of no abnormal postmerger performance. The strongest conclusions offered by Weston et al. (1999, 133 and 140) are that "It is *likely*, therefore, that value is created by M&As" and that "Some mergers perform well, others do not." So much for the brilliance of the academy!

If the academic literature seems ambivalent about judging the financial wisdom of M&A decisions, the popular business press shows no such hesitancy. In a 2002 special report, *BusinessWeek* carefully analyzed over 300 recent deals valued at $500 million or more and reported, "Fully 61% of buyers destroyed their own shareholders' wealth" (Henry and Jespersen 2002). This value destruction is primarily attributed to overpaying for the target. These dismal results hold for both the acquirer's short-term and long-term performance, and are by and large predicted by investors at the time of announcement. An early article exploring the same topic makes the point that poor performance is not a benign result, and places the blame squarely on corporate CEOs (Zweig et al. 1995).

> All this indicates that many large-company CEOs are making multibillion-dollar decisions about the future of their companies, employees, and shareholders in part by the seat of their pants. When things go wrong, as the evidence demonstrates that they often do, these decisions create unnecessary tumult, losses, and heartache. While there clearly is a role for thoughtful and well-conceived mergers in American business, all too many don't meet that description.
>
> Moreover, in merging and acquiring mindlessly and flamboyantly, dealmakers may be eroding the nation's growth prospects and global competitiveness. Dollars that are wasted needlessly on mergers that don't work might better be spent on research and new-product development. And in view of the growing number of corporate divorces, it's clear that the best strategy for most would-be marriage partners is never to march to the altar at all.
>
> —*BusinessWeek*, October 30, 1995

A 1996 survey of 150 companies by the *Economist* Intelligence Unit in London found that 70% of all acquisitions failed to meet the expectations of the initiator. Coopers &

Lybrand studied the postmerger performance of 125 companies and reported that 66% were financially unsuccessful. In summary, there is extensive evidence that most mergers benefit the acquired company at the expense of the buyer's shareholders.

We now turn our attention to three specific M&A transactions. (See Exhibits 17.5, 17.6, and 17.7.) While not the most recent deals, these are all well-known companies and brands, and as examples they very clearly highlight the all-too-common pitfalls. As the *BusinessWeek* articles painfully show, companies continue to make the same mistakes. And although this case study approach is unscientific, it is more informative and certainly more interesting than reviewing academic research. We purposely focus on failed deals in an attempt to learn where the acquirers went wrong. After discussing failed deals, in

---

Mercedes-Benz

CHRYSLER

Disaster Deal #1

The 1998 $130 billion megamerger between German luxury carmaker Daimler-Benz and the #3 U.S. automobile company, Chrysler Corporation, was universally hailed as a strategic coup for the two firms. An official at a rival firm simply said "This looks like a brilliant move on Mercedes-Benz's part."* The stock market agreed, as the two companies' shares rose by a combined $8.6 billion at the announcement. A 6.4% increase in Daimler-Benz's share price accounted for $3.7 billion of this total. The source of this value creation was simple: There was very little overlap in the two companies' product lines or geographic strengths. "The issue that excites the market is the global reach," said Stephen Reitman, European auto analyst for Merrill Lynch in London.* Daimler had less than 1% market share in the United States, and Chrysler's market share in Europe was equally minuscule. There would also be numerous cost-saving opportunities in design, procurement, and manufacturing.

The deal was billed as a true partnership, and the new firm would keep operational headquarters in both Stuttgart and Detroit and have "co-CEOs" for three years after the merger. In addition, each firm would elect half of the directors.

Aftermath: By the end of 2000, the new DaimlerChrysler's share price had fallen more than 60% from its postmerger high. Its market capitalization of $39 billion was 20% less than Daimler-Benz's alone before the merger! All of Chrysler's top U.S. executives had quit or been fired, and the company's third-quarter loss was an astounding $512 million. As if all of this weren't bad enough, DaimlerChrysler's third-largest shareholder, Kirk Kerkorian, was suing the company for $9 billion, alleging fraud when they announced the 1998 deal as a "merger of equals."

The merger struggled for the next few years, and even with the introduction of several so-called shared-platform vehicles in 2004, it was apparent to even the most ardent supporters of the deal that things had not gone according to plan. In May 2007, Daimler announced it would sell 80.1% of Chrysler to the private equity firm Cerberus Capital Management for $7.4 billion, effectively valuing all of Chrysler at $9.2 billion, or one-fifth its preacquisition value 10 years earlier. By late 2008, due in part to the global economic recession, Chrysler, along with GM and Ford, was teetering on the brink of bankruptcy.

*"Auto Bond: Chrysler Approves Deal with Daimler-Benz," *Wall Street Journal*, May 7, 1998.

Exhibit 17.5   Disaster deal #1: Mercedes-Benz/Chrysler.

Disaster Deal #2

Throughout 1994, Quaker Oats Co. was rumored to be a takeover target. It was relatively small ($6 billion in revenue) and its diverse product lines could be easily broken up and sold piece-meal. In November, Quaker announced an agreement to buy iced tea and fruit drink maker Snapple Beverage Corp. for $1.7 billion, or $14 per share. CEO William Smithburg dismissed the 10% drop in Quaker's stock price, arguing, "We think the healthy, good-for-you beverage categories are going to continue to grow." The hope was that Quaker could replicate the success of its national-brand exercise drink Gatorade, which held an extraordinary 88% market share.

Snapple, which had 27% of the ready-to-drink tea segment, was distributed mainly through smaller retail outlets and relied on offbeat advertising and a natural image to drive sales. Only about 20% of sales were from supermarkets, where Quaker's strength could be used to expand sales of Snapple's drinks.

Aftermath: In April 1997, Quaker announced it would sell Snapple for $300 million to Triarc Cos. Quaker took a $1.4 billion write-off and the sale price was less than 20% of what Quaker paid for Snapple less than three years earlier. Analysts estimated the company also incurred cash losses of approximately $100 million over the same period. Ending a 30-year career with the company, CEO Smithburg retired two weeks later at age 58.

Exhibit 17.6   Disaster deal #2: Quaker Oats/Snapple.

Disaster Deal #3

Between 1985 and 1990, AT&T's computer operations lost approximately $2 billion. The huge conglomerate seemed unable to compete effectively against the likes of Compaq, Hewlett-Packard, and Sun Microsystems. AT&T decided to buy rather than build and settled on NCR, a profitable, Ohio-based personal computer (PC) manufacturer with 1990 revenues of $6 billion. NCR did not want to be purchased, and this was made clear in a letter from CEO Chuck Exley to AT&T CEO Robert Allen: "We simply will not place in jeopardy the important values we are creating at NCR in order to bail out AT&T's failed strategy." Ouch! However, after a bitter takeover fight—and an increase of $1.4 billion in the offer price (raising the premium paid to more than 100%!)—AT&T acquired NCR in September 1991 for $7.5 billion.

Aftermath: In 1996, after operating losses exceeding $2 billion and a $2.4 billion write-off, AT&T spun off NCR in a transaction valued at about $4 billion, approximately half of what it had paid to acquire NCR less than five years before.

Exhibit 17.7   Disaster deal #3: AT&T/NCR.

the next section we examine the acquisition strategy and policies of Cisco Systems, the acquirer ranked number one in a recent survey of corporate M&A practices.

As you read about these dismal transactions, can you speculate on the reasons for failure? On their faces, they seemed like strategically sound transactions. While one might question AT&T's push into personal computers, the other two deals were simple horizontal mergers (i.e., an extension of the existing business into new product lines or geographic markets). In hindsight, each deal failed for different reasons, but there are some common issues. The lessons learned are critical for all managers considering growth by acquisition. We now examine these colossal failures in more detail.

In the Daimler/Chrysler merger, there were culture issues from the start, and it quickly became apparent that co-CEOs were not the way to manage a $130 billion global giant. Chrysler CEO Robert Eaton left quietly at the beginning of 2000, and there were other departures of high-level American executives. Morale suffered as employees in the United States realized that the so-called merger of equals was taking on a distinctive German flavor, and in November 2000 the last remaining Chrysler executive, James Holden, the company's U.S. president, was fired.

Rather than deal with these issues head-on, Daimler CEO Jürgen Schrempp took a hands-off approach as Chrysler's operations slowly spiraled downward. The company lost several top designers, delaying new product introductions and leaving Chrysler with an aging line of cars at a time when its competitors were firing on all cylinders. The delay in merging operations meant cost savings were smaller than anticipated, as were the benefits from sharing technology. Finally, analysts suggested that Daimler paid top dollar for Chrysler at a time when the U.S. automobile industry was riding a wave of unprecedented economic prosperity. As car sales began to sag at the end of 2000, all three U.S. manufacturers were facing excess capacity and offering huge incentives to move vehicles. This was not the ideal environment for quickly restructuring Chrysler's troubled operations, and Daimler was facing a 35% drop in projected operating profit between 1998 and 2001. Several shared-platform vehicles were introduced in 2004, including the Crossfire, which combined German engineering with American design. However, too much damage had already occurred and a single car was not going to fix it. DaimlerChrysler continued to lose money until 2007, when Daimler had finally had enough and sold 80% of Chrysler to Cerberus Capital Management. Cerberus could not turn Chrysler around, and in early 2009, the once-proud company filed for bankruptcy protection.

What doomed the Quaker/Snapple deal? One factor was haste. Quaker was so worried about becoming a takeover target in the rapidly consolidating food industry that it ignored evidence of slowing growth and decreasing profitability at Snapple. The market's concern was reflected in Quaker's stock price drop of 10% on the acquisition announcement. In spite of this, Quaker's managers proceeded, pushing the deal through on the promise that Snapple would be the beverage industry's next Gatorade. This claim unfortunately ignored the realities on the ground: Snapple had onerous contracts with its bottlers, fading marketing programs, and a distribution system that could not support a national brand. There was also a major difference between Snapple's quirky, offbeat corporate culture and the more structured environment at Quaker.

Most important, Quaker failed to account for the possible entrance of Coca-Cola and Pepsi into the ready-to-drink tea segment—and there were few barriers to entry—which ultimately increased competition and killed margins. In this case, Quaker's management was guilty of two mistakes: failure to analyze Snapple's products, markets, and competition correctly and overconfidence in their ability to deal with the problems. Either way, their lapses cost Quaker's shareholders billions.

Analysts believe that the merger between AT&T and NCR failed due to managerial hubris, overpayment, and a poor understanding of NCR's products and markets. A clash of culture between the two firms proved to be the final nail in the coffin. In 1990 AT&T's research division, Bell Labs, was one of the world's premier laboratories. With seven Nobel Prizes and countless patents to its name, it was where the transistor and the UNIX operating system had been invented. AT&T's executives mistakenly believed that this research prowess and $20 billion of annual long-distance telephone revenues, along with the NCR acquisition, would guarantee the company's success in the PC business. They were confident enough to increase their original offer price by $1.4 billion. The problem was that by this time, PCs had become a commodity and were being assembled at low cost around the world using off-the-shelf components. Unlike the microprocessor and software innovations of Intel and Microsoft, AT&T's research skills held little profit potential for the PC business.

AT&T hoped to use NCR's global operations to expand its core telecom business. But NCR's strengths were in developed countries, while the fastest-growing markets for communications equipment were third-world regions. And in many companies, the computer and telephone systems were procured and managed separately. Thus, the anticipated synergies never materialized.

Finally, the two companies had very different cultures. NCR was tightly controlled from the top, while AT&T was less hierarchical and more politically correct. When AT&T executive Jerre Stead took over at NCR in 1993, he billed himself as the "head coach," passed out T-shirts, and told all of the employees they were "empowered." This did not go over well in the conservative environment at NCR, and by 1994, only five of 33 top NCR managers remained with the company.

Conclusions: These three case studies highlight some of the difficulties firms face in achieving profitable growth through acquisitions. Rather than being unique situations, they are representative of the way many M&A transactions unfold. Managerial hubris and a competitive market make it easy to overestimate the merger's benefits and therefore overpay. A deal that makes sense strategically can still be a financial failure if the price paid for the target is too high. This is especially a problem when economic conditions are good and high stock prices make it easy to justify almost any valuation if the bidder's managers and directors really want to do a deal. Shrewd managers can sell deals that make little strategic sense to unsuspecting shareholders and then ignore signals from the market that the deal is not a good one.

The previous examples make it clear that it is easy to overstate the benefits that will come after the transaction is completed. Whatever their source, these benefits are elusive, expensive to find and implement, and subject to attack by competitors and economic conditions. Managers considering an acquisition should be conservative in their estimates of benefits and generous in the amount of time budgeted to achieve these benefits. The best way to accurately estimate the benefits of the merger is to have a thorough understanding of the target's products, markets, and competition. This takes time and can come only from careful due diligence, which must be conducted using a disciplined approach that fights the tendency for managers to become emotionally attached to a deal. In spite of the time pressures inherent in any merger transaction, this is truly a situation where haste makes waste.

A common factor in each of these transactions—and one often overlooked by managers and researchers in finance and accounting—is culture. Two types of culture can come into play in an acquisition. One is corporate or industry culture and the second is national culture, which is a factor in cross-border deals. If the target is in a different industry than the bidder, a careful analysis of the cultural differences between them is essential. Culture is especially critical in industries where the main assets being acquired are expertise or intellectual capital. Failure to successfully merge cultures in such industries can be particularly problematic because key employees will depart for better working conditions. When Microsoft withdrew its "friendly" $44 billion bid for Yahoo! in 2008, it did so partly out of fear that pursuing a hostile takeover would alienate Yahoo!'s most valuable asset, the employees.

However, these differences can be overcome, as illustrated by the successful 2001 combination of Hewlett-Packard Corporation (HP) and Compaq Computer. Since the deal closed, HP's share price has tripled. Later in this chapter, we discuss the keys to successful merger implementation. In the next section we examine the acquisition strategy of Cisco Systems Inc. We do this to make it clear that there are ways to increase your chances of success when planning and implementing an M&A strategy.

Anatomy of a Successful Acquirer: The Case of Cisco Systems Inc.

Cisco Systems, the Silicon Valley–based networking giant, is one of the world's most successful corporations. Since going public in 1990, Cisco has posted an eye-popping 35% compounded annual growth rate (CAGR). Revenues for the fiscal year ending July 2008 were up 13% to $39.5 billion, while net income grew to $8.0 billion, resulting in a healthy 20% net profit margin. What is behind such phenomenal results? Cisco decided early on that rapid growth was an important strategy and that acquisition was part of that strategy.

Since 1993, Cisco has acquired 132 companies, 16 of them in the 12-month period ending January 2008.[4] Most were small, privately held companies with technologies closely related to Cisco's core networking equipment business. Not every one of the deals has been a winner, and certainly some elements of Cisco's strategy are unique to the high-technology industry. However, in a recent survey of corporate M&A policies, Cisco was ranked number one in the world, and there are lessons for any potential acquirer in its practices.[5]

We will focus on two aspects of Cisco's acquisition strategy: the competitive and economic forces behind it and how new acquisitions are merged into the corporate fold. The strategic imperative behind Cisco's acquisition spree is simple. Each year the company gets 30% to 50% of its revenue from products that it did not sell 12 months before. Technological change means that Cisco cannot internally develop all of the products its customers need. The company has two choices: to limit its offerings or to buy the products and technology it can't or chooses not to develop. In this case, the strategy is driven by customer's demands and by the realities of the industry. Once CEO John Chambers and Cisco's board made rapid growth a priority, an effective M&A plan was the only way to accomplish this goal. This was the genesis for the company's "build, buy, partner" approach to innovation and growth. The "build" refers to Cisco's own internal research and development (R&D) efforts, on which the company spends approximately $5 billion per year. "Buy" and "partner" mean using investments in start-ups and partnerships with established firms to gain access to emerging sectors. To minimize risk, Cisco often begins with a small investment in order to get a better look at a potential acquisition and to assess its products, customers, and culture. Cisco believes "build," "buy," and "partner" are not independent, but that each plays a role in a successful growth strategy. Ned Hooper, Cisco's senior vice president of corporate development, notes, "Acquisition is not the strategy, it's the tool."[6]

When it comes to postacquisition integration, Cisco's M&A strategy is best captured by "consistent, repeatable, adaptable."[7] The "consistent" and "repeatable" parts are just recognition of the high number of deals Cisco does and the need for standardized procedures. The focus is on talent retention and making the acquired company's employees feel like part of the Cisco family, and Cisco strives to have a new acquisition fully integrated within two months. Cisco's acquisition of fiber-optic equipment maker Cerent Corporation is a good example of this strategy. Cisco purchased a 9% stake in Cerent in 1998 as a hedge against what analysts viewed as Cisco's lack of fiber-optic expertise. Through this small investment, Cisco CEO John Chambers got to know Cerent's top executive, Carl Russo. He quickly realized that they had both come up through the high-tech ranks as equipment salesmen and had built their companies around highly motivated and aggressive sales teams. Cerent's 266 employees included a 100-member sales team that had assembled a rapidly growing customer base. Cerent also favored sparse offices—a Cisco trademark—and Russo managed the company from an eight-foot-square cubicle. All of these factors gave Cisco important insights into Cerent's strengths and corporate culture.

When Chambers felt comfortable that Cerent could successfully become part of Cisco, he personally negotiated the $7 billion purchase price for the remaining 91% stake with Russo. The discussions took a total of two and a half hours over three days. When the deal was announced on August 25, 1999, the second—and arguably the most important—phase of Cisco's acquisition strategy kicked in. Over the years, including an occasional failure, Cisco had developed a finely tuned implementation plan for new acquisitions. The plan has three main pieces:

1. Don't forget the customer.
2. Salespeople are critical.
3. The small things garner loyalty.

There is often a customer backlash to merger announcements, as their perception of products and brands may change. In the recent spate of pharmaceutical industry mergers, only those firms that avoided pairing up experienced substantial sales growth. As part of the external environment, customers are easy to ignore in the short term when the tendency is to focus on the internal aspects of the implementation. This is a big mistake. To allay customer fears, in the weeks after Cerent was acquired, Russo and his top sales executive attended the annual Cisco sales convention meeting and Chambers joined sales calls to several of Cerent's main customers.

This lesson did not come cheaply. When Cisco acquired StrataCom in 1996, it immediately reduced the commission schedule of StrataCom's sales force and reassigned several key accounts to Cisco salespeople. Within a few months a third of StrataCom's sales team had quit; sales fell drastically, and Cisco had to scramble to retain customers. In the Cerent implementation, the sales forces of the two companies remained independent and Cerent's salespeople received pay increases of 15% to 20% to bring them into line with Cisco's compensation practices. As a result, there was little turnover, and sales grew.

Cisco executives realized early on that the strategic rationale for an acquisition and their grand plans for the future meant little to the target's mid- and low-level employees. They had more basic concerns like job retention and changes in their day-to-day activities. Cisco had also learned that quickly winning over these employees and keeping them focused on their jobs were critical to a successful implementation. This process begins weeks before the deal is done, as the Cisco transition team works to map each employee at the target into a Cisco job.

As Cerent employees left the meeting where the acquisition was announced, they were each given an information packet on Cisco, telephone and e-mail contacts for Cisco executives, and a chart comparing the vacation, medical, and retirement benefits of the two companies. There were follow-up sessions over the next several days to answer any lingering questions. Cisco also agreed to honor several aspects of Cerent's personnel policies that were more generous than their own (e.g., more generous expense allowances and permitting previously promised sabbaticals to be taken). Cisco understood that these were relatively small items in the larger context of a successful and timely transition.

When the merger was actually completed, Cerent employees had new IDs and business cards within days. By the following week, the e-mail and voice mail systems had been converted to Cisco's standards, and all of Cerent's computer systems were updated. By the end of September, one month after the acquisition announcement, the new employee mapping had been implemented. Most employees kept their original jobs and bosses; about 30 were reassigned because they had positions that overlapped directly with Cisco workers. Overall, there was little turnover.

The "adaptable" part of Cisco's integration strategy has manifested itself in the past five years, as Cisco has moved from small investments related to its core networking technology into large platform bets. Since 2003, Cisco has spent $2.5 billion on 44 companies in its core business, and over $11 billion on just four platform deals, including the 2006 $6.9 billion acquisition of set-top box manufacturer Scientific Atlanta.[8] These large deals for established companies have forced Cisco to adapt its integration approach, allowing the acquired firms to retain more autonomy, lengthening the integration time considerably (up to two years), and being careful not to damage existing brands and relationships. As a result, these platform deals have been largely viewed as successes and have become major contributors to Cisco's sales growth and profitability.

This section highlights some of the factors important to developing and implementing a successful acquisition strategy for one company. However, not all companies are like Cisco, and what works for Cisco may not guarantee you a winning acquisition plan. Cisco is fortunate to be in a rapidly growing industry in continuous need of new technologies and products. At the same time, the keys to successful implementation discussed earlier (i.e., concern for the customer, taking care of salespeople, and understanding what creates employee loyalty) are universal and must be part of any acquisition strategy. In the next section we look more closely at the question of value creation in M&A decisions.

Creating Value in Mergers and Acquisitions

We have already presented the dubious historical evidence on the financial performance of mergers and acquisitions. This record makes it clear that a significant number destroy shareholder value, some spectacularly. In this section, we more closely examine the issue of value creation, focusing on its sources in mergers and acquisitions. We begin the discussion with an assumption that the objective of managers in initiating these transactions is to increase the wealth of the bidder's shareholders. We will ignore the reality that managers may have personal agendas and ulterior motives for pursuing mergers and acquisitions, even those harmful to their shareholders. A discussion of these issues is beyond the scope of this chapter.[9]

To be very clear, recall the source of all value for holders of corporate equity. Stock prices are a function of two things: expected future cash flows and the risk of those flows. These cash flows may come as dividends, share price increases, or some combination of the two, but the important thing to understand is that changes in share prices simply reflect the market's expectations about future cash flows or their risk—nothing more and nothing less. If investors believe a company's cash flows in the future will be smaller or more risky, ceteris paribus, the share price will decline. If the expectation is for larger or less risky cash flows, the share price goes up. Thus, when we talk about M&A decisions creating value, there can only be two sources of that value: more cash flow or less risk. Our discussion focuses primarily on the former.

Consider two independent firms, A and B, with respective values V_A and V_B. Assume that the managers of firm A feel that the acquisition of firm B (i.e., the creation of a merged firm AB) would create value. That is, they believe $V_{AB} > V_A + V_B$. The difference between the two sides of this equation, $V_{AB} - (V_A + V_B)$, is the incremental value created by the acquisition, sometimes called the *synergy*. That is,

$$\text{Synergy} = V_{AB} - (V_A + V_B) \tag{1}$$

Clearly, positive synergy would be a prerequisite to going forward with the acquisition. In practice, things are a bit more complicated for two reasons: the costs of an acquisition and the target premium. The acquisition process carries significant direct costs for lawyers, consultants, and accountants. There is also the indirect cost caused by the distraction of the bidder's executives from their day-to-day operation of the existing business. Finally, the data presented earlier in the track record section shows that target shareholders in acquisitions typically receive a 30% to 40% premium over market price. Some transactions have smaller premiums, but in almost all cases, the acquirer pays a price above the preacquisition market value. All of these costs can be factored into the evaluation as follows:

$$\text{Net Advantage of Merging} = [V_{AB} - (V_A + V_B)] - \text{Merger Costs} - \text{Premium} \tag{2}$$

Example 3 Midland Motorcycles Inc. is considering the acquisition of Scotus Scooters. Midland's current market capitalization is $10 million, while Scotus has a market capitalization of $2 million. The executives at Midland feel the combined firm would be worth $14 million due to synergies. Current takeover premiums average 35%, and the total cost of the acquisition is estimated at $1.5 million. Should Midland proceed with the deal?

Using equation 2,

$$\text{Net Advantage of Merging} = [\$14 - (\$10 + \$2)] - \$1.5 - (35\% \times \$2) = -\$0.2\,\text{million}$$

The deal would destroy \$200,000 of value. Note that this is in spite of the fact that there are \$2 million of positive synergies created by the acquisition. The reality is that this synergy is more than offset by the costs of the transaction and the premium paid for the target, a typical problem in acquisitions. For example, consider Coca-Cola's 2001 interest in Quaker Oats, which Coke CEO Douglas Daft felt "fit perfectly into Coke's strategy of boosting growth by increasing its share of non-carbonated drinks. . . ."[10] Even Coke's directors felt that the strategic rationale behind the transaction was sound. But the deal was ultimately rejected because of the price. Warren Buffett, a major Coca-Cola shareholder, said, "Giving up $10\frac{1}{2}$% of the Coca-Cola Company was just too much for what we would get."[11]

Note that the bracketed term in equation 2 is just the synergy as defined in equation 1. Where does this synergy or incremental value originate? From the earlier discussion, we know that value can come from only two places—increased cash flows or reduced risk. In this case, the synergy can be computed as follows:

$$\text{Synergy} = \sum_{t=0}^{\infty} \frac{\Delta CF_t}{(1 + r)^t} \tag{3}$$

where ΔCF_t is the incremental cash flow in period t, and r is the appropriate risk-adjusted discount rate.

The total synergy is just the present value of all future cash flows. Equation 3 makes it clear that changes in future cash flows or their risk are at the root of any M&A synergies. Before considering how a merger might impact cash flows, recall how they are computed:

  Incremental revenues
 − Incremental costs
 − Incremental taxes
 − Incremental investment in net working capital
 − Incremental investment in fixed assets
 _____
 = Incremental cash flow

With this in mind, we can look more closely at potential sources of incremental cash flows—and therefore, value—in acquisitions. We focus on the following three areas:

1. Incremental revenue.
2. Cost reductions.
3. Tax savings.

Incremental Revenue

More revenue for the combined firm can come from marketing gains, strategic benefits, or market power. Increased revenue through marketing gains results from improvements in advertising, distribution, or product offerings. For example, when Citicorp and Travelers Inc. announced their merger in 1998, incremental revenue was a key factor:

> Finally, there is the central justification of the deal: cross-selling each other's products, mainly to retail customers. Over the next two years, Citigroup ought to be able to generate \$600 million more in earnings because of cross-selling.
>
> —*BusinessWeek*, April 20, 1998, 37

After acquiring Miller Brewing Company in 1970, Philip Morris used its marketing and advertising strength to move Miller from the #7 to the #2 U.S. beer maker by 1977.

Some acquisitions provide strategic benefits that act as insurance against or options on future changes in the competitive environment. As genetic research has advanced, pharmaceutical firms have used acquisitions to ensure they participate in the commercial potential offered by this new technology. The 2001 acquisition of SmithKline Beecham PLC by Glaxo Wellcome PLC was motivated by Glaxo's fear of missing out on this revolution in the industry. SmithKline had entered the genetic research field in 1993 by investing $125 million in Human Genome Sciences, a Rockville, Maryland, biotechnology company created to commercialize new gene-hunting techniques.

Finally, the acquisition of a competitor may increase market share and allow the merged firm to charge higher prices. By itself, this motive is not valid justification for initiating a merger, and any deal done solely to garner monopolistic power would be challenged by global regulators on antitrust grounds. However, market power may be a by-product of a merger done for other reasons. The XM-Sirius merger was a matter of financial survival, as neither company had the critical mass of subscribers needed to become profitable. The resultant near-monopoly market share of the merged corporation was a by-product of the economic reality.

Cost Reductions

Improved efficiency from cost savings is one of the most often cited reasons for mergers. This is especially true in the banking industry, as the 2000 merger between JPMorgan and Chase Manhattan makes clear.

> The key to executing the merger, say analysts, will be how quickly Chase can trim its expenses. It plans to save $500 million through job cuts, $500 million by consolidating the processing systems of the two institutions and $500 million by selling off excess real estate. In London, for example, the two banks have 21 buildings, and they won't need all of them.
>
> —*Wall Street Journal*, September 21, 2000, C22

In total, there was an estimated $1.5 billion of annual savings. The link between this and value creation is easy for investors to understand, and the benefits from cost reductions are relatively easy to quantify. These benefits can come from economies of scale, vertical integration, complementary resources, and the elimination of inefficient management.

Economies of scale result when a certain percentage increase in output results in a smaller increase in total costs, resulting in reduced average cost. It doesn't matter whether this increased output is generated internally or acquired externally. When the firm grows to its optimal size, average costs are minimized and no further benefits are possible. There are many potential sources of economies of scale in acquisitions, the most common being the ability to spread fixed overhead (e.g., corporate headquarters expenses, executive salaries, and the operating costs of central computing systems) over additional output.

Vertical integration acquisitions can reduce costs by removing supplier volatility, by reducing inventory costs, or by gaining control of a distribution network. Such benefits can come in any industry and for firms of all sizes. Waste Systems International, a regional trash hauler in the United States, acquired 41 collection and disposal operations between October 1996 and July 1999 with the goal of enhancing profitability.

> The business model is fairly straightforward. Waste Systems aims to own the garbage trucks that pick up the trash at curbside, the transfer stations that consolidate the trash and the landfills where it's ultimately buried. Such vertical integration is seen as crucial for success in the waste business. Owning landfill space gives a trash company control over its single biggest cost, disposal fees, and, equally important, produces substantial economies of scale.
>
> —*Wall Street Journal*/New England, July 28, 1999, NE3

One firm may acquire another to better utilize its existing resources. A chain of ski retailers might combine with golf or tennis equipment stores to better utilize warehouse and store space. These types of transactions—dependent upon complementary resources—are typical in industries with seasonal or very volatile revenue and earnings patterns.

Personnel reductions are often used to reduce costs after an acquisition. The savings can come from two sources, one being the elimination of redundancies and the second the replacement of inefficient managers. When firms combine, there may be overlapping functions (e.g., payroll, accounts payable, information systems, etc.). By moving some or all of the acquired firm's functions to the bidder, significant cost savings may be possible. In the second case, the target firm managers may actually be making decisions that limit or destroy firm value. By acquiring the firm and replacing them with managers who will take value-maximizing actions, or at least cease the ones that destroy value, the bidder can effect positive changes.

The U.S. oil industry in the late 1970s provides an excellent example of this. Excess production, structural changes in the industry, and macroeconomic factors resulted in declining oil prices and high interest rates. Exploration and development costs were higher than selling prices, and companies were losing money on each barrel of oil they discovered, extracted, and refined. The industry needed to downsize, but most oil company executives were unwilling to take such action and, as a result, continued to destroy shareholder value. T. Boone Pickens of Mesa Petroleum was one of the few industry participants who not only understood these trends, but was also willing to act. By acquiring several other oil companies and reducing their exploration spending, Pickens created significant wealth for his and the targets' shareholders.[12]

Tax Savings

Corporations in the United States pay billions of dollars each year in corporate income taxes. M&A activity may create tax savings that would not be possible absent the transaction. While acquisitions made solely to reduce taxes would be disallowed, substantial value may result from tax savings in deals initiated for valid business purposes. We consider the following three ways that tax incentives may motivate acquisition activity:

1. Unused operating losses.
2. Excess debt capacity.
3. Disposition of excess cash.

Operating losses can reduce taxes paid, provided that the firm has operating profits in the same period to offset. If this is not the case, the operating losses can be used to claim refunds for taxes paid in the three previous years or carried forward for 15 years. In all cases, the tax savings are worth less than if they were earned today due to the time value of money.

Example 4: Consider two firms, A and B, and two possible states of the economy, boom and bust, with the following outcomes:

	Firm A		Firm B	
	Boom	**Bust**	**Boom**	**Bust**
Taxable income	$1,000	$(500)	$(500)	$1,000
Taxes (@ 40%)	(400)	0	0	(400)
Net income	$ 600	$(500)	$(500)	$ 600

Notice that for each possible outcome, the firms together pay $400 of taxes. In this case, operating losses do not reduce taxes for the individual firms. Now consider the impact of an acquisition of firm B by firm A.

	Firm AB	
	Boom	**Bust**
Taxable income	$500	$500
Taxes (@ 40%)	(200)	(200)
Net income	$300	$300

The taxes paid have fallen by 50% to $200 under either scenario. This is incremental cash flow that must be considered when assessing the acquisition's impact on value creation. This calculation must be done with two caveats. First, only cash flows over and above what the independent firms would ultimately save in taxes should be included; second, the tax savings cannot be the main purpose of the acquisition.

Interest payments on corporate debt are tax deductible and can generate significant tax savings. Basic capital structure theory predicts that firms will issue debt until its additional tax benefits are offset by the increased likelihood of financial distress. Because most acquisitions provide some degree of diversification and reduce the variability of profits for the merged firms, they can also reduce the probability of financial distress. This diversification effect is illustrated in the previous example, where the postmerger net income is constant. The result is a higher debt-equity ratio, more interest payments, lower taxes, and value creation.

Many firms are in the enviable position of generating substantial operating cash flows and, over time, large cash surpluses. At the end of 2008, for example, Microsoft and Apple held a combined $45 billion in cash and short-term investments. Firms can distribute these funds to shareholders via a dividend or through a stock repurchase. However, both of these transactions have tax consequences for shareholders. A third option is to use the excess cash to acquire another company. This strategy would solve the surplus funds "problem" and carry tax benefits, as no tax is paid on dividends paid from the acquired firm to the acquiring firm. Again, the acquisition must have a business rationale beyond just saving taxes.

* * *

The following example summarizes the sources of value discussed in this section and illustrates how we might assess value creation in a potential acquisition.

Example 5: MC Enterprises Inc. manufactures and markets value-priced digital speakers and headphones. The firm has excellent engineering and design staffs and has won numerous awards from *High Fidelity* magazine for its most recent wireless bookshelf speakers. MC wants to enter the market for personal computer (PC) speakers, but does not want to develop its own line of new products from scratch. MC has three million outstanding shares trading at $30 per share.

Digerati Inc. is a small manufacturer of high-end speakers for PCs, best known for the technical sophistication of its products. However, the firm has not been well managed financially and has had recent production problems, leading to a string of quarterly losses. The stock recently hit a three-year low of $6.25 per share, with two million outstanding shares.

MC's executives feel that Digerati is an attractive acquisition candidate that would provide them with quick access to the PC market. They believe an acquisition would generate incremental after-tax cash flow from three sources:

1. *Revenue enhancement:* MC believes that Digerati's technical expertise will allow it to expand its current product line to include high-end speakers for home theater equipment. MC estimates these products could generate incremental annual cash flow of $1.25 million. Because this is a risky undertaking, the appropriate discount rate is 20%.

2. *Operating efficiencies:* MC is currently operating at full capacity with significant overtime. Digerati has unused production capacity and could easily adapt its equipment to produce MC's products. The estimated annual cash flow savings would be $1.5 million. MC's financial analysts are reasonably certain these results can be achieved and suggest a 15% discount rate.

3. *Tax savings:* MC can use Digerati's recent operating losses to reduce its tax liability. The tax accountant estimates $750,000 per year in cash savings for each of the next four years. Because these values are easy to estimate and relatively safe cash flows, they are discounted at 10%.

The premerger values of MC and Digerati are computed as follows:

Company	Number of Shares	Price per Share	Market Value
MC Enterprises	3,000,000	$30.00	$90 million
Digerati Inc.	2,000,000	6.25	$12.5 million

Assume that MC pays a 50% premium to acquire Digerati and that the costs of the acquisition total $3 million. What is the expected impact of the transaction on MC's share price?

Solution: We first compute the total value created by each of the incremental cash flows.

Source	Annual Cash Flow	Discount Rate	Value
Revenue enhancement	$1.25 million	20%	$ 6.25 million[13]
Operating efficiencies	1.50 million	15	10.0 million
Tax savings	0.75 million	10	2.38 million
Total value			$18.63 million

The total value created by the acquisition is $18.63 million. A 50% premium would give $6.25 million of this incremental value to Digerati's shareholders. After $3 million of acquisition costs, $9.38 million remains for MC's shareholders. Thus, each share should increase by $3.13 ($9.38 million divided by the three million shares outstanding) to $33.13.

Note that the solution to Example 5 assumes the market knows about and accepts the value creation estimates described. Investors will often discount management's estimates of value creation, believing them to be overly optimistic or doubting the timetable for their realization. In practice, estimating the synergistic cash flows and the appropriate discount rates is the analyst's most difficult task.

Summary: The sole motivation for initiating a merger or acquisition should be increased wealth for the acquirer's shareholders. We know from the empirical evidence presented earlier in the track record section that many transactions fail to meet this simple requirement. The main point of this section on creating value is that value can come from only two sources—incremental future cash flows or reduced risk. If we can estimate these parameters in the future, we can measure the acquisition's synergy, or potential for value creation. For the deal to benefit the acquirer's shareholders, management must do two things. The first is to make sure the premium paid is less than the potential synergy. Many acquisitions that make strategic sense and generate positive synergies fail financially simply because the bidder overpays for the target. The second task for the acquirer's management is to implement the steps needed after the transaction is completed to realize the deal's potential for value creation. This is a major challenge and is discussed further in the section on postmerger implementation. In the next section we briefly present some of the key issues managers should consider when initiating and structuring acquisitions.

Some Practical Considerations

In this section, we briefly discuss the following issues you may encounter in developing and executing a successful M&A strategy:

- Identifying candidates.
- Cash versus stock deals.

- Purchase accounting.
- Tax considerations.
- Antitrust concerns.
- Cross-border deals.

This is not meant to be a comprehensive presentation of these topics. Rather, the important aspects of each are described with the focus on how they can influence cash flows and synergy. The goal is to make sure that you are at least aware of how each item might affect your strategy and the potential for value creation.

Identifying and Screening Candidates

Bidders must first identify an industry or market segment they will target. This process should be part of a larger strategic plan for the company. The next step is to develop a screening process to rank the potential acquisitions in the industry and to eliminate those that do not meet the requirements. This first screen is typically done based on size, geographic area, and product mix. Each of the target's product lines should be assessed to see how it relates to (1) the bidder's existing target market, (2) markets that might be of interest to the bidder, and (3) markets that are of no interest to the bidder. Keep in mind that undesirable product lines may be sold.

It is also important to evaluate the current ownership and corporate governance structure of the target. If public, how dispersed is share ownership, and who are the majority stockholders? What types of takeover defenses are in place, and have there been previous acquisition attempts? If so, how have they fared? For a private company, there should be some attempt to discern how likely the owners are to sell. Information about the recent performance of the firm or the financial health of the owners may provide some insight.

The original list of potential acquisitions can be shortened considerably by using these criteria. Each company on this shortened list should first be analyzed assuming it would remain as a stand-alone business after the acquisition. This analysis should go beyond just financial performance and might include the criteria listed in Exhibit 17.8.

Other popular tools for this analysis include strengths, weaknesses, opportunities, and threats (SWOT) analysis, Porter's Five Forces model, and gap analysis.[14] Once this process is completed, the potential synergies of the deal should be assessed using the approach presented in the previous section. The result will be a list of potential acquisitions ranked by both their potential as stand-alone companies and the synergies that would result from a combination.

Cash versus Stock Deals

The choice of using cash or shares of stock to finance an acquisition is an important one. In making it, the following three factors should be considered:

1. *Risk sharing:* In a cash deal, the target firm shareholders take the money and have no continued interest in the firm. If the acquirer is able to create significant value after the merger, these gains will go only to its shareholders. In a stock deal, the target shareholders retain ownership in the new firm and therefore share in the risk of the transaction. Stock deals with Microsoft or Cisco in the 1990s made many target firm shareholders wealthy as the share prices of these two firms soared.

Exhibit 17.8   Criteria for analyzing a potential acquisition.

Future Performance Forecast	Financial Performance
Growth prospects	Profit growth
Future margin improvements	Profit margins
Future cash flows	Cash flow
Potential risk areas	Leverage
	Asset turnover
Key Strengths/Weaknesses	Return on equity
Products and brands	
Technology	**Business Performance**
Assets	Market share
Management	Product development
Distribution	Geographic coverage
	Research and development
Industry Position	Assets
Cost structure versus competitors	Employees
Competition	
Position in supply chain	

Source: Adapted from Coyle (2000, 32).

Chrysler Corporation stockholders, in contrast, saw the postmerger value of the Daimler-Benz shares they received fall by 60%.

2. *Overvaluation:* An increase in the acquirer's stock price, especially for technology firms, may leave its shares overvalued historically and even in the opinion of management. In this case, the acquirer can get more value using shares for the acquisition rather than cash. However, investors may anticipate this and view the stock acquisition as a signal that the acquirer's shares are overpriced.

3. *Taxes:* In a cash deal, the target firm's shareholders will owe capital gain taxes on the proceeds. Exchanging shares means the transaction is tax-free (at least until the target firm stockholders choose to sell their newly acquired shares of the bidder). Taxes may be an important consideration in deals where the target is private or has a few large shareholders, as Example 6 makes clear.

Often firms will make offers using a combination of stock and cash. In a 2001 study of U.S. mergers between 1973 and 1998, only 35.4% of the deals were cash-only. Stock-only (45.6%) and combination cash and stock (19%) accounted for approximately two-thirds of the deals.[15] This contrasts with the 1980s when many deals were cash offers financed by the issuance of junk bonds. The acquirer's financial adviser or investment banker can help sort through these factors to maximize the gains to shareholders.

Example 6: Sarni Inc. began operations 10 years ago as an excavating company. Jack Sarni, the principal and sole shareholder, purchased equipment (a truck and bulldozer) at that time for $40,000. The equipment had a six-year useful life and has been depreciated to a book value of zero. However, the machinery has been well maintained and because of inflation has a current market value of $90,000. The business has no other assets and no debt.

Pave-Rite Inc. makes an offer to acquire Sarni for $90,000. If the deal is a cash deal, Jack Sarni will immediately owe tax on $50,000, the difference between the $90,000 he receives and his initial investment of $40,000. If he instead accepts shares of Pave-Rite Inc. worth $90,000 in a tax-free acquisition, there is no immediate tax liability. He will owe tax only if and when he sells the Pave-Rite shares. Of course in this latter case, Sarni assumes the risk that Pave-Rite's shares may fall in value.

Purchase Accounting

Since 2001, only the purchase method of accounting has been accepted for acquisitions; the pooling of interests method is no longer permitted.[16] The *purchase method* requires the acquiring corporation to allocate the purchase price to the assets and liabilities it acquires. All identifiable assets and liabilities are assigned a value equal to their fair market value at the date of acquisition. The difference between the sum of these fair market values and the purchase price paid is called *goodwill*. Goodwill appears on the acquirer's books as an intangible asset and is *amortized*, or written off as a noncash expense for book purposes a period of not more than 40 years. The amortization of purchased goodwill is deductible for tax purposes and is taken over 15 years, although it must be evaluated annually for a loss in fair value or *impairment*. If the value of the goodwill has fallen, it is written down or impaired by the amount of the decrease. Time-Warner AOL's 2002 loss of $98.7 billion—the largest in corporate history—included $45 billion write-down of goodwill and was a clear admission that the merger two years earlier had been a dismal financial failure.

To illustrate the basics of purchase accounting, we offer the following simple example:

Example 7: Consider the predeal balance sheets for B.B. Lean Inc. and Dead End Inc., both clothing retailers (see Exhibit 17.9).

Now assume that B.B. Lean offers to purchase Dead End for $18 million worth of its stock. Assume further that Dead End's building has appreciated and has a current market value of $12 million. Under purchase accounting, B.B. Lean's balance sheet after the deal appears as shown in Exhibit 17.10.

Note that the acquired building has been written up to reflect its market value of $12 million and that the difference between the acquisition price ($18 million) and the market value of the assets acquired ($15 million) is booked as goodwill. B.B.

Exhibit 17.9   Predeal balance sheets.

B.B. Lean Inc.				Dead End Inc.			
($ millions)				($ millions)			
Cash	$ 6	Equity	$28	Cash	$ 3	Equity	$12
Land	22			Land	0		
Buildings	0			Buildings	9		
Total	$28		$28	Total	$12		$12

Exhibit 17.10   B.B. Lean Inc.: Postmerger balance sheet.

B.B. Lean Inc.			
($ millions)			
Purchase Method			
Cash	$ 9	Equity	$46
Land	22		
Buildings	12		
Goodwill	3		
Total	$46		$46

Lean's equity has increased by the $18 million of new shares it issued to pay for the deal.

*   *   *

Entire volumes have been written on the accounting treatment of acquisitions, and this is a very complex and dynamic issue. Because of this, it is important to get timely, expert advice on these issues from competent professionals.

Tax Issues

Taxes were discussed briefly in the paragraph comparing cash and stock deals. In a *tax-free transaction*, the acquired assets are maintained at their historical levels and target firm shareholders don't pay taxes until they sell the shares received in the transaction. To qualify as a tax-free deal, there must be a valid business purpose for the acquisition and the bidder must continue to operate the acquired business. In a *taxable transaction*, the assets and liabilities acquired are marked up to reflect current market values, and target firm shareholders are liable for capital gain taxes on the shares they sell.

In most cases, selling shareholders would prefer a tax-free deal. In the study by Weston and Johnson (1999), 65% of the transactions were nontaxable. However, there are situations where a taxable transaction may be preferred. If the target has few shareholders with other tax losses, their gain on the deal can be used to offset these losses. A taxable deal might also be optimal if the tax savings from the additional depreciation and amortization outweigh the capital gain taxes. In this case, the savings could be split between the target and bidder shareholders (at the expense of the government). Again, it is important to get current, expert advice from knowledgeable tax accountants when structuring any transaction.

Antitrust Concerns

Regulators around the world routinely review M&A transactions and have the power to disallow deals if they feel they are anticompetitive or will give the merged firm too much market power. More likely than an outright rejection are provisions that require the deal's participants to modify their strategic plan or to divest certain assets. When the Federal Trade Commission (FTC) approved the 2006 $27 billion acquisition of Guidant Corporation by Boston Scientific, it required the merged firm to divest its vascular business, which was sold to Abbott Laboratories for $4.1 billion. Such concessions can have important implications for cash flow and ultimately shareholder value.

The basis for antitrust laws in the United States is found in the Sherman Act of 1890, the Clayton Act of 1914, and the Hart-Scott-Rodino Act of 1976. Regulators assess market share concentration within the context of the economics of the industry. Factors such as ease of entry for competitors and the potential for collusion on pricing and production levels are also considered. In the end, antitrust enforcement is an inexact science that can have a major impact on M&A activity. When assessing potential acquisition candidates, the potential for regulatory challenges—and an estimate of the valuation impact of likely remedies—must be considered in the screening and ranking process.

Cross-Border Deals

In 2007, cross-border M&A transactions totaled $2 trillion and accounted for 41% of global M&A deal volume. Although total deal volume increased only 24%, the $2 trillion of cross-border deals was a staggering 78% increase over 2006. In addition, the value of deals with U.S. firms as the target was $100 billion greater than deals where U.S. firms were the acquirer ($360 vs. $254 billion).[17] By any measure, the level of international M&A activity is increasing as the globalization of product and financial markets continues. All of the issues discussed in this chapter apply to cross-border deals, in some cases with significant added complexities, which are discussed briefly next.

Each country has its own legal, accounting, and economic systems. This means that tax and antitrust rules may vary greatly from U.S. standards. While there is a move to standardized financial reporting via International Financial Reporting Standards (IFRS), there is still great variability in the frequency and reliability of accounting data around the world. Unfortunately, developing nations, which offer some of the best acquisition opportunities, have the most problems.

Doing M&A transactions across borders brings additional risks that have not been previously discussed. These include currency exchange risk, political risk, and the additional risk of national cultural differences. If a company is going to execute an effective international M&A strategy, all of these must be identified and quantified, as they can have a significant impact on synergies and the implementation timetable. It is critical for a bidder to have capable financial and legal advisers in each country where it is considering acquisitions.

Successful Postmerger Implementation

The section on track records makes it clear that most acquisitions fail to meet the expectations of corporate managers and shareholders. This dismal record is attributable to various causes, including ill-conceived acquisition strategies, poor target selection, overpayment, and failed implementation. In a study of 45 Forbes 500 firms, Smolowitz and Hillyer (1996) asked senior executives to rate a list of reasons for the poor performance record of acquisitions. The following were the five most frequently ranked factors:

1. Cultural incompatibility.
2. Clashing management styles and egos.
3. Inability to implement change.
4. Poor forecasting.
5. Excessive optimism with regard to synergy.

The last two are premerger problems, but the first three occur in the postmerger transition process. Deloitte & Touche Consulting estimates that 60% of mergers fail largely because of integration approach. Managers must understand that the acquisition closing dinner marks the end of one stage of the transaction and the beginning of the process that will determine the deal's ultimate success or failure. In this section we briefly discuss the following key components of a successful implementation plan:

- Expect chaos and a loss of productivity.
- Create a detailed plan *before* the deal closes.
- Keep your executives happy.
- Speed and communication are essential.
- Focus managerial resources on the sources of synergy.
- Culture, culture, culture.

The process of merging two firms creates havoc at every level of the organization. The moment the first rumors of a possible acquisition begin, an air of uncertainty and anxiety permeates the company. The first casualty in this environment is productivity, which grinds to a halt as the gossip network takes over. While the executives debate grand, strategic issues, the employees are concerned with more basic issues and need to know several key things about their new employers, their compensation, and their careers before productivity will resume. Managers must understand that this "me first" attitude is human nature and must be addressed—especially in transactions where the most important assets are people.

The first step in any postmerger implementation must be a detailed plan. We saw how Cisco maps the future of every employee in a soon-to-be-acquired firm. For those continuing on, their new positions and duties within Cisco are clearly defined from the beginning. The employees who will be relocated or terminated are also identified, and a separate plan for handling them is created. Relocation and severance packages must be generous to signal retained workers that their new employer is ethical and fair. The second reason for a detailed plan is that it allows transition costs to be accurately estimated. The costs to reconfigure, relocate, retrain, and sever employees must be budgeted, as they can have a significant impact on postmerger cash flows.

The detailed plan must start at the highest levels of the organization. If executives from the two firms are going to lead the transition, they must be confident of their future roles and comfortable with their compensation plans. In the Daimler-Benz/Chrysler deal, there was a good deal of animosity between executives as the German managers watched their American counterparts walk away with multimillion-dollar payoffs from their Chrysler stock options while simultaneously receiving equity in the newly merged firm. A fair incentive system must be in place at the corporation's executive suite before any implementation plan begins.

Once the key managers have been identified, retained, and given the proper incentives, they must carry the vision of the merger to the rest of the organization. To combat the productivity problems discussed earlier, managers have two critical weapons: speed and communication. Remember that the enemy from the employees' perspective is uncertainty, and absent timely information from above, they will usually assume the worst. Executives must move quickly to convey the vision for the merged entity and to assure key employees of their role in executing this vision.

While all employees should be part of this process, those who deal with the firms' customers should receive special attention. We saw how Cisco moves quickly to retain key salespeople and reassure important customers that the merger will only improve product offerings and services. In contrast, the 1997 merger between Franklin Planner and Covey Systems failed to heed this advice. Combining sales forces was seen as a key source of synergy, but the company was unsuccessful in merging the two compensation programs.

> Divisions were especially strong within the company's 1,700-person sales force, which marketed its seminars and training sessions. Former Covey salespeople got higher bonuses than Franklin staffers. Covey employees also kept their free medical coverage, while Franklin's had to pay part of their premiums.
>
> —*BusinessWeek*, November 8, 1999, 125

This situation created such sniping by sales reps on both sides that productivity plunged.

The implementation plan must focus management resources on those areas at the root of the deal's synergies. If value is going to be created, it will only be by executing on those aspects of the deal that were the original rationale for merging. Without a plan, it is too easy for managers to get bogged down in details of the implementation that have little marginal impact on shareholder wealth. In the failed AT&T/NCR merger, the hoped-for technological synergies between telecommunications and computers never materialized as managers worried more about creating a team environment.

In many cases, the disappointing performance of mergers can be traced to a failure to account for cultural differences between organizations. These differences can be based in corporate culture—or national culture in the case of cross-border deals. In many transactions, both corporate and national cultural differences are present. Because they are intangible and difficult to measure, cultural differences are often ignored in the preacquisition due diligence. This is unfortunate since they can ultimately be the most costly aspect of the implementation process. In mergers where the firms have similar cultures, the rapid combination of the two organizations can actually be easier. However, where there are large cultural differences, executives should consider keeping the entities separate for some time period. This allows each to operate comfortably within its own culture while at the same time learning to appreciate the strengths and weaknesses of the cultural differences between the organizations. Such an arrangement may delay the realization of certain synergies, but in the end is the most rational plan. The key is that culture can have a huge impact on value (both positive and negative), and therefore needs to be part of the planning process from the very beginning—even before any acquisition offer is made.

To ensure success, the postmerger implementation process must be carefully planned and executed. Even when this is done, there will undoubtedly be surprises and unanticipated problems. However, a well-thought-out plan should minimize their negative impact. The most important parts of the plan are speed and communication, which are critical weapons in the fight against successful implementation's main enemies—uncertainty, anxiety, and an inevitable drop in productivity. A plan conceived and implemented swiftly by the firms' executives, with their full and active leadership, improves the chances for a successful transition. As always, we urge acquirers to seek the advice of knowledgeable experts on the implementation process.

Summary and Conclusions

Mergers and acquisitions are a popular way for firms to grow, and as economic globalization continues, there is every reason to believe their size and frequency will increase. A 2008 study by consulting and accounting firm Grant Thornton International found that 44% of all surveyed firms had plans to grow by acquisition in the ensuing three years; that number rose to 60% for the rapidly growing BRIC (Brazil, Russia, India, and China) countries.[18] However, it is not the case that profitable growth by acquisition is easy. The empirical data presented in this chapter make it clear that corporate combinations have historically often failed to meet the operational and financial expectations of the acquiring firm's managers and shareholders. While target firm shareholders typically earn 30% to 40% premiums, M&A transactions do not create value on average for the acquirer's stockholders. This information should make it clear that a carefully designed acquisition strategy, realistic estimates of the potential synergies, and an efficient implementation plan are critical if the historical odds are to be overcome.

Managers must understand that the only sources of incremental value in corporate mergers and acquisitions are incremental future cash flows or reduced risk. These cash flows can come from increased revenues, reduced costs, or tax savings. The sum of the potential value created from these incremental cash flows is called synergy. For a deal to be successful financially, the premium paid and the costs of the transaction must be less than the deal's total synergy. Only then will the bidder's shareholders see their wealth increase. This sounds simple, but in a competitive market for corporate control, there must be a relatively unique relationship between the bidder and the target that other firms cannot easily match. The market must perceive the target as worth more as part of your firm than alone or with some other firm.

There are many practical details that potentially impact the creation of value in M&A transactions. These include the choice of payment (cash vs. stock), tax considerations, and antitrust concerns. Each of these may affect future cash flows and synergies and therefore must be part of the premerger due diligence process. We describe briefly how each factor can impact value creation, but refer potential bidders to investment bankers, professional accountants, tax experts, and attorneys for the most timely and customized advice.

The final and most important part of the process is the postmerger implementation plan. Managers often focus on completing the transaction, which is unfortunate since the transition to a single organization is where the keys to value creation lie. A detailed implementation plan must be developed *before* the transaction closes and communicated quickly and effectively to employees by the firm's new leadership. The plan must focus on the roots of synergy in the deal to ensure the successful creation of the anticipated shareholder value. In deals where there are major cultural differences, special attention must be paid to smoothly integrating these differences. Failure to do so can doom an otherwise sound transaction.

In the end, profitable growth by acquisition is possible, but difficult. The market for corporate control is competitive, and it is easy for bidders to overestimate potential synergies and therefore overpay for acquisitions. To avoid this, managers must develop and stick to an acquisition plan that makes strategic and financial sense. Only then can they hope to overcome history, human nature, and the odds against successfully creating shareholder value through mergers and acquisitions.

Internet Links

www.thedeal.com/blogs/	News and commentary on M&A activity and numerous other financial and economic topics.
www.stern.nyu.edu/~adamodar/	Academic site with numerous quantitative examples and spreadsheets that can be used to value potential synergies.
www.mergerstat.com	Comprehensive source of M&A data and deal alerts; many detailed reports require a subscription or payment, but there is some good free information.
http://dealbook.blogs.nytimes.com/	Up-to-date information on the latest M&A and bankruptcy news.
www.corporatefinancingweek.com/file/52239/ma-news.html	Good source for news on global M&A activity.

Notes

1. The term *private equity* refers to the sources of these firms' capital, not the type of companies in which they invest. Private equity firms raise capital from pension funds, endowments, foundations, hedge funds, and wealthy individuals—all nonpublic sources. Private equity firms invest in both public and private companies.
2. Chapter 7 of Weston et al. (1998) provides a concise summary of and more detail on empirical tests of M&A performance. More recent confirmation of these data is in Andrade et al. (2001) and Bhagat et al. (2005).
3. See, for example, Andrade, Mitchell, and Stafford (2001) and Rossi and Volpin (2004).
4. http://en.wikipedia.org/wiki/Cisco_Systems_acquisitions; data downloaded January 19, 2008.
5. *Merger & Acquisition Integration Excellence* (Chapel Hill, NC: Best Practices, LLC, 2000.
6. TheDeal.com, December 1, 2008, www.thedeal.com/corporatedealmaker/2008/12/two_kinds_of_integration.php (downloaded January 19, 2008).
7. Ibid.
8. "Cisco Changes Tack in Takeover Game," *Wall Street Journal*, April 17, 2008, A1.
9. For a more thorough discussion of this topic, see Weston et al. (1998), Chapter 5.
10. *Wall Street Journal*, November 30, 2000, B4.
11. Ibid.
12. See Harvard Business School Case 285053, *Gulf Oil Corp.—Takeover*, for a complete discussion of this value creation.

13. We assume all cash flows continue in perpetuity. To value a perpetual cash flow, simply divide the amount of the cash flow by the discount rate; in this case, $1.25 million per year ÷ 20% = $6.25 million.
14. For an explanation of Porter's Five Forces see www.quickmba.com/strategy/porter.shtml.
15. See Andrade, Mitchell, and Stafford (2001).
16. Prior to June 30, 2001, the *pooling of interests method* was also permissible. Under pooling, the assets of the two firms were combined, or pooled, at their historical book values. There was no revaluation of assets to reflect market value and therefore no creation of goodwill.
17. Stephen Grocer, "M&A in 2007: Inside the Numbers," Deal Journal, *Wall Street Journal*, January 3, 2008.
18. Grant Thornton International Ltd., "Mergers and Acquisitions: Opportunities for Global Growth," *International Business Report*, 2008.

References

Agrawal, Anup, Jeffrey F. Jaffe, and Gershon N. Mandelker. 1992. The post-merger performance of acquiring firms: A re-examination of an anomaly. *Journal of Finance* 47 (September): 1605–1621.

Andrade, Gregor, Mark Mitchell, and Erik Stafford. 2001. New evidence and perspectives on mergers. *Journal of Economic Perspectives* 15 (2): 103–120.

Bhagat, Sanjai, Ming Dong, David Hirshleifer, and Robert Noah. 2005. Do tender offers create value? New methods and evidence. *Journal of Financial Economics* 76 (1): 3–60.

Coyle, Brian. 2000. *Mergers and acquisitions*. Chicago: American Management Association, Glenlake Publishing Company, Ltd.

Henry, David, and Frederick F. Jespersen. 2002. Mergers: Why most big deals don't pay off. *BusinessWeek*, October 14, 60.

Rossi, Stefano, and Paolo F. Volpin. 2004. Cross-country determinants of mergers and acquisitions. *Journal of Financial Economics* 74 (2): 277–304.

Smolowitz, Ira, and Clayton Hillyer. 1996. Working paper. Bureau of Business Research, American International College, Springfield, MA.

Weston, J. Fred, Kwang S. Chung, and Juan A. Siu. 1998. *Takeovers, restructuring, and corporate governance*. 2nd ed. Upper Saddle River, NJ: Prentice Hall.

Weston, J. Fred, and Brian Johnson. 1999. What it takes for a deal to win stock market approval. *Mergers and Acquisitions* 34, no. 2 (September/October): 43–48.

Zweig, Phillip L., Judy Perlman Kline, Stephanie Anderson, and Kevin Gudridge. 1995. The case against mergers. *BusinessWeek*, October 30, 122.

For Further Reading

Morosini, Piero, *Managing Cultural Differences* (New York: Elsevier, 1997). A comprehensive discussion of culture's role in mergers and other corporate alliances. The focus is on cross-border deals, but the strategies for effective implementation can be used by all.

Sirower, Mark L., *The Synergy Trap: How Companies Lose the Acquisition Game* (New York: Free Press, 1997). Focuses on assessing the potential for synergies and value creation in mergers.

Vlasic, Bill, and Bradley A. Stertz, *Taken for a Ride: How Daimler-Benz Drove Off with Chrysler* (New York: HarperCollins, 2000). A fascinating behind-the-scenes look at the Daimler-Benz/Chrysler deal. Clearly shows the roles of culture, human nature, and managerial hubris in M&A transactions.

Weston, J. Fred, Kwang S. Chung, and Juan A. Siu, *Takeovers, Restructuring, and Corporate Governance*, 2nd ed. (Upper Saddle River, NJ: Prentice Hall, 1998). An excellent reference for developing and implementing an effective M&A strategy.

18

Outsourcing

Theodore Grossman

The 2008 financial crisis underscored the fragility of the economy. This event was not just domestic, but also global. Because of both the wild swings in the price of oil and the financial credit crisis, companies saw their bottom lines erode dramatically. It is especially during times of declining profits that companies look to shed costs and find more efficient ways of conducting business.

Outsourcing is not new. Outsourcing dates back to biblical times when the production of materials was outsourced to other tribes. Outsourcing as a business strategy, however, was first mentioned in 1979. Prior to that date, many companies "farmed out" a number of their needs. In the 1960s, many companies outsourced their data processing. Small companies utilized accounting firms to perform many of the functions that would normally be handled in-house. Publishing companies rarely performed their own composition, printing, and distribution. Yet, in the 1970s and 1980s, vertical integration became the trend. More and more companies believed that there were efficiencies in controlling all of the functions involved in producing and supporting their products. The recession in 1990, however, prompted businesses to closely evaluate what services should be performed in-house. Companies reviewed their organizations to determine their core competencies. Those functions that did not fit the model were considered for outsourcing. Thus, many companies eliminated departments such as legal services, information technology (IT), accounting, internal audit, product design, and even some manufacturing. If companies did not deem it strategic, many outsourced it.

Offshore outsourcing increased dramatically in the late 1990s as a result of the Y2K problem. Companies faced the daunting task of remediating millions of lines of COBOL code, a task far too large for companies' existing infrastructures, but one for which a booming workforce in India had capacity. India always possessed a wealth of technical talent. Because of the lack of demand within India, most of that talent tried to emigrate to the United States for employment. Yet, there were many who were not fortunate enough to overcome the U.S. immigration quotas. As a result, companies such as Tata Consulting Services, Wipro, and Infosys developed Y2K factories in India where thousands of skilled programmers modified the code to meet the requirements of the new millennium.

Then, with the growth of inexpensive broadband technology and the Internet, it no longer mattered where a company's support services were located. Almost any support services could be performed offshore. Law firms outsourced document examination and patent applications. Hospitals outsourced radiological interpretations during night-time hours. Call centers and technical support services were popular functions to be outsourced. Bangalore became the center of outsourcing services in India. In the United States, major American companies reinvented themselves as outsourcing companies. IBM and Hewlett-Packard became significant powers in providing outsourced services. For example, in the late 1990s, Sears outsourced all of its point-of-sale installation, maintenance, and call center support to IBM, which located 1,500 of its employees at various Sears facilities. (See Exhibit 18.1.)

Motivation to Outsource

What motivates a company to outsource some of the internal functions that do not fit its core competencies?

- *Cost reduction and cost control.* Most companies begin here. When business is booming, prices are stable, and credit is plentiful, companies become complacent. However, as soon as business turns down or competition increases, companies look for areas to trim costs and to increase margins. The last thing a company wishes to do is incur the wrath of Wall Street or its investors by not meeting their expectations. History has shown that the Street will penalize share price, and therefore market capitalization, if a company disappoints. Therefore, in times of stress, companies look to outsource any function that will produce cost savings.

- *Improved company focus.* At the turn of the millennium, Procter & Gamble had a separate services division to provide information technology, real estate, and human resources services to all of its operating divisions. It had determined in the early 1990s that a centralized service organization was more efficient than providing those services in each of the divisions. In the early 2000s, P&G reevaluated whether those services should continue to be provided in-house or should be outsourced to external entities.

After analyzing the alternatives, P&G awarded a $3 billion 10-year contract to Hewlett-Packard to manage P&G's IT infrastructure. It awarded IBM a long-term contract to manage the company's payroll, benefits, travel services, and relocation services, among other tasks. An estimated 700 Procter & Gamble employees would shift to being employed by IBM as part of the contract. In 2004, P&G increased its relationship with Hewlett-Packard to include processing its accounts payable systems.

Jones Lang LaSalle oversees 14 million square feet of real estate for P&G at 165 sites in 60 countries, 50 of which, including the corporate headquarters in Cincinnati, are located in North America. Sales offices and research facilities are located throughout the world.

- *Access to state-of-the-art talent or capabilities.* Many smaller companies can neither afford nor compete for world-class talent. Sometimes skills are in short supply in a specific geographical area or the issues of geographic relocation or immigration laws make it difficult to attract talent. Frequently, cultural differences prevent a company from taking advantage of resources. Labor shortages in the United States led to India's outsourcing market. How do you bring 50 top-notch people on board for a short-term project and then abandon them? Outsourcing provides an answer.

Exhibit 18.1 Outsourcing and offshoring industry overview.

Global Outsourcing Revenues	500	Bil. US$	2007	PRE
Global Outsourcing Contracts:				
Total TCV for Contracts with TCV > $25 Mil.	80.4	Bil. US$	2007	TPI
Americas	35.9	Bil. US$	2007	TPI
Europe, Middle East & Africa (EMEA)	33.4	Bil. US$	2007	TPI
Asia-Pacific	9.5	Bil. US$	2007	TPI
Average Contract Length for Contracts with TCV > $25 Mil.	5.55	Years	2007	TPI
Average TCV				
ITO Contract	135.4	Mil. US$	2007	TPI
BPO Contract	182.5	Mil. US$	2007	TPI
New Scope Contract	165.7	Mil. US$	2007	TPI
Restructuring Contract	166.8	Mil. US$	2007	TPI
Americas	139.7	Mil. US$	2007	TPI
Europe, Middle East & Africa (EMEA)	186.1	Mil. US$	2007	TPI
Asia-Pacific	175.7	Mil. US$	2007	TPI
TCV by Industry				
Business Services/Other	8.5	Mil. US$	2007	TPI
Energy	6.3	Mil. US$	2007	TPI
Financial Services	23.6	Mil. US$	2007	TPI
Healthcare & Pharmaceuticals	4.6	Mil. US$	2007	TPI
Manufacturing	11.5	Mil. US$	2007	TPI
Media & Entertainment	4.4	Mil. US$	2007	TPI
Restaurants & Retail	3.5	Mil. US$	2007	TPI
Telecommunications	13.2	Mil. US$	2007	TPI
Travel, Transportation & Hospitality	4.7	Mil. US$	2007	TPI
Annualized Market Revenues by Function				
IT Infrastructure	32.1	Bil. US$	2007	TPI
Full ITO (ADM bundled with Infrastructure)	19.1	Bil. US$	2007	TPI
Applications Development & Maintenance	8.5	Bil. US$	2007	TPI
Customer Relationship Management (CRM)	3.7	Bil. US$	2007	TPI
Financial Services Outsourcing	3.6	Bil. US$	2007	TPI
Human Resources	3.2	Bil. US$	2007	TPI
BPO Multi-Process	2.6	Bil. US$	2007	TPI
Fabrication & Assembly	1.7	Bil. US$	2007	TPI
Procurement	0.6	Bil. US$	2007	TPI
Service Provider Market Share, TCV of Contracts with TCV > $25 Mil.				

(*continued*)

Exhibit 18.1 *(Continued)*

Big 6*	37	%	2007	TPI
European Big 5*	9	%	2007	TPI
India-Based Service Provider	9	%	2007	TPI
Other Service Provider	44	%	2007	TPI
Indian IT Services Exports	18.0	Bil. US$	2007	NASSCOM
Projected	23.1	Bil. US$	2008	NASSCOM
Indian IT-Enabled Services & BPO Exports	8.4	Bil. US$	2007	NASSCOM
Projected	10.9	Bil. US$	2008	NASSCOM

PRE = Plunkett Research estimate; TPI = Technology Partners International; NASSCOM = National Association of Software and Service Companies; IDC = IDC Research Inc.; BPO = Business Process Outsourcing; ITO = Information Technology Outsourcing; HRO = Human Resources Outsourcing; TCV = Total Contract Value; ACV = Actual Contract Value.
*The Big 6 consists of Accenture, Affiliated Computer Services, Computer Sciences Corp., Electronic Data Systems, Hewlett-Packard, and IBM. The European Big 5 consists of Atos Origin, BT Global Services, Capgemini, Siemens, and T-Systems.
Source: Plunkett's Outsourcing & Offshoring Industry Almanac 2009. Copyright © 2008, Plunkett Research Ltd. All rights reserved. Reprinted by permission.

- *Ability to react quickly to rapidly changing business needs.* In the 1940 and 1950s, the life cycle of a business process lasted 15 to 20 years, and information systems lasted 10 to 20 years. At the turn of the millennium, the average life cycle of a business process decreased exponentially to a rate of near continuous change, and the life cycle for information technology was barely one or two years. How does a company support change that is occurring so rapidly? The Internet and electronic business have changed the operational landscape forever. Companies that cannot change overnight are left behind as industry laggards, constantly on the defensive. Outsourcing allows a company to corral the external resources necessary to overcome constant change.

- *Availability of internal resources.* When companies have limited resources to attack a problem or an opportunity, where should they apply those resources? All too often company resources are dedicated to fighting fires and not to exploiting opportunities. Companies are not like an accordion, able to expand and contract easily to meet the short-term demands of the marketplace. How does a company staff up to meet those demands? The cost of finding, training, and then disposing of that talent, along with the bad reputation that accompanies fickle hiring, is more expensive than outsourcing those functions.

Reasons for Outsourcing within the United States[1]	**% of Respondents**
Function not considered a core competency	42%
Reducing labor costs	35
Expanding the skill set of the labor pool	27

Of companies outsourcing, 44% reported increased productivity, 38% realized labor cost savings, and 26% retained competitive position.[2]

The most important reason cited for utilizing offshore outsourcing was reducing labor costs (29% of respondents).

Location of Offshore Outsourcing	% of Respondents
India	26%
China	16%
United Kingdom	16%

Of the companies outsourcing offshore, 61% reported that it allowed them to remain competitive, 54% reported a reduction in labor costs, and 36% benefited from increased labor pool skills.[3]

In the end, outsourcing is all strategic—minimizing risk, sharing risk with a partner, and getting the best return from the company's own resources.

Domestic versus Offshore Outsourcing

What are the pros and cons of the two alternatives? Clearly, cost is the main motivation for offshore outsourcing. Labor costs in India are typically one-third U.S. labor costs. However, as demand has increased, the cost of technical talent in India has as well. Though more expensive than before, Indian labor cost is still dwarfed by that of U.S. talent. In addition, the time difference of approximately 9 to 12 hours offers the strategic advantage of 24-hour productivity.

For example, many hospitals in the United States do not staff their radiology departments at night to read x-rays. Rather, because most radiological exams are now digital, the images are transmitted to facilities in countries such as India, where they are read immediately. When the hospitals' radiologists arrive in the morning, they verify the readings. IT maintenance can also now be scheduled during the overnight with database maintenance and optimization performed remotely from offshore sites.

To summarize:

Trends

- Large numbers of companies have cut in-house spending, but have increased offshore spending.
- The number of firms utilizing offshore providers has increased dramatically each year.

Why the Demand?

- Low cost—savings of greater than 25% and high return on investment (ROI).
- High quality.
- Speed to market.
- Reliability.

Issues with Using Offshore Providers

Periodically, terrorism impacts outsourcing regions, especially in India, where hostilities between Pakistan and India can erupt. The province of Kashmir provides a lightning rod for violence in cities such as Mumbai and Delhi. In 2005, there was a coup in Nepal, which has a small but substantial number of outsourcing providers. Communications, including the Internet, were cut off for several days. Also, the 9/11 terrorist attack has created challenges for offshore outsourcing, as representatives and temporary workers from offshore companies frequently cannot obtain visas for work in the United States.

Infrastructure issues can wreak havoc offshore. Whereas here in the United States power is generally not lost except during natural disasters, in Asia and the Caribbean inconsistent power is a way of life. Consequently, many of the offshore providers in India have their own generating sources to protect their infrastructures. Telephone service, even today, can also be inconsistent at times. In some countries, potable water supplies may frequently be turned off. In addition, developing countries do not necessarily have the necessary building codes and, therefore, physical infrastructures to withstand natural disasters. While the United States can withstand some significant disruptions caused by major floods and earthquakes, the devastation caused by disasters in developing countries is much worse, with many of the outsourcing companies lacking the necessary redundancies of facilities and staff.

There are a number of challenges associated with communication. Time zone differences, for example, while a boon for some projects, can be obstacles for others. Some of the larger outsourcing companies such as Wipro and Infosys provide on-site liaison personnel to assist in the communication issues. However, cultural differences can still drive the organization to distraction, and language differences even within the same country only complicate matters. There are 26 languages spoken in India, and each of the states within India has different laws and regulations. That said, India has been very successful in providing a plethora of outsourced services, including information technology, accounting, human resources management, and legal research.

Companies must also cope with the stigma of exploiting workers in the third world. Over the past 30 years sweatshop stories, many true, have circulated about children and women being forced to work long hours in subhuman conditions, while being paid subhuman wages. In the 1990s, Wal-Mart, in response to such criticism, created its "made in America" program in an effort to silence its critics. Although working conditions have improved offshore and there is less activism concerning this subject, it periodically becomes an issue for companies manufacturing or outsourcing in less developed countries.

Even if all of these issues have been resolved, companies still have to manage the expectations of their customers. Consumers resent the language differences and the perceived lower quality of service they receive when they speak with someone with a thick accent. As a result, some U.S. companies that have outsourced their call centers to places like India and Jamaica are bringing their centers back to the United States.

Last, there is the political backlash associated with offshore outsourcing. Dell Computer now offers consumers an option to pay for technical support from a U.S.-based call center. In times of recession or when Americans are losing jobs, politicians sound off about jobs being sent offshore. While consumers are happy about being able to buy inexpensive quality products from offshore manufacturers, the idea of sending high-skill jobs offshore is anathema to them.

Risks and Challenges of Outsourcing

There are numerous risks and challenges that businesses face when they decide to outsource, whether domestically or offshore. When a project or a process is conducted in-house, the company has total control over it. The company's internal controls, rules, and security govern the project or process. The moment it is outsourced, some level of intimacy and control is lost. Issues to be considered are:

- Privacy.
- Intellectual property (IP).
- Security.
- Loss of morale.
- Reliance on another company.
- Loss of control.
- Potential loss of internal knowledge.
- Potential loss of institutional knowledge.
- Cost containment.
- Differing objectives between vendor and company.

In today's legal and ethical environment, privacy is becoming a very important consideration. Outsourcing data preparation and medical record transcription are common applications. In light of various legal statutes, including the Health Insurance Portability and Accountability Act (HIPAA), a company must be careful who has access to health care data, and under what circumstances. Without the patient's permission, health care data cannot be shared with another party. Even with the patient's approval, the company must be very careful that the party with which it is sharing the data is not abusing that privilege. If the third party chooses to sell the data to yet another company, the original holder of the data could be liable. This issue is of great concern when dealing with companies in other countries that do not have data or health care privacy laws. Financial data is subject to the Gramm-Leach-Bliley Act. Under this law, consumers must be informed if any of their data is shared with third-party companies.

Companies are becoming increasingly concerned with protecting their intellectual property and ensuring that they do not infringe upon others' intellectual property. When outsourcing IT development, companies need to be vigilant about any third-party software that is included within the software being developed. Even open source code requires licensing of one sort or another. The mistake of infringing upon another company's intellectual property can be very expensive to litigate and can ultimately result in having to pay millions of dollars in licensing fees. Also, how do companies ensure that whatever trade secrets or other IP a third party is exposed to is not stolen? Intellectual property laws in many countries are lax. Can you imagine how to stop an employee of a company in Asia from selling your trade secrets?

In this day of the Internet, where companies' Web sites and networks are being attacked daily by various viruses and other hacking attempts from both within the United States and offshore, it is important for companies to be ever vigilant. Especially when software is being developed offshore, companies must ensure that backdoors are not

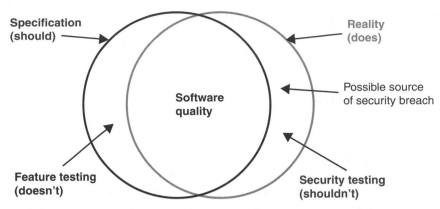

Exhibit 18.2 Verifying application software: Testing doesn't versus shouldn't.

left open to enable uninvited hacking. When software is developed, quality assurance generally tests to ensure that it conforms to the design specification.

Refer to Exhibit 18.2. The nonoverlap area to the left represents gaps between the design specification and the actual program. However, equally important is the nonoverlap area to the right, which represents features in the programs that were not in the original specification. While testing reveals the area to the left, very few companies test for the area to the right. The area to the right represents the potential backdoor for security weakness and hacking. Outsourcing providers usually are known for their high level of quality; however, companies that outsource software development have to be aware of the potential for security backdoors to be left open.

Organizational morale is an issue that needs to be addressed when contemplating outsourcing a function or project. When an entire function (e.g., human resources management) is being outsourced, frequently as part of the negotiations the outsourcing provider will hire the employees from the company. However, while this may sound like a win-win situation for both companies, it also presents its own challenges. Issues include potentially relocating transferred employees or reconciling the benefits offered by the two companies. Even those employees who remain in the old company might resent the treatment of any employees let go. In situations where projects require no layoffs but where functions are outsourced, employees might resent that the contracted employees are earning more than they are or are being given an opportunity to work on a new project that they would have preferred.

Companies and their outsourced partners have different and sometimes competing goals and objectives. As will be discussed later in this chapter, there are different business models for structuring the relationships between the two companies. Typically, the outsourcing provider wishes to make money, while the company contracting for the services wants to save money yet demand a high-quality, reliable product or service. How does one reconcile these differences while creating an effective business relationship that satisfies both parties?

Once a function or process is moved out-of-house, the potential for loss of knowledge and the reliance on others can become a concern. What if the company responsible for providing the outsourced functions were to go bankrupt? The outsourcing company might no longer have the internal skill set to take the outsourced function back. If it is a software project, every time a modification needs to be added, will the company have the institutional knowledge to make it on its own or will it be crippled?

Determining Success

The distinction between domestic and offshore outsourcing has become somewhat blurred. Even some domestic outsource providers have facilities in offshore areas. Some work might be performed in the United States and some performed offshore. Offshore outsourcers such as Wipro and Infosys have a 70/30 model whereby they provide for 70% of the work offshore and 30% on-site in the United States, which, at a minimum, helps to prevent communication issues.

Successful projects tend to be those that have well-defined requirements. Drafting requirements on the back of a napkin is no longer sufficient. Any outsourced project or service demands firm, well-defined specifications that ultimately become part of the contractual relationship. In software projects, those with less integration and fewer dependencies on other internal systems tend to be more successful. Boundaries between systems tend to create the most difficulties. Having few touch points between the system being developed and existing systems helps to guarantee the project's success.

Call centers providing customer and technical support have been a major area where companies have had success outsourcing. While, as discussed previously, consumers perceive a quality difference in the service between domestic and offshore call centers, many of the Indian call center providers now train their employees to speak English without an accent. Offshore call center employees are provided software to diagnose a problem that is identical to the software used in domestic centers. Still, there is a cultural difference that sometimes aggravates consumers. Many feel that the service offered is inferior to that provided domestically. To make it work, call center providers must create better experiences for consumers. Many companies are providing better training and expert systems for their call center operators.

Outsourcing a Process or a Project

What steps should a company follow once it decides to outsource a function? The company first considers the strategic implications of its actions and determines that the project or process does not fall within its core competencies. After doing so, the company should:

- Define the project.
- Select a list of qualified vendors.
- Create the request for proposal (RFP).
- Evaluate vendor responses.
- Evaluate each vendor's qualifications.
- Negotiate a contract.
- Manage the vendor and the project.

Defining the Project

The first step is to create a cross-functional team comprised of the various project stakeholders. The leadership of the project should be the ultimate users of the process or project. If it is an IT system being outsourced, the end users and the IT organization must partner together to manage the project. If a hospital outsources, for example, its radiological interpretation, managing the project will require an internal team of radiologists, radiological technicians, IT personnel for sending the digital images, financial analysts, and legal personnel. The project should be led by the radiology department. The team should be responsible for developing the specifications, drafting the RFP, evaluating the vendors and RFP responses, and, ultimately, managing the relationship with the outsourcing provider.

Clearly define the objectives of the project, including a detailed specification of the project, service, or process. Determine how to measure success and the specific metrics the company will use to determine whether the product or service is working properly. These metrics could be:

- Cost.
- Response time.
- Quality of service.
- Turnaround time.
- Accuracy.
- Reduction in staff.
- Facility usage.
- Return on investment.
- Customer satisfaction.

Without detailed specifications or defined metrics, the project is guaranteed to fail. No one, neither the vendor nor the customer, will know whether the project was successful, which will probably lead to dissatisfaction and, possibly, a lawsuit.

Selecting Appropriate and Qualified Vendors

There are a number of small as well as large vendors available to provide outsourcing services. Many specialize in vertical industries or in specific services (e.g., IT development). While small companies are usually more willing to negotiate than the larger ones, large companies like Hewlett-Packard, IBM, and Accenture are willing to assume responsibility for a plethora of services, from IT to human resources to accounting. Smaller companies are willing to perform more targeted services. If one chooses to outsource offshore, consider the major Indian companies (e.g., Tata Consulting Services, Wipro, or Infosys). Whichever route a company chooses, however, it needs to evaluate the strengths and weaknesses of the provider. Those include:

- Relevant experience.
- References.
- Price.

- Personnel.
- Available resources.
- Financial stability.
- Past lawsuits.
- Length of time performing outsourcing.
- Past successes.
- Past failures.

Request for Proposal (RFP) Content

In order for a provider to respond to an RFP with an accurate and complete proposal, it must be provided with a wealth of information, including:

- Company information (size, geography, products, public/private, etc.).
- Background on project (how the service is being performed currently).
- Guidelines for responding to the RFP.
- Detailed specifications for project to be developed.
- Testing criteria.
- Required response times (either for software or for service).
- Customer satisfaction requirements.
- Logistics.
- Selection criteria.
- Potential contract terms.

The RFP is the entry point into what will become a contractual relationship. If the company is to enter into a legally binding contract with the provider, it must provide that vendor with an accurate picture of its needs. If those needs are not well defined, both parties will be dissatisfied, which will most likely lead to a product that does not meet the company's needs or increased costs in doing so. The RFP is probably the most demanding part of the project, because it requires buy-in from all stakeholders. Investing time and effort up front pays dividends in the long-term success of the project.

RFP Evaluation

Once the RFPs have been submitted, they must be evaluated, which can be a daunting task. Most companies establish specific criteria and weigh the items so that the more important ones have greater influence on the overall score. Aside from the initial items requested in the RFP, the following should also be evaluated:

- Results of meetings with vendor references.
- Professionalism.
- Vendor stability.
- Vendor financials.
- Vendor staff to be assigned to project.

- Scope of vendor responses (not too narrow or broad).
- Willingness to compromise.
- Willingness to negotiate.

Vendor Selection

As the saying goes, let the buyer beware. Initially, everything might look great, but there is a series of danger points to be aware of. First, review the vendor's financials. If it is a public company, then the financials are readily available. However, if the company is private, you must obtain them from the vendor itself. Many will resist supplying their financials, but that is a red flag. In today's day and age, transparency is expected.

Is the company well funded? Look for negative working capital. Is the company dependent on progress payments from its customers in order to survive? Examine its sources of funds. Is the company generating positive cash from operations, or is it dependent on borrowings?

Have shareholder class action lawsuits been filed against the firm, or has the Securities and Exchange Commission (SEC) initiated an investigation into the firm? In the late 1990s and early 2000s, a few very large software firms were the target of both class action shareholder lawsuits and SEC investigations, resulting in significant fines, settlements, and, in at least one case, imprisonment of some of its officers. Such action would indicate stock price manipulation through possible financial fraud. In early 2009, Satyam, a major outsourcing company in India, confessed to falsifying its financials. It overstated its cash by $1 billion, its revenues by 20%, and its profits by 90%. This was a company that was audited by one of the major U.S. accounting firms and was listed on the New York Stock Exchange (NYSE). Its customers included the U.S. government, General Electric, Nestlé, and Cisco.

Has the company undergone a major restructuring, or have there been significant resignations at the executive level? During an economic boom, a number of sins are obscured by the success of the times, but during a recession, internal problems become more apparent. Companies must be aware that in tough economic times their vendors could be in jeopardy and the success of their project or outsourced service could be in peril.

Beware of bargain prices. They could indicate a company is willing to buy its way into the marketplace, but they could also be a signal of a company in distress. In either case, proceed carefully. Companies that lowball a quote could merely be planning price increases later on in the relationship. A company that wants to enter the market can be an interesting play. However, the outsourcer company must decide if it is comfortable being a guinea pig or a training ground for a vendor that wants to gain experience in the marketplace. Does it want to bear the risk in return for potentially substantial savings?

Beware of companies that do not want to provide a full customer list. It is unrealistic to assume that all customers are satisfied, and it is important to know what percentage were unhappy and what precipitated their dissatisfaction. It could have been caused by the client's lack of preparedness or inability to accurately define its needs or by the vendor's inability to successfully meet the terms of the contract. Remember the credo "no surprises." This relationship is like a marriage and should not be entered into unless both parties are prepared to weather all of the storms, and there will be storms.

Last, in some cases, outsourcing companies have made the poor decision to take equity positions in the provider's company. A company must never forget what business it is in. The company is outsourcing a function because it has determined the skill is not a core competency. Taking an equity position in the vendor is similar to bringing that skill set back in-house. A company should focus on its core competencies and not be distracted by ancillary activities.

Negotiating the Contract

There is a misconception in the industry that when a vendor like IBM presents a prospective customer with a contract the terms of the agreement are not negotiable. This is not the case. Regardless of a company's size, assuming the contract is of sufficient monetary value, any contract is negotiable. For a contract to be legal, each side must have some level of bargaining power; otherwise it might be considered a contract of adhesion, which is a legal term for a contract that might not be enforceable. A "take it or leave it" contract without one of the parties having any realistic opportunity to bargain is frequently considered a contract of adhesion.

Make sure that the contract includes the entire agreement between the parties. Most contracts are integrated agreements, which means that they exclude all other written and oral agreements between the parties. Therefore, everything must be in the contract. Be wary of handshake agreements. Remember, the contract is what the parties fall back on when something goes wrong. So be sure to cover your bases by considering everything that can go awry and making sure it is covered in the contract.

Some of the items that should be included in the contract and will be discussed in more detail are:

- Duration.
- Price.
- Payment terms.
- Incentives and penalties.
- Cost overruns.
- Renewal terms.
- Performance guarantees.
- Response time.
- Transition services.
- Necessary technology.
- Necessary personnel and nonsolicitation of personnel.
- Intellectual property.
- Confidentiality.
- Ownership of any developed products.
- Personnel to be assigned by vendor.
- Warranties (implied and express).
- Breach of contract and remedies.
- Limitation of liabilities.

- Termination.
- Assumption upon a sale.
- Transferability.
- Detailed specifications (technical or otherwise).
- Arbitration.
- Governing law.
- Notification.

While price is usually thought of to be straightforward, that is not always the case. The contract could be based on a fixed price or on time and materials. In a fixed price agreement, a company theoretically believes it knows the cost. However, for that to work, a very tight specification must be part of the contract. Anyone who has built or remodeled a house knows that the change orders can drive up the cost to a multiple of the original contract price. Frequently fixed price contracts have incentives and penalties for the vendor to deliver on time or to work to a specified customer service level. The risk clearly falls on the vendor to deliver at a fixed price, and the vendor is rewarded for doing so under cost.

In a time and materials agreement, the vendor is paid based on the efforts made and not any specific agreed-upon price. There are often no incentives for the vendor to deliver a certain price, and there is always the risk that the vendor will milk the job. Change orders become expensive add-ons. Also, in many cases, the company pays for the vendor's learning curve, as it is not unusual for a vendor to staff the project with new employees who lack experience with either the process or the project.

Payment terms are a point to be negotiated by the parties. For development contracts, there are usually progress payments tied to milestones. For service agreements, typical terms require payment on a regular basis (e.g., 30 days). Some contracts will include penalties for late payments. Conversely, some contracts call for payment penalties for late deliveries.

Performance guarantees and incentives clauses are key points in an outsourcing contract. Whether the agreement is for the development of a system or for providing a service (e.g., call centers or accounts payable), timetables and performance guarantees are critical. Performance guarantees are the most difficult aspect of the contract to negotiate, articulate, and monitor. There are a number of possible metrics (e.g., call center response times, number of invoices cleared in a time period, how long it takes to read an x-ray before responding, clearance of trouble tickets, how long a caller has to wait online before an operator answers, etc.), some of which can be measured using software tools. Others, such as quality of response, are much more difficult to measure. However the performance clause is written, it should be done in a manner that can truly be measured; otherwise it will be a source of contention between the parties.

In some cases, performance, or lack of performance, can trigger a termination or penalty, ultimately resulting in a lawsuit. For all of the obvious reasons, a vendor will resist including any penalty clauses for performance. Likewise, the vendor will frequently be motivated by a bonus for early delivery but will try to blame any delays in delivery on the company's inability to deliver a specification or other critical component necessary for the vendor to deliver the product or service. This contention may ultimately result in another potential lawsuit.

The specification of the project is the controlling document in the agreement and the most critical. Do not overlook anything. For example, if a software product is being developed, make sure issues such as response time, technology configuration, network configuration, software standards, testing standards, database standards, and documentation standards are included. If a specific hardware and network configuration is not specified in the contract, the responsibility for the added burden of the increased cost of the configuration will become a major source of contention.

When a company and vendor terminate a relationship, what obligations does a vendor have to assist the company in transitioning to either an in-house capability or another vendor? For example, when an outsourcing company takes over the data center of a company, it is common for the outsourcing company to purchase all of the data center assets of the company and to hire its employees. What happens at the end of the contract? The company no longer owns the technology, the employees, or in some cases the building. All of the institutional memory of the technology rests in the vendor. Does the vendor sell the equipment back to the company or its new vendor, and, if so, at what price? Do the employees return to the company? Companies must consider this issue before committing to outsourcing and must include language in the contract to protect themselves.

Under what circumstances can either party terminate the relationship? This, too, should be articulated in the agreement. Usually, the vendor can cancel for nonpayment of its fees. However, there should be a written notice provision with the opportunity to clear the default. Likewise, if the vendor defaults on its obligations, there should be an opportunity to cure. The vendor's obligations include warranties, service guarantees, timetables, personnel, and other obligations that are spelled out in the agreement.

Who owns the intellectual property (IP)? If a company contracts with a vendor to develop software or a product design, absent specific language to the contrary, ownership of the copyright for the software or design belongs to the creator of the code. Ensuring that the company is getting the fruits of its payments requires a "work for hire" clause in the contract that specifies which party will own the IP.

If the vendor uses some of its own IP to develop a software product for the company, who owns the derivative product? Without a license to use the new software, the company is out of luck. The vendor must grant at least a nonexclusive license to utilize the products that are embedded within the resulting software, even if the vendor uses freeware in the product. Freeware requires a license, and there is not one standard license for freeware. There are approximately three different license forms for freeware, depending on its source.

Also, make sure that the vendor indemnifies the company if it infringes another company's copyright or patent. Hold the vendor responsible for defending the company in the potential lawsuit, in addition to being responsible for damages. It is not unusual in today's environment for a company to infringe another's IP without intent. If a company receives a letter accusing it of infringing another company's patent or copyright, it is important for that notice to be taken seriously. The company must make an effort to determine if it is really infringing another's IP. Failure to do so could result in a judgment of willfulness with additional damages applied. Do not turn a blind eye to the notice letter. If it is determined that the company is infringing, it will be necessary to either cease infringing or negotiate a license to utilize the IP.

Assuming the project or service reveals any trade secrets or confidential information of either party, there needs to be an agreement that that information will not be released to any third party without the express permission of the parties.

The contract should also have specific language that requires that the personnel who were promised to be working on the project not be removed. The company should have the right to approve, at least, the key personnel assigned to the project. Do not allow a key person to be reassigned without permission. Also, if appropriate, list the specific minimum skill sets and competencies required of the personnel working on the project or providing the service. Last, it is not unusual to have a clause in the agreement that the company will not attempt to solicit any of the vendor's employees without the vendor's permission.

What warranties is the vendor offering? Usually the vendor attempts to offer as little as possible. The Uniform Commercial Code, which governs commercial contracts for the sale of goods and services, does not require that either implied or express warranties be part of the bargain. It does require that if they are disclaimed there must be specific language used to disclaim them. Express warranties are those that the vendor is willing to provide regarding issues such as product quality and the willingness to repair or replace the product for a period of time. Implied warranties are those of merchantability and fitness for a particular purpose. It seems obvious that when a company contracts for an accounts payable service that the company providing that service should warranty that the service qualifies as an accounts payable service and is fit for that purpose. However, although it sounds counterintuitive, the vendor could disclaim that implied warranty as part of the contract. The contracting company must ensure that the warranties reflect the understanding between the two parties.

There is usually a significant amount of contract language that seems unnecessary but is equivalent to a prenuptial agreement. It reflects the two parties' understanding of what will happen if things go awry or significant changes occur in one or both of the parties. For example, if the company is sold, what obligations does the vendor have to fulfill the contract? If the vendor is sold to a third party, must the company allow the acquirer to assume the fruits of the contract without the permission of the company? If the company does not want the third party to provide the service, must it grant permission if that occurs? In some cases, there is language that requires the vendor or company to grant permission, unless there are significant reasons not to. Permission to assign a contract by either party is a point of negotiation.

If there is a disagreement, where do the parties settle their differences? Normally, this is in court. In recent years, though, there has been a movement toward required arbitration, typically with representatives of the American Arbitration Association (AAA). In the most common form of AAA arbitration, each side picks an arbitrator, and the two arbitrators pick a third neutral arbitrator. The three hear the case and render a decision that is binding on the parties. This is a faster and less expensive method of dealing with conflict, but it sometimes produces results that are not amenable to at least one of the parties. In most cases, the results cannot be appealed to a state or federal court. This option should be negotiated. If this provision is left out of the contract, both parties can still select the arbitration or mediation route.

If there is a breach of the contract, what happens next? In many contracts there is a provision that allows the party breaching the contract to cure the breach. For example, if the vendor has not delivered the product by an agreed-upon date, there might be a provision that allows the vendor an additional 30 days to deliver the product. This again is a point of negotiation. If a vendor is constantly breaching the contract through poor performance or missed delivery dates, it might be best to terminate the agreement and move on to an alternative.

Despite the best intentions, sometimes the agreement between the two parties breaks down and results in a lawsuit. What are the possible damages? Frequently, there will be a limitation of liabilities clause in the agreement. The vendor will try to limit its liability to the amounts paid to the vendor under the contract. It is not unusual for a company to pay a vendor $500,000 and also, as a result of the contract, incur additional expenses of several million dollars in equipment, personnel, and software—potentially in addition to lost revenues and profits. If there is a limitation of liability clause in the agreement, then the company is out of luck and potentially several million dollars. This clause is a difficult one to negotiate, and the vendor will resist increasing its liability. Also, do not assume just because the vendor might have breached the agreement that the damages can continue accruing and that the company need not remediate its situation. The company has an obligation to mitigate its damages. Once it realizes that it is being damaged, it must do whatever is necessary to stop incurring damages.

Last, assuming there is litigation, where will it be litigated and what will the governing law be? The vendor, being the author of the agreement, will attempt to make its local state the venue for any litigation and that state's local laws the ones that govern. Many companies do not think this provision through carefully, and some jurisdictions have idiosyncratic local rules that can prove problematic.

What should be clear is that outsourcing, while it might be the correct strategy for the company to follow, must be carefully planned. It requires a team that includes all of the project's stakeholders, along with financial and legal representatives from the company.

Summary

A word of caution: Outsourcing is not a panacea for all ills. A company cannot outsource all of its processes. A number of companies made this strategic error in the e-commerce boom at the beginning of the millennium. Too many companies believed that they existed virtually and did not have any physical facilities or presence. Their strategy was to outsource practically all functions, including Web site development, Web hosting, distribution, customer service, delivery, and customer support. Companies learned that this did not work as planned. Amazon, the most successful e-commerce company, attempted to outsource almost all of its functions. Ultimately, it developed its own distribution centers to store and ship merchandise, and that, along with its developments in technology, became the company's core competency.

As economist Michael Munger states in his article "Bosses Don't Wear Bunny Slippers: If Markets Are So Great, Why Are There Firms?":

> In this essay, a serious question has been asked, and I want to make sure the reader sees why it is important. Outsourcing, either across town or across a huge ocean, is a form of transforming a transaction from one organized within a firm to one organized through a market. All firms use some combination of in-house work and outsourcing (no computer company makes its own furniture, grows the wheat for bread in the employee cafeteria, or makes waste paper baskets). Where is the line? How does the company decide what to buy and what to produce?

The answer is: profits. The company has to decide which approach, at every stage, costs less, improves quality, or in some other way increases profits. Price is an important consideration, of course, for managers. But the day-to-day activities of most employees, in most firms, are not directed by prices the way that price directs the choices of farmers. Workers are for the most part paid salaries, or by the hour.

In the current economic climate, with the very foundations of our financial system under attack and companies looking for strategies to minimize costs, it is natural for companies to look at outsourcing as that vehicle. Companies should weigh the risks of putting critical processes into a third party's hands and make informed choices. In doing so, it is essential that corporate executives keep their fingers on the ever-changing technological, financial, and legal landscapes.

Internet Links

http://scm.ncsu.edu/public/facts/facs060531.html

http://news.cnet.com/HP-seals-PG-outsourcing-deal/2100-1011_3-999971.html

www.boston.com/jobs/nehra/032706.shtml

www.acs-inc.com/pages_exp.aspx?id=206

http://h20219.www2.hp.com/services/cache/457080-0-0-225-121.html

http://northamerica.tata.com/businesses/it/index.aspx?sectid=ZACX2FP1m5c=

http://wipro.com/bpo/index.htm

www.econlib.org/library/Columns/y2008/Mungerfirms.html

www.outsourcing.com/

www.sourcingmag.com/content/what_is_outsourcing.asp

Notes

1. www.boston.com/jobs/nehra/032706.shtml.
2. Ibid.
3. Ibid.

For Further Reading

Alchian, Armen A., and Harold Demsetz, "Production, Information Costs, and Economic Organization," *American Economic Review* 62, no. 5 (1972), 777–795.

Chandler, Alfred, *The Visible Hand: The Managerial Revolution in American Business*, 2nd ed. (New York: Belknap, 1993).

Coase, Ronald H., "The Nature of the Firm," *Economica* 4 (1937): 386–405.

Friedman, Thomas, "The Other Side of Outsourcing: A Thomas Friedman/Discovery Channel Look at High Tech Outsourcing," YouTube, December 25, 2005, http://uk.youtube.com/watch?v=8quDb3FIUuo.

"The Future of Outsourcing: How It's Transforming Whole Industries and Changing the Way We Work," *BusinessWeek*, January 30, 2006.

Giridharadas, Anand, "Outsourcing Works, So India Is Exporting Jobs," *New York Times*, September 25, 2007.

Hira, Ron, and Anil Hira, "Outsourcing America: What's Behind Our National Crisis and How We Can Reclaim American Jobs" (New York: AMACOM, 2005).

Klein, Benjamin, Robert G. Crawford, and Armen Alchian, "Vertical Integration, Appropriable Rents, and the Competitive Contracting Process," *Journal of Law and Economics* (1978).

Munger, Michael, "Bosses Don't Wear Bunny Slippers: If Markets Are So Great, Why Are There Firms?" *Library of Economics and Liberty*, January 7, 2008.

Otterman, Sharon, *Trade: Outsourcing Jobs*, Council on Foreign Relations, February 20, 2004.

Williamson, Oliver E., *Markets and Hierarchies: Analysis and Antitrust Implications* (New York: Free Press, 1975).

Part VI

Advanced Topics

Information Technology and You

Dawna Travis Dewire

Of all the chapters in this book, the two dealing with information technology will have the shortest half-life.[1] Because of the constant flow of new technology, what is written about today will have changed somewhat by tomorrow. This chapter presents a snapshot of how technology is used today with particular focus on the finance and accounting functions. When you compare your experiences with the contents of this chapter, some of the information will no longer be applicable. Change means progress. Some companies will not have adapted; consequently, they will have lost opportunities and threatened their own future.

Information technology ... information systems ... computing ... do they all mean the same thing? Many people think so. Information systems use information technologies to deliver value to an organization. Information systems capture data, process it and/or store it, and output it as required or requested. Information technology is the technology used to build these information systems—a computer is only one example of information technology.

Consider an automated-teller machine (ATM): The information system uses the account on the card and the input password to verify the user; the withdrawal amount is compared to the account balance; if the funds are available, the information system instructs the cash counter to dispense the cash; the information system also instructs the card reader to return the card and instructs the printer to print the receipt; the information system records the transaction and updates the account balance. The ATM has a computer that is connected to the bank's network (which may redirect the transaction via a national network). Programs (software) are executed to accept the account, the password, and the amount of the withdrawal; to determine if the withdrawal request should be honored; to format and then print a receipt; to format and display the screen; to store the transaction data and update the balance. Data is stored and accessed on the account's bank's server computers. All this is done in a matter of seconds—24/7. ATM machines became the rage in the 1990s; now people can get cash back at a variety of retail locations, and can even pay bills online. This evolution of the banking industry has been driven by the use of technology and consumers' willingness (ultimately) to embrace the new technology.

This chapter focuses on the technologies that touch the users themselves. The next chapter, Information Technology and the Firm, looks at how an organization needs to view and manage information technology.

Introduction

Amazing as it may seem, the personal computer has only been around for about 30 years. Before 1980, the world of computing belonged to highly trained technical people who worked their wizardry in hermetically sealed rooms. Today, children use personal computers in kindergarten to learn the alphabet, grade school students use the Internet to research term papers, and on-the-go executives are always in touch using their laptop computer, beeper, Web-enabled smart cell phone (such as BlackBerry), and cellular personal digital assistant (PDA). But many people are not yet comfortable with these technologies. The range of people's acceptance and knowledge of information technology is wide, with the technical novice at one end and the techie at the other end of the continuum. Where you fall in this range will dictate what you gain from this chapter. If you fall near the techie side, skim this chapter for ideas that you might find interesting.

People's lives have been turned upside down as they learn to manage the latest technology in both their personal lives and work lives. E-mail has replaced handwritten letters and notes. Business communication happens instantly via e-mail or instant messages rather than messages left as voice mail or left with secretaries. Secretarial tasks are being done by workers themselves using personal productivity software such as word processing software, e-mail, and Internet-based calendaring. Documents are sent as e-mail attachments rather than sent as an overnight delivery or faxed—or they are posted on a corporate server to be downloaded by appropriate workers. Meetings are becoming virtual. Online chats—sometimes with video feeds—are replacing physical face-to-face meetings.

It used to be that when a new employee was hired, he or she was shown to a desk and given pen, pencil, paper, and a telephone. Today, a new hire is set up with a corporate login ID and a computer, usually attached to a network, and is possibly given a cellular phone, a beeper, and even a laptop computer for portable use.

The line between personal use of information technology and professional use is blurry. Most people have personal e-mail addresses as well as professional e-mail addresses. Personal letters are written using word processing software. Personal budgets are built using spreadsheet software. People use the Internet to shop 24/7.

Information technology has changed not only the way people work, but also, in some cases, the venue from which they perform their work. No longer are workers chained to their desks. People work from home via computer and telephone/cable communications. Businesspeople who travel with their portable computer have become so prevalent that hotels have installed wireless networks that allow guests to use their computer to communicate with their home office via the Internet. Air travelers can connect their laptop to an airplane's wireless network at their seat. Coffee cafés and restaurants promote their wireless networks. People can check their e-mail (business and personal) from their laptop, PDA, or smart phone using any wireless network they have access to.

How much do you need to understand about information technology to become technologically enabled? The answer to this question will depend on the job you hold and the organization for which you work. Since information technology is having a dramatic impact on the very definition of many industries, the material covered in this chapter and in Chapter 20 would have to be considered essential. To drive your car, you don't need to understand all the particulars of how your engine works, but having a general understanding is very helpful. Information technology is no different. These two chapters aim to give you that general understanding and introduction to the terms you should be comfortable with.

At the heart of information technology is a computer. Each computer has two components its users should understand—hardware and software—and has peripherals. Computers talk to each other via a network. What is passed among computers is data. This chapter is organized around these four concepts—hardware, software, networks, and data.

Hardware

Computer hardware comes in several shapes and sizes. Since this chapter is focusing on how technology affects users on a personal level, our treatment concentrates on personal computers (PCs) and smaller devices. Over the past 20 years, Microsoft and Intel have become so dominant in the software and hardware ends of the PC business that they have, de facto, set the worldwide standard for PCs, which is referred to as the *Wintel standard*, short for Microsoft *Windows* and the In*tel* CPU (central processing unit) chip. The Wintel standard continues to dominate the personal computer market, thus affecting both the hardware marketplace and the applications software that is developed. Currently, Hewlett-Packard/Compaq, Dell, and Acer Inc. are the largest producers of personal computers, with Apple Inc. a distant fourth. It's important to note that Apple computers use a different architecture than Wintel machines and their image in the marketplace is focused on graphics and such. In order to compete, Apple now offers a dual-boot machine so users can run software written for Windows as well as software written for Apple's own operating system on the same machine.

Personal computers come in two basic shapes: desktop and laptop. Regardless of their shape, all PCs have the same basic components. When you buy a computer, you usually have a choice on the size, the speed, and the amount of specific components that will make up your system. The basic components with which users must concern themselves are the CPU, RAM (random-access memory), hard disk, CD-ROM/DVD-ROM (read-only memory) drivers, monitor, modem, and various adapters. The rest of this section deals with these basic options.

Beyond personal computers, we are also seeing the emergence of a whole range of small digital products for supporting effective managers. These products, as a group, are called personal digital assistants (PDAs), and will be discussed separately.

Desktop Computers

Desktop computers generally have a tower that contains the drives and components of the computer itself, a separate monitor, a keyboard, and a mouse. The parts inside the tower of most desktop computers are very similar. Many of the manufacturers of desktop machines use parts from the same suppliers, as there are only a handful of companies that manufacture hard disk drives, for example. Before buying a machine, compare the attributes and capabilities of many different machines. Also, check the warranties offered by the different manufacturers. A one-year warranty is fairly typical; however, some computers come with two- or three-year warranties. Beware of hype advertising, and read the fine print. Many advertised specials do not include the monitor, which will cost upward of $100, depending on the size and quality.

Building on Apple's success with its desktop Macs that have the monitor, drives, and components all in one piece, Dell, Hewlett-Packard, and Sony have recently begun to offer all-in-one desktops. At present these machines are pricier than standard desktops, but consumers are attracted to their compact size without having to trade power for size.

Laptop Computers

The laptop computer (also called a notebook computer) has become a mainstay for the traveling worker. It provides all the functionality and most of the power of many desktop units in a package that weighs less than six pounds. A laptop is powered by standard electricity or for about four hours using its self-contained rechargeable battery. The keyboard and pointing device (usually controlled by the user's finger) are built into the laptop itself.

The display screen is one of the most important features of the laptop computer. Display quality and size are rapidly approaching the display qualities of monitors sold for desktop machines. They are discussed in more detail later in the monitor section.

Although laptops provide the luxury of portability, that is for the most part their *only* advantage over desktop machines. Desktops offer better displays, more memory, and higher speed—higher performance for far less money. A laptop computer could cost nearly twice as much as a comparable desktop unit.

Unlike desktop units, not all laptops are the same under the covers. The majority of the electronics are frequently custom designed. Consequently, servicing laptops is more complicated and more expensive, and laptop parts are not necessarily interchangeable.

It's important to mention two new types of laptops that are gaining in popularity. One is the tablet PC. This notebook has a touch screen or graphics tablet screen. The user can use a stylus or digital pen (or a fingertip) instead of a keyboard or mouse. The screen can rotate so that it can lie flat. Users can write on the screen using the stylus, saving the writing as an image file or having the writing converted to text by a word processing document. These machines weigh a little bit more than a traditional laptop.

The other is the netbook computer, sometimes called a mini laptop. These are lightweight, smaller, low-cost laptops that offer limited features (such as no DVD-ROM drive) and reduced processing power. They have either a hard drive or a solid-state drive. The machines are targeted toward users who only wish to do Web browsing, e-mail, and noncomplex uses of productivity tools. These machines will run Windows or Linux.

In recent years, there has been much talk about *cloud computing*. The Internet is always depicted as a cloud in network diagrams. The paradigm envisions that users will use primarily Internet services (software as a service, which is discussed in Chapter 20; Web 2.0, which is introduced in this chapter and expanded in Chapter 20; and Web-based applications via a browser) and that all the software and the data will be stored on servers (i.e., not stored on the user's machine).

Personal Digital Assistants (PDAs)

Personal digital assistants (PDAs) are small digital devices that can be used to take notes, to manage tasks, to keep track of appointments and addresses, and even to send and receive e-mail. Similar to PCs, a PDA has a CPU, RAM, a display screen, a keyboard of sorts, and possibly a modem. However, a PDA can typically fit easily into a pocket or purse. Most PDAs come with the ability to transfer appointments and contact information bidirectionally between the PDA and a PC, using software provided by the vendor. The most popular first-generation PDA was made by Palm, Inc.

Today's PDAs have a touch screen or set of keys for entering data, a memory card slot for data storage, and some sort of connectivity, such as IrDA, Bluetooth, and/or Wi-Fi. Those used primarily as telephones may use soft keys, a directional pad, and either a numeric keypad or a thumb keyboard instead of a touch screen. Those PDAs with touch screens also provide the user with a stylus to be used with the touch screen.

Currently there is a convergence of cellular and computer technologies, so we see smartphones with PDA features, most notably the BlackBerry from Research in Motion Limited. In addition to being a working telephone, a smartphone runs an operating system with a standardized interface and a platform for applications. Applications include e-mail, Web browsing, note organizer, instant messaging, Global Positioning System (GPS), and media player for video clips and music.

Hardware Components

Exhibit 19.1 shows a schematic rendition of how the components in a computer interact. This section explains the basic functioning of these components and presents some of the trade-offs that should be evaluated when deciding to buy a computer system.

Central Processing Unit (CPU)

All basic computers have a *central processing unit* (CPU). The CPU is the basic logical unit that is the "brain" in the computer. As mentioned earlier, it is often provided by Intel Corporation or one of the clone-chip manufacturers, such as Advanced Micro Devices (AMD). While Intel enjoys the lion's share of the market, the clones have recently made significant inroads based on lower prices for comparable products. Current state-of-the-art CPUs manage to integrate tens of millions of electronic components onto one thumbnail-sized silicon chip. CPUs such as the Intel Pentium brand come in different speeds, expressed in megahertz (MHz—million) or gigahertz (GHz—billion) cycles per second. Speed represents how fast the CPU is capable of performing calculations and data manipulations. Today's typical CPU operates at between 1 and 3 GHz. High-end

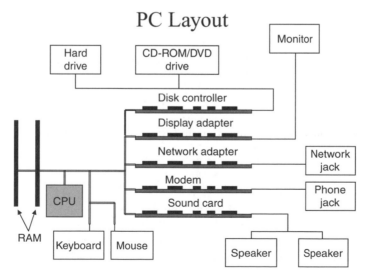

Exhibit 19.1   Interaction among computer components.

desktops come with multiple processing cores, in effect multiple processing units able to work together as one unit, resulting in higher speeds.

Random-Access Memory (RAM)

Random-access memory (RAM) is the space that the computer uses to execute programs. The amount of RAM required is dictated by the number of applications that the computer is asked to run simultaneously; for most average users, 2 gigabytes (GB) of RAM is an appropriate amount. Most software and hardware vendors recommend 4 gigabytes. You can never have too much RAM, so more is better.

Hard Disk

All programs and data are stored on the *hard disk* (also called the hard drive) of the computer. Disk technology has advanced greatly in the past decade. Recording density has enabled disk capacity to approach numbers previously unheard-of except in large mainframe commercial systems. In 1992, the typical disk stored 80 megabytes (MB) of data. Today, typical disk capacity on desktop machines is in the range of 200 to 300 gigabytes (GB) up to 10 terabytes (TB). Although it seems unimaginable to fill up an entire 200-gigabyte disk, it happens faster than one might think. Typical office applications require 750 megabytes of storage for the application alone, not including any associated data. Multimedia applications (sound and video) are very data intensive and quickly consume disk space. For example, CD quality music recordings consume roughly 10 megabytes per minute! Again, the more storage the better.

Solid-state drives (SSDs) are beginning to appear in the smaller machines. This is the technology that is used in flash drives that plug into USB ports. These drives start up faster and retrieval is quicker, since there is no read/write head to position. Current offerings are in the 2 GB range, although 512 GB drives are expected in the near future.

Reminder: Hard disk failures do occur. Always back up your data onto a removable disk, such as an external hard drive. Also worthy of mention is the use of USB flash drives, sometimes called thumb drives. These portable storage devices are small but can hold as much as 60 GB of data, programs, and so on. They allow the user to carry files in a briefcase or pocket, or store them off-site.

CD-ROM/DVD-ROM

In the 1990s, an increasing amount of data and applications was being supplied on compact disk (CD) technology, which can store large amounts of data (700 MB) inexpensively. Computers had CD-ROM drives to read CD-ROM. The original disks (CD-Rs) were sold as "read only," which actually meant they could be written on only once. As inexpensive recordable CD (CD-RW) drives became popular, people began to store massive databases or record music on their own. CD-ROM drives are sold with three different speed ratings: one speed for write-once operations, one for rewrite operations, and one for read-only operations. A 12×/10×/32× CD drive can write to CD-R disks at 12× speed, write to CD-RW disks at 10× speed, and read from CD disks at 32× speed.

Today, DVD-ROM disks, which have roughly six times the capacity of CD-ROM disks, are becoming popular and, in many cases, replacing CD-ROM disks. DVD popularity is being driven, at least in part, by the fact that a single DVD can accommodate the massive amount of data necessary to digitally store the sound and video images of a full-length feature movie. Recordable DVD drives are now becoming reasonably priced. With their ability to read both CDs and DVDs and their ability to record DVDs, recordable DVD drives are beginning to replace CD drives in newer computer systems.

There are numerous information databases available on CD that would be of interest to the accountant or finance executive. For example, most census data is available on CD. Also, historical data on stock and bond prices, copies of most trade articles, Internal Revenue Service (IRS) regulations, state tax regulations, tax forms, recent court decisions, tax services, generally accepted accounting principles and auditing standards (GAAP and GAAS), continuing education courses, and many other topics are available on CD.

Monitor

The first computer *monitor* was a cathode ray tube (CRT), which physically resembles a television. Flat-panel or LCD monitors have now become the norm. The major advantage of the flat-panel display is that it takes up much less space on a desk than does the CRT. Today's software supports dual screens—users can have different applications viewed on separate monitors and can move between the two applications without closing either one—so space on the desk becomes an issue.

There are significant advantages to having a display that is as large as space and budget allow. Some of the real power of windowing software is the ability to view several windows of data at the same time. Small display screens make such windowing much more difficult to view. A 19-inch display (diagonal measurement of the screen) is the minimum workable size.

On laptop computers and PDAs, the screen is an integral part of the machine itself. On laptops, screen sizes range from 13 to 20 inches. A tablet laptop allows the user to swivel the screen so it lies flat, thus allowing the user to write handwritten notes on the screen.

Peripherals

Every computer has to have hardware, software, and a monitor of some sort. To be able to communicate, a computer needs a network adapter and access to a modem. Most people would not consider their computer setup complete without a printer.

Modems

Modems are devices that allow computers to communicate with each other. The original modems were developed to use standard telephone lines and used dial-up access. Modem technology has increased the speed of data communications over standard telephone lines to speeds more than 10 times higher than those available in 1990. However, there is a practical limit to how fast computers can transmit data over ordinary telephone lines, and that limit has been reached at approximately 56 kilobits per second (KBps—thousands of bits per second).

Because of the limitations of telephone lines, alternatives have been developed—cable modems (broadband) transmit over cable television wires, and DSL (digital subscriber line) modems transmit over regular telephone wires using new technology. Both have the capability of transmitting data at rates higher than 1 megabit per second (MBps). Upload speeds are usually in the 128 to 768 KBps range. Although both technologies are spreading quickly, neither is yet available in all geographic locations. In addition, satellite data service, similar to satellite television service, is an available high-speed possibility for data communications.

To provide wireless access to devices with Wi-Fi capabilities (although actually a trademark of Wi-Fi Alliance, Wi-Fi has come to mean wireless Internet to users), a home office would also need a wireless modem. Either, a separate wireless modem connects directly to a cable or DSL modem, or the cable or DSL modem itself provides wireless support. Computers would use wireless access to reach this modem, which would in turn pass signals to the Internet via the cable/DSL modem. An area with Wi-Fi access is called a Wi-Fi hot spot. Organizations use wireless access points and wireless hubs and repeaters to provide wireless connectivity within their workspaces.

Network Adapter

Whereas modems connect computers together using phone/cable lines, *network adapters* allow computers to directly communicate with each other over wires that physically connect the computers. In most office environments, the various computers are interconnected through a local area network (LAN) so that they can share printers, data, access to the Internet, and other capabilities. Today, the dominant type of LAN is called an Ethernet network, and most network adapters are Ethernet adapters. Today's computers have built-in Ethernet adapters to support connection between PCs and cable/DSL modems as well as office environments.

Printers

Printer technology has stabilized in recent years, with two standards having emerged, *laser printers* and *inkjet printers.* Laser printers offer the best quality and speed. They are, for the most part, black and white (although color is available on high-end models) and offer high print resolution. Models range in price from $200 for personal use to several thousand dollars for a unit that offers printer sharing and color suitable for business. Employees route their work to printers that are connected to the organization's network.

Inkjet printers offer the lowest price. Models cost as little as $100 and are often offered as part of a new computer package. In higher-priced inkjet printers, print quality (color and black/white) is excellent. Today, many people are using inkjet printers (sometimes specialty printers) to print pictures taken with digital cameras; the results can be virtually indistinguishable from prints produced from film cameras and professional photo labs.

Laser printers are the clear choice for network sharing, while inkjets have become the mainstay for the individual user. Most people use a multifunction printer (printer, copier, scanner, and fax) for personal use. As more and more homes are being outfitted with wireless networks, users are also turning to wireless printers to allow them to print from anywhere that has access.

Software

The *operating system* is the basic software that makes the computer run. *Application software* is the software that executes a particular user function. The operating system is the software closest to the machine; the application software is the software closest to the user, as illustrated in Exhibit 19.2.

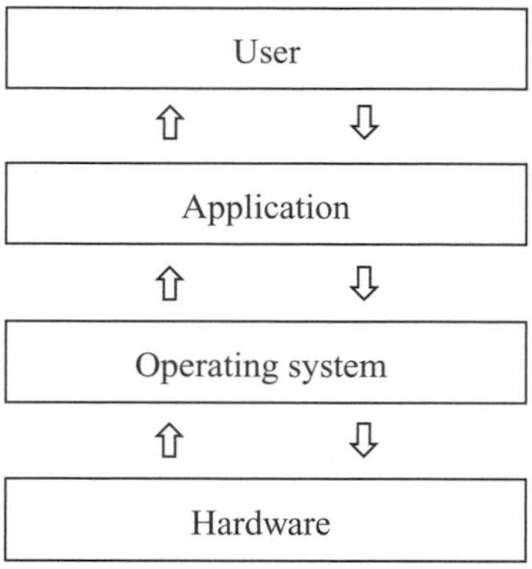

```
┌─────────────────────────────────┐
│              User               │
└─────────────────────────────────┘
         ⇧           ⇩
┌─────────────────────────────────┐
│           Application           │
└─────────────────────────────────┘
         ⇧           ⇩
┌─────────────────────────────────┐
│        Operating system         │
└─────────────────────────────────┘
         ⇧           ⇩
┌─────────────────────────────────┐
│            Hardware             │
└─────────────────────────────────┘
```

Exhibit 19.2   Layers of software on a computer.

Operating System

An *operating system* (OS) handles the management and coordination of activities and the sharing of resources of a computer. The OS handles the operation of the hardware, including disk drives, hard drives, and network communication. Almost all computers have some sort of operating system.

Microsoft Windows is the predominant operating system software for the personal computer. Microsoft has become the acknowledged leader in the development of both operating system and office automation software. The Windows operating system provides a graphical format for communicating between the computer and the user. The current state-of-the-art operating systems from Microsoft are, for individuals, Windows XP and now Windows Vista, and, for businesses, Windows Server 2008 (formerly Windows NT). Other operating systems in the marketplace, which can support various sizes of computers, are Mac OS X from Apple for use on its machines, and UNIX and Linux, which are freely available from The Open Group.

Application Software

Application software is the personal computer's raison d'être. Although there are a multitude of applications available for the PC, this chapter focuses on the following personal productivity categories of software:

- Word processing.
- Spreadsheets.
- Presentation.
- Databases.
- E-mail and instant messaging.
- Calendar.
- Personal finance.
- Project management.

The two most popular applications continue to be word processing and spreadsheet software. Most of the popular packages are available as application suites, which include word processing, spreadsheets, graphics, and sometimes database management software. Microsoft Office is one of the most widely used suites; it includes Word for Windows (word processing), Excel (spreadsheets), PowerPoint (presentation graphics), Access (database), Outlook (e-mail and calendaring), as well as several other applications. While Microsoft does own the market share of this market, there are other noteworthy alternatives. OpenOffice, open source software available from OpenOffice.org for free (at the time of publication), supports OpenDocument Format standards for data interchange with its own default file format as well as Microsoft Office formats. Organizations are evaluating using OpenOffice rather than upgrading to newer versions of Microsoft's suite. Another trend is toward online office suites that function as Web applications—as software as a service, which is discussed in Chapter 20. There is no software on the user's machine, nor is there any data. The most widely used online suite currently is Google Docs, which includes a word processor, a spreadsheet program, and a presentation editor. Users of such products need to keep in mind that their data is stored on the vendor's servers and they should be mindful of the issues that this creates.

Word Processing Software

Word processing software is by far the most used productivity software. Users can create, edit, and produce their own documents. Many users find that they compose online as well as finalize online—no more laboring over lined paper with handwriting that can't be read or additions/corrections that can't be deciphered. Users can control formatting for paragraphs, page layout, and headings, to name just a few features. Word processing software also provides spell-checking and grammar checking, tracking of changes, support for comment insertion, and creation of a table of contents and an index. The resulting document can be viewed on the screen in page layout or outline form, one page or two pages at a time, and with or without footnotes.

Today's word processing software includes many of the features of desktop publishing software, and it is so simple to use that any novice equipped with simple instructions can master the software. Not only can documents include text, but they can also contain spreadsheet tables, drawings, and pictures; be specially formatted; and be in black and white or color. Most word processing applications come with clip art, which consists of drawings, cartoons, symbols, or caricatures that can be incorporated into a document for emphasis. Word processing software has become the great business equalizer, making it difficult to decipher a small company or single practitioner from a large Fortune 500 company with a dedicated media department.

Spreadsheet Software

The original spreadsheet application was developed at the very beginning of the PC revolution and was called VisiCalc. It was later replaced by Lotus 1-2-3, which was the standard until the tremendous success of Microsoft Excel.

A spreadsheet is composed of a series of columns and rows (in Microsoft Excel 2008, 1,600 columns and one million rows). The intersection of a row and column is referred to as a *cell*. Columns have alphabetic letters, while rows have numbers. Cell reference (also called the cell address) B23 indicates the cell in column B and row 23. Formulas that use one of the many functions provided by the spreadsheet software together with cell addresses can be keyed into a cell. The formula isn't displayed in the cell; the result of the calculation of the formula is displayed in the cell.

For the accounting and finance executive, spreadsheet software has had the greatest impact on productivity at work. Imagine the controller of a company who has been asked to prepare the budget for the coming year. The company manufactures over 1,000 products with special pricing, depending on volume. The controller not only has to make assumptions about material costs, which might change over time, but also has a prior history of expense levels that must be factored into the analysis. Using pencil and paper (usually a columnar pad), the controller calculates and prepares all of the schedules necessary to produce the final page of the report, which contains the income statement and cash flow. The controller presents the findings to management, only to be asked to modify some of the underlying assumptions to reflect an unexpected change in the business. As a result, the controller must go back over all of the sheets, erasing and recalculating, then erasing and recalculating some more.

The creation of spreadsheet software rendered this process less painful. Spreadsheets allow the user to create the equivalent of those columnar sheets, but with embedded formulas. Consequently, any financial executive can create a financial simulation of any part of the business. By merely changing any of a multitude of assumptions, one can immediately see the ramifications of those changes. Spreadsheets allow for quick and easy what-if analyses. If the bank changes the interest rate on our loan by 1%, what will the impact be on our projected cash flow and income?

Spreadsheets also provide a "calculate backward" feature called *goal seeking*. The user might have a target value in mind. The spreadsheet software can calculate backward to determine what one (or more) of the input values needs to be in order to get that answer. For a simple example, consider debt financing in which the loan amount is known, the time is known, and there is a desired monthly payment in mind. What would the interest rate need to be in order to get that monthly payment for that loan amount for that time period?

Exhibit 19.3 provides an example of a simple spreadsheet application, a company's pro forma income statement. The spreadsheet is a plan for what the company expects its performance to be. In this example, the company expects to earn $85,361 (cell H18) after tax on $774,000 (cell H3) of sales revenues. At the bottom of the spreadsheet, there is a series of assumptions that are used in the calculations performed in this spreadsheet. For example, cost of goods sold will be 32.75% of sales, and advertising will be 12% of sales. Likewise, the income tax rate for this company is set at 25%. (Note: Some totals might be off due to rounding.)

Exhibit 19.4 shows the spreadsheet's formula infrastructure. For example, cell B4, which calculates the cost of goods sold for the month of January, contains a formula that requires the spreadsheet to multiply the cost of goods sold percentage that is shown in cell B21 by the sales shown in cell B3; the formula in cell B5, which calculates the gross profit, subtracts the cost of goods sold in cell B4 from the sales in cell B3; and cell H5, which calculates the total gross profit for the six months of January through June, contains the formula that adds the contents of cells in the range B5 through G5.

The spreadsheet is set up so that should the user wish to change any of the assumptions, such as the cost of goods sold percentage, the contents of that assumption cell could be changed to a new value, and any cell affected by this change would immediately display its new value. This is the power of the spreadsheet: the ability to recalculate once an input value has been changed.

Exhibit 19.3 Pro forma income statement.

	A	B	C	D	E	F	G	H
		Pro Forma Income Statement						
		January	February	March	April	May	June	Year to Date
1								
2								
3	Sales	$100,000	$125,000	$135,000	$127,000	$132,000	$155,000	$774,000
4	Cost of goods sold	32,750	40,938	44,213	41,593	43,230	50,763	253,485
5	Gross profit	67,250	84,063	90,788	85,408	88,770	104,238	520,515
6								
7	Operating expenses							
8	Salaries	22,800	28,500	30,780	28,956	30,096	35,340	176,472
9	Benefits	11,200	14,000	15,120	14,224	14,784	17,360	86,688
10	Rent	3,200	3,200	3,200	3,200	3,200	3,200	19,200
11	Utilities	4,300	4,750	3,790	4,100	3,100	2,800	22,840
12	Advertising	12,000	15,000	16,200	15,240	15,840	18,600	92,880
13	Supplies	1,300	1,400	1,270	1,500	1,550	1,600	8,620
14	Total operating expenses	54,800	66,850	70,360	67,220	68,570	78,900	406,700
15								
16	Net profit before taxes	12,450	17,213	20,428	18,188	20,200	25,338	113,815
17	Income taxes	3,113	4,303	5,107	4,547	5,050	6,334	28,454
18	Net profit after taxes	9,338	12,909	15,321	13,641	15,150	19,003	85,361
19								
20	Assumptions							
21	Cost of goods sold %	32.75%						
22	Salaries (% sales)	22.8%						
23	Benefits (% sales)	11.2%						
24	Advertising (% sales)	12%						
25	Income taxes %	25%						

Exhibit 19.4   Spreadsheet formula infrastructure.

	A	B	C	D	E	F	G	H
				Pro Forma Income Statement				
1								
2		January	February	March	April	May	June	Year to Date
3	Sales	100000	125000	135000	127000	132000	155000	=SUM(B3:G3)
4	Cost of goods sold	=$B$21*B3	=$B$21*C3	=$B$21*D3	=$B$21*E3	=$B$21*F3	=$B$21*G3	=SUM(B4:G4)
5	Gross profit	=B3−B4	=C3−C4	=D3−D4	=E3−E4	=F3−F4	=G3−G4	=SUM(B5:G5)
6								
7	Operating expenses							
8	Salaries	=$B$22*B3	=$B$22*C3	=$B$22*D3	=$B$22*E3	=$B$22*F3	=$B$22*G3	=SUM(B8:G8)
9	Benefits	=$B$23*B3	=$B$23*C3	=$B$3*D3	=$B$23*E3	=$B$23*F3	=$B$23*G3	=SUM(B9:G9)
10	Rent	=3200	=3200	=3200	=3200	=3200	=3200	=SUM(B10:G10)
11	Utilities	4300	4750	3790	4100	3100	2800	=SUM(B11:G11)
12	Advertising	=$B$24*B3	=$B$24*C3	=$B$24*D3	=$B$24*E3	=$B$24*F3	=$B$24*G3	=SUM(B12:G12)
13	Supplies	1300	1400	1270	1500	1550	1600	=SUM(B13:G13)
14	Total operating expenses	=SUM(B8:B13)	=SUM(C8:C13)	=SUM(D8:D13)	=SUM(E8:E13)	=SUM(F8:F13)	=SUM(G8:G13)	=SUM(B14:G14)
15								
16	Net profit before taxes	=B5−B14	=C5−C14	=D5−D14	=E5−E14	=F5−F14	=G5−G14	=SUM(B16:G16)
17	Income taxes	=$B$25*B16	=$B$25*C16	=$B$25*D16	=$B$25*E16	=$B$25*F16	=$B$25*G16	=SUM(B17:G17)
18	Net profit after taxes	=B16−B17	=C16−C17	=D16−D17	=E16−E17	=F16−F17	=G16−G17	=SUM(B18:G18)
19								
20	Assumptions							
21	Cost of goods sold %	32.75%						
22	Salaries (% sales)	2.28%						
23	Benefits (% sales)	1.12%						
24	Advertising (% sales)	12%						
25	Income taxes %	25%						

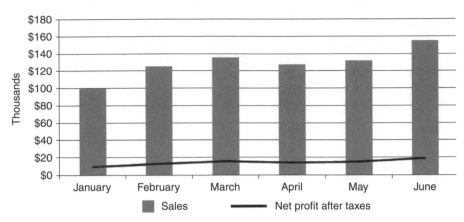

Exhibit 19.5   Pro forma sales and income graph.

Another powerful feature is the ability to copy formulas and have cell addresses in formulas either change relative to their original location or not change. In Exhibit 19.4, the formula in B4 is using relative addressing (change cell address when copied) as well as absolute addressing (don't change cell address when copied). The use of the dollar sign indicates absolute addressing. When the formula in B4 was copied to C4 through G4, the cell address of the cost of goods sold assumption cell should remain constant—so it is in the formula as $B$21. However, the percentage should be used against the sales numbers that are in that column. When the formula in B4 is copied, the B3 should become C3 in column C, and D3 in column D, and so on. That's relative addressing. Hence, when the formula shown in B4 ($B$21*B3) was copied to C4 through G4, the reference to the assumption cell didn't change, but the reference to the sales figure cell did.

In addition, most of the packages provide utilities for graphing results, which can be used independently or integrated into either a word processing report or a graphics presentation.

Exhibit 19.5 presents a graph of the information in our example spreadsheet. It contrasts sales and net profit over the six months.

The spreadsheet software currently on the market has over 50 financial functions, including net present value, future value, present value, accrued interest, depreciation, interest rate, internal rate of return, and yield for a Treasury bill, as well as logical functions, statistical functions, engineering functions, and data and time functions. A wizard leads the user through the arguments for the function. The arguments are usually cell addresses and can be indicated in the wizard by clicking on the appropriate cell. Exhibit 19.6 is a sample of the wizard for a net present value example using Microsoft Excel.

Presentation Software

Presentation software is used to create slide presentations. These presentations can include a variety of media through which information can be presented to an audience, such as text, graphs, pictures, video, and sound. Special effects are also available, such as animation that can be incorporated as the system transitions from one slide to the next, or within a slide itself. Slides can be printed in black and white or in color, as

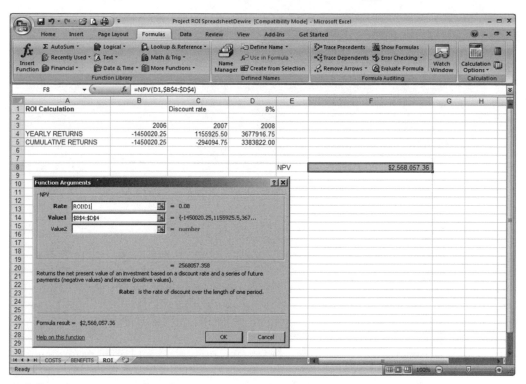

Exhibit 19.6   Example of net present value wizard in Microsoft Excel.

slides or handouts, and can be used on overhead projectors. Alternatively, a computer can be directly connected to a projection system for projection onto a screen or a television monitor, allowing the presenter to utilize the software's animation and sound features. Most of the presentation software comes equipped with various predeveloped background formats to help simplify the process of creating the presentation. Also, these software packages support the importing of both graphs and text from other software packages, such as word processing and spreadsheets. A set of slides for a presentation is often referred to as a *deck*. The most popular presentation graphics software is Microsoft PowerPoint.

Database Software

A *database* is a collection of data stored in such a way that the user may create and identify relationships among data. For example, a mailing list of one's customers might contain information about each customer, each of his or her purchases, and everything about the individual sales transactions themselves, including the price paid, who sold it, how paid, and so forth. This information can be retrieved in a variety of ways, usually specified by the user at the time of execution. The user might want a list of all customers who purchased a specific product between January and May, or possibly a list of all products a customer has purchased, in aggregate, that were sold by a particular salesperson. The number of possible combinations and permutations and ways in which one views the data is limited only by the collection of the data and the imagination of the user. Database technology has put the data of the firm in the hands of the worker. For example, using

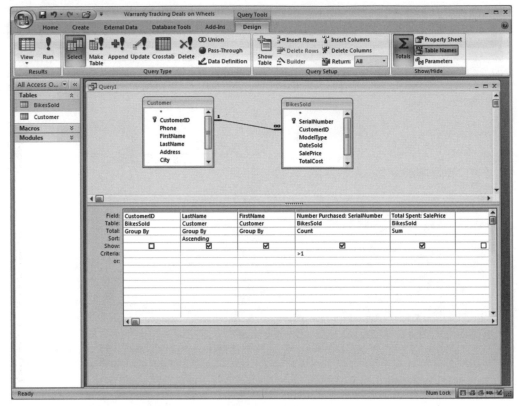

Exhibit 19.7   User-built query using Microsoft Access.

a database as just described (customer purchases), the worker might like to know the total amount spent, as well as the number of purchases for customers (from over 4,000 customers) who made more than one purchase. Exhibit 19.7 shows a user-developed query in Microsoft Access to extract that data, and Exhibit 19.8 shows the first 27 of 94 records returned by Microsoft Access.

Most current tools also offer the user a wizard that can be used to build a query. Exhibit 19.9 shows how a wizard in Microsoft Access might be used to build the query shown in the template in Exhibit 19.7. Users can pick the tables that contain the data they need and then pick the fields from those tables.

While knowledge workers are more and more often using databases and queries against databases in their jobs, database software is not yet commonplace in personal use. Most workers don't have that much personal data to manage or share, and often turn to a spreadsheet as a storage tool for such data. Databases and their use in organizations are discussed in more detail in Chapter 20, Information Technology and the Firm.

Electronic Mail (E-Mail) and Instant Messaging

E-mail is the most popular network application, as it has become the method of choice for communicating over both short distances (interoffice) and long distances. E-mail can be used to communicate with any other person on the local network or any other network within the organization's wide area network, as well as the Internet. (Networks

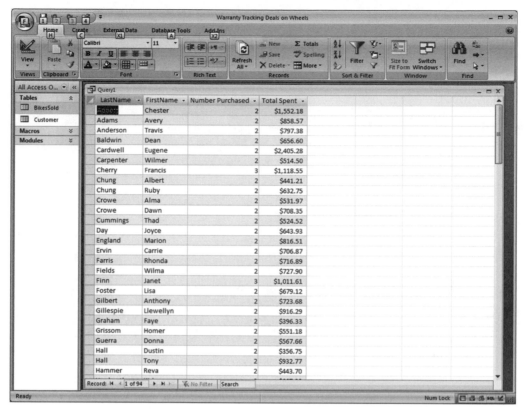

Exhibit 19.8   Results of user-built query in Microsoft Access.

are discussed in more detail later in this chapter as well as in Chapter 20.) E-mail has become so popular that overnight delivery services are being rendered obsolete for some types of communication.

Internet e-mail addresses often consist of a user name followed by the @ symbol, then a domain name (for example, the name of a company), then a period, then a domain type (frequently .com or .net). Thus, Jane Smith's e-mail address at GenRad might well be jsmith@genrad.com. If Jane also signed up for a free e-mail account with AOL, her address might be jane_smith@aol.com.

Most e-mail software packages include a basic word processing application to be used to generate messages (letters). In addition, these packages can be used to keep contact lists and to send a document to numerous people simultaneously. A document, once sent, can be received within seconds by people thousands of miles away. One of the more advantageous features of e-mail is that a file—a spreadsheet, a graphic presentation, a word processing document, an Adobe pdf file, a picture, a video, or even a database—can be attached to a message and sent with the e-mail.

Imagine that you have used a spreadsheet package to prepare a budget for your division in Boston. You print out your letter and spreadsheet and mail or ship it overnight to the main office in Chicago. You include an electronic copy of your spreadsheet on a CD-ROM so the individual in Chicago can merge it with the budgets from other divisions. Sometime within the next day or two, the recipient will receive the package. He or she

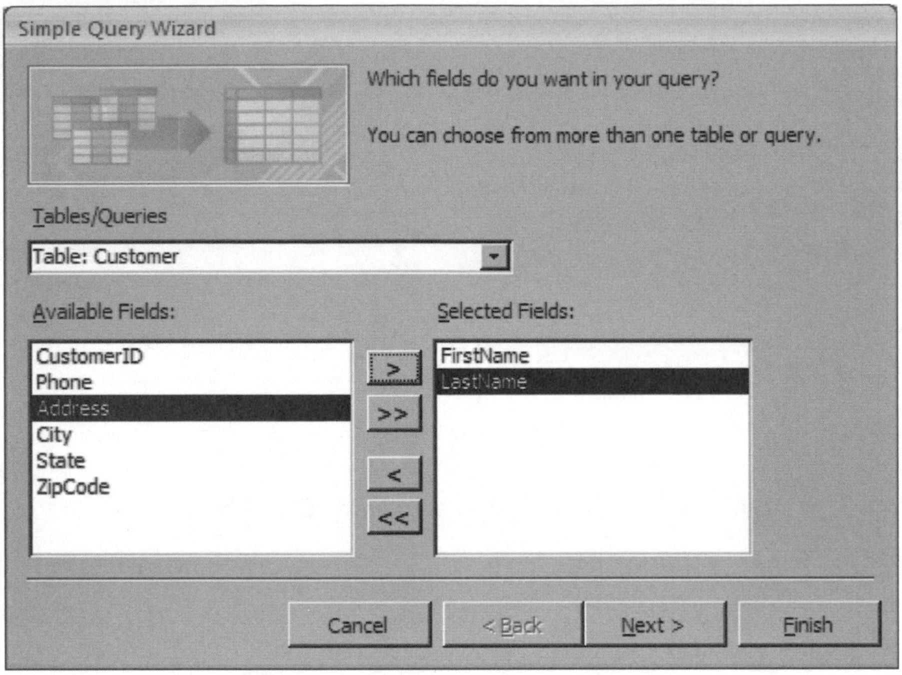

Exhibit 19.9   Query wizard in Microsoft Access.

will then read the information and use the file on the CD. Alternatively, using e-mail, you draft your thoughts as an e-mail message, electronically attach the spreadsheet file, and send it, via e-mail, to the individual in Chicago. Within a matter of seconds or minutes, he or she will receive the electronic package, read your message, and be able to extract your attachment and load it directly into a spreadsheet software package for processing.

Instant messaging (IM) (AIM is one of the most popular) is making its way from students to parents to the workplace. When a worker sends an e-mail, it's hard to know whether the recipient is at his or her desk. A read receipt can be added to the e-mail, but many users decline to send such receipts. Instant messaging allows users to see who in their network of IM "buddies" are online, or if not, when they might be back. A user can type a short message and send it immediately. The person online tends to respond immediately. For those who are "away" or not even logged on, the message will be delivered when they return or log on. IM tends to be more for personal than for business use, but that is beginning to change. Organizations are hosting their own internal instant messaging services so workers can communicate in real time with each other but aren't able to IM outside of the internal network.

Calendar

The feature of PDAs that fueled their success in the late 1990s was the way they allowed the user to maintain a calendar and contact list on the device. The device could then be synchronized to the owner's desktop using software provided by the PDA manufacturer. The power of that capability has been expanded to a corporate calendar, open calendars to facilitate setting meeting times, and integrating the calendar with e-mail. The software

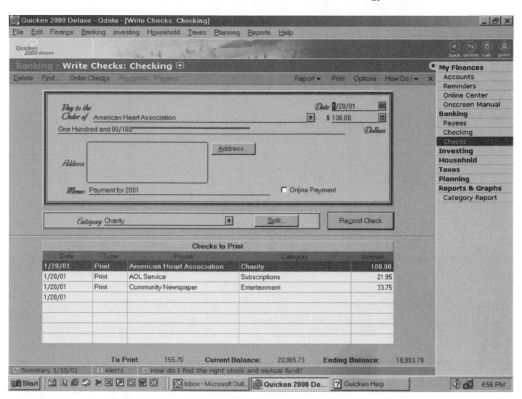

Exhibit 19.10   Check writing screen in Quicken 2000 from Intuit, Inc.

can issue alerts before scheduled meetings. Calendar software can also maintain tasks input by the owner of the calendar.

Personal Finance Software

There are several software packages that allow individuals or small businesses to manage finances, such as tracking bills paid, paying bills either electronically or by generating a check, and monitoring investments. The packages are relatively easy to use and yet fairly sophisticated in that they provide for secure communications for electronic bill paying and other online banking services such as account reconciliation, as well as the importing of current stock market quotes. The most widely used packages for personal finance are Quicken from Intuit and Microsoft Money. Small businesses use Quickbooks from Intuit, Microsoft Office Accounting, and Peachtree from Sage Software SB.

Exhibit 19.10 displays a sample screen that is used to enter bills to be paid. As you can see, the user input metaphor is that of a check, the very same document the user would use if the bill were to be paid manually. The difference is that, by using this method, data is collected for a host of other purposes:

- Tracking paid bills by category for budgeting purposes.
- Tracking payments for tax purposes.
- Reconciling the checking account.

The system has the capability to keep track of more than one account and to allow for interaccount transfers.

Project Management Software

Often, a manager is faced with the challenge of managing the many details concerned with a project, be it the construction of a building or pulling together a financial plan. With fairly simple projects, paper and pencil or a simple spreadsheet might be adequate tools for coordinating the people and steps involved in a project. But as the project gets complex, involving, say, more than a few people and/or more than a few dozen steps, one should consider using project management software to help with the planning and control of the activities.

Project management software allows a manager to plan for and then control the steps in a project with an eye toward managing the people and resources required for the project. Good project management software can help a manager foresee bottlenecks or constraints in a plan and can help the manager bring the project to completion in the shortest available time.

One popular tool for managing projects is called Microsoft Project. Exhibit 19.11 presents a typical screen from Microsoft Project. It shows the steps in a project along with a graphical representation of those steps in a format called a *Gantt chart*.

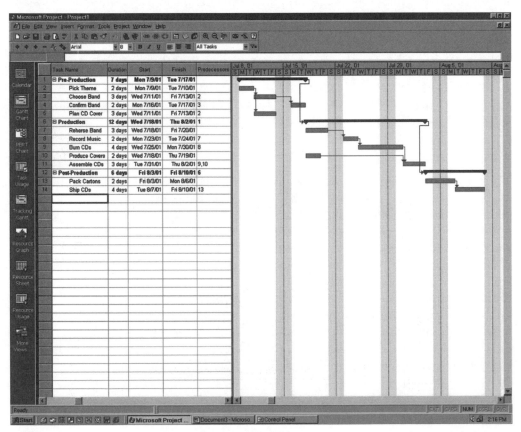

Exhibit 19.11   Gantt chart in Microsoft Project.

Networking

One of the advents of the recent decade was extensive *networking*, or interconnecting, of computers, which has facilitated the sharing and exchanging of data and information. The interconnecting may be directly through wires within a building; using modems via a public network (cable, DSL, or dial-up); or utilizing wireless modems that use radio frequency transmissions between the computers.

There are several different approaches, or *architectures*, for computer networks. In a small office environment with only a few computers, the computers might be connected in a *peer-to-peer* network. Here, all the computers function on the same level as peers or equals to each other. Peer-to-peer networking capability comes built into most of today's new computers, making it relatively easy to set up a peer-to-peer network between two or more PCs. All one needs is a network adapter card in each computer, along with some network access between or among them (wireless or cabled). The most notable peer-to-peer network is Napster, the online music file sharing service that allowed people to copy and distribute music files to each other and was forced to shut down by court order over copyright infringement issues.

However, in a larger networking environment (dozens, hundreds, or even thousands of computers hooked together), the situation is more complex. In this case, the most common network architecture used is called a *client-server* network. To deal with the added complexity, in a client-server network there is a hierarchy of computers, with one server acting as the traffic police directing the network traffic. This includes redirecting the traffic as well as accessing data from its server-based location. In this architecture, the user computer is referred to as the *client* in the network. A picture of a typical client-server network appears in Exhibit 19.12.

Networks are also covered in Chapter 20, Information Technology and the Firm.

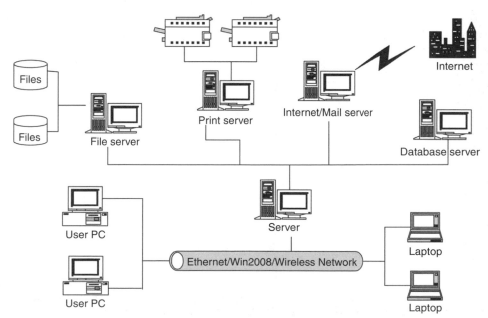

Exhibit 19.12   Diagram of client-server network.

Local and Wide Area Networks

Within a business, the typical network is called a *local area network* (LAN). Clients are connected to the network using wires or fiber-optic cabling to a hub. These hubs are interconnected to form the actual network. Transmission speeds are generally either 10 or 100 megabytes per second. Lines within a corporate network are usually T1 or T3 lines, which are fiber-optic lines used for long distance communications. The speed of a T3 line is about 28 times faster than the speed of a T1 line.

Just as in peer-to-peer networking, each PC on the network must have a network interface card if it will connect to a LAN, a wireless network, or a modem. When a series of LANs in different cities are interconnected, they form a *wide area network* (WAN). Large businesses, with facilities around the country or world, network their users' personal computers together in a series of LANs, which are further interconnected into a large WAN. The Internet is the world's largest WAN, connecting together millions of computers of commercial companies, government agencies, schools, colleges and universities, and not-for-profit agencies from around the world.

Preventing unauthorized people from accessing confidential information is one of the biggest challenges posed by networks. To do so, people and organizations use special security software. One technique, a *firewall*, allows outside users to obtain only that data that is outside the firewall of the network servers; only people inside the company may access information inside the firewall. Organizations also use *encryption* to make the transmitted information unreadable except to those who have the key to decipher the encryption algorithm.

World Wide Web

The terms *Internet*, *World Wide Web*, the *Web*, and *cyberspace* have become synonymous. It's important to understand that the Web is comprised of the network itself (the Internet) and software that provides the functionality we've come to expect from the Internet. It's also important to realize that the Internet is owned by no one company and is at present governed by no one group.

The Internet—the Network

The Internet is the worldwide WAN that has become the major growth area in technology and the business community. Although the Internet has been around for decades, its popularity exploded with the development of the necessary software programs that made the Web very user-friendly to explore.

Large organizations have a dedicated data link to the Internet using very fast data lines such as T1 or T3 lines. Individual users access the Internet using third-party companies called *Internet service providers* (ISPs). These ISPs allow users to connect to their servers, which are connected directly to the Internet. Some ISPs have started providing high-speed or broadband connectivity between users and the Internet with the use of cable modems or DSL technology (as discussed previously). High-speed connectivity will typically cost nearly $50 more than the normal $5 per month for dial-up speed (56K) access.

WWW—the Technology

One of the major attractions of the Web is that it is quite easy for the average person to use *Web browser* software to access any of the billions of sites on the Web. Web browsers are merely software programs that allow users to navigate the Web. The two most common browsers are Internet Explorer from Microsoft and Firefox from Mozilla. Internet Explorer comes free with Windows, and Firefox can be downloaded for free from Mozilla.com.

Every site that appears on the Internet has an address composed of a company or organization name, called a domain name, and a domain type. These addresses are referred to as *universal resource locators* (URLs). Each Web site displays its information using a series of Web pages. A Web page may contain text, drawings, pictures, and even audio and video. Text or images that contain links to other pages are called *hypertext links.*

The Internet has two standards that every user should be aware of: TCP/IP and HTML. Transmission-control protocol/Internet protocol (TCP/IP) enables computers to communicate over the Internet because each computer on the Internet has an IP address that is made up of a series of numbers. When a user sends an e-mail (for example), the message and its attachments are broken into small packets that contain content as well as the IP address of the sender, the IP address of the recipient, and the packet number. These packets are sent out to the network to their destination and sometimes take different routes depending on network traffic. When all packets arrive at the IP address of the recipient, they are reassembled into a complete message.

Hypertext markup language (HTML) allows data and images to be displayed on a user's screen. When a user types in a Web site address in the browser window, a request is sent to that IP address. The Web server at that address sends back HTML code, which is used by the browser to format the screen. To get a sense of what this code looks like, click on View, Source in any browser. To you and me it looks like gibberish, but, luckily for us, the browser software knows what to do with it.

Internet Search Engines

The Web has become so extensive, with so much information available to the user, that often one literally does not know where to look. Search engines were created to help users navigate the Web. Search engines like Yahoo! and Google constantly explore the Web, indexing each site using keywords as well as words found in text. Organizations are providing search capabilities inside their own Web sites to help users quickly find what they are looking for.

Privacy on the Internet

When using the Internet for e-mail, e-commerce, or other applications, it is essential to remember that the Internet is a public network. With the right skill, anyone who is on the Internet has the ability to "listen in" on your electronic transaction. While the transaction will appear to be processed normally, its confidentiality might well be compromised. Beware! Never send across the Web any confidential information that you would not want any other person or company to know.

Web browsers do have the ability to encrypt data that is transmitted between a user and a Web site. Most organizations conducting business on the Web will, therefore, send and receive confidential information only using encryption technology, which should provide adequate protection. Generally, Web sites that use a secure connection will notify you that they are using a secure methodology. In addition, whenever you are connected to a secure site, your Web browser will show a little icon of a closed padlock on the status bar at the bottom of your screen or in the address bar.

Beyond protecting data as it is transmitted, there is a significant privacy issue surrounding the use of data on a user's Internet activities. Whenever a user signs in to a Web site, the site can collect information about activities, such as purchases, address, and so on. At the moment, there is very little legislation at either the federal or the state level preventing Internet sites from selling or sharing information about users with third parties. Various industry groups are trying to encourage self-regulation, and many Web sites will post their privacy policy, usually as a link on the home page. However, at the moment there is little consistency or enforcement of privacy policy. We can expect that there will be significant legislation on privacy issues in the future, but until such legislation is in place, beware!

In addition, Internet sites may place small files, called *cookies*, on the computer's hard drive when a user is in contact with the site. In most cases, these cookies are innocuous, providing you with your favorite screen or allowing you to access the site without having to remember a password. However, cookies can also be used to help track Web actions and build a profile of user activities. Inexpensive or free software is available to help you manage or prevent cookies being placed on your computer, but blocking cookies may prevent you from being able to use certain Web sites.

E-Commerce

E-commerce (electronic commerce) is the ability to purchase goods and services over cyberspace. In cyberspace, though, the metaphors consumers use to shop are only two-dimensional representations of what they see when shopping in stores. Essentially, cyberspace consumers are only being supplied information (text and pictures) about products.

To add value, e-commerce retailers are trying to make the online visit itself more meaningful by customizing the shopping experience with suggestions based on earlier shopping, wish lists, and alerts. New mechanisms for Internet shopping are being developed, many of which include virtual reality and the appearance of three-dimensional venues. Retailers are providing their customers with the opportunity to have a three-dimensional computer model built from measurements of the customer's body. Once this model is built, the customer can "try on" clothing via his or her computer screen to see how the actual clothes will look on the customer's computer-based body. Try searching on "virtual clothes" to see some examples.

Web 2.0

While not a new version of the Web (as one might think by the 2.0), Web 2.0 is a change in the way that end users (and software developers) use the Web. The initial Web was focused on sharing data and information. Web 2.0 focuses on community and collaboration. Users participate in the site and feel a sense of community. Of all the concepts introduced in this chapter, this section is likely to have the shortest shelf life; when you read this, Web 2.0 will either have faded into the history books or be so widely used that it would need more than a few paragraphs to explain what it is and what impact it has had on professionals.

Web 2.0 sites generally allow their users to search, to act as author (blogs, wikis), to tag, to send alerts, and to provide syndication. Social network sites such as Facebook and

MySpace allow people to build communities of people who share similar interests and/or activities. Wikipedia is the best example of a *wiki* site—a collection of pages that enable anyone to contribute a posting or edit an existing posting. *Blogs* are running commentary on a subject. *Podcasts* are audio blogs. *Tagging* is assigning a keyword to an Internet bookmark, a computer file, or an image. The tags are assigned by the user (either creator or viewer). A collection of tags is called a *folksonomy*. Flickr and YouTube are examples of sites that use tags. When content is posted to a site, the creator assigns keywords to it so that users searching will find it. All of these sites provide powerful search engines to help users find content.

Really simple syndication (RSS) feeds publish frequently updated content in a standardized format (usually using XML). The RSS reader checks a user's subscribed feeds for updated material, and downloads what it finds. A hybrid use of this technology is Twitter, which is a social networking and microblogging site that allows its users to send updates and read updates posted by other users. The posts are short (140 characters) text-based posts. (One needs to register, but it is free—or at least was at publication.) Users can specify a circle of friends to receive posts, which are retrieved using the Twitter Web site, e-mail, text messaging on a mobile device, or applications such as Facebook.

Data

The reason information systems exist is to capture, manage, and share data and information. Data is an important strategic corporate asset.

Data versus Information

Data is captured and shared as information. Data is facts (e.g., a particular customer bought a red sweater on February 25 for $75). Information is insight gained from facts (e.g., 467 red sweaters were bought on February 25, more than any other color). Data is generally thought to be numbers and text. Today, data also includes multimedia files—a picture of that red sweater, an audio file that describes the red sweater for the sight-impaired, and a video clip that is a 360-degree view of the red sweater.

Database software was discussed earlier as the software used to manage all of this data and to provide tools for users to retrieve the data. That treatment was merely an overview of the features of database software. More detail is provided in Chapter 20, Information Technology and the Firm.

Multimedia

By the latter half of the 1990s, most personal computers came equipped to support *multimedia*, the ability to seamlessly display text, audio, and full-motion video. Computers were equipped with a high-resolution monitor and a CD drive, and had audio capabilities. Because of the amount of storage that video requires, full-motion video was somewhat difficult to accomplish on these personal computers. In order to manage the large amount of storage that video processing requires, the video data was compressed. Data compression examined the data, and, using an algorithm or formula, reduced the amount of necessary storage space by eliminating redundancies in the data. Then, before the data was displayed, it was inflated back to its original form with little or no loss of picture quality.

Today's personal computers with higher-resolution monitors, DVD drives, and fast processing speeds have very little trouble playing full-motion video from a DVD. Video clips can be viewed from a Web page or downloaded and played at a later time.

Internet Multimedia

The Internet provides an amazing plethora of information, and not just in text or still picture format. *Streaming media*, both video and audio, are becoming increasingly available on the Internet. There are several sites where one can obtain audio clips, listen to music, or listen to radio shows. For example, NFL football games and commentaries are available on the National Football League's or National Public Radio's respective Web pages. In addition, many music companies are allowing consumers to listen to music in the comfort of their homes before buying the CDs. Ruckus Network Inc. offered free and legal music downloads to college students from a library of nearly three million songs from various artists.

The site best known for video is YouTube (now owned by Google). Users can view any video in the YouTube library of hundreds of millions of videos. With a free YouTube account, a user can post videos (picture and sound) to the library and share its existence with friends. By tagging the video with keywords, the user increases the chances that others might uncover the video and view it as well. A search of "fix computer" found nearly 8,000 videos with those keywords. There are videos to help the viewer learn to play the piano, the guitar, or the drums. There are many music videos from artists trying to be discovered. Organizations are putting videos on YouTube as well. Edmunds.com posted a video of a test drive of a 2010 Ford Mustang. Infomercials (of sorts) are also posted on YouTube.

The Future—Today, Tomorrow, and Next Week

The industrial revolution occurred toward the beginning of the nineteenth century and we are still feeling its effects today. The computer revolution began about 1950, and the microprocessor—the heart of the PC revolution—has been exploited for only the past 30 years. But think about how our everyday lives have changed as a result of these innovations. Remember, the microprocessor, the main component of a computer, is part of so many of our appliances, computers, automobiles, watches, and so forth. The impact of the computer revolution is just as large as, if not larger than, its precursor, the industrial revolution, and has occurred over far less time. Moreover, the acceleration of change in our lives that results from the use of computer technology has been rapidly increasing. Technologists speak about the rapid changes in the development of the Internet and its allied products. They even joke that things are happening so fast that a three-month period is equivalent to an "Internet year." Funny, but true.

One of the biggest trends in the past several years has been the merging of heretofore separate technologies. As we mix computer technology with communication technology and throw in miniaturization for good measure, the products we may soon see are beyond imagining.

Mix together a PDA, a cell phone, and a Global Positioning System (GPS) satellite receiver—we already have such a device. Now consider: Such a device could remind you as you drive past the supermarket that you were supposed to pick up bread on the way home. You'd walk in the door to the market, and this pocket wonder would tell you, based on your past love of Snickers candy bars, that they are being sold three for $1 in aisle 2. As you move toward the checkout line, the clerk, who has never met you, greets you by name because your pocket wonder has announced your arrival to the screen on her cash register. While this scenario may sound fanciful, it is probably being tested somewhere in the world while you are reading this. Given the tremendous entrepreneurial potential for new products and services, how these technologies will be used in the future is wide open for the resourceful.

Why ". . . and Next Week"? The horizon for change in the world of technology is very short. Each year, major enhancements to both hardware and technology are released, rendering previous technology obsolete. Some people are paralyzed about buying computers, because they are concerned that the technology will change very soon. How right they are! The promise of technology is that it is constantly changing. Today's worker must recognize that and learn to adapt to the changing methods. Those who are technologically comfortable will be the first to gain strategic advantage in the work environment and succeed. A word to the wise:

Hold on to your hat, and enjoy the ride. Adapt and go with it.

Downloadable Resources for this chapter available at www.wiley.com/go/portablembainfinance

Information Technology and You

Information technology needs to be experienced, not just researched. The exercises for this chapter on the book's Web site gives the reader a chance to do exactly that—experience. Build a spreadsheet (or two or three) and see what happens when you copy formulas, use an assumption area, or make a chart. Build your own computer figuration to understand the options. Recognize some of the latest technologies in use when you visit your favorite Web sites.

Internet Links

Search Engines

www.yahoo.com	A good search site that organizes the Web into a hierarchy of categories.
www.google.com	A very extensive search site.

Computer Information Sites

www.cio.com	A site that provides news and white papers on topics that IT management should be aware of.
www.cnet.com	A site that provides product reviews and prices on a broad range of technology products.
www.computerworld.com	Online site for the hardcopy *ComputerWorld*.
www.zdnet.com	Web site of large technology publisher, with product reviews, software downloads, useful articles, and price comparisons.

Accounting Sites

www.aicpa.org	Home page of the American Institute of Certified Public Accountants, with lots of useful information and many links to other Web sites of interest to accountants.
www.aaahq.org	Home page of the American Accounting Association.

Financial Management Sites

www.fma.org	Home page of the Financial Management Association International, with lots of useful information and many links to other Web sites of interest to financial managers.
finance.yahoo.com	Very good home page for personal financial management, with many links to other personal finance Web sites

Note

1. Updated—based on work done by Edward G. Cale Jr. and Theodore Grossman.

For Further Reading

There are many excellent books on the personal use of computer systems. Titles cover the spectrum from books about individual software packages to books that explain how to program a computer. Many of these books come equipped with a DVD containing step-by-step examples and exercises. There are several popular series of these books. The following are but a few of the ones you might consider. You would probably find it worth your while to browse through a number of books at your local store, searching for those that meet your need for detail and that appear to be aimed at your current level of understanding. It is very difficult to get a sense of how closely a book meets your needs from the information that is available on the Internet.

John Wiley & Sons publishes a series of books titled "something" *Bible* where the "something" is the name of a software package (e.g., Microsoft Excel would be *Microsoft Excel 2007 Bible*).

Dummies Inc. has a series of books that are very noticeable with their yellow and black covers. They are all titled "something" *for Dummies*, where the "something" would again be the name of the software package (e.g., Microsoft Excel would be *Microsoft Excel for Dummies*). See books on individual products, product suites such as Office, the Internet, and so on.

Microsoft Press also publishes numerous titles for users. They are entitled "something" *Step-by-Step* where the "something" is the name of the software. There are books on individual products, product suites, and other product offerings (Vista, SQL Server).

20

Information Technology and the Firm

Dawna Travis Dewire

The information technology (IT) and its related topics that are discussed in Chapter 19, Information Technology and You, focus on the users—what technologies they use, what they need to understand about those technologies, and what they should expect on the horizon. This chapter discusses the firm's use of information technology.[1]

Historical Perspective

To understand the present and future of information technology, it is important to understand its past. In the 1960s and 1970s, most companies' information systems were enclosed in a so-called glass house. If you entered a company that had its own computer, the computer and all its peripherals (printers, tape drives, and disk drives) were located behind a glass wall with a security system that allowed only those people with access rights to enter the facility. One computer performed all of a company's data processing functions, and the transactions were processed one at a time. The computer in this host-centric environment was initially used for accounting purposes—check processing, order entry, accounts payable, accounts receivable, payroll, and the like. Some companies used an outside company (service bureau) to do its processing. By the late 1970s and early 1980s, most companies had brought their computing needs in-house and were running their own computer systems. Recognizing the power and potential of information technology, companies directed the use of their technology toward operations, marketing, and sales; and in the mid-1990s organizations started to create a new executive position, chief information officer (CIO), to oversee this process.

In the late 1980s, advances in technology prompted many companies to gradually change from host-centric computing to distributed computing. Instead of processing all of the information on one large mainframe computer, companies used minicomputers to act as dedicated processors for departments or specific applications. The minicomputers were, in many cases, networked together to share data. Databases became distributed, with data residing in different locations, yet accessible to all the machines in the network.

The personal computer had the greatest impact on the organization. It allowed true distributed processing. Each worker had a computer on their desk that was capable of performing feats that, until then, had been available only on the company's mainframe computer. This created both opportunities and headaches for the company, which will be addressed in the section on controls. By the early 2000s, minicomputers weren't dedicated but worked together to process the needs of the entire organization. The Internet allows customers and suppliers to communicate with the firm. Workers expect to be able to work from any location. Information technology management has gone from focusing on the processing needs of one machine and the applications running on that one machine to focusing on distributed applications, distributed hardware, distributed data, an internal network, worker productivity, security, and access 24/7.

To understand how information technology is used in a firm, this chapter is broken down into three basic components: information systems, organizational productivity, and management of technology resources. Technology is used to run the organization itself—the information systems that support the operations of the firm. Productivity of the workers also needs to be considered—e-mail, internal business process, portals, printing, and analytic tools, to name a few. The consumer buying experience is often online. Vendors can interact with internal inventory data. A corporate Web site needs to be maintained. The IT organization needs to support all aspects of technology's use within the organization. This chapter is designed to educate the reader on what the IT organization of the firm needs to deliver and what resources need to be considered for that delivery to be successful.

One of the most important resources that a firm needs to consider is its people—the users as well as the IT professionals. The best application will fail if the people it's built for won't use it. Users should be involved in the definition of an information system as well as the testing. Care should be taken to involve users in the training development and execution. Users should be aware of the reasons behind the adoption of new technology and its required new processes. Technology should never be adopted without a business reason behind the adoption. Implementation of any information system done without regard to the end user is headed for disaster.

Information Systems

Information systems support the firm's business endeavors. Simply put, information systems capture data, process it and/or store it, and output it. For most firms today, information technology is used to deliver information systems. The productivity tools mentioned in Chapter 19, Information Technology and You, could be used to build an information system, but these tools aren't information systems right out of the box. However, it's important not to get caught up in semantics. In the grand scheme of things, being able to categorize something you use as an information system isn't going to matter.

Types of Information Systems

Exhibit 20.1 represents the information systems paradigm. The original uses of information technology were focused on the lowest layer—the operational (transaction) systems. As technology evolved, firms began to look at higher levels in the paradigm. We start our discussion at the bottom.

Operational (Transaction) Systems

Operational (transaction) systems support the company's day-to-day operations, are typically used by workers in the lowest level of the organization, are run on a scheduled basis, usually contain large volumes of input data and generate numerous output reports.

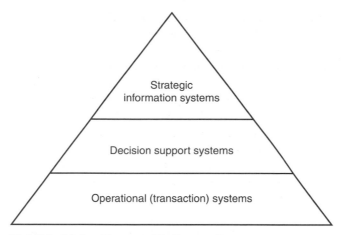

Exhibit 20.1 Types of information systems.

The processing rules are known and captured in programming code to be repeated over and over. These systems, typically called transaction processing systems, include check processing, order entry, accounts payable, accounts receivable, payroll, inventory control, and general ledger.

These systems are focused on how efficient the firm is. They create and manage large amounts of data. Output reports include a recap of the transactions that were handled as well as exception reports and variance reports. An aging report for accounts receivable is an example of a regularly processed report by an operational (transaction) system.

Today's organizations expect all of their operational systems to share data. Organizations are looking at enterprise resource planning (ERP) applications to manage their entire operation. Data is shared among functions—order entry, manufacturing, inventory management, human resources, and so on. ERP software is discussed in more detail later in this chapter.

Decision Support Systems

Decision support systems (DSSs) are generally used by middle-level managers to provide them with the data that they need to make decisions. The term was coined in the late 1970s and focused on giving decision makers the tools they needed to access and model data. Executive support systems also popular at the time focused on providing executives with snapshots of the firm's critical success factors and the ability to drill down to understand the underlying numbers.

The data used by these systems is scrubbed operational data, usually stored in a data warehouse. External data such as demographics might also be stored for retrieval in decision making. Online analytical processing (OLAP) gives users a powerful tool for analyzing data stored in the data warehouse.

In contrast to operational systems, the processing rules for decision systems are not known. Users turn to DSS tools when they are faced with semistructured decisions. As they begin to analyze the data, they aren't sure what steps they will take, what data they will need, or what tools they will use. They aren't sure where the analysis will take them.

This type of information system is focused on determining how effective the firm is against its goals. For example, while operational systems focus on how quickly an order can be filled, DSS systems focus on how many orders have been filled—by geographic area, by product line, by week/month, by retail store.

As technology has evolved, the term has morphed into *business intelligence* (BI) with key performance indicators. Software tools for workers are more powerful—database access is user friendly, data can be imported into a spreadsheet model, spreadsheet software now provides hundreds of functions that can be used in models, and dashboards are easily created with a variety of software tools. The line between the operational systems and DSS tools has become blurred.

Business intelligence is discussed in more detail later in this chapter.

Strategic Information Systems

Strategic information systems are used by senior management to make decisions on corporate strategy. For example, a retail company might use demographic census data, along with a computerized geographical mapping system, to evaluate the most appropriate locations for opening new stores, and then use historical performance data for similar stores to project overall impact on the bottom line. A manufacturing company, given its demands for both skilled and unskilled labor, might use a similar method to determine the optimal location for a new plant.

At this level in the organization, management is also looking for innovative ways to use technology. Technology can be used to improve internal operations, to improve communication with customers or with vendors, or to create a new product or service.

Today's Application Systems

In the 1970s and 1980s, application software systems were stand-alone. There was little sharing of data, leading to frequent redundancy of information. For example, in older systems, there might have been vendor data in both the inventory system and the accounts payable system, resulting in the possibility of multiple versions of the truth. Each system would contain address information, yet if the addresses were different for the same vendor, which one was right? Today, however, software applications are integrated across functional applications (accounts payable, accounts receivable, marketing, sales, manufacturing, etc.). Integrated applications contain only one vendor data location, which all applications utilize. These changes in software architecture better reflect the integration of functions that has occurred within most companies.

To understand how horizontally integrated systems can support a firm's strategic and competitive uses of information technology, let's look at an example.

Accounting systems, while used primarily for accounting data, can also be a source of data for sales and marketing. While retail stores' point-of-sale cash registers are used as a repository for cash and to account for it, they are also capturing data for inventory, sales, and customer marketing. As items are sold, the inventory management system gets updated numbers and can determine if an order needs to be placed with a vendor to replenish stock. The sales system gets updated numbers to understand how items are being sold across the country. Some major retailers ask customers for their zip codes when point-of-sale transactions are entered; that data is used by the company's marketing applications to assess how effective a particular marketing campaign was.

There is a host of software packages that can be used to integrate the functional needs of companies of all sizes. Smaller companies can find software selections that run on personal computers and networks, are integrated, and satisfy most of the companies' requirements. Quickbooks from Intuit, Microsoft Office Accounting, and Peachtree from Sage provide most of the necessary functional modules for small companies. These applications can be purchased through computer stores and software retailers usually for less than $200. Midsize organizations might look at more robust offerings such as those from Exact Software and Sage. Larger organizations look to enterprise resource planning (ERP) integrated software for their needs. ERP systems are discussed later in this chapter.

The offerings for midsize and large organization are often procured through a value-added reseller or licensed system integrator, who, for a fee, sell, install, and service the software. The practice of using third-party resellers began in the 1980s, when large hardware and software manufacturers realized that they were incapable of servicing all of the smaller companies that would be installing their products, many of whom required a lot of hand-holding. Consequently, a cottage industry of distributors and value-added dealers developed, in which companies earn profits on the sale of hardware and software and the ensuing consulting services.

Accounting Information Systems

As mentioned earlier, accounting systems were, for most companies, the first computerized applications. As the years progressed, these systems have become integrated and typically consist of the following modules:

- Accounts payable.
- Order entry and invoicing.
- Accounts receivable.
- Purchase order management and replenishment.
- Inventory control.
- Human resources management.
- Payroll.
- Fixed assets.
- General ledger and financial statements.

Whereas in past years organizations might have purchased some of these modules and developed others in-house, today most companies purchase packaged software that contains all these modules. Some companies do a phased implementation, however, starting with some modules with a future planned implementation of others.

Enterprise Resource Planning (ERP) Systems

While the software mentioned earlier (Quickbooks, Microsoft Accounting, Peachtree, AccPac, and Exact Systems) are indeed ERP offerings in that all modules are integrated and business processes are coded into the software, most business professionals think of large, integrated packages from companies like SAP, Oracle, and Infor when they hear the term ERP. These large packages integrate not only the accounting functions, but also the manufacturing, warehousing, sales, marketing, and distribution functions. Most ERP systems also interface with Web applications to enable e-commerce transactions.

ERP software implements what its vendor feels are best practices for business processes. Prior to ERP software, software was developed to fit the business processes of an individual firm or industry. Since that approach does not offer economies of scale, ERP vendors determine the most efficient steps for carrying out a particular business process and code those steps into their software. Organizations can choose either to modify their own business processes to match the best practices that are delivered in the software or to spend a great deal of time and money to customize the software to match their own business processes. A benefit of accepting so-called best practices is compliance with federal requirements such as Sarbanes-Oxley or International Financial Reporting Standards.

These packages have spawned an entire industry of consulting companies to assist large companies in implementing ERP software, a process that may take several years to complete. As in any software implementation, one must always factor into the timetable the process's cost and the distraction it causes the organization. In today's lean business environment, people have little extra time for new tasks. Implementing a major new system or, for that matter, any system requires a major time and effort commitment.

Information Technology in Banking and Financial Services

Information technology is mission critical for the banking and financial services industry. So it's no surprise that it is also the leading industry in its use of information technology. The industry has become a transaction processing industry that is information dependent. Very little real money is ever touched. Rather, all transactions, from stock purchases to the direct deposit of workers' checks, are processed electronically. Information technology has paved the way for innovations like the electronic trading systems used by NASDAQ and the New York Stock Exchange.

The financial services industry is also the leading industry to adopt new uses of information technology. Paperless check exchange, voice authentication, and secure messaging between banks are just a few of the innovative uses they have adopted.

Competitive advantage for banks has gone from having ATMs on every corner to having online banking features accessible on the Web. Customers can check balances, transfer funds, pay bills, and look at current credit card activity.

E-Commerce

E-commerce (electronic commerce) has changed the entire landscape of how business is transacted, as consumers are now able to purchase products (and sometimes services) over cyberspace. There is support for the entire selling cycle: product awareness, filling a "shopping cart," checking out, providing shipping information, processing payment, and sending confirmation to an e-mail address.

Retailers compete by trying to make the experience so pleasurable that consumers buy and come back often. A profile on a user is maintained with information on what products were purchased and/or viewed, allowing the Internet sites to create shopping experiences specific to the user's needs. E-commerce retailers turn to technology to compensate for the lack of touch-and-feel. Multiple views of a product are usually offered, including views of a product in different colors. Videos are available that show how a product might be used. Consumers can build their own 3-D models that can be used to virtually try on clothes.

When an organization makes the strategic decision to sell its products over the Internet, it is increasing the strategic importance of its information technology infrastructure and related data. With e-commerce, one's competition is a click away. It is critical for a firm to make sure that a consumer's shopping experience is a positive one. It becomes important to monitor ease of use, timeliness of data, speed (that a page takes to load), error-free operations, and working links, and to offer features to get the customer to return.

Traditional retailers (now called "bricks and mortar" because they have physical space) have become "clicks and mortar" retailers by also selling on the Internet. Customers are able to order over the Internet and have their purchases delivered to them or pick them up at a nearby store. They can also return merchandise to traditional stores.

The Internet has also made a significant difference for products such as music and software. Software that used to be purchased in a shrink-wrapped box with a CD and printed documentation now can be purchased online and the software itself downloaded instantly. Documentation can be downloaded to the user's computer or the user can use Web links when problems or questions occur. Music can be downloaded to a computer or a portable media device.

These new opportunities create new challenges for those involved in the operations, accounting, and finance functions of these virtual marketspace companies. Not only is the order being processed electronically, but it is also being shipped automatically, sometimes from a third party's fulfillment center. Also, the payment is being processed electronically. The electronic payment, usually through a third-party clearinghouse, must conform to various security standards in order to protect credit card information that is transmitted over the Web. Frequently the company selling the goods never receives the credit card number of the consumer, only an authorization number from the credit card clearinghouse. The tracking of the merchandise, as well as the payment, not to mention the processes for handling customer returns and credits, will present significant angst for the auditors and controllers of these firms.

Whereas most consumers think of e-commerce for physical goods, the financial services industry has embraced the concept and now offers most of its products over the Internet. Online services include, among others, the purchase of stocks and bonds, online mortgages, life insurance, and online banking.

Most of the focus of the investor community during the early 2000s was on the business-to-consumer (B2C) space, with millions of dollars made and lost as a result of people not understanding the business model. Most of the money raised in venture capital was used for advertising to gain brand recognition, while very little was invested in infrastructure. As a result, the B2C landscape is littered with the corpses of failed ventures—the dot-com bubble. Those that have survived are spending money on the traditional back-office functions that bricks-and-mortar retailers have developed over the years.

Business-to-Business E-Commerce

Although most consumers think just about business-to-consumer (B2C) e-commerce, the greatest potential lies in business-to-business (B2B) e-commerce. In a typical supply chain there are many B2B transactions involving raw materials or subcomponents. For example, a desktop computer manufacturer makes several B2B transactions to buy components for the tower—cords, monitor, keyboards, and mice.

Companies of every shape and size are realizing the opportunities for both ordering and selling their products over the Internet. Some companies are using their Internet sites to process orders, create and price custom configurations (similar to what Dell does on its site), track orders, and assist with customer service. Some industries are creating their own marketplaces for the cooperative purchase of goods and services. There are multitudes of B2B marketplaces and exchanges. Some are vertical, servicing specific industries. Others are horizontal marketplaces.

Procurement software is now being offered that automates the purchasing function of a firm. The software can approve and issue purchasing orders, receive and match an invoice with its order, and electronically pay the bill. This frees up the procurement department to work with suppliers to get better prices, and analyze the process itself. Current vendors of procurement software include SAP and Sage.

Organizational Productivity

Today's organizations have to understand their performance in real time and be able to communicate with all constituents (workers, vendors, customers, and investors). They need to manage their technology resources (hardware, software, network, and data) so that they support the productivity of their constituents and are still cost effective.

Business Intelligence and Business Analytics

Decision support systems, business intelligence, business analytics—the same or different? Business intelligence is the firm's understanding of the market behavior and its impact on the business. To get there, a firm uses tools to access, manipulate, and display data. It could be as simple as running user-generated queries against a database and generating reports from that data. It could be a little more complex using Online Analytical Processing (OLAP) to slice and dice "cubes" of data in a data warehouse. It could be using statistical routines to develop analytics about the data. It could be using data-mining techniques to learn more about relationships embedded in the data. It could be models that use the current data to predict future levels of performance. It could include dashboards that highlight organizational and personal performance factors. Business analytics refers to the use of the statistical tools.

A example of a dashboard is illustrated in Exhibit 20.2. The screen shot is from a demo provided by Information Builders. The idea of a dashboard is to give a snapshot of performance factors. The screen shot illustrates the metrics for sales. The dashboards for financials and quality would present metrics for those particular areas.

The notion of business intelligence and its family of tools has grown from earlier decision support systems applications. The idea behind both is how organizations gather and analyze data to make better business decisions and optimize business processes. Decision makers use data (data access and reporting), statistics, and predictive modeling. In some cases, the analysis could result in an automated decision that requires minimal human intervention. More often, the analysis provides input to the human decision maker. This evolution is a direct result of more robust user-friendly tools and the vast amounts of data that an organization now has available.

Key to the success of the resources used for business intelligence is the agility of the firm to react to new insights. There needs to be a strategic commitment to their importance. Workers need to be data-savvy and the organization must be committed to providing an integrated, cross-enterprise view of data and willing to fund the technology necessary to capture this data and make it accessible.

For example, Netflix, the movie rental company, uses business intelligence tools to recommend movies to a member based on previous rentals and its own inventory. When

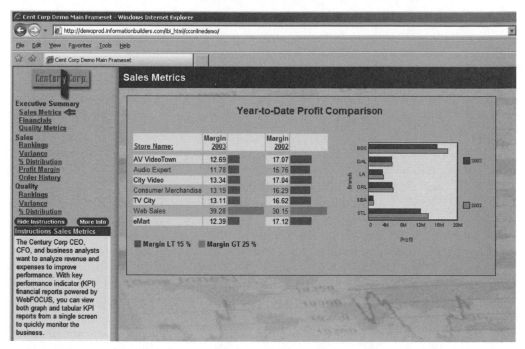

Exhibit 20.2   Sample dashboard from Information Builders' online demo.
Source: Information Builders.

consumers are customizing a computer online, Dell uses such tools to recommend upgrades based on what others have ordered and what Dell has in inventory.

Data Access and OLAP

Before the late 1980s, data in databases was accessible only via code that was typically written by a programmer in the IT organization. As database management software evolved to create user-friendly interfaces for building retrieval code, users began to build their own queries. (A query is an interrogation of data found in a database.) Rather than completely specify what data they wanted to see and how they wanted to see it formatted and then waiting for IT staff to get to the request (and there always seems to be a backlog), users could use a template or wizard to select their data and review the results, modify their request, review the results, and continue until the results were what they needed and were formatted appropriately.

Most databases used in organizations today are relational, and these queries are actually in Structured Query Language (SQL) code that is used against the database. More on SQL and relational databases can be found in the database section later in the chapter.

Organizations have begun to separate their operational data from their business intelligence data. The BI data are regularly written to the firm's data warehouse. Details as to how that process happens are discussed later in this chapter. Important to understand at this point is how a user can access this large volume of data that has been formatted to support business intelligence.

One important tool for BI is Online Analytical Processing (OLAP), which presents data as a virtual cube (think of a Rubik's cube) for analysis. The data could actually

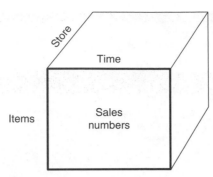

Exhibit 20.3 Business intelligence cube for actual sales.

have more than three dimensions, but in practice the visual is still referred to as a cube. The facts from operational systems is the data that are stored in the cube. The cube's dimensions are the categories of the data. An analyst can pick the dimensions that are of interest, and the software aggregates (such as average, count, sum, maximum, minimum) the remaining dimension within seconds.

Consider a BI model for a chain of 300 retail stores. One data element being modeled could be actual sales (the "facts"). The first dimension may be the company's merchandise items; second dimension may represent different points in time; and the third dimension may be the store locations. This cube is illustrated in Exhibit 20.3. Each of these dimensions is represented at the lowest detail level but could also be aggregated (items to product lines or items to department, store locations to districts, time to weeks/months/years). An executive might examine the men's department sales. She might then probe to learn what product lines of items sold better than others. After finding an underperforming product line, she may check how the product line did in different districts of stores. She might drill down, looking at individual items in individual stores, and compare their performance to that of a prior week or year. This process is like taking the Rubik's cube and continually rotating the levels, looking at each of the cube's faces. Each face represents data for a piece of merchandise for a store for a period of time. That is why this process is referred to as "slice and dice." You can slice and turn the data any which way you desire. The data can also be viewed and sorted in a tabular or graphical mode. The same theory applies, whether the database contains retailing data, stock market data, or accounting data.

OLAP features are beginning to be incorporated into the personal productivity products. Database tools can do cross-tab queries (aggregating data based on values in fields), and SQL, the language used to extract data from relational databases, has an OLAP function. Spreadsheet software is beginning to incorporate pivot tables (a blend of cross-tab functionality and OLAP aggregation) into their native offerings. Low-end data-analysis tools are rapidly becoming a commodity.

Exhibits 20.4 and 20.5 show examples of a decision support system's output. The output is from a demo from Information Builders that was also used in Exhibit 20.2, a sample dashboard.

Exhibit 20.4 illustrates how an analyst might customize a view of the data. The user picks from the drop-down lists at the top of the screen to slice and dice the cube. The

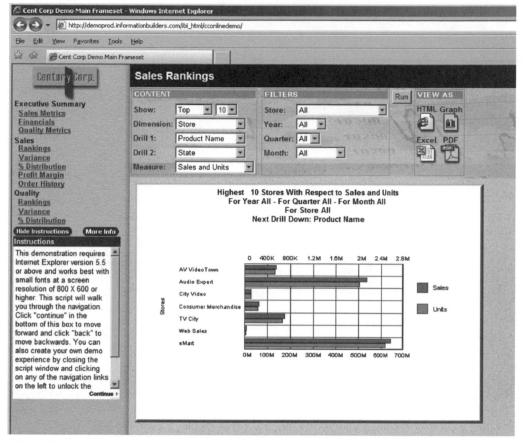

Exhibit 20.4   Custom view of data from Information Builders' online demo.

Source: Information Builders.

output can be viewed as a Web page (HTML), a graph (as illustrated), a spreadsheet, or a pdf file.

Exhibit 20.5 illustrates a different feature of this BI software. Once again, the user can specify specific values for the basic dimensions of the cube or aggregates of those dimensions. In this case, if the user clicks on a product name, the detailed data that makes up the displayed data would be shown.

Intranets, Extranets, and Portals

Organizations today are global; not just their customers, but also their own workers and vendors. Intranets and extranets are built with Internet technology to connect to employees (intranet) or vendors and customers (extranets). Portals are a hybrid technology.

An intranet allows employees from within a company to access data and services within the company's system. A firewall prevents outsiders from accessing any data that a company wishes to keep confidential. An intranet refers to those systems that are inside the firewall. Employees have the access authority to enter through the firewall and access information, even though they might be using a computer outside of the company. One manufacturing company has provided an intranet facility for its employees to learn

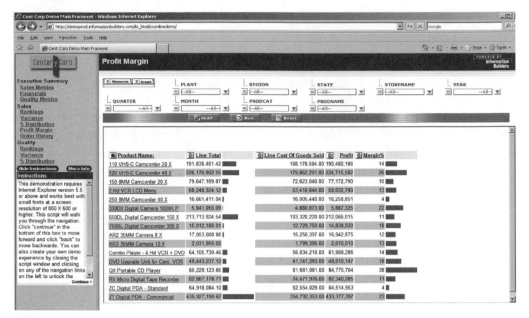

**Exhibit 20.5 Interface capable of drilling down, from Information Builders'
online demo.**

Source: Information Builders.

about their health, life, and disability insurance and their educational benefits. The system
allows them to sign up for these programs and to inquire about some of the most common
issues specific to the programs. When online, employees can also access and sign up for
a list of in-house training courses, read an employee newsletter, and check the current
price of the company's publicly traded stock.

An extranet allows external users to access data inside of the firewall but controls their
access. For example, part of Wal-Mart's ordering and logistics system allows its vendors
and suppliers to access Wal-Mart's store sales data stored on Wal-Mart's computer
systems. If these transactions occurred over the Internet, they would be referred to
as extranet transactions. Another example of an extranet is an application that allows a
consumer to track an order or a delivery, such as those offered by UPS and FedEx.

Extranets have evolved from earlier electronic data interchange (EDI) systems. EDI
allowed companies to communicate and conduct electronic commerce from one computer to another. EDI was one of the industry's growing uses for data communications,
and many companies used it to send purchase orders to their suppliers, thereby lessen-
ing the time it took for purchase orders to be received and then entered and processed
by the supplier. Organizations were able to maintain lower inventories by speeding up
the turnaround time of ordering and receiving goods and materials. On the flip side,
many suppliers used EDI to send their customers advance ship notifications, advising
them of what had been shipped so that they could prepare their warehouses for the
goods and materials. Some companies used EDI to transmit their invoices and then
to receive the subsequent payments. Early EDI specifications were not standard, and
a vendor working with multiple customers would have to maintain multiple versions
of EDI software. While industries used different versions of EDI in different ways,
their goals are always the same: to minimize the processing time and to lower inventory

costs and overhead expenses. EDI has been eclipsed by extranets and e-procurement software.

Organizations have begun building portals, which are Web-based gateways to the company's information and services. An organization might have multiple versions of the portal: one for those with access rights, and one for those without access rights. Most enterprise information portals are made up of small portlets that can be added or removed by a user. A portlet might be a link to e-mail, company announcements, company calendar, personal calendar, news feeds, stock feeds, collaboration sites, or areas within the company.

Productivity Tools

Workers expect to have productivity tools on their computers—desktop, laptop, notebook, netbook, PDA. Today's workers expect to be able to use e-mail and to have access to e-mail when away from the workplace. Having a word processor and presentation software is expected. Those workers who deal with numbers expect to have access to spreadsheet software.

There is a cost associated with these expectations since normally an organization has to buy individual copies of the software or buy a site license. The organization also has to support the software (help desk questions, training, etc.) and upgrade the software with patches or new releases. In addition, the organization has to evaluate whether to go through the time and cost of upgrading to new versions.

There are other options beginning to emerge in the marketplace. One is to supply these tools as software as a service (SaaS), which is discussed in more detail later in this chapter. This option does not require a copy of the software to be on the user's computer. The software and the data reside on the servers of the vendor of the software. Access is via the Internet. Data can be shared with others within the organization. The downside of this option is that the organization is at the mercy of the vendor and the vendor's servers. One of the more popular SaaS productivity tools is Google Docs, which provides word processing, spreadsheet software, and presentation software. Google also offers an online calendar and e-mail.

Another option is to use free (at time of publication) open source software, such as that offered by OpenOffice.org, which is sponsored by Sun Microsystems, Novell, IBM, and Google, to name a few. The suite of integrated products includes a word processor, spreadsheet software, presentation software, drawing software, and a database tool. These products can open (and save) other file formats, such as Microsoft's. Such software is loaded onto the user's computer either from a CD or via a download from the Internet. A discussion of open source software can be found in the software section of this chapter.

Knowledge Management

The notion of knowledge management (KM) continues to evolve as the power of technology evolves. Knowledge management is a set of processes or practices that an organization embraces that identify, create, store, and distribute knowledge—insights, experiences, best practices. The KM objectives are to reduce redundant work, to avoid reinventing the wheel, and to retain and share intellectual capital.

Knowledge that is easily shared is explicit knowledge. Tacit knowledge is not easily shared; it provides context and usually requires personal contact. Tacit knowledge often consists of norms that workers don't always recognize. A major goal of KM is to transform tacit knowledge into explicit knowledge—to codify it.

Early KM technologies included online expertise locators and document management systems. The technology evolved with the development and use of collaborative software. Social computing tools have taken this evolution to a new level, as the use of blogs and wikis allows for semistructured approaches to creating, storing, and distributing knowledge.

KM applications can be very elaborate and well structured; they can become part of the corporate culture and part of the corporate work process. Or KM applications can be the very opposite. Organizations have to let the grassroots efforts flourish while the organization begins to understand what knowledge needs to be managed and how it can best be managed.

Managing IT Resources

When all processing was done by one machine in one room with one operating system and run by professional technologists, managing the IT resources focused on maintaining that one machine and its peripherals, monitoring the air-conditioning of the "glass house" and making sure that the access system worked. Today, the IT organization within a firm has lots of machines of all sizes, lots of data to maintain and make available, lots of software, lots of connection nodes and firewalls, and lots of end users, not all of whom are technology-savvy, and some aren't even employees! Being held accountable by the end user—the person who is actually using the product offered by the IT organization—for many organizations was a new phenomenon.

Hardware

Most of the early computers were large, mainframe computers. Usually manufactured by IBM, they were powerful batch processing machines. Large numbers of documents (e.g., invoices or orders) were entered into the computer and then processed, producing various reports and special documents, such as accounts receivable aging statements.

In many companies, millions of lines of software were written to run on this mainframe technology. Generally, these machines were programmed in a language called COBOL and used an operating system that was proprietary for that hardware. The same program wouldn't necessarily run on computers from different manufacturers. Because there were slight differences in configurations and operating systems, it was even difficult to run the same software on different computers that were produced by the same manufacturer.

In the 1980s, technology evolved from proprietary operating systems to minicomputers with open operating systems. The first open operating systems were computers that used the UNIX operating system. Although in the 1970s Bell Labs actually developed UNIX as an operating system for scientific applications, it later became an accepted standard for commercial applications. The platform's independent operating system and its associated applications could run on a variety of manufacturers' computers, creating opportunities both for companies and for competition within the computer industry. Organizations were no longer inexorably tied to one manufacturer. UNIX became the standard in the early 1990s. However, standards changed rapidly, and UNIX lost ground due to the development of client-server technology. However, as organizations are now shifting toward Web-based applications, UNIX and its derivative, Linux, are becoming the operating systems of choice for servers as well as client machines.

Client-server technology is based on software on client machines making requests for services from server computers. The server accepts the request, processes it, and returns the requested information to the client machine. Client machines are typically PCs but could also be some of the other personal devices discussed in Chapter 19. Servers tend to be specialized. One might be the traffic cop directing requests to their appropriate destination server. Another might be a data server, an e-mail server, an application server, or a Web server. Many applications today use the technology of the Web to interface with their users, so the software used on the client computer is often a Web browser.

Servers tend to be "headless"—they don't have a monitor attached. They are usually in stacks and controlled via one machine that does have a monitor. They tend to stay on for long periods of time, and low failure rates are necessary for reliability. Servers are usually configured to do one thing well. The current operating systems of choice are Linux and Microsoft Windows Server 2008, an updated version of Windows NT.

Server technology has recently evolved into supporting the notion of virtual servers. In this case software can configure a server machine to think it is multiple servers, each with its own operating system and memory resources. Using virtual servers, a machine that has been configured to do calculations well can be home to multiple applications in the organization, rather than needing separate machines for each application. End users shouldn't know whether their requests are being processed by a stand-alone server or a virtual server.

Server technology is also heading toward a design in which processors are built around multiple, smaller processors, all operating at the same time. The goal of symmetrical multiprocessors (SMPs) and massively parallel processors (MPPs) is to split the processing load among the processors. In SMPs, there are between two and eight processors in a unit. SMPs are made available by a range of manufacturers and operating systems, and they provide processor power typically not available in a uniprocessor. SMPs share the same memory but split the processing; consequently, they are impacted by physical memory-addressing limitations and bus speed (how fast bytes can move between memory and the CPU). Laptops and desktops are being offered with dual-core devices (basically two processers inside the same CPU) and therefore providing multiprocessing capabilities. If a machine is used primarily for word processing and simple spreadsheet calculations, dual-core capability is overkill.

Faced with the demanding environment of multiple, simultaneous queries from databases that exceed hundreds of gigabytes, processors with massively parallel processors (MPPs) are being utilized more and more. MPPs are machines that have hundreds of smaller CPUs within one unit, each with its own memory. In this case, the processors work in parallel on the same request. Applications must be programmed to divide work in such a way that all the executing segments can communicate with each other.

In the early 1990s, Xerox's prestigious Palo Alto Research Center (Xerox PARC) introduced "ubiquitous computing," a model that it felt reflected the way companies and their employees would work in the future. At the time, the idea of small, inexpensive networked processing devices of a variety of sizes that would be used throughout everyday life seemed very farfetched. Not so today. Now the term that comes to mind is "pervasive computing." Devices with very tiny processes are in almost any type of object imaginable (cars, tools, appliances, consumer goods)—communicating through interconnected networks. They are becoming so prevalent in the environment that people don't realize when they are being used.

This trend toward smaller and smaller has been somewhat predictable. In the early 1960s, Gordon Moore, the inventor of the modern CPU at Intel, developed Moore's law, which predicts that the density of the components on a computer chip will double every 18 to 24 months, thereby doubling the chip's processing power. This hypothesis has proven to be very accurate. Intel recently announced that it expects that the downsizing of silicon chips with good economics will continue through 2029. It is interesting to note that Moore is also credited with a second law—that the cost to manufacturers (R&D, manufacturing, testing) to fulfill Moore's first law follows an opposite trend. The cost actually increases exponentially over time.

This trend toward smaller and smaller is very visible in the offerings for users—laptops, notebooks, tablets, netbooks, PDAs. Organizations have to determine how best to deliver technology to their users. Screens formatted for a laptop might not view well on a netbook or PDA. Users expect to have access to data that they need to make decisions. Users expect powerful software to allow them to excel at their jobs. Decisions made about user machines impact thousands of computers, not just hundreds. And while it might be relatively easy to just install a new upgrade of software to a machine, the organization has to consider the impact on the workers themselves. People tend to resist change; organizations have to plan for the resistance.

Software

While most older hardware has given way to newer and faster computers, most companies use a combination of newly acquired software and older, self-developed software. The latter was developed over a period of years, perhaps more than 25, using COBOL, which, until the early 1990s, was the standard programming language in business applications. Today, many companies' mission-critical systems still run on mainframe technology, using programs written in COBOL; in fact, there are billions of lines of COBOL programming code still functional in U.S. businesses. COBOL continues to be enhanced and more lines of code written each year.

These legacy systems have become a major issue for many, though, and were the key issue behind the Y2K (2000) problem, which centered on date arithmetic. Many systems stored date fields as MM/DD/YY and did subtraction to find out the number of days between dates (for example, the age of an accounts receivable account was the difference between the date of the invoice and the current date). Subtracting 10/04/99 from 01/04/00 would result in a negative number because the algorithm was to take the year's digits from one date and subtract them from the second date. Much noise was made about the Y2K problem, fueled by the fact that the programmers for these legacy systems were no longer with the firms and there was little or no documentation available for these legacy systems. Some firms used the "impending doom" as a reason to move to ERP systems, while others wrote work-arounds and still others decided to ride out the storm. When the new millennium rolled in, there were no significant computer failures and some countries that spent little on the Y2K bug fared as well as those that spent a great deal. The instant debate was whether the absence of computer failures was the result of the efforts to compensate for it or the problem itself was greatly overstated.

Today, most programmers write in C++ or C. C++ is an object-oriented programming language; object-oriented languages provide the programmer with a facility to create a programming object or module that may be reused in many applications. The widespread use of the Internet spawned a new category of languages. Perl, Java, and

PHP (which originally stood for Personal Home Page and is generally now considered to mean hypertext preprocessor, with the first "P" being recursive) are generally referred to as scripting languages and allow the application to behave according to the user's needs.

Tools were developed to be used by the end users themselves, thus freeing up IT professionals from simple tasks. These are called fourth-generation programming languages. There are a variety of types of 4GLs currently in use:

- *Report-generation tools.* These take a description of the data and the report to be generated and generate the report. They are usually data source dependent. Crystal Reports is an example of such a tool.

- *Statistical tools.* These 4GLs, such as SAS and SPSS, provide commands for data manipulation, selection, and reporting.

- *Data reporting tools.* These tools are usually provided with relational databases. They range from template input (as was illustrated in Chapter 19) to Structured Query Language (SQL). These tools retrieve data and can do some minor formatting.

Middleware

Middleware began to appear in the 1980s as a way to link newer applications to older legacy systems. The easiest way to think of middleware is as a translator. It takes the data from one application and converts it to a format and structure that a second application can use. They might be different types of application software, different operating systems, or different database structures.

The software has evolved into the technology that provides interoperability between distributed architectures and distributed applications. Middleware services provide application programming interfaces (APIs) to supply the interaction. Some types of middleware are remote procedure calls (RPCs) that do exactly that, message-oriented middleware (MOM) that sends messages but doesn't expect a response immediately (as is the case with RPCs), object request brokers that are used for object-oriented systems, and SQL-oriented data access middleware between applications and database servers.

Software as a Service

A new model of software deployment called software as a service (SaaS) has recently emerged. Software services from SaaS providers have been developed to leverage Web technologies and have been built with a multitenant back end that allows multiple users to access a shared data model. Customer access to the application is via the Internet. All processing happens on the vendor's hardware; all data is stored on the vendor's hardware. The SaaS provider takes care of software maintenance, ongoing operations of the hardware and network, and support for the application. However, the customer relinquishes control over the evolution of the software (upgrades happen when the SaaS vendor decides they should happen, whether or not it's disruptive to the customer). The cost of the application itself is an ongoing expense as part of the charge from the vendor rather than a one-time up-front cost. The cost of operation for the application is an ongoing expense, which may or may not be an advantage depending on the organization's current technology mix.

SaaS is considered a low-cost way for a business to use commercially licensed software without the associated high initial cost or manpower requirement. Applications that aren't mission critical but are processing heavy are good candidates for SaaS implementations.

Organizations are looking to SaaS vendors to supply services for customer relationship management, videoconferencing, human resources, e-mail, and call centers. An earlier model of deployment called application service providers (ASPs) also provided such services but were client-server implementations.

The downside of using an SaaS software solution is that the firm is placing its destiny in another company's hands and is dependent on that company's security and financial health. The upside is that the firm is not responsible for purchasing the application, maintaining it, and having to provide the computer power to process the data.

Open Source Software

The idea behind open source software is to develop software that makes its source code freely available for use, change, and/or distribution. The Open Source Initiative determines whether software can be considered open source, the major criteria being access to the source code itself and free redistribution of the source code itself. (Source code is the code that is translated into what the computer's CPU actually needs to do, which is called machine code.) Organizations have been slow to adopt open source software, worrying about the support, reliability, and viability of such products. The success of UNIX has begun to dispel these fears. Organizations are saving billions of dollars a year by installing open source software rather than licensed software.

Open source development has produced reliable and high-quality software quickly. There are many independent programmers testing and fixing bugs. Programmers can build custom interfaces and add new abilities. Organizations can adopt these new features as they see fit—they basically plug into existing source code. Larger successful projects enforce rules to facilitate teamwork and ensure system testing and documentation. Open source software does have its critics. Open source may allow hackers to determine weaknesses in the software. It is hard to build a sound business model around the open source development process, thus raising concerns about viability into the future.

Networks and Communications

It is becoming increasingly common in industry to create virtual wide area networks using multiple, interconnected local area networks. These networks also connect the older mainframe and midrange computers that industry uses for its older legacy systems to the client terminals on the users' desks. Exhibit 20.6 is a model of a typical company's wide area network, and it demonstrates how all of the older technology interconnects with the newer local area networks and the Internet.

In the early 1990s, there were numerous, competing network operating systems and protocols. Novell and its NetWare software held the largest market share at the time. As operating systems for computers themselves have evolved, newer operating systems such as Microsoft Windows Server 2008 have incorporated many features of the original network operating systems, in some cases making network operating systems themselves obsolete. Because of the Internet's overwhelming success, transmission-control protocol/Internet protocol (TCP/IP) has become the standard communications protocol.

The 1990s saw the advent of virtual organizations. Virtual organizations are formed when companies join together to create products or enterprises that they could not have created individually. In most cases, information technology allows companies to create these partnerships and share information as if they were one company. Using communications and collaborative software for e-mail, chat, instant messaging, file sharing, blogs,

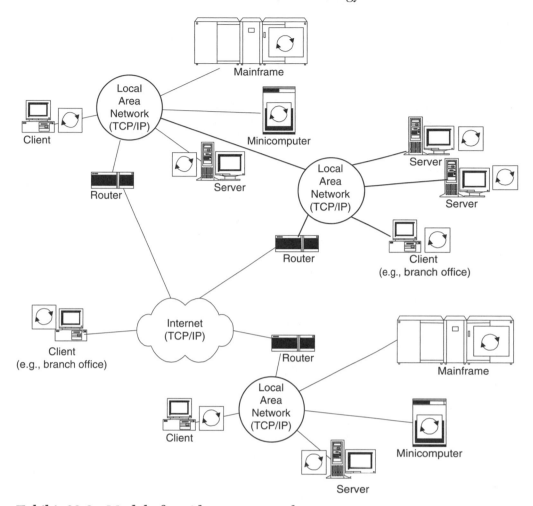

Exhibit 20.6   Model of a wide area network.

wikis, and online chats, the partners can communicate and share information with each other about their individual progress, in order to ensure the best possible success. This is discussed further in the section on IT strategy.

Database

The following scenario depicts what information systems looked like prior to the use of database management systems. Imagine a physical office in which each person has his or her own file cabinet. The information in the file cabinets belongs to the people whose desks are closest to them. They decide what information will be in their file cabinets and how it will be organized. For example, sales might refer to gross sales in one worker's cabinet and net sales in another's. Yet, the discrepancy would be unimportant, because there was actually very little sharing of data.

Database management systems assume that information is a corporate asset to be shared by all workers in the enterprise. Database technology, therefore, allows a company to have one integrated location for the storage of all company data. These systems create a standard vocabulary, or data dictionary, by which all references are consistent (e.g., "sales" always means "net sales"). They also enable each user to have a personalized view of the data, as if the information was still in the file cabinet next to the desk. Users need not concern themselves with the physical location or physical order of the data, either. Database management systems are capable of presenting the data as necessary. In fact, with distributed databases, the data does not even have to reside in the same location or computer. It can be spread around the world if necessary. Database systems are sufficiently intelligent and can find the data and process it as if it were located directly on the user's personal computer.

Most of the software that was developed in the earlier years relied on data structures called flat files. While some companies utilized database technology to store information, those database management systems were, in many cases, unwieldy and very expensive both to acquire and to maintain. They were usually hierarchical or network database systems, which were expensive and frequently required special database administrators just to constantly fine-tune the system.

Today's database technology is based on a relational model, and, on a very simplistic basis, it resembles a spreadsheet. In a relational database, there is a series of tables or files. Similar to a spreadsheet table, each table has columns with attributes and rows of data. There can be an almost unlimited number of tables in a database. While there is a practical limit to the size of a spreadsheet, databases can contain thousands and thousands of columns and millions and millions of rows of data. In addition, databases also allow users to relate or connect tables that share common columns of data.

Exhibit 20.7 is an example of a very simple portion of a payroll application. There are two different tables. The employee table contains data about each of the company's employees: name, marital status, number of dependents, and so on. The pay table contains data about every time each of the employees is paid: their gross payroll, Social Security taxes, federal withholding, state tax, and so on.

First, notice the common column between the two tables, the employee number. This column enables the database management system to relate the two tables. It allows the system, for example, to print a payroll journal that has both the weekly payroll information from the pay table and to access the employees' names from the employee table. Why not combine all the data into one table? Not only would the employees' names and Social Security numbers appear multiple times, requiring the unnecessary use of data storage, but also multiple versions of the truth might occur. If one of the employees should happen to change her name, the database would show one name for part of the year and another for the rest of the year. Redundant data creates opportunities for data corruption; just because data is changed in one table, that same data is not necessarily changed in all tables. Prudent systems design eliminates data field duplications wherever possible.

No treatment of relational database technology would be complete without mention of structured query language (SQL). SQL is used to retrieve, insert, update, and delete data and to manage data (such as add tables, fields, functions, and views) in relational database management systems. Standards for SQL are overseen by the International Standards Organization (ISO) but many vendors of database management software add their own proprietary extensions (additional functionality and/or commands). SQL queries allow a user to specify the desired results and let the database management system determine how to physically perform the necessary operations to produce the results.

Exhibit 20.7 Database data structures.

Employee Table

Employee Number	First Name	Initial	Last Name	Social Security Number	Marital Status	Number of Dependents	Date of Birth	Date of Hire	Date of Termination	Date of Last Pay Raise	Pay Rate	Hourly or Salary
1	Mary	E	Smith	123456789	M	4	4/1/63	7/21/91		9/1/96	8.505	H
2	Tom	T	Day	234567890	M	3	3/2/55	11/15/91		1/15/96	750.000	S
3	Harry	F	Jones	345678901	S	1	11/30/71	1/15/92	9/24/96	11/6/94	12.500	H
4	Sally	D	Kraft	456789012	S	0	10/5/65	3/6/92		3/5/96	14.755	H
5	Charlie		Malt	567890123	S	1	6/6/80	6/2/93		6/17/96	900.000	S
6	John	K	Free	678901234	M	5	8/5/49	11/1/94		12/15/95	17.500	H

Pay Table

Employee Number	Date	Number of Regular Hours	Number of Overtime Hours	Gross Payroll	Social Security Tax	Medicare Tax	Federal Withholding Tax	State Withholding Tax	Net Pay	Check Number
1	1/7/96	40.0	4.0	391.23	24.26	5.67	101.16425	21.52	238.62	1
2	1/7/96	40.0	0.0	750.00	46.50	10.88	193.935	41.25	457.44	2
3	1/7/96	40.0	0.0	500.00	31.00	7.25	129.29	27.50	304.96	3
4	1/7/96	40.0	4.0	678.73	42.08	9.84	175.506	37.33	413.97	4
5	1/7/96	40.0	0.0	900.00	55.80	13.05	232.722	49.50	548.93	5
6	1/7/96	40.0	2.5	765.63	47.47	11.10	197.97531	42.11	466.97	6
1	1/14/96	40.0	12.0	493.29	30.58	7.15	127.55493	27.13	300.87	7
2	1/14/96	40.0	0.0	750.00	46.50	10.88	193.935	41.25	457.44	8
3	1/14/96	40.0	8.0	650.00	40.30	9.43	168.077	35.75	396.45	9
4	1/14/96	40.0	7.9	765.05	47.43	11.09	197.82579	42.08	466.62	10
5	1/14/96	40.0	0.0	900.00	55.80	13.05	232.722	49.50	548.93	11
6	1/14/96	40.0	0.0	700.00	43.40	10.15	181.006	38.50	426.94	12
1	1/21/96	40.0	0.0	340.20	21.09	4.93	87.96916	18.71	207.49	13
2	1/21/96	40.0	0.0	750.00	46.50	10.88	193.935	41.25	457.44	14
3	1/21/96	40.0	2.4	545.00	33.79	7.90	140.9261	29.98	332.41	15
4	1/21/96	40.0	6.7	738.49	45.79	10.71	190.95816	40.62	450.42	16
5	1/21/96	40.0	0.0	900.00	55.80	13.05	232.722	49.50	548.93	17
6	1/21/96	40.0	5.0	831.25	51.54	12.05	214.94463	45.72	507.00	18

The most common SQL operation is a query. A query starts with the SELECT keyword followed by a list of columns from tables (that are also specified as part of the query). Clauses can be added to specify criteria for inclusion, aggregation, or sorting. The SQL code for the template query shown in Exhibit 19.7 is as follows:

```
SELECT Customer.LastName, Customer.FirstName,
    Count(BikesSold.SerialNumber) AS [Number Purchased],
    Sum(BikesSold.SalePrice) AS [Total Spent]
FROM Customer
  INNER JOIN BikesSold ON Customer.CustomerID = BikesSold.CustomerID
GROUP BY BikesSold.CustomerID, Customer.LastName, Customer.FirstName
HAVING (((Count(BikesSold.SerialNumber))>1))
ORDER BY Customer.LastName;
```

Field names are shown with syntax of *tablename.columnname*. The Count and Sum keyword perform aggregation based on the items listed in the GROUP BY clause. The AS keyword indicates that the column should be titled something other than its default caption. The FROM keyword is used to indicate the tables to be used. The INNER JOIN clause indicates how the data in the tables should be integrated (linked). The HAVING clause shows the restriction—in this case only customers whose count of bikes sold is >1. The ORDER BY clause is the sort order.

Data Warehouse

Data warehousing attempts to reconcile and integrate data from legacy applications software with today's newer technology. As mentioned earlier, industry is rife with older legacy systems that are currently cost prohibitive to replace. Most of these older systems are mission-critical operational transaction systems and satisfy most of the operational needs of the company. However, they are built on technology that cannot support the kinds of decision support tools that management requires. Many of these systems use older file structures or obsolete database management systems and are almost incapable of accessing and manipulating data.

As an alternative to replacing these systems, data warehousing provides a state-of-the-art database management system that is fed data from the older legacy systems. However, data does get duplicated, which can potentially cause a synchronization problem between the data in the warehouse and the data in the older legacy systems. Consequently, IT management must put stringent controls in place. Still, the benefits outweigh the potential problems, for the data warehouse comes with all of the high-tech tools that will enable management to create a plethora of queries and reports. Most of the newer business intelligence tools mentioned earlier require a storage capability similar to the data warehouse.

Any organization that implements a data warehouse must create a corporate data directory for the data that will reside in the data warehouse. This metadata includes attributes (name, size, data type, etc.); data about the data (where it is located, which application owns it, what data it is associated with); and descriptive information (context, quality, condition). Software tools follow these rules to extract, transform, and load operational data into the data warehouse. For example, the metadata will tell an end user

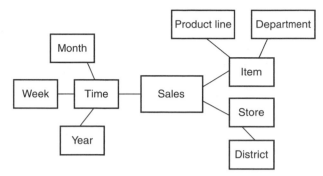

Exhibit 20.8   Snowflake schema.

that the data field called "sales" means "net sales" and comes from the general ledger application as the aggregate of all delivered orders for the period. Ideally, data elements should have names that are agreed to by those who work with the data—so maybe, in this example, the field would be called "net sales" to begin with.

Online analytical processing (OLAP) is a powerful tool for end users to use to access data. As discussed earlier, the data (the facts) is stored with its characteristics (called dimensions). The concept uses a cube as a visual to the end user. Of course, a cube can't be stored as such on a hard drive. The data for OLAP retrieval is stored using either a star schema or a snowflake schema. A star schema would include only the primary dimensions and fact table. When we expand our dimensions to include further details about the dimensions, the schema becomes more complicated—a snowflake schema. Illustrated in Exhibit 20.8 is the snowflake schema for the example used earlier in Exhibit 20.4.

New technologies have been developed to address the issue of information overload. In the 1970s, the average database was perhaps 100 megabytes in size. In the 1980s, databases were typically 20 gigabytes. Now, databases are in terabytes (trillions of bytes). Wal-Mart has a data warehouse that exceeds 4 petabytes (a petabype is a quadrillion bytes or 1,024 terabytes). With all that data, it is difficult for a user to know where to look. It is not the question that the user knows to ask that is necessarily important, but, rather, the question that the user does not know to ask that will come back to haunt him.

Data mining is a set of technologies that allow users to classify, cluster, learn about associations, and perform regressions. Classification uses algorithms to assign data into a predefined group. Clustering is similar to classification but the groups are not predefined. Regression analyzes the data to build a model that can be used for forecasting. Learning about associations searches for relationships between variables. Market basket analysis is used by supermarkets to analyze the data of what each customer buys to determine what products are frequently bought together. Data mining is used in customer relationship management software to identify prospects with a higher likelihood to respond to an offer.

Data mining can also be used to scan databases for any data that does not fit the business's model and identify any data that the user needs to examine further. For example, auditors might use data mining to scan client transaction detail to look for transactions that do not conform to company policies, and stock analysts can use it to scan data on stock prices and company earnings over a period of time in order to look for opportunities.

Internet Technology

Nothing has impacted technology and society in the past two decades more than the Internet. When Bill Clinton was inaugurated in January 1993, there were about 50 pages on the Internet. Today, there are more than 200 billion pages (and that's only an estimate—it's probably much higher than that!). The underlying technology behind the Internet has its roots in a project begun by the U.S. government in the early 1970s. The network was originally developed by a consortium of research colleges and universities and the federal government, which was looking for a way to share research data and provide a secure means of communicating and for backing up defense facilities. The original network was called ARPAnet. ARPAnet was sponsored by the Department of Defense's Advanced Research Projects Agency (ARPA). It was replaced in the 1980s by the current network, which originally was not very user friendly and was used mostly by techies. The Internet's popularity exploded with the development of the World Wide Web and the necessary software programs that made it much more user friendly to explore.

The Internet works on a set of software standards, the first of which, TCP/IP, was developed in the 1970s. The entire theory behind the Internet and TCP/IP, which enables computers to speak to each other over the Internet, was to create a network that had no central controller. The Internet is not like a string of Christmas lights, where if one light in the string goes out, the rest of the lights stop functioning. Rather, if one computer in the network is disabled, the rest of the network continues to perform because traffic is rerouted around it.

Each computer in the Internet has an Internet protocol (IP) address. Similar to one's postal address, it consists of a series of numbers (e.g., 155.48.178.21), and it tells the network where to leave e-mail messages and data. When a user types in a URL (e.g., www.babson.edu), computers on the Internet, called domain name servers (DNSs), convert the URL to an IP address. The message or data that is to be sent is broken into a series of packets. These packets contain the IP address of the sender, the IP address of the recipient, the packet number of the message (e.g., 7 of 23), and the data itself. Based on the Internet traffic, these packets could travel different routes to the destination IP address. The receiving computer then reassembles the packets into a complete message.

The second standard that makes the Internet work is Hypertext Mark-up Language (HTML). Using a Web browser, the computer converts the HTML or other programming language into the image that the user sees on the computer monitor. This language allows data to be displayed on the user's screen. It also allows a user to click on an Internet link and jump to a new page on the Internet. While HTML, along with its set of tags, remains the underlying programming language for the World Wide Web and is powerful in its own right, it is not dynamic and has its limitations—it was designed to display data. Therefore, languages such as JavaScript, Java, and Perl, which create animation, perform calculations, create dynamic Web pages, and access and update databases with information on the host's Web server, were developed to complement HTML. One such complementing language is extensible markup language (XML), which allows users to define tags for their documents to focus on what the data is. XML, an open standard overseen by the World Wide Web Consortium, allows a user to define the content (the data) in a document separately from the formatting of the document, which is done with HTML tags. Just as a browser is required to understand how to handle the HTML tags, an XML-aware application is necessary to know how to handle the XML tags. XML allows information to be shared between different computers, operating systems, and applications without requiring conversation.

Bringing the Use of Web Technologies In-House

Internet technology has radically changed the manner in which corporate information systems process their data. In the early and mid-1990s, corporate information systems used distributed processing techniques. Using this method, some of the processing would take place on the central computer (the server) and the rest on the users' (the clients') computers—hence the term *client-server computing*. Many companies implemented applications using this technology, which ensured that processing power was utilized at both ends and that systems were scalable. The problem with client-server processing was that different computers (even within the IBM-compatible PC family) used different drivers and required tweaking to make the systems work properly. Also, if the software needed to be changed at the client end and there were many clients (some companies have thousands of PC clients), maintaining the software on all of those clients could be a nightmare. Even with specialized tools developed for that purpose, it never quite worked perfectly.

As companies recognized the opportunity to send data over the Internet, whether for their customers, their suppliers, or their employees, they started to migrate all of their applications to a browser interface. This change has required companies to rethink where the locus of their processing will occur. Prior to the 1990s, companies' networks were host-centric, where all of their processing was conducted using one large mainframe. In the early 1990s, companies began using client-server architecture. Today, with the current browser technology and the Internet, the focus has shifted back to a host-centric environment. The difference, though, is that the browser on the users' computers is used to display and capture data, and the data processing actually occurs back at the central host on a series of specialized servers, not on one large mainframe computer. In this case, the only program a user needs is a standard browser, which solves the incompatibility problem presented by distributed data processing. No specialized software is stored on the users' computers.

Web 2.0 applications were introduced in Chapter 19, Information Technology and You. At first glance these applications seem personal, having no part in professional productivity. But a second glance reveals that this is not so. Imagine working on a project and needing someone who has worked on a similar project—social networking, or needing a copy of a diagram that was used in a similar project—tagging. Or a project team uses wiki software to develop a project report. Or a project team uses blogs to keep everyone informed. Organizations need to evaluate the newer uses of Internet technology as they become mainstream. End users are comfortable with the technology, so an organization needs to work on how to harness that comfort level to make its use improve end-user productivity.

Web Hosting

With such a business reliance on the Internet and many corporate applications using Web technologies, most companies host their own Web sites today. This allows the organization to maintain its internal Web-technology-based applications on-site but accessible from anywhere, anytime (with the right permissions, of course). It also allows the organization to be in control of its own Web presence and data. All of this, of course, comes at a price for the hardware, software, network capabilities and speed, and manpower.

For those companies that wish to not host their own Web presence, there are many vendors in the business of hosting Web sites. These companies provide the communications lines, Web servers, data backup, and, in some cases, Web design and maintenance services. Companies that choose to outsource their Web hosting are also protecting their main network from security breaches. However, they are still placing a great deal of their data on the Web hosting company's computer, which is still subject to security hackers.

Controls

Because the initial software applications that were developed in the 1960s and 1970s were accounting oriented, data processing (which is what the use of information technology was called at that time) typically reported to the chief financial officer, creating a control atmosphere consistent with accounting controls. A central group of trained data-entry operators was responsible for entering and verifying data. Access to the "glass house" was restricted, and, in some cases, access to the data entry and report distribution areas was also restricted. Because everything was self-contained, control was not a major issue.

In the late 1970s and early 1980s, online terminals began appearing on users' desks outside of the glass house, allowing them access to data. Initially, these terminals were used for information inquiry. Yet, even this limited function was tightly controlled by strict software access control and password protection. While workers were getting additional capabilities, they were also creating opportunities for lapses in control. This was just the beginning of the Trojan horse. Eventually, data entry moved out of the glass house to the warehouse receiving dock to be used for inventory receipts, to the order-entry desk to be used for new orders, to the purchasing department to be used for purchase orders, and, in the case of retailing, onto the sales floor for point-of-sale processing. No longer were trained data-entry operators responsible for the quality of the data; others were responsible for entering data, and it was just an ancillary part of their jobs, for which they were not necessarily even trained.

The control environment was breaking down, and the introduction of the personal computer only complicated the issue. No longer was control centralized. Although access to data could be controlled, control over the use of data and the content of reports was lost. For example, two people could each issue a report on sales, and the numbers could easily be different. Yet both reports could be accurate. How is this possible? It's simple. One of the reports may have been about gross sales and the other about net sales, or one may have been based on data through Friday and the other on data through Saturday.

When all programming was controlled by a small professional group, control was much easier. However, because today's spreadsheet programs are user friendly, and software does not require programming knowledge, everybody is his or her own programmer. Thus, it is difficult to control the consistency of the information that is being distributed.

The problems only become more complicated. Now companies allow their business partners, vendors, and even outsiders to access their internal computers, using the Internet. Data is interchanged, and moneys are exchanged electronically, often without paper backup. What was relatively simple to control before 1990 is now a nightmare. Accountants, systems professionals, and auditors must remain forever vigilant against both inadvertent and intentional unauthorized use and abuse of company data.

Information Technology Strategy

How do companies decide how to invest their IT budgets? What projects get funded? Which projects are of higher priority? Information technology strategy is not created in a vacuum. Rather, like all of the other operational departments within a corporation, IT must support the direction and goals of the company. Information technology architecture should be developed to support the corporate strategy as well as the IT strategy. If additional networks, workstations, or data warehouses are required, they are either acquired or developed. The chief information officer's job is to educate the rest of senior management about IT's ability to create opportunities for the company and help it move in directions that make sense.

Wal-Mart is known for its everyday low pricing strategy. To accomplish this goal, Wal-Mart had to change the manner in which it both conducted business with its suppliers and managed the inbound logistics, warehousing, and distribution of merchandise to its stores. It needed to abolish warehousing as much as possible and quicken the process by which stores ordered and received merchandise. Also, Wal-Mart needed to eliminate any unnecessary inventory in stores and allow stores to order merchandise only as needed. Last, lags in its distribution centers needed to be prevented, enabling goods to be received from their suppliers and immediately shipped to stores.

To accomplish this goal, Wal-Mart designed a systems and technology infrastructure that, through electronic data interchange (EDI), enables the stores to order goods, as needed, from their suppliers. Moreover, Wal-Mart permitted manufacturers to access computerized sales information directly from its computers, which, in turn, allowed them to gauge Wal-Mart's demand and then stage production to match it. Wal-Mart effectively shifted the burden of warehousing merchandise from its own warehouses to the vendors, eliminating the costs of both warehouse maintenance and surplus inventory. The distribution centers were automated, allowing cross-docking, whereby goods being received for specific stores were immediately sent to the shipping area designated for those stores, thus putting an end to time lags.

Wal-Mart currently has the lowest cost of inbound logistics in its industry. Its selling, general, and administrative expense is percentage points below that of its nearest competitor, enabling it to be the most aggressive retailer in its industry. Wal-Mart aligned its IT strategy and infrastructure to support the company's overall strategy. Information technology was the agent for change. Without the newer information technologies, none of the newer strategies and directions could have been successful.

Information Security and Compliance

A new role has begun appearing in organizations—chief information security officer (CISO). People in this position are responsible for IT-related governance, risk, and compliance issues. Organizations are realizing that data is a strategic asset and it should be protected. In some cases, organizations are coming to that realization on their own; in other cases, the realization is being driven by compliance requirements to such laws as Sarbanes-Oxley (often referred to as SOX), a federal law that spells out standards for all U.S. public companies and public accounting firms; the Payment Card Industry Data Security Standard (PCI DSS), a standard for processing card payments; the Health Insurance Portability and Accountability Act (HIPAA), national standards for health care transactions; and ISO/IEC 27002, an information security standard.

What this means for an IT organization is an additional requirement to understand the compliance rules and to put procedures and safeguards in place to secure data. With a global organization, there are cultural differences, informal and formal communication networks, and even different definitions of data privacy. Organizations need to explain compliance policies to end users so they understand why they need to do what must be done and will follow the necessary protocols. Wireless networks increase the need for encryption—data has to be protected in rest (stored) or in motion (transmitted). Laptop data has to be encrypted so if the laptop is lost or stolen, the data on the laptop is safe. Data loss prevention (sometimes referred to as data leak prevention) systems are designed to detect and prevent the unauthorized use and transmission of information. Breaches (unauthorized use) are costly and create a great deal of negative publicity.

It is an organization's duty to secure its data. Just because data is encrypted, that doesn't necessary mean it is secure. A breach of data at the TJX Companies, Inc. in 2007 compromised an estimated 90 million encrypted credit card records. Over 40 states have implemented breach notification laws that require organizations to report breaches to authorities and the persons affected by the breach. The state of Tennessee took privacy a step further with its Credit Security Act of 2007, which makes the use of a person's Social Security number in direct mailings or over the Internet a class B misdemeanor.

An organization is responsible for compliance by its outsourcing partners as well. These partners are responsible for the organization's data, and therefore the organization itself is responsible for the security of the data even if it resides on a computer owned by another company. When evaluating relationships with third parties, an organization must look at the security measures that are in place and audit their compliance.

Justifying the Cost of Information Technology

Should companies take that giant leap of faith and invest millions of dollars in new machines and software? Can the return on a company's investment in technology be measured using conventional metrics as are discussed in Chapter 4, Discounted Cash Flow.

These are questions that have concerned technology managers for years. Today, information technology consumes an increasing share of companies' budgets, but we cannot live without the technology. Thus, when a new version of the personal computer chip or Windows hits the market, companies must decide whether it is a worthwhile investment. Everyone wants the latest and greatest technology, believing that with it they will be more productive.

Although IT is the medium for change, its costs and soft benefits are difficult to measure. As technology gets disbursed throughout a company, it becomes increasingly difficult to track costs and determine benefits. As workers become their own administrative assistants, each company must determine whether its workers are more or less productive when they type their own documents and prepare their own presentations. These are many of the issues that companies are facing now and in the future as they struggle with new IT investments.

Conclusion

The world of business has changed dramatically in the past 10 years. What was unimaginable a decade ago is ordinary today. Product life cycle times have decreased from years to months. New technology is being introduced every day. An "Internet year" is equal to three or four calendar months. The manager who is comfortable with and understands the practical implications of technology will be one of the first to succeed. Imagination and creativity are vital. Don't be afraid of change. Understand it and embrace it.

Downloadable Resources for this chapter available at www.wiley.com/go/portablembainfinance

Information Technology and the Firm

It's important to understand what technology is already in use by your firm as well as what technology your firm might be evaluating. It's also important to understand how these technology choices affect you as a user. The exercises for this chapter in the book's Web site are directed toward that type of reflection. Do some research, ask questions, do more research. Evaluate what you hear and what you read. How does it impact you? How does it impact the effectiveness of the organization? How does it affect the bottom line? Be a knowledgeable user.

Internet Links

So many Web sites to choose from! Some of those listed here are also listed in Chapter 19, "Information Technology and You." Pick a topic from this chapter and use a search engine to find more information.

Search Engines

www.yahoo.com	A good search site that organizes the Web into a hierarchy of categories.
www.google.com	A very extensive search site.

Computer Information Sites

www.cio.com	A site that provides news and white papers on topics that IT management should be aware of.
www.cnet.com	A site that provides product reviews and prices on a broad range of technology products.
www.computerworld.com	An online site for the hardcopy *ComputerWorld*.
www.zdnet.com	Web site of a large technology publisher, with product reviews, software downloads, useful articles, and price comparisons.

General Information

frwebgate.access.gpo.gov/cgi-bin/getdoc.cgi?dbname=107_cong_public_laws&docid=f:publ204.107	This is a link to the Sarbanes-Oxley Act of 2002, as enacted. The legislation outlines standards that all U.S. public company boards, management, and public accounting firms have to abide by.

www.ifrs.com	This site is a source of information and resources on the International Financial Reporting Standards. The site is managed by the American Institute of Certified Public Accountants.
www.iso.org	The International Standards Organization is a network of national standards institutes from over 150 countries that forms a bridge between the public and private sectors. Members of ISO reach a consensus on solutions that meet requirements of business and the broader needs of society.
www.opensource.org	A nonprofit corporation, Open Source Initiative is a standards body that oversees the Open Source Definition. OSI also educates about and advocates for the benefits of open source software.
www.pcisecruitystandards.org	A council, founded by major credit card companies, whose mission is to oversee the development and implementation of security standards for account data protection.
www.w3c.org	The Web site for the World Wide Web Consortium.
www.web3schools.com	This site is a great source for explanations and examples of Web building tools.
www.webopedia.com	This site is an online encyclopedia dedicated to computer technology. Its discussion might be a bit more technical than Wikipedia. Webopedia is one of many Web sites owned and managed by Jupitermedia Corporation.
www.wikipedia.com	This free content encyclopedia is written collaboratively by volunteers from around the world. Anyone can edit any posting. It is hosted by the nonprofit Wikipedia Foundation.

Vendor Web Sites

www.crystalreportsstore.com	This software allows end users to build flexible reports from enterprise databases. Crystal Reports is now offered by Business Objects, which is an SAP company.
www.dell.com	One of the first computer manufacturers to allow customers to order online as well as customize their machines.
www.exactsoftware.com	This Netherlands-based company offers information systems needs for small and midsize companies. Its products support a wide range of industries.
www.google.com	In addition to being a powerful search engine, Google also offers SaaS software for productivity (Google Docs, calendaring, blogs, and collaboration software). From the home page, click on More and then More again to see the offerings.

www.infor.com	The strategy of this U.S.-based company was to build, acquire, and improve on enterprise software.
www.informationbuilders. com	The mission of this company is to help organizations access all of their information with tools that support the needs of the end users. In addition to its business intelligence software, it also offers integration software (middleware).
www.intuit.com	Intuit sells TurboTax for tax preparation, Quicken for managing personal finances, and Quickbooks for information systems needs for small businesses. Quickbooks can also be used as an SaaS.
www.microsoft.com	Microsoft has done a good job building a Web structure that supports all levels of users. You might need to do a lot of clicking to get exactly where you need to be, but it is there.
www.openoffice.org	This group offers open-source office suite software (currently for free) that can be downloaded from the site.
www.oracle.com	This U.S.-based company started out as a database company with its Oracle relational database. It has evolved into a full-service software company with middleware and enterprise software, all supported by the database product. In addition to its own suite of enterprise products, J.D. Edwards, PeopleSoft, Siebel, and Hyperion are all Oracle companies.
www.sage.com	This U.K.-based company offers information systems needs for small and midsize companies, with functional offerings as well as industry-specific offerings. Some of its better-known products include Peachtree, ACT!, and Accpac.
www.sap.com	This Germany-based company focuses on small and midsize companies as well as large companies. SAP terms its solutions as enterprise software applications. SAP is most noted for its ERP offerings, but it also has customer relationship management software, product life cycle management software, and supply chain management software, to name a few.
www.sas.com	This U.S.-based company has evolved into a provider of business intelligence software. SAS originally stood for statistical analysis software. SAS and SPSS both have their strengths and limitations; most companies compare them before deciding on one or the other. Some organizations use both.
www.spss.com	This U.S.-based company is noted for its business intelligence software. SPSS and SAS both have their strengths and limitations; most companies compare them before deciding on one or the other. Some organizations use both.

Note

1. Updated from a previous chapter written by Theodore Grossman.

For Further Reading

Bagranoff, Nancy A., Mark G. Simkin, and Carolyn Strand Norman, *Core Concepts of Accounting Information Systems*, 10th ed. (Hoboken, NJ: John Wiley & Sons, 2007).

Chaffey, Dave, *E-Commerce and E-Commerce Management*, 3rd ed. (Upper Saddle River, NJ: Prentice Hall, 2008).

English, Larry P., *Business Information Quality Applied: Best Practices for Improving Business Processes, Systems and Information* (Hoboken, NJ: John Wiley & Sons, 2009).

Huber, Mark W., Craig A. Piercy, and Patrick G. McKeown, *Information Systems: Creating Business Value* (Hoboken, NJ: John Wiley & Sons, 2006).

Jessup, Leonard, and Joseph Valacich, *Information Systems Today: Why IS Matters*, 2nd ed. (Upper Saddle River, NJ: Prentice Hall, 2005).

Meeker, Heather J., *The Open Source Alternative: Understanding Risks and Leveraging Opportunities* (Hoboken, NJ: John Wiley & Sons, 2008).

Mitra, A., and A. Gupta, *Creating Agile Business Systems with Reusable Knowledge* (New York: Cambridge University Press, 2007).

Pearlson, Keri E., and Carol S. Saunders, *Managing and Using Information Systems*, 4th ed. (Hoboken, NJ: John Wiley & Sons, 2009).

Tapscott, Don, and Anthony D. Williams, *Wikinomics: How Mass Collaboration Changes Everything* (New York: Portfolio, 2008).

Te'eni, Dov, Jane M. Carey, and Ping Zhang, *Human-Computer Interaction: Developing Effective Organizational Information Systems* (Hoboken, NJ: John Wiley & Sons, 2006).

Turner, Leslie, and Andrea Weickgenannt, *Accounting Information Systems: Controls and Processes* (Hoboken, NJ: John Wiley & Sons, 2008).

Vossen, Gottfried, and Stephan Hagemann, *Unleashing Web 2.0: From Concepts to Creativity* (San Francisco: Morgan Kaufmann, 2008).

21

Careers in Finance

Tracee Petrillo and Ralph J. Constantino

Unless you picked up this book at the airport for a long trip to Fiji, it's a safe bet you are interested in and/or already have an MBA as such. This is the perfect time for you to define, plan, and execute your end game. But just what do we mean by the "end game"? The end game is not a singular, unique, and magical final event; rather, it is a series of interconnected objectives that lead toward an end goal or goals.

For example, thinking about your future led you to your initial end game—exploring MBA programs. That effort in turn led you to another series of end games: taking the GMAT test, researching programs, completing applications, preparing for admissions interviews, and ultimately enrolling. Were these actions individual end games or a series of interconnected steps leading to a true end game? *Now* is when you define and take specific steps to reach your ultimate end game—employment.

For those who recognize that the ultimate end game is satisfying and rewarding, employment, this section is a must-read. It is intended to provide insight, overview, direction, and encouragement. We review career choices in finance popular among MBA graduates. In addition, we provide some tried-and-true strategies as well as "the road less traveled" advice. This chapter will complement your MBA program, hard work, and skills development, and assist you in attaining a satisfying and rewarding career.

Overview: What Is the Marketplace for MBAs?

Students choose to earn an MBA for different reasons. Some students simply want to round out their business skills, some are looking to advance in their current career/industry, some are sponsored by their companies and plan to return following completion of the degree, some hope to start a business, and some are hoping to change their career trajectory. In all of these cases, it is important for the students to begin to think about their careers prior to the start of the program. With this preprogram planning, students can identify the schools that will provide them with the right skills, network, and business connections to reach their goals following completion of the degree.

When considering the application process, prospective students should consider several factors as they compare business schools. Students look at size, location, strength of the alumni network, reputation, ranking, and specialty. Students interested in specializing in a specific discipline, such as finance or marketing, are best suited to consider schools with a reputation for placing students in these areas. Other schools are known for producing general managers. *U.S. News & World Report* is one well-known resource for reviewing rankings and can be found at http://grad-schools.usnews.rankingsandreviews.com/grad/mba/search.

Profile of Students' Pre-MBA Careers

It is also important to consider the pre-MBA industries and job functions ass well as the career functions and industries chosen upon graduation. In 2008, the Graduate Management Admission Council (GMAC) conducted its ninth annual survey of MBA graduates. There were 2,858 full-time MBA students who participated in the survey, approximately 41% of whom were non-U.S. citizens. According to the results of the survey, approximately 29% of pre-MBA students enter the program from the products and services industry and 18% enter from the finance/accounting industry. Although these two industries represent the two largest pre-MBA industries, pre-MBA students enter programs with experience across diverse industries and backgrounds. The most popular job functions upon entry into the MBA program include marketing/sales at 21% of the students and finance/accounting a close second with 20% of the entrants. Regardless of where students begin, there are a variety of industries and job functions where they launch their post-MBA careers.

Profile of Students' Post-MBA Careers

Post-MBA, students choose to enter various industries and job functions, often changing careers as a result of the MBA program. According to the GMAC survey, the number of students choosing the finance/accounting industry increased from 18% pre-MBA to 28% post-MBA. In fact, the finance/accounting industry represented the largest percentage of post-MBA students at 28%. Products/services represented 25% post-MBA versus 29% pre-MBA, followed by consulting (18% post-MBA versus 10% pre-MBA). MBA graduates choosing finance/accounting as a job function post-MBA also represented the largest group of respondents, 33%, followed by marketing/sales and consulting at 21% and 20%, respectively. Exhibit 21.1 presents two tables from the 2008 GMAC survey that represent the pre- and post-MBA job functions and industries.

It is important to note that the largest percentage of students post-MBA chose the finance/accounting industry and job function. The MBA degree is preferred, if not required, for many careers in this space. The next section focuses on career opportunities that are most popular with MBA graduates in finance and the financial services industry. Following this overview, we talk about how to plan your career before, during, and after your MBA to achieve the largest return on investment (ROI).

Career Opportunities in Finance

When considering a career in finance, there is an important question to ask: Do I want to perform a corporate finance job function, or do I want to work in the financial services industry? *Corporate finance* is the finance functional role within an existing company in any industry. *Financial services*, in contrast, is a broad term for the industry that includes highly diverse and evolving segments, markets, functions, and companies.

Careers in Corporate Finance

Graduates who enter into a career in corporate finance may find themselves in any industry; consumer products and services, health care, technology, and retail are some of the many industries. Finance managers and business analysts are two typical titles that MBA graduates secure in corporate finance. The corporate finance role is intended to help the company understand its budget and revenue stream and make strategic business decisions.

In addition, many companies across a variety of industries have implemented leadership development programs (LDPs). These leadership development rotation programs provide the opportunity for students to try a variety of positions throughout a company. LDPs in finance, also known as FLDPs, could include rotations in risk management, treasury, mergers and acquisitions, and financial planning and analysis, among others. FLDPs are found in many industries, including but not limited to insurance, construction, energy, and consumer products.

Exhibit 21.1   Pre-MBA and post-MBA job functions and industries.

Job Function	Pre-MBA (n = 2,215)	Post-MBA (n = 2,457)
Marketing/sales	21%	21%
Operations/logistics	17	8
Consulting	9	20
General management	15	11
Finance/accounting	20	33
Human resources	3	3
Information technology/MIS	11	2
Other	3	2
Total	100%	100%

Industry	Pre-MBA (n = 2,320)	Post-MBA (n = 2,537)
Consulting	10%	18%
Energy/utilities	3	4
Finance/accounting	18	28
Health Care/pharmaceuticals	5	7
Technology	16	9
Manufacturing	7	4
Non-Profit/government	13	4
Products/services	29	25
Other	0	1
Total	100%	100%

Source: "Global MBA Graduate Survey, 2008 Comprehensive Data Report: Full-Time MBA Programs." Graduate Management Admission Council, 2008.

Careers in Financial Services

Financial services is a term that includes a variety of segments and roles, each of which requires strong analytical skills. The economic financial crisis that surfaced in 2008 began a turbulent employment outlook in the financial services industry. It is more important than ever that MBA students do their homework on specific positions and firms that they are considering to truly understand the financial situation of the company and industry. Careers in financial services include, but are not limited to:

- Banking: retail, commercial, and investment.
- Traditional asset management: retail and institutional.
- Alternative investments: private equity/venture capital, hedge funds, real estate, commodities, derivatives, and currencies.
- Insurance: property and casualty, life insurance, annuities, and fund management.
- Consulting: management, asset planning, and financial advice.

Each of these career paths requires strong analytical, interpersonal, and communication skills. The following section highlights some of the specific careers available to MBAs. It is not all-inclusive, but instead serves as a sampling of opportunities that tend to be popular among MBA graduates.

Investment Banking

Investment banking refers to the raising of capital (money) for firms that allows them to expand, conduct mergers and acquisitions, or enter new markets. Investment banking can be a very prestigious opportunity for those who enter immediately upon graduation with an MBA degree, and competition for positions in investment banking can be very stiff. At the same time, investment bankers, especially at entry levels, can expect to work 80 to 100 hours per week.

Undergraduates typically enter into the *analyst* position in an investment bank. Analysts complete much of the financial modeling and entry-level tasks associated with completing deals. MBAs, in contrast, usually enter as *associates*, one level above the analysts. Associates also work long hours and spend much of their time on financial models and pitch books. Associates, however, unlike analysts, spend more time in client-facing activities.

The year 2008 proved to be a turbulent time in the financial services industry overall, with significant turmoil in the investment banking industry. Top investment banking firms, such as Lehman Brothers, found themselves in significant financial difficulties. This resulted in many mergers, acquisitions, and takeovers. The resulting downsizing and layoffs mean that the competition for positions in the surviving investment banks is even stiffer than it was before.

Vault.com is a great resource for up-to-date information on financial services firms.

Hedge Funds

A *hedge fund* is a private investment fund open to a limited range of investors that is permitted by regulators to undertake a wider range of activities than other investment funds and also pays a performance fee to its investment manager. Each fund will have its own strategy which determines the type of investments and the methods of investment it undertakes. Hedge funds as a class invest in a broad range of investments extending over shares, debt, commodities and beyond.[1]

Hedge funds employ various investment strategies, which guide the activities of the fund. The strategy outlines the techniques that the fund manager uses to create a positive

ROI for the fund. Specifically, hedge funds hedge their portfolios, use derivatives, short sell, and can use leverage to produce the desired results. Additional information about the specific strategies can be found in the *Vault Career Guide to Hedge Funds*.[2]

Specific titles and positions vary greatly from one hedge fund to another, depending on the size of the fund. In a smaller fund, MBA graduates with several years of experience may have the opportunity to compete for the director of operations role, overseeing a few direct reports and having direct client contact. In other hedge funds, MBAs may operate in a research or risk management role, providing support to the hedge fund manager.

Many larger banks have an area that manages hedge funds. For example, Bank of America and UBS each have hedge funds under their operations. HedgeWeek[3] has a Web site that covers the hedge fund industry globally and provides articles, company information, and job postings around the world.

Investment Management

Investment management refers to the management of assets through investment. The investment management industry, also called asset management, began with a focus on purely relationship-based investing. For example, a company might have looked to a bank where it had existing accounts to invest the pensions of its employees.

Today, however, individuals and firms look to specific asset management companies to manage their money. For example, these asset management companies often are looked upon to create wealth in the 401(k) plans (employee-based retirement plans) of specific companies. These asset management companies often use mutual funds as a safer and smarter investment tool for this wealth creation, as they provide a diversified portfolio of stocks and bonds. Individuals may choose to invest their money through firms such as Charles Schwab or TD Ameritrade, which allow investors to choose a portfolio of options for a fee, depending on the level of individual advisement the investor desires.

The portfolio management segment of the investment management industry tends to be highly sought after as a place for MBA graduates. There are three primary positions within the portfolio management structure: portfolio managers, associate portfolio managers, and portfolio manager assistants. The portfolio manager creates the investment strategy, oversees the implementation of that strategy, and interacts most often with the client. The associate portfolio manager (the position usually requires an MBA or CFA and several years of experience in the industry) works closely with the portfolio manager and interacts with the client, although less often than does the portfolio manager. The portfolio manager assistants provide day-to-day support to both the manager and the associate manager.

MBA graduates who are hoping to enter portfolio management but have little experience in the industry most often would begin in a research associate role. This role focuses on research (usually industry-specific) to create investment management recommendations to the portfolio management team. The MBAs usually spend three to five years in the research role before moving into the associate portfolio manager role.

Investment management in general requires not only strong analytical and quantitative skills, but also strong communication skills. Investment managers must have the ability to communicate clearly and concisely with colleagues and clients.

Additional information about specific investment management companies and industry specifics can be found in the *Vault Career Guide to Investment Management*.[4]

Private Wealth Management

Private wealth management is generally a smaller arm of an investment bank. It refers to the creation and execution of an overall strategy to create and manage wealth for individuals. This includes not only investment strategies, but also tax strategies, estate planning, and the protection of assets. Private wealth management usually involves many different segments of the firm to create the best strategy for each client. For example, the tax department may be called upon to ensure that the investment planning and estate planning utilize the correct strategies to ensure that clients are protecting their assets from unnecessary taxes.

Under the umbrella of private wealth management, one area that tends to be most attractive to MBAs is the role of financial adviser (also called a private banker). The entering position for one who aspires to work in this space is as an analyst, followed by an associate, then a vice president, and finally a managing director. The associate role would be the traditional entry point for an MBA graduate with some experience. Associates work closely with existing clients and in sales roles to attract new clients. Because of this, once again it is very important in this role to have not only a strong understanding of investments and a strong quantitative background, but also strong communication and sales skills.

Additional information about private wealth management can be found in the *Vault Career Guide to Private Wealth Management*.[5]

Real Estate

The real estate industry is one that is extremely volatile and subject to economic conditions. That being said, real estate will also be a part of a country's economic structure. Under the real estate umbrella, there are two distinct areas: residential and commercial. MBAs interested in the real estate industry most often will focus on the commercial segment. Within the commercial segment, there are many different types of opportunities available for MBAs. These include but are not limited to investment, brokerage, consulting, and development.[6]

Within commercial real estate, MBAs tend to be interested in firms that focus on funding commercial real estate. These firms include real estate investment trusts (REITs), mezzanine funds (combinations of private equity and fixed income), and private equity. These firms work with commercial real estate companies that are focused on developing new properties.

It is very difficult for MBAs without prior experience in real estate to enter the real estate industry, as competition is tough. Students should focus on networking—developing existing or new relationships with faculty, alumni, and other students who have experience in the industry—as well as on their curricular and extracurricular activities. Obtaining an internship in the real estate industry tends to help in the process. As is the case with the other financial services segments mentioned earlier, it is very important for MBAs to have strong quantitative and valuation abilities as well as extremely strong interpersonal skills in this space.

The MBA Jungle Web site is a great additional resource for the real estate industry, providing information on salary ranges, job descriptions, and career paths.[7]

Venture Capital

The National Venture Capital Association states that venture capital (VC) firms are "private partnerships or closely held corporations funded by private and public pension funds, endowment funds, corporations, wealthy individuals, foreign investors, and the venture capitalists themselves."[8]

Venture capital firms invest in companies with the goal of buying an equity interest in the company or the assets of the company. Usually, they hope to then sell their stake in the company or the assets of the company for a higher price than they paid—in other words, to achieve a positive return on investment (ROI). To achieve this, VCs spend a great deal of time analyzing the strengths and weaknesses of companies to determine which potential investments would create the largest ROI. Venture capital is about building the firm and then executing an exit strategy resulting in the highest ROI.

As is the case in the real estate industry, it is difficult for MBA graduates with no prior experience to immediately enter the venture capital industry. MBAs should focus on the following: building skills in financial analysis and valuation, obtaining experience in banking and financial services, and *networking*. MBAs should use the extensive network of their educational institution to help them make contacts in the industry. The network includes, but is not limited to: alumni, faculty, career center experts, fellow students, club members (in the VC or entrepreneurship club, for example) and personal networks. It is unlikely that VC firms will participate in on-campus recruiting or even that a resume and cover letter will be enough to get the interview. Networking is the key in VC.

For additional information on the venture capital industry, both MBA Jungle[9] and the *Vault Career Guide to Venture Capital*[10] are helpful resources.

Summary

Financial services opportunities for MBAs can be both lucrative and exciting. Each opportunity requires different skills, although some common skills across most financial services positions include strong analytical skills and the ability to communicate clearly and concisely both within the firm and externally with clients. MBAs can anticipate strong competition for positions within financial services and should focus on developing these skills.

In addition, MBAs hoping to enter financial services firms should be creative about identifying positions and firms of interest, as many firms will not participate in on-campus recruiting (especially in real estate or venture capital). Therefore, in addition to using the career services office, students should actively engage with alumni, fellow students, faculty, and club and association members. The following section provides a guide on how individuals can create and execute an individual career plan to help obtain a career in corporate finance or financial services.

Your Career Plan/*Your* End Game

Now that you have a sense of some opportunities in finance that are available to MBA graduates, it is essential to prepare and execute your career plan in a diligent, thorough, and creative manner. To help in that process, this section explores the critical elements, steps, and processes you will need to enhance your career search process. It is important to always balance the preparation and execution components.

As with any journey, you need to prepare. For example, an airplane pilot does not take the flight plan, hop into the cockpit, start the engines, and take off. The pilot meticulously reviews the flight plan, personally inspects the aircraft, talks with the tower, and may even re-review the weather forecasts. In fact, it is entirely likely that the pilot will also have some important and detailed conversations with the flight crew and others involved in the journey.

Why is this preparation so important? The best plan in the world cannot execute itself. No strategy, regardless of its brilliance, can offset an ineffectual implementation. As you read the following sections, consider how to adapt the concepts to your specific circumstances and situations.

Preparing for the Journey

In this section we explore the concepts of defining your value proposition and delivering the message effectively in written, verbal (oral), and digital forms.

IBM and BMW—these brand names are likely to trigger immediate and clear images and feelings. At this point, it is less important whether the reactions are positive or negative. More important, these brand names are successful because they convey knowledge, perceptions, and feelings of trust. This is the power of the brand. As you think about defining yourself, think about defining yourself as a *brand*. You should use this idea of branding as the basis for creating your career plan.

Creating Your Value Proposition

So what of your brand? Do you have one? Is it positive and compelling? More important, is it specific to you? For example, are you defined by your unique skills and abilities? Are you defined by more general factors such as attending a well-known business school? If you identify yourself solely as someone who graduated from an Ivy League institution, that's a good start, but it doesn't set you apart from the others who also are Ivy League graduates—you are still part of a broad population. You will need to portray a brand that is specific to you—that sets you apart from others. *What can you offer an employer that is meaningful, relevant, and significant? Is it a skill, an experience, unique knowledge, or a network of key contacts?* This is critical for you to determine and will help to set you apart in the face of ever-increasing competition.

For example, just as an advertising agency may use a multimarket multimedia strategy to promote its product, so must the MBA graduate! In addition, the best advertising firms integrate all the components of the campaign and brand. MBA graduates who want to make the largest impact will also seek to integrate all components of their brand.

Take a moment to consider the most effective advertising campaigns. What do they have in common? First and foremost, they caught your attention. Sometimes the ads are humorous; sometimes they include a catchy tune or cool celebrity. Capturing attention is valuable only if the ad is able to present a concise and compelling message that increases your desire to purchase the product. The leverage comes from the careful integration of the different media and ad versions used.

Let's take the example of a 1970s popular game show, *Name That Tune*. The object of the game was for contestants to identify a song by being provided with just a few musical notes. The contestant who was correct in the fewest number of notes was the champion. Imagine if these same concepts were employed to advertisements (instead of songs) and contestants needed to name the product or brand. Clearly, only those ads and brands that were most successful would be easily identified. Using this as an example, the key challenge for MBA students is to develop a concise, compelling, integrated, and effective personal branding strategy.

The foundation for building and communicating an effective brand message is comprised of the written resume, verbal resume, cover letter, e-mail communications, and networking. It is important to acknowledge that MBA graduates are assumed to have basic skills in analytics and communication. Building off this assumption, the remainder of this chapter focuses on packaging the unique skills, talents, and experiences that *you* bring to the table.

Written Resume—the Starting Point

Let's begin with the "I left it on the bus" test. Suppose you left your resume on a bus and it was found by either a well-known recruiter or an executive at a large financial services firm. Assuming that they took the time to look at your resume, would they know who you really are, what you are capable of doing, and what you want to do? In effect, does your resume convey *your story and brand* in a concise, compelling, and relevant way? If not, you will need to spend time to create an effective document that focuses on your accomplishments and the value you bring to a company.

Resumes remain a primary way that employers initially receive information from potential employees. MBA students need to create resumes that effectively reflect and differentiate their educations, experiences, accomplishments, and career goals. Resumes come in different formats, and opinions on effective resumes vary from expert to expert. However, most experts agree on the following tips for resume creation.

Your Resume Is Not Your Biography

Few people want to read a day-by-day account of your tasks and responsibilities. Many candidates, however, focus on this when creating a resume. Some then take this to the interview process and attempt to walk the interviewer through each line of the resume. Not only is this tactic not effective, but it doesn't serve to set you apart from the competition.

Your Resume Is a Marketing Tool—Treat It That Way!

As mentioned earlier, the most effective advertisements convey lots of information in a highly concise and compelling way. Their goal is to understand the customer's needs and then demonstrate the ability of the product or service to meet that need. Your resume faces the same challenge. Your resume should be created to match your skills and experiences to the needs of the employer. Therefore, resume writing is an ongoing interactive process where nuance and emphasis can mean a world of difference.

Target the Employer's Explicit and Perceived Needs and Preferences

At the end of the day, employers do not waste time and effort interviewing candidates they are not interested in. They are looking for specific experiences, skills, and accomplishments, as well as key intangibles such as job stability and personal attributes. Failure to focus on the needs of the employer means a lost opportunity. Employers are looking for candidates who can help them solve their problems and meet their needs.

Emphasize What You Can Contribute

Shift your resume from "This is who I am" to "This is what I bring to the table and how I can add value to your efforts."

Notice that this is all about using the same ingredients (education, jobs, etc.) and presenting them with the employer as the focus. It may be interesting to your grandmother that you were employed as an analyst at a small early stage firm, but unless she is hiring right now, you need to demonstrate how your experience as an analyst at a small early stage firm will benefit your future employer! How you present the information becomes as important as the information itself.

Your Resume Is Your Core Source Document

Beyond its popularity as the premier career search document, an effective resume defines your brand and provides the foundation that you will leverage in all subsequent activities and forms of communication. For that reason, your resume must be robust and adapted to current use. The message developed within your resume must be consistent with and carried through to all subsequent forms of communication.

Verbal (Oral) Resume

You may ask why we call your pitch the verbal or oral resume. (It is also known as an elevator pitch or rocket pitch.) The simple answer is that it's another part of your integrated branding system. As such, it should be designed to communicate orally what you have already compiled in written form (albeit in a more concise format).

An effective verbal resume should be engaging and informative. It should not sound like you are reading a shopping list or reporting your whereabouts to the police. It is essential to employ an informal delivery method to communicate a highly structured message. Clearly, to be effective your pitch needs to be delivered at a pace and in a tone consistent with your own style. Nonetheless, the goal of the message is to advance your job search efforts and therefore it needs to be highly structured with respect to the flow of information conveyed.

When should you use a verbal resume?

- Starting point in an interview.
- Networking opportunities.
- Accidental meeting with a prospective employer or key contact.
- Cold calls.
- Friends (yes, friends, and we will address this later).

Note that in any of these situations you could be asked, "So, MBA student, tell me about yourself." Consider the following possible responses:

MBA student: "Well, I go to [Great Reputation] College. I want to go into marketing. I worked with Allied Consumer Company and also the [Lesser-Known] Company."

Does this sound like you? Did the MBA student accomplish his goal of advancing his job search? Exactly what did the listener learn about him that would be compelling enough to engage with him further or recommend him to other influencers? Answer: very little. MBA student sounds unremarkable—so much so that it would be difficult for

someone to remember, much less convey, MBA student's story to others. Now consider the following:

Prospective employer: "So, Elizabeth, tell me about yourself."

Elizabeth: "Well, currently I am in the second year of my MBA program at [Great Rep] College, where I am concentrating in marketing. Prior to attending GRC I was a marketing analyst with Allied Consumer Company, where I analyzed consumer spending profiles and competitive strategies. I was also fortunate to be a marketing assistant with a smaller firm, the [Lesser-Known] Company, where I supported the East Coast regional manager in a variety of tracking activities. Because of these experiences, I knew I wanted a career in marketing, but I also recognized that to be successful I needed to obtain an advanced degree within a competitive program. So in addition to the reputation of GRC, I was very impressed by its curriculum and its emphasis on practical application of marketing concepts. As an example, I had the opportunity to work with the [Well-Known] Financial Services Group to help them address their new product launch. As a result of my experience and education, I am actively seeking challenging opportunities within a financial services firm where I can leverage my skills and experiences."

Which person do you know better? Which did a better job of differentiating himself/herself?

Verbal Resume Structure

In creating your verbal resume, you should focus on incorporating several of the following points into your pitch:

- Where are you now?
- Where have you been?
- What have you done?
- Why did you decide to go to school?
- What have you done at school?
- What are you looking for?

Your pitch should be tailored to your audience, the approximate amount of time allotted for the pitch, and the setting.

The Cover Letter

In many ways the cover letter can be more important than a resume because it serves as a first impression. A powerful cover letter not only encourages the reader to look at your resume, but it also creates a lens through which the person reads it. In effect, the cover letter leads the potential employer to want to learn more about you. What are the components of an effective cover letter?

- Who you are and what you are looking for.
- Validation: selected experiences and accomplishments.
- Call to action: how your value proposition will add value to the firm.

In contrast, the elements to be avoided in a cover letter are:

- Reproducing your resume—in total or in part.
- Failure to set the tone in the first paragraph.
- Repetition of skills by citing too many experiences.
- Telling the firm how this job will expand your learning.

Effective cover letters follow a standard business letter format, are free of grammatical and spelling errors, and convey a level of professionalism. It is important to focus on accomplishments and the value that you will bring to the position. Just as is true for your resume, you should tailor your cover letter to specific jobs and companies.

Digital Resume: Note about E-Mail Use

Use of e-mail is often convenient for the job seeker and for the recruiter. E-mail communication can help to expedite the sharing of information. However, it should not be assumed that every recruiter prefers to communicate electronically. Therefore, before engaging in job searching with a specific individual via e-mail, you should look for signals from the recruiter that e-mail is acceptable. One example of a signal that e-mail is acceptable is if the company provides its e-mail address verbally or within its presentation. Often, however, the signals may not be as clear. When in doubt, it is better to inquire: "May I contact you via e-mail?" Once you are certain that e-mail is acceptable, it is important to follow some basic guidelines to ensure that your e-mail communication will be well received and effective.

- Pay attention to grammar! Some tend to use slang terms when e-mailing. This is acceptable when communicating with friends, but for business purposes, always err on the side of formality.
- Be clear and concise in your messaging. People appreciate e-mail because it makes their job easier. You should not treat it as just an electronic alternative to a handwritten letter. In effect, pasting a traditional letter into an e-mail format may mean losing the benefits and advantages of e-mail communication.
- Use the subject line to your advantage. Let the recipient know right up front the purpose of the e-mail. Is this a follow-up, a thank-you, or an inquiry? Readers appreciate knowing the subject of the e-mail before opening and reading it.
- Avoid unprofessional stationery or special effects.
- Turn on the automatic spell-checker and read your e-mail several times prior to sending it.
- Place your signature and contact information at the bottom of your e-mail.

Remember: While they are different ways to communicate, resumes, cover letters, and e-mails all represent components that need to be integrated effectively to form a consistent message. Each needs to do its job, which is to advance you closer to your career goal.

Aiming for Your Goals

For career changers, identifying potential industries, companies, and professions is particularly difficult. It's simply hard to know what you don't know. So how do you get to know what you don't know?

Utilize All Possible Resources

Beginning with your college's career development office and expanding to faculty, friends, former colleagues, alumni, fellow students, and other networking, seek to learn as much as you can. Start with your areas of interest and experience. At the same time that you are looking at your likes and dislikes, you should be assessing your skills and experience. This process of assessment is iterative—as you learn about industries, companies, and careers, you will make assessments as to whether it makes sense for you to pursue them. It is just as helpful to learn about careers that are not a good fit—to rule them out—as it is to learn about opportunities that end up being a good fit.

Compile Initial Lists

Several lists may be helpful—lists of potential networking opportunities and contacts, lists of industries that may seem interesting, and lists of potential companies. To learn more about industries and companies, *Vault Career Guides* (which are often available through career development centers) and MBA Jungle's Web site may prove to be helpful resources.

Avoid Aiming at Sharply Different Targets

The earlier that you are able to focus in on specific industries, job functions, and companies, the easier it will be to compile and execute a plan for reaching your goals. Your plan will include curricular and noncurricular activities, internships and consulting projects, networking, and practicing your skills.

Refine, Maintain, and Update Target Lists

Your list will change throughout your MBA career as you learn and network, as the economic and market conditions change, and as other life changes happen. For example, following the economic turmoil of 2008, many investment banks ran into difficulties, as mentioned earlier. MBA students considering a career in investment banking were forced to adjust their plans and expand their target lists.

Implementing Your Strategy

If the prior preparation was done well, you are already in position to take the critical action steps. The very act of developing your resume caused you to think about your background and focus on potential industries/companies and roles where you can add the most value. By defining yourself you have also defined your (initial) area(s) of interest which in turn will propel you on your way. And so from this perspective, the Implementation Stage is neither separate nor distinct from the Getting Ready Stage. More importantly, it is essential to recognize it as part of an integrated strategy which in and of itself will be subject to revisions as you commence your actual search process.

Proactive versus Reactive Strategies

It does not take an MBA to recognize that it's easier to be reactive than proactive. It's easier to respond to a job posting than to uncover a job on your own. It is easier in this digital age to surf the Internet for hours instead of making a single exploratory phone call. Is it better to be proactive or reactive? In truth, both strategies are necessary.

Think of reactive strategies as being like farmers going into the fields seeking to harvest existing crops. Just as the farmer is dependent on external circumstances (in this case, nature) providing what is needed, if you are utilizing a reactive strategy, you are dependent on others providing what you need (in this case, a job opportunity). Like the farmer, you can plant seeds, but in the end you are highly dependent on things that are out of your control, and you can harvest only what has grown. In contrast, hunters are more in control of their own destinies. They make several calculated decisions, such as what to hunt, where to hunt, when and how to hunt. While hunters are still subject to forces outside of their control, they are in a better position to adjust their strategy as conditions change. Thinking about the analogy of the farmer versus the hunter for career seekers, the reactive career seeker will upload resumes, respond to job postings, and answer the phone, just like the farmer harvests the crops. The proactive job hunter will network with friends, alumni, fellow students, families, and others, proactively research industries and companies, and make proactive phone calls. Both approaches can prove to be successful, and the most successful job seekers use a combination of the two methods.

One of the keys to the hunter/proactive method is networking. Let's spend some time discussing this art and how to improve your skills in this area.

Networking

Networking is generally regarded as the most effective way to learn about and secure a new position. Yet it remains one of the most difficult things for any of us to do—even MBAs! So, given its importance, let's walk through the basics.

Networking is the process whereby you increase your knowledge of industries, companies, and professions, *and* others get to know more about you! If others know more about you, it will be easier for them to remember you, recommend you, and seek you out if or when opportunities arise. As with every strategy, it requires diligence and perseverance. Instead of waiting for opportunities passively, you must actively seek out opportunities. Also note that networking is a two-player game. To be successful, both parties need to benefit. It is important to identify how the other party benefits from helping you.

With Whom Should I Network? Everyone and Anyone!

A typical mistake occurs when people exclude potential conversations because the individual is not in the target industry or profession. Sometimes they avoid connecting with someone because they doubt the individual has the influence to help them. Wrong! Wrong! Wrong! Recall the concept of *Six Degrees of Separation*, which suggests that everyone on earth is separated by only six individuals. If that is true for everyone on the planet, just think of the odds when focusing on a specific industry or company within a limited geographic area.

While your ultimate goal is to connect with the right decision maker, it may take several steps to get there. For this reason, you need to recognize that each contact has the potential to help you move forward in your journey. Do not arbitrarily exclude people from your networking just because the connection is not immediately clear.

To start the process, prepare a list of at least 25 initial names to contact, categorized as follows.

Friends and Family

These are people you can contact at almost any time and say just about anything. They are incredibly important to you because you can be yourself and they will give you honest feedback.

Associations

These are people with whom you have some loose and/or undefined relationship, such as alumni, fellow pool club members, or neighbors. Associations can also include shared interest groups such as running clubs, book clubs, and fellow service club members. The specific association becomes less important as you begin to connect with that person on a different level. Any association provides the natural opportunity to connect with someone who may be able to help in your career search process.

First Stage Key Contacts

These are people you don't know and don't have any affiliation with, but you deem them important in their industry or company. They are critical in providing industry/company/professional insight and gaining access to the ultimate key contact.

Ultimate Key Contacts

By definition, these are critical individuals who are in the best possible position to connect you with key professionals. You may already know some, and others you will come to know through networking.

What Are the Goals of Networking?

Of course, it seems like a natural response to assume that there is one goal: to secure a great job. This is, of course, one of the end goals; however, the process is just as important for lifelong career development. In fact, some of the secondary goals can be invaluable. If securing a job is the top priority, a close second is obtaining critical information about industries, companies, and professions. For this reason, career changers in particular will benefit greatly from networking, because it provides them with unique, timely, firsthand, relevant information. Most important, networking also provides you with feedback and insight to determine if you are a good fit for a position, company, or industry.

Remember: Networking has multiple goals and opportunities. The primary goal is to secure a position, or more specifically, obtain the ideal career opportunity at a desired compensation rate.

Secondary goals are:

- Gain access to industries with significant barriers to entry.
- Acquire critical market intelligence about an industry, firm, or job function.
- Answer the pivotal question: "What do I want to do and where do I want to do it?"

What Do I Say and How Do I Approach Networking?

As with any marketing campaign, there is a key core message that remains consistent regardless of whom you are speaking with. However, the delivery of the message may change depending on the different audiences and situations. With this in mind, let's explore how to adapt your specific message(s) to each key constituent.

Let's begin with some key assumptions. Many find networking very challenging because we often do not like to talk about ourselves. It can be uncomfortable to ask for a job, and sometimes we simply do not know what to say. To reduce the stress and increase the effectiveness of your efforts, it is important to get into the proper state of mind.

- Do not ask for a job—that will be obvious.

- At the same time, let others know you are available by virtue of your networking efforts.

- Let the other person get to know your professional qualifications and make assessments on your potential fit with various opportunities.

Recall that every communication should contain your critical, powerful brand message. Equally important, do not assume that others know your qualifications. This is especially true of friends, family, and associations where people know you well as a person, but not necessarily in a professional context. For this reason, it is always best to err on the side of caution—use every encounter to reintroduce your skills, experience, and career goals.

With Friends and Family

Here are some sample approaches. You might say:

"You know me from the pool club, but it has been awhile, so let me give you a quick update. I am completing my MBA and am actively exploring career opportunities. My primary target is finance and I was hoping to get your perspective, given your experience in the industry and your familiarity with my background."

"You know me from Jane's book club, but it has been awhile, so let me give you a quick update. I am in the last stage of my MBA and am actively exploring career opportunities. Although I know that finance is not your field, I was hoping that you might know some people who work in finance that you might be willing to connect me to."

Associations

When reaching out to associations, recognize that your connection may be minimal and not obvious. You will need to educate them about your background—your elevator pitch will be invaluable in providing a quick summary. In preparing for your conversation, you should address the following:

- *Goal:* Understand that others need to know *early in the conversation* why you want to speak with them.

- *Validation:* Provide a justification for them to speak with you.

- *Call to action:* What can they do to help you move to the next level?

First Stage Key Contacts

In this case, you will be speaking with people you don't know and don't have any affiliation with. For this reason, you need to leverage your relationship with the individual who recommended you. It is critical to provide additional validation regarding your skills and experience. Be prepared to lead the conversation, but note that, ideally, the information flow should be two-way. Listen carefully, and adjust your messaging based on cues from the other person. Of course, do your homework about the firm and industry before the conversation—don't waste the person's time.

Ultimate Key Contact

If you have reached this stage, you've done well, so pause and build on this success. Before talking with the ultimate key contact, compile the notes of all previous conversations, craft your adjusted elevator pitch, research the firm and industry of this contact, and prepare questions and thoughts. Use all of this knowledge to craft your value proposition. You should also be prepared to add insight and information to the conversation.

Networking Summary

Recall what you are trying to accomplish:

- Acquire additional people to contact.
- Obtain market intelligence about industries, companies, and functions.
- Locate and gain access to the ultimate key contact.
- *Secure a position!*

Here is one final thought regarding networking: Remember to be gracious, polite, and professional in all of your interactions. Ask the person what would be the best time and the best way to speak—in person, over the phone, or via e-mail. Everyone and every conversation has the potential to help, and displaying a professional demeanor in every interaction will help make those with whom you are networking feel comfortable enough to open up their Rolodexes and connections to you. Also, remember to thank them for their time, insights, and assistance. Finally, update each person with your progress and keep in contact with them throughout your career.

Assessing Opportunities

While most of this discussion has been devoted to strategies to improve your career search efforts, it is also important to explore how to assess the opportunities that will arise as a result of your efforts.

It is vital to understand the complete value of an opportunity (beyond the monetary compensation). For example, job A offers a great starting salary as well as some other financial perks, but it also has some drawbacks. It is not the exact role you were hoping for, the firm is a bit larger than you would like, or moving ahead in the company may appear to be difficult. Job B, in contrast, provides a closer match to the job function you were hoping for and perhaps better opportunities, but the financial compensation is lower.

Unfortunately, there are no right or wrong answers to the question of job A or job B. The best you can do is to take stock of where you are and where you want to be and determine what are the most important and critical factors for *you*. If you look at the careers of the most successful people, they did not get to where they are by receiving 2% to 5% increases each year. The most successful people had irregular and exponential growth in the careers. These are people who seek jobs in which they constantly learn and increase their value to the company. So ultimately it's up to you.

As anxious as you might be about your first big job, you need to remember to keep in mind your long-term goals. Understand who you are and your preference for stability versus risk. For this reason, do not place too much emphasis on the salary level of your initial big job. Think about your initial job as part of a long-term strategy in which the each job is another step in a lifelong career pursuit. To help illustrate the point, ask yourself what distinguishes great pool players from the weekend variety. The casual player aims to get a single ball into a specific pocket. The truly great players choose their shots with an eye to setting up the next few shots. In adopting this approach, MBAs should think like the great pool player and assess a given position within the context of both immediate and long-term potential benefits.

Closing Thoughts: Coping with the Challenges

Recall the discussion of the end game, more specifically *your* end game. Well, now it's time to revisit that concept as you work through your career search process. As many of you have already experienced, a job search is demanding and can be frustrating. At times it can be overwhelming—unless you have a plan and stick to it. The thoughts presented here are designed to keep you engaged in a constructive way even when it seems like there is nothing happening. Each day you should be learning about yourself, and about potential companies and careers. When you hit a bump in the road, just get back on track as soon as possible, and continue the journey.

As noted earlier, the career search is a lifelong process, and as such it does not end with your first big MBA job. The suggestions presented help to ensure continual forward progress in your career search. A perpetual career search will provide the highest ROI!

Notes

1. Wikipedia, http://en.wikipedia.org/wiki/Hedge_fund.
2. Davare, Aditi, Holly Goodrich, Michael Martinez, and the Staff of Vault, *Vault Career Guide to Hedge Funds*, Vault.com, November 2007.
3. http://hedgeweek.com (HedgeMedia Ltd.).
4. Epstein, Adam, *Vault Career Guide to Investment Management*, Vault.com, July 2008.
5. Martinez, Mike, *Vault Career Guide to Private Wealth Management*, Vault.com, October 2006.
6. MBA Jungle (www.mbajungle.com), Industry Guides, Real Estate.
7. Ibid.
8. MBA Jungle (www.mbajungle.com), Industry Guides, Venture Capital, home page.
9. MBA Jungle (www.mbajungle.com), Industry Guides, Venture Capital/Private Equity.
10. Kaganovich, Oleg, James Currier, and Joe Bel Bruno, *Vault Career Guide to Venture Capital*, Vault.com, November 2008.

Glossary

Accrual accounting: An accounting method that recognizes revenues as they are earned and expenses as they are incurred. The timing of revenue and expense recognition is not tied to the timing of the inflow and outflow of cash. Accrual accounting is seen as essential in order to develop reliable measures of periodic financial performance and is a core concept of generally accepted accounting principles (GAAP).

Acid test ratio: *See* **Quick ratio**.

Acquisition: The purchase—not necessarily for cash—of a controlling interest in a firm.

AICPA (The American Institute of Certified Public Accountants): This is the national professional association of certified public accountants (CPAs).

Amortization: The periodic, noncash charge used to reduce an intangible asset.

Amortization schedule: The portion of the total initial cost of an intangible asset expensed each period.

Amortize: To repay principal and interest toward an amount borrowed over time.

Annuity: Equal payments, at a specific time interval, for a specific time period.

Annuity due: An annuity that pays installments at the beginning of each time interval.

Arbitration: A form of alternative dispute resolution. Its purpose is to resolve disputes outside of the court system using a negotiator or arbitrator. There are various organizations that provide such service (e.g., JAMS and the American Arbitration Association). There are other professionals, usually attorneys or retired judges, who perform these services.

Asset: An item owned by an enterprise and expected to provide future benefits to that enterprise. Examples of assets include cash, accounts receivable, inventories, property, plant and equipment, and intellectual property (such as patents, trademarks, and copyrights).

Asset acquisition: An acquisition executed by purchasing the assets of the target firm.

Asset approach: A general way of determining a value indication of a business, business ownership interest, or security by using one or more methods based on the value of the assets of that business net of liabilities.

Asymmetric information: A situation where an individual or group is better informed than another individual or group. If the managers of a company have better information about the company than outsiders, the managers have asymmetric information.

Audit committee: A committee of the board of directors required by Sarbanes-Oxley (SOX) for all U.S. public companies. The audit committee must include only outside directors (which excludes officers or employees of the corporation), and at least one audit committee member is required to have financial expertise. The purpose of the audit committee is to maintain communication with the independent audit firm and the corporation's internal audit function.

Balance sheet: A financial statement reporting a company's assets, liabilities, and equity, together with their respective dollar amounts, as of a given date at a specific point in time. The term *balance sheet* comes from the fact that a company's assets must equal its liabilities plus equity, thus balancing out (1) the total assets with (2) the combination of the liabilities incurred plus the equity capital raised to acquire the assets.

Beta: The measure of the systematic risk of any stock in the capital asset pricing model (CAPM). A stock's beta measures the correlation of the stock with the movements of the overall stock market, as well as the volatility of the stock compared to the volatility of the overall stock market.

Beta site: An unfinished Web site that is open to the public.

Bidder: The firm that initiates a merger or acquisition; the bidder usually retains control of the surviving firm.

Brand recognition: Customer awareness of a certain brand, company, or product.

Burn rate: The speed at which a company uses cash in excess of cash coming in.

Business valuation: The act or process of determining the value of a business enterprise or ownership interest therein.

Call center: A centralized office that places or receives telephone calls for the purpose of either marketing a device or service or providing a customer service function.

Capital asset pricing model (CAPM): A model in which the cost of capital for any security or portfolio of securities equals a risk-free rate plus a risk premium that is proportionate to the systematic risk of the security or portfolio.

Capital loss carryover: The excess of capital losses over capital gains that may not be deducted currently but may be carried forward and set off against future capital gains.

Capital structure: The composition of the invested capital of a business enterprise; the mix of long-term debt and equity financing.

Capitalization: A conversion of a single-period stream of benefits into value.

Capitalization factor: Any multiple or divisor used to convert anticipated benefits into value.

Capitalization rate: Any divisor (usually expressed as a percentage) used to convert anticipated benefits into value.

Cash flow: Cash that is spent or received over a period of time by an enterprise. It may be used in a general sense to encompass various levels of specifically defined cash flows. When the term is used, it should be supplemented by a qualifier (for example, "discretionary" or "operating") and a definition of exactly what it means in the given valuation context.

Cash flow statement: A financial statement reporting a company's inflows and outflows of cash for a period of time internally generated from operations plus externally obtained from financing, and minus cash used for investing in the business.

Changes in accounting estimates: Estimates are essential to the implementation of accrual accounting. A typical example would be the estimates of useful lives and salvage values that are necessary in computing depreciation. Changes in either useful lives or salvage values would represent changes in accounting estimates.

Changes in accounting principles: A change in the accounting treatment applied to a particular area of accounting. Most accounting changes are not discretionary but rather are the result of the mandatory adoption of new accounting standards. The most common example of a discretionary change is for inventory methods.

Charges: Commonly used in accounting in referring to expenses and losses.

Compound interest: Interest paid upon interest earned "and principal invested."

Comprehensive income: An expanded measure of income that includes items of other income in addition to traditional realized net income.

Conglomerate merger: A combination of firms in unrelated industries.

Consolidation: A merger in which an entirely new firm is created.

Control: The power to direct the management and policies of a business enterprise.

Control premium: An amount (expressed in either dollar or percentage form) by which the pro rata value of a controlling interest exceeds the pro rata value of a noncontrolling interest in a business enterprise, reflecting the power of control.

Core competency: A firm's key strength that meets the following three conditions, specified by Gary Hamel and C. K. Prahalad in "The Core Competence of the Corporation" (*Harvard Business Review*, May–June 1990): It provides consumer benefits, it is not easy for competitors to imitate, and it can be leveraged widely to many products and markets.

Core earnings: Earnings exclusive of the effects of nonrecurring items (*see* **Sustainable earnings base**). Also refers to earnings that derive from only the primary, or core, activities of the firm.

Correlation: A measure of the joint variation or association between two or more variables, such as the rates of return of two investments.

Cost approach: A general way of estimating a value indication of an individual asset by quantifying the amount of money that would be required to replace the future service capability of that asset.

Cost of capital: The expected rate of return (discount rate) that the market requires in order to attract funds to a particular investment.

Cost of capital: The cost to a company of the long-term capital it raises from debt and equity investors. Long-term investors provide capital expecting a rate of return, and this expected return is the company's cost of capital.

Cost-plus pricing: A pricing strategy where products and services are priced based on cost to develop plus a predetermined margin.

Country risk: The risk of conducting business in another country. Major components include repatriation risk, foreign exchange risk, and political risk.

Covariance: A product of the correlation between the rates of return of two investments, and the standard deviation of the rates of return of each of the two investments. Covariance captures the extent of association between the two investments and the volatility of each of the two investments.

Current: Generally means within a year.

Current ratio: Current assets divided by current liabilities.

Debt providers: Organizations that specialize in providing debt funding to businesses (e.g., banks).

Deferred tax valuation allowance: A portion of a deferred tax asset that is judged unlikely to be realized.

Demographic: Statistical characteristics of human populations (such as age, income, gender) used to identify markets.

Depreciation: The portion of the total initial cost of a tangible asset expensed each period to allow for wear, tear, and obsolescence.

Discontinued operations: Operations that constitute a separable business that are sold or otherwise ended.

Discount rate: A rate of return (cost of capital) used to convert a monetary sum, payable or receivable in the future, into present value.

Discounted cash flow: When discussing the time value of money, we assume that money invested or saved will earn interest; therefore, a known dollar amount today is worth more than that same dollar amount in the future.

Distribution channel: A chain of intermediaries that a firm's product must go through in order to reach the customer. Also known as *channel*. *See* **Multichannel distribution strategy**.

Diversification: The reduction of risk that occurs when an investor holds many different stocks or assets in a portfolio. This reduction of risk occurs due to variation in the rate or return earned by the different stocks or bonds in a portfolio.

Doriot, Georges: Founder of American Research and Development Corporation in 1946, the first publicly owned venture capital firm.

Economy of scale: The decrease in the marginal cost of production as a firm's output expands.

Effective income tax rate: Total income tax provision (expense) deducted from pretax income from continuing operations divided by pretax income from continuing operations.

Efficient search sequence: A pattern of searching for nonrecurring items that is designed to maximize their discovery and minimize search time.

Entrepreneurship: The practice of starting new organizations or revitalizing mature organizations in response to identified opportunities.

Equity: Interest or ownership in a business.

Equity risk premium: A rate of return in addition to a risk-free rate to compensate for investing in equity instruments because they have a higher degree of probable risk than risk-free instruments (a component of the cost of equity capital or equity discount rate).

Eurozone: The countries in Europe that have adopted the euro as their official currency.

Exchange rate: The amount of currency in one country that can be purchased by one unit of currency in another country.

Exchange rate risk: The risk of an adverse movement in exchange rates affecting prices of exports and the value of assets or liabilities.

Express warranty: A guarantee that is provided by a seller of a good or service to a buyer that the product or service will perform as required in the contract, and that, if not, it will repair or replace as necessary.

Extraordinary gains and losses: Revenues or gains and expenses or losses that are both unusual and nonrecurring.

Face or par value: The amount that is paid to bondholders when a bond matures and is retired. The interest paid to bondholders is also based on the face or par value.

Fair market value: The price, expressed in terms of cash equivalents, at which property would change hands between a hypothetical willing and able buyer and a hypothetical willing and able seller, acting at arm's length in an open and unrestricted market, when neither is under compulsion to buy or sell and when both have reasonable knowledge of the relevant facts.

FIFO: *See* **First in, first out (FIFO) inventory method**.

Financial Accounting Standards Board (FASB): A private-sector organization that plays the primary role in the formulation and promulgation of generally accepted accounting principles (GAAP).

Financial distress: The condition that exists when a company is experiencing problems and may be unable to pay, or has actually failed to pay, the interest and principal owed on its debt.

Financial leverage: The use of debt to finance by a company. A company that has borrowed money from long-term investors is using financial leverage.

First in, first out (FIFO) inventory method: A method of computing cost of sales that includes the oldest inventory costs first in the computation of cost of sales.

Fixed expense: Expenses or costs that do not change with sales volume.

Free cash flow: The cash flow generated by the company that is available to long-term investors. Free cash flow is calculated as after-tax operating profits, plus depreciation expense, minus capital expenditures, minus the increase in net working capital (or plus the decrease in net working capital).

Future value (FV): Value at the end of a time period.

FVA$_N$: Future value of an annuity.

GAAP: See **Generally accepted accounting principles**.

Generally accepted accounting principles (GAAP): The body of standards, rules, procedures, and practices that guide the required form and disclosures in the preparation of financial statements in the United States. For commercial firms, the primary bodies involved with adding to or modifying existing GAAP are the Financial Accounting Standards Board (FASB), and the Securities and Exchange Commission (SEC). For non-U.S. firms using International Financial Reporting Standards (IFRS), the primary source is the International Accounting Standards Board.

Generally accepted auditing standards (GAAS): The rules and regulations of the Public Company Accounting Oversight Board (PCAOB) regarding the planning, performance, recording, and reporting of public company audits. Not to be confused with GAAP.

Going private transaction: The conversion of a public firm into a private company, usually by either a leveraged buyout (LBO) or a management buyout (MBO), often initiated by a private equity firm.

Goodwill: As it relates to valuation, that intangible asset arising as a result of name, reputation, customer loyalty, location, products, and similar factors not separately identified. It is the excess of purchase price over fair market value of net assets acquired under the purchase method of accounting; goodwill appears on the acquirer's balance sheet as an intangible asset and is amortized over a period of not more than 40 years.

Gross margin: Difference between revenues and cost of goods sold.

Health Insurance Portability and Accountability Act (HIPAA): Enacted by Congress in 1996. As part of the act, Congress codified various privacy rights that are placed upon health care providers regarding the protection of patient health care information.

Horizontal merger: A merger of firms producing similar goods or services.

Hurdle rate: The cost of the capital used to fund an investment project. If the rate of return of the project clears the hurdle rate, the project should be accepted. If the rate of return of the project is less than the hurdle rate, the project should be rejected.

Impairment: Results from the loss in value of goodwill; impairment is the result of the write-down of goodwill.

Implied warranty: An implied guarantee that the good or service being sold is both merchantable (must be fit for the ordinary purpose for which such goods are sold) and fit for a particular purpose.

Income approach: A general way of determining a value indication of a business, business ownership interest, security, or intangible asset using one or more methods that convert anticipated benefits into a present single amount.

Income from continuing operations: A measure of financial performance for the period that excludes the effects of discontinued operations, extraordinary items, and the cumulative effect of accounting changes. All other revenues, gains, expenses, and losses are included in the computation of income from continuing operations.

Income statement: A financial statement reporting revenues (such as sales), expenses, and income, and their respective dollar amounts, for an enterprise over a given period of time.

Intangible assets: Nonphysical assets (such as franchises, trademarks, patents, copyrights, goodwill, equities, mineral rights, securities, and contracts as distinguished from physical assets) that grant rights, privileges, and have economic benefits for the owner.

Intellectual property (IP): The rights that a company or individual has over creations such as inventions or artistic creations. They are usually legalized in the form of a patent, copyright, trade secret, or trademark and are protected by law.

Interest rate: Compensation paid for use of money over a period of time.

Internal control: The policies and practices intended to protect assets and to assure accurate financial reporting and disclosure.

International Accounting Standards Board (IASB): A private-sector organization, located in London, that issues pronouncements and interpretations to formulate International Financial Reporting Standards.

International Financial Reporting Standards (IFRS): The international counterpart to U.S. GAAP, adopted by more than 100 countries and planned to replace GAAP within a few years.

Invested capital: The sum of equity and debt in a business enterprise. Debt is typically long-term debt.

Investment risk: The degree of uncertainty as to the realization of expected returns.

Investment value: The value to a particular investor based on individual investment requirements and expectations.

Irregular items of revenue, gain, expense, or loss: *See* **Nonrecurring items**.

Leverage: The proportion of long-term debt to common equity.

Liabilities: Obligations and debt that an enterprise must pay in the future.

Liability: An item, and its dollar amount, that is payable by the enterprise.

LIFO inventory method: A method of computing cost of sales that charges the most recent inventory costs into cost of sales. The most recent (last in) inventory items go into the cost of sales computation first (first out).

LIFO liquidation: A reduction in the physical quantity of inventory by a firm using the LIFO method. Typically, older and lower costs will be associated with the liquidated quantities. This has the effect of reducing cost of sales and increasing earnings. This earnings increase is treated as nonrecurring in the computation of sustainable earnings.

LIFO reserve: The excess (typically) of the replacement cost (or FIFO carrying value) of LIFO inventory over its LIFO carrying value.

Limitation of liability: An agreement in a contract that, in the event of a breach of the contract, the party breaching the contract cannot be held liable for a specific monetary amount, regardless of the damages that the other party has suffered. In many contracts, it is not unusual for the seller to have limited its liability to the amounts paid under the contract.

Liquidity: The ability to quickly convert property to cash or pay a liability.

Management's discussion and analysis (MD&A) of results of operations and financial condition: A required report under Securities and Exchange Commission regulations. The discussion of operations is required to include material nonrecurring items of revenue, gain, expense, and loss.

Market approach: A general way of determining a value indication of a business, business ownership interest, security, or intangible asset by using one or more methods that compare the subject to similar businesses, business ownership interests, securities, or intangible assets that have been sold.

Market capitalization: The total value at market prices of the securities in issue for a company, a stock market, or a sector of a stock market, calculated by multiplying the number of shares issued by the market price per share.

Market demand pricing: A pricing strategy where products services are priced based on current market prices.

Market segment: A subgroup of a population determined by shared characteristics and product/service needs. A market can be divided into segments through the use of demographic and psychographic characteristics.

Marketability: The ability to quickly convert property to cash at minimal cost.

Material: Significant in amount or in importance.

Material items: Items of sufficient size to have the potential to influence decision makers or other users of financial statements. Generally accepted accounting principles do not offer a specific quantitative definition of materiality.

MD&A: *See* **Management's discussion and analysis (MD&A) of results of operations and financial condition**.

Merger: The combination of two or more companies into a single entity.

Milestone: A significant point in development. Mostly used in business as a benchmark to gauge progress.

Minority discount: A discount for lack of control applicable to a minority interest.

Minority interest: An ownership interest less than 50% of the voting interest in a business enterprise.

Misstatements: Materially incorrect numbers in financial statements, due to error or fraud.

Multichannel distribution strategy: A distribution strategy that utilizes multiple channels to reach the customer (such as retail and online).

Multinational corporation: A company that does business in more than one country.

Multistep income statement: An income statement format that includes one or more profit subtotals such as gross profit and operating profit (*see also* **Single-step income statement**).

National Association of Securities Dealers Automated Quotation (NASDAQ) system: An electronic system set up by NASD for trading stocks. It is commonly referred to as the over-the-counter (OTC) market.

Net cash flow: Cash inflows less cash outflows. When the term is used, it should be supplemented by a qualifier (for instance, "to equity holders" or "to the firm") and a definition of exactly what it means in the given valuation context.

Net cash flows to equity holders: Those cash inflows less outflows flows available to pay out to equity holders (in the form of dividends) after funding operations of the business enterprise, making necessary capital investments, and reflecting increases or decreases in debt financing.

Net cash flows to the firm: Cash received by the firm less the associated cash expenditures.

Net operating loss carryforward: Under U.S. tax law, operating losses can be carried back and set off against profits in the previous three years. A refund of taxes can be obtained. If the loss is greater than the profits in the three previous years, then the loss can be carried forward for 20 years and set off against the profits of future years. The carrying forward of a loss may produce a future tax savings. In contrast, the carrying back of a loss produces a tax refund.

Net present value: Total present value of cash flows over a time period.

Noncurrent: Generally means longer than a year.

Nonrecurring items: Items of revenue, gain, expense, and loss that appear in earnings on only an infrequent or irregular basis, fluctuate significantly in terms of amount and/or sign, and are often not related to the core operational activities of the firm.

Nonsystematic risk: The risk associated with the unique or nonmarket factors that affect only a particular company. These factors are reduced or diversified when the company's common stock is held in a portfolio. Nonsystematic risk is not relevant and is not rewarded in stock investing, because it can be diversified away.

NPER or Nper: N = number of periods.

Offshore outsourcing: The outsourcing of a manufacture, process, design, or function to a third-party company located outside the company's base of operations in its own country.

Operating income: An intermediate, pretax measure of financial performance. Only operations-related items of revenue, gain, expense, and loss are included in the computation of operating income. Often considered equivalent to earnings before interest and taxes (EBIT).

Opportunity cost: A benefit forgone as a result of pursuing an alternative action.

Ordinary annuity: An annuity that pays installments at the end of each time interval.

Organization chart: A diagram illustrating the structure of an organization and positions within the organization.

Other comprehensive income: A set of unrealized income elements that are added to conventional net income to arrive at comprehensive income. The key other comprehensive income items are foreign currency translation adjustments, unrealized gains and losses on certain securities, and adjustments related to defined benefit pension plans.

Outsourcing: The subcontracting of a manufacture, process, design, or function to a third-party company.

Override: The noncompliance or bypassing or subversion of internal controls by top management.

Payment per period (PMT): Payment based on constant periodic amounts and a constant interest rate.

Pecking order theory: A theory of capital structure that holds that financial managers finance companies in a particular order: internal funds first, followed by safer debt securities, followed by riskier equity securities.

Perpetuity: A series of cash flows that go on forever.

Political risk: Risk arising from political change within a foreign country. This may include seizing the assets of a foreign company, changes in tax policy, changes in environmental and work regulations, or demands for bribes or other payments.

Pooling of interests method: A method not used since June 2001 in which after an acquisition the bidder and target firm balance sheets were combined simply by adding book values.

Portfolio: A collection of stocks or assets. Investors hold their stocks or assets in portfolios to reduce the overall risk of their investments.

Premise of value: An assumption regarding the most likely set of transactional circumstances that may be applicable to the subject valuation (e.g., going concern, liquidation).

Premium: The amount over current market price paid to the target to execute an acquisition.

Present value (PV): Value today of a future amount of money.

Primary target audience (PTA): A group of potential customers identified by demographic and psychographic data that will be the focus of the company's early marketing and sales efforts.

Proxy contest: An attempt to gain control of a corporation by soliciting shareholder votes.

Psychographic data: Information that categorizes customers based on their personalities, psychological traits, lifestyles, values, and social memberships.

Purchase method: After the acquisition, the target firm's assets are put on the bidder's balance sheet at their fair market value; often creates the intangible asset goodwill.

PVA$_N$: Present value of an annuity.

Quick ratio: (Current Assets − Inventories)/Current Liabilities. Also known as the acid test ratio.

Rate of return: An amount of income (loss) and/or change in value realized or anticipated on an investment, expressed as a percentage of that investment.

Regulation D: Under the Securities Act of 1933, all offers to sell securities must either be registered with the SEC or meet an exemption. Regulation D contains three rules (Rules 504, 505, and 506) offering exemptions from registration requirements, allowing smaller companies to offer and sell securities without having to register the securities with the SEC.

Repatriation risk: The risk that governments will not allow money to flow out of a country.

Request for proposal (RFP): A request made by a company to a vendor or supplier to submit a proposal for a specific product or service.

Required return: The return required by a corporation to invest in a project. It is weighted average cost of capital (WACC), adjusted for risk.

Residual value: The prospective value as of the end of the discrete projection period in a discounted benefit streams model.

Restatements: Corrected financial statements, usually to replace financial statements that have been materially misstated—or more rarely to allow for mergers or other legitimate factors (as opposed to error or fraud).

Restructuring charges: Expenses typically recognized in conjunction with downsizings, reengineerings, reorganizations, and comparable activities. The expenses are usually made up of cash costs, accruals of obligations for future expenditures, as well as the write-down of assets.

Risk premium: A rate of return in addition to a risk-free rate to compensate the investor for accepting risk.

Risk-free rate: The rate of return available in the market on an investment free of default risk.

Secondary target audience (STA): A group of potential customers identified by demographic and psychographic data that will be a secondary or alternative focus of the company's early marketing and sales efforts. *See also* **Primary target audience**.

Securities and Exchange Commission (SEC): The federal government regulatory authority over U.S. financial markets.

Shareholder class action: A lawsuit brought by a group of shareholders of a public company against usually the officers and directors of the company for breach of their fiduciary duties or fraud.

Simple interest: Interest paid only on the principal.

Single-step income statement: An income statement format that simply deducts expenses and losses from revenues and gains in arriving at a single measure of income from continuing operations.

Solvency: The ability to pay the bills and to meet all financial commitments.

SOX: The Sarbanes-Oxley Act of 2002.

Standard of value: The identification of the type of value being utilized in a specific engagement (e.g., fair market value, fair value, investment value).

Statement of Financial Accounting Standards (SFAS): A pronouncement of the Financial Accounting Standards Board; these statements are the central elements of generally accepted accounting principles (GAAP).

Stock acquisition: The purchase of a controlling interest in a firm by buying its outstanding equity.

Sustainable earnings base: A revised historical earnings series from which the effects of all nonrecurring items have been removed (*see* **Core earnings**).

Sustainable earnings worksheet: A worksheet used to organize and summarize nonrecurring items so that their effects can be removed from as-reported net income in order to arrive at a sustainable earnings base.

Synergy: The incremental value generated by the combination of two or more firms; sources may include cost savings and revenue enhancement.

Systematic risk: The risk associated with common or market factors that affect all of the companies in an economy. These factors cannot be diversified away by holding a portfolio, because all of the assets or stocks in the portfolio are affected by these factors. When using the capital asset pricing model, systematic risk is measured by beta.

Takeover: The transfer of corporate control from one group of shareholders to another.

Target: A firm that is the subject of takeover or acquisition activities.

Taxable transaction: An acquisition in which the target firm shareholders are immediately subject to capital gains on their sale of shares.

Tax-adjusted nonrecurring items: Pretax nonrecurring items of revenue, gain, expense, and loss that are multiplied by 1 minus a representative income tax rate. The result is the after-tax effect of each of these items on net income.

Tax-free transaction: An acquisition in which the primary consideration paid to the target's shareholders is the acquirer's common stock, thereby deferring capital gain taxes until the new shares are sold.

Tender offer: A public, open offer to shareholders to buy their stock at a certain price during a specific time, subject to getting a minimum number of shares.

Terminal value: The value of a company once it matures and attains a constant and perpetual growth rate. Calculating terminal value captures the value of all the cash flows to investors in all of the company's constant and perpetual growth years.

Tertiary target audience (TTA): A group of potential customers identified by demographic and psychographic data that will be the focus of the company's later marketing and sales efforts. *See also* **Primary target audience**.

Time value of money: Value of a dollar today (present value) versus what the value of that same dollar will be in the future (future value).

Trade-off theory: A theory of capital structure holding that financial managers choose the capital structure that minimizes the company's cost of capital. This minimum point occurs when the debt tax shield benefits from new debt are exactly offset by the costs of financial distress from new debt.

Unsystematic risk: The portion of total risk specific to an individual security that can be avoided through diversification.

Valuation (of a company): The market value of a company. (*See* **Market capitalization**.)

Valuation date: The specific point in time to which the valuator's opinion of value applies (also referred to as "effective date" or "appraisal date").

Value proposition: The value of a business's products and services to its customers.

Variance and standard deviation: Variance is a measure of the dispersion of individual observed returns around the mean of the individual observed returns, and standard deviation is the square root of variance.

Vendor: A seller of goods.

Venture capitalist: A financial institution specializing in the provision of equity and other forms of long-term capital to enterprises, usually to firms with a limited track record but with the expectation of substantial growth. The venture capitalist may provide both funding and varying degrees of managerial and technical expertise. Venture capital has traditionally been associated with start-ups; however, venture capitalists have increasingly participated in later-stage projects.

Vertical merger: A merger in which the two firms are from different stages from the same industry or production process; for example, an automobile manufacturer purchases a steel-maker.

Weighted average cost of capital (WACC): The cost of capital (discount rate) determined by the weighted average, at market value, of the cost of all financing sources in the business enterprise's capital structure.

Whistle-blower: Person who reports or reveals apparent irregularities.

Willfulness: In an IP context, willfulness is deliberate disregard for the ownership of another's IP rights. If a finding of willfulness is determined, then treble (triple) damages may be assessed by the courts.

Work for hire: A clause in a contract that legally assigns the intellectual property developed as part of a project to the contracting party. Absent this clause, copyright law provides for the ownership of a copyright to reside with the author of the product.

Working capital: Current assets less current liabilities.

Yield to maturity: The rate of return investors will earn if they purchase a bond at its current price and hold the bond until maturity. The cost of debt for a company is the current yield to maturity of its bonds, because if investors are willing to buy and hold the bonds, earning the yield to maturity, then this rate must be investors' required rate of return.

Y2K: The year 2000 problem was the result of legacy software not capable of processing dates past 12/31/99. As a result, companies spent millions of dollars to retrofit their software to accurately process dates in the new millennium.

Index

589